A TREASURY
OF IRISH POETRY

THE MACMILLAN COMPANY
NEW YORK · BOSTON · CHICAGO · DALLAS
ATLANTA · SAN FRANCISCO

MACMILLAN & CO., Limited
LONDON · BOMBAY · CALCUTTA
MELBOURNE

THE MACMILLAN COMPANY
OF CANADA, Limited
TORONTO

A TREASURY

OF

IRISH POETRY

IN THE ENGLISH TONGUE

EDITED BY

STOPFORD A. BROOKE

AND

T. W. ROLLESTON

REVISED AND ENLARGED

NEW YORK
THE MACMILLAN COMPANY
1932

𝔗𝔬

SIR CHARLES GAVAN DUFFY

Aᴍᴏɴɢ ᴡʜᴏꜱᴇ ᴍᴀɴʏ ꜱᴇʀᴠɪᴄᴇꜱ ᴛᴏ Iʀᴇʟᴀɴᴅ ᴡᴀꜱ ᴛʜᴇ

ᴘᴜʙʟɪᴄᴀᴛɪᴏɴ ᴏꜰ ᴛʜᴇ ꜰɪʀꜱᴛ ᴡᴏʀᴛʜʏ ᴄᴏʟʟᴇᴄᴛɪᴏɴ

ᴏꜰ Iʀɪꜱʜ ɴᴀᴛɪᴏɴᴀʟ ᴘᴏᴇᴛʀʏ, ᴛʜᴇ ᴇᴅɪᴛᴏʀꜱ

ᴡɪᴛʜ ᴅᴇᴇᴘ ʀᴇꜱᴘᴇᴄᴛ

Dᴇᴅɪᴄᴀᴛᴇ ᴛʜɪꜱ ᴠᴏʟᴜᴍᴇ

ACKNOWLEDGEMENTS TO THE REVISED EDITION

Thanks are due to the following for the poems listed below:

To the author for permission to reprint *The Blind Man at the Fair* and *The Old Woman*, by Joseph Campbell.

To The Viking Press for permission to reprint *Chamber Music XIV* and *Chamber Music XXXV*, by James Joyce. From CHAMBER MUSIC by James Joyce; New York, The Viking Press; copyright 1918 by B. W. Huebsch.

To the author and to Shakespeare & Co. for permission to reprint *A Memory of the Players in a Mirror at Midnight* and *She Weeps over Rahoon*, by James Joyce.

To The Right Honorable Lord Dunsany, literary executor, and to Brentano's for permission to reprint *To a Linnet in a Cage*, *The Little Boy in the Morning*, and *The Home-Coming of the Sheep*, by Francis Ledwidge.

To The Talbot Press for permission to reprint *John-John* and *A Woman*, by Thomas MacDonagh; MacDonagh's translation of *Ideal*, by Padraic Pearse; *The Dark Palace*, by Alice Milligan; and *The Spark*, by Joseph Plunkett.

To Mr. James Starkey and to Norman, Remington & Co. for permission to reprint *The Sheep*, *The Herdsman*, and *The Others*, by Seumas O'Sullivan.

To Edward Synge, Esq., for permission to reprint *The Passing of the Shee* and *Queens*, by the late J. M. Synge; copyright 1909 by John Quinn.

To The Macmillan Company for *The Coolin*, *The Daisies*, and *Bessie Bobtail*, by James Stephens; and for *The Deer of Ireland* and *The Landing*, by Padraic Colum.

INTRODUCTION

THE position which Ireland holds in the literature of the world is beginning to be understood at last. In the nineteenth century, Ireland, slowly relieved from the oppression which forbade her very speech and denied education to her native intelligence, made known to scholars and the friends of literature the imaginative work she had done in the past. England, who for many years encouraged the cry — Can any good come out of Ireland? — has shown little interest in that work, and the class which in Ireland calls itself cultivated has shown even less interest than England. A few Celtic scholars, many of whom are quite unknown to fame; and a few 'rebellious persons,' who having no chance with the sword grasped the pen — began this labour of love. They awakened little excitement in Trinity College, Dublin, but they did stir up Continental scholars; and that which an Irish University on the whole neglected, was done by German and French professors and students with system, accuracy, and enthusiasm. Moreover, the modern school of critical historians in England and the Continent soon recognised and proclaimed the originating and inspiring work by which Ireland, in ancient days, had awakened England and Europe into intellectual, artistic, and religious life.

The people who from our little island did so much for the civilisation of the nations wrote and spoke at home the Irish tongue, and all their poetical work up to the beginning of this century is in that tongue. But England naturally wished to get rid of the Irish tongue and was naturally careless of its literature. Ireland herself, and that was a pity, did not care enough about her own tongue to preserve it as a vehicle for literature; and finally her poets and thinkers were steadily driven to use the English language. Much has been lost by this destruction of a literary language, but much has also been gained. If Irish can again be used as a vehicle for literature, so much the better. A few are now making that endeavour, and all intelligent persons will wish them good luck and success. It is no disadvantage to a man or a country to be bilingual, and the teaching and use of the Irish tongue will throw light upon the ancient form of it, enable scholars to understand it better, and increase our knowledge of its treasures Moreover, there are many realms of imaginative feeling in Ireland which can only be justly put into poetic form in the tongue of the country itself. No other vehicle can express them so well.

On the other hand, the gain to Irishmen of speaking and writing in English is very great. It enables them to put their national aspirations, and the thoughts and passions which are best expressed in poetry, into a language which is rapidly becoming universal. It enables them to tell the world of literature of the ancient myths, legends, and stories of Ireland, and to represent them, in a modern dress, by means of a language which is read and understood by millions of folk in every part of the world. These considerations lie at the root of the matter, and if Irish writers do not deviate into an imitation of English literature, but cling close to the spirit of their native land, they do well for their country when they use the English tongue.

The use of English by national poets and versifiers may be said to have begun towards the end of the eighteenth century; it has continued ever since, and this book is a history and Anthology of that poetry. We have divided it into six books, representing on the whole distinct phases, but these divisions must not be too sharply separated. They overlap one another, and there will sometimes arise, in the midst of a new phase, a poet who will revert to the types of the past or make a forecast into the future. The short introductions to these books discuss the characteristics and the historical sequence of the general movement of Irish poetry during the nineteenth century. The arrangement of the selections in these six books illustrates that movement.

When the book was first projected, I wished to include nothing in it which did not reach a relatively high standard of excellence. But I soon discovered — and this was strongly urged by my brother Editor — that the book on those lines would not at all represent the growth or the history of Irish poetry in the English language. Moreover, our original purpose had already been carried out by Mr. Yeats in his too brief Anthology, and it was advisable that we should adopt a different aim. It must also be said, with some sorrow, that the Irish poetry of the first sixty years of this century would not reach, except in a very few examples, the requirements of a high standard of excellence. Art is pleased with the ballads, war songs, political and humorous poetry, and with the songs of love and of peasant life, but she does not admit them into her inner shrine. It is only quite lately that modern Irish poetry can claim to be fine art. But as it has now, in what is called the Celtic Revival, reached that point, the history of the poetry that preceded it, and examples from it, are of value and of interest, at least to Irishmen. We laid aside then our original intention, and our book is a systematic record of the best poems we can cull from the writers of the nineteenth century. It is also a history of the development of a special national art, and as such has a real place in the history of literature. The modern as well as the earlier forms of that art stand completely apart from the English poetry of their time. Moreover the book illustrates very vividly the history of Ireland and of her movement towards a national existence.

We do not claim for the poetry a lofty place. That would be unwise and untrue. But I have given reasons in the second part of this Introduction why we claim for it not only the affection and reverence of Irishmen, but a distinct place in the temple of Poetry, and a bland and sympathetic interest from the students, the critics and the lovers of literature. They will find here a school of poetry in the making, a child growing into a man ; and a slight sketch of its progress may not be out of place in this Introduction.

Goldsmith and other Irishmen had written poems in the English tongue before the close of the eighteenth century, but they were English in matter and manner, and belonged to the English tradition. The national poetry of Ireland, written in English, began towards the close of the eighteenth century with the ballads and songs made by the peasants, by the hedge-school-masters and their scholars, and by the street beggars. Nearly all those distinctive marks of the Irish poetry of the first half of the nineteenth century on which I shall hereafter dwell make in these a first and rude appearance. Even before 1798 William Drennan, a cultivated gentleman, beat the big patriotic drum in English verse ; and the *United Irish* movement, together with the influence of Grattan and his Parliament, strengthened that conception of an Irish nation which was now embodied by the ballad-makers, and sung in drawing-rooms by fine ladies, and by ragged minstrels from street to street of the towns. Wrath and sorrow alike filled these ballads, and pride in Ireland. 'When Erin first rose from the dark swelling tide' was the first of a multitude of poems with the same motive; and it was sung all over Ireland. It was followed by the 'Wearin' of the Green,' a song which has glided into a national anthem, and by the 'Shan Van Vocht,' which celebrated the sailing of the French to Ireland to help the revolt of Lord Edward FitzGerald. Thomas Moore struck the same national note, and forced it into prominence in English society.

Along with this patriotic poetry, and always accompanying it in Ireland, the elegiac pipe was heard, and Moore in his best songs played upon it with a grace and tenderness in comparison with which his other poetry fades from our hearing. Callanan and Gerald Griffin continued this strain, but it was partly accompanied and partly succeeded, in an eminently Irish revolt from sadness, by songs like those of Lever, Lover, and Father Prout, in which the wit, fun, and wildness of the Irish nature were displayed.

Before this amusing phase was exhausted, and in a grave reaction from the elements of the stage Irishman contained in it, the poets of the *Nation* newspaper, indignant that the light gaiety of the Irish character (though they justly appreciated the courage and charm of this gaiety in the days of misery) should alone represent their people, and moved by the spirit which soon passed into action when Europe rose for liberty and justice in 1848, again set forth the national aspirations of Ireland. They called on Protestant and Catholic alike, on the Orange and the Green, to unite for the deliverance and nationality of Ireland. Gavan Duffy, who founded and edited the

Nation, Thomas Davis and their comrades, united literature to
their politics and civic morality to literature. Indeed, the
Nation poets are sometimes too ethical for poetry. Their
work inspired, almost recreated, Ireland; and it still continues
to inspire Irishmen all over the world with its nationalising
spirit. Its poetry could not naturally be of a high class, but
it may be said to have made the poetic literature of Ireland.
The editors of this newspaper received and published poems
sent to them by peasants and struggling folk, hitherto voiceless; and extended in this way a love of literature, a knowledge of its ideals, and an opportunity to make it, over the
country. Those Irish also who had fled to foreign lands felt
the impulse given by this journal, and poetry awoke among the
emigrants. It became impossible, after the Songs of the
Nation were collected and published, for England or Europe
or America to either forget or ignore the passion for nationality
in the hearts of the Irish.

The Famine years in which the Death-keen of a whole
people was listened to by the indignation and pity of the
world, produced its own terrible poetry. A vast emigration
succeeded the Famine. A third of the population found it
impossible to live in Ireland; and then a poetry of exile and
of passionate remembrance of their land took form among
Irish poets, and melted into sorrow men whose hearts had
been hot with wrath. It was no wonder, after this dreadful
suffering, that political poetry lost the temperance of the Songs
of the *Nation* and took a ferocious turn in men like McCarroll;
but of that kind of fierce poetry there is far less in Ireland
than we might expect.

Of the men who succeeded[1] the poets of the *Nation,* Man-

---

[1] I say 'succeeded,' but only in the sense of succession of one phase of
poetry to another. In reality, the beginning of the Gaelic movement was
contemporaneous with the rise of the political poetry of the *Nation.*

gan, whose genius was as wayward and as unequal as his life, was the chief. He too, beyond his interest in foreign literature, was a political poet. But he was so with a difference, a difference which brought a new and vitalising element not only into Irish song, but into Ireland's struggle to be a nation. Acquainted with the past history of Irish chiefs and their wars, and also with Gaelic tradition, he derived from this wild and romantic source a thrill of new enthusiasm, and began that return to Gael-dom for inspiration which is so constant an element in the Celtic revival of our own day. He brought again into prominence, and with astonishing force, the historical ballad, and gave it a new life. His impulse descended to Ferguson, and together they originated a new Celtic movement.

In the midst of this political poetry of the present and this fresh poetry of the past, some tender little poems, always appearing in the turmoil and pain of Ireland, celebrate with quiet and graceful feeling the idylls of peasant life. This element also has passed into our modern poetry, and fills it with the stories of the lowly life and love of Ireland.

The Fenian movement which, hopeless of justice from constitutional means, called Ireland to arms, did not produce much poetry; and what it produced was feebler, as a whole, than the Songs of the *Nation*, but some lyrics included in our book have a passionate intensity which I look for in vain among the *Nation* poets. After '67, patriotic rage seldom recurs as a separate motive for poetry. There were a few Land League poets, but they were even less vigorous than the Fenians. Political indignation lasts in modern poetry only as part of the aspiration to nationality. Its fury is now no longer heard. It flashes for a moment out of death or failure in the poems of Fanny Parnell, but she is the last writer who was passionately inspired by politics.

The modern movement, justly occupied more with poetry for its own sake than with poetry in aggression against England, has passed into a quieter land, with wider horizons. Its indwellers have larger aims and aspirations than the poets who preceded them. What is universal in poetry is greater to them than any particular; what belongs to human nature all over the world is more to them than what belongs to any special nation. Nevertheless, they remain, as they ought to remain, distinctively Irish. But they pass beyond Ireland also. They desire to do work which may be united with the great and beautiful Song of the whole world. While they love Ireland dearly and fill their work with the spirit of Ireland, they also wish to be inhabitants of that high Land of Art, where there is neither English nor Irish, French nor German, but the spirit of loveliness alone.

This new movement took two lines, which ran parallel to one another, like two lines of railway. But now and again, as lines of railway meet and intersect at stations, these two mingled their motives, their subjects, and their manner. But, on the whole, they ran without touching; and one followed the English and the other the Irish tradition. The poets who kept the first line, and who are placed in Book VI., have been so deeply influenced by Wordsworth, Keats, and in part by Shelley, that even when they write on Irish subjects the airs of England breathe and the waters of England ripple in their poetry. It is impossible not to admire the subtlety, tenderness, and love of nature of these poets, but their place is apart in an Anthology of Irish poetry. They have not kept, along with their devotion to their art, the spirit of their native land. They are descended from the English poets; and if they were to read out their poems on Knocknarea, Queen Meave, and with her the Fairy Race of Ireland, would drive them from her presence,

V. DRAMA

VI. SPEECHES, PAMPHLETS, AND LETTERS

VII. BIOGRAPHY

AUTOBIOGRAPHY

SOCIAL ESSAYS

CULTURAL ESSAYS

PERSONAL ESSAYS

APPENDIX

gently, for they are bards, but inevitably, and transport them on the viewless winds to England.

The other line on which Irish verse ran was backward to the recovery of the old Celtic stories and their modernising in poetry, and forward to the creation of a new form of the Celtic spirit. The poets who did and are doing this work, while they have studied and honoured the great masters of song, and, as they write in English, the English masters, have yet endeavoured to secure and retain in their poetry not only the national and spiritual elements of the character of the Irish people, but also that appealing emotion which lives like a soul in the natural scenery of Ireland, and makes it, at least for Irishmen, transcend all other scenery by depth and range of sentiment.

I have said that Mangan began the return to Celtic tradition, but as it were by chance, with no deliberate hand. Even before him Callanan and Walsh had fallen back, out of their stormy poetry, on the silent record of Irish story, and had put into English verse some Gaelic poems. The translations Miss Brooke had made in the last century were indeed the first of all, but they were as English in manner as Goldsmith's verses. Mangan was the true precursor of the revival of the passion and thought of ancient and mediæval Ireland. But the leader of the choir was Sir Samuel Ferguson, whose 'Lays of the Western Gael,' 1867, established the Celtic movement. In his own time few cared to drink of the forgotten fountains he struck from the rock where they were hidden, nor did he gain the interest or gratitude of any wide society, but the waters he delivered have swelled into fertilising streams. His restoration of the sagas of Ireland has made a new realm for romantic poetry, and given it fresh impulse and fresh subjects. He has done this not only for Ireland, but for the literary world. English, French, Germans, Americans have begun to enter into and enjoy that enchanted land. Even Tennyson, English of the English, could not resist its attraction. Moreover, its Cycle of Tales has proved its right to be one of the great Subject-matters of poetry by its adaptability. The later Irish poets who have modernised its tales or episodes have been able to treat it with the same freedom and individuality as the romantic poets did the legend of Arthur. A great Cycle of Tales fits itself into the individual temper of each poet, and calls on him, as it were imperiously, to make new matter out of it. It desires no slavish following of its ancient lines; it begs for fresh creation. Ferguson, Sigerson, Aubrey de Vere, Larminie, Todhunter, Russell, Nora Hopper, and William Yeats have invented new representations of the old Celtic stories, and the work of each of these poets stands apart.

Another phase of the Celtic movement, illustrated in this book, tends to accurate translations, preserving the original metres, of old Irish poetry into English verse. This has been done with great enthusiasm and success by Dr. Hyde and Dr. Sigerson. It has its interest : it adds to our knowledge ; but the original poetry is curiously unequal, and the scientific metres no more an excellence in Irish poetry than they are in Icelandic. They limit both passion and freedom.

One would have thought that in this Celtic revival, faery poetry would have occupied a large place. In Ireland the fairies are still alive, and faery-land is still real. But they scarcely live in the modern poets of Ireland. William Allingham's fairies are of English origin. One Irish poet actually takes refuge with Oberon and Titania, who, though they may trace their far-off origin to Ireland, are creatures wholly different from the Irish fairies, in whose atmosphere they could not breathe. Oberon and Titania have never crossed the Channel. The Irish fairies, who are descended from the great Nature

Gods and the under-deities of flood and fell and lake and angry sea, are of a double nature, kindly and terrible ; and in their fall from their high estate the terrible has, more than the kindly, become their abiding temper. They do not therefore come easily into subjects for modern verse, except when the Irish poet is attacked by pessimism. Fortunately that disease is not common in Ireland, and those who do suffer from it at times in Ireland soon break out into laughter at themselves. Indeed, the Fairy Race of Ireland themselves are not at all pessimistic. They live their own life ; are very ancient in temper ; are quite un-affected by science, art, and literature ; carry off beautiful human girls and children, as their women carried off lovers of old from the race of men ; avenge a slight or any want of reverence with great promptitude and a native sense of justice ; dance, and play music of their own making ; and even mingle a rare gamesome-ness with their dignity and severity. It is a pity nothing has yet in poetry been written about them with full insight and knowledge. It is true their acquaintance or friendship is not easily made, and the greater personages among them are very haughty and reticent. But the lesser folk are more approach-able, and are delightful company. There is but one poet in Ireland who has been admitted to this retired and difficult society, who knows a little of its terrible, mysterious, and spiritual charm.

That charm has partly to do with a new phase of the Celtic movement in poetry — the last which has come into being, and perhaps the most fruitful. For certain young poets, either looking deeper into that mysterious world, or driven by a spirit in themselves, have seen beneath the myths and legends of Ireland, and in the hidden regions where the Nature Gods of the Irish still dwell afar, the images and symbols of those remoter states of the human soul, which only live on the borderland between the worlds of matter and spirit, and share in the nature of both.   And out of this has arisen a mystic school of modern poets, who, if they do not isolate themselves too much in that, will awaken a new power in Irish literature.   But to dwell only in that land, and never to emerge into the open country where the great simplicities of human nature quietly abide, will in the end weaken that type of poetry, and may bring it to nothing.   I am glad that some of the mystical poets, having seen that truth, have written poems, as Blake did, full of a natural humanity.

There has also been recovered, with a new note attached to it, and with more of fine art than before, the poetry of Irish humour and of its companion, pathos; and poems, like those of Mr. Graves, are as gracious and gay as they are national.   Correlative with these, and passing into them, are the idylls of the poor.   Peasant life in Ireland is radically different from peasant life in England ; it has its own Celtic qualities and of the best ; and it holds a multitude of tender, gay, sweet, courageous, and natural subjects for Irish poets who love their countrymen and enjoy their temper.   Many such poems will be found in this book, and I hope that many more will be written.   There are plenty of remote and romantic subjects in Irish life and legend, of wars, adventures, raidings, sieges, of tragic loves and sorrows, of spells and enchantments, of the gods and mortals in love and battle with one another, of a hundred passionate and mystic things, and this com-mercial modern world will welcome them, if they are not moralised ; but the better food and pleasanter delights of poetry will be found in the daily life of men and women spiritualised by natural passion into that eternal world of Love where the unseen things are greater than the seen.   It is in that return to natural love that poetry when athirst drinks fresh dew, and rises into a new life ; and in it will be found the true mysticism, the vital spirituality, the passion, and that noble sensuousness which, when it is thrilled through and through by the spiritual, becomes, and especially in contact with nature, itself a part of spirit.

This slight history of Irish poetry during a century is necessarily inadequate. An introduction is limited : many things must be omitted, many points left undeveloped, and criticism of living poets must be left alone. These omissions are filled up by the introductions and the criticisms in this book. I have dwelt on tendencies rather than on men. It remains to say something of the reason for publishing a separate Anthology of Irish poetry, and of the distinctive elements of that poetry. That there are distinctive elements in it is the main reason for publishing its Anthology.

The first of these is its nationality. That, right or wrong, is the deepest thing in Ireland, and it is a multitudinous absurdity for England to try to ignore it. Even if it were wrong, as it is not, all laws or any government which do not take it into the highest consideration are bound to fail dismally in Ireland. This stands to reason, but reason rarely influences Cabinets or lawyers. It stands also to reason that if Irish nationality be so deep a thing, the Irish literature which ignores it is bound to be inferior in life and originality to that which is inspired by it. And such is the case. The Irish poetry which follows the English tradition too often wears an imitative look, languishes into subtleties, or dreams into commonplace. Were it possible that Irish literature should be anglicised, there would soon be no literature worth the name in Ireland. It has not been anglicised. No one can be deaf to the national note in the greater part of the poetry here published. It is everywhere distinctive,

from the 'Wearin' of the Green' to the 'Wanderings of Oisin';
and there are so many forms of it that they alone give interest
to this book.

English poetry is national enough, but it is a national
poetry of pride (not ignoble pride), of victory and of joy.
Irish national poetry has its own pride, not ignoble either, but
different from English pride. It is the pride of the will
unconquered by trouble, of courage to endure ill-fate to the
end, of the illimitable hope for the future which is a child of
the imaginative powers. Nor is her national poetry of victory
and joy, but of defeat and sorrow and hope. The poems here
are in all points different from the national poems of England.
So sorrowful are they that English seems no fitting vehicle for
their emotions.

When the English embody their nation, she sits by the seashore, crowned; with the triple fork of Poseidon to rule the waves;
helmeted, and her shield by her side like Athena; Queen of
her own isle, and in her mind, Queen of all the seas. She is a
poetic figure, but belongs more to the pride of life than the
passion of poetry. But when Irish poets imagined Ireland, she
sits, an uncrowned queen, on the wild rocks of the Atlantic
coast, looking out to the west, and the sorrow of a thousand
years makes dark her ever youthful eyes. Her hair, wet with
the dews, is her helmet, and her robe she has herself woven from
the green of her fields and the purple of her hills. This Virgin
Lady of Ireland, in the passion of her martyrdom, was the
subject, after her conquest by England, of a crowd of Gaelic
poems, and is the subject still of English poems by Irish poets.
And many names are hers, names under which she was hidden
from the English oppressors. *Dark Rosaleen, Silk of the Kine,
Innisfail,* the *Little Black Rose,* the *Rose of the World,* and others
too long to number; but all of them belong to immortal beauty.

One hardly wishes, for the sake of Art, that this Lady should lose all the sorrow by which her loveliness is veiled, but yet, joy would make her lovelier; and the national symbol of Ireland may yet have that enchanting light in her eyes. If Irish poetry could so image her now, it would be well. That which is conceived with imaginative truth often fulfils itself in reality.

Another distinctive mark of this poetry is its religion. Ireland's religion is linked closely to her nationality, and has been as much oppressed. The note of the poetry is nearly always Catholic, and Catholic with the pathos, the patience, and the passion of persecution added to its religious fervour. English poetry, on the other hand, is a poetry of many forms of religion; men of all churches and sects can find their spiritual sympathies represented in it. But it has no specialised, no isolated religious note, because persecution such as existed in Ireland did not deepen its music into a cry.

The religious poetry of England (there are only a few exceptions, like Southwell) is comfortable and at peace. It plays its pleasant, quaint, or solemn flute in quiet vicarages, or Bishops' palaces, or in the classic gardens of the Universities. Even the Nonconformist verse breathes the settled consolations of a warless land. But the Irish religious poetry of the early nineteenth century was written in prisons, under sentence of exile or death, on the wild moor and in the mountain cave. Its writers lived under the ban of Government, crushed by abominable laws; and the mercy given to the wolf was the only mercy given to men whose crime was the love of their own religion. Their religious poetry gained from that experience a passionate love for the Catholic Church, and well the Church deserved it. And we have in this book only too few of the poems which image and record this love, expressed with an intensity and devotion which, though it has but little art, has much of nature.   Things have changed since then ; persecution has ceased, and the present Catholic poetry is written by comfortable persons.   Yet the old savour clings to, and the ancient passion rings in, the modern poems.   The memories of martyrdom are as powerful in song as its realities.

The matter and the manner have both changed.   The sacred legends of Irish saints are now told, and the glories of the ancient Church of Ireland.   The mystic elements, so deep in Catholicism, are selected for the music of verse ; and their intense spirituality, white and rose-red with the heavenly flames of wisdom and love, is a vital part of the mysticism which is one of the powers of the Celtic revival.

Nor was the Church of Ireland left of old, nor is she now left, without her imagined personality.   As the Lady of Ireland was created by the poets, so was the Lady of the Church.   She sits on the shore of Irish Romance, hand in hand with her who personifies Ireland as a nation, and two more pathetic figures — in their indomitable resistance to oppression, in their sorrow and their hope, in their claim to the love of their people because of their own undying love, in their eternal youth to which no oppression has given one stain of age — do not exist in the world of literature.   They are clothed with the beauty of their land, and the martyrdom of their people is their crown of light.   A thousand poems are hidden as yet in this conception.

Another distinctive mark of this poetry is what England calls Rebellion.   Rebellion, even when its motive is only pride or the support of an immoral cause, much more when it is waged by sword or pen against legalised oppression and iniquitous laws, is always a poetic motive.   It is the weak against the strong, independence against tutelage, the love of one's own land in her hour of sorrow and danger.   And all these motives are vivid in Irish poetry. It is a poor country that can make no songs in a struggle for freedom ; it is not worth its freedom.

Then, when the fierce songs of rebellious war are still, and the rebels, defeated, suffer the penalties of the victor, songs of pity and wrath awake together, and these are even more poetic than marching and battle songs. And further, when the struggle of the spirit goes on, though the bodily powers are enslaved, and the soul of the people will not yield, but still in silence breathes revolt — the poetry of rebellion takes to itself moral sanctions, and then, moral passion for justice is mingled in that poetry with the finer passions of the spirit.

Nor does the matter end here. It is pitiful, but it is one of the curses that are bred by injustice, that among the injured people Revenge then claims to be Justice, and the law, being identified with injustice by the people, is despised and scorned. Sympathy with the legal criminal then arises in song. The oppressed peasant who illegally rights his own wrong is counted a martyr ; the outlaw and the prisoner are made into knights of romance. Unjust law produces these revolts against it, and where they are, the law is in fault, not the people. In a well-governed country, except among the degraded classes, they are not found. In Ireland, they were found among men of high intelligence, of gentle manners, of cultivated affections, of high and noble aims, of deep religious fervour, and of poetic imagination. Many of these rose to high offices in the State in other lands than Ireland, and some were tender and graceful poets. It is worth while to read the idyllic poems of Charles Kickham, the Fenian, and to ask if one who felt thus was worthy of penal servitude. The fact is that the greater number of Irishmen were proud to take the hand of the ' treason-felons,' and thought their imprisonment their crown of honour. That could not have occurred in

England ; and the reason was, not that these Irishmen were bad, but that England was tolerably well-governed and Ireland intolerably ill-governed. Well, in this long rebellion of body and soul the poetry of rebellion grew up, and it is a distinctive note in Irish poetry. There is not a trace of this kind of poetry in English verse, but England created it in Ireland.

In the realm of Art in which I write, I am glad to have poetry of this kind in the English language. Whether it be rebellious or not does not matter to Art. The only questions Art asks are : 'Is it well done? was it worth the doing?' and the readers of this book may answer the questions for themselves. In the early Irish poetry rebellion, with all its 'motives,' flames out incessantly. There is little good work in it, but it is original, and its very rudeness attracts like early sculpture. It has a daring, lilting, fine, and savage swing, and sets, with great joy, the Saxon and the Celt in battle array. It has an inspiration which breathes of the people, and it calls for slaughter, revenge, and ruin with an energy Art will not disdain. But pitiless poetry of this kind seldom reaches a high level. Since the days of the Hebrew prophets, who do possess the pitiless poetry in its highest form — for their fierce religion uplifted into strength the natural weakness of vengeance — I do not know any fine poetry which calls for merciless slaughter and revenge.

The best rebel poetry of Ireland is not found among such songs, but is found in those which are based on pity for the imprisoned rebel, sorrow for the exile, and sympathy with the outlaw. There is no class of poetry in England that celebrates the first or the second of these motives. There is in Scotland, and the Jacobite songs have the same air of romance as the Irish songs of those who were hunted, like Prince Charlie, from cave to cave, and who died for the cause. They are numerous in the Irish records, and though few are of fine poetic quality, yet their circumstances enhance them. As to sympathy with the outlaw, we have poetry of that kind in English literature, but we must go back, in order to find it, for several centuries. The songs which concreted themselves, year after year, round the names of Robin Hood and his wild-wood followers bear, in their sympathy with the outlaw, some analogy to the Irish poems with the same subject. But there is a difference. The English ballads are happy, the forest life is enjoyed, the outlaws get the better of the law, and they are received into royal favour at the end. The Irish songs are drenched in sorrow, the life of the outlaw is wretched, the law chases him like a fox, and when he is caught, he is slaughtered without mercy. We have, for the most part, left those days behind us, and no rebellious poetry, save a few scattered songs, now appears. But in the realm of Art, in whose quiet meadows we now read poems of this class, we may be glad to have them in the English tongue.

The poetry of Misery also arose, a wild and melancholy cry. Here and there a song of misery—the misery of a class, like the 'Song of the Shirt'—is found in England ; but this Irish poetry was for the misery of a whole country, for the misery of millions. The sword had passed over Ireland, and torture was added to the work of the sword. Then famine came, a famine that concentrated into itself and doubled and trebled the misery of former famines, a famine that awakened horror in the whole of the civilised world. Men, women, and children died by thousands of starvation. They fell dead in the streets of the towns and on the moors and mountains, and their bodies were given for meat to the fowls of the air and the beasts of the field. On the top of that, pestilence arrived, and those

whom famine had spared plague destroyed. England sub-
scribed, when the mischief was done, a huge sum for Ireland's
relief, but the administration of it was marked by that absolute
want of common sense which till quite lately has always
characterised the government of Ireland by England. The
food given was totally unfit for creatures wasted with famine
and fever ; and the starving peasants, weak as new-born children,
had often to walk miles to the centres of distribution. There
was plenty of good food in Ireland, but the poor could not
buy it. It was a famine of poverty, not of want of food. More
cattle, it is said, were exported to England that year from Ireland
than in any previous year. The misery of exile followed on
the pestilence. The number of those who, unable to find any
means of life in Ireland, left the country, carrying with them
hatred of England, runs into millions. Such a history is un-
exampled in Europe during the last hundred years. Indeed,
there is no indictment of past English rule in Ireland, even
when made by those who hate England most, so terrible as the
silent indictment of the miseries by which Ireland was deci-
mated. They could not have occurred in a decently governed
country.

Well, the misery had its poetry — a kind of poetry unknown
before in literature written in the English tongue, and though,
as usual, its poetic excellence is not high, it has a passionate,
strange note, an astonished horror and dismay, a wild wail of
utterance, which Art, now that time has mellowed the memories
of the pain, accepts with gratitude, and would not willingly let
die. Ireland has added to English literature this poetry of the
Sword, the Famine, and the Pestilence. England could not
produce it, for centuries have passed away since she was
devastated from end to end by these dreadful sisters. Nor
has England any of the poetry of exile — a pathetic and fruitful

motive. Its songs are among the best that the lyric poets of Ireland have produced. They are simple, natural, direct, and rapid. They seldom err, as so many Irish poems err, by over-length, that is, by the poet's incapacity to select the suggestive and cast away the superfluous. And they also have at their root that poetic image of Ireland, as a Lady of Sorrow, whose tragic fate has deepened for her the passionate love of her people. Many of these songs are written in prison, in convict ships, in the far lands into which the youth of Ireland fled to gain bread to eat and raiment to put on, and they breathe the hopeless desire to see again the hills and skies of Ireland. Others, however banished, might return, and hope might be in their songs, but the Irish exile had no hope. And many of these songs are of visits to a native land in dreams, and have the spiritual note of dreams. This then is another distinctive-ness in Irish poetry, and even to the present day this motive is continued. But the hopelessness of return, the woe of the exile have departed. There is nothing now to prevent a man returning to Ireland, and political exile, we may hope, has ceased to be. But the memory of what has been still lives in Art, and is used by Art.

Another class of poems are only distinctive from the dis-tinctive character of the Irish peasant. The idylls of the poor, the loves and sorrows of the poor, belong to all countries, and are excellent subjects for poetry, when they are naturally felt. Any distinctiveness the Irish poems of this kind possess, many of which are contained in this book, arises from a special doubleness in the Irish character, which indeed exists in other peoples, but is nowhere, I think, so clear in its divisions, and so extreme in its outward forms, as in Ireland. The peasant meets overwhelming trouble with the courage and the endurance of a fatalism which is only modified by his profound religion.

He dies in silence and submission, but as long as there is a shadow of hope that fate will lift her hand, the uncomplaining courage with which he stems misfortune, the steady affection with which he defends those he loves against it, is as intelligent and of as high a morality as it is simple and unconscious. The peasant idylls of sorrow and trouble met with courage and love, and then with simple fatalism, have their own peculiar touch — a touch whose note is deepened by the underlying thought of the vast misfortune of their country. All personal trouble is only an incident in Ireland of the vaster trouble of the whole land — an element in poetry which cannot belong to English poetry. Along with this are the poems which represent a contrasted feature in the Irish character. The moment the weight of trouble is removed — or if in the midst of the worst trouble a sudden impulse of joy or love should come, or of physical excitement or of intellectual humour — a sudden reaction sets in; the elastic heart forgets for the time its pain; the acuteness of the trouble ministers to the acuteness of the gaiety, and a wild, gay, witty, sometimes turbulent joy leaps into life, during which the world is filled with laughter and brightness and satisfied affection. This is the source of the witty and delightful songs which, even in the darkness of famine and pestilence, emerged in Irish literature, and which are apart from all other songs in the English language. They celebrate the ideal pleasure of fanciful intoxication, the mutual games and fun of two sweethearts, the joys of fighting, the rapture of making a fool of a man and telling him of it, and even the wild and wicked daring of the 'Night before Larry was Stretched.' Nowhere in English, since the days of 'Golias,' can such songs be found, and I dare say the English are glad that they are impossible. But Art, in its bold young moods, may not be sorry to possess them.

I have already described how, when the worst stress of these woes was over, the Irish poets ceased to express themselves in political poetry, but nevertheless—save in those poets who followed the English tradition—consecrated their verse towards the support of a vigorous and vital nationality : first, by the representation in a modern dress of the Irish myths and sagas ; and secondly, by the representation of the spiritual elements of the modern world from an Irish standpoint, and in an Irish spirit. The subject makes the first distinctively Irish, but recommends itself to the use of poets and story-tellers in all nations that love literature. When art and criticism have cleared the Celtic stories from their early coarseness and rudeness and their later extravagance of diction and ornament, they will be a treasure-house of subjects for those who love the past, or for those who love to modernise the past. But those who work at them in these ways in Ireland will have to possess or to sympathise with the Celtic spirit, must understand and feel its distinctiveness. The material, when modernised, seems to demand that condition, at least from Irishmen. Men of other countries may use the stories as they please, as the Normans, French, and Germans used the Tales of Arthur. But the Irish poets must embody their ancient story in verse that breathes the spirit of Ireland, or fall below their true vocation. They may fill it with modern motives, symbolise and spiritualise its tales ; they may change its robes ; they may animate it with the passions and thoughts of our own time, and express it with the fine and careful delicacy of poetic art. But the living and distinctive soul in it will be born in Ireland. Of the fulfilment of this no better or shorter example can be given than Mr. Yeats' poem of the ' Hosting of the Sidhe.'

The other tendency of Irish poetry is towards a more spiritual view of the world than now prevails in fine literature.

In this, however, it does not stand alone. Such a reaction from mere sensuousness or materialism or from the commonplaces of natural description and love, has visited French poetry, and the wave of it has reached England. In France both the mystic and religious elements of this spiritual movement are represented in combination; and there is one class of Irish poets who have added to their religious work not only the mysticism which, as I have said, lies so deep in the Catholic Church, but also a lively leaven of Neo-Platonism, with a modern Celtic addition of their own. The result of this admixture is a curious, difficult, symbolic, and interesting type of poetry, charged with motives of serene but somewhat austere beauty. And the austerity in the beauty is not the least charm in the poetry. We can claim for this Catholic and mystic poetry, of which Mr. Lionel Johnson is the chief singer, a real distinctiveness. With the exception of Francis Thompson, himself a Catholic, English poetry is without it at present. It used to exist in England, in work like that of Henry Vaughan and other Platonists, but even there the difference between the present Irish poetry, with its Celtic element like a fresh wind within it, is clearly marked.

Other poets, of whom Mr. Russell is chief, have made mysticism alone their subject. The powers which spiritually move under the visible surface of human life, and lead it, in its blindness, on to goals of which it knows nothing; the powers which invisibly move under the forces and forms of the natural world, and which create and recreate it day by day by Thought and Love — these are the subjects of the song of these poets, and though we have had purely mystic poets in England, yet we have none now, and it is well to recover this element for Art. Only, if it were possible for them to write about universal human life as well, as all the greater poets have done, and about Nature as she seems to the senses as well as to the soul, it were better. Shelley, who was mystic enough on one side of his being, was in full sympathy with the common life of men and women on another side. Otherwise the purely mystic poetry, with all its charm and art, hands on no torch. It is then a childless woman.

Other writers, both men and women, have written on religious matters without any admixture of mysticism, and their poetry approaches more nearly to imaginative work than the distinctly religious poetry of England. The religious poets of Ireland are almost altogether Catholic, and it is well for poetry that it is so. The Church of England poetry is weighted away from Art by doctrinal and ecclesiastical formula, by a diluted scepticism of the supernatural, and by a distrust and reprobation of enthusiasm which has its source in the temper of the universities — a temper which Trinity College has inadequately imitated. As to the Nonconformists, they cherish a most sorrowful want of imagination. Beauty has no temple among their shrines, and it seems a pity that so large and influential a body of citizens should be incapable of producing any fine religious poetry. In Ireland, however, the immense store of poetic subjects which belong to the Catholic Church, the living faith in the legendary world of the saints and in miracle, the multitude of thoughts, stories, and passions which cluster round the vast antiquity of the Church of Rome, and the poetic image (of which I have spoken) of the young and virgin beauty of the persecuted Church of Ireland, present to the poetic religious temper beautiful and innumerable motives for song, and create incessant emotion round them. I wonder there is not more religious poetry written in Ireland, and in the Irish spirit. At present, we are not likely to have it in England. Christina Rossetti is its only imaginative representative in modern English, and she was at root Italian. Her work has that high, pure, keen spiritual note which the Celtic Catholic poetry loves to hear. And in it also is that mingling of earthly sorrow with celestial joy, of sweetness and austerity, in an atmosphere of mystic ecstasy, which is vital, but not yet fully developed, in the Celtic revival.

As yet, in modern Ireland, the larger religion is untouched, the religion of the greater poets — not their personal religion which is often limited — but that which poetry of its own will creates; which answers to the unformulated aspirations of the soul towards the eternal love; which is neither Catholic nor Protestant, but includes both; which has no fixed creed, no necessary ritual, no formulas; and no Church but that invisible Church with which the innumerable spirits of the universe are in communion, and whose device bears these words: 'The Letter killeth, but the Spirit giveth life.' It is my hope that the spiritual tendency of Irish poetry will embody that conception.

These three tendencies in Irish poetry — each with its distinctive Celtic touch, towards religion, towards mysticism, and towards a mingling of both into one, have been united in the poems of Mr. Yeats. He has added to them a spiritualised representation of the ancient Celtic stories, and he has also done some work, direct, simple, and humane, on actual life. His poetry has therefore a wider range than that of his fellow-poets. Moreover, he has suffused these various kinds of verse with an imaginative spirituality which has borne their subjects, while they belong to this world, into the invisible world of which this is the shadow. I hope that, having proved his universality, he will not fasten down into any one of these several forms of poetry and abandon the rest. He has a natural turn for mysticism and its symbolic ways, and it would be a great loss if he gave up to this particular form what was meant for mankind; if, like Aaron's serpent, it swallowed up the other forms of poetry.

Amid the varied aims of these poets there is one element common to them all. It is their Nationalism. That nationalism has on the whole ceased to be aggressive against England, and that is all the better. Poetry has no national feuds. But the nationalism which, in love of Ireland, sets itself in poetry towards the steady evolution of the Celtic nature, and the full representation of its varied elements — that is vital in these poets, and is vital to the life, growth, and flowering of Irish poetry. Irish poetry, if it is to be a power in literature, must be as Irish as English poetry is English. It has now gained what of old it wanted. It has gained art. Its work is no longer the work of amateurs. Its manner and melody are its own. Its matter is not yet as great as it ought to be for the creation of poetry of the higher ranges. The Subject-matter of mankind has been only lightly or lyrically treated in Ireland, or only in such side issues as mysticism or religion or re-animation of the past. A graver, larger, and more impassioned treatment of those weighty human issues which live in the present, but are universal in the nature of man, is necessary before Irish poetry can reach maturity.

As to the other great Subject-matter — outward Nature as seen and felt by man — that, I am surprised to find, considering the feeling of the Celt for natural scenery, has received no adequate treatment from the Irish poets. What they have as yet done in this way is not to be compared with the work of English or French poets; moreover, the aspects of nature in Ireland, the special sentiment and soul of natural scenery in Ireland, so varied from sky to sea and from sea to land, so distinguished and so individual, have not, save in a few scattered lines, been expressed — I had almost said, have not been perceived — by the poets who live in that scenery. A vast subject-matter, then, almost untouched, lies before the future Irish poets.

I have said that Art has only shown itself of late in the Irish poetry of this century; nor is there any attempt on my part to claim for the poems in this book a lofty place in literature. The river of Irish poetry in the English language is yet in its youth. It rose a hundred years ago in the far-off hills, and wrought its turbulent way down the channelled gorge it carved for its stream out of its own mountains. Other streams have joined it, bearing with them various waters; and it has only just now issued from the hills, and begun to flow in quieter and lovelier lands, glancing from ripple to pool and from pool to ripple, among woods and meadows, happy, and making its lovers happy. It is the youngest child of the Goddess Poesy. Let it be judged as a youth. In time, if it remain true to its country's spirit, the stream that has just emerged from the mountain torrent will become a noble river.

STOPFORD A. BROOKE.

October 1900.

To the living authors who have kindly sanctioned the inclusion of writings of theirs in this collection we desire to express our sincere thanks. We also gratefully acknowledge permission given by the undernamed publishing houses to make extracts from the works set opposite their names:

John Lane — BALLADS IN PROSE, and UNDER QUICKEN BOUGHS by Miss Nora Hopper; THE EARTH-BREATH, by A. E.

J. M. Dent & Co. — THREE BARDIC TALES, by John Todhunter.

Cameron & Ferguson, Glasgow — POEMS by 'Leo' (J. K. Casey), by Lady Wilde, and T. C. Irwin.

William McGee, Dublin — KOTTABOS.

Blackwood & Sons — SONGS OF THE ANTRIM GLENS, by Moira O'Neill.

Elkin Mathews — POEMS, by Lionel Johnson; ROSES AND RUE, by Miss Alice Furlong.

Kegan Paul, Trench, Trübner & Co. — ST. AUGUSTINE'S HOLIDAY AND OTHER POEMS, by the Most Rev. Dr. Alexander, Primate.

Macmillan & Co. — POEMS, by Mrs. Alexander.

T. Fisher Unwin — BARDS OF THE GAEL AND GALL, by George Sigerson, M.D., F.R.U.I.; POEMS, by W. B. Yeats.

We have also to thank Lady Ferguson and Mrs. Allingham for permission to include extracts from the works of Sir Samuel Ferguson and of William Allingham, and the Rev. H. Wynne for a similar favour in regard to our extract from Mrs. Wynne's volume 'Whisper.'

It would be impossible to enumerate here all the works which have been of use to us in the compilation of this anthology, but special acknowledgment must be made to the editors of previous anthologies whose labours have lightened ours. Among works which have been of special service to us are Sir Charles Gavan Duffy's SPIRIT OF THE NATION, and BALLAD POETRY OF IRELAND; THE HARP OF ERIN, and other collections edited by 'Duncathail' (R. Varian); POETS AND POETRY OF IRELAND, by Alfred M. Williams; THE BALLADS OF IRELAND, by Edward Hayes; IRISH MINSTRELSY, by Halliday Sparling; A BOOK OF IRISH VERSE, by W. B. Yeats; THE NEW SPIRIT OF THE NATION, by M. MacDermott. Mr. D. J. O'Donoghue's DICTIONARY OF IRISH POETRY has of course rendered us great service as a work of reference. We have also to thank its author for the willingness with which he has placed at our disposal his unrivalled knowledge of Irish literature. Mr. John O'Leary has also kindly permitted us to draw upon his valuable library of Irish works, as well as upon his no less valuable store of judgment and information. The late Mr. John Kelly lent us a very extensive collection made by him of fugitive verse from Irish periodicals, for which we regret that we cannot now thank him.

THE EDITORS.

PUBLISHER'S NOTE

THE biographical notes throughout the book have been brought up to date, and a new section of recent poems has been added. It has been thought wise, however, to leave untouched the signed critical comments by such men as Yeats, Rolleston, A. E., Brooke, Sigerson, and Hyde, which preceded the work of a great number of the poets included in the earlier sections. These appreciations have undoubted value as contemporary evaluations.

CONTENTS

A TREASURY
OF IRISH POETRY

IRISH POETS

BOOK I

THERE are two classes of anonymous poems—those which seem to have grown up among the people, often perhaps the work of more than one hand, and reflecting the spirit rather of a class or of a race than of an individual ; and those which are distinctly individual and are only anonymous by the accident that no author's name has ever been affixed to them. The former class of poems are represented in the first and briefest book of this Anthology. They represent, mainly, the earliest attempts of the Irish peasantry to express themselves in poetic form in the English language.

Multitudes of such attempts must have been made and lost. Now and then a stray line or two has by virtue of its pathetic music caught the ear of some man of letters and found its way into print. Sir Charles Duffy has recorded his early recollection of a rude ballad of this description, at the singing of which he saw a whole dinner company dissolved in tears, and in which the warm-hearted reception given by Belfast to Wolfe Tone and the Catholic envoys of 1793 on their way to plead for the freedom of their faith was thus spoken of :

> The Lord in His mercy be kind to Belfast:
> The poor Irish exile she soothed as he passed.

Many such things there must have been, many more than ever found their way into print, and many which were printed as ballad sheets and are now lost for ever. But some have survived in chapbooks, anthologies, old newspapers, stray records of every kind, and of these a selection is here given. In some the grandiloquent phrase of the hedge-schoolmaster is noticeable, some are pieces of wild irresponsible humour, some have a tender and unconscious grace, or are animated by a grotesque vitality, or express with rude fervour the patriotic devotion of the peasant. A peasant-poetry of far greater beauty and elevation was in process of creation at the time when the majority of these pieces were written—the eighteenth century and the beginning of the nineteenth—but this was in the Gaelic tongue, then the language of the masses of the people. In his "Love Songs" and "Religious Songs" of Connacht, Dr. Douglas Hyde has turned much of this popular poetry into English verse, retaining the characteristic traits of the original. Specimens of this will be found under his name in Book V. Here, however, we present only the first stammerings of the Irish spirit in the new tongue which, about the beginning of this century, began to be the language of Irish literature.

THE WEARIN' O' THE GREEN

The finest of Irish street-ballads, and described by a writer in the *Athenæum* in 1887 as probably the finest street-ballad ever written. One of its numerous variants sung in a play of Boucicault's has given rise to the belief that he wrote it, but it appears to date from about the year 1798. It deserves to be called the Irish National Anthem, if any piece of poetry can claim that title.

OH, Paddy dear! an' did ye hear the news that's goin' round?
The shamrock is by law forbid to grow on Irish ground!
No more St. Patrick's Day we'll keep, his colour can't be seen,
For there's a cruel law agin the wearin' o' the green!
I met wid Napper Tandy, and he took me by the hand,
And he said, 'How's poor Ould Ireland, and how does she stand?'
She's the most disthressful country that iver yet was seen,
For they're hangin' men and women there for wearin' o' the green.

An' if the colour we must wear is England's cruel red,
Let it remind us of the blood that Ireland has shed;
Then pull the shamrock from your hat, and throw it on the sod,—
And never fear, 'twill take root there, tho' under foot 'tis trod!

When law can stop the blades of grass from growin' as they grow,
And when the leaves in summer-time their colour dare not show,
Then I will change the colour, too, I wear in my caubeen,
But till that day, plaze God, I'll stick to wearin' o' the green.

THE SORROWFUL LAMENTATION OF CALLAGHAN, GREALLY AND MULLEN

KILLED AT THE FAIR OF TURLOUGHMORE

A STREET-BALLAD

This is a genuine ballad of the people, written and sung among them. The reader will see at once how little resemblance it bears to the *pseudo* Irish songs of the stage, or even to the street-ballads manufactured by the ballad-singers. It is very touching, and not without a certain unpremeditated grace. The vagueness, which leaves entirely untold the story it undertook to recount, is a common characteristic of the Anglo-Irish songs of the people. The circumstance on which it is founded took place in 1843, at the fair of Darrynacloughery, held at Turloughmore. A faction-fight having occurred at the fair, the arrest of some of the parties led to an attack on the police ; after the attack had abated or ceased, the police fired on the people, wounded several, and killed the three men whose names stand at the head of the ballad. They were indicted for murder, and pleaded the order of Mr. Brew, the stipendiary magistrate, which was admitted as a justification. Brew died before the day appointed for his trial.—Note by Sir Charles Gavan Duffy, *Ballad Poetry of Ireland*.

' COME, tell me, dearest mother, what makes my father stay,
Or what can be the reason that he's so long away ?'
' Oh ! hold your tongue, my darling son, your tears do grieve me
     sore ;
I fear he has been murdered in the fair of Turloughmore.

Come, all you tender Christians, I hope you will draw near ;
It's of this dreadful murder I mean to let you hear,
Concerning those poor people whose loss we do deplore
(The Lord have mercy on their souls) that died at Turloughmore.

It is on the First of August, the truth I will declare,
Those people they assembled that day all at the fair ;
But little was their notion what evil was in store,
All by the bloody Peelers at the fair of Turloughmore.

Were you to see that dreadful sight 'twould grieve your heart, I
    know,
To see the comely women and the men all lying low ;
God help their tender parents, they will never see them more,
For cruel was their murder at the fair of Turloughmore.

It's for that base bloodthirsty crew, remark the word I say,
The Lord He will reward them against the judgment-day ;
The blood they have taken innocent, for it they'll suffer sore,
And the treatment that they gave to us that day at Turloughmore.

The morning of their trial as they stood up in the dock,
The words they spoke were feeling, the people round them flock :
'I tell you, Judge and Jury, the truth I will declare,
It was Brew that ordered us to fire that evening at the fair.'

Now to conclude and finish this sad and doleful fray,
I hope their souls are happy against the judgment-day ;
It was little time they got, we know, when they fell like new-mowed
    hay,
May the Lord have mercy on their souls against the judgment-
    day.

The Lamentation of Hugh Reynolds

A STREET-BALLAD

    I copied this ballad from a broad-sheet in the collection of Mr. Davis ;
but could learn nothing of its date, or the circumstances connected with it. It
is clearly modern, however, and founded on the story of an abduction, which
terminated differently from the majority of these adventures. The popular
sympathy in such cases is generally in favour of the gallant, the impression
being that an abduction is never attempted without at least a tacit consent on the
part of the girl. Whenever she appears as a willing witness for the prosecution it
is said she has been tampered with by her friends, and public indignation falls
upon the wrong object. The 'Lamentation' was probably written for or by
the ballad-singers ; but it is the best of its bad class.
    The student would do well to compare it with the other street-ballads in the
collection ; and with the simple old traditional ballads, such as ' Shule Aroon '
and ' Peggy Bawn,' that he may discover, if possible, where the charm lies
that recommends strains so rude and naked to the most cultivated minds.
These ballads have done what the songs of our greatest lyrical poets have *not*

done—delighted both the educated and the ignorant.   Whoever hopes for an equally large and contrasted audience must catch their simplicity, directness, and force, or whatever else constitutes their peculiar attraction. —Note by Sir Charles Gavan Duffy, *Ballad Poetry of Ireland*.

My name it is Hugh Reynolds, I come of honest parents ;
  Near Cavan I was born, as plainly you may see ;
By loving of a maid, one Catherine MacCabe,
  My life has been betrayed ; she's a dear maid to me.[1]

The country were bewailing my doleful situation,
  But still I'd expectation this maid would set me free ;
But, oh ! she was ungrateful, her parents proved deceitful,
  And though I loved her faithful, she's a dear maid to me.

Young men and tender maidens, throughout this Irish nation,
  Who hear my lamentation, I hope you'll pray for me ;
The truth I will unfold, that my precious blood she sold,
  In the grave I must lie cold ; she's a dear maid to me.

For now my glass is run, and the hour it is come,
  And I must die for love and the height of loyalty :
I thought it was no harm to embrace her in my arms,
  Or take her from her parents ; but she's a dear maid to me.

Adieu, my loving father, and you, my tender mother,
  Farewell, my dearest brother, who has suffered sore for me ;
With irons I'm surrounded, in grief I lie confounded,
  By perjury unbounded ! she's a dear maid to me.

Now, I can say no more ; to the Law-board [2] I must go,
  There to take the last farewell of my friends and counterie ;
May the angels, shining bright, receive my soul this night,
  And convey me into heaven to the blessed Trinity.

---

[1] ' A dear maid to me.'   An Irish idiom ; meaning, not that she was much beloved by him, but that his love for her brought a heavy penalty with it—cost him dearly.   Observe the effect of this idiom at the close of the second verse.

[2] Gallows.

Willy Reilly

Willy Reilly was the first ballad I ever heard recited, and it made a pain-
fully vivid impression on my mind.   I have never forgotten the smallest incident
of it.   The story on which it is founded happened some sixty years ago; and
as the lover was a young Catholic farmer, and the lady's family of high
Orange principles, it got a party character, which, no doubt, contributed to its
great popularity.   There is no family under the rank of gentry, in the inland
counties of Ulster, where it is not familiarly known.   Nurses and sempstresses,
the honorary guardians of national songs and legends, have taken it into
special favour, and preserved its popularity.—Note by Sir Charles Gavan Duffy,
Ballad Poetry of Ireland.

'Oh! rise up, Willy Reilly, and come along with me,
I mean for to go with you and leave this counterie,
To leave my father's dwelling, his houses and free land;'
And away goes Willy Reilly and his dear *Coolen Ban.*

They go by hills and mountains, and by yon lonesome plain,
Through shady groves and valleys, all dangers to refrain;
But her father followed after with a well-armed band,
And taken was poor Reilly and his dear *Coolen Ban.*

It's home then she was taken, and in her closet bound;
Poor Reilly all in Sligo jail lay on the stony ground,
Till at the bar of justice, before the Judge he'd stand,
For nothing but the stealing of his dear *Coolen Ban.*

'Now in the cold, cold iron my hands and feet are bound,
I'm handcuffed like a murderer, and tied unto the ground.
But all the toil and slavery I'm willing for to stand,
Still hoping to be succoured by my dear *Coolen Ban.*'

The jailor's son to Reilly goes, and thus to him did say:
'Oh! get up, Willy Reilly, you must appear this day,
For great Squire Foillard's anger you never can withstand,
I'm afeer'd you'll suffer sorely for your dear *Coolen Ban.*

'This is the news, young Reilly, last night that I did hear:
The lady's oath will hang you or else will set you clear.'
'If that be so,' says Reilly, 'her pleasure I will stand,
Still hoping to be succoured by my dear *Coolen Ban.*'

Now Willy's drest from top to toe all in a suit of green,
His hair hangs o'er his shoulders most glorious to be seen ;
He's tall and straight, and comely as any could be found ;
He's fit for Foillard's daughter, was she heiress to a crown.

The Judge he said : ' This lady being in her tender youth,
If Reilly has deluded her she will declare the truth.'
Then, like a moving beauty bright, before him she did stand,
' You're welcome there, my heart's delight and dear *Coolen Ban.*'

' Oh, gentlemen,' Squire Foillard said, ' with pity look on me,
This villain came amongst us to disgrace our family,
And by his base contrivances this villainy was planned ;
If I don't get satisfaction I'll quit this Irish land.'

The lady with a tear began, and thus replied she :
' The fault is none of Reilly's, the blame lies all on me ;
I forced him for to leave his place and come along with me ;
I loved him out of measure, which wrought our destiny.'

Out bespoke the noble Fox,[1] at the table he stood by :
' Oh, gentlemen, consider on this extremity ;
To hang a man for love is a murder, you may see :
So spare the life of Reilly, let him leave this counterie.'

' Good my lord, he stole from her her diamonds and her rings,
Gold watch and silver buckles, and many precious things,
Which cost me in bright guineas more than five hundred pounds,
I'll have the life of Reilly should I lose ten thousand pounds.'

' Good my lord, I gave them him as tokens of true love,
And when we are a-parting I will them all remove ;
If you have got them, Reilly, pray send them home to me.'
' I will, my loving lady, with many thanks to thee.'

' There is a ring among them I allow yourself to wear,
With thirty locket diamonds well set in silver fair,
And as a true-love token wear it on your right hand,
That you'll think on my poor broken heart when you're in foreign
    land.'

---

[1] The prisoner's counsel, afterwards a judge.

Then out spoke noble Fox : ' You may let the prisoner go ;
The lady's oath has cleared him, as the Jury all may know.
She has released her own true love, she has renewed his name ;
May her honour bright gain high estate, and her offspring rise to
 fame ! '

The Night before Larry was Stretched

The authorship of this extraordinary piece of poetic ribaldry has been much
discussed, but the name of the modern Villon who uttered such an authentic
strain from *Là Bas* has never been discovered, if indeed it had any single
author. Probably it was mainly a sense of humorous contrast which led it for
a long time to be attributed to a dignitary of the Established Church, Dean
Burrowes. It is written in Dublin slang of the end of last century.

THE night before Larry was stretched,
 The boys they all paid him a visit ;
A bait in their sacks, too, they fetched ;
 They sweated their duds till they riz it :
For Larry was ever the lad,
 When a boy was condemned to the squeezer,
Would fence all the duds that he had
 To help a poor friend to a sneezer,
  And warm his gob 'fore he died.

The boys they came crowding in fast,
 They drew all their stools round about him,
Six glims round his trap-case were placed,
 He couldn't be well waked without 'em.
When one of us asked could he die
 Without having duly repented,
Says Larry, ' That's all in my eye ;
 And first by the clargy invented,
  To get a fat bit for themselves.'

' I'm sorry, dear Larry,' says I,
 ' To see you in this situation ;
And, blister my limbs if I lie,
 I'd as lieve it had been my own station.'
'Ochone ! it's all over,' says he,
 ' For the neckcloth I'll be forced to put on,

And by this time to-morrow you'll see
  Your poor Larry as dead as a mutton,
    Because, why, his courage was good.

'And I'll be cut up like a pie,
  And my nob from my body be parted.'
'You're in the wrong box, then,' says I,
  'For blast me if they're so hard-hearted :
A chalk on the back of your neck
  Is all that Jack Ketch dares to give you ;
Then mind not such trifles a feck,
  For why should the likes of them grieve you ?
    And now, boys, come tip us the deck.'

The cards being called for, they played,
  Till Larry found one of them cheated ;
A dart at his napper he made
  (The boy being easily heated) :
'Oh, by the hokey, you thief,
  I'll scuttle your nob with my daddle !
You cheat me because I'm in grief,
  But soon I'll demolish your noddle,
    And leave you your claret to drink.'

Then the clergy came in with his book,
  He spoke him so smooth and so civil ;
Larry tipped him a Kilmainham look,
  And pitched his big wig to the devil ;
Then sighing, he threw back his head
  To get a sweet drop of the bottle,
And pitiful sighing, he said :
  'Oh, the hemp will be soon round my throttle
    And choke my poor windpipe to death.

'Though sure it's the best way to die,
  Oh, the devil a better a-livin' !
For, sure, when the gallows is high
  Your journey is shorter to Heaven :
But what harasses Larry the most,
  And makes his poor soul melancholy,

Is to think of the time when his ghost
　　Will come in a sheet to sweet Molly—
　　　Oh, sure it will kill her alive !'

So moving these last words he spoke,
　　We all vented our tears in a shower ;
For my part, I thought my heart broke,
　　To see him cut down like a flower.
On his travels we watched him next day ;
　　Oh, the throttler ! I thought I could kill him ;
But Larry not one word did say,
　　Nor changed till he come to ' King William '—
　　　Then, *musha !* his colour grew white.

When he came to the nubbling chit,
　　He was tucked up so neat and so pretty,
The rumbler jogged off from his feet,
　　And he died with his face to the city ;
He kicked, too—but that was all pride,
　　For soon you might see 'twas all over ;
Soon after the noose was untied,
　　　And at darky we waked him in clover,
　　　And sent him to take a ground sweat.

' JOHNNY, I HARDLY KNEW YE '

While going the road to sweet Athy,
　　　　Hurroo ! hurroo !
While going the road to sweet Athy,
　　　　Hurroo ! hurroo !
While going the road to sweet Athy,
A stick in my hand and a drop in my eye,
A doleful damsel I heard cry :
　　' Och, Johnny, I hardly knew ye !

　　With drums and guns, and guns and drums
　　　The enemy nearly slew ye ;
　　My darling dear, you look so queer,
　　　Och, Johnny, I hardly knew ye !

' Where are your eyes that looked so mild ?
   Hurroo ! hurroo !
Where are your eyes that looked so mild?
   Hurroo ! hurroo !
Where are your eyes that looked so mild,
When my poor heart you first beguiled?
Why did you run from me and the child?
  Och, Johnny, I hardly knew ye !
       With drums, &c.

' Where are the legs with which you run ?
   Hurroo ! hurroo !
Where are the legs with which you run?
   Hurroo ! hurroo !
Where are the legs with which you run
When you went to carry a gun ?
Indeed, your dancing days are done !
  Och, Johnny, 1 hardly knew ye !
       With drums, &c.

' It grieved my heart to see you sail,
   Hurroo ! hurroo !
It grieved my heart to see you sail,
   Hurroo ! hurroo !
It grieved my heart to see you sail,
Though from my heart you took leg-bail ;
Like a cod you're doubled up head and tail.
  Och, Johnny, I hardly knew ye !
       With drums, &c.

' You haven't an arm and you haven't a leg,
   Hurroo ! hurroo !
You haven't an arm and you haven't a leg,
   Hurroo ! hurroo !
You haven't an arm and you haven't a leg,
You're an eyeless, noseless, chickenless egg ;
You'll have to be put wid a bowl to beg :
  Och, Johnny, I hardly knew ye !
       With drums, &c.

'I'm happy for to see you home,
     Hurroo ! hurroo !
I'm happy for to see you home,
     Hurroo ! hurroo !
I'm happy for to see you home,
All from the island of Sulloon,[1]
So low in flesh, so high in bone ;
     Och, Johnny, I hardly knew ye !
                    With drums, &c.

'But sad as it is to see you so,
     Hurroo ! hurroo !
But sad as it is to see you so,
     Hurroo ! hurroo !
But sad as it is to see you so,
And to think of you now as an object of woe,
Your Peggy 'll still keep ye on as her beau ;
     Och, Johnny, I hardly knew ye !

     With drums and guns, and guns and drums,
          The enemy nearly slew ye ;
     My darling dear, you look so queer,
          Och, Johnny, I hardly knew ye !'

THE CRUISKEEN LAWN

It would be difficult to imagine a more jovial, sly, rollicking and altogether irresistible bacchanalian song than the immortal 'Cruiskeen Lawn.' The English words and the Irish blend together most happily. The chorus is pronounced something like

     Grá-ma-chree ma crooskeen,
     Shlántya gal ma-voorneen
     'S grá-ma-chree a cooleen bán, &c.

á being pronounced as in 'shawl.' The meaning is :

     Love of my heart, my little jug !
     Bright health to my darling !
     The love of my heart is her fair hair, &c.

The origin of the poem is lost in obscurity. It probably sprang up, in its present form, in the convivial circles of eighteenth-century Ireland, and no doubt has a reminiscence of some Gaelic original. *Lán* = full.

---

[1] Ceylon.

LET the farmer praise his grounds,
Let the huntsman praise his hounds,
 The shepherd his dew-scented lawn ;
But I, more blest than they,
Spend each happy night and day
 With my charming little crúiscín lán, lán, lán,
 My charming little crúiscín lán.

Grádh mo chroidhe mo crúiscín,—
Sláinte geal mo mhúirnín.
 Is grádh mo chroidhe a cúilin bán.
Grádh mo chroidhe mo crúiscín,—
Sláinte geal mo mhúirnín,
 Is grádh mo chroidhe a cúilin bán, bán, bán,
 Is grádh mo chroidhe a cúilin bán.

Immortal and divine,
Great Bacchus, god of wine,
 Create me by adoption your son ;
In hope that you'll comply,
My glass shall ne'er run dry,
 Nor my smiling little crúiscin lán, lán, lán,
 My smiling little crúiscín lán.

And when grim Death appears,
In a few but pleasant years,
 To tell me that my glass has run ;
I'll say, Begone, you knave,
For bold Bacchus gave me lave
 To take another crúiscín lán, lán, lán,
 Another little crúiscín lán.

Then fill your glasses high,
Let's not part with lips adry,
 Though the lark now proclaims it is dawn ;
And since we can't remain,
May we shortly meet again,
 To fill another cruiscin lán, lán, lán,
 To fill another crúiscín lán.

SHULE AROON

A BRIGADE BALLAD

The date of this ballad is not positively known, but it appears to be early in the eighteenth century, when the flower of the Catholic youth of Ireland were drawn away to recruit the ranks of the Brigade. The inexpressible tenderness of the air, and the deep feeling and simplicity of the words, have made the ballad a popular favourite, notwithstanding its meagreness and poverty.—Note by Sir Charles Gavan Duffy, *Ballad Poetry of Ireland.*

I WOULD I were on yonder hill,
'Tis there I'd sit and cry my fill,
And every tear would turn a mill,
Is go d-teidh tu, a mhúrnín, slán!

    Siubhail, siubhail, siubhail, a rúin!
    Siubhail go socair, agus siubhail go ciúin,
    Siubhail go d-ti an doras agus eulaigh liom,
    Is go d-teidh tu, a mhúrnín, slán! [1]

I'll sell my rock, I'll sell my reel,
I'll sell my only spinning-wheel,
To buy for my love a sword of steel,
Is go d-teidh tu, a mhúrnín, slán!

    Siubhail, siubhail, siubhail, a rúin!
    Siubhail go socair, agus siubhail go ciúin,
    Siubhail go d-ti an doras agus eulaigh liom,
    Is go d-teidh tu, a mhúrnín, slán!

I'll dye my petticoats, I'll dye them red,
And round the world I'll beg my bread,
Until my parents shall wish me dead,
Is go d-teidh tu, a mhúrnín, slán!

    Siubhail, siubhail, siubhail, a rúin!
    Siubhail go socair, agus siubhail go ciúin,
    Siubhail go d-ti an doras agus eulaigh liom,
    Is go d-teidh tu, a mhúrnín, slán!

---

[1] In Mr. Halliday Sparling's IRISH MINSTRELSY Dr. Sigerson versifies this chorus gracefully, and almost literally, as follows :

    ' Come, come, come, O Love !
    Quickly come to me, softly move ;
    Come to the door, and away we'll flee,
    And safe for aye may my darling be ! '

I wish, I wish, I wish in vain,
I wish I had my heart again,
And vainly think I'd not complain,
Is go d-teidh tu, a mhúrnín, slán !

>   *Siubhail, siubhail, siubhail, a rúin !*
>   *Siubhail go socair, agus siubhail go ciúin*
>   *Siubhail go d-ti an doras agus eulaigh liom,*
>   *Is go d-teidh tu, a mhúrnín, slán !*

But now my love has gone to France,
To try his fortune to advance ;
If he e'er come back, 'tis but a chance,
Is go d-teidh tu, a mhúrnín, slán !

>   *Siubhail, siubhail, siubhail, a rúin !*
>   *Siubhail go socair, agus siubhail go ciúin,*
>   *Siubhail go d-ti an doras agus eulaigh liom,*
>   *Is go d-teidh tu, a mhúrnín, slán !*

IRISH MOLLY O

A STREET-BALLAD

Like ' Shule Aroon,' this ballad has been largely kept alive by virtue of the
beautiful and pathetic air to which it is sung.

OH ! who is that poor foreigner that lately came to town,
And like a ghost that cannot rest still wanders up and down ?
A poor, unhappy Scottish youth ; — if more you wish to know,
His heart is breaking all for love of Irish Molly O !

>   She's modest, mild, and beautiful, the fairest I have known—
>   The primrose of Ireland—all blooming here alone —
>   The primrose of Ireland, for wheresoe'er I go,
>   The only one entices me is Irish Molly O !

When Molly's father heard of it, a solemn oath he swore,
That if she'd wed a foreigner he'd never see her more.
He sent for young MacDonald and he plainly told him so—
' I'll never give to such as you my Irish Molly O ! '

>   She's modest, &c.

MacDonald heard the heavy news—and grievously did say—
'Farewell, my lovely Molly, since I'm banished far away,
A poor forlorn pilgrim I must wander to and fro,
And all for the sake of my Irish Molly O !'
                                She's modest, &c.

'There is a rose in Ireland, I thought it would be mine :
But now that she is lost to me, I must for ever pine,
Till death shall come to comfort me, for to the grave I'll go,
And all for the sake of my Irish Molly O !'
                                She's modest, &c.

'And now that I am dying, this one request I crave,
To place a marble tombstone above my humble grave !
And on the stone these simple words I'd have engraven so—
" MacDonald lost his life for love of Irish Molly O !"'
                                She's modest, &c.

THE MAID OF CLOGHROE

Air : 'Cailín deas cruithi-na-mbo.'
          (The Pretty Girl milking the Cows.)

As I roved out, at Faha, one morning,
    Where Adrum's tall groves were in view—
When Sol's lucid beams were adorning,
    And the meadows were spangled with dew—
Reflecting, in deep contemplation,
    On the state of my country kept low,
I perceived a fair juvenile female
    On the side of the hill of Cloghroe.

Her form resembled fair Venus,
    That amorous Cyprian queen ;
She's the charming young sapling of Erin,
    As she gracefully trips on the green ;
She's tall, and her form is graceful,
    Her features are killing also ;
She's a charming, accomplished young maiden,
    This beautiful dame of Cloghroe.

Fair Juno, Minerva, or Helen,
  Could not vie with this juvenile dame ;
Hibernian swains are bewailing,
  And anxious to know her dear name.
She's tender, she's tall, and she's stately,
  Her complexion much whiter than snow ;
She outrivals all maidens completely,
  This lovely young maid of Cloghroe.

At Coachfort, at Dripsey, and Blarney
  This lovely young maid is admired ;
The bucks, at the Lakes of Killarney,
  With the fame of her beauty are fired.
Her image, I think, is before me,
  And present wherever I go ;
Sweet, charming young maid, I adore thee,
  Thou beautiful nymph of Cloghroe.

Now aid me, ye country grammarians !
  Your learned assistance I claim,
To know the bright name of this fair one—
  This charming young damsel of fame.
Two mutes and a liquid united,
  Ingeniously placed in a row,
Spell part of the name of this phœnix,
  The beautiful maid of Cloghroe.

A diphthong and three semivowels
  Will give us this cynosure's name—
This charming Hibernian beauty,
  This lovely, this virtuous young dame.
Had Jupiter heard of this fair one,
  He'd descend from Olympus, I know,
To solicit this juvenile phœnix—
  This beautiful maid of Cloghroe.

C

JENNY FROM BALLINASLOE

This reads remarkably like a conscious burlesque on the hedge schoolmaster's style of love poem.

YOU lads that are funny, and call maids your honey,
　　Give ear for a moment ; I'll not keep you long.
I'm wounded by Cupid ; he has made me stupid ;
　　To tell you the truth now, my brain's nearly wrong.
A neat little posy, who does live quite cosy,
　　Has kept me unable to go to and fro ;
Each day I'm declining, in love I'm repining,
　　For nice little Jenny from Ballinasloe.

It was in September, I'll ever remember,
　　I went out to walk by a clear river side
For sweet recreation, but, to my vexation,
　　This wonder of Nature I quickly espied ;
I stood for to view her an hour, I'm sure :
　　The earth could not show such a damsel, I know,
As that little girl, the pride of the world,
　　Called nice little Jenny from Ballinasloe.

I said to her : ' Darling ! this is a nice morning ;
　　The birds sing enchanting, which charms the groves ;
Their notes do delight me, and you do invite me,
　　Along this clear water some time for to rove.
Your beauty has won me, and surely undone me ;
　　If you won't agree for to cure my sad woe,
So great is my sorrow, I'll ne'er see to-morrow,
　　My sweet little Jenny from Ballinasloe.'

' Sir, I did not invite you, nor yet dare not slight you ;
　　You're at your own option to act as you please :
I am not ambitious, nor e'er was officious ;
　　I am never inclined to disdain or to tease.
I love conversation, likewise recreation ;
　　I'm free with a friend, and I'm cold with a foe ;
But virtue's my glory, and will be till I'm hoary,'
　　Said nice little Jenny from Ballinasloe.

' Most lovely of creatures ! your beautiful features
   Have sorely attracted and captured my heart ;
If you won't relieve me, in truth you may b'lieve me,
   Bewildered in sorrow till death I must smart;
I'm at your election, so grant me protection,
   And feel for a creature that's tortured in woe.
One smile it will heal me ; one frown it will kill me ;
   Sweet, nice little Jenny from Ballinasloe ! '

' Sir, yonder's my lover ; if he should discover
   Or ever take notice you spoke unto me,
He'd close your existence in spite of resistance ;
   Be pleased to withdraw, then, lest he might you see.
You see, he's approaching ; then don't be encroaching
   He has his large dog and his gun there also.
Although you're a stranger, I wish you from danger,
   Said nice little Jenny from Ballinasloe.

I bowed then genteelly, and thanked her quite freely ;
   I bid her adieu, and took to the road ;
So great was my trouble my pace I did double ;
   My heart was oppressed and sank down with the load.
For ever I'll mourn for beauteous Jane Curran,
   And ramble about in affection and woe,
And think on the hour I saw that sweet flower,
   My dear little Jenny from Ballinasloe !

THE BOYNE WATER

   Sir Charles Gavan Duffy rightly observes that these fragments of the
original ' Boyne Water ' are far more racy and spirited than the song by
Colonel Blacker which has superseded them.

July the First, of a morning clear, one thousand six hundred and
   ninety,
King William did his men prepare—of thousands he had thirty—
To fight King James and all his foes, encamped near the Boyne
   Water ;
He little fear'd, though two to one, their multitudes to scatter.

King William call'd his officers, saying : 'Gentlemen, mind your
station,
And let your valour here be shown before this Irish nation ;
My brazen walls let no man break, and your subtle foes you'll
scatter,
Be sure you show them good English play as you go over the
water.'

. . . . . .

Both foot and horse they marched on, intending them to batter,
But the brave Duke Schomberg he was shot as he crossed over
the water.
When that King William did observe the brave Duke Schomberg
falling,
He rein'd his horse with a heavy heart, on the Enniskilleners
calling :

' What will you do for me, brave boys—see yonder men retreating ?
Our enemies encourag'd are, and English drums are beating.'
He says, ' My boys, feel no dismay at the losing of one com-
mander,
For God shall be our king this day, and I'll be general under.'

. . . . . .

Within four yards of our fore-front, before a shot was fired,
A sudden snuff they got that day, which little they desired ;
For horse and man fell to the ground, and some hung in their
saddle :
Others turn'd up their forked ends, which we call *coup de ladle.*

Prince Eugene's regiment was the next, on our right hand ad-
vanced,
Into a field of standing wheat, where Irish horses pranced—
But the brandy ran so in their heads, their senses all did scatter,
They little thought to leave their bones that day at the Boyne
Water.

Both men and horse lay on the ground, and many there lay
bleeding,
I saw no sickles there that day—but, sure, there was sharp
shearing.

Now, praise God, all true Protestants, and heaven's and earth's
   Creator,
For the deliverance that He sent our enemies to scatter.
The Church's foes will pine away, like churlish-hearted Nabal
For our deliverer came this day like the great Zorobabel.

So praise God, all true Protestants, and I will say no further,
But had the Papists gain'd the day, there would have been open
   murder.
Although King James and many more were ne'er that way in-
   clined,
It was not in their power to stop what the rabble they designed.

By Memory Inspired

Said to have been composed by J. Kearney, a Dublin street-singer, but
believed by Mr. D. J. O'Donoghue to have been merely popularised by him.
It is a fair example of the modern street-ballad.

BY memory inspired
   And love of country fired,
The deeds of MEN I love to dwell upon ;
   And the patriotic glow
   Of my Spirit must bestow
A tribute to O'Connell that is gone, boys—gone.
Here's a memory to the friends that are gone !

In October 'Ninety-Seven—
   May his soul find rest in Heaven !—
William Orr to execution was led on :
   The jury, drunk, agreed
   That IRISH was his creed :
For perjury and threats drove them on, boys—on.
Here's the memory of John Mitchel that is gone !

In 'Ninety-Eight—the month July—
   The informer's pay was high ;
When Reynolds gave the gallows brave MacCann ;
   But MacCann was Reynolds' first—
   One could not allay his thirst ;
So he brought up Bond and Byrne that are gone, boys—gone.
Here's the memory of the friends that are gone !

We saw a nation's tears
Shed for John and Henry Shears ;
Betrayed by Judas, Captain Armstrong ;
We may forgive, but yet
We never can forget
The poisoning of Maguire [1] that is gone, boys—gone :
Our high Star and true Apostle that is gone !

How did Lord Edward die ?
Like a man, without a sigh !
But he left his handiwork on Major Swan !
But Sirr, with steel-clad breast
And coward heart at best,
Left us cause to mourn Lord Edward that is gone, boys—
gone.
Here's the memory of our friends that are gone !

September, Eighteen-Three,
Closed this cruel history,
When Emmet's blood the scaffold flowed upon.
Oh, had their spirits been wise,
They might then realise
Their freedom—but we drink to Mitchel that is gone, boys—
gone.
Here's the memory of the friends that are gone !

THE SHAN VAN VOCHT

One of the most popular of Irish street-ballads.   Written in 1796, when the French fleet arrived in Bantry Bay.   The 'Shan Van Vocht' (Sean Bhean Bhocht) means 'The Poor Old Woman '—a name for Ireland.

OH ! the French are on the sea,
Says the Shan Van Vocht ;
The French are on the sea,
Says the Shan Van Vocht ;

---

[1] Father Tom Maguire, the well-known Catholic controversialist, who with other members of his family was poisoned, it was alleged, by his housekeeper, 1847.

Oh ! the French are in the Bay,
They'll be here without delay,
And the Orange will decay,
    Says the Shan Van Vocht.

  Oh ! the French are in the Bay,
  They'll be here by break of day,
  And the Orange will decay,
      Says the Shan Van Vocht.

And where will they have their camp ?
    Says the Shan Van Vocht ;
Where will they have their camp ?
    Says the Shan Van Vocht ;
On the Curragh of Kildare,
The boys they will be there,
With their pikes in good repair,
    Says the Shan Van Vocht.

  To the Curragh of Kildare
  The boys they will repair,
  And Lord Edward will be there,
      Says the Shan Van Vocht.

Then what will the yeomen do ?
    Says the Shan Van Vocht ;
What will the yeomen do ?
    Says the Shan Van Vocht ;
What should the yeomen do,
But throw off the red and blue,
And swear that they'll be true
    To the Shan Van Vocht ?

  What should the yeomen do,
  But throw off the red and blue,
  And swear that they'll be true
    To the Shan Van Vocht ?

And what colour will they wear ?
    Says the Shan Van Vocht ;
What colour will they wear ?
    Says the Shan Van Vocht ;

What colour should be seen
Where our fathers' homes have been,
But their own immortal Green?
    Says the Shan Van Vocht.

    What colour should be seen
    Where our fathers' homes have been,
    But their own immortal Green?
        Says the Shan Van Vocht.

And will Ireland then be free?
    Says the Shan Van Vocht;
Will Ireland then be free?
    Says the Shan Van Vocht;
Yes! Ireland shall be free,
From the centre to the sea;
Then hurrah for Liberty!
    Says the Shan Van Vocht.

    Yes! Ireland shall be free,
    From the centre to the sea;
    Then hurrah for Liberty!
        Says the Shan Van Vocht.

BOOK II

WILLIAM DRENNAN

THIS writer, the best of the poets of the 1798 Rebellion, was born in Belfast on May 23, 1754, and died on February 5, 1820. He was one of the strongest supporters of the Society of United Irishmen, whose original manifesto he wrote. In 1794 he was tried for sedition, but was acquitted. His verses, which are very few in number, are perhaps rhetoric rather than poetry, but the rhetoric is always strong and sincere. Most of them, apart from the national lyrics, appeared first in Joshua Edkin's COLLECTION OF POEMS, Dublin 1801 (restricted to Irish writers). He published FUGITIVE PIECES in Belfast, 1815, and a translation of 'The Electra' of Sophocles in 1817. He took particular pride in the fact of having invented the phrase 'Emerald Isle,' which occurs in a song highly extolled by Moore, but hardly deserving of his extravagant eulogy. His best piece is unquestionably 'The Wake of William Orr,' commemorating the execution of a respectable Ulster farmer who was convicted on perjured evidence, and whose name has never been forgotten in Ireland. The toast ' Remember Orr ' was for some years one of the watchwords of the aristocratic Whig party in England.   D. J. O'DONOGHUE.

ERIN

WHEN Erin first rose from the dark swelling flood
God bless'd the green Island, and saw it was good ;
The em'rald of Europe, it sparkled and shone—
In the ring of the world the most precious stone.

In her sun, in her soil, in her station thrice blest,
With her back towards Britain, her face to the West,
Erin stands proudly insular on her steep shore,
And strikes her high harp 'mid the ocean's deep roar.

But when its soft tones seem to mourn and to weep,
The dark chain of silence is thrown o'er the deep ;
At the thought of the past the tears gush from her eyes,
And the pulse of her heart makes her white bosom rise.
Oh ! sons of green Erin, lament o'er the time
When religion was war and our country a crime ;
When man in God's image inverted His plan,
And moulded his God in the image of man ;

When the int'rest of State wrought the general woe,
The stranger a friend and the native a foe ;
While the mother rejoiced o'er her children oppressed,
And clasp'd the invader more close to her breast ;
When with Pale for the body and Pale for the soul,
Church and State joined in compact to conquer the whole
And as Shannon was stained with Milesian blood,
Ey'd each other askance and pronounced it was good.

By the groans that ascend from your forefathers' grave
For their country thus left to the brute and the slave,
Drive the demon of Bigotry home to his den,
And where Britain made brutes now let Erin make men.
Let my sons, like the leaves of the shamrock, unite—
A partition of sects from one footstalk of right ;
Give each his full share of the earth and the sky,
Nor fatten the slave where the serpent would die.

Alas ! for poor Erin that some are still seen
Who would dye the grass red from their hatred to Green ;
Yet, oh ! when you're up and they're down, let them live,
Then yield them that mercy which they would not give.
Arm of Erin, be strong ! but be gentle as brave !
And, uplifted to strike, be as ready to save !
Let no feeling of vengeance presume to defile
The cause or the men of the Emerald Isle.

The cause it is good, and the men they are true,
And the Green shall outlive both the Orange and Blue !
And the triumphs of Erin her daughters shall share
With the full swelling chest and the fair flowing hair.
Their bosom heaves high for the worthy and brave,
But no coward shall rest in that soft-swelling wave.
Men of Erin ! awake, and make haste to be blest !
Rise, Arch of the Ocean and Queen of the West !

THE WAKE OF WILLIAM ORR

THERE our murdered brother lies ;
Wake him not with woman's cries ;
Mourn the way that manhood ought—
Sit in silent trance of thought.

Write his merits on your mind ;
Morals pure and manners kind ;
In his head, as on a hill,
Virtue placed her citadel.

Why cut off in palmy youth ?
Truth he spoke, and acted truth.
' Countrymen, UNITE,' he cried,
And died for what our Saviour died.

God of peace and God of love !
Let it not Thy vengeance move—
Let it not Thy lightnings draw—
A nation guillotined by law.

Hapless Nation, rent and torn,
Thou wert early taught to mourn ;
Warfare of six hundred years !
Epochs marked with blood and tears !

Hunted thro' thy native grounds,
Or flung *reward* to human hounds,
Each one pulled and tore his share,
Heedless of thy deep despair.

Hapless Nation ! hapless Land !
Heap of uncementing sand !
Crumbled by a foreign weight :
And by worse, domestic hate.

God of mercy ! God of peace !
Make this mad confusion cease ;
O'er the mental chaos move,
Through it SPEAK the light of love.

Monstrous and unhappy sight !
Brothers' blood will not unite ;
Holy oil and holy water
Mix, and fill the world with slaughter.

Who is she with aspect wild ?
The widow'd mother with her child—
Child new stirring in the womb !
Husband waiting for the tomb !

Angel of this sacred place,
Calm her soul and whisper peace—
Cord, or axe, or guillotine,
Make the sentence—not the sin.

Here we watch our brother's sleep :
Watch with us, but do not weep :
Watch with us thro' dead of night—
But expect the morning light.

MY FATHER

WHO took me from my mother's arms,
And, smiling at her soft alarms,
Showed me the world and Nature's charms ?

Who made me feel and understand
The wonders of the sea and land,
And mark through all the Maker's hand ?

Who climbed with me the mountain's height,
And watched my look of dread delight,
While rose the glorious orb of light?

Who from each flower and verdant stalk
Gathered a honey'd store of talk,
And filled the long, delightful walk?

Not on an insect would he tread,
Nor strike the stinging nettle dead—
Who taught, at once, my heart and head?

Who fired my breast with Homer's fame,
And taught the high heroic theme
That nightly flashed upon my dream?

Who smiled at my supreme desire
To see the curling smoke aspire
From Ithaca's domestic fire?

Who, with Ulysses, saw me roam,
High on the raft, amidst the foam,
His head upraised to look for home?

'What made a barren rock so dear?'
'My boy, he had a country there!'
And who then dropped a precious tear?

Who now in pale and placid light
Of memory gleams upon my sight,
Bursting the sepulchre of night?

Oh! teach me still thy Christian plan,
For practice with thy precept ran,
Nor yet desert me, now a man.

Still let thy scholar's heart rejoice
With charm of thy angelic voice;
Still prompt the motive and the choice—

For yet remains a little space
Till I shall meet thee face to face,
And not, as now, in vain embrace.

JOHN PHILPOT CURRAN

THE famous wit and orator was born at Newmarket, County
Cork, July 24, 1750, and died in London on October 14,
1817.   He wrote few poems, and the following sombre lament,
with its cry like that of the wind in a ruined house, is by far
the best of them.   It was founded on a chance encounter and
conversation with a deserting soldier whom he met on a
journey.

THE DESERTER'S MEDITATION

IF sadly thinking, with spirits sinking,
  Could more than drinking my cares compose,
A cure for sorrow from sighs I'd borrow,
  And hope to-morrow would end my woes.
But as in wailing there's nought availing,
  And Death unfailing will strike the blow,
Then for that reason, and for a season,
  Let us be merry before we go.

To joy a stranger, a way-worn ranger,
  In every danger my course I've run ;
Now hope all ending, and death befriending
  His last aid lending, my cares are done.
No more a rover, or hapless lover,
  My griefs are over—my glass runs low ;
Then for that reason, and for a season,
  Let us be merry before we go.

RICHARD BRINSLEY SHERIDAN

THE great Irish wit, orator and dramatist was born in Dublin,
1751 ; a son of Thomas Sheridan, an actor.   After a stormy life,
much of which belongs to English literature and much to
English history, he died in 1816, and was buried in Westminster

Abbey. The following graceful lyric, 'Dry be that Tear,' illustrates the well-known love of intricate verbal melody, and the taste for cunning devices of chiming sound which mark Gaelic poetry, and which frequently appear in Anglo-Irish verse.

DRY BE THAT TEAR

DRY be that tear, my gentlest love,
  Be hushed that struggling sigh ;
Nor seasons, day, nor fate shall prove,
  More fixed, more true, than I.
Hushed be that sigh, be dry that tear ;
  Cease, boding doubt ; cease, anxious fear—
     Dry be that tear.

Ask'st thou how long my love shall stay,
  When all that's new is past ?
How long ? Ah ! Delia, can I say,
  How long my life shall last ?
Dry be that tear, be hushed that sigh ;
  At least I'll love thee till I die—
     Hushed be that sigh.

And does that thought affect thee, too,
  The thought of Sylvio's death,
That he, who only breathed for you,
  Must yield that faithful breath ?
Hushed be that sigh, be dry that tear,
  Nor let us lose our heaven here—
     Dry be that tear.

SONG

HAD I a heart for falsehood framed,
  I ne'er could injure you ;
For, tho' your tongue no promise claimed,
  Your charms would make me true ;
Then, lady, dread not here deceit,
  Nor fear to suffer wrong,
For friends in all the aged you'll meet,
  And lovers in the young.

But when they find that you have blessed
    Another with your heart,
They'll bid aspiring passion rest,
    And act a brother's part.
Then, lady, dread not here deceit,
    Nor fear to suffer wrong,
For friends in all the aged you'll meet,
    And brothers in the young.

GEORGE NUGENT REYNOLDS

Born at Letterfyan, County Leitrim, about 1770 ; the son of a landowner in that county. He wrote numerous songs and poems for the Dublin magazines between 1792–95 ; published a musical piece called 'Bantry Bay' in 1797, which was performed at Covent Garden, and a poem in four cantos in 1791. The following is his best song. Several pieces have been attributed to him which he did not write. He died at Stowe, in Buckinghamshire, in 1802.

KATHLEEN O'MORE

My love, still I think that I see her once more,
But alas ! she has left me her loss to deplore,
    My own little Kathleen, my poor little Kathleen,
        My Kathleen O'More !

Her hair glossy black, her eyes were dark blue,
Her colour still changing, her smiles ever new—
    So pretty was Kathleen, my sweet little Kathleen,
        My Kathleen O'More !

She milked the dun cow that ne'er offered to stir ;
Though wicked to all, it was gentle to her—
    So kind was my Kathleen, my poor little Kathleen,
        My Kathleen O'More !

She sat at the door one cold afternoon,
To hear the wind blow and to gaze on the moon—
   So pensive was Kathleen, my poor little Kathleen,
     My Kathleen O'More !

Cold was the night-breeze that sighed round her bower ;
It chilled my poor Kathleen ; she drooped from that hour,
   And I lost my poor Kathleen, my own little Kathleen,
     My Kathleen O'More !

The bird of all birds that I love the best
Is the robin that in the churchyard builds its nest ;
   For he seems to watch Kathleen, hops lightly o'er Kathleen,
     My Kathleen O'More !

ANONYMOUS

KITTY OF COLERAINE [1]

Often wrongly attributed to Lysaght.

As beautiful Kitty one morning was tripping
   With a pitcher of milk for the fair of Coleraine,
When she saw me she stumbled, the pitcher down tumbled,
   And all the sweet buttermilk watered the plain.
'Oh, what shall I do now ? 'Twas looking at you now !
   I'm sure such a pitcher I'll ne'er see again.
'Twas the pride of my dairy. Oh, Barney McCleary,
   You're sent as a plague to the girls of Coleraine.'

I sat down beside her, and gently did chide her
   That such a misfortune should give her such pain ;
A kiss then I gave her, and before I did leave her
   She vowed for such pleasure she'd break it again.
'Twas the haymaking season—I can't tell the reason—
   Misfortunes will never come single, 'tis plain !
For very soon after poor Kitty's disaster
   The devil a pitcher was whole in Coleraine.

---

[1] Coleraine is generally pronounced in Ireland *Col'raine.*

D

THOMAS MOORE

THOMAS MOORE was born under the gloom of the Penal Laws.
His parents were Catholic, and he clung all his life to the
Church of his fathers. His patriotism he wore rather lightly,
but not his religion. That lay deep, and perhaps the best of
all his songs—'The Irish Peasant to his Mistress'—records the
love and honour he gave to the martyred church of Ireland.
He suffered from the laws against Catholics as a boy and a
young man. All avenues to distinction, even to education,
were closed against him. It was not till the Act of 1793 did
away with the worst of the remaining sanctions of the Penal
Code that he could even enter Trinity College, and he was
still excluded from its honours and emoluments. No wonder,
then, that he hailed, even as a boy, the French Revolution,
and seemed to see in it the dawn of deliverance for himself
and his people. He tells, in one of his Prefaces, how he was
taken by his father in 1792 to a dinner given in Dublin to
celebrate that great event, and how he sat on the knee of the
chairman while the toast went round—'May the breezes from
France fan our Irish Oak into verdure.'

These early experiences influenced his life and work as a
poet. They made him, as we should now say, a Liberal ; they
kept him a lover of Ireland even in the midst of the fashionable
society which he amused, enjoyed, and sometimes endured ;
they often intruded into the brilliant wit of his political satires
a passionate intensity which surprises the reader, as when in a
green grove full of flowers and butterflies a dark pine rises ;
and they were at the root of the power of the IRISH MELODIES.
All his life he waged war against intolerance and oppression,
and for this he deserves our gratitude. But he carried out the
war in his own way. It was not the way of the martyr, nor of
the stern patriot. The spirit of the writers of the ballads of
the *Nation* was not his. He was too light, too gay, too social
a creature to live or to write in that fashion ; and English

Society, with flattery and good living, laid its chains upon him. Had he resisted this Dalilah, even though he was not a Samson, he might have found that grave, indignant passion, that steady sincerity which would have chastened his lightness, reduced his exuberance, and drawn him down into those depths of feeling where the unnecessary in poetry is consumed. We see what might have been in a song like 'At the mid hour of night, when stars are weeping, I fly.' But he was led away from these impassioned regions, not only by the flattery of society, by the circumstances of the time which forbade to an Irish patriot all the means of fame, but also by his own nature. He was one to whom Anacreon was dearer than Sophocles, and his translations of that poet reveal the gay, witty, pleasure-loving character of the man. Their note remained an element in his poetry for the greater part of his life. How he could wed some of the spiritual Irish music to the bacchanalian words with which he degrades its Elfin mysticism, I have never been able to understand. And the worst of it is that these songs of wine and women were not, as poetry, true. He was neither a frank convivialist, nor much of a wandering lover. Had he been either one or the other with any force, the poetry would have been better. He only played with these subjects, flitting over them like a humming-bird. Anacreon, who was really in earnest, loses his reality in Moore's translations. There is not a trace of true passion, sensual or otherwise, in the 'poems of Mr. Little,' and the love scenes where Moore tries to be serious in LALLA ROOKH or the LOVES OF THE ANGELS resemble vital love as much as the sugar wreaths on a wedding-cake resemble living flowers. There are tender passages in his songs, of a sweet and natural emotion, but they belong to the friends and the wife he loved, and have nothing to do with the rest of his shallow, brilliant, and sometimes tinsel poetry. The man was thin, and, fortunately for his success, he did not know it. On the contrary, he believed himself, even though he was modest about it, to be a poet of substantial power. Such a faith enabled him to go on writing thousands of verses, with loose fertility, on every kind of subject. The society in which he lived was even more unreal than himself, and it saw all that it lazily cared for represented by Moore with a dazzling lightness and an insincere sentiment which exactly suited it. They turned, amazed and frightened by Byron's revolutionary force, repelled by Wordsworth's simplicity, to a poet who did not disturb them or indict their life, and who adorned the hours of their indifferent leisure with a filagree of sentiment, philosophy, classical and Oriental imagery, of women and wine and wit. It was a society which loved bric-à-brac, and Moore gave it bric-à-brac poetry of the best kind. Never was it better done ; and the verse had a melodious movement, as of high-bred and ignorant ladies dancing on enamelled meadows, which pleased the ear and almost seemed to please the eye. He was quite, then, in harmony with the society for which he wrote, and it would be rather surly of us if we judged him altogether from our standard of poetry and abused him for complying with the taste of his time. No one dreams of comparing him with the greater men, or of giving his poetry too important a place in the history of English song. But the man whose work Byron frankly admired ; whom Scott did not dispraise ; who received letters of thanks and appreciation from readers in America, Europe, and Asia ; who fulfilled Matthew Arnold's somewhat foolish criterion of a poet's greatness by being known and accepted on the Continent ; whom the Italians, French, Germans, Russians, Swedes, and Dutch translated ; whose LALLA ROOKH was partly put into Persian, and became the companion of Persians on their travels and in the streets of Ispahan ; to whom publishers like Longmans gave 3,000*l.* for a poem before they had even seen it, 'as a tribute to reputation already acquired'—can scarcely be treated with the indifferent contempt which some have lavished upon him. He pleased, and he pleased a very great number. Time has altered that contemporary verdict, and rightly—but when it is almost universal, not merely the verdict of a clique, it counts. It does not permit us, in judging of a poet, to throw his reputation altogether overboard. And indeed what he did, within his own range and at his lower poetical level, was well done

and original. The graver satires, such as ' Corruption' and
' Intolerance,' written in imitation of Pope, have neither weight,
humour, felicity of phrase, nor savage bitterness. He had no
more capacity for grave or cruel poetry than a butterfly has for
making honey or using a sting. But the lighter satirical poetry,
the TWOPENNY POST-BAG, the SATIRICAL AND HUMOROUS
POEMS, could not be bettered. They stand alone in their
excellence. They have a roguish happiness in their own wit,
and their wit is honestly brilliant. They are severe, but there
is so much gaiety in the severity that even those most sharply
attacked had no desire to revenge themselves. Even the Prince-
Regent—whom Moore, who was no toady, scarified—laughed
at the picture of himself, and enjoyed the mockery. We can
scarcely imagine, we whom no such wit illumines, how society
was charmed, tickled, and seasoned by *jeux d'esprit* which hit
the moment with such sagacity and mirth, and which, continued
for nearly thirty years, kept their freshness ; and even now
furnish weapons against 'that spirit of monopoly by which,
under all its various impersonations—commercial, religious,
and political—these satires were first provoked.'

A worthier subject for his song now occurred to him. It
was bound up with the associations of his childhood and the
patriotic and religious passion of his youth, with his sympathy
for the Irish rising and his friendship for Emmet. It was
mingled with his love of music and his talent for singing ; and
the music he fitted with lyrics was the creation of his native
land. All the depths which, though shallow enough, existed
in his nature, were stirred by this work, and among the songs
he wrote to Ireland's music his best poetry lies—the only
poetry of his which will continue to justly please mankind. ' It
was,' he says, ' in working the rich mine of my country's melodies
that my humble labours as a poet have derived their sole lustre
and value.' These songs have variety ; they touch both
tragedy and comedy. They drink, they dance and sing ; they
march to battle, they mourn over the dead ; they follow the
patriot to the scaffold and to exile ; they sing the scenery, the
legends, the sorrows, and the mirth of Ireland. They do this

work not in the best way possible. They have not the true Celtic touch either in joy or in sorrow. They are entirely devoid of mysticism ; they never belong to fairy-land ; and Moore did not conceive for a moment the haunted, obscure, and majestic darkness of the Celtic ancientry. Their patriotism is mostly on the surface—a sympathy more dainty than passionate, nurtured more by soft music than by salt tears. But a certain amount of patriotic feeling they do reach, as much as Moore, cossetted by English society, was capable of supporting. To as much of it as he felt, he was faithful, and openly faithful ; and this is a courage for which we may give him credit. He did more for Ireland than we think. He made her music charm the world. He brought by his singing of the Melodies (and though he had no power in his voice, he had a manner of singing which enchanted and thrilled his hearers) the wrongs and sorrows of Ireland into the ears and consideration of that class in society which had not listened to or cared for them before. It is not too much to say that Moore hastened Catholic Emancipation by his Melodies. Moreover, a natural sweet tenderness which was of the very essence of the man, but which rarely appears in his poetry, emerges and surprises in some of the IRISH MELODIES. How far this naturalness, sincerity, and pathos were due to the effect of the music upon him I cannot quite determine. 'I only know,' he says, 'that in a strong and inborn feeling for music lies the source of whatever talent I may have shown for poetical composition, and that it was the effort to translate into language the emotions and passions which music appeared to me to express that first led to my writing any poetry at all deserving the name.' This is as modest as it is true, and it supplies us with the best definition and criticism of all his serious poetry. That poetry is the translation of music into as pretty and melodious words as possible ; and the poetry varied in form, thought, and emotion as the music varied. LALLA ROOKH is the representation in words of the florid, fanciful music which pleased his time. When in the Irish music he touched a sadder, wilder, tenderer, and more imaginative music—which in its mirth was broken into plaintiveness, and in its plaintiveness turned on itself with laughter, which mingled with its note of joyous defiance the passionate pain of the exile for the home where so many brave men had died under oppression—he was lifted by the music into a higher region of poetry. What he heard, he wrote. Music was first, and poetry followed. This is not the case with a great poet. Music may illustrate his work, not create it. Poetry is first. That it was not first with Moore places him in a unique position among the poets, and accounts for that strangeness in his work which differentiates it from all the poetry which appeared in his time—indeed, from any other English poetry. It had no resemblance to Scott; it was wholly unaffected by the revival of naturalism in Wordsworth and Coleridge. The influence of Byron may be traced in it and in its subjects, but it was devoid of Byron's power and of his poetic passion. It was like nothing else ; and we may at least grant him the praise of originality. To this strangeness may perhaps be traced some of his amazing popularity ; LALLA ROOKH ran in a short time through twenty editions. His tragedies are absurd. The 'Veiled Prophet' is transpontine. Where the 'Fire Worshippers' has power, it is derived from his Irish hatred of intolerance and the remembrance of the oppression of his country. 'Paradise and the Peri' is melodious, but curiously insincere ; and 'Nourmahal' just suited Moore's prattling tenderness in love and his delight in ornamental description. It is a really pretty story of true love, told sometimes with grace and charm, and sometimes with irritating sentimentality. As to the prose insertions, which weave the various poems into a romance, they are not unworthy. They have the gilded quality of the poetry, but, like the poetry, they are readable in certain moods. It is easy to criticise LALLA ROOKH, like Fadladeen ; but it is pleasanter far, when the temper seizes us for that sort of thing, to pass into another age and listen to it, not for long, as the Princess listened to Feramorz.

In 1817 his visit to Paris awoke again his satirical Muse,

and the Fudge Family had nearly as much success as Lalla Rookh. He travelled then, and his Rhymes on the Road are only ' bad prose fringed with rhyme.' Owing to pecuniary difficulties, he lived in Paris till 1822, when the Loves of the Angels, the Fables for the Holy Alliance, and the kindness of some friends freed him from his trouble. The Epicurean, a prose tale, originally conceived as a poem—in which Egyptian, Greek and Christian philosophy are pounded together, as in a mortar, with Athenian gardens, pyramids, Nile temples, the Thebaid desert and mystic marvels—ended his poetic career. He lived to write a few more songs, the Life of Lord Byron, and an almost worthless History of Ireland.

Moore is neither a truly Celtic nor a truly English poet. The deep things in the Irish nature were not in him. No mysticism made him dream ; no hunger for the spiritual world beset him ; no fairyland, sometimes gracious, but chiefly terrible, was more real to him than the breathing world. No sadness without a known cause, no joy whose source was uncomprehended, influenced him. Nature did not speak to him of dreadful and obscure powers, or of beauty and love and eternal youth beyond mortal reach but not beyond immortal desire. The love of his country was no passion ; it was more that political hatred of intolerance and oppression which any honest Whig might feel, but which Moore felt deeply as a Catholic. None of these Celtic elements belonged to him, and they and others are at the roots of Irish imagination. Nor did he replace them by the elements of English imagination. His poetry is no more English than Irish in character. It does not grow naturally out of the tree of English poetry ; it is a graft upon it. He does not descend from any poetical ancestors in England, and he has had no influence on any of the English poets that followed him. He stands, as I have said, curiously alone. Had he had imagination, he would have been in brotherhood with either English, Scottish, or Irish poets. But he is a curious instance of a poet who never, save perhaps in one or two songs, deviates into imaginative work. On the other hand, he is a master in fancy, a poet so full of that power which plays with grace and brightness on the surface of Nature and man but which never penetrates, that few if any have ever showed so well what fancy could do, when quite alone, and enjoying herself, apart from her nobler sister, imagination. And Moore helped his fancy by collecting, with infinite care, heaps of material on which she could work. He ransacked classical and Oriental history, philosophy, botany, legendary lore, religion, dress, jewels ; everything to supply his fancy with illustrations, with subjects which she could entertain herself with ornamenting. No copiousness, no fertility is greater, in this region, than Moore's. And he brought to the help of his fancy a wit, an *esprit*, which made everything he touched with it sparkle and sing. Lastly, owing to his love of music, he gave to his poetry all the tenderness of which fancy is capable, and a melodious movement. a metrical flexibility, which delighted his contemporaries, and which has the power still of pleasing our later and more fastidious time.

STOPFORD A. BROOKE.

Thomas Moore was born in Dublin, 1779. His father was a native of County Kerry, his mother of Wexford. He was educated, like Sheridan before him, mainly at Samuel Whyte's excellent grammar-school. He entered Trinity College in 1794, the year after the partial repeal of the Penal Laws permitted a Roman Catholic to do so. Here Robert Emmet was one of his closest friends, and he was very nearly being involved with him in the United Irish conspiracy. In 1799 he went to London, bringing with him the reputation which his wonderful singing and playing had gained for him in Dublin society and the volume of translations from Anacreon which was his first published work. The introduction to the Prince of Wales set him on the high road to success, and his POETICAL WORKS OF THE LATE THOMAS LITTLE (1801) was much applauded and admired. He was appointed Admiralty Registrar at the Bermudas in 1803, and after a short visit to the island placed the duties of the office, after the usual practice of the day, in the hands of a deputy, and went on a tour through the United States and Canada. He returned to London in the winter of 1804. In 1806 appeared the ODES AND EPISTLES, which, on a severe review in the *Edinburgh*, led to an abortive duel with Jeffrey, afterwards one of Moore's closest friends. In the following year, 1807, began the publication of the IRISH MELODIES with music, arranged by Stevenson. The airs were taken chiefly from the collections of Bunting and Holden, and were mercilessly altered

(whether by Moore or his collaborator is unknown) to suit the musical taste
of the day. In the admirable edition of the MELODIES in which the
original airs have been at last restored by the hand of Dr. C. Villiers
Stanford it is suggested in the preface that Stevenson, who was much
under the influence of Haydn, 'imported into his arrangements a dim echo
of the style of the great Austrian composer. He could scarcely,' adds
Dr. Stanford, 'have chosen a model more unsuited for the wildness and
ruggedness of the music with which he had to deal. This probably led to
the alterations of scales and characteristic intervals (such as the flat
seventh) which are the life and soul of Irish melodies.' The publication
of the MELODIES went on at irregular intervals till 1834, Moore receiving
a hundred guineas for each song, or 12,810*l.* in all. In 1811 he married
a young actress, Miss Bessie Dyke. Save for the untimely death of all
the five children born of their union, his domestic life appears to have
been one of unclouded happiness, as it was certainly one of enduring
affection on both sides. The young couple settled first at Keyworth in
Leicestershire ; afterwards at other places in the country. About this time
Moore engaged to write a long narrative poem for Longmans, and that
publisher, before a line of the work was written, undertook to pay 3,000*l.*
for it—the highest sum ever as yet offered for a single poem. Moore shut
himself up with a library of Eastern books, and in 1815, after many
unsuccessful attempts, had written enough of LALLA ROOKH to submit to
the opinion of the publisher, who however declined to read it. In 1816,
the year following the battle of Waterloo, when England was passing
through an epoch of the deepest commercial depression, Moore with the
scrupulous honour which he carried into all business transactions
volunteered to let the publisher off his bargain. The latter, however,
refused to accept the offer, and LALLA ROOKH came out in 1817, achieving
an immediate and striking success and winning for its author a European
fame. Shortly afterwards a severe financial disaster befell him. His
deputy at the Bermudas turned out a rogue, and Moore found himself liable
to the Admiralty for 6,000*l.* of defalcations. Ultimately the debt was
reduced to 1,000*l.*, which was settled by a wealthy friend of the poet, Lord
Lansdowne, and shortly afterwards repaid to him by Moore. His NATIONAL
AIRS (1815) and SACRED SONGS (1816) had begun to rival the success of
the MELODIES. In 1817 a trip to the Continent gave the motive for
he FUDGE FAMILY IN PARIS and the other satires of the same series.

The LOVES OF THE ANGELS appeared in 1822, and FABLES FOR THE
HOLY ALLIANCE in 1823. In the following year Moore was the chief
actor in one of the most singular and mysterious episodes of literary history.
During a visit to Venice in 1819 Byron had presented Moore with his
memoirs, a striking testimony to the honour and discretion of his friend.
The death of Byron occurred in April 1824. Moore had in 1821 sold the

memoirs to John Murray for 2,000 guineas. It was evidently con-
templated both by Byron and by Moore that the memoirs should be
published after the death of their author. Yet immediately after that
event Moore repaid Murray the 2,000 guineas with interest, and induced
him to return the manuscripts, which he at once put in the fire. The only
thing we can feel certain of in regard to this strange transaction is that the
motive of it must have been honourable both to Moore and to his
publisher. Moore, however, did not eventually suffer by it, as he undertook
a LIFE OF BYRON (published in 1830), for which Murray paid him 4,000
guineas. About the same year the LIFE OF LORD EDWARD FITZGERALD
and the MEMOIRS OF CAPTAIN ROCK testified to the constant affection for
his native land which time and circumstances never weakened. His LIFE OF
SHERIDAN had appeared in 1825. During the later years of his life Moore
unwisely undertook to write a HISTORY OF IRELAND for Lardner's CABINET
CYCLOPÆDIA. The work, for which he eventually discovered himself to
be wholly unfitted, spread to four times the bulk originally intended, and
his intellect and energy sank under the burden. It turned out to be the
solitary failure of an unusually successful literary career. He died in 1852,
and was buried at Bromham near Devizes. His wife survived him for a
few years, and part of the literary pension of 300*l.* a year which Moore
had enjoyed since 1835 was continued to her for her lifetime.

THE SONG OF FIONNUALA

SILENT, O Moyle, be the roar of thy water ;
    Break not, ye breezes, your chain of repose,
While, murmuring mournfully, Lir's lonely daughter
    Tells to the night-star her tale of woes.
When shall the swan, her death-note singing,
    Sleep, with wings in darkness furl'd ?
When will heaven, its sweet bells ringing,
    Call my spirit from this stormy world ?

Sadly, O Moyle, to thy winter-wave weeping,
    Fate bids me languish long ages away ;
Yet still in her darkness doth Erin lie sleeping,
    Still doth the pure light its dawning delay.
When will that day-star, mildly springing,
    Warm our isle with peace and love ?
When will heaven, its sweet bells ringing,
    Call my spirit to the fields above ?

The Irish Peasant to his Mistress[1]

Through grief and through danger thy smile hath cheer'd my
way
Till hope seem'd to bud from each thorn that round me lay;
The darker our fortune, the brighter our pure love burn'd,
Till shame into glory, till fear into zeal was turn'd;
Yes, slave as I was, in thy arms my spirit felt free,
And bless'd even the sorrows that made me more dear to thee.

Thy rival was honour'd, while thou wert wrong'd and scorn'd,
Thy crown was of briars, while gold her brows adorn'd;
She woo'd me to temples, whilst thou lay'st hid in caves,
Her friends were all masters, while thine, alas! were slaves;
Yet cold in the earth, at thy feet, I would rather be
Than wed what I lov'd not, or turn one thought from thee.

They slander thee sorely, who say thy vows are frail—
Hadst thou been a false one, thy cheek had look'd less pale.
They say, too, so long thou hast worn those lingering chains,
That deep in thy heart they have printed their servile stains.
Oh! foul is the slander—no chain could that soul subdue—
Where shineth *thy* spirit, there liberty shineth too!

---

[1] The peculiar metre of this and the following poem is not uncommon
in Gaelic verse : *e.g.*

An raib tu 'g an g-Carraig, nó b-raca tú féin mo ġráò?
Nó a b-raca tú ġile, finne, 'gur rġéiṁ na mná?

From this source it seems to have found its way into English literature,
Shelley used it, dividing the lines differently, and with double rhymes, in
the lines written in 1822:

When the lamp is shattered,
The light in the dust lies dead;
When the cloud is scattered,
The rainbow's glory is fled.

and Swinburne in his Songs before Sunrise:

Who is this that sits by the way, by the wild wayside,
In a rent stained raiment, the robe of a cast-off bride?

At the Mid Hour of Night

At the mid hour of night, when stars are weeping, I fly
To the lone vale we lov'd, when life shone warm in thine eye ;
 And I think oft, if spirits can steal from the regions of air,
 To revisit past scenes of delight, thou wilt come to me there,
And tell me our love is remember'd, even in the sky.

Then I sing the wild song 'twas once such pleasure to hear !
When our voices commingling breath'd, like one, on the ear ;
 And, as Echo far off through the vale my sad orison rolls,
 I think, O my love ! 'tis thy voice from the Kingdom of Souls,
Faintly answering still the notes that once were so dear.

When He Who Adores Thee

When he who adores thee has left but the name
 Of his faults and his sorrows behind,
Oh ! say wilt thou weep, when they darken the fame
 Of a life that for thee was resign'd ?
Yes, weep, and however my foes may condemn,
 Thy tears shall efface their decree :
For Heaven can witness, though guilty to them,
 I have been but too faithful to thee.

With thee were the dreams of my earliest love ;
 Every thought of my reason was thine ;
In my last humble prayer to the Spirit above,
 Thy name shall be mingled with mine,
Oh ! blest are the lovers and friends who shall live
 The days of thy glory to see ;
But the next dearest blessing that Heaven can give
 Is the pride of thus dying for thee.

After the Battle

Night clos'd around the conqueror's way
 And lightnings show'd the distant hill
Where those who lost that dreadful day
 Stood few and faint, but fearless still.

The soldier's hope, the patriot's zeal,
 For ever dimm'd, for ever crost —
Oh ! who shall say what heroes feel,
 When all but life and honour's lost ?

The last sad hour of freedom's dream
 And valour's task mov'd slowly by,
While mute they watch'd till morning's beam
 Should rise and give them light to die.
There's yet a world where souls are free,
 Where tyrants taint not Nature's bliss : —
If death that world's bright opening be,
 Oh ! who would live a slave in this ?

THE LIGHT OF OTHER DAYS

OFT, in the stilly night,
 Ere Slumber's chain hath bound me,
Fond Memory brings the light
 Of other days around me ;
  The smiles, the tears,
  Of boyhood's years,
 The words of love then spoken ;
  The eyes that shone,
  Now dimm'd and gone,
 The cheerful hearts now broken !
Thus, in the stilly night,
 Ere Slumber's chain hath bound me,
Sad Memory brings the light
 Of other days around me.

When I remember all
 The friends, so link'd together,
I've seen around me fall,
 Like leaves in wintry weather,
  I feel like one
  Who treads alone
Some banquet-hall deserted,
  Whose lights are fled,
  Whose garlands dead,
 And all but he departed !

Thus, in the stilly night,
  Ere Slumber's chain hath bound me,
Sad Memory brings the light
  Of other days around me.

ON MUSIC

WHEN thro' life unblest we rove,
  Losing all that made life dear,
Should some notes we used to love
  In days of boyhood meet our ear,
Oh ! how welcome breathes the strain,
  Wakening thoughts that long have slept,
Kindling former smiles again
  In faded eyes that long have wept.

Like the gale that sighs along
  Beds of Oriental flowers
Is the grateful breath of song
  That once was heard in happier hours ;
Fill'd with balm, the gale sighs on,
  Though the flowers have sunk in death ;
So, when pleasure's dream is gone,
  Its memory lives in Music's breath.

Music ! oh how faint, how weak
  Language fades before thy spell !
Why should Feeling ever speak,
  When thou canst breathe her soul so well ?
Friendship's balmy words may feign,
  Love's are e'en more false than they ;
Oh ! 'tis only Music's strain
  Can sweetly soothe and not betray.

ECHO

HOW sweet the answer Echo makes
  To music at night,
When, rous'd by lute or horn, she wakes,
And far away, o'er lawns and lakes,
  Goes answering light !

Yet Love hath echoes truer far,
  And far more sweet,
Than e'er beneath the moonlight's star,
Of horn, or lute, or soft guitar,
  The songs repeat.

'Tis when the sigh in youth sincere—
  And only then—
The sigh that's breath'd for one to hear
Is by that one, that only dear,
   Breath'd back again !

As Slow Our Ship

As slow our ship her foamy track
  Against the wind was cleaving,
Her trembling pennant still look'd back
  To that dear Isle 'twas leaving,
So loath we part from all we love,
  From all the links that bind us ;
So turn our hearts as on we rove,
  To those we've left behind us.

When round the bowl of vanish'd years
  We talk, with joyous seeming—
With smiles that might as well be tears,
  So faint, so sad their beaming ;
While mem'ry brings us back again
  Each early tie that twined us,
Oh, sweet's the cup that circles then
  To those we've left behind us.

And when, in other climes, we meet
  Some isle or vale enchanting,
Where all looks flow'ry, wild and sweet,
  And nought but love is wanting ;
We think how great had been our bliss,
  If Heav'n had but assign'd us
To live and die in scenes like this,
  With some we've left behind us !

As travellers oft look back at eve,
  When eastward darkly going,
To gaze upon that light they leave,
  Still faint behind them glowing—
So, when the close of pleasure's day
  To gloom hath near consign'd us,
We turn to catch one fading ray
  Of joy that's left behind us.

NO, NOT MORE WELCOME

No, not more welcome the fairy numbers
  Of music fall on the sleeper's ear,
When, half-awaking from fearful slumbers,
  He thinks the full choir of heaven is near—
Than came that voice, when, all forsaken,
  This heart long had sleeping lain,
Nor thought its cold pulse would ever waken
  To such benign, blessed sounds again.

Sweet voice of comfort! 'twas like the stealing
  Of summer wind thro' some wreathed shell—
Each secret winding, each inmost feeling
  Of all my soul echoed to its spell;
'Twas whisper'd balm—'twas sunshine spoken
  I'd live years of grief and pain
To have my long sleep of sorrow broken
  By such benign, blessed sounds again.

MY BIRTHDAY

'My birthday!' What a different sound
  That word had in my youthful ears!
And how, each time the day comes round,
  Less and less white its mark appears!

When first our scanty years are told,
It seems like pastime to grow old;

E

And as youth counts the shining links
    That time around him binds so fast,
Pleased with the task, he little thinks
    How hard that chain will press at last.

Vain was the man, and false as vain,
    Who said, ' Were he ordained to run
His long career of life again,
    He would do all that he *had* done.'
Ah ! 'tis not thus the voice that dwells
    In sober birthdays speaks to me ;
Far otherwise—of time it tells
    Lavished unwisely, carelessly ;
Of counsel mocked ; of talents made
    Haply for high and pure designs,
But oft, like Israel's incense, laid
    Upon unholy, earthly shrines ;
Of nursing many a wrong desire ;
    Of wandering after Love too far,
And taking every meteor fire
    That crossed my pathway for his star !
All this it tells, and could I trace
    The imperfect picture o'er again,
With power to add, retouch, efface
    The lights and shades, the joy and pain,
How little of the past would stay !
How quickly all should melt away—
All—but that freedom of the mind
    Which hath been more than wealth to me ;
Those friendships in my boyhood twined,
    And kept till now unchangingly ;
And that dear home, that saving ark
    Where Love's true light at last I've found,
Cheering within when all grows dark
    And comfortless and stormy round.

CHARLES WOLFE

THE world is often spoken of as dull and blind to true excellence. It is a shallow view. Humanity bristles with sensitive tentacles which rarely fail to grasp and draw in anything that will nourish it, even if they sometimes, for a time, lay hold of things useless and unwholesome. Even thus the world's tentacles get hold of things, like the DISCOURSES of Epictetus or the RELIGIO MEDICI, that never were intended for publicity, nor do they fail to search out minuter things too. The Rev. Charles Wolfe, an obscure Irish clergyman, writes a short poem which a friend who had learned it recites to a casual travelling acquaintance. The latter publishes it in the *Newry Telegraph.* Soon it is on the lips of Shelley and Byron, and now there is hardly a reader of the English language who has not read the 'Burial of Sir John Moore.' Few indeed are the 'occasional' poems that possess so enduring a power to move the heart. Its note of pride and sorrow is tuned to that of all the lofty sorrows of the world, and the very music of the lines, with their long, deep vowel sounds, like the burst of solemn passion in Beethoven's Funeral March, will carry their meaning and emotion to readers of many generations hence.

Wolfe wrote but little poetry in his short life, and little of what he wrote can compare with the 'Burial Ode.' But the 'Song' which he wrote under the influence of a strain of Irish music, to which he was keenly sensitive, has a remarkable intensity of feeling and sweetness of melody. He had a keen affection for his native land and all that it produced, and though a descendant of the dominant class, and what we should now call an Imperialist, he could write lines like the following from his long poem on 'Patriotism':

> O Erin ! O my mother ! I will love thee !
> Whether upon thy green Atlantic throne
> Thou sitt'st august, majestic and sublime ;

E 2

> Or on thy empire's last remaining fragment
> Bendest forlorn, dejected and forsaken,—
> Thy smiles, thy tears, thy blessings and thy woes,
> Thy glory and thy infamy, be mine !

The selection here given includes one poem—a sonnet—not previously printed.   It is taken from a manuscript insertion bound up in a volume of the LIFE AND REMAINS OF THE REV. C. WOLFE (third edition, 1827) which was purchased in a second-hand bookshop in Dublin in 1888.   The volume has also bound up with it a leaf from *Bentley's Magazine*, vol. v., containing a German version of the ' Burial Ode,' and a copy of a note from Mr. Edmund Gosse in Ward's ENGLISH POETS, vol. iv. (1880), on the history of the Ode.   After these come two quarto leaves of older paper, and written in a quite differ-ent and evidently earlier handwriting.   They contain three hitherto unknown pieces alleged to be by Wolfe.   The first is entitled 'The Contrast : Lines written by the Rev. C. Wolfe while standing under Windsor Terrace.'   It is a poem on George III., reading like a hasty impromptu sketch of what might have been made a powerful piece of verse.   I may quote two stanzas :

> We have fought the fight.   From his lofty throne
>   The foe to our land we tumbled,
> And it gladdened each heart, save his alone
>   For whom that foe was humbled :
> His silver beard o'er a bosom spread
>   Unvaried by life's emotion,
> Like a yearly lengthening snowdrift spread
>   On the calm of a frozen ocean.
>
> Still o'er him Oblivion's waters lay,
>   Though the tide of life kept flowing ;
> When they spoke of the King, 'twas but to say,
>   ' The old man's strength is going.'
> At intervals thus the waves disgorge,
>   By weakness rent asunder,
> A piece of the wreck of the ' Royal George,'
>   For the people's pity and wonder.

Then comes the sonnet given below, and finally a poem

On hearing ' The Last Rose of Summer'—a melody on which
Wolfe wrote a prose story now extant.　The last stanza runs :

> Sweet mourner, cease that melting strain,
>> Too well it suits the grave's cold slumbers ;
> Too well—the heart that loved in vain
>> Breathes, lives, and weeps in those wild numbers.

T. W. ROLLESTON.

Charles Wolfe was the son of Theobald Wolfe, a landowner of the
County Kildare, of the same family as the hero of Quebec, now represented
by Richard Wolfe, Esq., of Forenaghts, County Kildare.　One of Theobald
Wolfe's tenants was Peter Tone, a coachmaker of Dublin, who called his
eldest son after his landlord — Theobald Wolfe—and thus caused the
name to be written deep in Irish history.　Charles Wolfe was born
in 1791, and was educated at Winchester, and Trinity College, Dublin,
where he was distinguished for high intellectual attainments and successes.
He took orders in 1817 (the year in which the ' Burial Ode ' was published),
and held curacies at Drumclog and Castle Caulfield, County Tyrone.　He
was intensely beloved by all conditions of people among his flock, for whom
he ruined his weak constitution in devoted work.　He died of consumption
in 1823, after a vain attempt to restore his health by a voyage to France.
His LIFE AND REMAINS have been published (1825) by the Rev. Archdeacon Russell.

THE BURIAL OF SIR JOHN MOORE

I

Not a drum was heard, not a funeral note,
　As his corse to the rampart we hurried ;
Not a soldier discharged his farewell shot
　O'er the grave where our hero we buried.

II

We buried him darkly at dead of night,
　The sods with our bayonets turning ;
By the struggling moonbeam's misty light,
　And the lantern dimly burning.

III

No useless coffin enclosed his breast,
　Not in sheet or in shroud we wound him
But he lay like a warrior taking his rest,
　With his martial cloak around him.

IV

Few and short were the prayers we said,
  And we spoke not a word of sorrow ;
But we steadfastly gazed on the face that was dead,
  And we bitterly thought of the morrow.

V

We thought, as we hollow'd his narrow bed,
  And smooth'd down his lonely pillow,
That the foe and the stranger would tread o'er his head,
  And we far away on the billow !

VI

Lightly they'll talk of the spirit that's gone,
  And o'er his cold ashes upbraid him ;
But little he'll reck, if they let him sleep on
  In the grave where a Briton has laid him.

VII

But half of our heavy task was done
  When the clock struck the hour for retiring,
And we heard the distant and random gun
  That the foe was sullenly firing.

VIII

Slowly and sadly we laid him down
  From the field of his fame fresh and gory ;
We carved not a line, and we raised not a stone—
  But we left him alone with his glory !

SONNET WRITTEN DURING HIS RESIDENCE IN COLLEGE

MY spirit's on the mountains, where the birds
  In wild and sportive freedom wing the air,
Amidst the heath-flowers and the browsing herds,
  Where Nature's altar is, my spirit's there.
It is my joy to tread the pathless hills,
  Though but in fancy—for my mind is free,
And walks by sedgy ways and trickling rills,
  While I'm forbid the use of liberty.

This is delusion, but it is so sweet
   That I could live deluded.   Let me be
Persuaded that my springing soul may meet
   The eagle on the hills—and I am free.
Who'd not be flatter'd by a fate like this?
To fancy is to feel our happiness.

LINES WRITTEN TO MUSIC

IF I had thought thou couldst have died
   I might not weep for thee ;
But I forgot, when by thy side,
   That thou couldst mortal be :
It never through my mind had past
   The time would e'er be o'er,
And I on thee should look my last,
   And thou shouldst smile no more.

And still upon that face I look,
   And think 'twill smile again ;
And still the thought I will not brook,
   That I must look in vain !
But when I speak—thou dost not say
   What thou ne'er left'st unsaid ;
And now I feel, as well I may,
   Sweet Mary, thou art dead !

If thou wouldst stay e'en as thou art,
   All cold and all serene,
I still might press thy silent heart,
   And where thy smiles have been.
While e'en thy chill bleak corse I have,
   Thou seemest still mine own :
But there I lay thee in thy grave—
   And now I am alone !

I do not think, where'er thou art,
   Thou hast forgotten me,
And I perhaps may soothe this heart
   In thinking too of thee :

Yet there was round thee such a dawn
Of light, ne'er seen before,
As Fancy never could have drawn,
And never can restore.

LUKE AYLMER CONOLLY

THE following poem is frequently printed as anonymous. It was written by Conolly, and is in his LEGENDARY TALES IN VERSE, published anonymously in Belfast in 1813. He was born at Ballycastle, County Antrim, graduated at Trinity College, Dublin, in 1806, and entered the Church. He died in or about 1833.

THE ENCHANTED ISLAND

To Rathlin's Isle I chanced to sail
When summer breezes softly blew,
And there I heard so sweet a tale
That oft I wished it could be true.

They said, at eve, when rude winds sleep,
And hushed is ev'ry turbid swell,
A mermaid rises from the deep,
And sweetly tunes her magic shell.

And while she plays, rock, dell, and cave,
In dying falls the sound retain,
As if some choral spirits gave
Their aid to swell her witching strain.

Then, summoned by that dulcet note,
Uprising to th' admiring view,
A fairy island seems to float
With tints of many a gorgeous hue.

And glittering fanes, and lofty towers,
All on this fairy isle are seen :
And waving trees, and shady bowers,
With more than mortal verdure green.

And as it moves, the western sky
  Glows with a thousand varying rays ;
And the calm sea, tinged with each dye,
  Seems like a golden flood of haze.

They also say, if earth or stone
  From verdant Erin's hallowed land
Were on this magic island thrown,
  For ever fixed it then would stand.

But when for this some little boat
  In silence ventures from the shore
The mermaid sinks—hushed is the note—
  The fairy isle is seen no more.

MARGUERITE A. POWER

NIECE of Lady Blessington, and a clever writer of verse.
Landor praised her poems on more than one occasion. She
was born about 1815, and died in July 1867. She wrote much
poetry for periodicals (such as *The Irish Metropolitan Magazine*, 1857–8) edited by herself, her aunt, and others, and also
several novels and a book of travel. The following is from
her best poem, 'Virginia's Hand,' which was separately published
in 1860 :

A HIDDEN ROSE-TREE

. . . . LATE at morning's prime I roved,
Where erst a garden bloomed, where now a waste
Of tangled vegetation, rank and wild,
Held sole pre-eminence—or so I deemed—
Till, turning from an alley long untrod,
And densely sheltered by o'er-arching boughs,
From whence, scarce half a foot above my head,
The shrieking blackbirds darted from the nest
My presence had invaded, I arrived
Upon a little space hedged closely round

With dark-leaved evergreens, but at the top
The blue sky spread its canopy, unbarred
By crossing boughs, and in his daily course
From east to west the genial sun would still
Grant it a smile in passing. 'Mid the shrubs
A strong white forest-rose had taken root
(Perchance been planted by a hand mine knew,
Now mouldering—O my heart, thou knowest where !)
And all the stem and lower boughs concealed
Amid the thicker evergreens, its top
Had struggled upwards towards the heaven above
'Gainst obstacles incredible, till now
Far o'er my head, among dark, polished leaves
Of laurel and stiff holly, it outspread
Its clusters exquisite of bud and bloom,
Some yet green-sheathed, some tinted at the heart
With faintest yellow, others shedding down
Their petals white, that lay like pearly shells
Receding waves have left on lonely shores.

GEORGE DARLEY

THE poems of George Darley are among the most curious
phenomena of literature. There are surely few as yet unacquainted with him who can read the verses here given
as specimens of his work without eagerly desiring to know
more of the writer. There are probably none who would
not be disappointed with the result of further researches.
Darley—the recluse, the poet, the mathematician, living
without distraction the ardent life of the spirit—could, as at
times in NEPENTHE, breathe forth a strain of such glorious
music that one might think it could only have been uttered
by a poetic genius of the highest order. But we read on,
and the brain becomes exhausted and benumbed. Dazzled
and weary, we seek a refuge from the unvarying blaze of

verbal splendour ; and there is no refuge but to shut the book. The Celtic intoxication of sounding rhythm and glittering phrase was never better illustrated than by George Darley. Frequently it happens that his verse, though always preserving in some curious way the outward characteristics of fine poetry, becomes a sort of *caput mortuum* ; the glow of life fades out of it. Or, again, it gives us only 'splendours that perplex' and leaves the spirit faint and bewildered. But when, as sometimes happens, spirit and sound, light and life, come together in their miraculous accord and form a living creation of spiritual ecstasy, then indeed we can yield ourselves wholly to the spell of the Celtic enchantment.

George Darley's work of course won cordial recognition from his brother-poets of the day. Tennyson offered to pay the expenses of publishing his verse ; Browning was inspired by SYLVIA ; Carey, the translator of Dante, thought that drama the finest poem of the day. But Darley, misanthropic, wayward, and afflicted with an exceptionally painful impediment in his speech which drove him from society in morbid isolation, seems never to have met his peers in wholesome human contact, and lived alone, burying himself in the study of mathematics, of Gaelic, and what not, weaving his rich and strange fancies, apparently indifferent to public approval or criticism, which indeed the public spared him by entirely ignoring him. He was author of several mathematical works said to show remarkable merit and originality.

T. W. ROLLESTON.

George Darley was born in Dublin, 1795 ; the eldest son of Arthur Darley, of the Scalp, County Wicklow. His family is believed to have come into Ireland with the Ulster Plantation. He entered Trinity College, Dublin, in 1815, and graduated in 1820. In 1822 he settled in London, and in the same year produced his ERROURS OF ECSTACIE (a dialogue with the moon), which was no doubt written in Ireland. Then followed THE LABOURS OF IDLENESS (prose and verse) by Guy Penseval, 1826 ; SYLVIA, a fairy drama, in 1827 ; and NEPENTHE, an indescribable rhapsody, in 1839. 1840 and 1841 saw respectively the publication of two tragedies, THOMAS À BECKET and ETHELSTAN, dramas in which the light of poetry plays but fitfully. He died in London in 1846.

A memorial volume of his poems containing several till then unprinted pieces has been published for private circulation by R. and M. J. Livingstone (A. Holden, Church Street, Liverpool).

From NEPENTHE

OVER hills and uplands high
   Hurry me, Nymphs ! O hurry me !
Where green Earth from azure sky
   Seems but one blue step to be ;
Where the Sun in wheel of gold
Burnishes deeply in her mould,
And her shining walks uneven
Seem declivities of Heaven.
Come ! where high Olympus nods,
Ground-sill to the hill of Gods !
Let me through the breathless air
Soar insuperable, where
Audibly in mystic ring
The angel orbs are heard to sing ;
And from that bright vantage ground,
Viewing nether heaven profound,
Mark the eagle near the sun
Scorching to gold his pinions dun ;
With fleecy birds of paradise
Upfloating to their native skies ;
Or hear the wild swans far below
Faintly whistle as they row
Their course on the transparent tide
That fills the hollow welkin wide.

HYMN TO THE SUN

BEHOLD the world's great wonder,
   The Sovereign Star arise !
'Midst Ocean's sweet dead thunder,
   Earth's silence and the skies.

The sea's rough slope ascending,
   He steps in all his beams,
Each wave beneath him bending
   His throne of glory seems.

Of red clouds round and o'er him
His canopy is roll'd,
The broad ooze burns before him,
A field of cloth of gold.

Now strike his proud pavilion !
He mounts the blue sublime,
And throws in many a million
His wealth from clime to clime.

True Loveliness[1]

It is not beauty I demand,
A crystal brow, the moon's despair,
Nor the snow's daughter, a white hand,
Nor mermaid's yellow pride of hair.

Tell me not of your starry eyes,
Your lips that seem on roses fed,
Your breasts, where Cupid tumbling lies,
Nor sleeps for kissing of his bed.

A bloomy pair of vermeil cheeks,
Like Hebe's in her ruddiest hours,
A breath that softer music speaks
Than summer winds a-wooing flowers,

These are but gauds.   Nay, what are lips ?
Coral beneath the ocean-stream,
Whose brink, when your adventurer slips,
Full oft he perisheth on them.

And what are cheeks, but ensigns oft
That wave hot youths to fields of blood ?
Did Helen's breast, though ne'er so soft,
Do Greece or Ilium any good ?

Eyes can with baleful ardour burn ;
Poison can breathe, that erst perfumed ;
There's many a white hand holds an urn
With lovers' hearts to dust consumed.

---

[1] In the first edition of the Golden Treasury this poem was printed
as anonymous among the seventeenth-century writers in Book II.

For crystal brows there's nought within,
  They are but empty cells for pride ;
He who the Siren's hair would win
  Is mostly strangled in the tide.

Give me, instead of beauty's bust,
  A tender heart, a loyal mind,
Which with temptation I would trust,
  Yet never linked with error find—

One in whose gentle bosom I
  Could pour my secret heart of woes,
Like the care-burthened honey-fly
  That hides his murmurs in the rose.

My earthly comforter ! whose love
  So indefeasible might be,
That when my spirit wonn'd above,
  Hers could not stay for sympathy.

THE FALLEN STAR

A STAR is gone ! a star is gone !
  There is a blank in Heaven,
One of the cherub choir has done
  His airy course this even.

He sat upon the orb of fire
  That hung for ages there,
And lent his music to the choir
  That haunts the nightly air.

But when his thousand years are passed
  With a cherubic sigh
He vanished with his car at last—
  For even cherubs die !

Hear how his angel-brothers mourn—
  The minstrels of the spheres—
Each chiming sadly in his turn
  And dropping splendid tears.

The planetary sisters all
  Join in the fatal song,
And weep this hapless brother's fall
  Who sang with them so long.

But deepest of the choral band
  The Lunar Spirit sings,
And with a bass-according hand
  Sweeps all her sullen strings.

From the deep chambers of the dome
  Where sleepless Uriel lies
His rude harmonic thunders come
  Mingled with mighty sighs.

The thousand car-borne cherubim
  The wandering Eleven,
All join to chant the dirge of him
  Who fell just now from Heaven.

From THE FIGHT OF THE FORLORN

THE CHIEF *loquitur:*

BARD! to no brave chief belonging,
  Hath green Eire no defenders?
See her sons to battle thronging,
  Gael's broad-swords and Ir's bow-benders!

Clan Tir-oer! Clan Tir-conel!
  Atha's royal sept of Connacht!
Desmond red! and dark O'Donel!
  Fierce O'More! and stout MacDonacht

Hear the sounding spears of Tara [1]
  On the blue shields how they rattle!
Hear the reckless Lord of Lara
  Humming his short song of battle! [2]

---

[1] Darley has a note deriving ' Tara,' originally ' Teamur,' from *Teach-mor*, or ' Great House '—the palace of the Irish Kings.

[2] This phrase evidently refers to the metrical structure of the Gaelic *Rosg-catha*, or battle-song.

Ullin's chief, the great O'Nial,
    Sternly with his brown axe playing,
Mourns for the far hour of trial
    And disdains this long delaying !

Gray O'Ruark's self doth chide me,
    Thro' his iron beard and hoary,
Murmuring in his breast beside me—
    ' On to our old fields of glory ! '

Red-branch crests, like roses flaming,
    Toss with scorn around Hi-Dallan,
Battle, blood, and death proclaiming—
    Fear'st thou still for Inisfallan ?

SAMUEL LOVER

THE versatility of Lover is one of the stock examples in Irish biography, and it is somewhat difficult to say in which of his various capacities he best succeeded. I am inclined to think that it is as a humorous poet that he ranks highest. He has many competitors in other branches of intellectual activity, but there are very few indeed who can be placed on the same level as a humorist in verse. His work as a miniature painter, as a composer, and as a novelist, excellent as it is, is likely to be forgotten long before such racy songs as ' Widow Machree,' ' Molly Carew,' ' Barney O'Hea,' and ' Rory O'More,' to name but a few of his best-known pieces, have become obsolete. There is an archness, an irresistible gaiety in these effusions to which it is difficult to find a parallel even among Irish writers. When he attempts the serious or sentimental, he generally fails lamentably. Humour is his most legitimate quality—he is the arch-humorist among Irish poets. He was born in Dublin on February 24, 1797, and gave early indication of his literary and musical gifts, to the annoyance of his father, a worthy stockbroker, whose intention it was to train him in business, and who disliked the arts. Finally his scruples were overcome, but the result was a permanent estrangement. The younger Lover began his career as a painter, and obtained very considerable reputation by his admirable miniatures of Paganini, Thalberg, and others, which were declared by competent judges to be worthy of the best professors of the art. Weakness of sight compelled him to turn to another means of livelihood, and he wrote many clever short stories, afterwards collected together in the two volumes of LEGENDS AND STORIES OF IRELAND. Subsequently he produced the longer stories known to most readers as HANDY ANDY ; RORY O'MORE ; and TREASURE TROVE : OR, HE WOULD BE A GENTLEMAN. These were illustrated by capital comic etchings of his own. Meanwhile his songs, nearly three hundred of which were set to music as well as written by himself, extended his fame far and wide. His more ambitious poetical efforts are weak, and the same thing may be practically said of his stories. He has never done anything in fiction better than BARNEY O'REARDON THE NAVIGATOR, and certainly his richly humorous songs are the only tolerable efforts of his Muse. He was granted a Civil List pension of 100*l*. in 1856, and after a long and prosperous life died in Jersey on July 6, 1868. In person he was almost as diminutive as his country-men, Tom Moore and Crofton Croker ; and, like them, he was very popular with all who had the pleasure of meeting him.

D. J. O'DONOGHUE.

WIDOW MACHREE

WIDOW MACHREE, it's no wonder you frown,
 Och hone ! Widow Machree,
Faith, it ruins your looks, that same dirty black gown,
 Och hone ! Widow Machree.
  How altered your air
  With that close cap you wear,
  'Tis destroying your hair
  That should be flowing free ;
  Be no longer a churl
  Of its black silken curl,
Och hone ! Widow Machree.

Widow Machree, now the summer is come,
 Och hone ! Widow Machree,
When everything smiles, should a beauty look glum ?
 Och hone ! Widow Machree.
   See, the birds go in pairs,
   And the rabbits and hares—
   Why, even the bears
   Now in couples agree—
   And the mute little fish,
   Though they can't spake, they wish—
 Och hone ! Widow Machree.

Widow Machree, and when winter comes in,
 Och hone ! Widow Machree,
To be poking the fire all alone is a sin,
 Och hone ! Widow Machree.
   Sure the shovel and tongs
   To each other belongs,
   While the kettle sings songs
   Full of family glee !
   Yet alone with your cup,
   Like a hermit you sup,
 Och hone ! Widow Machree.

And how do you know, with the comforts I've towld,
 Och hone ! Widow Machree,
But you're keeping some poor fellow out in the cowld ?
 Och hone ! Widow Machree.
   With such sins on your head
   Sure your peace would be fled,
   Could you sleep in your bed
   Without thinking to see
   Some ghost or some sprite
   That would wake you at night,
 Crying, ' Och hone ! Widow Machree !'

Then take my advice, darling Widow Machree,
 Och hone ! Widow Machree,
And, with my advice, faith, I wish you'd take me,
 Och hone ! Widow Machree.

You'd have me to desire
Then to stir up the fire ;
And sure Hope is no liar
In whisp'ring to me
That the ghosts would depart
When you'd me near your heart,
Och hone ! Widow Machree !

BARNEY O'HEA

Now let me alone, though I know you won't,
    Impudent Barney O'Hea !
        It makes me outrageous
        When you're so contagious,
And you'd better look out for the stout Corney Creagh ;
        For he is the boy
        That believes I'm his joy,
So you'd better behave yourself, Barney O'Hea !
        Impudent Barney,
        None of your blarney,
        Impudent Barney O'Hea !

I hope you're not going to Bandon Fair,
For indeed I'm not wanting to meet you there,
        Impudent Barney O'Hea !
        For Corney's at Cork,
        And my brother's at work,
And my mother sits spinning at home all the day,
        So no one will be there
        Of poor me to take care,
So I hope you won't follow me, Barney O'Hea !
        Impudent Barney,
        None of your blarney,
        Impudent Barney O'Hea !

But as I was walking up Bandon Street,
Just who do you think that myself should meet,
        But impudent Barney O'Hea !
        He said I looked killin',
        I called him a villain,

F 2

And bid him that minute get out of the way,
  He said I was joking,
  And grinned so provoking,
I couldn't help laughing at Barney O'Hea!
  Impudent Barney,
  None of your blarney,
  Impudent Barney O'Hea!

He knew 'twas all right when he saw me smile,
For he was the rogue up to ev'ry wile,
  Impudent Barney O'Hea!
  He coaxed me to choose him,
  For if I'd refuse him
He swore he'd kill Corney the very next day;
  So, for fear 'twould go further,
  And just to save murther,
I think I must marry that madcap, O'Hea!
  Bothering Barney,
  'Tis he has the blarney
  To make a girl Mistress O'Hea.

RORY O'MORE

YOUNG Rory O'More courted Kathleen bawn,
He was bold as a hawk, and she soft as the dawn;
He wish'd in his heart pretty Kathleen to please,
And he thought the best way to do that was to tease.
'Now, Rory, be aisy,' sweet Kathleen would cry,
Reproof on her lips, but a smile in her eye;
'With your tricks I don't know, in troth, what I'm about,
Faith, you've teased till I've put on my cloak inside out.'
'Oh! jewel,' says Rory, 'that same is the way
You've thrated my heart for this many a day,
And 'tis plaz'd that I am, and why not, to be sure?
For 'tis all for good luck,' says bold Rory O'More.

'Indeed, then,' says Kathleen, 'don't think of the like,
For I half gave a promise to soothering Mike;
The ground that I walk on he loves, I'll be bound.'
'Faith,' says Rory, 'I'd rather love you than the ground.'

'Now, Rory, I'll cry, if you don't let me go ;
Sure I dream ev'ry night that I'm hating you so !'
'Oh !' says Rory, 'that same I'm delighted to hear,
For dhrames always go by contrairies, my dear !
Oh ! jewel, keep dreaming that same till you die,
And bright morning will give dirty night the black lie ;
And 'tis plaz'd that I am, and why not, to be sure?
Since 'tis all for good luck,' says bold Rory O'More.

'Arrah, Kathleen, my darlint, you've teaz'd me enough,
Sure I've thrash'd, for your sake, Dinny Grimes and Jim Duff ;
And I've made myself, drinking your health, quite a baste,
So I think, after that, I may talk to the priest.'
Then Rory, the rogue, stole his arm round her neck,
So soft and so white, without freckle or speck,
And he look'd in her eyes that were beaming with light,
And he kiss'd her sweet lips,—don't you think he was right?
'Now, Rory, leave off, sir ; you'll hug me no more ;
That's eight times to-day that you've kiss'd me before.'
'Then here goes another,' says he, ' to make sure,
For there's luck in odd numbers,' says Rory O'More.

CHARLES JAMES LEVER

SCATTERED through Lever's novels are numerous songs, often
as brilliant and racy as his inimitable prose. Unlike his later
prose, however, which in novels like THE O'DONOGHUE and
THE KNIGHT OF GWYNNE showed a power responsive to the
deepening intellectual interest of his work, his verse, when
he tried to be serious, rarely achieved more than sentimentality. The pieces here given seem as good as things of
the kind can be. Their gay humour is irresistible, and their
language and rhythm are handled by a veritable master of his
craft.

Lever was born in Dublin in 1806, and was the son of an
English contractor. He graduated in Trinity College, Dublin,

1827, and afterwards became an M.D. of Louvain. He did much journalistic work in Dublin, besides practising successfully as a physician, and edited *The Dublin University Magazine*— with which so many distinguished Irish men of letters have been connected—from 1842 to 1845. He received a Consular appointment at Spezzia in 1858, and died Consul at Trieste in 1872.

LARRY M'HALE

OH, Larry M'Hale he had little to fear,
  And never could want when the crops didn't fail ;
He'd a house and demesne and eight hundred a year,
  And a heart for to spend it, had Larry M'Hale !
The soul of a party, the life of a feast,
  And an illigant song he could sing, I'll be bail ;
He would ride with the rector, and drink with the priest,
  Oh ! the broth of a boy was old Larry M'Hale.

It's little he cared for the Judge or Recorder ;
  His house was as big and as strong as a gaol ;
With a cruel four-pounder he kept in great order
  He'd murder the country, would Larry M'Hale.
He'd a blunderbuss too ; of horse-pistols a pair !
  But his favourite weapon was always a flail ;
I wish you could see how he'd empty a fair,
  For he handled it nately, did Larry M'Hale.

His ancestors were kings before Moses was born,
  His mother descended from great Grana Uaile :
He laughed all the Blakes and the Frenches to scorn ;
  They were mushrooms compared to old Larry M'Hale.
He sat down every day to a beautiful dinner,
  With cousins and uncles enough for a tail ;
And, though loaded with debt, oh ! the devil a thinner
  Could law or the sheriff make Larry M'Hale.

With a larder supplied and a cellar well stored,
  None lived half so well, from Fair-Head to Kinsale ;
As he piously said, ' I've a plentiful board,
  And the Lord He is good to old Larry M'Hale.'

So fill up your glass, and a high bumper give him,
  It's little we'd care for the tithes or Repale ;
For Ould Erin would be a fine country to live in,
  If we only had plenty like LARRY M'HALE.

THE WIDOW MALONE

DID ye hear of the widow Malone,
                  Ohone !
Who lived in the town of Athlone,
                  Alone ?
Oh ! she melted the hearts
Of the swains in them parts—
So lovely the widow Malone,
                  Ohone !
So lovely the widow Malone.

Of lovers she had a full score
                  Or more ;
And fortunes they all had galore,
                  In store ;
From the minister down
To the Clerk of the Crown,
All were courting the widow Malone,
                  Ohone !
All were courting the widow Malone.

But so modest was Mistress Malone,
                  'Twas known
No one ever could see her alone,
                  Ohone !
Let them ogle and sigh,
They could ne'er catch her eye—
So bashful the widow Malone,
                  Ohone !
So bashful the widow Malone.

Till one Mr. O'Brien from Clare—
                  How quare !
It's little for blushing they care
                  Down there—

Put his arm round her waist,
Took ten kisses at laste—
'Oh,' says he, 'you're my Molly Malone—
        My own !'
'Oh,' says he, 'you're my Molly Malone !'

And the widow they all thought so shy,
        My eye !
Ne'er thought of a simper or sigh —
        For why ?
But, ' Lucius,' says she,
'Since you've now made so free,
You may marry your Molly Malone,
        Ohone !
You may marry your Molly Malone.'

There's a moral contained in my song,
        Not wrong,
And, one comfort, it's not very long,
        But strong :
If for widows you die,
Learn *to kiss*, not to sigh,
For they're all like sweet Mistress Malone !
        Ohone !
Oh ! they're very like Mistress Malone !

FRANCIS SYLVESTER MAHONY
('FATHER PROUT ')

THE well-known scholar and wit was born in Cork in 1804, and
died in Paris on May 18, 1866. He became a Jesuit priest,
but concerned himself more with literature and journalism than
with a religious calling. He wrote the famous 'Reliques of
Father Prout' for *Fraser's Magazine*, and afterwards became
Roman correspondent of *The Daily News* and Paris
correspondent of *The Globe*. Most of his writings have been
collected. The following is his nearest approach to poetry :

THE BELLS OF SHANDON

WITH deep affection and recollection
  I often think of the Shandon bells,
Whose sounds so wild would, in days of childhood,
  Fling round my cradle their magic spells.
On this I ponder, where'er I wander,
  And thus grow fonder, sweet Cork, of thee ;
      With thy bells of Shandon,
      That sound so grand on
  The pleasant waters of the river Lee.

I have heard bells chiming full many a clime in,
  Tolling sublime in cathedral shrine ;
While at a glib rate brass tongues would vibrate,
  But all their muśic spoke nought to thine ;
For memory dwelling on each proud swelling
  Of thy belfry knelling its bold notes free,
      Made the bells of Shandon
      Sound far more grand on
  The pleasant waters of the river Lee.

I have heard bells tolling ' old Adrian's mole' in,
  Their thunder rolling from the Vatican,
With cymbals glorious, swinging uproarious
  In the gorgeous turrets of Notre Dame ;
But thy sounds were sweeter than the dome of Peter
  Flings o'er the Tiber, pealing solemnly.
      Oh ! the bells of Shandon
      Sound far more grand on
  The pleasant waters of the river Lee.

There's a bell in Moscow, while on tower and Kiosko
  In St. Sophia the Turkman gets,
And loud in air calls men to prayer
  From the tapering summit of tall minarets.
Such empty phantom I freely grant 'em,
  But there's an anthem more dear to me :
      'Tis the bells of Shandon,
      That sound so grand on
  The pleasant waters of the river Lee.

JOHN FRANCIS WALLER

BORN in Limerick in 1809, and graduated LL.D. at Trinity College, Dublin, in 1852. He was called to the Irish Bar, but mainly occupied himself with literature. He wrote much verse and prose for *The Dublin University Magazine*, which he edited for a time, and received an official appointment in Dublin in 1867. He has written many poems, including some excellent lyrics, and is also the author and editor of other works. His poems are to be found in five different volumes—RAVENS-CROFT HILL, 1852 ; THE DEAD BRIDAL, 1854 ; POEMS, 1854 ; OCCASIONAL ODES, 1864 ; PETER BROWN, 1872.

THE SPINNING-WHEEL

MELLOW the moonlight to shine is beginning,
Close by the window young Eileen is spinning ;
Bent o'er the fire her blind grandmother, sitting,
Is crooning, and moaning, and drowsily knitting :—
' Eileen, *achora*, I hear some one tapping.'
' 'Tis the ivy, dear mother, against the glass flapping.'
' Eily, I surely hear somebody sighing.'
' 'Tis the sound, mother dear, of the summer wind dying.'
   Merrily, cheerily, noiselessly whirring,
     Swings the wheel, spins the wheel, while the foot's stirring ;
   Sprightly, and brightly, and airily ringing
     Thrills the sweet voice of the young maiden singing.

' What's that noise that I hear at the window, I wonder ?'
' 'Tis the little birds chirping the holly-bush under.'
' What makes you be shoving and moving your stool on,
And singing, all wrong, that old song of " The Coolun " ?'
There's a form at the casement—the form of her true love—
And he whispers, with face bent, ' I'm waiting for you, love ;
Get up on the stool, through the lattice step lightly,
We'll rove in the grove while the moon's shining brightly. '
   Merrily, cheerily, noiselessly whirring, &c.

The maid shakes her head, on her lips lays her fingers,
Steals up from her seat—longs to go, and yet lingers ;
A frightened glance turns to her drowsy grandmother,
Puts one foot on the stool, spins the wheel with the other.
Lazily, easily, swings now the wheel round,
Slowly and lowly is heard now the reel's sound ;
Noiseless and light to the lattice above her
The maid steps—then leaps to the arms of her lover.

Slower—and slower—and slower the wheel swings ;
Lower—and lower—and lower the reel rings ;
Ere the reel and the wheel stopped their ringing and
  moving,
Through the grove the young lovers by moonlight are
  roving.

KITTY NEIL

AH, sweet Kitty Neil, rise up from that wheel,
  Your neat little foot will be weary from spinning.
Come, trip down with me to the sycamore-tree ;
  Half the parish is there, and the dance is beginning.
The sun is gone down, but the full harvest moon
  Shines sweetly and cool in the dew-whitened valley ;
While all the air rings with the soft loving things
  Each little bird sings in the green-shaded alley.

With a blush and a smile Kitty rose up the while,
  Her eye in the glass, as she bound her hair, glancing ;
'Tis hard to refuse when a young lover sues—
  So she couldn't but choose to go off to the dancing.
And now on the green the glad couples are seen,
  Each gay-hearted lad with the lass of his choosing ;
And Pat without fail leads out sweet Kitty Neil—
  Somehow, when he asked, she ne'er thought of refusing.

Now Felix Magee puts his pipes to his knee,
  And with flourish so free sets each couple in motion ;
With a cheer and a bound the boys patter the ground,
  The maids move around just like swans on the ocean,

Cheeks bright as the rose, feet light as the doe's,
  Now coyly retiring, now boldly advancing ;
Search the world all around, from the sky to the ground,
  No such sight can be found as an Irish lass dancing.

Sweet Kate, who could view your bright eyes of deep blue,
  Beaming humidly through their dark lashes so mildly,
Your fair-turned arm, heaving breast, rounded form,
  Nor feel his heart warm, and his pulses throb wildly ?
Young Pat feels his heart, as he gazes, depart,
  Subdued by the smart of such painful, yet sweet love ;
The sight leaves his eye, as he cries with a sigh,
  ' Dance light, for my heart it lies under your feet, love.'

WILLIAM CARLETON

THE great Irish novelist was born at Prillisk, County Tyrone, in 1794 ; the son of a small farmer. He was educated chiefly by one Patrick Frayne, whose unfading portrait as Mat Kavanagh was afterwards drawn in ' The Hedge School.' He was at first, like many of the clever sons of Irish peasant families, intended for the priesthood. The experiences of his schooldays, the story how he became a Ribbonman, the Orange and Catholic disturbances, the merry-makings of the people, Carleton's fights, loves, early marriage, and adventures in search of education and livelihood, are told in his own inimitable manner in the AUTOBIOGRAPHY, lately edited by Mr. D. J. O'Donoghue. Having become a Protestant, he made his *début* in literature as a contributor of stories of Irish peasant life to *The Christian Examiner*, lately started by Cæsar Otway. He contributed a few poems to the same magazine. ' Sir Turlough ' appeared in 1839 in *The National Magazine*, edited by Charles Lever. After a life in which there was much of gaiety, much of gloom, and in spite of his literary success much struggle with penury, he died, famous and beloved, in 1869. Since 1848 he had been in receipt of a Civil List pension of 200*l.* a year.

SIR TURLOUGH; OR, THE CHURCHYARD BRIDE [1]

In the churchyard of Erigle Truagh, in the barony of Truagh, County Monaghan, there is said to be a Spirit which appears to persons whose families are there interred. Its appearance, which is generally made in the following manner, is uniformly fatal, being an omen of death to those who are so unhappy as to meet with it. When a funeral takes place, it watches the person who remains last in the graveyard, over whom it possesses a fascinating influence. If the loiterer be a young man, it takes the shape of a beautiful female, inspires him with a charmed passion, and exacts a promise to meet in the churchyard on a month from that day; this promise is sealed by a kiss, which communicates a deadly taint to the individual who receives it. It then disappears, and no sooner does the young man quit the churchyard than he remembers the history of the spectre—which is well known in the parish—sinks into despair, dies, and is buried in the place of appointment on the day when the promise was to have been fulfilled. If, on the contrary, it appears to a female, it assumes the form of a young man of exceeding elegance and beauty. Some years ago I was shown the grave of a young person, about eighteen years of age, who was said to have fallen a victim to it: and it is not more than ten months since a man in the same parish declared that he gave the promise and the fatal kiss, and consequently looked upon himself as lost. He took a fever, died, and was buried on the day appointed for the meeting, which was exactly a month from that of the interview. There are several cases of the same kind mentioned, but the two now alluded to are the only ones that came within my personal knowledge. It appears, however, that the spectre does not confine its operations to the churchyard, as there have been instances mentioned of its appearance at weddings and dances, where it never failed to secure its victims by dancing them into pleuritic fevers. I am unable to say whether this is a strictly local superstition, or whether it is considered peculiar to other churchyards in Ireland or elsewhere. In its female shape it somewhat resembles the Elle maids of Scandinavia; but I am acquainted with no account of fairies or apparitions in which the sex is said to be changed, except in that of the Devil himself. The country people say it is Death.—*Author's note.*

> The bride she bound her golden hair—
>   *Killeevy, O Killeevy!*
> And her step was light as the breezy air
> When it bends the morning flowers so fair,
>   By the bonnie green woods of Killeevy.

---

[1] 'The "Sir Turlough" of Carleton is perhaps the most successful legendary ballad of modern times.'—Mr. Theodore Martin, in *The Dublin University Magazine*, 1839.

And oh, but her eyes they danc'd so bright,
   Killeevy, O Killeevy !
As she longed for the dawn of to-morrow's light,
Her bridal vows of love to plight,
   By the bonnie green woods of Killeevy.

The bridegroom is come with youthful brow,
   Killeevy, O Killeevy !
To receive from his Eva her virgin vow ;
' Why tarries the bride of my bosom now ? '
   By the bonnie green woods of Killeevy.

A cry ! a cry !—'twas her maidens spoke,
   Killeevy, O Killeevy !
' Your bride is asleep—she has not awoke ;
And the sleep she sleeps will be never broke,'
   By the bonnie green woods of Killeevy.

Sir Turlough sank down with a heavy moan,
   Killeevy, O Killeevy !
And his cheek became like the marble stone—
' Oh, the pulse of my heart is for ever gone ! '
   By the bonnie green woods of Killeevy.

The *keen* is loud ; it comes again,
   Killeevy, O Killeevy !
And rises sad from the funeral train,
As in sorrow it winds along the plain,
   By the bonnie green woods of Killeevy.

And oh, but the plumes of white were fair
   Killeevy, O Killeevy !
When they flutter'd all mournful in the air,
As rose the hymn of the requiem prayer,
   By the bonnie green woods of Killeevy.

There is a voice but one can hear,
   Killeevy, O Killeevy !
And it softly pours, from behind the bier,
Its note of death on Sir Turlough's ear,
   By the bonnie green woods of Killeevy.

The *keen* is loud, but that voice is low,
   Killeevy, O Killeevy !
And it sings its song of sorrow slow,
And names young Turlough's name with woe
   By the bonnie green woods of Killeevy.

Now the grave is closed, and the mass is said,
   Killeevy, O Killeevy !
And the bride she sleeps in her lonely bed,
The fairest corpse among the dead,
   By the bonnie green woods of Killeevy.

The wreaths of virgin-white are laid,
   Killeevy, O Killeevy !
By virgin hands, o'er the spotless maid ;
And the flowers are strewn, but they soon will fade,
   By the bonnie green woods of Killeevy.

' Oh ! go not yet—not yet away,
   Killeevy, O Killeevy !
Let us feel that *life* is near our clay,'
The long-departed seem to say,
   By the bonnie green woods of Killeevy.

But the tramp and the voices of *life* are gone,
   Killeevy, O Killeevy !
And beneath each cold forgotten stone
The mouldering dead sleep all alone,
   By the bonnie green woods of Killeevy.

But who is he that lingereth yet ?
   Killeevy, O Killeevy !
The fresh green sod with his tears is wet
And his heart in the bridal grave is set,
   By the bonnie green woods of Killeevy.

Oh, who but Sir Turlough, the young and brave,
   Killeevy, O Killeevy !
Should bend him o'er that bridal grave,
And to his death-bound Eva rave ?
   By the bonnie green woods of Killeevy.

' Weep not—weep not,' said a lady fair,
   Killeevy, O Killeevy !
' Should youth and valour thus despair,
And pour their vows to the empty air ? '
   By the bonnie green woods of Killeevy.

There's charmed music upon her tongue,
   Killeevy, O Killeevy !
Such beauty—bright, and warm and young—
Was never seen the maids among,
   By the bonnie green woods of Killeevy.

A laughing light, a tender grace,
   Killeevy, O Killeevy !
Sparkled in beauty around her face,
That grief from mortal heart might chase,
   By the bonnie green woods of Killeevy.

' The maid for whom thy salt tears fall,
   Killeevy, O Killeevy !
Thy grief or love can ne'er recall ;
She rests beneath that grassy pall,
   By the bonnie green woods of Killeevy.

' My heart it strangely cleaves to thee,
   Killeevy, O Killeevy !
And now that thy plighted love is free
Give its unbroken pledge to me,
   By the bonnie green woods of Killeevy.'

The charm is strong upon Turlough's eye,
   Killeevy, O Killeevy !
His faithless tears are already dry,
And his yielding heart has ceased to sigh,
   By the bonnie green woods of Killeevy.

' To thee,' the charmèd chief replied,
   Killeevy, O Killeevy !
' I pledge that love o'er my buried bride ;
Oh ! come, and in Turlough's hall abide,
   By the bonnie green woods of Killeevy.'

Again the funeral voice came o'er
  Killeevy, O Killeevy !
The passing breeze, as it wailed before,
And streams of mournful music bore,
  By the bonnie green woods of Killeevy.

' If I to thy youthful heart am dear,
  Killeevy, O Killeevy !
One month from hence thou wilt meet me here
Where lay thy bridal Eva's bier,
  By the bonnie green woods of Killeevy.'

He pressed her lips as the words were spoken,
  Killeevy, O Killeevy !
And his *banshee's* wail—now far and broken—
Murmured ' Death,' as he gave the token
  By the bonnie green woods of Killeevy.

' Adieu ! adieu !' said the lady bright,
  Killeevy, O Killeevy !
And she slowly passed like a thing of light,
Or a morning cloud, from Sir Turlough's sight,
  By the bonnie green woods of Killeevy.

Now Sir Turlough has death in every vein,
  Killeevy, O Killeevy !
And there's fear and grief o'er his wide domain,
And gold for those who will calm his brain,
  By the bonnie green woods of Killeevy.

' Come, haste thee, leech ; right swiftly ride,
  Killeevy, O Killeevy !
Sir Turlough the brave, Green Truagha's pride,
Has pledged his love to the churchyard bride,
  By the bonnie green woods of Killeevy.'

The leech groaned loud : ' Come, tell me this,
  Killeevy, O Killeevy !
By all thy hopes of weal and bliss,
Has Sir Turlough given the fatal kiss
  By the bonnie green woods of Killeevy ?'

G

‘ The *banshee's* cry is loud and long,
    Killeevy, O Killeevy !
At eve she weeps her funeral song,
And it floats on the twilight breeze along,
    By the bonnie green woods of Killeevy.’

‘ Then the fatal kiss is given.   The last
    Killeevy, O Killeevy !
Of Turlough’s race and name is past ;
His doom is seal’d, his die is cast,
    By the bonnie green woods of Killeevy.’

‘ Leech, say not that thy skill is vain ;
    Killeevy, O Killeevy !
Oh, calm the power of his frenzied brain,
And half his lands thou shalt retain,
    By the bonnie green woods of Killeevy.’

The leech has failed, and the hoary priest,
    Killeevy, O Killeevy !
With pious shrift his soul released,
And the smoke is high of his funeral feast,
    By the bonnie green woods of Killeevy.

The *shanachies* now are assembled all,
    Killeevy, O Killeevy !
And the songs of praise, in Sir Turlough’s hall,
To the sorrowing harp’s dark music fall,
    By the bonnie green woods of Killeevy.

And there is trophy, banner, and plume,
    Killeevy, O Killeevy !
And the pomp of death, with its darkest gloom,
O’ershadows the Irish chieftain’s tomb,
    By the bonnie green woods of Killeevy.

The month is clos’d, and Green Truagha’s pride,
    Killeevy, O Killeevy !
Is married to death—and, side by side,
He slumbers now with his churchyard bride,
    By the bonnie green woods of Killeevy.

A Sigh for Knockmany

Take, proud ambition, take thy fill
   Of pleasures won through toil or crime ;
Go, learning, climb thy rugged hill,
   And give thy name to future time.
Philosophy, be keen to see
   Whate'er is just, or false, or vain ;
Take each thy meed, but oh, give me
   To range my mountain glens again.

Pure was the breeze that fanned my cheek,
   As o'er Knockmany's brow I went ;
When every lovely dell could speak
   In airy music, vision-sent.
False world, I hate thy cares and thee ;
   I hate the treacherous haunts of men ;
Give back my early heart to me,
   Give back to me my mountain glen.

How light my youthful visions shone
   When spanned by Fancy's radiant form !
But now her glittering bow is gone,
   And leaves me but the cloud and storm ;
With wasted form and cheek all pale,
   With heart long seared by grief and pain,
Dunroe, I'll seek thy native gale,
   I'll tread my mountain glens again.

Thy breeze once more may fan my blood,
   The valleys all are lovely still ;
And I may stand as once I stood,
   In lonely musings on thy hill.
But ah ! the spell is gone.   No art
   In crowded town, or native plain,
Can teach a crushed and breaking heart
   To pipe the songs of youth again.

GERALD GRIFFIN

GERALD GRIFFIN [1] was born in 1803 at Limerick, and his youth was spent not far from the Shannon, at Fairy Lawn, Adare, and Pallas Kenry. The historical monuments and memories around gave direction to his work, and the pastoral calm reappears in his poetry. Though a home-lover, he was adventurous. At twenty he went to London to seek his fortune in letters, inspired by the success of Banim, who befriended him. He endured privations courageously for some years, and finally got anchorage in the Press. His principal and most popular works are his novels, one of which, THE COLLEGIANS, was dramatised by Dion Boucicault and remains a favourite, under the name of THE COLLEEN BAWN. He himself had written for the stage. He took with him to London a piece called AGUIRE, and three other tragedies. GISIPPUS survives. Charles Kean read it, and 'was fully impressed with the beauty of the language and the high talent displayed throughout,' but feared for its success as an acting play. Macready, however, was decidedly favourable. It was warmly received when produced at Drury Lane in 1842, two years after the author's death. In Dublin it was repeatedly acted by T. C. King, with great effect. It belongs to the classic school. Had he given to the stage the tragic realities of life around him, such as he gave to his novels, he might have formed a successful national drama. His riper mind found fresher paths. It should be counted to him that he was the first to present several of our folk-customs, tales, and ancient legends in English prose. In poetry his longer pieces fail in freshness, vigour, and local colour ; they are conventional compositions, carefully worked, with pleasing imagery and pensive reflections. In his lyrics, however, where his native genius is free, he is at his best, impassioned at times (though never passionate), tender, delicate, yet strong with a certain

---

[1] *Rectè* O'Griobta (O'Greeva).

dramatic grasp of his subject. There is a curious prudence, somewhat Edgeworthian, in certain of his verses, which controls passion and may be due to the influence of a Quaker lady whose friend he was. Even the Shannon suggests that he should fulfil his appointed course 'with tranquil breast and ordered will.' The tender and delicate feeling displayed in ' A Place in thy Memory, Dearest,' 'Old Times ! Old Times ! ' ' I love my Love in the Morning,' and others have won them a wide popularity. He also, like Callanan, but more often than he, introduces Gaelic terms and lines : thus, he embodies the old ballad refrain of 'Siubal a rúin ' (Shule Aroon) in ' My Mary of the Curling Hair.' ' Gile machree' (Brightness of my Heart) is his most characteristic ballad. ' Eileen Aroon,' composed after an Irish model, but without its passion, is perfect of its kind, and was a prime favourite with Tennyson. The 'Sister of Charity' is a pæan on self-denial. In several poems, such as 'Sleep that like a Couched Dove,' 'The Bridal Wake,' 'The Wake without a Corpse,' he commemorates incidents of custom and folk-lore not yet passed away. ' Folta volla ' and ' O'Driscoll's War-song' show his more vigorous moods. In ' Céad Míle Fáilte' the last of the pagan Gael welcome, with grave pathos, their Christian supplanter. His love of Nature and aërial fancy are shown in ' Lines to a Sea-gull seen off the Cliffs of Moher.' Gerald Griffin retired in 1838 from active literary work, became a Christian Brother, and devoted himself to the teaching of the poor ; he died of fever in 1840, at the early age of thirty-six, in the North Monastery, Cork, where he lies at peace.

GEORGE SIGERSON.

The LIFE OF GERALD GRIFFIN was written by his brother (1842). THE POETICAL AND DRAMATIC WORKS OF GERALD GRIFFIN was published by Duffy, Dublin, 1895.

GILE MACHREE

GILE MACHREE,
Sit down by me,
We now are joined and ne'er shall sever ;

This hearth's our own,
Our hearts are one,
And peace is ours for ever !

When I was poor,
Your father's door
Was closed against your constant lover ;
With care and pain
I tried in vain
My fortunes to recover.
I said, ' To other lands I'd roam,
Where fate may smile on me, love ;'
I said, ' Farewell, my own old home !'
And I said, ' Farewell to thee, love !'
Sing, *Gile machree*, &c.

I might have said,
My mountain maid,
Come live with me, your own true lover—
I know a spot,
A silent cot,
Your friends can ne'er discover,
Where gently flows the waveless tide
By one small garden only ;
Where the heron waves his wings so wide,
And the linnet sings so lonely !
Sing, *Gile machree*, &c.

I might have said,
My mountain maid,
A father's right was never given
True hearts to curse
With tyrant force
That have been blest in heaven.
But then I said, ' In after years,
When thoughts of home shall find her,
My love may mourn with secret tears
Her friends thus left behind her.'
Sing, *Gile machree*, &c.

Oh no, I said,
My own dear maid,
For me, though all forlorn, for ever
That heart of thine
Shall ne'er repine
O'er slighted duty—never.
From home and thee, though wandering far,
A dreary fate be mine, love ;
I'd rather live in endless war
Than buy my peace with thine, love.
Sing, *Gile machree*, &c.

Far, far away,
By night and day,
I toiled to win a golden treasure ;
And golden gains
Repaid my pains
In fair and shining measure.
I sought again my native land,
Thy father welcomed me, love ;
I poured my gold into his hand,
And my guerdon found in thee, love.

Sing, *Gile machree*,
Sit down by me,
We now are joined and ne'er shall sever ;
This hearth's our own,
Our hearts are one,
And peace is ours for ever !

CÉAD MÍLE FÁILTE, ELIM !

(SONG FROM ' THE INVASION ')

CÉAD míle fáilte ! child of the Ithian !
Céad míle fáilte, Elim !
Aisneach, thy temple in ruins is lying,
In Druim na Druid the dark blast is sighing.
Lonely we shelter in grief and in danger,
Yet have we welcome and cheer for the stranger.
Céad míle fáilte ! child of the Ithian !
Céad míle fáilte, Elim !

Woe for the weapons that guarded our slumbers,
Tamreach, they said, was too small for our numbers ;
Little is left for our sons to inherit,
Yet, what we have, thou art welcome to share it.
          Céad míle fáilte ! child of the Ithian !
                    Céad míle fáilte, Elim !

Corman, thy teachers have died broken-hearted ;
Voice of the Trilithon, thou art departed !
All have forsaken our mountains so dreary—
All but the spirit that welcomes the weary.
          Céad míle fáilte ! child of the Ithian !
                    Céad míle fáilte, Elim !

Vainly the Draithe, alone in the mountain,
Looks to the torn cloud or eddying fountain ;
The spell of the Christian has vanquished their power,
Yet is he welcome to rest in our bower.
          Céad míle fáilte ! child of the Ithian !
                    Céad míle fáilte, Elim !

Wake for the Christian your welcoming numbers !
Strew the dry rushes to pillow his slumbers.
Long let him cherish, with deep recollection,
The eve of our feast, and the Druids' affection.
          Céad míle fáilte ! child of the Ithian!
                    Céad míle fáilte, Elim !

LINES ADDRESSED TO A SEAGULL, SEEN OFF THE CLIFFS
OF MOHER, IN THE COUNTY OF CLARE

WHITE bird of the tempest ! O beautiful thing !
With the bosom of snow and the motionless wing,
Now sweeping the billow, now floating on high,
Now bathing thy plumes in the light of the sky,
Now poising o'er ocean thy delicate form,
Now breasting the surge with thy bosom so warm,
Now darting aloft with a heavenly scorn,
Now shooting along like a ray of the morn,
Now lost in the folds of the cloud-curtained dome,
Now floating abroad like a flake of the foam,

Now silently poised o'er the war of the main,
Like the spirit of Charity brooding o'er pain,
Now gliding with pinion all silently furled,
Like an angel descending to comfort the world !
Thou seem'st to my spirit, as upward I gaze,
And see thee, now clothed in mellowest rays,
Now lost in the storm-driven vapours that fly
Like hosts that are routed across the broad sky,
Like a pure spirit true to its virtue and faith,
'Mid the tempests of Nature, of passion, and death !

Rise, beautiful emblem of purity, rise !
On the sweet winds of heaven to thine own brilliant skies ;
Still higher—still higher—till lost to our sight,
Thou hidest thy wings in a mantle of light ;
And I think, how a pure spirit gazing on thee,
Must long for the moment—the joyous and free—
When the soul disembodied from nature shall spring
Unfettered at once to her Maker and King ;
When the bright day of service and suffering past,
Shapes fairer than thine shall shine round her at last,
While, the standard of battle triumphantly furled,
She smiles like a victor, serene on the world !

THE WAKE OF THE ABSENT

THE dismal yew and cypress tall
    Wave o'er the churchyard lone,
Where rest our friends and fathers all,
    Beneath the funeral stone.
Unvexed in holy ground they sleep,
    Oh ! early lost ! o'er thee
No sorrowing friend shall ever weep,
    Nor stranger bend the knee.
        Mo Chuma ! [1] lorn am I !
Hoarse dashing rolls the salt sea wave
Over our perished darling's grave.

---

[1] *Mo Chuma :* My grief ; or, Woe is me.

The winds the sullen deep that tore
   His death-song chanted loud,
The weeds that line the clifted shore
   Were all his burial shroud.
For friendly wail and holy dirge,
   And long lament of love,
Around him roared the angry surge,
   The curlew screamed above.
        Mo Chuma! lorn am I !
My grief would turn to rapture now,
Might I but touch that pallid brow.

The stream-born bubbles soonest burst
   That earliest left the source ;
Buds earliest blown are faded first
   In Nature's wonted course.
With guarded pace her seasons creep,
   By slow decay expire ;
The young above the aged weep,
   The son above the sire.
        Mo Chuma! lorn am I !
That death a backward course should hold,
To smite the young and spare the old.

EILEEN AROON [1]

When, like the early rose,
   Eileen aroon !
Beauty in childhood blows,
   Eileen aroon !
When, like a diadem,
   Buds blush around the stem,
   Which is the fairest gem ?
   Eileen aroon !

Is it the laughing eye ?
   Eileen aroon !
Is it the timid sigh ?
   Eileen aroon !

---

[1] *Eibhlín a rúin :* Eileen, my treasure.

Is it the tender tone,
Soft as the stringed harp's moan?
Oh! it is Truth alone,
   Eileen aroon!

When, like the rising day,
   Eileen aroon!
Love sends his early ray,
   Eileen aroon!
What makes his dawning glow
Changeless through joy or woe?—
Only the constant know,
   Eileen aroon!

I know a valley fair,
   Eileen aroon!
I knew a cottage there,
   Eileen aroon!
Far in that valley's shade
I knew a gentle maid,
Flower of a hazel glade,
   Eileen aroon!

Who in the song so sweet?
   Eileen aroon!
Who in the dance so fleet?
   Eileen aroon!
Dear were her charms to me,
Dearer her laughter free,
Dearest her constancy,
   Eileen aroon!

Youth must with time decay,
   Eileen aroon!
Beauty must fade away,
   Eileen aroon!
Castles are sacked in war,
Chieftains are scattered far
Truth is a fixéd star,
   Eileen aroon!

JEREMIAH [1] JOSEPH CALLANAN

CALLANAN'S nature was sensitive, scrupulous, and shifting, if not shiftless : a Bohemian of a good type, honourable and refined. Intended for the priesthood of a yet unemancipated people, he withdrew from Maynooth on finding himself inapt ; then he gave attention to medicine, remained a student of Trinity College, Dublin, for two years, won two prizes in verse and retired. Some fertile years he spent ('wasted,' say biographers) amid the romantic mountains of West Cork, which were the true university that moulded his mind and endowed it with the seeds of enduring life. Here his living poetry had birth. Other years he passed teaching in schools (one being that of Mr. Maginn, father of the well-known writer), and the last two of his existence as a tutor in Lisbon, for the sake of its milder climate, which led him gently to death. Born in Cork in 1795, he died at Lisbon on September 19, 1829.

It was inevitable, perhaps, that the influence of Byron should suggest and shape THE RECLUSE OF INCHIDONY, that of Scott THE REVENGE OF DONAL COMM, and that of Moore some of his lyrics. They are fine compositions, but the first fails through the young man's non-knowledge of life's greater agonies. All would have been failure, so far as good verse may be, had he not known Irish and drunk at the high head-fountains of his race. This gave his genius a youth and freedom of its own. To this we owe his vigorous, stirring, and thoroughly original poem on 'Gougaune Barra,' with its resonant double-rimes, so characteristic of the Gael. His pride was to have awakened the ancient harp and mingled with the voice of southern waters the songs that even Echo had forgotten, he says, invoking the 'Least Bard of the Hills.' The claim was

---

[1] It may be noted that 'Jeremiah' is for some slight resemblance in sound the English form into which the Irish peasantry transpose the Gaelic name ' Diarmuid.'

justified. Moore unquestionably revived the spirit of Irish melody and first infused into poetry the legends of the land. It is Callanan's distinction—a great one, though ignored till now—that he was the first to give adequate versions of Irish Gaelic poems. Compared with preceding and many subsequent attempts, they are marvellously close and true to their originals. Take, for example, the passionate vehemence of the 'Dirge of O'Sullivan Bear,' the native simplicity of 'The Girl I love' and 'Brown Drimin,' the strain of weirdness in 'The Outlaw of Loch Lene,' given in a metre unusual in English, but known in Irish, and the pure ballad pathos of 'The Convict of Clonmel.' The 'Lament of O'Gnive' is a paraphrase and somewhat Byronised : Ferguson's more faithful rendering is more effective. Callanan was among the first (after the popular balladists) to introduce a Gaelic refrain into English poetry, as witness his verses entitled 'Tusa ta measg na reultan mōr' ('Thou who art among the greater planets'). He is not, indeed, one of the greater planets, but yet shines with a clear light.

GEORGE SIGERSON.

THE RECLUSE OF INCHIDONY was published in 1830, and a volume of collected poems in 1861, since when there have been several reprints.

DIRGE OF O'SULLIVAN BEAR

FROM THE IRISH

One of the Sullivans of Bearhaven, who went by the name of Morty Oge, fell under the vengeance of the law. He had long been a very popular character in the wild district which he inhabited, and was particularly obnoxious to the local authorities, who had good reason to suspect him of enlisting men for the Irish Brigade in the French service, in which it was said he held a captain's commission. Information of his raising these 'wild geese' (the name by which recruits were known) was given by a Mr. Puxley, on whom in consequence O'Sullivan vowed revenge, which he executed by shooting him on Sunday while on his way to church. This called for the interposition of the higher powers, and accordingly a party of military was sent round from Cork to attack O'Sullivan's house. He was daring and well armed ; and the house was fortified, so that he made an obstinate defence. At last a confidential servant of his, named Scully, was bribed to wet the powder in the guns and pistols prepared for his defence, which rendered him powerless. He attempted to escape, but while springing over a high wall in the rear of his house he received a mortal wound in the back. They tied his body to a boat, and dragged it in that manner through the sea from Bearhaven to Cork, where his head was cut off and fixed on the county gaol, where it remained for several years. Such is the story current among the people of Bearhaven. The dirge is supposed to have been the composition of O'Sullivan's aged nurse.—*Author's note.*

THE sun on Ivera
　　No longer shines brightly,
The voice of her music
　　No longer is sprightly,
No more to her maidens
　　The light dance is dear,
Since the death of our darling
　　O'Sullivan Bear.

Scully ! thou false one,
　　You basely betrayed him,
In his strong hour of need,
　　When thy right hand should aid him ;
He fed thee—he clad thee—
　　You had all could delight thee :
You left him—you sold him—
　　May Heaven requite thee !

Scully ! may all kinds
　　Of evil attend thee !
On thy dark road of life
　　May no kind one befriend thee !
May fevers long burn thee,
　　And agues long freeze thee !
May the strong hand of God
　　In His red anger seize thee !

Had he died calmly
　　I would not deplore him,
Or if the wild strife
　　Of the sea-war closed o'er him ;
But with ropes round his white limbs
　　Through ocean to trail him,
Like a fish after slaughter—
　　'Tis therefore I wail him.

Long may the curse
　Of his people pursue them :
Scully that sold him,
　And soldier that slew him !
One glimpse of heaven's light
　May they see never !
May the hearthstone of hell
　Be their best bed for ever !

In the hole which the vile hands
　Of soldiers had made thee,
Unhonour'd, unshrouded,
　And headless they laid thee;
No sigh to regret thee,
　No eye to rain o'er thee,
No dirge to lament thee,
　No friend to deplore thee !

Dear head of my darling,
　How gory and pale
These aged eyes see thee,
　High spiked on their gaol !
That cheek in the summer sun
　Ne'er shall grow warm ;
Nor that eye e'er catch light,
　But the flash of the storm.

A curse, blessed ocean,
　Is on thy green water,
From the haven of Cork
　To Ivera of slaughter :
Since thy billows were dyed
　With the red wounds of fear,
Of Muiertach Oge,
　Our O'Sullivan Bear !

The Convict of Clonmel

from the irish

How hard is my fortune,
  And vain my repining !
The strong rope of fate
  For this young neck is twining.
My strength is departed,
  My cheek sunk and sallow,
While I languish in chains
  In the gaol of Clonmala.[1]

No boy in the village
  Was ever yet milder.
I'd play with a child,
  And my sport would be wilder ;
I'd dance without tiring
  From morning till even,
And the goal-ball I'd strike
  To the lightning of heaven.

At my bed-foot decaying,
  My hurlbat is lying ;
Thro' the boys of the village
  My goal-ball is flying ;
My horse 'mong the neighbours
  Neglected may fallow,
While I pine in my chains
  In the gaol of Clonmala.

Next Sunday the patron
  At home will be keeping,
And the young active hurlers
  The field will be sweeping ;
With the dance of fair maidens
  The evening they'll hallow,
While this heart, once so gay,
  Shall be cold in Clonmala.

---

[1] *Cluain meala* (' Field of honey ') : Irish of ' Clonmel.'

GOUGAUNE BARRA

THERE is a green island in lone Gougaune Barra,
Where Allua of songs rushes forth as an arrow,
In deep-vallied Desmond—a thousand wild fountains
Come down to that lake from their home in the mountains.
There grows the wild ash, and a time-stricken willow
Looks chidingly down on the mirth of the billow,
As, like some gay child that sad monitor scorning,
It lightly laughs back to the laugh of the morning.

And its zone of dark hills—oh ! to see them all bright'ning,
When the tempest flings out its red banner of lightning,
And the waters rush down, 'mid the thunder's deep rattle
Like clans from the hills at the voice of the battle ;
And brightly the fire-crested billows are gleaming,
And wildly from Mullagh the eagles are screaming,
Oh ! where is the dwelling, in valley or highland,
So meet for a bard as this lone little island ?

How oft when the summer sun rested on Clara,
And lit the dark heath on the hills of Ivera,
Have I sought thee, sweet spot, from my home by the ocean,
And trod all thy wilds with a minstrel's devotion,
And thought of thy bards when, assembling together
In the clefts of thy rocks or the depth of thy heather,
They fled from the Saxon's dark bondage and slaughter
And waked their last song by the rush of thy water.

High sons of the lyre, oh ! how proud was the feeling,
To think while alone through that solitude stealing,
Though loftier minstrels green Erin can number,
I only awoke your wild harp from its slumber,
And mingled once more with the voice of those fountains
The songs even Echo forgot on her mountains ;
And glean'd each grey legend that darkly was sleeping
Where the mist and the rain o'er their beauty were creeping.

Least bard of the hills ! were it mine to inherit
The fire of thy harp and the wing of thy spirit,

H

With the wrongs which, like thee, to our country have bound me,
Did your mantle of song fling its radiance around me,
Still, still in those wilds might young Liberty rally,
And send her strong shout over mountain and valley,
The star of the West might yet rise in its glory,
And the land that was darkest be brightest in story.

I too shall be gone ; but my name shall be spoken
When Erin awakes and her fetters are broken ;
Some minstrel will come, in the summer eve's gleaming,
When Freedom's young light on his spirit is beaming,
And bend o'er my grave with a tear of emotion,
Where calm Avon-Bwee seeks the kisses of ocean,
Or plant a wild wreath from the banks of that river
O'er the heart and the harp that are sleeping for ever.

THE OUTLAW OF LOCH LENE

FROM THE IRISH

OH, many a day have I made good ale in the glen,
That came not of stream or malt, like the brewing of men.
My bed was the ground, my roof the greenwood above,
And the wealth that I sought, one fair kind glance from my love.

Alas ! on that night when the horses I drove from the field,
That I was not near from terror my angel to shield.
She stretched forth her arms—her mantle she flung to the wind—
And swam o'er Loch Lene her outlawed lover to find.

Oh, would that a freezing, sleet-winged tempest did sweep,
And I and my love were alone far off on the deep !
I'd ask not a ship, or a bark, or pinnace to save ;
With her hand round my waist I'd fear not the wind or the wave.

'Tis down by the lake where the wild tree fringes its sides
The maid of my heart, the fair one of heaven, resides ;
I think as at eve she wanders its mazes along
The birds go to sleep by the sweet, wild twist of her song.

EDWARD WALSH

EDWARD WALSH was born in Londonderry, 1805, and became
a school-teacher. He was appointed a schoolmaster to convicts
on Spike Island, and died in 1850. When John Mitchel was
on his way to penal servitude at the Bermudas he stopped at
Spike Island and saw Walsh there, 'a tall gentleman-like
person in black but rather over-worn clothes. . . . I knew his
face, but could not at first remember who he was ; he was
Edward Walsh, author of " Mo craoibhin cno " and other sweet
songs, and of some very musical translations from old Irish
ballads. Tears stood in his eyes as he told me he had
contrived to get an opportunity of seeing and shaking hands
with me before I should leave Ireland. . . . He stooped down
and kissed my hands. " Ah ! " said he, " you are now the man
of all Ireland most *to be envied.*" ' Mitchel certainly did not
envy Walsh, whose life was a constant struggle with penury, and
who must have found a daily torture in the cruelly inappropriate
employment forced on his fine genius and sensitive nature.

Walsh's chief mission as a poet was to collect and make
known the waifs and strays of Gaelic poetry preserved among
the people. He was a frequent contributor to *The Nation* up
to 1848, but is, on the whole, rather to be ranged with
Callanan in this book than placed among the poets whose fame
is closely identified with that of the organ of Young Ireland.

RELIQUES OF IRISH JACOBITE POETRY, 1844 ; IRISH POPULAR
SONGS, with translations and notes, 1847.

MO CRAOIBHIN CNO [1]

MY heart is far from Liffey's tide
 And Dublin town ;
It strays beyond the southern side
 Of Cnoc-maol-Donn,[2]

---

[1] *Mo craoibhin cno* literally means ' my cluster of nuts ' ; but it figura-
tively signifies ' my nut-brown maid.' It is pronounced *Ma Creeveen Kno.*

[2] *Cnoc-maol-Donn* (the ' brown bare hill '), Knockmealdown : a lofty
mountain between the county of Tipperary and that of Waterford, com-
manding a glorious prospect.

Where Cappoquin hath woodlands green,
    Where Amhan-mhor's [1] waters flow,
Where dwells unsung, unsought, unseen,
    Mo craoibhín cno,
Low clustering in her leafy screen,
    Mo craoibhín cno!

The high-bred dames of Dublin town
    Are rich and fair,
With wavy plume, and silken gown,
    And stately air ;
Can plumes compare thy dark brown hair ?
    Can silks thy neck of snow ?
Or measur'd pace, thine artless grace,
    Mo craoibhín cno,
When harebells scarcely show thy trace,
    Mo craoibhín cno ?

I've heard the songs by Liffey's wave
    That maidens sung—
They sung their land the Saxon's slave,
    In Saxon tongue.
Oh ! bring me here that Gaelic dear
    Which cursed the Saxon foe,
When thou didst charm my raptured ear,
    Mo craoibhín cno !
And none but God's good angels near,
    Mo craoibhín cno !

I've wandered by the rolling Lee,
    And Lene's green bowers ;
I've seen the Shannon's widespread sea
    And Limerick's towers—
And Liffey's tide, where halls of pride
    Frown o'er the flood below ;
My wild heart strays to Amhan-mhor's side,
    Mo craoibhín cno !
With love and thee for aye to bide,
    Mo craoibhín cno !

---

[1] *Amhan-mhor* (the ' Great River ') : the Blackwater, which flows into the sea at Youghal.   The Irish name is uttered in two sounds : *Oan-Vore.*

HAVE YOU BEEN AT CARRICK? [1]

FROM THE IRISH

HAVE you been at Carrick, and saw you my true-love there,
And saw you her features, all beautiful, bright and fair?
Saw you the most fragrant, flowery, sweet apple-tree?
Oh! saw you my loved one, and pines she in grief like me?

'I have been at Carrick, and saw thy own true-love there;
And saw, too, her features, all beautiful, bright and fair;
And saw the most fragrant, flowering, sweet apple-tree—
I saw thy loved one—she pines *not* in grief like thee.'

Five guineas would price every tress of her golden hair—
Then think what a treasure her pillow at night to share!
These tresses thick-clust'ring and curling around her brow—
O Ringlet of Fairness! I'll drink to thy beauty now!

When, seeking to slumber, my bosom is rent with sighs—
I toss on my pillow till morning's blest beams arise;
No aid, bright beloved! can reach me save God above,
For a blood-lake is formed of the light of my eyes with love!

Until yellow autumn shall usher the Paschal day,
And Patrick's gay festival come in its train alway—
Until through my coffin the blossoming boughs shall grow,
My love on another I'll never in life bestow!

.   .   .   .   .   .

Lo! yonder the maiden illustrious, queen-like, high,
With long-flowing tresses adown to her sandal-tie—
Swan, fair as the lily, descended of high degree,
A myriad of welcomes, dear maid of my heart, to thee!

---

[1] The translator remarks: 'This is a song of the South, but there are so many places of the name of Carrick, such as Carrick-on-Shannon, Carrick-on-Suir, &c., that I cannot fix its precise locality. In this truly Irish song, when the pining swain learns that his absent mistress is not love-sick like himself, he praises the beauty of her copious hair, throws off a glass to her health, enumerates his sufferings, and swears to forego the sex for ever; but she suddenly bursts upon his view, his resolves vanish into thin air, and he greets his glorious maid.'

THE DAWNING OF THE DAY

FROM THE IRISH

An extremely close rendering of the beautiful Gaelic song, *Fáinne geal an Lae*. Contrary to his usual custom Walsh has preserved some of the internal chimes characteristic of Irish verse : *e.g.* —

> ' At early dawn I once had *been*
> Where *Lene's* blue waters flow.'

The ancient melody, which the words fit so well, is one of exquisite tenderness and wistfulness.

I

AT early dawn I once had been
  Where Lene's blue waters flow,
When summer bid the groves be green,
  The lamp of light to glow.
As on by bower, and town, and tower,
  And widespread fields I stray,
I meet a maid in the greenwood shade
  At the dawning of the day.

II

Her feet and beauteous head were bare,
  No mantle fair she wore ;
But down her waist fell golden hair,
  That swept the tall grass o'er.
With milking-pail she sought the vale,
  And bright her charms' display ;
Outshining far the morning star
  At the dawning of the day.

III

Beside me sat that maid divine
  Where grassy banks outspread.
' Oh, let me call thee ever mine,
  Dear maid,' I sportive said.
' False man, for shame, why bring me blame ? '
  She cried, and burst away—
The sun's first light pursued her flight
  At the dawning of the day.

Lament of the *Mangaire Sugach*

from the irish

Andrew Magrath, commonly called the *Mangaire Sugach* (or ' Jolly Merchant '), having been expelled from the Roman Catholic Church for his licentious life, offered himself as a convert to the doctrines of Protestantism ; but, the Protestant clergyman having also refused to accept him, the unfortunate *Mangaire* gave vent to his feelings in this lament.—*Author's note.*

I

Beloved, do you pity not my doleful case,
Pursued by priest and minister in dire disgrace?
The churchmen brand the vagabond upon my brow—
Oh ! they'll take me not as Protestant or Papist now !

II

The parson calls me wanderer and homeless knave ;
And though I boast the Saxon creed with aspect grave.
He says that claim my Popish face must disallow,
Although I'm neither Protestant nor Papist now !

III

He swears (and oh, he'll keep his oath) he's firmly bent
To hunt me down by penal Acts of Parliament ;
Before the law's coercive might to make me bow,
And choose between the Protestant and Papist now !

IV

The priest me deems a satirist of luckless lay,
Whose merchant-craft hath often led fair maids astray,
And, worse than hunted fugitive all disavow,
He'll take me not a Protestant or Papist now !

V

That, further, I'm a foreigner devoid of shame,
Of hateful, vile, licentious life and evil name ;
A ranting, rhyming wanderer, without a cow,
Who now is deem'd a Protestant—a Papist now !

VI

Alas ! it was not charity or Christian grace
That urged to drag my deeds before the Scotic race.
What boots it him to write reproach upon my brow,
Whether they deem me Protestant or Papist now ?

VII

Lo ! David, Israel's poet-king, and Magdalene,
And Paul, who of the Christian creed the foe had been—
Did Heaven, when sorrow fill'd their heart, reject their vow
Though they were neither Protestant nor Papist now ?

VIII

Oh ! since I weep my wretched heart to evil prone,
A wanderer in the paths of sin, all lost and lone,
At other shrines with other flocks I fain must bow.
Who'll take me, whether Protestant or Papist, now ?

IX

Beloved, whither can I flee for peace at last,
When thus beyond the Church's pale I'm rudely cast?
The Arian creed, or Calvinist, I must avow,
When severed from the Protestant and Papist now !

THE SUMMING-UP

Lo, Peter th' Apostle, whose lapses from grace were three,
Denying the Saviour, was granted a pardon free ;
O God ! though the *Mangaire* from him Thy mild laws cast,
Receive him, like Peter, to dwell in THY HOUSE at last !

GEORGE FOX

GEORGE FOX was born in Belfast; graduated in Trinity
College, Dublin, 1842 ; and not long after went to America.
Very little more is known of him except that Ferguson dedi-
cated to him his POEMS of 1880 : 'Georgio, Amico, Con-
discipulo, Instauratori.'

THE COUNTY OF MAYO [1]

FROM THE IRISH

This specimen of our vernacular literature, written to a beautiful old melody, is one of the most popular songs of the peasantry of the counties of Mayo and Galway, and is doubtless a composition of the seventeenth or early eighteenth century. The original Irish has been published by Mr. Hardiman, in his IRISH MINSTRELSY. This translation, one of the supremely good things in that line of literature, was first published by Samuel Ferguson in a review of Hardiman's work (*Dublin University Magazine*, June 1834).

ON the deck of Patrick Lynch's boat I sat in woeful plight,
Through my sighing all the weary day and weeping all the night.
Were it not that full of sorrow from my people forth I go,
By the blessed sun, 'tis royally I'd sing thy praise, Mayo.

When I dwelt at home in plenty, and my gold did much abound,
In the company of fair young maids the Spanish ale went round.
'Tis a bitter change from those gay days that now I'm forced to go,
And must leave my bones in Santa Cruz, far from my own Mayo.

---

[1] The following passage from an article by Mr. Standish O'Grady appeared in *The All-Ireland Review*, while the proofs of this Anthology were being read. It seems to demand quotation here :—

' Our last Irish aristocracy was Catholic, intensely and fanatically Royalist and Cavalier, and compounded of elements which were Norman-Irish and Milesian-Irish. They worshipped the Crown when the Crown had become a phantom or a ghost, and the god whom they worshipped was not able to save them or himself. They were defeated and exterminated. They lost everything, but they never lost honour ; and because they did not lose that, their overthrow was bewailed in songs and music which will not cease to sound for centuries yet :

" Shaun O'Dwyer o'Glanna,
We're worsted in the game."

' Worsted they were, for they made a fatal mistake ; and they had to go ; but they carried their honour with them, and they founded noble or princely families all over the Continent.

' Who laments the destruction of our present Anglo-Irish aristocracy ? Perhaps in broad Ireland not one. They fail from the land while innumerable eyes are dry, and their fall will not be bewailed in one piteous dirge or one mournful melody.'

They're altered girls in Irrul now ; 'tis proud they're grown and
   high,
With their hair-bags and their top-knots—for I pass their buckles
   by.
But it's little now I heed their airs, for God will have it so,
That I must depart for foreign lands, and leave my sweet Mayo.

'Tis my grief that Patrick Loughlin is not Earl in Irrul still,
And that Brian Duff no longer rules as Lord upon the Hill ;
And that Colonel Hugh MacGrady should be lying dead and low,
And I sailing, sailing swiftly from the county of Mayo.

JOHN BANIM

JOHN BANIM, who was born in Kilkenny on April 3, 1798, is
chiefly known through the powerful stories 'by the O'Hara
Family,' which he wrote in conjunction with his brother
Michael ; but he published also a couple of volumes of verse
—namely, THE CELT'S PARADISE : a Poem in Four Duans
(London, 1821) and CHAUNT OF THE CHOLERA : Songs for
Ireland (London, 1831).   His tragedy, DAMON AND PYTHIAS,
was also published in London in 1821.

With the exception of one or two lyrics, these volumes
contain nothing worthy of note.   Where his songs are
at all tolerable, they are full of fire and feeling, and written
with a quite natural simplicity and strength.   Such are the
pieces here quoted.   His chief fault is his general disregard of
metrical laws.

Banim's health failed while he was still a young man, and
his later years were passed in pain and misery.   He was
granted a small Civil List pension, but did not long enjoy it,
dying on August 1, 1842.   His 'Soggarth Aroon'[1] is one of
the most popular of Irish poems, and has found a place in
many anthologies.

D. J. O'DONOGHUE.

[1] *Sagart* (sacerdos) *a rúin* : Priest, dear.

Soggarth Aroon

Am I the slave they say,
   Soggarth aroon ?
Since you did show the way,
   Soggarth aroon,
Their slave no more to be,
While they would work with me
Old Ireland's slavery,
   Soggarth aroon !

Loyal and brave to you,
   Soggarth aroon,
Yet be not slave to you,
   Soggarth aroon,
Nor, out of fear to you,
Stand up so near to you—
Och ! out of fear to *you,*
   Soggarth aroon !

Who, in the winter's night,
   Soggarth aroon,
When the cold blast did bite,
   Soggarth aroon,
Came to my cabin door,
And, on the earthen floor,
Knelt by me, sick and poor,
   Soggarth aroon ?

Who, on the marriage day,
   Soggarth aroon,
Made the poor cabin gay,
   Soggarth aroon ?
And did both laugh and sing,
Making our hearts to ring,
At the poor christening,
   Soggarth aroon ?

Who, as friend only met,
    Soggarth aroon,
Never did flout me yet,
    Soggarth aroon?
And when my heart was dim
Gave, while his eye did brim,
What I should give to him,
    Soggarth aroon?

Och, you and only you,
    Soggarth aroon!
And for this I was true to you,
    Soggarth aroon;
In love they'll never shake,
When for Old Ireland's sake
We a true part did take,
    Soggarth aroon!

HE SAID THAT HE WAS NOT OUR BROTHER

This ferocious attack was provoked by some utterances of the Duke of Wellington about Ireland.

HE said that he was not our brother—
    The mongrel! he said what we knew.
No, Eire! our dear Island-mother,
    He ne'er had his black blood from you!
And what though the milk of your bosom
    Gave vigour and health to his veins?
He was but a foul foreign blossom,
    Blown hither to poison our plains!

He said that the sword had enslaved us—
    That still at its point we must kneel.
The liar!—though often it braved us,
    We cross'd it with hardier steel!
This witness his Richard—our vassal!
    His Essex—whose plumes we trod down!
His Willy—whose peerless sword-tassel
    We tarnish'd at Limerick town!

No ! falsehood and feud were our evils,
　　While force not a fetter could twine.
Come Northmen—come Normans—come Devils !
　　We give them our *Sparth* [1] to the chine !
And if once again he would try us,
　　To the music of trumpet and drum,
And no traitor among us or nigh us—
　　Let him come, the Brigand ! let him come !

THE IRISH MOTHER IN THE PENAL DAYS

NOW welcome, welcome, baby-boy, unto a mother's fears,
The pleasure of her sufferings, the rainbow of her tears,
The object of your father's hope, in all he hopes to do,
A future man of his own land, to live him o'er anew !

How fondly on thy little brow a mother's eye would trace,
And in thy little limbs, and in each feature of thy face,
His beauty, worth, and manliness, and everything that's his,
Except, my boy, the answering mark of where the fetter is !

Oh ! many a weary hundred years his sires that fetter wore,
And he has worn it since the day that him his mother bore ;
And now, my son, it waits on you, the moment you are born,
The old hereditary badge of suffering and scorn !

Alas, my boy so beautiful !—alas, my love so brave !
And must your gallant Irish limbs still drag it to the grave?
And you, my son, yet have a son, foredoomed a slave to be,
Whose mother still must weep o'er him the tears I weep o'er thee !

---

[1] Battle-axe.

BOOK III

THE POETS OF *THE NATION*

The Nation newspaper was founded in the autumn of 1842, and its first proprietor and editor, Charles Gavan Duffy, emigrated to Australia in 1855. These fourteen years fell into two distinct periods—the first ending with the imprisonment of Duffy in 1848, the second with his emigration. They were certainly the most eventful years that Ireland had experienced since the Union. They witnessed the rise and fall of O'Connell's Repeal movement ; the insurrection of '48 ; the Famine ; the introduction into the British Parliament of Duffy's scheme of Independent Opposition, and its failure ; and the consequent wreck of the Tenant Right movement, through the treachery of the 'Brigadiers' and the madness of the people. It is a record of heroic effort, of crushing disaster, and of miserable defeat. Yet if these years were among the most calamitous in Irish history, it is none the less true that they were the most fertile in the seeds of future success. Almost everything that Ireland has since gained in the practical field— and she has gained much—has been won by developing and applying the ideas struck out at that time. And *The Nation* newspaper was the forge of thought in which the most active and ardent minds of the country wrought indefatigably at the fabric of her freedom and prosperity. But it was not only ideas and suggestions that were bequeathed to the future from these fourteen years, it was also passion and inspiration. The body of National poetry produced at this period—first as fugitive verse in the columns of the newspaper, afterwards collected and reprinted in countless editions—entered profoundly into the heart and mind of Irishmen of that and subsequent generations.[1] Other writers have produced poetic work of a loftier order ; but of this it may be said, and of this alone, that no one who is unacquainted with it can understand the contemporary history of Ireland.

The story of the foundation and early career of *The Nation* has been told so fully in so accessible a book as Sir Charles Gavan Duffy's YOUNG IRELAND, that it is not necessary here to describe these transactions at any length. Seldom, if ever, has any journal exercised so great and so worthy an effect on the political education of a people. The founders of *The Nation* found the masses of their countrymen just emerging from serfdom, unconscious of their power, ignorant of their history ; the sense of nationality, such as there was, the monopoly of one religious faction and the scorn of another ; their aspirations either fantastically vague or crudely material. On the ears of such a people fell sentences like these :

This country of ours is no sand-bank, thrown up by some recent caprice of earth. It is an ancient land, honoured in the archives of civilisation, traceable into antiquity by its piety, its valour and its sufferings. Every great European race has sent its stream to the river of Irish mind. Long wars, vast organisations, subtle codes, beacon crimes, leading virtues, and self-mighty men were here. If we live influenced by wind and sun and tree, and not by the passions and deeds of the PAST, we are a thriftless and hopeless people.—DAVIS'S ESSAYS.

Thus, and in a hundred essays, articles, and poems, elaborating these conceptions in detail, did Thomas Davis, Duffy, and their colleagues point their countrymen to their past. And as for the future, we may recognise in the following passage the kernel of multitudes of similar articles, essays, poems, holding up before the Irish people a noble and severe ideal of self-cultivation, of discipline and preparation, for great

[1] ' Deep down in the heart of every young Irishman,' says Mr. William O'Brien, with absolute truth, ' you will find the spirit of *The Nation*.'

destinies which in those golden days seemed nearer at hand
than they can to the most sanguine now :

The elements of Irish nationality are not only combining —in fact,
they are growing confluent in our minds. Such nationality as merits a
good man's help, and awakens a true man's ambition—such nationality
as could stand against internal faction and foreign intrigue—such
nationality as would make the Irish hearth happy, and the Irish name
illustrious, is becoming understood. It must contain and represent all
the races of Ireland. It must not be Celtic ; it must not be Saxon ; it
must be Irish. The Brehon law, and the maxims of Westminster—the
cloudy and lightning genius of the Gael, the placid strength of the Sacsanach, the marshalling insight of the Norman —a literature which shall
exhibit in combination the passions and idioms of all, and which shall
equally express our mind in its romantic, its religious, its forensic, and
its practical tendencies—finally, a native government, which shall
know and rule by the might and right of all, yet yield to the arrogance
of none—these are the components of such a nationality.— DAVIS'S
ESSAYS.

The keynote of all the poetry which gave wings to the
purposes and propaganda of *The Nation*, and which has served
more than anything else to keep the fame of the Young
Irelanders fresh to day, was the doctrine of Irish nationality.
Nationality is indeed the diapason of all worthy imaginative
literature,[1] but in the case of *The Nation* poets—at least, those
of the first period, up to 1848—it was generally also the
immediate theme or motive of their writings. They wrote for
a directly political purpose—to inspire their countrymen with
national pride, and faith in the cause of Repeal, and also with
hatred of English rule. Lyrics of pure emotion like ' My
Grave,' by Davis, or Judge O'Hagan's beautiful poem, ' The
Old Story,' were rather by-products of their toil ; their direct
object was to influence opinion and action. Poetry produced
under this stimulus may not take rank with the creation of the
artist dreaming on eternal truths, eternal beauty, and expressing
them in the rich and arduous harmonies of music and thought

[1] 'Der stärkste Antrieb zu geistigem und wirtschaftlichem Schaffen.'—
*Petition of German Authors and Professors to the Czar for the Liberties of
Finland.*

which we call poetry. Yet if the Young Irelanders worked for an immediate practical aim, none the less did high truth and noble passion inspire and inform their work, and their influence on the mind and heart of their readers was altogether for good. They awakened the intellect of Ireland from slumber, and they made the written word a power in the land.

How, it may be asked, did all this poetic talent spring up so suddenly ? One hardly knows. Duffy originated the idea of publishing National songs and ballads in *The Nation*, and Davis inaugurated the scheme with the finest poem he ever wrote, the 'Lament for Owen Roe.' Other writers—some of them peasants, some artisans, some exiles who had made their homes in far-distant lands—whose gift for verse or sympathy with their country would otherwise perhaps never have found utterance, were inspired by the example of Davis and the passion of the time. *The Nation* went far and wide through the country; it reached the priest, the student, the schoolmaster, the Repeal Committee man. Soon it found its way to the artisan and the peasant ; it was read aloud in the chapel-yard on Sundays, or round the forge fire of an evening. It told the people of an Ireland they had never heard of before ; not the Ireland of burlesque, or of bigoted misrepresentation, inhabited by Handy Andies and Scullabogue murderers, but ' an old historic island, the mother of soldiers and scholars, whose name was heard in the roar of onset on a thousand battlefields, for whose dear love the poor homesick exile in the garret or cloister of some foreign city toiled or plotted . . . the one mother country which a man loves as he loves the mother who held him to her breast.' [1] To express the throng of new ideas, emotions, aspirations, which crowded on the mind of the people, the Irish genius turned naturally to song. From wholly new and unsuspected quarters poems began to pour in upon *The Nation* —now it was some student who in a flame of patriotic passion wrought a lyric to which the hearts of Irishmen will quiver for all time ; now it was some gifted lady of the dominant classes who stepped from her pride of place to become the stormy

[1] C. G. Duffy.

voice of an oppressed and perishing people ; now it was some schoolboy in a provincial town who sent up, in a scarcely legible manuscript, verses throbbing with fiery energy ; or a girl nurtured in seclusion and in an atmosphere of tender piety who added a strain of delicate sweetness to the martial music which came most frequently and naturally to the poets of *The Nation.*

Intensely patriotic as this poetry was, there was yet one important aspect of patriotism which found, and perhaps could find, no distinct expression in it ; it had little or nothing of the Gaelic note. In reading Mangan, whose orbit coincided for a while with that of *The Nation*, but who must, on the whole, be considered as a star that dwelt apart, and Ferguson, who was united to *The Nation* writers by ties of friendship and of political sympathy, but not by literary association, one feels that these writers have behind them the moulding influences of a body of literature quite other than the English— a literature marked by a peculiar strain of mingled homeliness and grandeur, of simplicity and elaboration, of sensuousness and mysticism. This was the ancient literature of the Gael —the one literature of modern Europe which grew up spontaneously, untouched by the mighty influences of classic culture. And Mangan and Ferguson are the progenitors of those writers of our own day, like Standish O'Grady and Yeats, who are the representatives of the old Gaelic tradition, though they hand it forward in the English tongue. *The Nation* writers, however, recall not the Gaelic but the English tradition. Davis's ' Lament for Owen Roe ' has a certain Gaelic *afflatus*, and Edward Walsh knew how to 'turn a simple verse true to the Gaelic ear' ; but for the most part, though the poets of *The Nation* loved to sprinkle their verses with Irish phrases, the qualities which remind us that there was once a Gaelic literature lie rather on the surface than in the substance of their work. Nor at that time could it well have been otherwise. The ancient tongue was still living ; but Nationalist opinion, represented by O'Connell, regarded it as a sort of incubus, and of the old literature little was known or understood.

With this general introduction the poets of *The Nation*
may now be left to speak for themselves. The selections
which follow are taken from the two excellent collections of
The Nation poetry, the SPIRIT OF THE NATION (Jas. Duffy,
Dublin) and the NEW SPIRIT OF THE NATION (T. Fisher
Unwin, London), and also in some cases from the other
writings of authors who are represented in these volumes, and
who won their earliest or principal distinction as writers for
The Nation during the editorship of Charles Gavan Duffy.
After his emigration the paper was ably conducted, and with
special care for its literary repute, by Mr. A. M. Sullivan ; but
no poetic movement comparable to that which is illustrated in
the two volumes I have mentioned has ever again been
associated with politics or journalism in Ireland.

T. W. ROLLESTON.

THOMAS DAVIS

THE poetical work of Thomas Davis fell within the last three
years of his short life, from the date when he joined *The
Nation* enterprise in 1842 to his death in 1845. He never
put forth his full strength in this direction, and his history,
which has been fully written by his friend and colleague,
Sir Charles Gavan Duffy, is the history of a man of action, not
of a *littérateur*. His songs were things which he paused to do—
often hastily, and by the way—as he was pressing forward to his
aim. Yet his poetry, written as it was straight from the heart
and on the themes that vitally interested and moved him, was
not only a powerful auxiliary to his work as a political guide
and teacher, but has high and enduring attractions of its own,
and has added peculiar fragrance to a memory worthy on so
many grounds of being cherished by his countrymen. It was
in his poetry that he most intimately revealed himself. And
though Thomas Davis was extraordinarily fertile in ideas, and
indefatigable in methodic industry, the best thing he gave to

the Irish people was not an idea or an achievement of any sort, but simply the gift of himself. He was the ideal Irishman. North and south, east and west, the finest qualities of the population that inhabit this island seemed to be combined in him, developed to their highest power, and coloured deeply with whatever it is in character and temperament that makes the Irish one of the most separate of races. The nation saw itself transfigured in him, and saw the dreams nourished by its long memories and ancestral pride coming true. Hence the intense personal devotion felt towards Davis by the ardent and thoughtful young men who were associated with him, and the sense of irreparable loss caused by his early death. He stood for Ireland—for all Ireland—as no other man did, and it was hardly possible to distinguish the cause from his personality. Yet perhaps the best evidence of the potency and the nobility of his influence was the fact that this sense of loss was overcome by the recollection of the ideals he had held up, and that his memory was honoured by the undaunted pursuance of his work, and the maintenance of the pure and lofty ardour with which he wrought.

Thomas Davis was born in 1814 at Mallow, County Cork. His father was a surgeon in the Royal Artillery, of Welsh origin ; his mother belonged to a well-known Irish family, the Atkins of Firville. As a boy he is said to have been shy, very sensitive, and not at all quick at learning ; but at Trinity College the passion of the student took possession of him, and though he never competed for honours and prizes he became, and remained all his life, a diligent and omnivorous reader. He was called to the Bar in 1838, but speedily abandoned that profession for literature and journalism. With Charles Gavan Duffy and John Blake Dillon he took part in the founding of *The Nation* and in its subsequent management. His 'Lament of Owen Roe' was among the first of the National poems and ballads which soon formed so marked a feature in the propaganda carried on by that paper. On September 16, 1845, he died of scarlet fever, and was followed to his grave by the lamentations of his countrymen of every creed and every political party.　' Beloved and honoured,' as his friend O'Hagan wrote,

> '. . . With a sphere
> Of proud exertion widening near,
> In manhood's power and might arrayed,
> Cold in the grave we saw him laid.

> Not dying, as he yearned to die,
> Keened his country's victor-cry;
> But struck by swift and stern disease.
> How strange to man are God's decrees!

Davis's prose writings were edited in 1845 by C. G. Duffy, and in 1889 an enlarged edition was brought out by Walter Scott, London.　His poems have been collected and edited by T. Wallis, with an excellent introduction (James Duffy, Dublin).　His Life has been written by Sir Charles Gavan Duffy (Kegan Paul).

Celts and Saxons

We hate the Saxon and the Dane,
　We hate the Norman men—
We cursed their greed for blood and gain,
　We curse them now again.
Yet start not, Irish-born man!
　If you're to Ireland true,
We heed not blood, nor creed, nor clan—
　We have no curse for you.

We have no curse for you or yours,
　But Friendship's ready grasp,
And Faith to stand by you and yours
　Unto our latest gasp—
To stand by you against all foes,
　Howe'er or whence they come,
With traitor arts, or bribes, or blows,
　From England, France, or Rome.

What matter that at different shrines
　We pray unto one God?
What matter that at different times
　Our fathers won this sod?

In fortune and in name we're bound
  By stronger links than steel ;
And neither can be safe nor sound
  But in the other's weal.

As Nubian rocks and Ethiop sand,
  Long drifting down the Nile,
Built up old Egypt's fertile land
  For many a hundred mile :
So Pagan clans to Ireland came,
  And clans of Christendom,
Yet joined their wisdom and their fame
  To build a nation from.

Here came the brown Phœnician,
  The man of trade and toil—
Here came the proud Milesian,
  A-hungering for spoil ;
And the Firbolg and the Cymry,
  And the hard, enduring Dane,
And the iron Lords of Normandy,
  With the Saxons in their train.

And oh ! it were a gallant deed
  To show before mankind,
How every race and every creed
  Might be by love combined—
Might be combined, yet not forget
  The fountains whence they rose,
As, filled by many a rivulet,
  The stately Shannon flows.

Nor would we wreak our ancient feud
  On Belgian or on Dane,
Nor visit in a hostile mood
  The hearths of Gaul or Spain ;
But long as on our country lies
  The Anglo-Norman yoke,
Their tyranny we'll stigmatise,
  And God's revenge invoke.

We do not hate, we never cursed,
   Nor spoke a foeman's word
Against a man in Ireland nursed,
   Howe'er we thought he erred.
So start not, Irish-born man !
   If you're to Ireland true,
We heed not race, nor creed, nor clan—
   We've hearts and hands for you.

LAMENT FOR THE DEATH OF EOGHAN RUADH O'NEILL [1]

Time.—November 10, 1649.   *Scene.*—Ormond's Camp, County Waterford.
Speakers.—A veteran of Eoghan O'Neill's clan, and one of the horsemen, just
arrived with an account of his death.

' DID they dare—did they dare, to slay Owen Roe O'Neill ? '
'Yes, they slew with poison him they feared to meet with steel.' [2]
' May God wither up their hearts !   May their blood cease to flow !
May they walk in living death who poisoned Owen Roe!

'Though it break my heart to hear, say again the bitter words.'
'From Derry, against Cromwell, he marched to measure swords ;
But the weapon of the Sacsanach met him on his way,
And he died at Cloch Uachtar [3] upon St. Leonard's Day.

' Wail, wail ye for the Mighty One !   Wail, wail, ye for the Dead !
Quench the hearth, and hold the breath—with ashes strew the head.
How tenderly we loved him !   How deeply we deplore !
Holy Saviour ! but to think we shall never see him more !

' Sagest in the council was he, kindest in the hall :
Sure, we never won a battle—'twas Owen won them all.
Had he lived—had he lived, our dear country had been free ;
But he's dead—but he's dead, and 'tis slaves we'll ever be.

---

[1] Commonly called Owen Roe O'Neill. The Life of this great general
and noble Irishman has been admirably written for the ' New Irish Library '
by Mr. J. F. Taylor, Q.C. (Fisher Unwin).

[2] This is an anachronism. Poison was freely employed against the
Irish in Elizabethan but not in Cromwellian times. Yet the suspicion
lives among the people even to the present day—witness the street-ballad
' By Memory Inspired,' Book I.

[3] Clough Oughter.

'O'Farrell and Clanrickarde, Preston and Red Hugh,
Audley and MacMahon, ye are valiant, wise, and true ;
But what—what are ye all to our darling who is gone?
The Rudder of our ship was he—our Castle's corner-stone!

'Wail, wail him through the island ! Weep, weep for our pride !
Would that on the battlefield our gallant chief had died !
Weep the victor of Beinn Burb—weep him, young men and old !
Weep for him, ye women—your Beautiful lies cold !

'We thought you would not die—we were sure you would not go,
And leave us in our utmost need to Cromwell's cruel blow—
Sheep without a shepherd, when the snow shuts out the sky—
Oh ! why did you leave us, Owen? Why did you die?

'Soft as woman's was your voice, O'Neill ! Bright was your eye.
Oh ! why did you leave us, Owen? Why did you die?
Your troubles are all over ; you're at rest with God on high :
But we're slaves, and we're orphans, Owen ! Why did you die?'

THE SACK OF BALTIMORE [1]

This was the last poem written by Thomas Davis. As a specimen of his power in a narrative poem it seems far superior to his perhaps better-known ballad on Fontenoy. Miss Mitford in her MEMOIRS wrote of it : 'Not only is it full of spirit and melody . . . but the artistic merit is so great. . . . There is no careless line or a word out of place ; and how the epithets paint—"fibrous sod," "heavy balm," "shearing sword"!'

THE summer sun is falling soft on Carbery's hundred isles ;
The summer sun is gleaming still through Gabriel's rough defiles ;

---

[1] Baltimore is a small seaport in the barony of Carbery, in South Munster. It grew up round a castle of O'Driscoll's, and was, after his ruin, colonised by the English. On June 20, 1631, the crew of two Algerine galleys landed in the dead of the night, sacked the town, and bore off into slavery all who were not too old or too young or too fierce for their purpose. The pirates were steered up the intricate channel by one Hackett, a Dungarvan fisherman, whom they had taken at sea for the purpose. Two years after he was convicted and executed for the crime. Baltimore never recovered from this. To the artist, the antiquary, and the naturalist, its neighbourhood is most interesting. (See THE ANCIENT AND PRESENT STATE OF THE COUNTY AND CITY OF CORK, by Charles Smith, M.D.)

Old Inisherkin's crumbled fane looks like a moulting bird ;
And in a calm and sleepy swell the ocean tide is heard ;
The hookers lie upon the beach ; the children cease their play ;
The gossips leave the little inn ; the households kneel to pray ;
And full of love and peace and rest—its daily labour o'er—
Upon that cosy creek there lay the town of Baltimore.

A deeper rest, a starry trance, has come with midnight there ;
No sound, except that throbbing wave, in earth or sea or air.
The massive capes and ruined towers seem conscious of the
    calm ;
The fibrous sod and stunted trees are breathing heavy balm.
So still the night, these two long barques round Dunashad that
    glide
Must trust their oars—methinks not few—against the ebbing tide.
Oh ! some sweet mission of true love must urge them to the
    shore—
They bring some lover to his bride, who sighs in Baltimore !

All, all asleep within each roof along that rocky street,
And these must be the lover's friends, with gently gliding feet—
A stifled gasp ! a dreamy noise !   ' The roof is in a flame !'
From out their beds, and to their doors, rush maid and sire and
    dame—
And meet, upon the threshold stone, the gleaming sabre's fall,
And o'er each black and bearded face the white or crimson shawl ;
The yell of ' Allah ' breaks above the prayer and shriek and roar—
Oh, blessed God ! the Algerine is lord of Baltimore !

Then flung the youth his naked hand against the shearing sword ;
Then sprung the mother on the brand with which her son was
    gored ;
Then sunk the grandsire on the floor, his grand-babes clutching
    wild ;
Then fled the maiden, moaning faint, and nestled with the child.
But see, yon pirate strangled lies, and crushed with splashing
    heel,
While o'er him in an Irish hand there sweeps his Syrian steel—
Though virtue sink and courage fail, and misers yield their store,
There's *one* hearth well avengéd in the sack of Baltimore !

Midsummer morn, in woodland nigh, the birds began to sing—
They see not now the milking-maids—deserted is the spring !
Midsummer day—this gallant rides from distant Bandon's town—
These hookers crossed from stormy Skull, that skiff from Affa-
    down ;
They only found the smoking walls, with neighbours' blood
    besprent,
And on the strewed and trampled beach awhile they wildly went—
Then dashed to sea, and passed Cape Clear, and saw five leagues
    before
The pirate galleys vanishing that ravaged Baltimore.

Oh ! some must tug the galley's oar, and some must tend the
    steed—
This boy will bear a Scheik's chibouk, and that a Bey's jerreed.
Oh ! some are for the arsenals, by beauteous Dardanelles ;
And some are in the caravan to Mecca's sandy dells.
The maid that Bandon gallant sought is chosen for the Dey—
She's safe—he's dead—she stabbed him in the midst of his Serai.
And when to die a death of fire that noble maid they bore,
She only smiled—O'Driscoll's child—she thought of Baltimore.

'Tis two long years since sunk the town beneath that bloody band,
And all around its trampled hearths a larger concourse stand,
Where, high upon a gallows-tree, a yelling wretch is seen—
'Tis Hackett of Dungarvan—he who steered the Algerine !
He fell amid a sullen shout, with scarce a passing prayer,
For he had slain the kith and kin of many a hundred there.
Some muttered of MacMurchadh, who brought the Norman o'er—
Some cursed him with Iscariot, that day in Baltimore.

THE GIRL OF DUNBWY

'Tis pretty to see the girl of Dunbwy
Stepping the mountain statelily—
Though ragged her gown and naked her feet,
No lady in Ireland to match her is meet.

Poor is her diet, and hardly she lies—
Yet a monarch might kneel for a glance of her eyes ;

The child of a peasant—yet England's proud Queen
Has less rank in her heart and less grace in her mien.

Her brow 'neath her raven hair gleams, just as if
A breaker spread white 'neath a shadowy cliff—
And love and devotion and energy speak
From her beauty-proud eye and her passion-pale cheek.

But, pale as her cheek is, there's fruit on her lip,
And her teeth flash as white as the crescent moon's tip,
And her form and her step, like the red-deer's, go past—
As lightsome, as lovely, as haughty, as fast.

I saw her but once, and I looked in her eye,
And she knew that I worshipped in passing her by.
The saint of the wayside—she granted my prayer
Though we spoke not a word ; for her mother was there.

I never can think upon Bantry's bright hills,
But her image starts up, and my longing eye fills ;
And I whisper her softly : ' Again, love, we'll meet !
And I'll lie in your bosom, and live at your feet.'

NATIONALITY

A NATION'S voice, a nation's voice—
    It is a solemn thing !
It bids the bondage-sick rejoice—
    'Tis stronger than a king.
'Tis like the light of many stars,
    The sound of many waves ;
Which brightly look through prison-bars
    And sweetly sound in caves.
Yet is it noblest, godliest known,
When righteous triumph swells its tone.

A nation's flag, a nation's flag—
    If wickedly unrolled,
May foes in adverse battle drag
    Its every fold from fold.

But in the cause of Liberty,
  Guard it 'gainst Earth and Hell ;
Guard it till Death or Victory—
  Look you, you guard it well !
No saint or king has tomb so proud
As he whose flag becomes his shroud.

A nation's right, a nation's right—
  God gave it, and gave, too,
A nation's sword, a nation's might,
  Danger to guard it through.
'Tis freedom from a foreign yoke,
  'Tis just and equal laws,
Which deal unto the humblest folk
  As in a noble's cause.
On nations fixed in right and truth
God would bestow eternal youth.

May Ireland's voice be ever heard
  Amid the world's applause !
And never be her flag-staff stirred
  But in an honest cause !
May freedom be her very breath,
  Be Justice ever dear :
And never an ennobled death
  May son of Ireland fear !
So the Lord God will ever smile,
With guardian grace, upon our isle.

JOHN DE JEAN FRAZER

Born in the King's County about 1809, and wrote largely
for *The Nation, The Irish Felon,* &c. He was a cabinet-
maker by trade. Died in Dublin 1852. His 'Song for
July 12th' represents with much literary grace and skill the
form of thought prevalent among *The Nation* writers towards
Orangeism.

SONG FOR JULY 12TH, 1843

Air—'Boyne Water'

COME ! pledge again thy heart and hand—
   One grasp that ne'er shall sever ;
Our watchword be—'Our native land !'
   Our motto—' Love for ever !'
And let the Orange lily be
   Thy badge, my patriot-brother—
The everlasting Green for *me* ;
   And we for one another.

Behold how green the gallant stem
   On which the flower is blowing ;
How in one heavenly breeze and beam
   Both flower and stem are glowing.
The same good soil, sustaining both,
   Makes both united flourish ;
But cannot give the Orange growth,
   And cease the green to nourish.

Yea, more—the hand that plucks the flow'r
   Will vainly strive to cherish ;
The stem blooms on—but in that hour
   The flower begins to perish.
Regard them, then, of equal worth
   While lasts their genial weather ;
The time's at hand when into earth
   The two shall sink together.

Ev'n thus be, in our country's cause,
   Our party feelings blended ;
Till lasting peace, from equal laws,
   On both shall have descended.
Till then the Orange lily be
   Thy badge, my patriot-brother—
The everlasting Green for *me* ;
   And—we for one another.

JOHN O'HAGAN

O'HAGAN (born at Newry 1822) entered the ranks of *The Nation* writers when a young barrister fresh from Trinity College, Dublin, and contributed to that journal much spirited verse over the signature 'Sliabh Cuilinn' (Slieve Cullan—a mountain near Newry). 'A boyish face, a frank smile, and a readiness to engage in badinage' were, according to Sir C. G. Duffy, the first characteristics that impressed themselves on his associates; but he soon showed gifts of character and intellect that made him one of the most influential and trusted members of the Young Ireland party. After a distinguished career at the Bar he was appointed by Mr. Gladstone first chairman of the Irish Land Commission, and died in 1890.

THE SONG OF ROLAND, translated from the French, 1880; THE CHILDREN'S BALLAD ROSARY, 1890.

OURSELVES ALONE

THE work that should to-day be wrought,
   Defer not till to-morrow;
The help that should within be sought,
   Scorn from without to borrow.
Old maxims these—yet stout and true—
   They speak in trumpet tone,
To do at once what is to do,
   And trust OURSELVES ALONE.

Too long our Irish hearts we schooled
   In patient hope to bide,
By dreams of English justice fooled
   And English tongues that lied.
That hour of weak delusion's past—
   The empty dream has flown:
Our hope and strength, we find at last,
   Is in OURSELVES ALONE.

Aye ! bitter hate or cold neglect,
　　Or lukewarm love at best,
Is all we've found, or can expect,
　　We Aliens of the West.
No friend, beyond our own green shore,
　　Can Erin truly own ;
Yet stronger is her trust, therefore,
　　In her brave sons ALONE.

Remember, when our lot was worse—
　　Sunk, trampled to the dust—
'Twas long our weakness and our curse
　　In stranger aid to trust.
And if, at length, we proudly trod
　　On bigot laws o'erthrown,
Who won that struggle ?   Under God,
　　Ourselves—OURSELVES ALONE.

Oh ! let its memory be enshrined
　　In Ireland's heart for ever !
It proves a banded people's mind
　　Must win in just endeavour ;
It shows how wicked to despair,
　　How weak to idly groan—
If ills at *others'* hand ye bear,
　　The cure is in YOUR OWN.

The foolish word 'impossible'
　　At once, for aye, disdain !
No power can bar a people's will,
　　A people's right to gain.
Be bold, united, firmly set,
　　Nor flinch in word or tone—
We'll be a glorious nation yet,
　　REDEEMED—ERECT—ALONE !

THE OLD STORY

' Old as the universe, yet not outworn.'—The Island.

HE came across the meadow-pass,
  That summer eve of eves ;
The sunlight streamed along the grass
  And glanced amid the leaves ;
And from the shrubbery below,
  And from the garden trees,
He heard the thrushes' music flow,
  And humming of the bees.
The garden-gate was swung apart—
  The space was brief between ;
But there, for throbbing of his heart,
  He paused perforce to lean.

He leaned upon the garden-gate ;
  He looked, and scarce he breathed ;
Within the little porch she sate,
  With woodbine overwreathed ;
Her eyes upon her work were bent
  Unconscious who was nigh ;
But oft the needle slowly went,
  And oft did idle lie ;
And ever to her lips arose
  Sweet fragments faintly sung,
But ever, ere the notes could close,
  She hushed them on her tongue.

' Why should I ever leave this spot,
  But gaze until I die ? '
A moment from that bursting thought
  She felt his footstep nigh.
One sudden lifted glance—but one,
  A tremor and a start,
So gently was their greeting done
  That who would guess their heart ?

Long, long the sun had sunken down,
  And all his golden trail

K

Had died away to lines of brown,
    In duskier hues that fail.
The grasshopper was chirping shrill—
    No other living sound
Accompanied the tiny rill
    That gurgled underground—
No other living sound, unless
    Some spirit bent to hear
Low words of human tenderness,
    And mingling whispers near.

The stars, like pallid gems at first,
    Deep in the liquid sky,
Now forth upon the darkness burst,
    Sole kings and lights on high
In splendour, myriad-fold, supreme—
    No rival moonlight strove,
Nor lovelier e'er was Hesper's beam,
    Nor more majestic Jove.
But what if hearts there beat that night
    That recked not of the skies,
Or only felt their imaged light
    In one another's eyes?

And if two worlds of hidden thought
    And fostered passion met,
Which, passing human language, sought
    And found an utterance yet ;
And if they trembled like to flowers
    That droop across a stream,
The while the silent starry hours
    Glide o'er them like a dream ;
And if, when came the parting time,
    They faltered still and clung ;
What is it all ?—an ancient rhyme
    Ten thousand times besung—
That part of paradise which man
    Without the portal knows—
Which hath been since the world began,
    And shall be till its close.

PROTESTANT ASCENDENCY

'A Protestant King, a Protestant House of Lords and Commons, a Protestant Hierarchy ; the courts of Justice, the army, the navy, and the revenue, in all their branches and details, Protestant – and this system fortified and maintained by a connection with the Protestant State of Great Britain.

'The Protestants of Ireland will never relinquish their political position, which their fathers won with their swords, and which they, therefore, regard as their birthright.'—*Letter of the Dublin Corporation*, 1793.

GREAT fabric of oppression
 By tyrant plunderers planned,
So giant-vast, so iron-fast,
That were not God's great fiat pass'd
That man's injustice shall not last
 Thou might'st eternal stand ;
Black fortress of Ascendency,
 Beneath whose wasting sway
Sprang crime and strife, so deadly rife—
 What rests of thee to-day ?

A few unsightly fragments,
 The scoff and scorn of all,
Long pierc'd and rent by freedom's power
They rot and crumble hour by hour,
And wait the lightest storm to lour,
 In hapless wreck to fall.
What show of faded banners,
 What shouts of angry men,
Or doughty threat or sullen fret,
 Will raise that pile again ?

Vain ! vain ! go seek the charnel
 Where haughty Clare lies low ;
Tell him how ruin darkens o'er
The cause he sav'd in flames and gore,
How his strong will is needed sore
 In this your day of woe—
Rouse bloody Toler, summon all
 Clan Beresford to gorge and prey,
And acrid Saurin's heart of gall
 And serpent Castlereagh.

And those dry bones shall hearken
    And smite with ghastly fear
This isle once more, ere ye restore
    Their dead dominion here.

Vain ! vain ! can ye roll backward
    The world for fifty years ?
From thrice three glowing millions drain
Their strength and substance, heart and brain ?
Where thought and daring impulse reign,
    Plant old derided fears ?
Get their strong limbs your yoke to bear,
    Your grasp upon their purse ?
Your maddest madman would not dare
    So wild a dream to nurse—
Awake ! awake ! your paths to take
    For better or for worse.

The better lies before you,
    The noblest ever trod ;
To meet your brothers face to face,
Quell idle feuds of creed or race,
And take your gallant grandsires' place
    To free your native sod.
Make recreant statesmen tremble,
    And ingrate England quail,
And win and wear the proudest share
    In Ireland's proudest tale.

The worse—'tis yours to choose it—
    In helpless rage to stand :
To see the gulf and, trembling, wait—
To writhe beneath o'ermastering fate,
Repelling with a scowl of hate
    Your brother's outstretched hand—
In history known as tigers
    Whose teeth and fangs were drawn,
Whose heart and will were murderous still
    When means and strength were gone.

> Know, Protestants of Ireland,
>   That, doomed among mankind—
> Marked with the fatal mark—are they
> Who will not know their place or day,
> But cling to phantoms pass'd away,
>   And sow the barren wind.
> Life's ever-shifting currents
>   Brave men put forth to try ;
> *They* wait beside the ebbing tide
>   Till darkness finds them dry.

SIR CHARLES GAVAN DUFFY

C. G. DUFFY was born in Monaghan, 1816.   He was educated
in that town, and entered journalism in Dublin at a very early
age.   In 1842 he launched *The Nation* newspaper.   In the
words of Mr. Martin MacDermott, the great gift which he
brought to the National movement was 'the power of initiation
and organisation, without which, notwithstanding Davis's
splendid talents, there never would have been a *Nation* newspaper or a Young Ireland party.'   THE LIBRARY OF IRELAND
and in later days THE NEW IRISH LIBRARY were originated
by him, and his BALLAD POETRY OF IRELAND is an
invaluable collection of Irish verse.   He was arrested in
1848, but after several abortive trials, in which the anxiety of
the Crown to obtain a conviction overreached itself, he was
released.   After the Famine, he projected and carried out a
national agitation for land reform, in which political differences
on other questions were laid aside, and entered Parliament in
connection with this movement.   It failed when apparently on
the eve of success, owing largely to the opposition of Cardinal
Cullen and some of the Catholic hierarchy, who supported
Sadlier and Keogh—deserters from the Tenant League camp.
Duffy then emigrated to Australia, where he became Premier of
Victoria and subsequently Speaker, and received the honour
of K.C.M.G. in 1873.   In his later years he lived at Nice,

and busied himself chiefly in recording—in volumes as fascinating as they are instructive—the history of the Irish movements in which he was engaged. He died in 1903.

None of the Young Irelanders wrote in rhyme and metre with more sinewy force than Duffy. His lines smite home, like the axe of an Irish Gallowglass ; and though his mind, as his whole career shows, was eminently that of a statesman, he clearly thought and felt as a reckless fighter when he faced the enemies of his cause with the keen blade of verse in his hand. The rising of 1641 and the brigandage of the Rapparees were among the features of the secular resistance of Ireland with which the National cause was most often reproached, and for which its leaders were expected to apologise. And those were the very things that Duffy chose to flaunt before his shocked (or delighted) readers, for the apologetic attitude then so prevalent in Ireland, the tacit admission that the English conquest was in any sense a triumph of civilisation over barbarism, was utterly repugnant to him and his colleagues, and their first object was to make their countrymen understand the whole truth about their history and be proud of it. Duffy's lyre had other strings too, which he touched with skill, as in the 'Lay Sermon' and other poems collected in the NEW SPIRIT OF THE NATION, but it is in these warlike strains that his verse has most strength and character.

Sir Charles Duffy's principal works are : YOUNG IRELAND ; THE LEAGUE OF THE NORTH AND SOUTH (the Tenant League) ; LIFE OF THOMAS DAVIS ; A SHORT LIFE OF THOMAS DAVIS (' New Irish Library ') ; and an edition of IRISH BALLAD POETRY (1843). He also published his reminiscences, MY LIFE IN TWO HEMISPHERES.

THE MUSTER OF THE NORTH
A.D. 1641

We deny and have always denied the alleged massacre of 1641. But that the people rose under their chiefs, seized the English towns and expelled the English settlers, and in doing so committed many excesses, is undeniable—as is equally their desperate provocation. The ballad here printed is not meant as an apology for these excesses, which we condemn and lament, but as a true representation of the feelings of the insurgents in the first madness of success.—*Author's note.*

Joy! joy! the day is come at last, the day of hope and pride—
And see! our crackling bonfires light old Bann's rejoicing tide,
And gladsome bell and bugle-horn from Newry's captured towers,
Hark! how they tell the Saxon swine this land is ours—is OURS!

Glory to God! my eyes have seen the ransomed fields of Do√n,
My ears have drunk the joyful news, 'Stout Phelim hath his own.'
Oh! may they see and hear no more!—oh! may they rot to clay!—
When they forget to triumph in the conquest of to-day.

Now, now we'll teach the shameless Scot to purge his tnievish
maw;
Now, now the Court may fall to pray, for Justice is the Law;
Now shall the Undertaker[1] square, for once, his loose accounts—
We'll strike, brave boys, a fair result, from all his false amounts.

Come, trample down their robber rule, and smite its venal spawn,
Their foreign laws, their foreign Church, their ermine and their
lawn,
With all the specious fry of fraud that robbed us of our own;
And plant our ancient laws again beneath our lineal throne.

Our standard flies o'er fifty towers, o'er twice ten thousand men;
Down have we plucked the pirate Red, never to rise again;
The Green alone shall stream above our native field and flood—
The spotless Green, save where its folds are gemmed with Saxon
blood!

Pity![2] no, no, you dare not, priest—not you, our Father, dare
Preach to us now that godless creed—the murderer's blood to
spare;
To spare his blood, while tombless still our slaughtered kin implore
'Graves and revenge' from Gobbin cliffs and Carrick's bloody
shore![3]

---

[1] The Scotch and English adventurers planted in Ulster by James I.
were called 'Undertakers.'

[2] Leland, the Protestant historian, states that the Catholic priests
'laboured zealously to moderate the excesses of war,' and frequently
protected the English by concealing them in their places of worship and
even under their altars.

[3] The scene of the massacre of the unoffending inhabitants of Island
Magee by the garrison of Carrickfergus.

Pity ! could we 'forget, forgive,' if we were clods of clay,
Our martyred priests, our banished chiefs, our race in dark decay,
And, worse than all—you know it, priest—the daughters of our
    land—
With wrongs we blushed to name until the sword was in our hand ?

Pity ! well, if you needs must whine, let pity have its way—
Pity for all our comrades true, far from our side to-day :
The prison-bound who rot in chains, the faithful dead who poured
Their blood 'neath Temple's lawless axe or Parsons' ruffian sword.

They smote us with the swearer's oath and with the murderer's
    knife ;
We in the open field will fight fairly for land and life ;
But, by the dead and all their wrongs, and by our hopes to-day,
One of us twain shall fight their last, or be it we or they.

They banned our faith, they banned our lives, they trod us into
    earth,
Until our very patience stirred their bitter hearts to mirth.
Even this great flame that wraps them now, not *we* but *they* have
    bred :
Yes, this is their own work ; and now their work be on their head !

Nay, Father, tell us not of help from Leinster's Norman peers,
If we shall shape our holy cause to match their selfish fears—
Helpless and hopeless be their cause who brook a vain delay !
Our ship is launched, our flag's afloat, whether they come or stay.

Let silken Howth and savage Slane still kiss their tyrant's rod,
And pale Dunsany still prefer his master to his God ;
Little we'd miss their fathers' sons, the Marchmen of the Pale,
If Irish hearts and Irish hands had Spanish blade and mail !

Then let them stay to bow and fawn, or fight with cunning words ;
I fear me more their courtly arts than England's hireling swords ;
Nathless their creed, they hate us still, as the despoiler hates ;
Could they love us, and love their prey, our kinsmen's lost estates ?

Our rude array's a jagged rock to smash the spoiler's pow'r—
Or, need we aid, His aid we have who doomed this gracious hour ;
Of yore He led His Hebrew host to peace through strife and pain,
And us He leads the self-same path, the self-same goal to gain.

Down from the sacred hills whereon a saint [1] communed with God,
Up from the vale where Bagenal's blood manured the reeking sod,
Out from the stately woods of Truagh, M'Kenna's plundered home,
Like Malin's waves, as fierce and fast, our faithful clansmen come.

Then, brethren, *on !*   O'Neill's dear shade would frown to see you
     pause—
Our banished Hugh, our martyred Hugh, is watching o'er your
     cause—
His generous error lost the land—he deemed the Norman true ;
Oh, forward ! friends, it must not lose the land again in you !

The Irish Rapparees

A PEASANT BALLAD

   When Limerick was surrendered and the bulk of the Irish army took
service with Louis XIV., a multitude of the old soldiers of the Boyne, Aughrim
and Limerick, preferred remaining in the country at the risk of fighting for
their daily bread ; and with them some gentlemen, loath to part from their
estates or their sweethearts.   The English army and the English law drove
them by degrees to the hills, where they were long a terror to the new and old
settlers from England, and a secret pride and comfort to the trampled peasantry,
who loved them even for their excesses.   It was all they had left to take pride
in.—*Author's note.*

RIGH SHEMUS he has gone to France and left his crown behind :—
Ill-luck be theirs, both day and night, put runnin' in his mind !
Lord Lucan [2] followed after, with his slashers brave and true,
And now the doleful *keen* is raised—' What will poor Ireland do ?
             ' What must poor Ireland do ?
Our luck, they say, has gone to France.   What *can* poor Ireland
     do ? '

Oh, never fear for Ireland, for she has so'gers still,
For Remy's boys are in the wood, and Rory's on the hill ;

---

   [1] St. Patrick, whose favourite retreat was Lecale, in the County
Down.
   [2] After the Treaty of Limerick, Patrick Sarsfield, Lord Lucan, sailed
with the Brigade to France, and was killed while leading his countrymen
to victory at the battle of Landen, in the Low Countries, July 29, 1693.

And never had poor Ireland more loyal hearts than these—
May God be kind and good to them, the faithful Rapparees !
        The fearless Rapparees !
The jewel waar ye, Rory, with your Irish Rapparees !

Oh, black's your heart, Clan Oliver, and coulder than the clay !
Oh, high's your head, Clan Sassenach, since Sarsfield's gone away !
It's little love you bear to us for sake of long ago —
But howld your hand, for Ireland still can strike a deadly blow—
        Can strike a mortal blow—
Och ! *dar-a-Chriost !* 'tis she that still could strike the deadly blow !

The master's bawn, the master's seat, a surly *bodach* [1] fills ;
The master's son, an outlawed man, is riding on the hills ;
But, God be praised, that round him throng, as thick as summer
    bees,
The swords that guarded Limerick walls—his faithful Rapparees !
        His lovin' Rapparees !
Who daar say ' No' to Rory Oge, who heads the Rapparees !

Black Billy Grimes, of Latnamard, he racked us long and sore—
God rest the faithful hearts he broke ; we'll never see them moie !
But I'll go bail he'll break no more while Truagh has gallows-trees,
For why ? he met one lonesome night the awful Rapparees !
        The angry Rapparees !
They never sin no more, my boys, who cross the Rapparees.

Now, Sassenach and Cromweller, take heed of what I say—
Keep down your black and angry looks that scorn us night and
    day ;
For there's a just and wrathful Judge that every action sees,
And He'll make strong, to right our wrong, the faithful Rapparees !
        The fearless Rapparees !
The men that rode at Sarsfield's side, the changeless Rapparees !

---

[1] *Bodach* : a severe, inhospitable man ; a churl.

WILLIAM B. McBURNEY

VERY little is known of this writer, who was an early contributor to *The Nation*. He is said to have died about 1900 in the United States. He also wrote under the name of 'Carroll Malone.'

THE CROPPY BOY

A BALLAD OF '98

'GOOD men and true ! in this house who dwell,
To a stranger *bouchal*, I pray you tell
Is the Priest at home ? or may he be seen ?
I would speak a word with Father Green.'

'The Priest's at home, boy, and may be seen ;
'Tis easy speaking with Father Green ;
But you must wait, till I go and see
If the holy Father alone may be.'

The youth has entered an empty hall—
What a lonely sound has his light foot-fall !
And the gloomy chamber's chill and bare,
With a vested Priest in a lonely chair.

The youth has knelt to tell his sins.
'*Nomine Dei*,' the youth begins :
At '*mea culpa*' he beats his breast,
And in broken murmurs he speaks the rest.

' At the siege of Ross did my father fall,
And at Gorey my loving brothers all.
I alone am left of my name and race ;
I will go to Wexford and take their place.

' I cursed three times since last Easter Day—
At Mass-time once I went to play ;
I passed the churchyard one day in haste,
And forgot to pray for my mother's rest.

'I bear no hate against living thing ;
But I love my country above my King.
Now, Father ! bless me, and let me go
To die, if God has ordained it so.'

The Priest said nought, but a rustling noise
Made the youth look above in wild surprise ;
The robes were off, and in scarlet there
Sat a yeoman captain with fiery glare.

With fiery glare and with fury hoarse,
Instead of blessing, he breathed a curse :
''Twas a good thought, boy, to come here and shrive ;
For one short hour is your time to live.

'Upon yon river three tenders float ;
The Priest's in one, if he isn't shot ;
We hold his house for our Lord the King,
And—" Amen," say I—may all traitors swing !'

At Geneva barrack that young man died,
And at Passage they have his body laid.
Good people who live in peace and joy,
Breathe a prayer and a tear for the Croppy boy.

THE GOOD SHIP *CASTLE DOWN*

A REBEL CHAUNT, A.D. 1776

OH, how she plough'd the ocean, the good ship *Castle Down*,
That day we hung our colours out, the Harp without the Crown !
A gallant barque, she topp'd the wave, and fearless hearts were
    we,
With guns and pikes and bayonets, a stalwart company.
'Twas a sixteen years from THUROT ; and sweeping down the
    bay
The ' Siege of Carrickfergus ' so merrily we did play :
And by the old castle's foot we went, with three right hearty
    cheers,
And wav'd aloft our green cockades, for we were Volunteers,
                                        Volunteers !
Oh, we were in our prime that day, stout Irish Volunteers.

'Twas when we heav'd our anchor on the breast of smooth
    Garmoyle.
Our guns spoke out in thunder : ' Adieu, sweet Irish soil !
At Whiteabbey and Greencastle, and Holywood so gay,
Were hundreds waving handkerchiefs and many a loud huzza.
Our voices o'er the water struck the hollow mountains round—
Young Freedom, struggling at her birth, might utter such a sound.
By that green slope beside Belfast, we cheer'd and cheer'd it still—
For they had chang'd its name that year, and they call'd it
    Bunker's Hill—
                        Bunker's Hill !
Oh, were our hands but with our hearts in the trench at Bunker's
    Hill !

Our ship clear'd out for Quebec ; but thither little bent,
Up some New England river, to run her keel we meant ;
So we took a course due north as round the old Black Head we
    steer'd,
Till Ireland bore south-west by south, and Fingal's rock appear'd.
Then on the poop stood Webster, while the ship hung flutteringly,
About to take her tack across the wide, wide ocean sea—
He pointed to th' Atlantic, ' Sure, yon's no place for slaves :
Haul down these British badges, for Freedom rules the waves—
                        Rules the waves ! '
Three hundred strong men answered, shouting ' Freedom rules
    the waves ! '

Then all together rose and brought the British ensign down,
And up we haul'd our Irish Green, without the British Crown.
Emblazoned there a Golden Harp like a maiden undefiled,
A shamrock wreath around her head, look'd o'er the sea and
    smiled.
A hundred days, with adverse wind, we kept our course afar,
On the hundredth day came bearing down a British sloop of war.
When they spied our flag they fired a gun, but as they near'd us
    fast,
Old Andrew Jackson went aloft and nailed it to the mast—
                        To the mast !
A soldier was old Jackson, and he made our colours fast.

Patrick Henry was our captain, as brave as ever sailed.
' Now we must do or die,' said he, ' for the Green Flag is nailed.
Silently came the sloop along ; and silently we lay
Flat, till with cheers and loud broadside the foe began the fray.
Then the boarders o'er the bulwarks, like shuttlecocks, we cast ;
One close discharge from all our guns cut down the tapering mast.
' Now, British tars ! St. George's Cross is trailing in the sea—
How d'ye like the greeting and the handsel of the Free ?—
                                        Of the Free !
How like you, lads, the greeting of the men who will be free ? '

They answer'd us with cannon, as befitted well their fame ;
And to shoot away our Irish flag each gunner took his aim ;
They ripp'd it up in ribbons till it fluttered in the air,
And riddled it with shot-holes till no Golden Harp was there ;
But through the ragged holes the sky did glance and gleam in
    light,
Just as the twinkling stars shine through God's unfurled flag at
    night.
With dropping fire we sang, ' Good-night, and fare ye well, brave
    tars !'
Our captain looked aloft : ' By Heaven ! the flag is Stripes and
    Stars !'
                                        Stripes and Stars !
So into Boston port we sailed, beneath the Stripes and Stars.

JOHN KELLS INGRAM

(See J. K. Ingram, Book VI.)

THE MEMORY OF THE DEAD

WHO fears to speak of Ninety-Eight ?
    Who blushes at the name ?
When cowards mock the patriot's fate,
    Who hangs his head for shame ?

He's all a knave or half a slave
  Who slights his country thus :
But a true man, like you, man,
  Will fill your glass with us.

We drink the memory of the brave,
  The faithful and the few—
Some lie far off beyond the wave,
  Some sleep in Ireland, too ;
All, all are gone—but still lives on
  The fame of those who died ;
And true men, like you, men,
  Remember them with pride.

Some on the shores of distant lands
  Their weary hearts have laid,
And by the stranger's heedless hands
  Their lonely graves were made ;
But though their clay be far away
  Beyond the Atlantic foam,
In true men, like you. men,
  Their spirit's still at home.

The dust of some is Irish earth ;
  Among their own they rest ;
And the same land that gave them birth
  Has caught them to her breast ;
And we will pray that from their clay
  Full many a race may start
Of true men, like you, men,
  To act as brave a part.

They rose in dark and evil days
  To right their native land ;
They kindled here a living blaze
  That nothing shall withstand.
Alas ! that Might can vanquish Right—
  They fell, and passed away ;
But true men, like you, men,
  Are plenty here to-day.

Then here's their memory—may it be
    For us a guiding light,
To cheer our strife for liberty,
    And teach us to unite !
Through good and ill, be Ireland's still,
    Though sad as theirs, your fate ;
And true men, be you, men,
    Like those of Ninety-Eight.

MARTIN MacDERMOTT

MARTIN MacDERMOTT was born in Dublin in 1823. He
contributed much graceful verse to *The Nation*, and was
the editor of the NEW SPIRIT OF THE NATION, a volume
which has been of much help towards this Anthology. He
took part in the political movements of the '48 period, being
deputed to represent the leaders of the attempted insurrection
in Paris. He served for some years as Chief Architect to the
Office of Works of the Khedive of Egypt, and later lived in
England. He also took some part in the work of the Irish
Literary Society of London. He died in 1905.

GIRL OF THE RED MOUTH

GIRL of the red mouth,
    Love me ! Love me !
Girl of the red mouth,
    Love me !
'Tis by its curve, I know,
Love fashioneth his bow,
And bends it—ah, even so !
    Oh, girl of the red mouth, love me !

Girl of the blue eye,
    Love me ! Love me !
Girl of the dew eye,
    Love me !

Worlds hang for lamps on high ;
And thought's world lives in thy
Lustrous and tender eye—
    Oh, girl of the blue eye, love me !

Girl of the swan's neck,
    Love me ! Love me !
Girl of the swan's neck,
    Love me !
As a marble Greek doth grow
To his steed's back of snow,
Thy white neck sits thy shoulder so,—
    Oh, girl of the swan's neck, love me !

Girl of the low voice,
    Love me ! Love me !
Girl of the sweet voice,
    Love me !
Like the echo of a bell,—
Like the bubbling of a well—
Sweeter ! Love within doth dwell,—
    Oh, girl of the low voice, love me !

RICHARD DALTON WILLIAMS

THE ' Munster War-Song ' was sent to *The Nation* by Williams
when a schoolboy at Carlow. He was born in the city of
Dublin in 1822. He was tried for treason-felony in 1848, but
acquitted. In 1849 he took his medical degree in Edinburgh,
practised in Dublin for a couple of years, and then emigrated
to the U.S.A. He became Professor of *Belles Lettres* in
Mobile (Ala.), and in 1856 took up practice as a physician at
New Orleans. He died in 1862. A monument has been raised
to him by a regiment of Irish-American soldiers who happened
to encamp near his grave during the Civil War. Williams wrote
a great deal of humorous as well as patriotic verse for *The
Nation*. With much grace, pathos, and energy, he had the

L

'fatal facility' of many Irish verse-writers, and never achieved all that he was capable of. His 'Dying Girl' is, however, a piece of verse which will not easily be forgotten. His poems have been collected and published by P. A. Sillard, Dublin.

The Munster War-Song

BATTLE OF AHERLOW, A.D. 1190

CAN the depths of the ocean afford you not graves,
That you come thus to perish afar o'er the waves—
To redden and swell the wild torrents that flow
Through the valley of vengeance, the dark Aherlow?[1]

The clangour of conflict o'erburthens the breeze,
From the stormy Slieve Bloom to the stately Galtees ;
Your caverns and torrents are purple with gore,
Slievenamon, Glen Colaich, and sublime Galtee Mor !

The Sunburst that slumbered, embalmed in our tears,
Tipperary ! shall wave o'er thy tall mountaineers !
And the dark hill shall bristle with sabre and spear
While one tyrant remains to forge manacles here.

The riderless war-steed careers o'er the plain
With a shaft in his flank and a blood-dripping mane ;
His gallant breast labours, and glare his wild eyes ;
He plunges in torture—falls—shivers—and dies.

Let the trumpets ring triumph ! The tyrant is slain !
He reels o'er his charger deep-pierced through the brain ;
And his myriads are flying, like leaves on the gale—
But who shall escape from our hills with the tale ?

For the arrows of vengeance are show'ring like rain,
And choke the strong rivers with islands of slain,
Till thy waves, lordly Shannon, all crimsonly flow,
Like the billows of hell, with the blood of the foe.

---

[1] Aherlow Glen, County Tipperary.

Ay ! the foemen are flying, but vainly they fly—
Revenge with the fleetness of lightning can vie ;
And the septs of the mountains spring up from each rock
And rush down the ravines like wolves on the flock.

And who shall pass over the stormy Slieve Bloom,
To tell the pale Saxon of tyranny's doom,
When, like tigers from ambush, our fierce mountaineers
Leap along from the crags with their death-dealing spears ?

They came with high boasting to bind us as slaves,
But the glen and the torrent have yawned on their graves.
From the gloomy Ardfinnan to wild Temple Mor—
From the Suir to the Shannon—is red with their gore.

By the soul of Heremon ! our warriors may smile,
To remember the march of the foe through our isle ;
Their banners and harness were costly and gay,
And proudly they flashed in the summer sun's ray ;

The hilts of their falchions were crusted with gold,
And the gems of their helmets were bright to behold ;
By Saint Bride of Kildare ! but they moved in fair show—
To gorge the young eagles of dark Aherlow !

THE DYING GIRL

FROM a Munster vale they brought her,
   From the pure and balmy air ;
An Ormond peasant's daughter,
   With blue eyes and golden hair—
They brought her to the city,
   And she faded slowly there.
Consumption has no pity
   For blue eyes and golden hair.

When I saw her first reclining
   Her lips were mov'd in pray'r,
And the setting sun was shining
   On her loosen'd golden hair.

When our kindly glances met her,
   Deadly brilliant was her eye ;
And she said that she was better,
   While we knew that she must die.

She speaks of Munster valleys,
   The *pattern*, dance and fair,
And her thin hand feebly dallies
   With her scattered golden hair.
When silently we listen'd
   To her breath with quiet care,
Her eyes with wonder glisten'd—
   And she asked us, ' What was there ? '

The poor thing smiled to ask it,
   And her pretty mouth laid bare,
Like gems within a casket,
   A string of pearlets rare.
We said that we were trying
   By the gushing of her blood
And the time she took in sighing
   To know if she were good.

Well, she smil'd and chatted gaily,
   Though we saw in mute despair
The hectic brighter daily,
   And the death-dew on her hair.
And oft her wasted fingers
   Beating time upon the bed :
O'er some old tune she lingers,
   And she bows her golden head.

At length the harp is broken ;
   And the spirit in its strings,
As the last decree is spoken,
   To its source exulting springs.
Descending swiftly from the skies,
   Her guardian angel came,
He struck God's lightning from her eyes,
   And bore Him back the flame.

Before the sun had risen
   Thro' the lark-loved morning air,
Her young soul left its prison,
   Undefiled by sin or care.
I stood beside the couch in tears
   Where pale and calm she slept,
And tho' I've gaz'd on death for years,
   I blush not that I wept.
I check'd with effort pity's sighs
   And left the matron there,
To close the curtains of her eyes
   And bind her golden hair.

ELLEN MARY PATRICK DOWNING

KNOWN as 'Mary of *The Nation*,' her poems in that journal being generally signed by the name 'Mary' alone. She was born in Cork on March 19, 1828, and died on January 27, 1869. In 1849 she entered a convent. Her poetry has the simplicity and unconscious grace of a bird's song.

VOICES OF THE HEART, 1868, 1880 ; POEMS FOR CHILDREN, 1881.

MY OWEN

PROUD of you, fond of you, clinging so near to you,
Light is my heart now I know I am dear to you !
Glad is my voice now, so free it may sing to you
All the wild love that is burning within for you !
Tell me once more, tell it over and over,
The tale of that eve that first saw you my lover.
   Now I need never blush
   At my heart's hottest gush ;
The wife of my Owen her heart may discover.

Proud of you, fond of you, having all right in you !
Quitting all else through my love and delight in you !
Glad is my heart, since 'tis beating so nigh to you !
Light is my step, for it always may fly to you !
Clasped in your arms, where no sorrow can reach to me,
Reading your eyes till new love they shall teach to me,
　　　Though wild and weak till now,
　　　　By that blessed marriage vow,
More than the wisest know your heart shall preach to me.

The Old Church at Lismore

This poem, inscribed in the MS. ' My Last Verses,' was the last written by
' Mary ' before entering on her novitiate in 1849.

Old Church, thou still art Catholic !—e'en dream they as they
　　may
That the new rites and worship have swept the old away ;
There is no form of beauty raised by Nature, or by art,
That preaches not God's saving truths to man's adoring heart !

In vain they tore the altar down ; in vain they flung aside
The mournful emblem of the death which our sweet Saviour died ;
In vain they left no single trace of saint or angel here—
Still angel-spirits haunt the ground, and to the soul appear.

I marvel how, in scenes like these, so coldly they can pray,
Nor hold sweet commune with the dead who once knelt down as
　　they ;
Yet not as they, in sad mistrust or sceptic doubt—for, oh,
They looked in hope to the blessèd saints, these dead of long ago.

And, then, the churchyard, soft and calm, spread out beyond the
　　scene
With sunshine warm and soothing shade and trees upon its green ;
Ah ! though their cruel Church forbid, are there no hearts will
　　pray
For the poor souls that trembling left that cold and speechless
　　clay ?

My God! I am a Catholic! I grew into the ways
Of my dear Church since first my voice could lisp a word of
  praise ;
But oft I think though my first youth were taught and trained
  awrong,
I still had learnt the one true faith from Nature and from song!

For still, whenever dear friends die, it is such joy to know
They are not all beyond the care that healed their wounds below,
That we can pray them into peace, and speed them to the shore
Where clouds and cares and thorny griefs shall vex their hearts no
  more.

And the sweet saints, so meek below, so merciful above ;
And the pure angels, watching still with such untiring love ;
And the kind Virgin, Queen of Heaven, with all her mother's care,
Who prays for earth, because she knows what breaking hearts are
  there !

Oh, let us lose no single link that our dear Church has bound,
To keep our hearts more close to Heaven, on earth's ungenial
  ground ;
But trust in saint and martyr yet, and o'er their hallowed clay,
Long after we have ceased to weep, kneel faithful down to pray.

So shall the land for us be still the Sainted Isle of old,
Where hymn and incense rise to Heaven, and holy beads are
  told ;
And even the ground they tore from God, in years of crime and
  woe,
Instinctive with His truth and love, shall breathe of long ago !

ARTHUR GERALD GEOGHEGAN

AUTHOR of THE MONKS OF KILCREA, a collection of stories
in verse, which for many years remained anonymous, and was
much spoken of. It was first published in 1853, and a second

edition was issued, with other poems, in 1861. It was translated into French in 1858.   Its author was born in Dublin on
June 1, 1810, and entered the Excise in 1830.   He became a
collector of Inland Revenue in 1857, and retired in 1877.   He
died in Kensington on November 29, 1889, and was buried at
Kensal Green.   His poems appeared chiefly in *The Nation*
and in other Dublin papers and magazines.

AFTER AUGHRIM

Do you remember, long ago,
Kathaleen?
When your lover whispered low,
' Shall I stay or shall I go,
Kathaleen ? '
And you answered proudly, ' Go !
And join King James and strike a blow
For the Green ! '

Mavrone, your hair is white as snow,
Kathaleen ;
Your heart is sad and full of woe.
Do you repent you made him go,
Kathaleen ?
And quick you answer proudly, ' No !
For better die with Sarsfield so
Than live a slave without a blow
For the Green ! '

DENNY LANE

BORN in Cork in 1818, and died 1896 in that city, where he
was a successful merchant and manufacturer.   He is only
known as a poet by two pieces, both of which appeared in
The Nation in 1844 and 1845.   The metrical structure of this
poem, whether intentionally or otherwise, is curiously close to
that of Gaelic verse.

The Lament of the Irish Maiden

On Carrigdhoun the heath is brown,
　The clouds are dark o'er Ardnalee,
And many a stream comes rushing down
　To swell the angry Ownabwee.
The moaning blast is sweeping past
　Through many a leafless tree,
And I'm alone—for he is gone—
　My hawk is flown—*Ochone machree !*

The heath was brown on Carrigdhoun,
　Bright shone the sun on Ardnalee,
The dark green trees bent, trembling, down
　To kiss the slumbering Ownabwee.
That happy day, 'twas but last May—
　'Tis like a dream to me—
When Donnell swore—aye, o'er and o'er—
　We'd part no more—*astor machree !*

Soft April showers and bright May flowers
　Will bring the summer back again,
But will they bring me back the hours
　I spent with my brave Donnell then ?
'Tis but a chance, for he's gone to France,
　To wear the *fleur-de-lis*,
But I'll follow you, my Donnell Dhu,
　For still I'm true to you, *machree !*

MARY KELLY

Better known as 'Eva,' most of her poems having appeared during the early years of *The Nation* over that name. Born at Headfort, County Galway, about 1825, she later lived in Australia, where her husband, Dr. Kevin Izod O'Doherty, was a successful physician. Her poems were published in a volume at San Francisco in 1877.

Tipperary

Were you ever in sweet Tipperary, where the fields are so sunny
    and green,
And the heath-brown Slieve-bloom and the Galtees look down
    with so proud a mien?
'Tis there you would see more beauty than is on all Irish ground—
God bless you, my sweet Tipperary, for where could your match
    be found?

They say that your hand is fearful, that darkness is in your eye:
But I'll not let them dare to talk so black and bitter a lie.
Oh! no, *macushla storin!* bright, bright, and warm are you,
With hearts as bold as the men of old, to yourselves and your
    country true.

And when there is gloom upon you, bid them think who has
    brought it there—
Sure, a frown or a word of hatred was not made for your face so
    fair;
You've a hand for the grasp of friendship—another to make them
    quake,
And they're welcome to whichsoever it pleases them most to take.

Shall our homes, like the huts of Connaught, be crumbled before
    our eyes?
Shall we fly, like a flock of wild geese, from all that we love and
    prize?
No! by those who were here before us, no churl shall our tyrant be;
Our land it is theirs by plunder, but, by Brigid, ourselves are free.

No! we do not forget the greatness did once to sweet Eire belong;
No treason or craven spirit was ever our race among;
And no frown or no word of hatred we give—but to pay them back;
In evil we only follow our enemies' darksome track.

Oh! come for a while among us, and give us the friendly hand,
And you'll see that old Tipperary is a loving and gladsome land;
From Upper to Lower Ormond, bright welcomes and smiles will
    spring—
On the plains of Tipperary the stranger is like a king.

JOHN KEEGAN

BORN in Queen's County about 1809, and died in 1849. He was a frequent contributor to *The Nation* and other periodicals. He was of peasant origin, and was educated at one of those hedge-schools which have done more than is commonly recognised for the cultivation of Irish intellect. His poems are usually more distinguished for the simplicity and pathetic grace of the 'Dark Girl' than for the rough energy which marks this 'Harvest Hymn.'

THE IRISH REAPER'S HARVEST HYMN

ALL hail ! Holy Mary, our hope and our joy !
Smile down, blessed Queen ! on the poor Irish boy
Who wanders away from his dear beloved home ;
O Mary ! be with me wherever I roam.
      Be with me, O Mary !
      Forsake me not, Mary !
But guide me and guard me wherever I roam !

From the home of my fathers in anguish I go,
To toil for the dark-livered, cold-hearted foe,
Who mocks me, and hates me, and calls me a slave,
An alien, a savage—all names but a knave.
      But, blessed be Mary !
      My sweet, holy Mary !
The *bodach*, he never dare call me a knave.

From my mother's mud sheeling an outcast I fly,
With a cloud on my heart and a tear in my eye ;
Oh ! I burn as I think that if *Some One* would say,
' Revenge on your tyrants !'—but Mary ! I pray,
      From my soul's depth, O Mary !
      And hear me, sweet Mary !
For union and peace to Old Ireland I pray.

The land that I fly from is fertile and fair,
And more than I ask or I wish for is there,
But *I* must not taste the good things that I see—
' There's nothing but rags and green rushes for me.' [1]
                    O mild Virgin Mary !
                    O sweet Mother Mary !
Who keeps my rough hand from red murder but thee ?

But, sure, in the end our dear freedom we'll gain,
And wipe from the green flag each Sassanach stain.
And oh ! Holy Mary, your blessing we crave !
Give hearts to the timid, and hands to the brave ;
                    And then, Mother Mary !
                    Our own blessed Mary !
Light liberty's flame in the hut of the slave !

THE ' DARK GIRL ' BY THE ' HOLY WELL '

I think it was in the midsummer of 1832 that I joined a party of the peasantry of my native village, who were *en route* to a ' pilgrimage ' at St. John's
Well, near the town of Kilkenny.   The journey (about twenty-five Irish miles)
was commenced early in the afternoon, and it was considerably after sunset
when we reached our destination.   My companions immediately set about the
fulfilment of their vows, whilst I, who was but a mere boy, sat down on the green
grass, tired and in ill-humour, after my long and painful tramp over a hundred
stony hills and a thousand rugged fields, under the burning sun of a midsummer afternoon.   I was utterly unable to perform any act of devotion, nor, I
must confess, was I very much disposed to do so, even were I able ; so I seated
myself quietly amid the groups of beggars, cripples, ' dark people,' and the
other various classes of pilgrims who thronged around the sacred fountain.
Among the crowd I had marked two pilgrims, who, from the moment I saw
them, arrested my particular attention.   One of these was an aged female,
decently clad—the other was a very fine young girl, dressed in a gown, shawl
and bonnet of faded black satin.   The girl was of a tall and noble figure—
strikingly beautiful, but *stone blind*.   I learned that they were natives of the
county of Wexford ; that the girl had lost her sight in brain fever, in her
childhood ; that all human means had been tried for her cure, but in vain ; and
that now, as a last resource, they had travelled all the way to pray at the
shrine of St. John, and bathe her sightless orbs in the healing waters of his
well.   It is believed that when Heaven wills the performance of cures, the sky
opens above the well, at the hour of midnight, and Christ, the Virgin Mother,
and St. John descend in the form of three snow-whites, and descend with the

---

[1] Taken literally from a conversation with a young peasant on his way
to reap the harvest in England.

rapidity of lightning into the depths of the fountain. No person but those destined to be cured can *see* this miraculous phenomenon, but everybody can *hear* the musical sound of their wings as they rush into the well and agitate the waters ! I cannot describe how sad I felt myself, too, at the poor girl's anguish, for I had almost arrived at the hope that, though another ' miracle ' was never wrought at St. John's Well, Heaven would relent on this occasion, and restore that sweet Wexford girl to her long-lost sight. She returned, however, as she came—a ' Dark Girl '—and I heard afterwards that she took ill and died before she reached home. —*Author's note.*

'MOTHER ! is that the passing bell ?
  Or, yet, the midnight chime ?
Or, rush of Angel's golden wings ?
  Or is it near *the Time*—
The time when God, *they say*, comes down
  This weary world upon,
With Holy Mary at His right
  And, at His left, St. John !

'I'm dumb ! my heart forgets to throb ;
  My blood forgets to run ;
But vain my sighs—in vain I sob—
  God's will must still be done.
I hear but tone of warning bell,
  For holy priest or nun ;
On earth, God's face I'll never see !
  Nor Mary ! nor St. John !

' Mother ! my hopes are gone again ;
  My heart is black as ever ;—
Mother ! I say, look forth *once more*,
  And see can you discover
God's glory in the crimson clouds—
  See does He ride upon
That perfumed breeze—or do you see
  The Virgin, or St. John ?

'Ah, no ! ah, no ! Well, God of Peace,
  Grant me Thy blessing still ;
Oh, make me patient with my doom
  And happy at Thy will ;

And guide my footsteps so on earth,
    That, when I'm dead and gone,
My eyes may catch Thy shining light,
    With Mary! and St. John?

'Yet, mother, could I see *thy* smile,
    Before we part, below—
Or watch the silver moon and stars
    Where Slaney's ripples flow;
Oh! could I see the sweet sun shine
    My native hills upon,
I'd never love my God the less,
    Nor Mary, nor St. John!

' But no, ah no! it cannot be!
    Yet, mother! do not mourn—
Come, kneel again, and pray to God,
    In peace, let us return;
The Dark Girl's doom must aye be mine—
    But Heaven will light me on,
Until I find my way to God,
    And Mary, and St. John!'

MICHAEL JOSEPH BARRY

MICHAEL JOSEPH BARRY was born in Cork about 1817, and
wrote much verse for *The Nation* up to the time of the '48
insurrection. He treated the result of that attempt as final,
and ceased his connection with the National movement. He
became a police magistrate in Dublin, but after a time
relinquished the appointment and went to live on the
Continent. He died in 1889. His poems are spirited and
energetic, but do not show signs of the brilliant wit which, as

Sir Charles G. Duffy tells us, used to delight his colleagues in *The Nation* office. While he was a police magistrate, a constable giving evidence before him against an Irish-American suspected of seditious designs swore that the prisoner wore 'a Republican hat.' 'A Republican hat !' exclaimed the counsel for the prisoner ; 'does your worship know what that means ?' 'I presume,' said his worship, 'a Republican hat means a hat without a crown.'

Wrote 'The Kishoge Papers' for *The Dublin University Magazine.* Published in 1854 A WATERLOO COMMEMORATION FOR 1854 ; LAYS OF THE WAR, 1856 ; HEINRICH AND LENORE, 1886. Edited SONGS OF IRELAND, 1845.

THE SWORD

WHAT rights the brave ?
The sword !
What frees the slave ?
The sword !
What cleaves in twain
The despot's chain,
And makes his gyves and dungeons vain ?
The sword !

CHORUS

Then cease thy proud task never
While rests a link to sever !
Guard of the free,
We'll cherish thee,
And keep thee bright for ever !

What checks the knave ?
The sword !
What smites to save ?
The sword !
What wreaks the wrong
Unpunished long,
At last, upon the guilty strong ?
The sword !

What shelters Right?
                    The sword !
What makes it might?
                    The sword !
What strikes the crown
Of tyrants down,
And answers with its flash their frown?
                    The sword !

CHORUS

Then cease thy proud task never, &c.

Still be thou true,
                    Good sword !
We'll die or do,
                    Good sword !
Leap forth to light
If tyrants smite,
And trust our arms to wield thee right,
                    Good sword !

CHORUS

Yes ! cease thy proud task never
While rests a link to sever !
        Guard of the free,
        We'll cherish thee,
And keep thee bright for ever !

MICHAEL TORMEY

THE REV. MICHAEL TORMEY was born in Westmeath 1820, and died in 1893. He edited *The Tablet* at one time, and was keenly interested in the Tenant League movement which succeeded the Famine, and was partly evoked by it. He was not distinguished as a poet, but 'The Ancient Race' has in it a surge of heartfelt anguish and wrath which renders not unfitly the master passion of the Irish peasant.

THE ANCIENT RACE

This poem was written at the era of the Irish Tenant League (1850–56), when the principles of the land struggle were first formulated.

WHAT shall become of the ancient race,
The noble Keltic island race?
Like cloud on cloud o'er the azure sky,
When winter storms are loud and high,
Their dark ships shadow the ocean's face—
What shall become of the Keltic race?

What shall befall the ancient race—
The poor, unfriended, faithful race?
Where ploughman's song made the hamlet ring,
The hawk and the owlet flap their wing;
The village homes, oh, who can trace—
God of our persecuted race!

What shall befall the ancient race?
Is treason's stigma on their face?
Be they cowards or traitors? Go—
Ask the shade of England's foe;
See the gems her crown that grace;
They tell a tale of the ancient race.

They tell a tale of the ancient race—
Of matchless deeds in danger's face;
They speak of Britain's glory fed
With blood of Kelts, right bravely shed;
Of India's spoil and Frank's disgrace—
Such tale they tell of the ancient race.

Then why cast out the ancient race?
Grim want dwelt with the ancient race,
And hell-born laws, with prison jaws;
And greedy lords, with tiger maws,
Have swallowed—swallow still apace—
The limbs and blood of the ancient race.

Will no one shield the ancient race?
They fly their fathers' burial place;

M

The proud lords with the heavy purse,
Their fathers' shame—their people's curse—
Demons in heart, nobles in face—
They dig a grave for the ancient race !

What shall befall the ancient race ?
Shall all forsake their dear birthplace,
Without one struggle strong to keep
The old soil where their fathers sleep?
The dearest land on earth's wide space—
Why leave it so, O ancient race ?

What shall befall the ancient race ?
Light up one hope for the ancient race ;
Oh, priest of God—Soggarth Aroon !
Lead but the way, we'll go full soon ;
Is there a danger we will not face,
To keep old homes for the Irish race ?

They shall not go, the ancient race—
They must not go, the ancient race !
Come, gallant Kelts, and take your stand—
And form a league to save the land ;
The land of faith, the land of grace,
The land of Erin's ancient race !

They must not go, the ancient race !
They shall not go, the ancient race !
The cry swells loud from shore to shore,
From emerald vale to mountain hoar,
From altar high to market-place—
'THEY SHALL NOT GO, the ancient race !'

THOMAS D'ARCY McGEE

OF all the rhetorical qualities of poetry—rhythm and phrase
and picturesque diction—McGee possessed a greater measure
than any other of *The Nation* poets. But he wrote with a

careless energy which, if it always produced something remarkable, yet rarely left it strong and finished in every part. He was born in Carlingford, County Louth, in 1825. After much success as a journalist in America, where he edited *The Boston Pilot*, he came home and joined *The Nation* and its political movement in 1844. He escaped, with a price on his head, after the outbreak of 1848, and eventually settled in Canada, where he entered the legislature and became a Minister of the Crown. He took a leading part in the federation of the Canadian States. He revisited Ireland during the time of the Fenian movement, which he denounced with a fervour which, in view of his own antecedents, caused intense bitterness of feeling, and led to the dreadful crime of his assassination in Ottawa in 1868.

McGee was a prolific and versatile writer. He published in 1847 IRISH WRITERS OF THE SEVENTEENTH CENTURY ; HISTORY OF THE IRISH SETTLERS IN AMERICA, 1851; MEMOIRS OF C. G. DUFFY, 1849 ; LIFE OF BISHOP MAGIN, 1856 ; LIFE OF ART MCMURROUGH, 1847 ; HISTORY OF IRELAND ; and contributed numberless poems to *The Nation* and other periodicals. A collected edition of his poems has been edited by Mrs. J. Sadleir, New York, 1869.

THE DEAD ANTIQUARY O'DONOVAN

FAR are the Gaelic tribes and wide
Scattered round earth on every side,
    For good or ill ;
They aim at all things, rise or fall,
Succeed or perish—but, through all,
    Love Erin still.

Although a righteous Heaven decrees [1]
'Twixt us and Erin stormy seas
    And barriers strong—
Of care, and circumstance, and cost—
Yet count not all your absent lost,
    Oh, Land of Song !

---

[1] These lines were written in America.

Above *your* roofs no star can rise
That does not lighten in *our* eyes ;
          Nor any set,
That ever shed a cheering beam
On Irish hillside, street or stream,
          That we forget.

And thus it comes that even I,
Though weakly and unworthily,
          Am moved by grief
To join the melancholy throng
And chant the sad entombing song
          Above the Chief.

I would not do the dead a wrong :
If graves could yield a growth of song
          Like flowers of May,
Then Mangan from the tomb might raise
One of his old resurgent lays—
          But, well-a-day !

He, close beside his early friend,
By the stark shepherd safely penned,
          Sleeps out the night ;
So his weird numbers never more
The sorrow of the isle shall pour,
          In tones of might.

Though haply still, by Liffey's tide,
That mighty master must abide,
          Who voíced our grief
O'er Davis lost ; [1] and he who gave
His free frank tribute to the grave
          Of Eire's Chief ; [2]

---

[1] Samuel Ferguson.
[2] Denis Florence McCarthy, whose poem on the death of O'Connell
was one of the noblest tributes paid to the memory of the great Tribune.—
Author's note.

Yet must it not be said that we
Failed in the rites of minstrelsy,
    So dear to souls
Like his whom lately death had ta'en,
Altho' the vast Atlantic main
    Between us rolls !

Too few, too few, among our great,
In camp or cloister, Church or State,
    Wrought as he wrought ;
Too few, of all the brave we trace
Among the champions of our race,
    Gave us his thought.

He toiled to make our story stand,
As from Time's reverent, Runic hand
    It came undecked
By fancies false ; erect, alone,
The monumental Arctic stone
    Of ages wrecked.

He marshalled Brian on the plain,
Sailed in the galleys of the Dane ;
    Earl Richard too,
Fell Norman as he was and fierce—
Of him and his he dared rehearse
    The story true.

O'er all low limits still his mind
Soared catholic and unconfined,
    From malice free.
On Irish soil he only saw
One State, One People, and One Law,
    One Destiny.

Truth was his solitary test,
His star, his chart, his east, his west ;
    Nor is there aught
In text, in ocean, or in mine,
Of greater worth, or more divine
    Than this he sought.

With gentle hand he rectified
The errors of old bardic pride,
And set aright
The story of our devious past.
And left it, as it now must last,
Full in the light.

To Duffy in Prison

'Twas but last night I traversed the Atlantic's furrow'd face—
The stars but thinly colonised the wilderness of space—
A white sail glinted here and there, and sometimes o'er the swell,
Rang the seaman's song of labour or the silvery night-watch bell ;
I dreamt I reached the Irish shore and felt my heart rebound
From wall to wall within my breast, as I trod that holy ground ;
I sat down by my own hearth-stone, beside my love again—
I met my friends, and him the first of friends and Irish men.

I saw once more the dome-like brow, the large and lustrous eyes ;
I mark'd upon the sphinx-like face the cloud of thoughts arise,
I heard again that clear quick voice that as a trumpet thrill'd
The souls of men, and wielded them even as the speaker will'd—
I felt the cordial-clasping hand that never feigned regard,
Nor ever dealt a muffled blow, or nicely weighed reward.
My friend ! my friend !—oh, would to God that you were here
    with me—
A-watching in the starry West for Ireland's liberty !

Oh, brothers, I can well declare, who read it like a scroll,
What Roman characters were stamp'd upon that Roman soul.
The courage, constancy and love—the old-time faith and truth—
The wisdom of the sages—the sincerity of youth —
Like an oak upon our native hills, a host might camp there-under,
Yet it bare the song-birds in its core, amid the storm and thunder;
It was the gentlest, firmest soul that ever, lamp-like, showed
A young race seeking freedom up her misty mountain road.

Like a convoy from the flag-ship our fleet is scattered far,
And you, the valiant Admiral, chained and imprisoned are—
Like a royal galley's precious freight flung on sea-sunder'd strands,
The diamond wit and golden worth are far-cast on the lands,

And I, whom most you lov'd, am here, and I can but indite
My yearnings and my heart-hopes, and curse *them* while I write.
Alas ! alas ! ah, what are prayers, and what are moans or sighs,
When the heroes of the land are lost—of the land that will not
    RISE ?

They will bring you in their manacles beneath their blood-red rag,
They will chain you like the conqueror to some sea-moated crag,
To their slaves it will be given your great spirit to annoy,
To fling falsehood in your cup, and to break your martyr joy ;
But you will bear it nobly, as Regulus did of eld,
The oak will be the oak, and honoured e'en when fell'd.
Change is brooding over earth ; it will find you 'mid the main,
And, throned between its wings, you'll reach your native land again.

INFELIX FELIX

    Phelim or Felix O'Neill, leader of the rising of 1641, which began the Nine
Years' War.   He was executed in Dublin by Cromwell, after having refused
to purchase liberty by implicating Charles I. in the rebellion.

WHY is his name unsung, O minstrel host ?
Why do ye pass his memory like a ghost ?
Why is no rose, no laurel, on his grave ?
Was he not constant, vigilant and brave ?
Why, when that hero-age ye deify,
Why do ye pass *Infelix Felix* by ?

He rose the first—he looms the morning-star
Of the long, glorious, unsuccessful war.
England abhors him !   Has she not abhorr'd
All who for Ireland ventured life or word ?
What memory would she not have cast away
That Ireland hugs in her heart's heart to-day ?

He rose in wrath to free his fetter'd land.
' There's blood—there's Saxon blood—upon his hand.'
Ay, so they say !   Three thousand, less or more,
He sent untimely to the Stygian shore.
They were the keepers of the prison-gate—
He slew them his whole race to liberate.

O clear-eyed poets ! ye who can descry
Through vulgar heaps of dead where heroes lie—
Ye, to whose glance the primal mist is clear —
Behold, there lies a trampled noble here !
Shall we not leave a mark ? shall we not do
Justice to one so hated and so true ?

If ev'n his hand and hilt were so distain'd—
If he was guilty, as he has been blamed—
His death redeem'd his life.   He chose to die
Rather than get his freedom with a lie.
Plant o'er his gallant heart a laurel-tree,
So may his head within the shadow be.

I mourn for thee, O hero of the North—
God judge thee gentler than we do on earth !
I mourn for thee, and for our land, because
She dare not own thee martyr in our cause ;
But they, our poets, they who justify—
They will not let thy memory rot or die !

SALUTATION TO THE KELTS

HAIL to our Keltic brethren, wherever they may be,
In the far woods of Oregon or o'er the Atlantic sea ;
Whether they guard the banner of St. George in Indian vales,
Or spread beneath the nightless North experimental sails—
             One in name and in fame
             Are the sea-divided Gaels.

Though fallen the state of Erin, and changed the Scottish land,
Though small the power of Mona, though unwaked Lewellyn's
   band,
Though Ambrose Merlin's prophecies are held as idle tales,
Though Iona's ruined cloisters are swept by northern gales :
             One in name and in fame
             Are the sea-divided Gaels.

In Northern Spain and Italy our brethren also dwell
And brave are the traditions of their fathers that they tell :

The Eagle or the Crescent in the dawn of history pales
Before the advancing banners of the great Rome-conquering
Gaels.

One in name and in fame
Are the sea-divided Gaels.

A greeting and a promise unto them all we send ;
Their character our charter is, their glory is our end,—
Their friend shall be our friend, our foe whoe'er assails
The glory or the story of the sea-divided Gaels.

One in name and in fame
Are the sea-divided Gaels.

DENIS FLORENCE McCARTHY

DENIS FLORENCE McCARTHY was born in Dublin in 1817. He began to write for *The Nation* in 1843 and was a frequent and valued contributor to it, both in prose and poetry. He also wrote for *The Dublin University Magazine* and other periodicals of the day. He was appointed Professor of English Literature and Poetry in the Catholic University of Ireland in 1854, and died in 1882.

He was an industrious writer, having produced five volumes of original verse as well as numerous translations from Calderon, and his work was always on a high level. The strain of indignant satire in 'Cease to do Evil' does not often recur— his imagination dwelt rather on the sweet and gracious aspects of life and Nature, and these he rendered in verse marked by sincere feeling, wide culture, and careful though unpretentious art.

BALLADS, POEMS, AND LYRICS was published in Dublin, 1850 ; ODE ON THE DEATH OF THE EARL OF BELFAST, 1854 ; UNDER-GLIMPSES AND OTHER POEMS, 1857 ; THE BELL-FOUNDER AND OTHER POEMS, 1857 ; THE CENTENARY OF MOORE, 1880. His collected poems have been published (with many omissions) in Dublin 1884. He was the editor of THE BOOK OF IRISH BALLADS and THE POETS AND DRAMATISTS OF IRELAND.

'CEASE TO DO EVIL—LEARN TO DO WELL.'[1]

O THOU whom sacred duty hither calls,
　　Some glorious hours in freedom's cause to dwell,
Read the mute lesson on thy prison walls—
　　' Cease to do evil—learn to do well !'

If haply thou art one of genius vast,
　　Of generous heart, of mind sublime and grand,
Who all the spring-time of thy life hast passed
　　Battling with tyrants for thy native land—
If thou hast spent thy summer, as thy prime,
　　The serpent brood of bigotry to quell,
Repent, repent thee of thy hideous crime—
　　' Cease to do evil—learn to do well !'

If thy great heart beat warmly in the cause
　　Of outraged man, whate'er his race might be—
If thou hast preached the Christian's equal laws,
　　And stayed the lash beyond the Indian sea—
If at thy call a nation rose sublime—
　　If at thy voice seven million fetters fell,
Repent, repent thee of thy hideous crime—
　　' Cease to do evil—learn to do well !'

If thou hast seen thy country's quick decay,
　　And, like a prophet, raised thy saving hand,
And pointed out the only certain way
　　To stop the plague that ravaged o'er the land—
If thou hast summoned from an alien clime
　　Her banished senate here at home to dwell,
Repent, repent thee of thy hideous crime—
　　' Cease to do evil—learn to do well !'

---

[1] Inscription on the prison where O'Connell, his son John, T. M. Ray, Thomas Steele, Richard Barrett, John Grey, and Charles Gavan Duffy were imprisoned on the verdict for conspiracy, afterwards quashed by the House of Lords.

Or if, perchance, a younger man thou art,
   Whose ardent soul in throbbings doth aspire,
Come weal, come woe, to play the patriot's part
   In the bright footsteps of thy glorious sire !
If all the pleasures of life's youthful time
   Thou hast abandoned for the martyr's cell,
Do thou repent thee of thy hideous crime—
   'Cease to do evil—learn to do well !'

Or art thou one [1] whom early science led
   To walk with Newton through the immense of heaven,
Who soared with Milton and with Mina bled,
   And all thou hadst in Freedom's cause hast given ?
Oh ! fond enthusiast—in the after-time
   Our children's children of your worth shall tell !
England proclaims thy honesty a crime—
   'Cease to do evil—learn to do well !'

Or art thou one [2] whose strong and fearless pen
   Roused the young isle, and bade it dry its tears,
And gathered round thee ardent, gifted men,
   The hope of Ireland in the coming years—
Who dares in prose and heart-awakening rhyme
   Bright hopes to breathe, and bitter truths to tell ?
Oh ! dangerous criminal, repent thy crime—
   'Cease to do evil—learn to do well !'

'Cease to do evil'—aye ! ye madmen, cease !
   Cease to love Ireland, cease to serve her well,
Make with her foes a foul and fatal peace,
   And quick will ope your darkest, dreariest cell.
'Learn to do well'—aye ! learn to betray—
   Learn to revile the land in which you dwell ;
England will bless you on your altered way—
   'Cease to do evil—learn to do well !'

---

[1] Thomas Steele, 'a young Protestant of Cromwellian descent, whose enthusiasm for liberty led him to volunteer among the Spanish revolutionists under Mina.'

[2] C. G. Duffy.

Spring Flowers from Ireland

ON RECEIVING AN EARLY CROCUS AND SOME VIOLETS IN A SECOND LETTER FROM IRELAND

Mr. Aubrey de Vere has written the following criticism on this poem :— ' It seems to me to be one of singular—indeed, of extraordinary—beauty. It has that union of pathos and moral thought, with fineness of execution, which belongs to some of Wordsworth's later poems. The love of our native land has never been expressed with finer feeling, or with a finer handling, than in this poem.'

WITHIN the letter's rustling fold
   I find, once more—a glad surprise :
A little tiny cup of gold—
   Two lovely violet eyes ;—
A cup of gold with emeralds set,
   Once filled with wine from happier spheres ;
Two little eyes so lately wet
   With spring's delicious dewy tears.

Oh ! little eyes that wept and laughed,
   Now bright with smiles, with tears now dim ;
Oh ! little cup that once was quaffed
   By fay-queens fluttering round thy rim.
I press each silken fringe's fold—
   Sweet little eyes, once more ye shine ;
I kiss thy lip, oh ! cup of gold,
   And find thee full of memory's wine.

Within their violet depths I gaze,
   And see, as in the camera's gloom,
The Island with its belt of bays,
   Its chieftain'd heights all capped with broom ;
Which, as the living lens it fills,
   Now seems a giant charmed to sleep—
Now a broad shield embossed with hills,
   Upon the bosom of the deep.

When will the slumbering giant wake?
   When will the shield defend and guard ?
Ah, me ! prophetic gleams forsake
   The once rapt eyes of seer or bard.

Enough if, shunning Samson's fate,
   It doth not all its vigour yield ;
Enough if plenteous peace, though late,
   May rest beneath the sheltering shield.

I see the long and lone defiles
   Of Keimaneigh's bold rocks uphurled ;
I see the golden-fruited isles
   That gem the queen-lakes of the world ;
I see—a gladder sight to me—
   By soft Shangánagh's silver strand
The breaking of a sapphire sea
   Upon the golden-fretted sand.

Swiftly the tunnel's rock-hewn pass,
   Swiftly, the fiery train runs through—
Oh ! what a glittering sheet of glass !
   Oh ! what enchantment meets my view !
With eyes insatiate I pursue,
   Till Bray's bright headland bounds the scene—
'Tis Baiæ by a softer blue !
   Gaeta by a gladder green !

By tasselled groves, o'er meadows fair,
   I'm carried in my blissful dream,
To where—a monarch in the air—
   The pointed mountain reigns supreme ;
There, in a spot remote and wild,
   I see once more the rustic seat
Where Carrigoona, like a child,
   Sits at the mightier mountain's feet.

There by the gentler mountain's slope—
   That happiest year of many a year,
That first swift year of love and hope—
   With her then dear and ever dear,
I sat upon the rustic seat—
   The seat an aged bay-tree crowns—
And saw outspreading from our feet
   The golden glory of the Downs.

The furze-crowned heights, the glorious glen,
  The white-walled chapel glistening near,
The house of God, the homes of men,
  The fragrant hay, the ripening ear ;
There, where there seemed nor sin, nor crime,
  There in God's sweet and wholesome air—
Strange book to read at such a time—
  We read of Vanity's false Fair.

We read the painful pages through—
  Perceived the skill, admired the art,
Felt them if true, not wholly true—
  A truer truth was in our heart.
Save fear and love of ONE, hath proved
  The sage, how vain is all below ;
And one was there who feared and loved,
  And one who loved that she was so.

The vision spreads, the memories grow,
  Fair phantoms crowd the more I gaze.
Oh ! cup of gold, with wine o'erflow,
  I'll drink to those departed days :
And when I drain the golden cup
  To them, to those, I ne'er can see,
With wine of hope I'll fill it up,
  And drink to days that yet may be.

I've drunk the future and the past,
  Now for a draught of warmer wine—
One draught the sweetest and the last—
  Lady, I'll drink to thee and thine.
These flowers that to my breast I fold,
  Into my very heart have grown—
To thee I drain the cup of gold,
  And think the violet eyes thine own.

———————

MICHAEL DOHENY

DOHENY was born at Brookhill, County Tipperary, in 1805. He was a frequent contributor to *The Nation*. Like most of his colleagues, he acted the lessons he had tried to teach in 1848, and after the failure of the insurrection was 'on his keeping' in Ireland, with a reward of £300 on his head, for some time, during which the following poem may have been written. He at last succeeded in evading the police and escaping to New York, where he became a lawyer, and subsequently fought in the Civil War. A small prose work of his, THE FELON'S TRACK, attained much popularity. He died in 1863.

A CUSHLA GAL MO CHREE.[1]

THE long, long wished-for hour has come,
    Yet come, *astor*, in vain ;
And left thee but the wailing hum
    Of sorrow and of pain ;
My light of life, my only love !
    Thy portion, sure, must be
Man's scorn below, God's wrath above—
    A cuisle geal mo chroidhe !

I've given for thee my early prime,
    And manhood's teeming years ;
I've blessed thee in my merriest time,
    And shed with thee my tears ;
And, mother, though thou cast away
    The child who'd die for thee,
My fondest wishes still should pray
    For *cuisle geal mo chroidhe !*

For thee I've tracked the mountain's sides,
    And slept within the brake,
More lonely than the swan that glides
    On Lua's fairy lake.

---

[1] ' Bright vein of my heart.'

The rich have spurned me from their door,
　　Because I'd make thee free ;
Yet still I love thee more and more,
　　A cuisle geal mo chroidhe !

I've run the outlaw's wild career,
　　And borne his load of ill ;
His rocky couch—his dreamy fear—
　　With fixed, sustaining will ;
And should his last dark chance befall,
　　Even that shall welcome be ;
In death I'd love thee best of all,
　　A cuisle geal mo chroidhe !

'Twas told of thee the world around,
　　'Twas hoped for thee by all,
That with one gallant sunward bound
　　Thou'dst burst long ages' thrall ;
Thy faith was tried, alas ! and those
　　Who perilled all for thee
Were cursed and branded as thy foes,
　　A cuisle geal mo chroidhe !

What fate is thine, unhappy Isle,
　　When even the trusted few
Would pay thee back with hate and guile,
　　When most they should be true !
'Twas not my strength or spirit quailed,
　　Or those who'd die for thee—
Who loved thee truly have not failed,
　　A cuisle geal mo chroidhe !

LADY WILDE

Jane Francesca Elgee, the daughter of an archdeacon of
the Church of Ireland, was born in Wexford about 1820, and
began to write for *The Nation* in 1844. Her contributions

were usually signed 'Speranza.' In 1851 she married Mr. (afterwards Sir) W. R. Wilde, a distinguished oculist and antiquary. The passionate rhetoric of her verse, which reflected her own fearless and generous character, helped in no small degree to make *The Nation* a political force, but, as in the case of many other Irish writers of both prose and verse, she won her true literary success in the former medium. Her translation of the AMBER-WITCH and her ANCIENT LEGENDS OF IRELAND are work of the highest order of their class. She died in London in 1896.

THE FAMINE YEAR

WEARY men, what reap ye ?—'Golden corn for the stranger.'
What sow ye ?—'Human corses that await for the Avenger.'
Fainting forms, all hunger-stricken, what see you in the offing ?
'Stately ships to bear our food away amid the stranger's scoffing.'
There's a proud array of soldiers—what do they round your
    door ?
'They guard our master's granaries from the thin hands of the
    poor.'
Pale mothers, wherefore weeping ?—'Would to God that we were
    dead—
Our children swoon before us, and we cannot give them bread ! '

Little children, tears are strange upon your infant faces,
God meant you but to smile within your mother's soft embraces.
'Oh ! we know not what is smiling, and we know not what is
    dying ;
But we're hungry, very hungry, and we cannot stop our crying ;
And some of us grow cold and white—we know not what it means.
But as they lie beside us we tremble in our dreams.'
There's a gaunt crowd on the highway—are ye come to pray to
    man,
With hollow eyes that cannot weep, and for words your faces wan ?

'No; the blood is dead within our veins ; we care not now for life ;
Let us die hid in the ditches, far from children and from wife ;
We cannot stay to listen to their raving, famished cries—
Bread ! Bread ! Bread !—and none to still their agonies.

N

We left an infant playing with her dead mother's hand :
We left a maiden maddened by the fever's scorching brand : '
Better, maiden, thou wert strangled in thy own dark-twisted
    tresses !
Better, infant, thou wert smothered in thy mother's first caresses.

' We are fainting in our misery, but God will hear our groan ;
Yea, if fellow-men desert us, He will hearken from His throne !
Accursed are we in our own land, yet toil we still and toil ;
But the stranger reaps our harvest— the alien owns our soil.
O Christ, how have we sinned, that on our native plains
We perish houseless, naked, starved, with branded brow, like
    Cain's ?
Dying, dying wearily, with a torture sure and slow—
Dying as a dog would die, by the wayside as we go.

' One by one they're falling round us, their pale faces to the sky ;
We've no strength left to dig them graves— there let them lie.
The wild bird, when he's stricken, is mournèd by the others,
But we, we die in Christian land — we die amid our brothers—
In the land which God has given—like a wild beast in his cave,
Without a tear, a prayer, a shroud, a coffin, or a grave.
Ha ! but think ye the contortions on each dead face ye see,
Shall not be read on judgment-day by the eyes of Deity?

' We are wretches, famished, scorned, human tools to build your
    pride,
But God will yet take vengeance for the souls for whom Christ
    died.
Now is your hour of pleasure, bask ye in the world's caress ;
But our whitening bones against ye will arise as witnesses,
From the cabins and the ditches, in their charred, uncoffined
    masses,
For the ANGEL OF THE TRUMPET will know them as he passes.
A ghastly, spectral army before great God we'll stand
And arraign ye as our murderers, O spoilers of our land !'

END OF POETS OF *THE NATION*

ANONYMOUS[1]

A Lay of the Famine

Hush ! hear you how the night wind keens around the craggy
    reek ?
Its voice peals high above the waves that thunder in the creek.

'Aroon ! aroon ! arouse thee, and hie thee o'er the moor !
Ten miles away there's bread, they say, to feed the starving poor.

' God save thee, Eileen *bawn astor*, and guide thy naked feet,
And keep the fainting life in us till thou come back with meat.

' God send the moon to show thee light upon the way so drear,
And mind thou well the rocky dell, and heed the rushy mere.'

She kissed her father's palsied hand, her mother's pallid cheek,
And whirled out on the driving storm beyond the craggy reek.

All night she tracks, with bleeding feet, the rugged mountain way,
And townsfolks meet her in the street at flushing of the day.

But God is kinder on the moor than man is in the town,
And Eileen quails before the stranger's harsh rebuke and frown.

Night's gloom enwraps the hills once more and hides a slender
    form
That shudders o'er the moor again before the driving storm.

No bread is in her wallet stored, but on the lonesome heath
She lifts her empty hands to God, and prays for speedy death.

Yet struggles onward, faint and blind, and numb to hope or fear,
Unmindful of the rocky dell or of the rushy mere.

But, ululu ! what sight is this ?—what forms come by the reek ?
As white and thin as evening mist upon the mountain's peak.

Mist-like they glide across the heath—a weird and ghostly band ;
The foremost crosses Eileen's path, and grasps her by the hand.

---

[1] Now known to be the work of Rosa Mulholland (Lady Gilbert).

'Dear daughter, thou hast suffered sore, but we are well and free ;
For God has ta'en our life from us, nor wills it long to thee.

'So hie thee to our cabin lone, and dig a grave so deep,
And underneath the golden gorse our corpses lay to sleep—

'Else they will come and smash the walls upon our mould'ring
      bones,
And screaming mountain birds will tear our flesh from out the
      stones.

'And, daughter, haste to do thy work, so thou mayst quickly come,
And take with us our grateful rest, and share our peaceful home.'

.   .   .   .   .   .

The sun behind the distant hills far-sinking down to sleep ;
A maiden on the lonesome moor, digging a grave so deep ;

The moon above the craggy reek, silvering moor and wave,
And the pale corpse of a maiden young stretched on a new-made
      grave.

JAMES McCARROLL

BORN at Lanesborough, County Longford, on August 3, 1814,
and died in New York in 1891. He was an active journalist,
and possessed much musical knowledge, and was also a
successful inventor and patentee. His collected poems were
published in 1889. He lived many years in America and
Canada.

THE IRISH WOLF

The Times once used this term to designate the Irish people.

SEEK music in the wolf's fierce howl
    Or pity in his blood-shot eye,
When hunger drives him out to prowl
    Beneath a rayless northern sky :

But seek not that we should forgive
   The hand that strikes us to the heart,
And yet in mockery bids us live
   To count our stars as they depart.

We've fed the tyrant with our blood ;
   Won all his battles—built his throne—
Established him on land and flood,
   And sought his glory next our own.

We raised him from his low estate ;
   We plucked his pagan soul from hell,
And led him pure to heaven's gate,
   Till he, for gold, like Judas fell.

And when in one long, soulless night
   He lay unknown to wealth or fame,
We gave him empire—riches—light,
   And taught him how to spell his name.

But now, ungenerous and unjust,
   Forgetful of our old renown,
He bows us to the very dust ;
   But wears our jewels in his crown.

JOHN SAVAGE

JOHN SAVAGE was born in Dublin 1828 and died in New York 1888. After taking some part in the '48 movement he emigrated to America and adopted the profession of journalism there. In 1879 he received the honorary degree of LL.D. from St. John's College, Fordham. He published several volumes of poetry : LAYS OF THE FATHERLAND, 1850 ; SYBIL, 1850 ; FAITH AND FANCY, 1864 ; POEMS, 1870. The following powerful ballad has appeared in many Irish collections of verse. A feeble first verse, apparently added as an afterthought, in which passion froths over into rant, has been here omitted, to the great gain of the poem in dramatic energy.

SHANE'S HEAD

Scene.—*Before Dublin Castle.*　Night.　A clansman of Shane O'Neill's
　　discovers his Chief's head on a pole.

Is it thus, O Shane the haughty ! Shane the valiant ! that we
　　meet—
Have my eyes been lit by Heaven but to guide me to defeat ?
Have *I* no Chief, or *you* no clan, to give us both defence,
Or must I, too, be statued here with thy cold eloquence ?
Thy ghastly head grins scorn upon old Dublin's Castle Tower ;
Thy shaggy hair is wind-tossed, and thy brow seems rough with
　　power ;
Thy wrathful lips like sentinels, by foulest treachery stung,
Look rage upon the world of wrong, but chain thy fiery tongue.

That tongue, whose Ulster accent woke the ghost of Columbkill ;
Whose warrior-words fenced round with spears the oaks of Derry
　　Hill ;
Whose reckless tones gave life and death to vassals and to knaves,
And hunted hordes of Saxons into holy Irish graves.
The Scotch marauders whitened when his war-cry met their ears,
And the death-bird, like a vengeance, poised above his stormy
　　cheers ;
Ay, Shane, across the thundering sea, out-chanting it, your tongue
Flung wild un-Saxon war-whoopings the Saxon Court among.

Just think, O Shane ! the same moon shines on Liffey as on
　　Foyle,
And lights the ruthless knaves on both, our kinsmen to despoil ;
And you the hope, voice, battle-axe, the shield of us and ours,
A murdered, trunkless, blinding sight above these Dublin towers !

Thy face is paler than the moon ; my heart is paler still—
My heart ?　I had no heart—'twas yours—'*twas* yours ! to keep
　　or kill.
And you kept it safe for Ireland, Chief—your life, your soul, your
　　pride ;
But they sought it in thy bosom, Shane—with proud O'Neill it
　　died.

You were turbulent and haughty, proud and keen as Spanish
    steel—
But who had right of these, if not our Ulster's Chief, O'Neill,
Who reared aloft the ' Bloody Hand ' until it paled the sun,
And shed such glory on Tyrone as chief had never done?

He was 'turbulent' with traitors ; he was 'haughty' with the
    foe ;
He was 'cruel,' say ye, Saxons ! Ay ! he dealt ye blow for blow !
He was ' rough ' and 'wild'—and who's not wild to see his hearth-
    stone razed ?
He was 'merciless as fire'—ah, ye kindled him—he blazed !
He was 'proud'—yes, proud of birthright, and because he flung
    away
Your Saxon stars of princedom, as the rock does mocking spray.
He was wild, insane for vengeance—ay ! and preached it till
    Tyrone
Was ruddy, ready, wild, too, with ' Red hands' to clutch their
    own.

' The Scots are on the border, Shane ! ' Ye Saints, he makes no
    breath ;
I remember when that cry would wake him up almost from death.
Art truly dead and cold? O Chief ! art thou to Ulster lost ?
' Dost hear—*dost hear*? By Randolph led, the troops the Foyle
    have crossed ! '
He's truly dead ! He must be dead ! nor is his ghost about—
And yet no tomb could hold his spirit tame to such a shout :
The pale face droopeth northward—ah ! his soul must loom up
    there,
By old Armagh, or Antrim's glynns, Lough Foyle, or Bann the
    Fair !
I'll speed me Ulster-wards—your ghost must wander there, proud
    Shane,
In search of some O'Neill, through whom to throb its hate again.

JOHN WALSH

This poet has been greatly neglected by his countrymen, and he appears in very few Irish anthologies. Yet he wrote some admirably simple and touching pieces. Many of his poems appeared in *The Nation* and the Waterford papers. He was a schoolmaster, like Edward Walsh, and was born at Cappoquin, County Waterford, on April 1, 1835, and died at Cashel, County Tipperary, in February 1881.

To My Promised Wife

Dear maiden, when the sun is down,
And darkness creeps above the town,
The woodlands' green is changed to brown,
  And the mild light
Melting beneath the tall hills' frown
  Steals into night,

I don an honest coat of grey,
And, setting stupid care at bay,
Across the fields of scented hay
  I stroll along,
Humming some quaint old Irish lay
  Or simple song.

And when, dear maid, I come to you,
A laughing eye of brightest blue,
And flushing cheek of crimson hue,
  Tell whom I greet,
And bounds a little heart as true
  As ever beat.

The green grass on the river-side,
The full moon dancing on the tide,
The half-blown rose that tries to hide
  Her blush in dew,
Are fair ; but none, my promised bride,
  As fair as you.

And though, dear love, our gathered store
Of gold is small, the brighter ore
Of love's deep mine we'll seek the more,
    And truth shall be
The guard beside our cottage-door,
    Astor mo chroidhe!

DRIMIN DONN DILIS [1]

OH! *drimin donn dilis!* the landlord has come,
Like a foul blast of death has he swept o'er our home;
He has withered our roof-tree—beneath the cold sky,
Poor, houseless, and homeless, to-night must we lie.

My heart it is cold as the white winter's snow;
My brain is on fire, and my blood's in a glow.
Oh! *drimin donn dilis,* 'tis hard to forgive
When a robber denies us the right we should live.

With my health and my strength, with hard labour and toil,
I dried the wet marsh and I tilled the harsh soil;
I moiled the long day through, from morn until even,
And I thought in my heart I'd a foretaste of heaven.

The summer shone round us above and below,
The beautiful summer that makes the flowers blow:
Oh! 'tis hard to forget it, and think I must bear
That strangers shall reap the reward of my care.

Your limbs they were plump then—your coat it was silk,
And never was wanted the mether of milk;
For freely it came in the calm summer's noon,
While you munched to the time of the old milking croon.

How often you left the green side of the hill,
To stretch in the shade and to drink of the rill!
And often I freed you before the grey dawn
From your snug little pen at the edge of the bawn.

---

[1] 'Dear brown cow.'

But they racked and they ground me with tax and with rent,
Till my heart it was sore and my life-blood was spent :
To-day they have finished, and on the wide world
With the mocking of fiends from my home I was hurled.

I knelt down three times for to utter a prayer,
But my heart it was seared, and the words were not there ;
Oh ! wild were the thoughts through my dizzy head came,
Like the rushing of wind through a forest of flame.

I bid you, old comrade, a long last farewell ;
For the gaunt hand of famine has clutched us too well ;
It severed the master and you, my good cow,
With a blight on his life and a brand on his brow.

D. MacALEESE

BORN in 1833 at Randalstown, County Antrim, Mr. MacAleese
worked for some time at his father's trade—that of a shoe-
maker—but his taste for letters led him into journalism,
where he began as printer's reader on a Belfast paper.   He was
at one time editor and proprietor of *The People's Advocate*,
Monaghan, and was returned to Parliament for North Monaghan in 1895.

A MEMORY

ADOWN the leafy lane we two,
  One brown October eve, together sped ;
  The clustered nuts were hanging overhead,
And ever and anon, the deep woods through,
The grey owl piped his weird ' Tu-whut ! tu-whoo ! '

Adown the leafty lane we two
  Strolled on and on, till sank the setting sun
  In sapphire beauty round Tyleden dun,
And shadows long and longer round us grew ;
Had earth a pair so happy as we two ?

Adown the leafy lane we two
  Loitered and laughed, and laughed and loitered more,
  And talked of ' gentle folk ' and fairy lore.
Till, one by one, from out the vaulted blue,
The diamond stars came softly forth to view.

Adown the leafy lane we two
  Saw figures flitting 'mong the quicken trees,
  Tall Finian forms, holding high revelries,
And dogs, like Bran in sinew and in thew,
Chased shadowy deer the vista'd woodlands through.

Adown the leafy lane we two
  Heard fairy pipes play fairy music sweet,
  And now and then the tramp of fairy feet,
And screams of laughter 'mong the fairy crew—
The elves and fays that haunt old Corradhu.

Adown the leafy lane no more
  We two go loitering in the Autumn eves,
  When merry reapers tie the golden sheaves,
And kine come lowing to the cottage door,
Where ready pails await the milky store.

Astoireen, no, far, far away,
  Secluded lies that golden-memoried lane,
  Where ceaseless flows the bright and sparkling Main
Through scenes of beauty to the storied Neagh—
Here by the Hudson's banks we two grow grey.

JOSEPH SHERIDAN LE FANU

Le Fanu was certainly one of the most remarkable of Irish
writers. In Uncle Silas, in his wonderful tales of the supernatural, and in a short and less known but most masterly story,
The Room in the Dragon Volant, he touched the springs of
terror and suspense as perhaps no other writer of fiction in the

language has been able to do. His fine scholarship, poetic sense, and strong yet delicate handling of language and of incident give these tales a place quite apart among works of sensational fiction. But perhaps the most interesting of all his novels is THE HOUSE BY THE CHURCHYARD—a wonderful mixture of sensationalism, humour, tragedy, and romance. In poetry his 'Shemus O'Brien,' a capital piece written for recitation, is a well-known favourite, and has been made the basis of a fine Irish opera by C. Villiers Stanford. It is noteworthy, by the way, that Le Fanu, the son of a Dean of the Established Church, and proprietor and editor of a Tory newspaper, became a rebel whenever he wrote verse.

The piece from 'The Legend of the Glaive' here given shows the weird and romantic touch which Le Fanu had at command, and 'The Address to the Bottle' has much of the almost savage energy which he showed more in certain scenes of THE HOUSE BY THE CHURCHYARD than anywhere else.

From Mr. Alfred Perceval Graves's introduction to Le Fanu's poems we may take the following picture of his habits and character in later years :

'Those who possessed the rare privilege of Le Fanu's friendship, and only they, can form any idea of the true character of the man ; for after the death of his wife, to whom he was most deeply devoted, he quite forsook general society, in which his fine features, distinguished bearing, and charm of conversation marked him out as the beau-ideal of an Irish wit and scholar of the old school.

'From this society he vanished so entirely that Dublin, always ready with a nickname, dubbed him 'The Invisible Prince'; and, indeed, he was for long almost invisible, except to his family and most familiar friends, unless at odd hours of the evening, when he might occasionally be seen stealing, like the ghost of his former self, between his newspaper office and his home in Merrion Square. Sometimes too he was to be encountered in an old, out-of-the-way bookshop, poring over some rare black-letter Astrology or Demonology.'

Le Fanu was born in Dublin in 1814, and graduated at Trinity College, Dublin, in 1837. About 1838 he purchased *The Warder*, a Conservative journal, and afterwards became editor and owner of *The Dublin Evening Mail* and of *The Dublin University Magazine.* Most of his poetic and prose work appeared first in the last-named periodical. His POEMS appeared for the first time in a collected edition, edited by Mr. Alfred Perceval Graves, in 896. He died in 1873.

FIONULA

How to this hour she is sometimes seen by night in Munster

From THE LEGEND OF THE GLAIVE

BY the foot of old Keeper, beside the *bohreen*,
In the deep blue of night the thatched cabin is seen ;
Neath the furze-covered ledge, by the wild mountain brook,
Where the birch and the ash dimly shelter the nook,
And many's the clear star that trembles on high
O'er the thatch and the wild ash that melt in the sky.
'Shamus Oge' and old Teig are come home from the fair,
And the car stands up black with its shafts in the air,
A warbling of laughter hums over the floor,
And fragrant's the flush of the turf through the door.
Round the glow the old folk and the colleens and boys
Wile the hour with their stories, jokes, laughter, and noise ;
Dogs stretched on the hearth with their chins on their feet lie,
To her own purring music the cat dozes sweetly ;
Pretty smiles answer, coyly, while soft spins the wheel,
The bold lover's glances or whispered appeal.
Stealing in, like the leather-wings under the thatch,
A hand through the dark softly leans on the latch,
An oval face peeps through the clear deep of night,
From her jewels faint tremble blue splinters of light.
There's a stranger among us, a chill in the air,
And an awful face silently framed over there ;
The green light of horror glares cold from each eye,
And laughter breaks shivering into a cry.
A flush from the fire hovers soft to the door,
In the dull void the pale lady glimmers no more.
The cow'ring dogs howl, slowly growls the white cat,
And the whisper outshivers, 'God bless us ! what's that ?'

The sweet summer moon o'er Aherlow dreams,
And the Galtees, gigantic, loom cold in her beams ;
From the wide flood of purple the pale peaks uprise,
Slowly gliding like sails 'gainst the stars of the skies ;
Soft moonlight is drifted on mountain and wood,
Airy voices sing faint to the drone of the flood,
As the traveller benighted flies onward in fear,
And the clink of his footsteps falls shrill on his ear.
There's a hush in the bushes, a chill in the air,
While a breath steals beside him and whispers, ' Beware !'
While aslant by the oak, down the hollow ravine,
Like a flying bird's shadow smooth-gliding, is seen
Fionula the Cruel, the brightest, the worst,
With a terrible beauty the vision accurst,
Gold-filleted, sandalled, of times dead and gone—
Far-looking, and harking, pursuing, goes on :
Her white hand from her ear lifts her shadowy hair,
From the lamp of her eye floats the sheen of despair ;
Her cold lips are apart, and her teeth in her smile
Glimmer death on her face with a horrible wile.
Three throbs at his heart—not a breath at his lip,
As the figure skims by like the swoop of a ship ;
The breeze dies and drops like a bird on the wing,
And the pulse of the rivulet ceases to sing ;
And the stars and the moon dilate o'er his head,
As they smile out an icy salute to the dead.

The traveller—alone—signs the cross on his breast,
Gasps a prayer to the saints for her weary soul's rest ;
His ' gospel' close pressed to the beat of his heart,
And fears still to linger, yet dreads to depart.
By the village fire crouched, his the story that night,
While his listeners around him draw pale with affright ;
Till it's over the country—'God bless us, again !'
How he met Fionula in Aherlow Glen.

Abhrain an Bhuideil

From what dripping cell, through what fairy glen,
Where 'mid old rocks and ruins the fox makes his den,
Over what lonesome mountain,
   Acuishle mo chroidhe !
  Where gauger never has trod,
  Sweet as the flowery sod,
  Wild as the breath
  Of the breeze on the heath,
And sparkling all o'er like the moon-lighted fountain,
   Are you come to me—
   Sorrowful me ?

   Dancing—inspiring—
   My wild blood firin' ;
   Oh ! terrible glory—
    Oh ! beautiful siren—
   Come, tell the old story—
    Come, light up my fancy, and open my heart.
   Oh, beautiful ruin—
   My life—my undoin'—
   Soft and fierce as a pantheress,
    Dream of my longing, and wreck of soul,
I never knew love till I loved you, enchanthress !

At first, when I knew you, 'twas only flirtation,
  The touch of a lip and the flash of an eye ;
But 'tis different now—'tis desperation !
   I worship before you,
   I curse and adore you,
  And without you I'd die.
   Wirrasthrue ! [1]
   I wish 'twas again
   The happy time when

---

[1] *Wirrasthrue* = Mhuire ir truagh : ' O Mary, 'tis pity.'

I cared little about you,
Could do well without you,
But would just laugh and view you ;
'Tis little I knew you !

Oh ! terrible darling,
How have you sought me,
Enchanted, and caught me ?
See, now, where you've brought me—
To sleep by the roadside, and dress out in rags.
Think how you found me ;
Dreams come around me—
The dew of my childhood and life's morning beam ;
Now I sleep by the roadside, a wretch all in rags.
My heart that sang merrily when I was young
Swells up like a billow and bursts in despair ;
And the wreck of my hopes on sweet memory flung,
And cries on the air,
Are all that is left of the dream.

Wirrasthrue !
My father and mother,
The priest, and my brother—
Not a one has a good word for you.
But I can't part you, darling ; their preaching's all vain ;
You'll burn in my heart till these thin pulses stop ;
And the wild cup of life in your fragrance I'll drain—
To the last brilliant drop.
Then oblivion will cover
The shame that is over,
The brain that was mad, and the heart that was sore ;
Then, beautiful witch,
I'll be found—in a ditch,
With your kiss on my cold lips, and never rise more.

SHEMUS O'BRIEN:

A TALE OF 'NINETY-EIGHT, AS RELATED BY AN IRISH PEASANT

PART I

JIST after the war, in the year 'Ninety-Eight,
As soon as the Boys wor all scattered and bate,
'Twas the custom, whenever a peasant was got,
To hang him by trial—barrin' such as was shot.

There was trial by jury goin' on by daylight,
And the martial law hangin' the lavings by night :
It's them was hard times for an honest gossoon ;
If he missed in the judges, he'd meet a Dragoon !
An' whether the sojers or judges gave sentence,
The devil a much time they allowed for repentance ;
An' the many a fine Boy was then on his keepin',
With small share of restin', or sittin', or sleepin' !
An' because they loved Erinn, and scorned to sell it,
A prey for the bloodhound, a mark for the bullet—
Unsheltered by night, and unrested by day,
With the heath for their barrack, revenge for their pay.

An' the bravest an' honestest Boy of thim all
Was Shemus O'Brien, from the town of Glingall ;
His limbs wor well set, an' his body was light,
An' the keen-fangéd hound had not teeth half as white.
But his face was as pale as the face of the dead,
An' his cheek never warmed with the blush of the red ;
An', for all that, he wasn't an ugly young Boy—
For the devil himself couldn't blaze with his eye—
So droll an' so wicked, so dark an' so bright,
Like a fire-flash that crosses the depth of the night.
An' he was the best mower that ever has been,
An' the elegantest hurler that ever was seen :
In fencin' he gave Patrick Mooney a cut,
An' in jumpin' he bate Tom Molony a foot ;
For lightness of foot there was not his peer,
For, by Heavens ! he'd almost outrun the red deer ;

O

An' his dancin' was such that the men used to stare,
And the women turn crazy, he did it so quare ;
An' sure the whole world [1] gave in to him there !

An' it's he was the Boy that was hard to be caught ;
An' it's often he ran, an' it's often he fought ;
An' it's many the one can remember quite well
The quare things he did ; and it's oft I heerd tell
How he frightened the magistrates in Cahirbally,
An' escaped through the sojers in Aherlow valley,
An' leathered the yeomen, himself agen four,
An' stretched the four strongest on ould Galteemore.

But the fox must sleep sometimes, the wild deer must rest,
And treachery prey on the blood of the best ;
An' many an action of power an' of pride,
An' many a night on the mountain's bleak side,
And a thousand great dangers an' toils overpast,
In darkness of night he was taken at last.

Now, Shemus, look back on the beautiful moon,
For the door of the prison must close on you soon ;
An' take your last look at her dim misty light,
That falls on the mountain an' valley to-night.
One look at the village, one look at the flood,
An' one at the sheltering far-distant wood ;
Farewell to the forest, farewell to the hill,
An' farewell to the friends that will think of you still.
Farewell to the patthern, the hurlin' an' wake,
An' farewell to the girl that would die for your sake !

An' twelve sojers brought him to Maryborough jail,
An' with irons secured him, refusin' all bail.
The fleet limbs wor chained, and the sthrong hands wor
    bound,
An' he lay down his length on the cold prison ground ;

---

[1] In Gaelic the consonant *r* is given its full value before another consonant, producing the effect of a dissyllable, *e.g.* *tarbh* pronounced 'thorruv' (a bull). This practice, like many other Gaelic locutions, has been carried into English : hence 'worruld' for 'world'; 'firrum' for 'firm,' &c.

And the dhrames of his childhood kem over him there,
As gentle and soft as the sweet summer air ;
An' happy remimbrances crowdin' in ever,
As fast the foam-flakes dhrift down on the river,
Bringin' fresh to his heart merry days long gone by,
Till the tears gathered heavy an' thick in his eye.

But the tears didn't fall ; for the pride iv his heart
Wouldn't suffer one dhrop down his pale cheek to start ;
An' he sprang to his feet in the dark prison cave,
An' he swore with a fierceness that misery gave,
By the hopes iv the good an' the cause iv the brave,
That, when he was mouldering in the cowld grave,
His inimies never should have it to boast
His scorn iv their vengeance one moment was lost :
His bosom might bleed, but his cheek should be dhry ;
For undaunted he lived, and undaunted he'd die.

PART II

Well, as soon as a few weeks were over an' gone,
The terrible day of the trial came on ;
There was such a crowd, there was scarce room to stand,
An' sojers on guard, an' Dragoons sword in hand ;
An' the court-house so full that the people were bothered,
An' attornies and criers on the point o' bein' smothered ;
An' counsellors almost gev' over for dead,
An' the jury sittin' up in the box overhead ;
An' the judge settled out so determined an' big,
An' the gown on his back, an' an elegant wig ;
An' silence was call'd, an' the minute 'twas said,
The court was as still as the heart of the dead.

An' they heard but the opening of one prison-lock,
An' Shemus O'Brien kem into the dock ;
For one minute he turned his eyes round on the throng,
An' then looked on the bars, so firm and so strong.
An' he saw that he had not a hope nor a friend,
A chance to escape, nor a word to defend ;
An' he folded his arms, as he stood there alone,
As calm an' as cold as a statue of stone.

An' they read a big writin', a yard long at laste,
An' Shemus didn't see it, nor mind it a taste ;
An' the judge took a big pinch of snuff, an' he says :
' Are you guilty or not, Jim O'Brien, if you plaise ? '
An' all held their breath in silence of dread,
An' Shemus O'Brien made answer an' said :
' My lord, if you ask me if in my lifetime
I thought any treason, or did any crime,
That should call to my cheek, as I stand alone here,
The hot blush of shame or the coldness of fear,
Though I stood by the grave to receive my death-blow,
Before God an' the world I would answer you No !
But if you would ask me, as I think it like,
If in the Rebellion I carried a pike,
An' fought for Ould Ireland, from the first to the close,
An' shed the heart's blood of her bitterest foes—
I answer you YES ; an' I tell you again,
Though I stand here to perish, it's my glory that then
In her cause I was willin' my veins should run dry,
An' that now for her sake I am ready to die.'

Then the silence was great, and the jury smiled bright ;
An' the judge wasn't sorry the job was made light ;
By my soul, it's himself was the crabbed ould chap !
In a twinkling he pulled on his ugly black cap.
Then Shemus's mother, in the crowd standin' by,
Called out to the judge with a pitiful cry :
' Oh ! judge, darlin', don't—oh ! don't say the word !
The crathur is young—have mercy, my lord !
You don't know him, my lord ; oh ! don't give him to ruin !
He was foolish—he didn't know what he was doin' ;
He's the kindliest crathur, the tinderest-hearted-—
Don't part us for ever, we that's so long parted !
Judge mavourneen, forgive him—forgive him, my lord !
An' God will forgive you—oh ! don't say the word ! '

That was the first minute O'Brien was shaken,
When he saw that he was not quite forgot or forsaken !
An' down his pale cheek, at the word of his mother,
The big tears were running, one after the other ;

An' two or three times he endeavoured to spake,
But the strong manly voice used to falter and break.
But at last, by the strength of his high-mounting pride,
He conquer'd an' master'd his grief's swelling tide ;
An' says he, ' Mother, don't—don't break your poor heart !
Sure, sooner or later, the dearest must part.
An' God knows it's better than wand'ring in fear
On the bleak trackless mountain among the wild deer,
To be in the grave, where the heart, head, an' breast,
From labour and sorrow for ever shall rest.
Then, mother, my darlin', don't cry any more—
Don't make me seem broken in this my last hour ;
For I wish, when my heart's lyin' under the raven,
No true man can say that I died like a craven.'

Then towards the judge Shemus bent down his head,
An' that minute the solemn death-sentence was said.

PART III

The mornin' was bright, an' the mists rose on high,
An' the lark whistled merrily in the clear sky ;
But why are the men standing idle so late ?
An' why do the crowd gather fast in the street ?
What come they to talk of ? What come they to see ?
An' why does the long rope hang from the cross-tree ?
Oh ! Shemus O'Brien, pray fervent an' fast—
May the saints take your soul, for this day is your last.
Pray fast, an' pray strong, for the moment is nigh,
When, strong, proud, an' great as you are, you must die !—

At last they drew open the big prison gate,
An' out came the Sheriffs an' sojers in state.
An' a cart in the middle, and Shemus was in it—
Not paler, but prouder than ever, that minit ;
An' as soon as the people saw Shemus O'Brien,
Wid prayin' and blessin', an' all the girls cryin',
A wild wailin' sound kem on all by degrees,
Like the sound of the lonesome wind blowin' through trees.

On, on to the gallows the Sheriffs are gone,
An' the car an' the sojers go steadily on,
An' at every side swellin' around of the cart,
A wild sorrowful sound that would open your heart.

Now under the gallows the cart takes its stand,
An' the hangman gets up with a rope in his hand,
An' the priest, havin' blest him, gets down on the ground,
An' Shemus O'Brien throws one look around.
Then the hangman drew near, and the people grew still,
Young faces turn sickly, an' warm hearts turn chill ;
An' the rope bein' ready, his neck was made bare,
For the gripe of the life-strangling cords to prepare ;
An' the good priest has left him, havin' said his last prayer.

But the good priest did more—for his hands he unbound !
An' with one daring spring Jim has leaped on the ground !

Bang ! bang ! go the carbines, an' clash go the sabres ;
He's not down ! he's alive ! Now attend to him, neighbours !

By one shout from the people the heavens are shaken—
One shout that the dead of the world might awaken.
Your swords they may glitter, your carbines go bang,
But if you want hanging, 'tis yourselves you must hang !
To-night he'll be sleepin' in Aherlow Glen,
An' the divil's in the dice if you catch him agin.
The sojers run this way, the Sheriffs run that,
An' Father Malone lost his new Sunday hat ;
An' the Sheriffs were, both of them, punished severely,
An' fined like the divil, because Jim done them fairly !

CHARLES J. KICKHAM

KICKHAM was above all things 'kindly Irish of the Irish, neither Saxon nor Italian'—a patriot first and a poet after. Still, a true poet he was whether in verse or in prose, with a note both simple and strong, if not deep or varied; a keen lover and observer of Nature, in deep and tender sympathy with the men and women about him, and with a knowledge of the manners, customs, feelings and moods of the Irish peasant greater, I think, than was possessed by any other man I ever met. If this sympathy and knowledge were shown in larger measure in his novels than in his poems, it was that in the former he had ampler room for their display, for, whether by chance or by design, he wrote much in prose and but little in verse. But in prose or in verse he showed clearly how well he knew and loved his country. He may be reckoned as the chief of the Fenian poets—a smaller and weaker band of *littérateurs* than the poets of *The Nation*, but one which accomplished something of considerable note in the domain of practical affairs. For some twenty years before we went to prison in 1865, while in prison, and after we left it, I knew Kickham as probably no other man did. The better I knew him, the more highly I valued his character and his intellect. Maimed and disfigured by an accident which would have crushed all spirit out of most men, he worked to his last day with an unselfish devotion that no man has ever surpassed. And, uncompromising rebel though he was from the beginning to the end, the spirit in which he worked was one of love, not of hate. A man endowed with his gifts of observation, humour, and romantic feeling—and with his humane, sincere and lovable character, might in happier circumstances have rivalled Carleton as a delineator of Irish peasant life. But his steps were led in other and more perilous paths, and the writings he has left are but evidence of what he might have accomplished if his whole strength had been turned in the direction of literature. He found other and what he deemed

more pressing work to do for Ireland ; and it is certainly not
for me to quarrel with his choice.

JOHN O'LEARY.

Charles Joseph Kickham was born at Mullinahone, County Tipperary,
in 1828.   He began at about twenty years of age to write verse and prose
for various periodicals.   His stories of Irish life—SALLY KAVANAGH ;
FOR THE OLD LAND ; and KNOCKNAGOW—all appeared first in serial form.
In 1863 he joined the staff of *The Irish People*, the organ of the Fenian
movement, edited by his friend and colleague Mr. John O'Leary, and was
arrested with him in that year, and sentenced to fourteen years' penal servitude—O'Leary receiving twenty.   His eyesight and hearing had been
seriously injured by a gunpowder accident in youth, and though during his
imprisonment he almost lost the use of both senses he remained after his
release, as he had been formerly, one of the guiding spirits of the Fenian
movement.   He died at Blackrock, near Dublin, in 1882, and was buried at
Mullinahone.   A fine statue by Mr. John Hughes has been erected to his
memory in the town of Tipperary.

RORY OF THE HILL

'THAT rake up near the rafters,
    Why leave it there so long ?
The handle, of the best of ash,
    Is smooth and straight and strong ;
And, mother, will you tell me,
    Why did my father frown
When to make the hay, in summer-time,
    I climbed to take it down ? '
She looked into her husband's eyes,
    While her own with light did fill,
' You'll shortly know the reason, boy ! '
    Said Rory of the Hill.

The midnight moon is lighting up
    The slopes of Sliav-na-man,—
Whose foot affrights the startled hares
    So long before the dawn ?
He stopped just where the Anner's stream
    Winds up the woods anear,
Then whistled low and looked around
    To see the coast was clear.

The sheeling door flew open—
    In he stepped with right good-will—
'God save all here and bless your WORK,'
    Said Rory of the Hill.

Right hearty was the welcome
    That greeted him, I ween,
For years gone by he fully proved
    How well he loved the Green ;
And there was one amongst them
    Who grasped him by the hand—
One who through all that weary time
    Roamed on a foreign strand ;
He brought them news from gallant friends
    That made their heart-strings thrill—
'My *sowl !* I never doubted them !'
    Said Rory of the Hill.

They sat around the humble board
    Till dawning of the day,
And yet not song nor shout I heard—
    No revellers were they :
Some brows flushed red with gladness,
    While some were grimly pale ;
But pale or red, from out those eyes
    Flashed souls that never quail !
'And sing us now about the vow,
    They swore for to fulfil—'
'You'll read it yet in history,'
    Said Rory of the Hill.

Next day the ashen handle
    He took down from where it hung,
The toothed rake, full scornfully,
    Into the fire he flung ;
And in its stead a shining blade
    Is gleaming once again—
(Oh ! for a hundred thousand of
    Such weapons and such men !)

Right soldierly he wielded it,
   And—going through his drill—
'Attention'—'charge'—'front, point'—'advance!'
   Cried Rory of the Hill.

She looked at him with woman's pride,
   With pride and woman's fears;
She flew to him, she clung to him,
   And dried away her tears;
He feels her pulse beat truly,
   While her arms around him twine—
'Now God be praised for your stout heart,
   Brave little wife of mine.'
He swung his first-born in the air,
   While joy his heart did fill—
'You'll be a FREEMAN yet, my boy,'
   Said Rory of the Hill.

Oh! knowledge is a wondrous power,
   And stronger than the wind;
And thrones shall fall, and despots bow,
   Before the might of mind;
The poet and the orator
   The heart of man can sway,
And would to the kind heavens
   That Wolfe Tone were here to-day!
Yet trust me, friends, dear Ireland's strength—
   Her truest strength—is still
The rough-and-ready roving boys,
   Like Rory of the Hill.

MYLES O'HEA

HIS locks are whitened with the snows of nigh a hundred years,
And now with cheery look and step the journey's end he nears;
He feared his God, and bravely played the part he had to play,
For lack of courage never stained the soul of Myles O'Hea.

A young man 'lighted from his steed, and by that old man stood.
'Good friend,' he asked, 'what see you in yon castle by the wood?

I've marked the proud glare of your eye and of your cheek the
    glow.'
' My heart,' the old man said, ' went back to eighty years ago !

' I was a beardless stripling then, but proud as any lord :
And well I might—in my right hand I grasped a freeman's sword ;
And, though an humble peasant's son, proud squires and even peers
Would greet me as a comrade—we were the Volunteers !

' That castle was our colonel's. On yonder grassy glade
At beat of drum our regiment oft mustered for parade,
And from that castle's parapets scarfs waved and bright eyes
    shone
When our bugles woke the echoes with the march of " Garryowen."

' Oh ! then 'twas never thought a shame or crime to love the land,
For freedom was the watchword, nerving every heart and hand ;
And Grattan, Flood, and Charlemont were blessed by high and
    low
When our army won the Parliament of eighty years ago.'

' And what of him, your colonel ? ' ' He, good old colonel, died
While the nation's heart was pulsing with the full and flowing tide
Of liberty and plenteousness that coursed through every vein.
How soon it ebbed, that surging tide ! Will it ever flow again ?

' Who owned the castle after him ? ' ' His son—my friend and foe.
You see yon rocks among the gorse in the valley down below.
We leaped among them from the rocks, and through their ranks
    we bore ;
I headed the United men, he led my yeoman corps.

' They reeled before our reddened pikes ; his blood had dyed my
    blade,
But I spared him for his father's sake ; and well the debt he paid !
For how, when right was trampled down, 'scaped I the tyrant's
    ban ?
The yeoman captain's castle, sir, contained an outlawed man !

' Yes, England was his glory—the mistress of the sea,
" William," " Wellington," and " Wooden Walls," his toasts would
    ever be.

I'd pledge "Green Erin and her Cause," and then he'd laugh and
say
That he knew one honest traitor—the "rebel" Myles O'Hea.

'In after-years he threatened hard to pull our roof-trees down
If we failed to vote at his command. Some quailed before his
frown.
Then I seized the old green banner and I shouted "Altars free !"
The gallant Forties,[1] to a man, left him to follow me !

'Well, God be with him. He was forced from home and lands to
part,
But to think 'twas England robbed him—it was that that broke his
heart.
"Old friend," he said, and grasped my hand, "I'm loyal to my
Queen,
But would such a law, at such a time, be made in College
Green ?"

'And while the tears rolled down his cheeks, his grandson, a brave
youth,
Clung to that tree beside the brook (good sir, I tell you truth),
And, sobbing, kissed it like a child ; nor tears could I restrain.'
The young man turned and hid his face in his hunter's flowing
mane.

'And Myles O'Hea,' he spake at length, 'have tropic suns and time
So changed the boy who weeping clung to yon old spreading lime ?
I was that boy. My father's home and lands are mine again :
But for every pound he paid for them I paid the Scotchman ten.'

High wassail in the castle halls. The wealthy bride is there,
And gentlemen and tenantry, proud dames and maidens fair,
And there—like Irish bard of old—beside the bridegroom gay
A white-haired peasant calmly sits ; 'tis poor old Myles O'Hea.

---

[1] The forty-shilling freeholders, whose votes won Catholic Emancipation, and who were themselves disfranchised in consequence.

With swimming eyes the bridegroom grasps that noble rustic's
    hand,
While round the board, with brimming cups, the wassailers all
    stand,
And louder swelled the harper's strains and wilder rose the cheers
When he pledged ' Your comrades long ago—the Irish Volunteers.'

' Now, God be praised,' quoth Myles O'Hea, ' they foully lie who
    say
That poor Old Ireland's glory's gone, for ever passed away.
But, gentlemen, what say you ?   Were not this a braver show
If sword-hilts clanked against the board like eighty years ago?'

THE IRISH PEASANT GIRL

SHE lived beside the Anner,
    At the foot of Slievenamon,
A gentle peasant girl,
    With mild eyes like the dawn—
Her lips were dewy rose-buds ;
    Her teeth of pearls rare ;
And a snow-drift 'neath a beechen bough,
    Her neck and nut-brown hair.

How pleasant 'twas to meet her
    On Sunday, when the bell
Was filling, with its mellow tones,
    Lone wood and grassy dell !
And when at eve young maidens
    Stray'd the river bank along,
The widow's brown-haired daughter
    Was loveliest of the throng.

Oh, brave, brave Irish girls—
    We well may call you brave !—
Sure the least of all your perils
    Is the stormy ocean wave,
When you leave your quiet valleys
    And cross the Atlantic foam,
To hoard your hard-won earnings
    For the helpless ones at home.

'Write word to my own dear mother,
　　Say we'll meet with God above ;
And tell my little brothers
　　I send them all my love.
May the angels ever guard them
　　Is their dying sister's prayer '—
And folded in the letter
　　Was a braid of nut-brown hair.

Ah, cold and well-nigh callous
　　This weary heart has grown
For thy helpless fate, dear Ireland,
　　And for sorrows of my own ;
Yet a tear my eye will moisten,
　　As by Anner's side I stray,
For the lily of the mountain foot
　　That withered far away.

St. John's Eve

' Do you remember that St. John's Eve, three years ago, when we walked round by Ballycullen to see the bonfires ? '—*Letter to Kickham in Woking Convict Prison.*

Yes, Gertrude, I remember well
　　That St. John's Eve, three years ago,
When, as the slanting sunbeams fell
　　Across the mountains all aglow,
Upon the lonely bridge we turned
　　To watch the roseate, russet hue,
Till faint and fainter still it burned
　　As if 'twere quenched by falling dew.

Then up the sloping hill we clomb,
　　And backward looked with pensive eyes,
Along the vale, our own sweet home,
　　The dearest spot beneath the skies ;
Dear for the golden hours that were
　　When life's glad morn all radiant shone,
Fondly dear for loved ones there,
　　And dearer still for loved ones gone.

The sun glides down behind the hill ;
   The shadows deepen while we gaze ;
The chapel, the Old Home, the mill,
   Are hidden in the twilight haze.
The wayside shepherd on the height
   Waits our approach, nor seems to heed
His vagrant flock throng out of sight—
   Adown the winding road they speed.

Deep learn'd was he in Gaelic lore,
   And loved to talk of days gone by;
(A saddening theme, those days of yore !)
   And still he turned with sparkling eye
From Druid rites and Christian fane,
   From champion bold and monarch grand,
To tell of fray and foray when
   His sires were princes in the land.

When to the Well-mile bridge we came,
   You pointed where the moonbeams white
Silvered the stream ; when, lo ! a flame,
   A wavy flame of ruddy light,
Leaped up, the farmyard fence above,
   And, while his children's shout rang high,
His cows the farmer slowly drove
   Across the blaze, he knew not why.[1]

Soon round the vale—above, below,
   And high upon the blue hills' brows
The bonfires shine with steady glow,
   Or blink through screening orchard boughs.
And now, in my lone dismal cell,
   While I that starry scene recall—
The fields, the hills, the sheltered dell—
   I close my eyes and see them all.

My dear-loved land must it be mine
   No more, except in dreams, to see ?

---

[1] A relic of ancient fire-worship practised on St. John's Eve, and still lingering in some parts of Ireland.

Yet think not, friends, that I repine
　At my sad fate—if sad it be.
Think not the captive weåkly pines,
　That from his soul all joy hath flown.
Oh, no ! the 'solemn starlight' shines
　As brightly as it ever shone.

And though I've had my share of pain,
　And sunken is my cheek and pale,
Yet, Gertrude, were it ours again
　On St. John's Eve, in Compsey vale,
While loitering by the Anner stream
　To view the mountain's purpled dome—
Waiting to see the bonfires gleam
　All round our quiet hill-claspéd home—

We'd talk of bygone blissful hours—
　And oh ! what blissful hours I've known !
It was a world of smiles and flowers,
　That little home-world of our own.
And happy thoughts each heart would fill—
　What else but happy could we be,
While Hope stood smiling on the hill
　And in the valley, Memory ?

ROBERT DWYER JOYCE

A vigorous ballad-poet, who was born at Glenosheen, County
Limerick, in 1830, and died in Dublin on October 24, 1883.　He
practised as a physician with much success in Boston.　His
poems are very numerous, and he published four volumes of
verse, as well as a couple of volumes of stories.　Some of his
songs and ballads have much power.　He was a frequent contributor to *The Irish People*, and may be reckoned as one of
the poets of the Fenian movement.　His most ambitious work
is a version of the tale of 'Deirdre,' which had an immense
success in America.　He was brother of Dr. P. W. Joyce, the
well-known educationalist and collector of Irish music.

FINEEN THE ROVER

AN old castle towers o'er the billow
   That thunders by Cleena's green land,
And there dwelt as gallant a rover
   As ever grasped hilt by the hand.
Eight stately towers of the waters
   Lie anchored in Baltimore Bay,
And over their twenty score sailors,
   Oh ! who but the Rover holds sway ?
      Then, ho ! for Fineen the Rover !
        Fineen O'Driscoll the free !
      Straight as the mast of his galley,
        And wild as the wave of the sea !

The Saxons of Cork and Moyallo,
   They harried his lands with their powers ;
He gave them a taste of his cannon,
   And drove them like wolves from his towers.
The men of Clan London brought over
   Their strong fleet to make him a slave ;
They met him by Mizen's wild highland,
   And the sharks crunched their bones 'neath the wave.
      Then, ho ! for Fineen the Rover,
        Fineen O'Driscoll the free ;
      With step like the red stag of Beara,
        And voice like the bold sounding sea.

Long time in that old battered castle,
   Or out on the waves with his clan,
He feasted and ventured and conquered,
   But ne'er struck his colours to man.
 a fight 'gainst the foes of his country
   He died as a brave man should die ;
And he sleeps 'neath the waters of Cleena,
   Where the waves sing his *caoine* to the sky.
      Then, ho ! for Fineen the Rover,
        Fineen O'Driscoll the free ;
      With eye like the osprey's at morning,
        And smile like the sun on the sea.

P

The Blacksmith of Limerick

He grasped his ponderous hammer ; he could not stand it more,
To hear the bombshells bursting and the thundering battle's roar.
He said : ' The breach they're mounting, the Dutchman's murder-
            ing crew—
I'll try my hammer on their heads and see what *that* can do !

' Now, swarthy Ned and Moran, make up that iron well ;
'Tis Sarsfield's horse that wants the shoes, so mind not shot or
            shell.'
' Ah, sure,' cried both, ' the horse can wait—for Sarsfield's on the
            wall,
And where you go we'll follow, with you to stand or fall ! '

The blacksmith raised his hammer, and rushed into the street,
His 'prentice boys behind him, the ruthless foe to meet—
High on the breach of Limerick, with dauntless hearts they stood
Where the bombshells burst and shot fell thick, and redly ran the
            blood.

' Now look you, brown-haired Moran, and mark you, swarthy Ned ;
This day we'll prove the thickness of many a Dutchman's head !
Hurrah ! upon their bloody path they're mounting gallantly ;
And now the first that tops the breach, leave him to this and me ! '

The first that gained the rampart, he was a captain brave !
A captain of the Grenadiers, with blood-stained dirk and glaive ;
He pointed and he parried, but it was all in vain,
For fast through skull and helmet the hammer found his brain !

The next that topp'd the rampart, he was a colonel bold,
Bright thro' the murk of battle his helmet flashed with gold.
' Gold is no match for iron ! ' the doughty blacksmith said,
As with that ponderous hammer he cracked his foeman's head !

' Hurrah for gallant Limerick ! ' black Ned and Moran cried,
As on the Dutchmen's leaden heads their hammers well they
            plied ;
A bombshell burst between them—one fell without a groan,
One leaped into the lurid air, and down the breach was thrown !

'Brave smith! brave smith!' cried Sarsfield, 'beware the
treacherous mine—-
Brave smith! brave smith! fall backward, or surely death is
thine!'
The smith sprang up the rampart and leaped the blood-stained wall,
As high into the shuddering air went foemen, breach and all!

Up like a red volcano they thundered wild and high,
Spear, gun, and shattered standard, and foemen thro' the sky;
And dark and bloody was the shower that round the blacksmith
fell—
He thought upon his 'prentice boys, they were avenged well!

On foemen and defenders a silence gathered down,
'Twas broken by a triumph-shout that shook the ancient town;
As out its heroes sallied, and bravely charged and slew,
And taught King William and his men what Irish hearts can do!

Down rushed the swarthy blacksmith unto the river side,
He hammered on the foes' pontoon, to sink it in the tide;
The timber it was tough and strong, it took no crack or strain—
'Mavrone, 'twon't break,' the blacksmith roared; 'I'll try their
heads again!'

    .   .   .   .   .   .

The blacksmith sought his smithy, and blew his bellows strong;
He shod the steed of Sarsfield, but o'er it sang no song:
· Ochon! my boys are dead,' he cried; 'their loss I'll long deplore,
But comfort's in my heart—their graves are red with foreign
gore!'

JOHN KEEGAN CASEY

Son of a peasant farmer, born near Mullingar, County
Westmeath. He was imprisoned as a Fenian in 1867, and in
consequence of his sufferings died in 1870, aged twenty-three.
His funeral at Glasnevin is said to have been attended by
fifty thousand people. He was one of the few poets produced

by the Fenian movement. That his poetry had fire and sweetness the following verses show, and these, with his youth and
his fate, have greatly endeared him to his countrymen.

His POEMS have been published by Cameron Ferguson & Co., Glasgow.

THE RISING OF THE MOON

A.D. 1798

‘ OH, then, tell me, Shawn O’Ferrall,
      Tell me why you hurry so ? ’
‘ Hush ! *ma bouchal*, hush, and listen ; ’
      And his cheeks were all a-glow :
‘ I bear ordhers from the Captain—
      Get you ready quick and soon ;
For the pikes must be together
      At the risin’ of the moon.’

‘ Oh, then, tell me, Shawn O’Ferrall,
      Where the gath’rin’ is to be ? ’
‘ In the ould spot by the river,
      Right well known to you and me ;
One word more—for signal token
      Whistle up the marchin’ tune,
With your pike upon your shoulder,
      By the risin’ of the moon.’

Out from many a mud-wall cabin
      Eyes were watching thro’ that night :
Many a manly chest was throbbing
      For the blessed warning light.
Murmurs passed along the valleys,
      Like the *banshee’s* lonely croon,
And a thousand blades were flashing
      At the risin’ of the moon.

There, beside the singing river,
      That dark mass of men were seen—
Far above the shining weapons
      Hung their own beloved ‘ Green.’

'Death to ev'ry foe and traitor !
  Forward ! strike the marchin' tune,
And hurrah, my boys, for freedom !
  'Tis the risin' of the moon.'

Well they fought for poor Old Ireland,
  And full bitter was their fate ;
(Oh ! what glorious pride and sorrow
  Fill the name of 'Ninety-Eight !)
Yet, thank God, e'en still are beating
  Hearts in manhood's burning noon,
Who would follow in their footsteps
  At the risin' of the moon !

MAIRE MY GIRL

Air—' Mairgread ni Chealleadh '

OVER the dim blue hills
  Strays a wild river,
Over the dim blue hills
  Rests my heart ever.
Dearer and brighter than
  Jewels and pearl,
Dwells she in beauty there,
  Maire [1] my girl.

Down upon Claris heath
  Shines the soft berry,
On the brown harvest tree
  Droops the red cherry.
Sweeter thy honey lips,
  Softer the curl
Straying adown thy cheeks,
  Maire my girl.

'Twas on an April eve
  That I first met her ;
Many an eve shall pass
  Ere I forget her.

---

[1] Pronounced, *Maurya.*

Since my young heart has been
　　Wrapped in a whirl,
Thinking and dreaming of
　　Maire my girl.

She is too kind and fond
　　Ever to grieve me,
She has too pure a heart
　　E'er to deceive me.
Were I Tyrconnell's chief
　　Or Desmond's earl,
Life would be dark, wanting
　　Maire my girl.

Over the dim blue hills
　　Strays a wild river,
Over the dim blue hills
　　Rests my heart ever ;
Dearer and brighter than
　　Jewels or pearl,
Dwells she in beauty there,
　　Maire my girl.

ELLEN O'LEARY

THE Fenian movement differed from that of 1848 in being
singularly unproductive of poetry—a fact which is all the more
remarkable because one of the leaders of the movement and
editor of its journal, *The Irish People*, was a born lover of
letters.   This was Mr. John O'Leary, brother of Ellen O'Leary,
from whose small volume—LAYS OF COUNTRY, HOME AND
FRIENDS (1891)—two pieces are here given.   Miss O'Leary
was born in Tipperary, 1831, and from about her twentieth year
was a contributor to various periodicals, including of course
her brother's journal.   She took an active part in the Fenian
conspiracy after the arrest of Stephens, whose escape she
materially assisted.   Her brother was sentenced to twenty years'

penal servitude in 1865, and returned to Ireland after five years of imprisonment and fourteen of exile. She then joined him in Dublin. She died in 1889, after a painful illness borne with her wonted gentleness and fortitude. Her poems have been described by the editor of her volume as 'simple field-flowers which blossomed above the subterranean workings of a grim conspiracy.'

To God and Ireland True

I SIT beside my darling's grave,
  Who in the prison died,
And tho' my tears fall thick and fast,
  I think of him with pride :
Ay, softly fall my tears like dew,
For one to God and Ireland true.

' I love my God o'er all,' he said,
  ' And then I love my land,
And next I love my Lily sweet,
  Who pledged me her white hand :
To each—to all—I'm ever true ;
To God—to Ireland—and to you.'

No tender nurse his hard bed smoothed
  Or softly raised his head ;
He fell asleep and woke in heaven
  Ere I knew he was dead ;
Yet why should I my darling rue ?
He was to God and Ireland true.

Oh ! 'tis a glorious memory ;
  I'm prouder than a queen
To sit beside my hero's grave,
  And think on what has been :
And, oh, my darling, I am true
To God—to Ireland—and to you.

My Old Home

LADY LODGE

A POOR old cottage tottering to its fall ;
Some faded rose-trees scattered o'er the wall ;
Four wooden pillars all aslant one way ;
A plot in front, bright green, amid decay,
Where my wee pets, whene'er they came to tea,
Laughed, danced, and played, and shouted in high glee ,
A rusty paling and a broken gate
Shut out the world and bounded my estate.

Dusty and damp within, and rather bare ;
Chokeful of books, here, there and everywhere ;
Old-fashioned windows, and old doors that creaked,
Old ceilings cracked and grey, old walls that leaked ;
Old chairs and tables, and an ancient lady
Worked out in tapestry, all rather shady ;
Bright pictures, in gilt frames, the only colour,
Making the grimy wallpaper look duller.

What was the charm, the glamour that o'erspread
That dingy house and made it dear?　The dead—
The dead—the gentle, loving, kind and sweet,
The truest, tenderest heart that ever beat.
While she was with me 'twas indeed *a home*,
Where every friend was welcome when they'd come.
Her soft eyes shone with gladness, and her grace
Refined and beautified the poor old place.

But she is gone who made home for me there,
Whose child-like laugh, whose light step on the stair
Filled me with joy and gladness, hope and cheer.
To heaven she soared, and left me lonely here.
The old house now has got a brand-new face ;
The roses are uprooted ; there's no trace
Of broken bough or blossom—no decay—
The past is dead—the world wags on alway.

JOHN FRANCIS O'DONNELL

BORN in Limerick, 1837, J. F. O'Donnell plunged very early into journalism, writing for innumerable papers in Ireland, England, and the United States of America. He was one of the prominent contributors to Mr. O'Leary's *Irish People*, and was a warm sympathiser with the Fenian movement. In 1873 he obtained an appointment in the office of the Agent-General for New Zealand, but died in the following year, aged thirty-seven. His POEMS were published by the Southwark Irish Literary Club, with an introduction by Richard Dowling, in 1891. He wrote apparently with great energy and at lightning speed, throwing his idea into the first words that came. The general level of his work is therefore not so high as one might expect from the following song, in which the impetuosity and spirit of the impromptu are happily united with a beautiful technique.

A SPINNING SONG

MY love to fight the Saxon goes,
　　And bravely shines his sword of steel ;
A heron's feather decks his brows,
　　And a spur on either heel ;
His steed is blacker than the sloe,
　　And fleeter than the falling star ;
Amid the surging ranks he'll go
　　And shout for joy of war.

Tinkle, twinkle, pretty spindle ; let the white wool drift and
　　dwindle.
Oh ! we weave a damask doublet for my love's coat of steel.
Hark ! the timid, turning treadle crooning soft, old-fashioned
　　ditties
To the low, slow murmur of the brown round wheel.

　My love is pledged to Ireland's fight ;
　　My love would die for Ireland's weal,
　To win her back her ancient right,
　　And make her foemen reel.

> Oh! close I'll clasp him to my breast
>   When homeward from the war he comes;
> The fires shall light the mountain's crest,
>   The valley peal with drums.

Tinkle, twinkle, pretty spindle; let the white wool **drift and**
    dwindle.
Oh! we weave a damask doublet for my love's coat of steel.
Hark! the timid, turning treadle crooning soft, old-fashioned
    ditties
To the low, slow murmur of the brown round wheel.

THOMAS CAULFIELD IRWIN

IRWIN possessed many of the essential qualities of a poet; he
had imagination and music, and he had gained wide culture by
education and travel.   But for a strain of mental derangement
he might have left behind him a very distinguished name.   In
his later days, as he used to be seen in the Dublin streets, he
presented a weird and uncouth but venerable figure.   The
gentle mania which had then descended upon him had, however, occasionally made its appearance much earlier.   The
great Irish antiquary, O'Donovan, has left a picture of him and
his ways in a note to Sir Samuel Ferguson:

> I understand that the mad poet who is my next-door neighbour
> claims acquaintance with you.   He says I am his enemy, and watch him
> through the thickness of the wall which divides our houses.   He threatens
> in consequence to shoot me.   One of us must leave.   I have a houseful
> of books and children; he has an umbrella and a revolver.   If, under the
> circumstances, you could use your influence and persuade *him* to remove
> to other quarters, you would confer a great favour on, yours sincerely,
> JOHN O'DONOVAN.

Irwin's besetting sin was diffuseness.   He published six
volumes, and much of them is a waste of words.   But perhaps
there is scarcely one of his poems in which one may not find

lines that ring with the unmistakable note of true poetry. The 'mad poet' was a keen observer both of men and Nature, delighting in life wherever he found it, and capable of rendering what he saw and felt in verse—now charged with tragic solemnity, and now coloured with a delicate fancy. He must be reckoned as a great but unrealised possibility in modern Irish literature.

Thomas Caulfield Irwin was born in the County Down, 1823. He wrote much in various periodicals, and was on the staff of *The Irish People*, the organ of the Fenian movement, edited by John O'Leary. In an essay on his writings in *Tinsley's Magazine* he is described as the 'Irish Keats.' He published his VERSICLES in 1856, and followed it with IRISH POEMS AND LEGENDS, 1869 ; SONGS AND ROMANCES, 1878 ; WINTER AND SUMMER STORIES (prose), 1879 ; PICTURES AND SONGS, 1880 ; SONNETS ON THE POETRY AND PROBLEM OF LIFE, 1881 ; POEMS, SKETCHES AND SONGS, 1889. He had been intended for the medical profession, but lost all his private means in 1848, and from this time lived a desultory and, at least in outward circumstances, rather unhappy life. He died in Dublin in 1892.

A WINDOW SONG

WITHIN the window of this white,
  Low, ivy-roofed, retired abode,
We look through sunset's sinking light
  Along the lone and dusty road
That leads unto the river's bridge,
  Where stand two sycamores broad and green,
Whence from their rising grassy ridge
  The low rays lengthen shade and sheen.
The village panes reflect the glow,
  And all about the scene is still,
Save, by the foamy dam below,
  The drumming wheel of the whitewashed mill :

    A radiant quiet fills the air,
    And gleam the dews along the turf :
      While the great wheel, bound
      On its drowsy round,
    Goes snoring through the gusts of surf.

A-south, beyond the hamlet lie
   The low, blue hills in mingling mist,
With furl of cloud along the sky,
   And ravines rich as amethyst,
And mellow edges golden-ored
   As sinks the round sun in the flood,
And high up wings the crow line toward
   Old turrets in the distant wood ;
Awhile from some twilighted roof
   The blue smoke rises o'er the thatch ;
By cots along the green aloof
   Some home-come labourer lifts the latch ;

     Or housewife sings her child to sleep,
     Or calls her fowl-flock from the turf,
       While the mill-wheel, bound
       On its drowsy round,
     Goes snoring through the gusts of surf.

Still at our open window, where
   Gleams on the leaves the lamp new lit,
For hours we read old books, and share
   Their thoughts and pictures, love and wit :
As midnight nears, its quiet ray
   Thrown on the garden's hedges faint,
Pales, as the moon, from clouds of grey,
   Looks down serenely as a saint.
We hear a few drops of a shower,
   Laying the dust for morning feet,
Patter upon the corner bower,
   Then, ceasing, send an air as sweet.

     And as we close the window down,
     And close the volumes read so long,
       Even the wheel's snore
       Is heard no more,
     And scarce the runnel's swirling song.

A Character

As from the sultry town, oppressed,
  At eve we pace the suburb green,
There, at his window looking west,
  Our good old friend will sure be seen :
Upon the table, full in light,
  Backgammon box and Bible lie :
Behind the curtain, hid from sight,
  A wine-glass no less certainly ;
    A finger beckons—nothing loath
      We enter—ah ! his heart is low,
    His flask is brimming high, but both
      Shall change their level ere we go.

We sit, and hour on hour prolong,
  For memory loves on wine to float ;
He tells old tales, chirps scraps of song,
  And cracks the nut of anecdote ;
Tells his best story with a smile—
  'Tis his by fifty years of right ;
And slowly rounds his joke, the while,
  With eye half closed, he trims the light :
    The clock hand marks the midnight's date,
      But blithe is he as matin wren ;
    His grasp is firm, his form dilate
      With wine, and wit of vanished men.

He reads each morn the news that shook
  The days of Pitt and Nelson, too,
But little cares for speech or book,
  Or battle after Waterloo ;
The present time is lost in haze,
  The past alone delights his eye ;
He deems the men of these poor days
  As worthless all of history ;
    Who dares to scorn that love of thine,
      Old friend, for vanished men and years ?
    'Tis youth that charms thee—pass the wine—
      The wine alone is good as theirs.

Each morn he basks away the hours
In garden nooks, and quaffs the air ;
Chats with his plants, and holds with flowers
A tender-toned communion there ;
Each year the pleasant prospect shrinks,
And houses close the olden view ;
The world is changing fast ; he thinks
The sun himself is failing too.
    Ah ! well-a-day, the mists of age
      May make these summer seasons dim ;
    No matter—still in Chaucer's page
      The olden summers shine for him.

From CÆSAR

I

WITHIN the dim museum room,
'Mid dusty marbles, drowsed in light,
Black Indian idols, deep-sea bones,
Gods, nymphs, and uncouth skeletons,
One statua of stately height
Shines from an old nook's shifting gloom.

II

Mark well : as from a turret tall
Droops some victorious flag, the wreath
Of conquest tops him ; keenly nigh
Gleam the worn cheek and falcon eye,
Whose fixed spirit flames beneath
That bony crown pyramidal.

III

'Tis he whose name around the earth
Has rolled in History's echoing dreams ;
An antique shape of Destiny,
A soul dæmonic, born to be
A king or nothing—moulded forth
From giant Nature's fierce extremes.

IV

His was a policy like fate
   That shapes to-day for future hours ;
      The sov'reign foresight his to draw
      From crude events their settled law,
To learn the soul, and turn the weight
   Of human passions into powers.

V

His was the mathematic might
   That moulds results from men and things—
      The eye that pierces at a glance,
      The will that wields all circumstance,
The star-like soul of force and light,
   That moves etern on tireless wings.

VI

Keen as some star's magnetic rays,
   His judgment subtle and sublime
      Unlocked the wards of every brain,
      Till, clothed in gathered might amain,
Scorning the inferior Destinies,
   He burst the palace gates of Time.

VII

Bright, swift, resistless as the sun,
   He scorned the track of traversed sky ;
      Though throned in empery supreme,
      Still held the mighty past a dream,
Self-emulative, storming on
   To vaster fields of Victory.

VIII

Thus upward ever, storm and shade
   Flew past, but till he reached the goal
      He paused not ; on one height intent,
      But from the clouds of blind event,
That severed to his gaze, re-made
   The wings of his triumphant soul.

To a Skull

SILENT as thou, whose inner life is gone,
  Let me essay thy meaning if I can,
Thou ghostly, ghastly moral carved in bone,
  Old Nature's quiet mockery of man.

I place thee in the light ; the orient gold
  Falls on thy crown, and strikes each uncouth line ;
Strange shape ! the earth has ruins manifold,
  But none with meaning terrible as thine.

For here beneath this bleak and sterile dome
  Did hatred rage, and silent sorrow mourn—
A little world, an infinite spirit's home,
  A heaven or hell abandoned and forlorn.

Here thought on thought arose, like star on star,
  And love, deemed deathless, habited ; and now
An empty mausoleum, vainer far
  Than Cheops' mountain pyramid, art thou.

Once on that forehead, radiant as the day,
  Imagination flamed in trancéd mood :
Once on thy fleshy mask, now fallen away,
  Rippled the pulses of a bridegroom's blood ;

And laughter wrinkled up those orbs with fun,
  And sorrow furrowed channels as you prayed—
Well, now no mark is left on thee but one,
  The careless stroke of some old sexton's spade.

Lost are thy footprints ; changeful as the air
  Is the brown disc of earth whereon we move ;
The bright sun looks for them in vain.   Ah, where
  Is now thy life of action, thought, and love ?

Where are thy hopes, affections, toil, and gain ?
  Lost in the void of all-surrounding death.
And does this pound of lime alone remain
  To tell of all thy passion, pride, and faith ?

'Where is the soul?' we cry—and swift the sound
    Dies in the morning depth of voiceless light ;
'The structure where?' Oh, bend unto the ground,
    And ask the worm that crawls the mould at night.

The brown leaf rots upon the Autumn breeze,
    The empty shell is washed upon the shore,
The bubble glitters on the morning seas,
    And bursting in the vast is seen no more.

Like mist thy life has melted on the air,
    And what thy nature, history, or name,
No sorcery now of science or of prayer
    Can make the voiceless infinite proclaim.

Dumb are the heavens ; sphere controlling sphere
    Chariot the void through their allotted span ;
And man acts out his little drama here
    As though the only Deity were man.

Cold Fate, who sways creation's boundless tides,
    Instinct with masterdom's eternal breath,
Sits in the void invisible, and guides
    The huge machinery of life and death,

Now strewing seeds of fresh immortal bands
    Through drifts of universes deepening down ;
Now moulding forth with giant spectral hands
    The fire of suns colossal for his crown ;

Too prescient for feeling, still enfolds
    The stars in death and life, in night and day,
And, clothed in equanimity, beholds
    A blossom wither or a world decay ;

Sleepless, eternal, labouring without pause,
    Still girds with life his infinite abode,
And moulds from matter by developed laws
    With equal ease the insect or the God !

Poor human skull, perchance some mighty race,
　　The giant birth of never-ceasing change,
Winging the world, may pause awhile to trace
　　Thy shell in some re-orient Alpine range ;

Perchance the fire of some angelic brow
　　May glow above thy ruin in the sun,
And higher shapes reflect, as we do now
　　Upon the structure of the Mastodon.

LADY DUFFERIN

Daughter of Thomas Sheridan and granddaughter of
R. B. Sheridan the dramatist. She was born in 1807, and
married first the Hon. Pryce Blackwood, who became Earl of
Dufferin ; but just before her death, which occurred on June 13,
1867, married her second husband, the Earl of Gifford. She
has written some of the most beautiful and touching of Irish
songs and ballads.

Lament of the Irish Emigrant

I'm sittin' on the stile, Mary,
　　Where we sat side by side,
On a bright May mornin', long ago,
　　When first you were my bride :
The corn was springin' fresh and green,
　　And the lark sang loud and high—
And the red was on your lip, Mary,
　　And the lovelight in your eye.

The *place* is little changed, Mary ;
　　The day is bright as then ;
The lark's loud song is in my ear,
　　And the corn is green again ;

But I miss the soft clasp of your hand,
   And your breath, warm on my cheek,
And I still keep list'nin' for the words
   You never more will speak.

'Tis but a step down yonder lane,
   And the little church stands near—
The church where we were wed, Mary ;
   I see the spire from here.
But the graveyard lies between, Mary,
   And my step might break your rest—
For I've laid you, darling ! down to sleep
   With your baby on your breast.

I'm very lonely now, Mary,
   For the poor make no new friends :
But, oh ! they love the better still,
   The few our Father sends !
And you were all *I* had, Mary—
   My blessin' and my pride !
There's nothin' left to care for now,
   Since my poor Mary died.

Yours was the good, brave heart, Mary,
   That still kept hoping on
When the trust in God had left my soul
   And my arm's young strength was gone.
There was comfort ever on your lip,
   And the kind look on your brow—
I bless you, Mary, for that same,
   Though you cannot hear me now.

I thank you for the patient smile
   When your heart was fit to break,
When the hunger-pain was gnawin' there
   And you hid it for *my* sake ;
I bless you for the pleasant word
   When your heart was sad and sore—
Oh ! I'm thankful you are gone, Mary,
   Where grief can't reach you more !

I'm biddin' you a long farewell,
  My Mary—kind and true !
But I'll not forget *you*, darling,
  In the land I'm goin' to :
They say there's bread and work for all,
  And the sun shines always there—
But I'll not forget Old Ireland,
  Were it fifty times as fair !

And often in those grand old woods
  I'll sit and shut my eyes,
And my heart will travel back again
  To the place where Mary lies ;
And I'll think I see the little stile
  Where we sat side by side,
And the springin' corn, and the bright May morn,
  When first you were my bride.

Terence's Farewell

So, my Kathleen, you're going to leave me
  All alone by myself in this place,
But I'm sure you will never deceive me—
  Oh no, if there's truth in that face.
Though England's a beautiful city,
  Full of illigant boys—oh, what then ?
You would not forget your poor Terence ;
  You'll come back to Ould Ireland again.

Och, those English, deceivers by nature,
  Though maybe you'd think them sincere,
They'll say you're a sweet charming creature,
  But don't you believe them, my dear.
No, Kathleen, *agra* ! don't be minding
  The flattering speeches they'll make :
Just tell them a poor boy in Ireland
  Is breaking his heart for your sake.

It's folly to keep you from going,
　　Though, faith, it's a mighty hard case—
For, Kathleen, you know, there's no knowing
　　When next I shall see your sweet face.
And when you come back to me, Kathleen—
　　None the better will I be off then—
You'll be spáking such beautiful English,
　　Sure, I won't know my Kathleen again.

Eh, now, where's the need of this hurry?
　　Don't flutter me so in this way!
I've forgot, 'twixt the grief and the flurry,
　　Every word I was maning to say.
Now just wait a minute, I bid ye—
　　Can I talk if you bother me so?—
Oh, Kathleen, my blessing go wid ye
　　Ev'ry inch of the way that you go.

ANONYMOUS

MUSIC IN THE STREET

This striking poem appeared in an Irish-American paper about 1864, and was suggested by hearing the 69th Irish regiment play Irish airs through the New York streets.

IT rose upon the sordid street,
　　A cadence sweet and lone;
Through all the vulgar din it pierced,
　　That low melodious tone.
It thrilled on my awakened ear
　　Amid the noisy mart,
Its music over every sound
　　Vibrated in my heart.

I've heard full oft a grander strain
　　Through lofty arches roll,
That bore on the triumphant tide
　　The rapt and captive soul.

In this the breath of my own hills
  Blew o'er me soft and warm,
And shook my spirit, as the leaves
  Are shaken by the storm.

As sounds the distant ocean wave
  Within a hollow shell,
I heard within this far-off strain
  The gentle waters swell
Around my distant island shore,
  And glancing through the rocks,
While o'er their full and gliding wave
  The sea-birds wheeled in flocks.

There, through the long delicious eves
  Of that old haunted land
The Naiads, in their floating hair,
  Yet dance upon the strand ;
Till near and nearer came the sound,
  And swelled upon the air,
And still strange echoes trembled through
  The magic music there.

It rose above the ceaseless din,
  It filled the dusty street,
As some cool breeze of freshness blows
  Across the desert's heat.
It shook their squalid attic homes—
  Pale exiles of our race—
And drew to dingy window-panes
  Full many a faded face,

And eyes whose deep and lustrous light
  Flashed strangely, lonely there,
And many a young and wistful brow
  Beneath its soft brown hair ;
And other eyes of fiercer fire,
  And faces rough and dark—
Brave souls ! that bore thro' all their lives
  The tempests on their bark.

In through the narrow rooms it poured,
    That music sweeping on,
And perfumed all their heavy air
    With flowers of summers gone,
With waters sparkling to the lips,
    With many a summer breeze,
That woke into one rippling song
    The shaken summer trees.

In it, along the sloping hills
    The blue flax-blossoms bent ;
In it, above the shining streams
    The ' Fairy Fingers ' leant ;
In it, upon the soft green Rath,
    There bloomed the Fairy Thorn ;
In their tired feet they felt the dew
    Of many a harvest morn.

In it, the ripe and golden corn
    Bent down its heavy head ;
In it, the grass waved long and sweet
    Above their kindred dead ;
In it, the voices of the loved
    They might no more behold
Came back and spoke the tender words
    And sang the songs of old.

Sometimes there trembled through the strain
    A song like falling tears,
And then it rose and burst again
    Like sudden clashing spears ;
And still the faces in the street
    And at the window-panes
Would cloud or lighten, gloom or flash
    With all its changing strains.

But, ah ! too soon it swept away,
    That pageantry of sound—
Again the parted tide of life
    Closed darkly all around,

As in the wake of some white bark,
   In sunshine speeding on,
Close in the dark and sullen waves,
   The darker where it shone.

The faces faded from my view,
   Like faces in a dream ;
To its dull channel back again
   Crept the subsiding stream.
And I, too, starting like the rest,
   Cast all the spell aside,
And let the fading music go—
   A blossom down the tide.

DION BOUCICAULT

THIS noted actor and dramatist was born in Dublin, of French parentage, on December 26, 1822. His Irish plays were extremely popular, but he wrote an enormous number of other dramas, comedies, and farces. He lived in America during the latter part of his life, and died there in September 1890.

THE EXILED MOTHER

I'M very happy where I am,
   Far across the say—
I'm very happy far from home,
   In North Amerikay.

It's lonely in the night when Pat
   Is sleeping by my side.
I lie awake, and no one knows
   The big tears that I've cried.

For a little voice still calls me back
   To my far, far counthrie,
And nobody can hear it spake–
   Oh ! nobody but me.

There is a little spot of ground
  Behind the chapel wall ;
It's nothing but a tiny mound,
  Without a stone at all ;

It rises like my heart just now,
  It makes a dawny hill ;
It's from below the voice comes out,
  I cannot kape it still.

Oh ! little Voice, ye call me back
  To my far, far counthrie,
And nobody can hear ye spake—
  Oh ! nobody but me.

TIMOTHY DANIEL SULLIVAN

MR. T. D. SULLIVAN, born 1827 at Bantry, County Cork, distinguished himself as journalist, politician, and poet. His verse consisted in a great measure of racy political pasquinades, whose satire and humour, tuned to catching rhythms, have won them much popularity. He also wrote patriotic poems of a higher and more serious class, and tried his hand, like most other Irish poets of his day, on themes taken from the legendary romances of Ireland. His ' God save Ireland,' which may be said to dispute the position of Irish national anthem with ' The Wearing of the Green,' has the misfortune to be written to a commonplace and quite un-Irish air. Mr. Sullivan's best work is to be found in simple ballads of fatherland and home. His style when dealing with congenial themes is clear, direct, and sincere.

Mr. Sullivan published in 1868 DUNBOY AND OTHER POEMS. This was followed in 1879 by GREEN LEAVES, and in 1887 by LAYS OF THE LAND LEAGUE. POEMS was published in 1888; PRISON POEMS AND LAYS OF TULLAMORE in the same year; BLANAID AND OTHER POEMS in 1892; and a volume of selections in 1899. Mr. Sullivan was a member of Parliament for several years, and sat successively for County Westmeath, for Dublin (College Green Division), and County Donegal. He became a contributor to *The Nation* in 1854, and ultimately owned and edited that journal on the death of his brother, Mr. A. M. Sullivan. He was Lord Mayor of Dublin in 1886 and 1887, and died in 1914.

STEERING HOME

FAR out beyond our sheltered bay,
  Against the golden evening sky,
A brown speck rises ; then away
  It sinks—it dwindles from my eye.
  Again it rises ; drawing nigh,
Its well-known shape grows sharp and clear—
It is his bark, my Donal dear.
  And oh ! though small a speck it be,
Kind Heaven, that knows my hope and fear,
  Can tell the world it holds for me.

My boat of boats is steering home—
  She bends and sways before the wind ;
I cannot see the milky foam
  Beneath her bows and far behind.
  But oh ! I know my love will find—
Howe'er the evening current flows,
Howe'er the rising night wind blows—
  The shortest course his keel can dart
From where he is to where he knows
  I wait to clasp him to my heart.

Come, Donal, home ! See by my side
  Your little sons, impatient too.
All day they loitered by the tide,
  And prattled of your boat and you ;
  Into the glancing waves they threw
Some little chips—the surges bore
Their tiny vessels back to shore ;
  Then would they clap their hands, and say
The first was yours ; then, o'er and o'er,
  Would ask me why you stayed away.

Come, Donal, home !   The red sun sets ;
　Come to your children dear, and me ;
And, bring us full or empty nets,
　A scene of joy our hearth shall be.
　You'll tell me stories of the sea ;
And I will sing the songs you said
Were sweet as wild sea-music made
　By mermaids on the weedy rocks—
When in some sheltered quiet shade,
　They sit and comb their dripping locks.

He comes ! he comes !   My boat is near ;
　I know her mainsail's narrow peak.
They haul her flowing sheets—I hear
　The dry sheaves on their pivots creak.
　He waves his hand—I hear him speak—
Come to the beach, my sons, with me ;
He'll greet us from her side, and we
　Shall meet him when he leaps to shore ;
Then take him home, and bid him see
　Our brighter deck—our cottage floor.

You and I

　I KNOW what will happen, sweet,
　　When you and I are one ;
　Calm and bright and very fleet,
　　All our days will run.
　Fond and kind our words will be,
　　Mixed no more with sighs ;
　Thoughts too fine for words we'll see
　　Within each other's eyes.

　Sweet, when you and I are one,
　　Earth will bloom anew—
　Brighter then the stars and sun,
　　Softer then the dew.
　Sweeter scents will then arise
　　From the fields and flowers ;
　Holier calm will fill the skies
　　In the midnight hours.

Music now unheard, unknown,
 Then will reach our ears ;
Not a plaint in any tone,
 Not a hint of tears.
In a round of bliss complete
 All our days will run—
That is what will happen, sweet,
 When you and I are one.

DEAR OLD IRELAND

IRISH AIR

I

DEEP in Canadian woods we've met,
 From one bright island flown ;
Great is the land we tread, but yet
 Our hearts are with our own.
And ere we leave this shanty small,
 While fades the Autumn day,
  We'll toast Old Ireland !
  Dear Old Ireland !
  Ireland, boys, hurrah !

II

We've heard her faults a hundred times,
 The new ones and the old,
In songs and sermons, rants and rhymes,
 Enlarged some fifty-fold.
But take them all, the great and small,
 And this we've got to say :
  Here's dear Old Ireland !
  Good Old Ireland !
  Ireland, boys, hurrah !

III

We know that brave and good men tried
 To snap her rusty chain—
That patriots suffered, martyrs died—
 And all, 'tis said, in vain.

But no, boys, no ! a glance will show
　How far they've won their way—
　　Here's good Old Ireland !
　　Brave Old Ireland !
　　Ireland, boys, hurrah !

IV

We've seen the wedding and the wake,
　The patron and the fair ;
And lithe young frames at the dear old games
　In the kindly Irish air ;
And the loud ' hurroo,' we have heard it too,
　And the thundering ' Clear the way !'
　　Here's gay Old Ireland !
　　Dear Old Ireland !
　　Ireland, boys, hurrah !

V

And well we know in the cool grey eves,
　When the hard day's work is o'er,
How soft and sweet are the words that greet
　The friends who meet once more ;
With ' Mary machree !' ' My Pat ! 'tis he !'
　And ' My own heart night and day !'
　　Ah, fond Old Ireland !
　　Dear Old Ireland !
　　Ireland, boys, hurrah !

VI

And happy and bright are the groups that pass
　From their peaceful homes, for miles
O'er fields and roads and hills, to Mass,
　When Sunday morning smiles ;
And deep the zeal their true hearts feel
　When low they kneel and pray.
　　Oh, dear Old Ireland !
　　Blest Old Ireland !
　　Ireland, boys, hurrah !

VII

But deep in Canadian woods we've met,
    And we never may see again
The dear old isle where our hearts are set
    And our first fond hopes remain !
But come, fill up another cup,
    And with every sup we'll say,
        ' Here's dear Old Ireland !
        Loved Old Ireland !
        Ireland, boys, hurrah !

FANNY PARNELL

SISTER of the late C. S. Parnell, M.P. She was born in
County Wicklow in 1854, and wrote poems for *The Irish
People* (1864–5) before she reached her teens. She was
afterwards closely connected with her brother's political work,
and died in America in 1882. She was a fervent speaker and
organiser, and had much poetical ability.

POST-MORTEM

SHALL mine eyes behold thy glory, O my country ?
    Shall mine eyes behold thy glory ?
Or shall the darkness close around them, ere the sun-blaze
    Break at last upon thy story ?

When the nations ope for thee their queenly circle,
    As a sweet new sister hail thee,
Shall these lips be sealed in callous death and silence
    That have known but to bewail thee ?

Shall the ear be deaf that only loved thy praises
    When all men their tribute bring thee ?
Shall the mouth be clay that sang thee in thy squalor
    When all poets' mouths shall sing thee ?

Ah ! the harpings and the salvos and the shoutings
   Of thy exiled sons returning
I should hear, though dead and mouldered, and the grave
     damps
   Should not chill my bosom's burning.

Ah ! the tramp of feet victorious ! I should hear them
   'Mid the shamrocks and the mosses,
And my heart should toss within the shroud and quiver,
   As a captive dreamer tosses.

I should turn and rend the cere clothes round me,
   Giant-sinews I should borrow,
Crying, ' O my brothers, I have also loved her,
   In her lowliness and sorrow.

' Let me join with you the jubilant procession,
   Let me chant with you her story ;
Then contented I shall go back to the shamrocks,
   Now mine eyes have seen her glory.'

BOOK IV

JAMES CLARENCE MANGAN

James Clarence Mangan fills the most tragic place in the Irish literature of this century ; and even if he be not its greatest poet, at least he has only equals, no superiors. His fame has been obscured and injured—in part by his own fault, in part by the indiscretion of friends and admirers, in part by the pressure of inevitable circumstance. Born to unhappiness, dowered with a melancholy temperament and a drifting will, he never found natural joy save, like Thomas à Kempis, ' in a nook with a book ' and in the exercise of his art. Like sundry other unhappy poets, he found joys less natural and sane in opium and alcohol. It is not essential for our present purpose to examine the kind, the extent, the gravity of his indulgence in these methods of obliviousness or exaltation : the evidence of his contemporaries is conflicting : enough, to say that in whatever degree Mangan must share the reproach of Coleridge, De Quincey, Poe, of the Scottish Ferguson and Burns, he yet claims our compassion rather than our contempt. His weakness never marred the purity, in all senses, of his poetry : he made no Byronic parade or boast of his own worst side. From cradle to coffin ' Melancholy marked him for her own,' and his heart always knew its own bitterness. Infinitely sensitive, of a fragile and tremulous spirit, the harshness of the world was his master, and from the first he succumbed to whatever miseries, real or imagined, came his way. The story of his life is a story of persistent gloom and grayness, peopled by

R

phantoms and phantasies of sorrow : he was a born dreamer of
dreams, and passed his days in a kind of *penumbra*. He was
gentle and grotesque, eccentric and lovable : but much of a
mystery to all and to himself. Fit for nothing but literature,
and passionately enamoured of it, he was a desultory, uncertain, capricious writer : always a student with a true love
of learning, his knowledge was casual, imperfect, hardly a
scholar's. Further, it was a part of his strange nature to
be innocently insincere, or inventive, or imaginative, about
himself and his : there was 'a deal of Ariel, just a streak of
Puck' in his composition, and he throws dust in the eyes of
his readers, who vainly try to ascertain the precise measure
of truth and actuality in his personal or literary statements.
With all his devotion to letters and learning, he was incapable
of exercising a prolonged and constant energy : it was not in
him to concentrate and control his powers. When he wrote
without inspiration, but in obedience to some external call or
need, he wrote either with a strong and arid rhetoric or with
a somewhat ghastly air of mocking merriment and jesting
cynicism : and so little could he command his imagination
that almost the whole of his greatest and most perfect work
owes its inception to the work—often the inferior work—of
others. The poet of the 'Dark Rosaleen' is a great original
poet : such splendour of verse is not translation, but a new
creation. And yet, but for the Gaelic poet, Costello of
Ballyhaunis, Mangan would not have written his masterpiece.

The poetry of this unique man falls under four chief heads :
paraphrases or translations from the Gaelic ; those from the
German, and sometimes from other modern languages ; poems
which profess to spring from Turkish and Oriental originals ;
poems avowedly and indisputably original. His collected poems,
of every description, would compose a considerable volume in
point of size : and it would contain little that is of no value —
little without some touch, if not of genius, yet assuredly of a
singular talent. But were we to exclude from such a collection
some twenty or thirty famous pieces, the residue would not be
of such a rare and distinguished quality as entitles a cunning

versifier to claim the higher rank of poet. Mangan's great work has never been overpraised : not so his less great. He was an Irishman writing English verse during the first half of the century : his wide and genuine if straggling culture, his range of literary interest, his technical mastery of verse, filled his audience with a feeling of novelty. It was a portent, a presage, of an outburst of Irish poetry in English verse such as had not before been heard : and it is not unnatural that Mangan's poetry was received, is often still received, with too lavish an applause, too indiscriminate a welcome. Again : Mangan, though nothing of a politician, was much of a patriot ; and national pride tended to exalt the merits of whatever came from Mangan the accomplished, the specially inspired. It is largely a question of date and period : Mangan was a pioneer, and became a source of inspiration. Others have entered into his labours, and Ireland has borne poets of far deeper and more patient culture, and of a technical skill sometimes not far beneath his own at its finest. The mass of Mangan's poetry seems less miraculous and immaculate now than it seemed half a century ago : then, he had scarce a rival ; since then, he has had many and worthy rivals, though none has surpassed him. Only his master-work need be considered here, and our brief selections illustrate every aspect of it.

There are few who question the supremacy, among his poems, of those derived from Gaelic sources. Doubtless to the struggling, starving Irish poet, who never dreamed of winning English praise and writing for an English public, Ireland and her history and her hope were natural themes : but patriotism and love of country are insufficient to explain the poetical excellence of these poems. Passionate patriotism can make execrable poetry. Something else there must be to account for this superiority : and it can surely be found in the truth that to Mangan, essentially the poet of dreams and sorrows and longings, of an ideal rapture and a perfect beauty, the history of Ireland appealed with a personal force. In that beautiful and tragic history he found what

profoundly moved him, not only as an Irishman who loved
Ireland, but as the sad and stricken man who fed on dreams,
was haunted by memories, lived in an infinite desire. The
laments, the prophecies, the dauntless defiances, the radiant
hopes, in a word the various *passions* which he found in the
history and literature of the Gael came home to him : he felt
them as he could not feel the emotions of German poets. He
therefore brought to his Irish versions such a wealth of
unfeigned emotion, such a profusion of artistic cunning, as to
make them verily the fresh expression of his own soul and the
fine flower of his genius. With but four or five exceptions, he
leaves aside the Gaelic poetry of love or laughter, and fills his
page with the cry of battle, the wail for the dead, the dirge of
departed glory. The note of sorrow—noble and proud sorrow—
appears in almost all his Irish poems : nothing so appealed to
his sad heart as tears. As he broods over the lamentations
of ancient bards, raising the *keen* over Ireland desolate and
derelict, over Irish princes exiled or dead, over Irish hopes
frustrated and Irish chivalry in defeat, his own immense
melancholy kindles into a melancholy of majestic music. He
transmutes the mourning Irish music of Owen Ward into
English verse of monumental magnificence and monotony in
woe as he chants the lament for the lords of Tyrone and
Tyrconnell, The O'Neill and The O'Donnell, dead exiles
sleeping together in holy Rome : each of the eighteen stanzas,
with its elaborate structure, is like a funeral march, full of deep
repeated chords, and a wailing cry that pierces up through the
heavier tones of sorrow. These poems are starred with the
lovely and great names of the princes, the provinces, the
pleasant places of Ireland, vanquished, dead, fugitive, ruined,
vanished. Where is Brian's fair palace of Kinkora ? Whither
are flown the Wild Geese ? Where is ' the Young Deliverer of
Kathaleen Ny-Houlahan ' ? And, ' alas, for the once proud
people of Banba ! ' Weep, Ireland, for Owen Roe ! and hear
the Banshee crying for the Knight of Kerry ! Take your farewell
of Patrick Sarsfield ! Mourn for glory gone from the Castle of
Donegal ! Be sad for the soul of O'Sullivan Beara, the betrayed

and murdered !   'Through the long drear night I lie awake for the sorrows of Inisfail,' the 'Mother of light and song !' Thus run the greater part of these poems : and the two master-pieces, which transcend the rest, are 'Dark Rosaleen' and 'O'Hussey's Ode to The Maguire.' The 'Dark Rosaleen' ranks with the great lyrics of the world ; it is one of the fairest and fiercest in its perfection of imagery and rhythm : here is the chivalry of a nation's faith, struck of a sudden into the immortality of music. The 'Ode to The Maguire' burns with a noble ferocity in lines of the highest Homeric simplicity and grandeur. Here is the true Mangan of greatness and of genius. His quieter Irish poems are less successful, for all their charm : both 'Ellen Bawn' and 'The Fair Hills of Eire' have found better renderings than his. In the 'Woman of Three Cows' Mangan is more at home with the racy sarcasm of his original. But the Irish portion of his poems, viewed as a whole, is that to which he brought most of the sincere passion, the artistic instinct and capacity, the high poetic seriousness that he possessed ; more than all his other poems, they bear a severe and critical scrutiny : for which reason, and not merely because they *are* Irish, we place them in the forefront of his work.

Next to these in importance stand Mangan's poems of the East, which are practically his own, though he studied Eastern poetry in translations, and was in part drawn Eastward by his favourite Germans, with whom, as with Byron, Moore, Hugo, Heine, there was a fashion of Orientalism ; and he followed them in the imitation of Eastern rhythms. In many of his Oriental poems Mangan has poured, out of his darkness of the shadow, all a captive's wistful longing for the sunlight, for the fragrance of roses, for the burning blue : and also his half-sad, half-smiling sense of life's fleetness and illusion. He loved the thought of the East, and to indulge in the dreams of such Irish scholars as Vallancey about the Oriental origin of the Gael : he loved, as FitzGerald loved, an Orient largely of his own creation. What Davis has called Mangan's 'perfect mastery of versification ; his flexibility of passion, from loneliest grief to the maddest humour,' appear profusely in these glowing poems attributed to fictitious Turks and impossible Persians. Mangan, who loved to dream of colour and light and golden visions, is brilliantly felicitous in some of these pieces : but he is more nobly inspired, and not less glowingly, when he sings of the ' Little Black Rose ' (the *Roisin Dubh*) than when he moralises upon the roses of Shiraz. Yet, certainly, these ardent poems of the East, with their voluptuous music and imagination, their wise and trite and venerable philosophy, their vigour of dramatic movement, constitute Mangan's second glory : they are of greater value than all but the very finest things in his vast ANTHOLOGIA GERMANICA. There is power of a rare kind in the ' Karamanian Exile,' the ' Wail and Warning of the Three Khalandeers,' the ' Time of the Roses,' the ' Howling Song of Al Mohara,' the ' Time of the Barmecides.' Even some of Mangan's least unfortunate fooling is done in Oriental disguise.

The ANTHOLOGIA GERMANICA, with which are grouped Mangan's renderings or adaptations from sundry other modern tongues, constitutes the larger part of his work. He was born at a time when German poetry and philosophy were receiving due attention at the hands of English writers, and his receptive literary temperament was influenced by that circumstance : further, much German sentiment of romanticism, of reverie, of personal passion, appealed to him with singular force. Yet, with a few exceptions, his work in this kind is of little more than a fine and interesting mediocrity : and for the most part it is at its best when he frankly deserts his originals to embroider or embellish them with beauties of his own devising. He is happiest when concerned with poets not of the first order : with Schiller, Rückert, Körner, Freiligrath, Uhland, Bürger, rather than with Goethe and Heine. Rückert, in especial, called forth his great gifts of rhythmical beauty : but in the main we must lament the hard necessities, material and spiritual, which led him to this task of echoing or improving a mass of poetry often poor in quality and ephemeral. The chief value of this collection lies in its copious illustration of Mangan's technical excellence in his art, of his lyrical dexterity : but twice or thrice does it reveal him flushed and enraptured with the poetic passion of his work inspired from Irish sources. Mangan's wholly original poems, like those taken from or suggested by German or Oriental literature, would hardly have entitled him to a high rank among poets : a small portion of them is admirable, a larger portion has a certain effectiveness and power, the greatest portion is stiff or stilted with a forced rhetoric—the rhetoric of the poet writing upon political occasion, who has declamation at his command, but scant beauty of imagination. Of the original poems, the most famous and most moving is the terrible 'Nameless One' : a burst of Byronism more profoundly sincere than all but a very few of Byron's most embittered dirges over his own wretched soul. Most drearily imaginative also is 'Siberia,' a lyric of despair and dereliction : and in some other pieces there is a strain of felicitous melancholy, a true pathetic touch. It is, however, not to be denied that in Mangan we have a poet hampered, let and hindered, by inborn physical and spiritual sensitiveness ; a visionary seldom capable of arresting his fairest visions ; a self-tormentor void of that interior peace whence comes the assured impulse of poetry. His perturbed and vagrant mind wandered in dry places and in the dark, longing vainly for consolation and light : he could always write mockingly, spasmodically, forcibly, fiercely, but only at rare seasons beautifully. Shrinking from the world, cursed with real and imagined curses, he was never 'master of his fate' nor 'captain of his soul': and poetry, so great a solace to many poets of unhappiness, visited him from regions not of gladness but of gloom. Ireland alone, with her mingling of misery and heroic pride, woke in him the joy of poetry and the passion of art triumphant.

Few poets more imperatively demand to have their lives considered in any estimate of their poems. Over Mangan's life is writ large the inscription of hopelessness and incapacity to be strong : he let go the helm, to drift through life and through

the worlds of poetry, metaphysics, curious lore of many kinds,
finding no anchorage in any harbour. He squandered his
power and mastery over verse upon matter mediocre or worse ;
and even that in a desultory, capricious fashion, as the humour
of the hour took him. An alien in the world, he had desires,
but no ambitions ; he cared nothing for literary fame, and
everything for some indefinable ideal with which his daily life
was in fearful contrast. Before his latter years he knew no
positive definite suffering but such as a firm will could have
overcome ; but, without incurring Dante's curse upon those
who 'wilfully live in sadness,' he would seem from the first
to have persuaded himself that the valley of the shadow was
to be his way through life. Hence the imperfection, the conscious carelessness, that mark so much of his work ; hence
his content to earn his bread by work comparatively unworthy
of his genius, though he might have earned it by worthier
labours. It was not worth while—what did it matter ? That
was his attitude ; and so, dreaming his unattainable and inexpressible dreams, he resigned into the hands of Fate and Chance
both his self-control and the control of his art. Words, rhymes,
rhythms, were always ready at his call, and he fashioned of
them things ingenious, things betraying infinite resource ; the
ability to create by their means things of the highest beauty,
unspoiled by freak or whim, undulled by conventional rhetoric,
things poetically pure, was his but once and again. It would
be cruel to judge such a man by anything but his supreme
achievements ; to exalt unduly his lesser achievements is to
endanger the just glory of the poet at his loftiest and loveliest
height. Mangan wrote much that must always delight lovers
of poetry and of Mangan, which is yet but a small part of his
title to greatness ; he wrote a little which is a possession for
evermore of all who 'love the highest when they see it.' It
was as cruel as uncritical to forget that Mangan was a weak-
ling, lovable and to be compassionated, whose piteous necessities
found expression in writings often unvalued by himself and
not meant for remembrance. Excellent dexterities of rhyme,
audacities of phrase, masteries of metre, though testifying to

great accomplishment, do not testify to anything more ; and those who confound Mangan's best with his second-best verse do him a grave disservice. *Non tali auxilio nec defensoribus istis* will Mangan maintain his station and his title to greatness. Happily, in this case, criticism and patriotism can go hand-in-hand : Mangan's flight is highest, his music is noblest, when ancient Ireland speaks to him of her glories, her sorrows, her hopes. He is the poet of much else that is imperishable ; but above all he is the poet of a poem foremost among the world's poems of inspired patriotism. It were enough for Mangan's fame that he is the poet of the ' Dark Rosaleen.'

LIONEL JOHNSON.

James Mangan, who for literary purposes assumed the name of Clarence, was born in Dublin upon May 1, 1803. His father was a tradesman, of irascible temper, and of improvident ways which impoverished the family. Before the age of fifteen Mangan was educated in various schools, at one of which, thanks to a learned priest, he laid the foundations of his multifarious linguistic scholarship. At the age of fifteen he was put to a scrivener's office, where he remained for seven years : he then served in an attorney's office for three more. These ten years, though his accounts of them may be in some measure exaggerated, were a time of uncongenial drudgery. Upon finally quitting this kind of employment he entered upon an erratic and uncertain literary life : the only posts that he ever held, and that for no long time, being successively a post in the Ordnance Survey Office, through the kindness of Dr. Petrie, and in the Library of Trinity College, through the kindness of Dr. Todd. Eventually, thanks to the growth upon him of incorrigible irregularities of life, about which the evidence of his contemporaries and surviving friends is conflicting, he was cast upon the world to live by his pen. From first to last all his published works appeared in Dublin magazines and journals : we need only mention *The Dublin University Magazine, The Nation,* and *The Dublin Penny Journal.* The one collection of his work that appeared in his lifetime is the ANTHOLOGIA GERMANICA, published in 1845. His latter life was miserable and precarious ; and in 1849 he died in the Meath Hospital, of cholera—as seems probable ; of starvation and exhaustion, as some say—aged forty-six. He was buried in Glasnevin Cemetery. His life in its details is hard to follow and ascertain ; his own statements are clearly coloured by his imaginative habit of mind, which itself was affected by the use of stimulants or narcotics, or both : the evidence of those who knew him is discordant. But that life, whatever be the precise truth concerning it, was wholly lived in Dublin, and, sad though it were, was not marked by incidents or adventures of a notable kind. Its uniform sadness is perhaps its one sure and clear fact. After his death there appeared POETS AND POETRY OF MUNSTER, translations edited by John O'Daly, in 1850; in 1859 the celebrated John Mitchel published an edition of the POEMS, with a fine and generous introduction ; in 1884 the Rev. C. P. Meehan, Mangan's friend and benefactor, issued ESSAYS IN PROSE AND VERSE ; in 1897 Miss Guiney published her SELECTIONS from the poems, and in the same year Mr. D. J. O'Donoghue published a probably final LIFE AND WRITINGS. There is no complete edition of Mangan's works, nor is such a thing desirable ; the volumes here mentioned contain all, perhaps more than all, that is required for an appreciation of his genius and a knowledge of his life.—L. J.

DARK ROSALEEN

FROM THE IRISH

OH ! my dark Rosaleen,
    Do not sigh, do not weep !
The priests are on the ocean green,
    They march along the deep.
There's wine from the royal Pope
    Upon the ocean green,
And Spanish ale shall give you hope,
    My dark Rosaleen !
    My own Rosaleen !
Shall glad your heart, shall give you hope,
Shall give you health, and help, and hope,
    My dark Rosaleen !

Over hills and through dales
    Have I roamed for your sake ;
All yesterday I sailed with sails
    On river and on lake.
The Erne, at its highest flood,
    I dashed across unseen,
For there was lightning in my blood,
    My dark Rosaleen !
    My own Rosaleen !
Oh ! there was lightning in my blood,
Red lightning lightened through my blood,
    My dark Rosaleen !

All day long, in unrest,
  To and fro do I move.
The very soul within my breast
  Is wasted for you, love !
The heart in my bosom faints
  To think of you, my Queen,
My life of life, my saint of saints,
  My dark Rosaleen !
  My own Rosaleen !
To hear your sweet and sad complaints,
My life, my love, my saint of saints,
  My dark Rosaleen !

Woe and pain, pain and woe,
  Are my lot, night and noon,
To see your bright face clouded so,
  Like to the mournful moon.
But yet will I rear your throne
  Again in golden sheen ;
'Tis you shall reign, shall reign alone,
  My dark Rosaleen !
  My own Rosaleen !
'Tis you shall have the golden throne,
'Tis you shall reign, and reign alone,
  My dark Rosaleen !

Over dews, over sands,
  Will I fly for your weal :
Your holy delicate white hands
  Shall girdle me with steel.
At home in your emerald bowers,
  From morning's dawn till e'en,
You'll pray for me, my flower of flowers,
  My dark Rosaleen !
  My own Rosaleen !
You'll think of me through daylight's hours,
My virgin flower, my flower of flowers,
  My dark Rosaleen !

I could scale the blue air,
   I could plough the high hills,
Oh ! I could kneel all night in prayer,
   To heal your many ills !
And one beamy smile from you
   Would float like light between
My toils and me, my own, my true,
   My dark Rosaleen !
   My own Rosaleen !
Would give me life and soul anew,
A second life, a soul anew,
   My dark Rosaleen !

Oh ! the Erne shall run red
   With redundance of blood,
The earth shall rock beneath our tread,
   And flames wrap hill and wood,
And gun-peal and slogan-cry
   Wake many a glen serene,
Ere you shall fade, ere you shall die,
   My dark Rosaleen !
   My own Rosaleen !
The Judgment Hour must first be nigh,
   Ere you can fade, ere you can die,
   My dark Rosaleen !

A VISION OF CONNAUGHT IN THE THIRTEENTH CENTURY

'Et moi, j'ai été aussi en Arcadie.'

I WALKED entranced
   Through a land of morn ;
The Sun, with wond'rous excess of light
   Shone down and glanced
   Over seas of corn,
And lustrous gardens a-left and right.
   Even in the clime
   Of resplendent Spain

Beams no such sun upon such a land ;
　　But it was the time,
　　　'Twas in the reign,
Of Cáhal Mór of the Wine-red Hand.

　　Anon stood nigh
　　　By my side a man
Of princely aspect and port sublime.
　　Him queried I,
　　　'Oh, my Lord and Khan,
What clime is this, and what golden time ?'
　　When he—' The clime
　　　Is a clime to praise ;
The clime is Erin's, the green and bland ;
　　And it is the time,
　　　These be the days,
Of Cáhal Mór of the Wine-red Hand !'

　　Then I saw thrones,
　　　And circling fires,
And a dome rose near me, as by a spell,
　　Whence flowed the tones
　　　Of silver lyres,
And many voices in wreathéd swell ;
　　And their thrilling chime
　　　Fell on mine ears
As the heavenly hymn of an angel-band—
　　' It is now the time,
　　　These be the years,
Of Cáhal Mór of the Wine-red Hand !'

　　I sought the hall,
　　　And, behold ! a change
From light to darkness, from joy to woe !
　　Kings, nobles, all,
　　　Looked aghast and strange ;
The minstrel-group sate in dumbest show !
　　Had some great crime
　　　Wrought this dread amaze,

This terror ?   None seemed to understand !
'Twas then the time,
We were in the days,
Of Cáhal Mór of the Wine-red Hand.

I again walked forth !
But lo ! the sky
Showed fleckt with blood, and an alien sun
Glared from the north,
And there stood on high,
Amid his shorn beams, A SKELETON !

It was by the stream
Of the castled Maine,
One autumn eve, in the Teuton's land,
That I dreamed this dream
Of the time and reign
Of Cáhal Mór of the Wine-red Hand !

LAMENT FOR THE PRINCES OF TIR-OWEN AND TIRCONNELL

FROM THE IRISH

O WOMAN of the Piercing Wail,
Who mournest o'er yon mound of clay
With sigh and groan,
Would God thou wert among the Gael !
Thou wouldst not then from day to day
Weep thus alone.
'Twere long before, around a grave
In green Tirconnell, one could find
This loneliness ;
Near where Beann-Boirche's banners wave,
Such grief as thine could ne'er have pined
Companionless.

Beside the wave, in Donegal,
In Antrim's glen, or fair Dromore,
Or Killillee,
Or where the sunny waters fall
At Assaroe, near Erna's shore,
This could not be.

On Derry's plains—in rich Drumcliff—
  Throughout Armagh the Great, renowned
      In olden years,
No day could pass but woman's grief
  Would rain upon the burial-ground
      Fresh floods of tears !

Oh no !—from Shannon, Boyne, and Suir,
  From high Dunluce's castle-walls,
      From Lissadill,
Would flock alike both rich and poor.
  One wail would rise from Cruachan's halls
      To Tara's hill ;
And some would come from Barrow-side,
  And many a maid would leave her home
      On Leitrim's plains,
And by melodious Banna's tide,
  And by the Mourne and Erne, to come
      And swell thy strains !

Oh ! horse's hoofs would trample down
  The mount whereon the martyr-saint
      Was crucified.
From glen and hill, from plain and town,
  One loud lament, one thrilling plaint,
      Would echo wide.
There would not soon be found, I ween,
  One foot of ground among those bands
      For museful thought,
So many shriekers of the *keen*
  Would cry aloud, and clap their hands,
      All woe-distraught !

Two princes of the line of Conn
  Sleep in their cells of clay beside
      O'Donnell Roe.
Three royal youths, alas ! are gone,
  Who lived for Erin's weal, but died
      For Erin's woe !

Ah ! could the men of Ireland read
  The names these noteless burial stones
    Display to view,
Their wounded hearts afresh would bleed,
  Their tears gush forth again, their groans
    Resound anew !

The youths whose relics moulder here
  Were sprung from Hugh, high Prince and Lord
    Of Aileach's lands ;
Thy noble brothers, justly dear,
  Thy nephew, long to be deplored
    By Ulster's bands.
Theirs were not souls wherein dull Time
  Could domicile Decay or house
    Decrepitude !
They passed from Earth ere Manhood's prime,
  Ere years had power to dim their brows
    Or chill their blood.

And who can marvel o'er thy grief,
  Or who can blame thy flowing tears,
    That knows their source ?
O'Donnell, Dunnasana's chief,
  Cut off amid his vernal years,
    Lies here a corse
Beside his brother Cathbar, whom
  Tirconnell of the Helmets mourns
    In deep despair—
For valour, truth, and comely bloom,
  For all that greatens and adorns,
    A peerless pair.

Oh ! had these twain, and he, the third,
  The Lord of Mourne, O'Niall's son,
    Their mate in death—
A prince in look, in deed and word—
  Had these three heroes yielded on
    The field their breath ;

Oh ! had they fallen on Criffan's plain,
 There would not be a town or clan
  From shore to sea
But would with shrieks bewail the slain,
 Or chant aloud the exulting *rann*
  Of jubilee.

When high the shout of battle rose
 On fields where Freedom's torch still burned
  Through Erin's gloom,
If one, if barely one of those
 Were slain, all Ulster would have mourned
  The hero's doom !
If at Athboy, where hosts of brave
 Ulidian horsemen sank beneath
  The shock of spears,
Young Hugh O'Neill had found a grave,
 Long must the north have wept his death
  With heart-wrung tears !

If on the day of Ballachmyre,
 The Lord of Mourne had met, thus young,
  A warrior's fate,
In vain would such as those desire
 To mourn, alone, the champion sprung
  From Niall the Great !
No marvel this—for all the dead,
 Heaped on the field, pile over pile,
  At Mullach-brack,
Were scarce an *eric* for his head,
 If Death had stayed his footsteps while
  On victory's track !

If on the Day of Hostages
 The fruit had from the parent bough
  Been rudely torn
In sight of Munster's bands—Mac-Nee's—
 Such blow the blood of Conn, I trow,
  Could ill have borne.

S

If on the day of Balloch-boy,
  Some arm had laid, by foul surprise,
    The chieftain low,
Even our victorious shout of joy
  Would soon give place to rueful cries
    And groans of woe !

If on the day the Saxon host
  Were forced to fly—a day so great
    For Ashanee—
The Chief had been untimely lost,
  Our conquering troops should moderate
    Their mirthful glee.
There would not lack on Lifford's day,
  From Galway, from the glens of Boyle,
    From Limerick's towers,
A marshalled file, a long array,
  Of mourners to bedew the soil
    With tears in showers !

If on the day a sterner fate
  Compelled his flight from Athenree,
    His blood had flowed,
What numbers all disconsolate
  Would come unasked, and share with thee
    Affliction's load !
If Derry's crimson field had seen
  His life-blood offered up, though 'twere
    On Victory's shrine,
A thousand cries would swell the *keen*,
  A thousand voices of despair
    Would echo thine !

Oh ! had the fierce Dalcassian swarm,
  That bloody night on Fergus' banks,
    But slain our Chief ;
When rose his camp in wild alarm,
  How would the triumph of his ranks
    Be dashed with grief !

How would the troops of Murbach mourn,
    If on the Curlew Mountains' day—
        Which England rued—
Some Saxon hand had left them lorn :
    By shedding there, amid the fray,
        Their prince's blood !

Red would have been our warriors' eyes,
    Had Roderick found on Sligo's field
        A gory grave.
No Northern Chief would soon arise,
    So sage to guide, so strong to shield,
        So swift to save.
Long would Leith-Cuinn have wept if Hugh
    Had met the death he oft had dealt
        Among the foe ;
But, had our Roderick fallen too,
    All Erin must, alas ! have felt
        The deadly blow.

What do I say?   Ah, woe is me—
    Already we bewail in vain
        Their fatal fall !
And Erin, once the Great and Free,
    Now vainly mourns her breakless chain,
        And iron thrall !
Then, daughter of O'Donnell, dry
    Thine overflowing eyes, and turn
        Thy heart aside ;
For Adam's race is born to die,
    And sternly the sepulchral urn
        Mocks human pride.

Look not, nor sigh, for earthly throne,
    Nor place thy trust in arm of clay :
        But on thy knees
Uplift thy soul to God alone,
    For all things go their destined way,
        As He decrees.

S 2

Embrace the faithful Crucifix,
  And seek the path of pain and prayer
      Thy Saviour trod ;
Nor let thy spirit intermix
  With earthly hope and worldly care
      Its groans to God.

And Thou, O mighty Lord ! whose ways
  Are far above our feeble minds
      To understand ;
Sustain us in these doleful days,
  And render light the chain that binds
      Our fallen land !
Look down upon our dreary state—
  And through the ages that may still
      Roll sadly on,
Watch thou o'er hapless Erin's fate,
  And shield at least from darker ill
      The blood of Conn !

THE DAWNING OF THE DAY

'TWAS a balmy summer morning,
    Warm and early,
  Such as only June bestows ;
Everywhere the earth adorning,
    Dews lay pearly
  In the lily-bell and rose.
Up from each green leafy bosk and hollow
  Rose the blackbird's pleasant lay,
And the soft cuckoo was sure to follow—
  'Twas the Dawning of the Day.

Through the perfumed air the golden
    Bees flew round me,
  Bright fish dazzled from the sea ;
Till medreamt some fairy olden
    World spell-bound me
  In a trance of witcherie.

Steeds pranced round anon with stateliest housings,
　　Bearing riders prankt in rich array,
Like flushed revellers after wine carousings—
　　'Twas the Dawning of the Day.

Then a strain of song was chanted,
　　　　And the lightly
　　　Floating sea-nymphs drew anear.
Then again the shore seemed haunted
　　　　By hosts brightly
　　　Clad, and wielding shield and spear !
Then came battle shouts, an onward rushing—
　　Swords, and chariots, and a phantom fray :
Then all vanished.　The warm skies were blushing
　　In the Dawning of the Day.

Cities girt with glorious gardens,
　　　　Whose immortal
　　　Habitants in robes of light
Stood, methought, as angel-wardens
　　　　Nigh each portal,
　　　Now arose to daze my sight.
Eden spread around, revived and blooming,
　　When lo ! as I gazed, all passed away—
I saw but black rocks and billows looming
　　In the dim chill Dawn of Day.

KATHALEEN NY-HOULAHAN [1]

A JACOBITE RELIC—FROM THE IRISH

LONG they pine in weary woe—the nobles of our land—
Long they wander to and fro, proscribed, alas ! and banned ;
Feastless, houseless, altarless, they bear the exile's brand,
　　But their hope is in the coming-to of Kathaleen Ny-Houlahan.

Think not her a ghastly hag, too hideous to be seen ;
Call her not unseemly names, our matchless Kathaleen ;
Young she is, and fair she is, and would be crowned a queen,
　　Were the king's son at home here with Kathaleen Ny-Houlahan.

---

[1] One of the numerous poetic names for Ireland.

Sweet and mild would look her face—Oh ! none so sweet and mild—
Could she crush the foes by whom her beauty is reviled ;
Woollen plaids would grace herself and robes of silk her child,
　If the king's son were living here with Kathaleen Ny-Houlahan.

Sore disgrace it is to see the Arbitress of thrones
Vassal to a Saxoneen of cold and sapless bones !
Bitter anguish wrings our souls—with heavy sighs and groans
　We wait the Young Deliverer of Kathaleen Ny-Houlahan.

Let us pray to Him who holds life's issues in His hands,
Him who formed the mighty globe, with all its thousand lands :
Girding them with sea and mountains, rivers deep, and strands,
　To cast a look of pity upon Kathaleen Ny-Houlahan.

He who over sands and waves led Israel along—
He who fed, with heavenly bread, that chosen tribe and throng ;
He who stood by Moses when his foes were fierce and strong,
　May He show forth His might in saving Kathaleen Ny-Houlahan !

THE WOMAN OF THREE COWS

FROM THE IRISH

O WOMAN of Three Cows, *agra* ! don't let your tongue thus
　rattle !
Oh, don't be saucy, don't be stiff, because you may have cattle.
I have seen—and, here's my hand to you, I only say what's true—
A many a one with twice your stock not half so proud as you.

Good luck to you, don't scorn the poor, and don't be their despiser ;
For worldly wealth soon melts away, and cheats the very miser ;
And death soon strips the proudest wreath from haughty human
　brows—
Then don't be stiff, and don't be proud, good Woman of Three
　Cows.

See where Momonia's heroes lie, proud Owen Mór's descendants.
'Tis they that won the glorious name, and had the grand atten-
　dants ;
If they were forced to bow to Fate, as every mortal bows,
Can you be proud, can you be stiff, my Woman of Three Cows ?

The brave sons of the Lord of Clare, they left the land to mourning ;
Mavrone ! for they were banished, with no hope of their returning.
Who knows in what abodes of want those youths were driven to
   house ?
Yet you can give yourself these airs, O Woman of Three Cows.

Oh, think of Donnel of the Ships, the Chief whom nothing daunted,
See how he fell in distant Spain unchronicled, unchanted ;
He sleeps, the great O'Sullivan, where thunder cannot rouse—
Then ask yourself, should you be proud, good Woman of Three
   Cows ?

O'Ruark, Maguire, those souls of fire, whose names are shrined in
   story :
Think how their high achievements once made Erin's greatest
   glory.
Yet now their bones lie mouldering under weeds and cypress
   boughs—
And so, for all your pride, will yours, O Woman of Three Cows.

Th' O'Carrolls, also, famed when fame was only for the boldest,
Rest in forgotten sepulchres with Erin's best and oldest ;
Yet who so great as they of yore in battle or carouse ?
Just think of that, and hide your head, good Woman of Three
   Cows.

Your neighbour's poor ; and you, it seems, are big with vain ideas,
Because, *inagh* ! you've got three cows—one more, I see, than she
   has ;
That tongue of yours wags more at times than charity allows ;
But if you're strong, be merciful—great Woman of Three Cows.

AVRAN

Now, there you go ; you still, of course, keep up your scornful
   bearing,
And I'm too poor to hinder you ; but, by the cloak I'm wearing,
If I had but four cows myself, even though you were my spouse,
I'd thwack you well, to cure your pride, my Woman of Three Cows.

The Karamanian Exile

I SEE thee ever in my dreams,
        Karaman !
Thy hundred hills, thy thousand streams,
        Karaman ! O Karaman !
As when thy gold-bright morning gleams,
As when the deepening sunset seams
With lines of light thy hills and streams,
        Karaman !
So thou loomest on my dreams,
        Karaman ! O Karaman !

The hot bright plains, the sun, the skies,
        Karaman !
Seem death-black marble to mine eyes,
        Karaman ! O Karaman !
I turn from summer's blooms and dyes ;
Yet in my dreams thou dost arise
In welcome glory to my eyes,
        Karaman !
In thee my life of life yet lies,
        Karaman !
Thou still art holy in mine eyes,
        Karaman ! O Karaman !

Ere my fighting years were come,
        Karaman !
Troops were few in Erzerome,
        Karaman ! O Karaman !
Their fiercest came from Erzerome,
They came from Ukhbar's palace dome,
They dragged me forth from thee, my home,
        Karaman !
Thee, my own, my mountain home,
        Karaman !
In life and death, my spirit's home,
        Karaman ! O Karaman !

Oh, none of all my sisters ten,
    Karaman !
Loved like me my fellow-men,
    Karaman !
I was mild as milk till then,
I was soft as silk till then ;
Now my breast is as a den,
    Karaman !
Foul with blood and bones of men,
    Karaman !
With blood and bones of slaughtered men,
    Karaman ! O Karaman !

My boyhood's feelings newly born,
    Karaman !
Withered like young flowers uptorn,
    Karaman ! O Karaman !
And in their stead sprang weed and thorn ;
What once I loved now moves my scorn ;
My burning eyes are dried to horn,
    Karaman !
I hate the blessed light of morn,
    Karaman !
It maddens me, the face of morn,
    Karaman ! O Karaman !

The Spahi wears a tyrant's chain,
    Karaman !
But bondage worse than this remains,
    Karaman ! O Karaman !
His heart is black with million stains :
Thereon, as on Kaf's blasted plains,
Shall never more fall dews and rains,
    Karaman !
Save poison-dews and bloody rains,
    Karaman !
Hell's poison-dews and bloody rains,
    Karaman ! O Karaman !

But life at worst must end ere long,
   Karaman !
Azreel avengeth every wrong,
   Karaman ! O Karaman !
Of late my thoughts rove more among
Thy fields ; o'ershadowing fancies throng
My mind, and texts of bodeful song,
   Karaman !
Azreel is terrible and strong,
   Karaman !
His lightning sword smites all ere long,
   Karaman ! O Karaman !

There's care to-night in Ukhbar's halls,
   Karaman !
There's hope, too, for his trodden thralls,
   Karaman ! O Karaman !
What lights flash red along your walls?
Hark ! hark !—the muster-trumpet calls !—
I see the sheen of spears and shawls,
   Karaman !
The foe ! the foe !—they scale the walls,
   Karaman !
To-night Muràd or Ukhbar falls,
   Karaman ! O Karaman !

THE TIME OF THE BARMECIDES

MY eyes are filmed, my beard is grey,
 I am bowed with the weight of years ;
I would I were stretched in my bed of clay
 With my long-lost Youth's compeers !
For back to the past, though the thought brings woe,
 My memory ever glides—
To the old, old time, long, long ago,
 The time of the Barmecides !
To the old, old time, long, long ago,
 The time of the Barmecides !

Then youth was mine, and a fierce wild will
  And an iron arm in war,
And a fleet foot high upon Ishkar's hill,
  When the watch-lights glimmered afar,
And a barb as fiery as any I know
  That Khoord or Beddaween rides,
Ere my friends lay low—long, long ago,
  In the time of the Barmecides ;
Ere my friends lay low—long, long ago,
  In the time of the Barmecides.

One golden goblet illumed my board,
  One silver dish was there ;
At hand my tried Karamanian sword
  Lay always bright and bare.
For those were the days when the angry blow
  Supplanted the word that chides —
When hearts could glow—long, long ago,
  In the time of the Barmecides ;
When hearts could glow—long, long ago,
  In the time of the Barmecides.

Through city and desert my mates and I
  Were free to rove and roam,
Our diapered canopy the deep of the sky
  Or the roof of the palace dome —
Oh ! ours was that vivid life to and fro
  Which only sloth derides—
Men spent Life so, long, long ago,
  In the time of the Barmecides ;
Men spent Life so, long, long ago,
  In the time of the Barmecides.

I see rich Bagdad once again,
  With its turrets of Moorish mould,
And the Kailif's twice five hundred men,
  Whose binishes flamed with gold ;
I call up many a gorgeous show
  Which the Pall of Oblivion hides—

All passed like snow, long, long ago,
　　With the time of the Barmecides ;
All passed like snow, long, long ago,
　　With the time of the Barmecides.

But mine eye is dim, and my beard is grey,
　　And I bend with the weight of years—
May I soon go down to the House of Clay,
　　Where slumber my Youth's compeers !
For with them and the Past, though the thought
　　　　wakes woe,
　　My memory ever abides ;
And I mourn for the times gone long ago—
　　For the times of the Barmecides !
I mourn for the times gone long ago,
　　For the times of the Barmecides.

SIBERIA

In Siberia's wastes
　　The ice-wind's breath
Woundeth like the toothéd steel.
Lost Siberia doth reveal
　　Only blight and death.

Blight and death alone.
　　No Summer shines.
Night is interblent with Day.
In Siberia's wastes alway
　　The blood blackens, the heart pines.

In Siberia's wastes
　　No tears are shed,
For they freeze within the brain.
Nought is felt but dullest pain,
　　Pain acute, yet dead ;

Pain as in a dream,
　　When years go by
Funeral-paced, yet fugitive—
When man lives and doth not live
　　Doth not live—nor die.

In Siberia's wastes
 Are sands and rocks.
Nothing blooms of green or soft,
But the snowpeaks rise aloft
 And the gaunt ice-blocks.

And the exile there
 Is one with those ;
They are part, and he is part,
For the sands are in his heart,
 And the killing snows.

Therefore in those wastes
 None curse the Czar ;
Each man's tongue is cloven by
The North Blast, who heweth nigh
 With sharp scimitar.

And such doom each drees,
 Till, hunger-gnawn
And cold slain, he at length sinks there,
Yet scarce more a corpse than ere
 His last breath was drawn.

O'HUSSEY'S ODE TO THE MAGUIRE

FROM THE IRISH

WHERE is my Chief, my Master, this bleak night, *mavrone* !
 Oh, cold, cold, miserably cold, is this bleak night for Hugh ;
 Its showery, arrowy, speary sleet pierceth one through and
  through—
Pierceth one to the very bone !

Rolls real thunder ? Or was that red, livid light
 Only a meteor ? I scarce know ; but through the midnight dim
 The pitiless ice-wind streams. Except the hate that persecutes
  him,
Nothing hath crueller venomy might.

An awful, a tremendous night is this, meseems !
   The flood-gates of the rivers of heaven, I think, have been burst
      wide—
   Down from the overcharged clouds, like unto headlong ocean's
      tide,
Descends grey rain in roaring streams.

Though he were even a wolf raging the round green woods,
   Though he were even a pleasant salmon in the unchainable sea,
   Though he were a wild mountain eagle, he could scarce bear, he,
This sharp, sore sleet, these howling floods.

Oh ! mournful is my soul this night for Hugh Maguire !
   Darkly, as in a dream he strays !   Before him and behind
   Triumphs the tyrannous anger of the wounding wind,
The wounding wind that burns as fire !

It is my bitter grief – it cuts me to the heart—
   That in the country of Clan Darry this should be his fate !
   Oh, woe is me, where is he ?   Wandering, houseless, desolate,
Alone, without or guide or chart !

Medreams I see just now his face, the strawberry-bright,
   Uplifted to the blackened heavens, while the tempestuous winds
   Blow fiercely over and round him, and the smiting sleet-shower
      blinds
The hero of Galang to-night !

Large, large affliction unto me and mine it is,
   That one of his majestic bearing, his fair, stately form,
   Should thus be tortured and o'erborne—that this unsparing
      storm
Should wreak its wrath on head like his !

That his great hand, so oft the avenger of the oppressed,
   Should this chill, churlish night, perchance, be paralysed by
      frost—
   While through some icicle-hung thicket—as one lorn and lost—
He walks and wanders without rest.

The tempest-driven torrent deluges the mead ;
  It overflows the low banks of the rivulets and ponds —
  The lawns and pasture-grounds lie locked in icy bonds,
So that the cattle cannot feed.

The pale bright margins of the streams are seen by none ;
  Rushes and sweeps along the untamable flood on every side—
  It penetrates and fills the cottagers' dwellings far and wide—
Water and land are blent in one.

Through some dark wood, 'mid bones of monsters, Hugh now
        strays,
  As he confronts the storm with anguished heart, but manly
        brow—
  Oh ! what a sword-wound to that tender heart of his were now
A backward glance at peaceful days !

But other thoughts are his—thoughts that can still inspire
  With joy and an onward-bounding hope the bosom of MacNee—
  Thoughts of his warriors charging like bright billows of the sea,
Borne on the wind's wings, flashing fire !

And though frost glaze to-night the clear dew of his eyes,
  And white gauntlets glove his noble fine fair fingers o'er,
  A warm dress is to him that lightning-garb he ever wore,
The lightning of the soul, not skies.

AVRAN

Hugh marched forth to the fight—I grieved to see him so depart ;
  And lo ! to-night he wanders frozen, rain-drenched, sad,
        betrayed—
  But the memory of the lime-white mansions his right hand hath
        laid
In ashes warms the hero's heart.

The Nameless One

  Roll forth, my song, like the rushing river
      That sweeps along to the mighty sea ;
  God will inspire me while I deliver
          My soul to thee !

Tell thou the world, when my bones lie whitening
　　Amid the last homes of youth and eld,
That there once was one whose veins ran lightning
　　　　No eye beheld.

Tell how his boyhood was one drear night-hour,
　　How shone for him, through his griefs and gloom,
No star of all heaven sends to light our
　　　　Path to the tomb.

Roll on, my song, and to after-ages
　　Tell how, disdaining all earth can give,
He would have taught men from wisdom's pages
　　　　The way to live.

And tell how trampled, derided, hated,
　　And worn by weakness, disease and wrong,
He fled for shelter to God, who mated
　　　　His soul with song—

With song which alway, sublime or vapid,
　　Flowed like a rill in the morning beam,
Perchance not deep, but intense and rapid—
　　　　A mountain stream.

Tell how the Nameless, condemned for years long
　　To herd with demons from hell beneath,
Saw things that made him, with groans and tears, long
　　　　For even death.

Go on to tell how, with genius wasted,
　　Betrayed in friendship, befooled in love,
With spirit shipwrecked, and young hopes blasted
　　　　He still, still strove.

Till, spent with toil, dreeing death for others,
　　And some whose hands should have wrought for him
(If children live not for sires and mothers),
　　　　His mind grew dim.

And he fell far through that pit abysmal,
　The gulf and grave of Maginn and Burns,
And pawned his soul for the Devil's dismal
　　Stock of returns.

But yet redeemed it in days of darkness,
　And shapes and signs of the final wrath,[1]
When death, in hideous and ghastly starkness,
　　Stood in his path.

And tell how now, amid wreck and sorrow,
　And want, and sickness, and houseless nights,
He bides in calmness the silent morrow
　　That no ray lights.

And lives he still, then ?　Yes !　Old and hoary
　At thirty-nine, from despair and woe,
He lives, enduring what future story
　　Will never know.

Him grant a grave to, ye pitying noble,
　Deep in your bosoms !　There let him dwell !
He, too, had tears for all souls in trouble,
　　Here and in hell.

SHAPES AND SIGNS

I SEE black dragons mount the sky,
　I see earth yawn beneath my feet—
　I feel within the asp, the worm
That will not sleep and cannot die,
　Fair though may show the winding-sheet !
　I hear all night as through a storm
　Hoarse voices calling, calling
　　My name upon the wind—
　All omens monstrous and appalling
　　Affright my guilty mind.

---

[1] The ' shapes and signs of the final wrath ' are described in two terrible
stanzas printed below from a hitherto unknown poem given in O'Donoghue's
LIFE OF MANGAN.

T

I exult alone in one wild hour—
　　That hour in which the red cup drowns
　　The memories it anon renews
In ghastlier guise, in fiercer power—
　　Then Fancy brings me golden crowns,
　　　　And visions of all brilliant hues
　　　　Lap my lost soul in gladness,
　　　　　　Until I wake again,
　　　　And the dark lava-fires of madness
　　　　　　Once more sweep through my brain.

GONE IN THE WIND [1]

I

SOLOMON ! where is thy throne ?   It is gone in the wind.
Babylon ! where is thy might ?   It is gone in the wind.
Like the swift shadows of Noon, like the dreams of the Blind,
Vanish the glories and pomps of the earth in the wind.

II

Man ! canst thou build upon aught in the pride of thy mind ?
Wisdom will teach thee that nothing can tarry behind ;
Though there be thousand bright actions embalmed and enshrined,
Myriads and millions of brighter are snow in the wind.

III

Solomon ! where is thy throne?   It is gone in the wind.
Babylon ! where is thy might ?   It is gone in the wind.
All that the genius of man hath achieved or designed
Waits but its hour to be dealt with as dust by the wind.

---

[1] With one of Mangan's usual mystifications this magnificent threnody was described by him as a translation from the German of Rückert, and has hitherto always been printed as such.   It has, however, no German original—the phrase 'gone in the wind' being practically all that it possesses in common with a certain poem of Rückert's, and there the phrase is used differently.   We therefore restore the poem to its true author.

IV

Say, what is Pleasure ! A phantom, a mask undefined.
Science ? An almond, whereof we can pierce but the rind.
Honour and Affluence ? Firmans that Fortune hath signed,
Only to glitter and pass on the wings of the wind.

V

Solomon ! where is thy throne ? It is gone in the wind.
Babylon ! where is thy might ? It is gone in the wind.
Who is the Fortunate ? He who in anguish hath pined !
He shall rejoice when his relics are dust in the wind !

VI

Mortal ! be careful with what thy best hopes are entwined ;
Woe to the miners for Truth—where the Lampless have mined !
Woe to the seekers on earth for—what none ever find !
They and their trust shall be scattered like leaves on the wind.

VII

Solomon ! where is thy throne ? It is gone in the wind.
Babylon ! where is thy might ? It is gone in the wind.
Happy in death are they only whose hearts have consigned
All Earth's affections and longings and cares to the wind.

VIII

Pity, thou, reader ! the madness of poor humankind,
Raving of knowledge—and Satan so busy to blind !
Raving of glory,—like me,—for the garlands I bind
(Garlands of Song) are but gathered, and strewn in the wind.

IX

Solomon ! where is thy throne ? It is gone in the wind.
Babylon ! where is thy might ? It is gone in the wind.
I, Abul-Namez, must rest ; for my fire hath declined,
And I hear voices from Hades like bells on the wind.

Written in a Nunnery Chapel [1]

ME hither from moonlight
A voice ever calls,
    Where pale pillars cluster
    And organ tones roll—
Nor sunlight nor moonlight
E'er silver these walls ;
    Lives here other lustre,
    The Light of the Soul.

Here budded and blossomed,
Here faded and died,
    Like brief-blooming roses,
    Earth's purest of pure !
Now ever embosomed
In bliss they abide—
    Oh, may, when life closes,
    My meed be as sure !

SIR SAMUEL FERGUSON

OMITTING living writers, of whom it is too early to speak with confidence, Ferguson was unquestionably the Irish poet of the past century who has most powerfully influenced the literary history of his country. It was in his writings that the great work of restoring to Ireland the spiritual treasure it had lost in parting with the Gaelic tongue was decisively begun. He was, however, no mere antiquarian. He was also a man of affairs, and a patriot in the highest sense of the word. He had friends in all parties, and yet was in no respect a political trimmer. Indeed, though with strong National proclivities—of which he gave evidence in some of his earlier ballads, and which came to the front in his successful defence of Richard Dalton Williams, the Young Ireland poet, when tried for treason-

---

[1] From O'Donoghue's LIFE OF MANGAN.

felony—he felt that the highest duty he owed his country was that of a poet and prose writer above party. As Mr. Yeats points out, 'he was wiser than Young Ireland in the choice of his models ; for while drawing not less than they from purely Irish sources, he turned to the great poets of the world for his style,' and notably to Homer : and the result is that, as Roden Noël puts it, 'CONGAL and his shorter Irish heroic poems combine in a striking manner the vague, undefined shadowy grandeur, the supernatural glamour of northern romance, with the self-restraint, distinct symmetrical outline, ordered proportion and organic construction of the Greek classic.' More than this, as Mr. Aubrey De Vere observes, 'its qualities are those characteristic of the noble, not the ignoble poetry—viz. passion, imagination, vigour, an epic largeness of conception, wide human sympathies, vivid and truthful description—while with them it unites none of the vulgar stimulants for exhausted or morbid poetic appetite, whether the epicurean seasoning, the sceptical, or the revolutionary.' Again, Ferguson differs from those who regard the poetical life as another world detachable from this—a life mystical, non-human, non-moral— the life, if you will, of faëry, demon, or demi-god. These men do not seem able to grasp the fact that the noblest poetic work of all, that of Shakespeare and Dante and the great Greek tragedians, possesses all the elusive glamour of genius and that something besides which makes it human—or, rather, divine—because it catches and inflames the divine spark in the human heart, and thereby satisfies and saves.

No doubt the attitude of the poetic school who would thus pen off poetry from practice is the not unnatural revolt of young Celtic idealists against the Anglo-Saxon materialism of a great deal of modern British life. But are they not thereby promoting an intellectual error as dangerous as the mediæval one which isolated learning and piety in the monastery and the desert ? Will not its limitation by a literary coterie lead them into a worse isolation ?

Ferguson was in no danger of falling into this illusion. He was absolutely human and practical, broad and sympathetic-minded both. Yet for entire success as a poet in his particular day he had to struggle against difficulties constitutional, accidental, and of his own seeking. His very versatility rendered difficult that entire devotion of his energies to his art of which Tennyson is the great modern example. He could not spare the time, even had he the taste, for that fastidious word-for-word finish in verse to which the late Laureate accustomed the critics, and through them the educated public. Then Ferguson was deliberately facing the fact that the Irish themes he had set his heart upon had no public to greet them. A generation before, they would have had the support of a cultured and unprovincialised Irish upper class ; a generation later they would have claimed attention, in Ferguson's hands, as the noblest outcome of the Irish literary revival. He was therefore both before and after his time, and realised his position to the full. Indeed, when the writer once spoke to him with regret of the neglect of all but Irish literature other than political, he acknowledged it, but with the quiet expression of his confidence that ' his time would come.'

Professor Dowden has called Ferguson an eighteenth-century poet. It would be interesting to see him develop this theme. Perhaps his point of view may be surmised from the following passage in a letter addressed by him to Ferguson : ' You say CONGAL has not been a success. I think, whether on " broad rumour " or not, a success it has been, estimated by the "perfect witness of all-judging Jove."

' A poem with epic breadth and thews is not likely to be popular now. A diseased and over-sensitive nerve is a qualification for the writing of poetry at present, much more than a thoughtful brain or strength of muscle. Some little bit of novel sensibility, a delight in such colours as French milliners send over for ladies' bonnets, or the nosing of certain curious odours, is enough to make the fortune of a small poet. What seems to me most noteworthy in your poems is the union of culture with simplicity and strength. Their refinement is large and strong, not curious and diseased ; and they have spaces and movements which give one a feeling like the

sea or the air on a headland.   I had not meant to say anything
of CONGAL, but somehow this came and said itself.'

Nothing could be more largely appreciative of Ferguson's
work than this.   That fine saying, 'Your poems have spaces
and movements which give one a feeling like the sea or the
air on a headland,' may be here illustrated by one of the
greatest passages in CONGAL ; indeed, it in all probability
suggested the criticism to Dr. Dowden.   It may be quoted,
moreover, as a telling example of how Ferguson's careless
or rough treatment of detail is carried off by the largeness of
his conception and movement:

He looking landward from the brow of some great sea-cape's head,
Bray or Ben-Edar—sees beneath, in silent pageant grand,
Slow fields of sunshine spread o'er fields of rich, corn-bearing land ;
Red glebe and meadow margin green commingling to the view
With yellow stubble, browning woods, and upland tracts of blue ;
Then, sated with the pomp of fields, turns, seaward, to the verge
Where, mingling with the murmuring wash made by the far-down surge,
Comes up the clangorous song of birds unseen, that, low beneath,
Poised off the rock, ply underfoot ; and, 'mid the blossoming heath,
And mint-sweet herb that loves the ledge rare-air'd, at ease reclined,
Surveys the wide pale-heaving floor crisped by a curling wind ;
With all its shifting, shadowy belts, and chasing scopes of green,
Sun-strown, foam-freckled, sail-embossed, and blackening squalls between,
And slant, cerulean-skirted showers that with a drowsy sound,
Heard inward, of ebullient waves, stalk all the horizon round ;
And—haply, being a citizen just 'scaped from some disease
That long has held him sick indoors, now, in the brine-fresh breeze,
Health-salted, bathes ; and says, the while he breathes reviving bliss,
'I am not good enough, O God, nor pure enough for this ! '

The ear educated to Tennyson's or Swinburne's verse would
be jarred by the heavy aggregation of consonants in 'Red
glebe,' 'Poised off the rock, ply,' 'loves the ledge rare-aired,
'just 'scaped from some disease' ; by the rough metrical effect
of 'made by' in the seventh line ; and by the necessity for
pausing after 'birds' in the next, if it is to be made to scan at
all.   But as a presentment of country, cliff, and ocean, it is
alike so broad and delicate in colour and movement that it

rises visibly before us, till the sough of the sea is in our ears, and we breathe and smell its keen savours. Then the human note with which it closes is inexpressibly touching.

It is not, however, implied that Ferguson is wanting in the musical ear or the appreciation of fine poetical craftsmanship, but rather suggested that, unlike Tennyson and other writers, he is not *sectus ad unguem* in everything he attempts, because he is not careful to be so. Moreover, like Wordsworth, he did not always write when his best mood was upon him.

'The Forging of the Anchor' is a remarkably finished achievement for a young man of one-and-twenty, and 'The Fairy Thorn,' another early poem, is exquisite wizardry itself. True, it appears to have been conceived and executed with a rapidity which was inspiration, and is indeed one of Ferguson's gems without flaw. But the fact remains that very little of Ferguson's has this absolute verbal felicity.

His translations from the Irish are among the best of the kind. They differ from Miss Brooke's and Miss Balfour's versions, and those of other translators preceding him, by their assimilation of Irish idioms and Irish measures into English verse without violence—indeed, with a happy judgment which lends a delightful effect to these lyrics. Edward Walsh has scarcely excelled Ferguson in this field ; and Dr. Sigerson and Dr. Hyde, though they come closer to the original metres, rarely go past him in poetical passion.

But the very character of the originals calls for simple treatment, and high polish would have spoilt Ferguson's verse-translations from the Irish.

Ferguson was casting round for nobler themes to work upon, whilst keeping his hand in at these translations. Patriotic to the core, he was above all things eager to achieve something lofty in literature for Ireland's sake—something that might help to lift her from the intellectual flats upon which she had fallen.

In his own delightful epistle to his friend Dr. Gordon, written in Burns's measure, as from one descendant of the Scot to another, he thus puts it :

And, aiblins though at times mislasted
Wi' grievous thochts o' moments wasted,
Auld frien's estranged, and green hopes blasted,
    As birkies will
When the 'mid line o' life they've crossed it,
    I'm happy still.

For ilka day I'm growin' stronger
To speak my mind in love or anger ;
And, hech ! ere it be muckle longer,
    You'll see appearin
Some offerin's o' nae cauld haranguer
    Put out for Erin.

Lord, for ane day o' service done her !
Lord, for ane hour's sunlight upon her !
Here, Fortune, tak' warld's wealth and honour,
    You're no' my debtor,
Let me but rive ane link asunder
    O' Erin's fetter !

Let me but help to shape the sentence
Will put the pith o' independence,
O' self-respect in self-acquaintance,
    And manly pride
Intil auld Eber-Scot's descendants—
    Take a' beside !

Let me but help to get the truth
Set fast in ilka brother's mouth,
Whatever accents, north or south,
    His tongue may use,
And there's ambition, riches, youth,
    Take which you choose.

But dinna, dinna take my frien's ;
And spare me still my dreams at e'ens,
And sense o' Nature's bonny scenes,
    And a' above ;
Leave me, at least, if no' the means
    The thocht o' love !

But before he had ripened for the full outcome of his genius Ferguson anticipated it by one of the noblest laments in our language—'Thomas Davis : an Elegy, 1845 '—a poignant

expression of his grief at the death of his friend, the famous
young National leader.

Sir Charles Gavan Duffy tells us that 'Ferguson, who lay on
a bed of sickness when Davis died—impatient that for the
moment he could take no part in public—asked me to come
to him, that he might ease his heart by expressing his sense of
what he had lost. He read me fragments of a poem written
under these circumstances, the most Celtic in structure and
spirit of all the elegies laid on the tomb of Davis. The last
verse sounded like a prophecy—it was, at any rate, a powerful
incentive to take up our task anew.'

The Irish potato famine now intervened, and drove Ferguson into the *sæva indignatio* of Juvenal at the Government
mismanagement, which had multiplied its horrors a hundredfold.

No one knew this better than himself, for he was secretary
to the Irish Council whose wise advice, tendered to the English
Parliament, was rejected in favour of futile experimental legis-
lation. Convinced that a Parliament after Grattan's model
would have saved the country, he became a Repealer and one
of the poets of Repeal.

> Deem not, O generous English hearts, who gave
> Your noble aid our sinking Isle to save,
> This breast, though heated in its Country's feud,
> Owns aught towards *you* but perfect gratitude.
>
> .   .   .   .
>
> But, frankly while we thank you all who sent
> Your alms, so thank we not your Parliament,
> Who, what they gave, from treasures of our own
> Gave, if you call it giving, this half loan,
> Half gift from the recipients to themselves
> Of their own millions, be they tens or twelves ;
> Our own as well as yours : our Irish brows
> Had sweated for them ; though your Commons' House,
> Forgetting your four hundred millions debt,
> When first in partnership our nations met,
> Against our twenty-four (you then twofold
> The poorer people), call them British Gold.
> No ; for these drafts on our United Banks
> We owe no gratitude and give no thanks !

More than you'd give to us, if Dorsetshire
Or York a like assistance should require ;
Or than you gave us when, to compensate
Your slave-owners, you charged our common state
Twice the amount : no, but we rather give
Our curses, and will give them while we live,
To that pernicious blind conceit, and pride,
Wherewith the aids we asked you misapplied.

. . . . .

Sure, for our wretched Country's various ills
We've got, a man would think, enough of bills,—
Bills to make paupers, bills to feed them made ;
Bills to make sure that paupers' bills are paid ;
Bills in each phrase of economic slang ;
Bills to transport the men they dare not hang
(I mean no want of courage physical,
' 'Tis Conscience doth make cowards of us all ').

Ferguson, however, lived to turn this fine power of literary invective against the successors of the Young Ireland poets and patriots with whom he had sympathised, when he found them descending from the high aspirations of Davis and Duffy to what he believed to be ' a sordid social war of classes carried on by the vilest methods.'

In his satiric poems ' The Curse of the Joyces ' and ' At the Polo Ground '—an analysis in Browning's manner of Carey's frame of mind before giving the fatal signal to the assassins of Mr. Burke and Lord Frederic Cavendish—and in his Dublin eclogue ' In Carey's Footsteps,' he attacks the cruelties of the then existing system of political agitation with unsparing severity.

Ferguson's LAYS OF THE WESTERN GAEL, which appeared in 1864, was a gratifying surprise even to many of his friends, owing to the inclusion in it of fresh and finer work than he had yet achieved. Their point of departure is thus well described by Mr. A. M. Williams, the American critic :

' The LAYS OF THE WESTERN GAEL are a series of ballads founded on events in Celtic history, and derived from the Early Chronicles and poems. They are original in form and substance, the ballad form and measure being unknown to

the early Celtic poets of Ireland ; but they preserve in a
wonderful degree the ancient spirit, and give a picture of
the ancient times with all the art of verity. They have a
solemnity of measure like the voice of one of the ancient bards
chanting of

> Old forgotten far-off things
> And battles long ago,

and they are clothed with the mists of a melancholy age.
They include such subjects as "The Tain Quest," the search
of the bard for the lost lay of the great cattle-raid of Queen
Maeve of Connaught, and its recovery, by invocation, from the
voice of its dead author, who rises in misty form above his
grave ; "The Healing of Conall Carnach," a story of violated
sanctuary and its punishment ; "The Welshmen of Tirawley,"
one of the most spirited and original, and which has been
pronounced by Mr. Swinburne as amongst the finest of modern
ballads, telling of a cruel mulct inflicted upon the members of
a Welsh Colony and its vengeance ; and other incidents in
early Irish history. In his poems, rather than in Macpherson's
"Ossian" or in the literal translations, will the modern reader
find the voice of the ancient Celtic bards speaking to the
intelligence of to-day in their own tones, without false change
and dilution, or the confusion and dimness of an ancient
language.'

Of the longer lays thus far published, 'The Tain Quest'
found the greatest acceptance with his poetic compeers, and
the most notable criticism of it was that of Thomas Aird. 'In
all respects "The Tain Quest" is one of the most striking
poems of our day. Specially do I admire the artistic skill
with which you have doubled the interest of the Quest itself
by introducing in the most natural and unencumbering way
so many of the best points of the "Great Cattle Foray," the
subject-matter of the "Tain." The shield has long been grand
in poetry ; you have made it grander. The refusal of Fergus to
stir to the force of private sympathy, but his instantaneous
recognition of the patriotic necessity of song, is a just and
noble conception.

'The power of the Bard over the rude men of Gort ; the filial piety of the sons of Sanchan, and their brotherly love ; that mysterious Vapour, and that terrible blast of entrance, and the closing malediction by the Maiden, are all very notable towards the consummation of effect. As for the kissing of the champions in the pauses of the fight, I know of nothing in the reaches of our human blood so marvellously striking and sweet ; you have now made it immortal in song. However admirably expressed, the last stanza is an error in art. Surely you spoil the grand close, and the whole piece, by appending your own personality of interference as a commentator on the malediction. Might I not further say (with a peculiar smile) you make the preordained fulfilment of Malison a sublime apology for Irish Grub Street ? ' The sting in the tail of this fine judgment is deserved, and it is curious to observe that Ferguson has been similarly unlucky in 'The Welshmen of Tirawley' in this attempt to tag a comment on to the end of a tale which he has so nobly adorned. That magnificently savage lay should end with the ante-penultimate stanza.

This tendency to act at times as a commentator on his own work and to present it at others in a too ponderously Latinised form are, with the careless, not to say bluff, disregard for verbal delicacies into which he now and again lapses, the only proclivities to which exception can be taken in Ferguson's technique. But his method is uniformly manly, and his occasional periods of majestic inspiration sweep our minor critical objections before them, as the blast from his Mananan's mantle swept the chieftain and his hound into the valley like leaves before the wind. We have taken Ferguson to our hearts as we take our best brother, cherishing his very ponderosities and carelessnesses as part and parcel of his greatness, as we cherish the kindred qualities in Samuel Johnson—for the love of the man and the gentleman behind the bluff exterior.

In 1872 appeared CONGAL, which Ferguson describes in a letter to Father Russell as an epic poem of greater length and higher literary pretension than his LAYS OF THE WESTERN GAEL.

An epic requires a great subject, and he who writes it must have vision and manliness closely allied in his nature, else how can he realise the heroic ideal? These are Ferguson's pre-eminent qualities. He is manly. His heroes proclaim it in their every action, their every utterance; and his tender portrait of Lafinda could only have been drawn by a gallant gentleman. He has vision. The terrible shapes and Celtic superstitions— the Giant Walker, the Washer of the Ford—loom monstrously before us as he sings; and he marshals the contending hosts at Moyra with a magnificent realism to which we know no modern parallel.

His subject is a great old-world tale of love and hate, and ambition and jealousy, and craft and courage—a splendid story of the last heroic stand made by Celtic Paganism against the Irish Champions of the Cross. An epitome of it with illustrative passages is annexed.

But great though much of CONGAL undoubtedly is, Ferguson's genius was to break into finest flower at the last.

The volume of 1880 contains some striking verse of a religious, philosophical, and personal kind, including the searching 'Two Voices,' the trenchant and yet more touching 'Three Thoughts,' the noble lines entitled 'The Morning's Hinges,' and the lofty 'Hymn of the Fishermen'—a poem written after a surmounted danger of shipwreck. But in 'Deirdré' and 'Conary' he reaches his fullest height as a poet, and the best that has been said or could well be said about them comes from William Allingham and Aubrey De Vere—the two men of his time whose opinion should interest, if not influence, us most.

Allingham wrote on receipt of the volume: 'Many thoughts of my own swarmed about the pages as I turned them, like bees in a lime-tree. In your style high culture is reconciled with simplicity, directness, and originality; and nothing can be happier than your enrichment of English speech with Irish forms without the least violence. All the Irish poems are very remarkable, but "Deirdré" I count the chief triumph. Its peculiar form of unity is perfectly managed, while in general effect it recalls nothing so much as a Greek play.'

Mr. Aubrey De Vere and Mr. Yeats, and perhaps the larger proportion of the other leading Irish critics, prefer ' Conary ' to ' Deirdré.'

' It would be difficult,' writes De Vere, 'to find, amid our recent literature, a poem which at once aims as high as "Conary" and as adequately fulfils its aim. . . . Novel to English readers as is such a poetic theme, and embarrassing as are a few of the Gaelic names, the work belongs to the " great " style of poetry —that style which is characterised by simplicity, breadth of effect, a careless strength full of movement, but with nothing of the merely "sensational" about it, and an entire absence of those unclassic tricks that belong to meaner verse. It has caught thoroughly that epic character so remarkable in those Bardic Legends which were transmitted orally through ages when Homer must have been a name unknown in Ireland.'

To sum up : though at times over-scholarly and nodding now and again—as all the great unconscious poets, from Homer down, will occasionally nod, as opposed to the little self-con-scious ones who are never caught napping—Ferguson is always human, always simple, always strong. Sense ever goes before sound with him. He is no mere reed for blowing music through. He takes you into no gorgeous jungle of colour and scent, and stealing serpent and ravening beast, where per-spective is lost and will paralysed, and passion riots unrestrained.

No ! what Mr. W. B. Yeats finely wrote in 1886 is still true to-day :

' The author of these poems is the greatest poet Ireland has produced, because the most central and most Celtic. Whatever the future may bring forth in the way of a truly great and national literature—and now that the race is so large, so widely spread, and so conscious of its unity, the years are ripe – will find its morning in these three volumes of one who was made by the purifying flame of national sentiment the one man of his time who wrote heroic poety—one who, among the somewhat sybaritic singers of his day, was like some

aged sea-king sitting among the inland wheat and poppies—
the savour of the sea about him and its strength.'

A. P. GRAVES.

Sir Samuel Ferguson, sixth and youngest child of John Ferguson and
his wife Agnes Knox, was born in Belfast, in the house of his maternal
grandfather, on March 10, 1810.

The Ferguson family had migrated to the North of Ireland from
Scotland about the year 1640, and we find Samuel Ferguson, Sir Samuel's
grandfather, resident at Standing Stone, in the County of Antrim. The
younger Samuel was educated in Belfast and at Trinity College, Dublin.
He was called to the Irish Bar in 1838, and to the Inner Bar in 1859.

In 1867 he retired from the practice of his profession to become the
first Deputy Keeper of the Records of Ireland. But while only in his
twenty-first year he wrote ' The Forging of the Anchor' and ' Willy
Gilliland,' and contributed prose such as ' The Wet Wooing' and ' The
Return of Claneboy' to *Blackwood*. A little later, in the early thirties, he
published ' The Fairy Thorn,' ' The Forester's Complaint,' and a series of
papers on Hardiman's IRISH MINSTRELSY, containing verse-translations
from the Gaelic. A long series of historic tales—the Hibernian Nights
Entertainments—followed in *The Dublin University Magazine*. Over-
wrought at the Bar, he recruited his health by spending the year 1845-46
on the Continent, employing much of his time in a diligent examination of
the museums, libraries, and architectural remains of the principal places in
Europe where traces of the early Irish scholars and missionaries might be
looked for. His notebooks are in consequence enriched with exquisite
sketches of scenery and antiquities and pen-and-ink etchings of foreign
cathedrals.

Thus his travels added largely to his knowledge of art, archæology, and
history.

He married in 1848 Mary Catherine, eldest daughter of Mr. Robert R.
Guinness, and soon settled permanently at 20 North Great George's Street,
Dublin. In the same year he founded the Protestant Repeal Association
to aid the Young Ireland movement, but subsequently withdrew altogether
from active politics. In 1865, after the publication of his LAYS OF THE
WESTERN GAEL, he received the degree of LL.D. *honoris causâ* from
Dublin University, and in 1874 was made an honorary member of the
Society of Antiquaries of Scotland. His knighthood was conferred on him
in 1878, he was made president of the Royal Irish Academy in 1881, and
at the tercentenary of the University of Edinburgh in 1884 he received
the honorary degree of LL.D.

During these years he was a busy writer on literary and archæological
questions, and as an evidence of the variety of his work at this time may
be mentioned his famous *jeu d'esprit* ' Father Tom and the Pope,' afterwards

reprinted in ' Tales from *Blackwood*,' and his letter to Hallam the historian, which appeared in *The Dublin University Magazine* and led to the erection of a statue in the new Houses of Parliament to Henri de Londres, Archbishop of Dublin in the thirteenth century, whose just claim to that distinction would otherwise have been overlooked.

Many of Ferguson's articles in magazines and reviews at the time deal with such general subjects as the poetry of Burns and Mrs. Browning, Ruskin's STONES OF VENICE and SEVEN LAMPS OF ARCHITECTURE, Layard's NINEVEH, and Chesney's volume on Artillery.

But the work which was distinctly his, and to which his best faculties were given, was concerned with Ireland, and covered a wide field.   For we find him dealing now with Irish music, now with Irish architecture ; or again with Irish annals, Irish law, and Irish antiquities—Pagan and Christian —and yet attending to such subjects of modern importance as the attractions and capabilities of his country.   And here it may be said that he was an ardent explorer of Irish scenery as well as of the remains of the old Irish ecclesiastical establishments, as his two charming papers—the results of a tour made by him to Clonmacnois, Clare, and Aran—convincingly prove. To these prose works he was meantime adding his ' Lament for Thomas Davis,' his ' Inheritor and Economist,' ' Dublin : a Satire after Juvenal,' ' Westminster Abbey,' and his ' Cromlech on Howth,' exquisitely illustrated and illuminated with initial letters from the Book of Kells by his friend Miss Margaret Stokes.   Ferguson published his epic CONGAL (founded on the ancient bardic tale of the Battle of Moy-Rath)—which he himself considered his *magnum opus*—in 1872, though a subsequent volume of poems containing ' Conary ' and ' Deirdré ' and ' The Naming of Cuchullin,' and published in 1880, has met with more popular acceptance. A small book, SHAKESPEREAN BREVIATES—condensations of some of Shakespere's plays for the use of Shakespere Reading Societies, the broken plots being skilfully woven together, with explanatory verses—was also brought out during Ferguson's lifetime.   Two posthumously published volumes are OGHAM INSCRIPTIONS IN IRELAND, WALES, AND SCOTLAND, and THE REMAINS OF ST. PATRICK, a verse rendition of the writings of our national saint.   LAYS OF THE RED BRANCH, published after his death by Lady Ferguson, is a collection from different volumes of all the poems dealing with the Conorian cycle of Irish heroic literature, arranged in historical order and furnished with an historical introduction.

Sir Samuel Ferguson after an illness of some months' duration—a failure of the heart's action—passed away on August 9, 1886, at Shand Lodge, Howth.   His personal popularity. attested to by many friendships formed through life amongst old and young of every persuasion and party, was confirmed at his death by the commingling of all classes and creeds a' his funeral as it passed to St. Patrick's Cathedral.   For thither, besides

many private friends, followed the officers and members of the Royal Irish
Academy, with their mace draped in crape for their dead President ; whilst
the staff of the Record Office, down to the humblest workman connected
with it, joined the procession.

The Archbishop of Dublin, Lord Plunket, delivered a touching address
after the service, which contained these words : ' Do we not all feel that
by the death of our dear brother departed in the Lord we have all of us as
Irishmen suffered an irreparable loss ?　In whatever light we may regard
the character of him who has been taken from us—whether as a scholar, a
poet, or a patriot, or a God-fearing servant of his Master—we must all
feel that Ireland has suffered a loss which it will be impossible to repair, and
which cannot be confined merely to those who belong to any one class or
any one creed amongst us.'

SELECTIONS FROM 'CONGAL,' WITH AN ARGUMENT

The Pagan Prince, Congal (7th century A.D.), son of the famous Scallan
Broadshield, by his prowess sets Domnal on the throne of Erin under
promise to restore him his ancestral realm of Ulster, which had been in
great part torn from his forefathers by other sub-Kings.　Domnal tem-
porises, and only restores Congal part of this territory.　Congal is bound to
Domnal by fosterage, and desires peace for a tender reason, being betrothed
to Lafinda, Princess of Donn, who has been brought up a Christian by the
nuns of St. Brigid.　But Congal, who is of an imperious nature, takes
umbrage at what he believes to be an insult offered to him by King Domnal
at a royal banquet at Dunangay.　He breaks from the feast, followed by his
Ulster champions, and seeks his uncle Kellach in the mountains of Mourne.
Here lived that implacable old Pagan, surrounded by all that were left of the
great company of the lords of Erin, who as heathens had been condemned
and banished at the synod of Drumkeat under King Aed, Domnal's father.
Kellach hails his insulted nephew with delight, and successfully urges him
to seek assistance from the Kings of Scotland and Wales.　But before
starting Congal visits Lafinda :—

The Princess with her women-train without the fort he found,
Beside a limpid running stream, upon the primrose ground ;
In two ranks seated opposite, with soft alternate stroke
Of bare, white, counter-thrusting feet, fulling a splendid cloak
Fresh from the loom : incessant rolled athwart the fluted board
The thick web fretted, while two maids, with arms uplifted, poured
Pure water on it diligently, and to their moving feet
In answering verse they sang a chaunt of cadence clear and sweet.

Princess Lafinda stood beside—her feet in dainty shoes
Laced softly, and her graceful limbs in robes of radiant hues
Clad delicately, keeping time : on boss of rushes made,
Old nurse Levarcam near them sat, beneath the hawthorn shade.
A grave experienced woman she, of reverend years, to whom
Well known were both the ends of life—the cradle and the tomb —
Whose withered hands had often smoothed the wounded warrior's
    bed,
Bathed many new-born babes, and closed the eyes of many dead.
      The merry maidens, when they spied the warlike King in
          view,
Beneath their robes in modest haste their gleaming feet withdrew
And laughing all surceased their task.   Lafinda blushing stood,
Elate with conscious joy to see so soon again renewed
A converse — ah, how sweet compared with that of nurse or maid !
But soon her joy met cruel check.

  Congal tells how he has been insulted, that war is imminent, and that
their approaching marriage must await its issue.
  She endeavours to dissuade him from his purpose, but Congal is
inexorable. He obtains hoped-for aid from abroad, and with a vast fleet
of auxiliaries sets sail for Erin. But evil omens await him, and at first
affright his allies. But the invading host, re-inspirited, marches inland and
pitches its tents for the night, but they get no rest in their encampment.
Mananan the Sea-God, figured as the Warder of Erin, marches round and
round the encamping army of invaders :

          For all the night around their echoing camp
Was heard continuous from the hills a sound as of the tramp
Of giant footsteps ; but so thick the white mist lay around,
None saw the Walker save the King.   He, starting at the sound,
Called to his foot his fierce red hound ; athwart his shoulders cast
A shaggy mantle, grasped his spear, and through the moonlight
    passed
Alone up dark Ben-Boli's heights, towards which, above the woods
With sound as when at close of eve the noise of falling floods
Is borne to shepherd's ear remote on stilly upland lawn,
The steps along the mountain-side with hollow fall came on.
Fast beat the hero's heart ; and close down-crouching by his knee
Trembled the hound, while through the haze, huge as through
    mists at sea

The week-long sleepless mariner descries some mountain-cape,
Wreck-infamous, rise on his lee, appeared a monstrous Shape,
Striding impatient, like a man much grieved, who walks alone,
Considering of a cruel wrong ; down from his shoulders thrown
A mantle, skirted stiff with soil splashed from the miry ground,
At every stride against his calves struck with as loud rebound
As makes the mainsail of a ship brought up along the blast,
When with the coil of all its ropes it beats the sounding mast.
So, striding vast, the giant passed ; the King held fast his breath—
Motionless, save his throbbing heart ; and chill and still as death
Stood listening while, a second time, the giant took the round
Of all the camp : but when at length, for the third time, the sound
Came up, and through the parting haze a third time huge and dim
Rose out the Shape, the valiant hound sprang forth and challenged
      him.
And forth, disdaining that a dog should put him so to shame,
Sprang Congal, and essayed to speak : ' Dread Shadow, stand !
      Proclaim
What wouldst thou, that thou thus all night around my camp
      shouldst keep
Thy troublous vigil, banishing the wholesome gift of sleep
From all our eyes, who, though inured to dreadful sounds and
      sights
By land and sea, have never yet in all our perilous nights
Lain in the ward of such a guard.'
                                    The Shape made answer none,
But with stern wafture of its hand went angrier striding on,
Shaking the earth with heavier steps.   Then Congal on his track
Sprang fearless.
                  ' Answer me, thou churl ! ' he cried.   ' I bid thee back ! '
But while he spoke the giant's cloak around his shoulders grew
Like to a black bulged thunder-cloud, and sudden out there flew
From all its angry swelling folds, with uproar unconfined,
Direct against the King's pursuit, a mighty blast of wind.
Loud flapped the mantle tempest-lined, while fluttering down the
      gale,
As leaves in autumn, man and hound were swept into the vale ;
And, heard o'er all the huge uproar, through startled Dalaray
The giant went, with stamp and clash, departing south away.

At the ford of Moy-Linny they encounter a still more terrible spectre, the Washer of the Ford.

>   Mid-leg deep she stood
> Beside a heap of heads and limbs that swam in oozing blood,
> Whereon, and on a glittering heap of raiment rich and brave,
> With swift, pernicious hands she scooped and poured the crimson wave.

Congal addresses her :

>   Who art thou, hideous one ?   And from what curst abode
> Comest thou thus in open day the hearts of men to freeze ?
> And whose lopped heads and severed limbs and bloody vests are these ? '
> ' I am the Washer of the Ford,' she answered ; ' and my race
> Is of the Tuath de Danann line of Magi ; and my place
> For toil is in the running streams of Erin ; and my cave
> For sleep is in the middle of the shell-heaped cairn of Maev,
> High up on haunted Knocknarea; [1] and this fine carnage-heap
> Before me, and these silken vests and mantles which I steep
> Thus in the running waters, are the severed heads and hands
> And spear-torn scarfs and tunics of these gay-dressed, gallant bands
> Whom thou, O Congal ! leadest to death.   And this,' the Fury said,
> Uplifting by the clotted locks what seemed a dead man's head,
> ' Is thine own head, O Congal ! '

The two foregoing passages may stand as types of the manner in which Ferguson has fitted the English language to the wild shapes of Gaelic mythology, and re-peopled the imaginative world of the Irish people with the divine and mysterious figures that faded from it with the loss of the ancient tongue.   After these episodes there follows an affecting but vain attempt on the part of Lafinda and the spirit of St. Brigid to turn Congal from his hostile purpose.   He marches to battle against King Domnal and his Irish hosts.   One after another of the contending champions falls in single combat with a rival hero, till the Christian champion, Prince Conal, encounters Congal himself.   After a fierce struggle Conal prevails, but Congal is rescued from him—only to fall, by a strange irony of fate, by an

---

[1] This huge cairn on the mountain of Knocknarea, overlooking the town of Sligo, is a landmark visible for many leagues around.

unexpected stroke of the idiot Prince Cuanna. This is the beginning of
the end. Congal fights on, though his life-blood is flowing fast, until his
fall causes the panic and flight of the Pagan forces.

Then dire was their disorder, as the wavering line at first
Swayed to and fro irresolute ; then, all disrupted, burst
Like waters from a broken dam effused upon the plain,
The shelter of Kilultagh's woods and winding glens to gain.

A fine episode is here introduced. Kellach, the old paralysed Pagan
Bard, who has been watching the battle from his *tolg* or litter, upraised on a
hill, cannot fly with the ' heavy-rolling tide of ruin and despair ' which
streams past him.

But keen-eyed Domnal, when he stood to view the rout, ere long
Spying that white, unmoving head amid the scattering throng,
Exclaimed : ' Of all their broken host one only man I see
Not flying ; and I therefore judge him impotent to be
Of use of limb. ' Go ; take alive,' he cried, ' and hither fetch
The hoary-haired unmoving man . . . . '
                    . . . . A swift battalion went
And, breaking through the hindmost line, where Kellach sat
        hard by,
Took him alive ; and, chair and man uphoisting shoulder-high,
They bore him back, his hoary locks and red eyes gleaming far,
The grimmest standard yet displayed that day o'er all the war ;
And grimly, where they set him down, he eyed the encircling ring
Of Bishops and of chafing Chiefs who stood about the King.
        Then, with his crozier's nether end turned towards him,
            Bishop Erc
Said : ' Wretch abhorred, to thee it is we owe this bloody work ;
By whose malignant counsel moved, thy hapless nephew first
Sought impious aid of foreigners ; for which be thou accurst.'
And turned and left them.
                    Senach then approaching, mildly said :
' No curse so strong but in the blood for man's redemption shed
May man dissolve ; and also thou, unhappy, if thou wilt
Mayst purchase peace and pardon now, and every stain of guilt
That soils thy soul may'st wash away, if but with heart sincere
Thou wilt repent thee and embrace the heavenly boon which here
I offer.'

'Speak him louder, sir,' said harsher Ronan Finn.
'Kellach, repent thy sins,' he cried ; 'and presently begin,
For few the moments left thee now ; and, ere the hour be past,
Thy lot may, for eternity, in heaven or hell be cast.'
          'Repent thy sins,' said Domnal, 'and implore the Church's
                grace ;
So shall thy life be spared thee yet a little breathing-space.'
          Then Kellach from the Bishops' gaze withdrew his wavering
                glance,
And, fixing his fast-glazing eyes on Domnal's countenance,
Said : 'I am old, and mainly deaf ; and much of what they say
I hear not. But I tell thee this : we'd not be here to-day
But for this trick of cursing, wherein much more expert
Are these front shaven Druids than in any manly art.'
          'Injurious Kellach,' said the King, 'beware the chastening rod
The Church of Christ reserves for those who mock the priests of
                God.'
          'Of no good God are these the priests,' said Kellach ; 'and,
                for me,
I ne'er sought evil Spirit's aid 'gainst any enemy :
But what I've learned in better times among my noble peers,
That I have practised and upheld for well-nigh fourscore years ;
And never asked from clerk or witch, by sacrifice or charm,
To buy a demon's venal help to aid my own right arm :
But in my house good Poets, men expert in song and lay,
I've kept in bounteous sort, to teach my sons the prosperous way
Of open truth and manliness : for ever since the time
When Cathbad smothered Usnach's sons in that foul sea of slime
Raised by abominable spells at Creeveroe's bloody gate
Do ruin and dishonour still on priest-led Kings await.
Wherefore, by Fergus, son of Roy, ere that year passed away,
Emania was left bare and black ; and so lies at this day :
And thou in desert Tara darest not thyself to dwell,
Since that other bald magician, of Lorrah, from his bell
Shook out his maledictions on the unoffending hill.'
          Said Domnal : 'By my valour, old man, thou doest ill,
Comparing blessed saints of Christ with Pagan priests of Crom.'
          'Crom or whomever else they serve,' said Kellach ; 'them
                that come

Cursing, I curse.'

　　　　　　　Then Ronan Finn, upheaving high his bell,
Rang it, and gave the banning word ; and Kellach therewith fell
Off his *tolg* side upon the ground, stone dead.　The Poets there
Next night, in secret, buried him upon his brazen chair.

　　　　　Brass-armed complete for standing fight, in Cahir-Laery,
　　　　　wall,
Sun-smitten Laery,[1] rampart-tomb'd, awaits the judgment-call,
Facing the Leinstermen.　Years roll, and Leinster is no more
The dragon-den of hostile men it was in days of yore ;
Still, constant till the day of doom, while the great stone-work
　　　lasts,
Laery stands listening for the trump, at whose wall-bursting
　　　blasts
He leaps again to fire thy plain, O Liffey, with the glare
Of that dread golden-bordered shield.　Thus ever, on his chair,
Kellach awaits, from age to age, the coming of the time
Will bring the cursers and the curs'd before the Judge sublime.

　　　Congal has meantime been whirled from the flying host by the giant
Warder, Mananan, who figures strangely and dimly in the background of
the tale both as the protector of Erin and the patron of heroes.　True to the
Irish conception of the supernatural, he remains as a rule half merged in
Nature—not completely disengaged from it, and taking firm and distinct
shape like a Greek deity, but rather communicating to what is natural and
visible the sense of the divinity behind it.　Congal finds himself in his
native vale in Antrim, and laments his shame and grief :

'But more than for myself I mourn my generous friends deceived,
And all their wives and little ones of lord and sire bereaved.'
Tears, sent from whence the thought had come—let faith divine
　　　their source—
Rose at the thought to Congal's eyes, and pressed with tender
　　　force

---

　　[1] Laoghaire MacNeill, King of Ireland in the days of St. Patrick, had
made a peace with the Leinstermen and ratified it with a vow by the Sun and
Wind.　When he broke his compact, say the chroniclers, the Sun and Wind
slew him.　He desired to be buried, standing and armed, in the rampart of
his *cahir* or fort, with his face towards Leinster.

Unwonted passage ; and he wept, with many bitter sighs
In sudden vision of his life and all its vanities.
As when a tempest—which all day, with whirlwind, fire, and hail
Vexing mid-air, has hid the sight of sunshine from the vale—
Towards sunset rolls its thunderings ; fast as it mounts on high,
A flood of placid light refills the lately troubled sky ;
Shine all the full down-sliding streams, wet blades, and quivering
    sprays,
And all the grassy-sided vales with emerald lustre blaze ;
So, in the shower of Congal's tears, his storms of passion passed,
So o'er his long-distempered soul came tranquil light at last.

    Ere wonder in his calming mind had found reflection's aid,
There came across the daisied lawn a veiled religious maid,
From wicket of a neighbouring close ; and, as she nearer drew,
The peerless gesture and the grace indelible he knew.

Then follows a tender and touching conversation with Lafinda, after
which a marvellous vision rises before the sight of Congal – Mananan, with
his mantle flashing like a summer sea, now appearing, not in anger, but as
a symbol of peace and regeneration for the distracted land.

    Even as he spoke, soft rustling sounds to all their ears were
    borne,
Such as warm winds at eve excite 'mongst brown-ripe rolling corn.
All, but Lafinda, looked ; but she, behind a steadfast lid,
Kept her calm eyes from that she deemed a sight unholy, hid.
And Congal reck'd not if the Shape that passed before his eyes
Lived only on the inward film, or outward 'neath the skies.
    No longer soiled with stain of earth, what seemed his mantle
    shone
Rich with innumerable hues refulgent, such as one
Beholds, and thankful-hearted he, who casts abroad his gaze
O'er some rich tillage-countryside when mellow Autumn days
Gild all the sheafy foodful stooks ; and broad before him spread—
He looking landward from the brow of some great sea-cape's head,
Bray or Ben-Edar—sees beneath, in silent pageant grand,
Slow fields of sunshine spread o'er fields of rich, corn-bearing
    land ;
Red glebe and meadow-margin green commingling to the view
With yellow stubble, browning woods, and upland tracts of blue ;—

Then, sated with the pomp of fields, turns, seaward, to the verge
Where, mingling with the murmuring wash made by the far-down
    surge,
Comes up the clamorous song of birds unseen, that, low beneath,
Poised off the rock, ply underfoot; and, 'mid the blossoming
    heath,
And mint-sweet herb that loves the ledge rare-air'd, at ease
    reclined,
Surveys the wide pale-heaving floor crisped by a curling wind;
With all its shifting, shadowy belts, and chasing scopes of green,
Sun-strown, foam-freckled, sail-embossed, and blackening squalls
    between,
And slant, cerulean-skirted showers that with a drowsy sound,
Heard inward, of ebullient waves, stalk all the horizon round;
And—haply, being a citizen just 'scaped from some disease
That long has held him sick indoors, now, in the brine-fresh
    breeze,
Health-salted, bathes; and says, the while he breathes reviving
    bliss,
'I am not good enough, O God, nor pure enough for this!'—
Such seemed its hues.   His feet were set in fields of waving grain;
His head, above, obscured the sun: all round the leafy plain
Blackbird and thrush piped loud acclaims: in middle air, breast-
    high,
The lark shrill carolled; overhead, and halfway up the sky,
Sailed the far eagle: from his knees, down dale and grassy steep,
Thronged the dun, mighty upland droves, and mountain-mottling
    sheep,
And by the river-margins green, and o'er the thymy meads
Before his feet, careered, at large, the slim-knee'd, slender steeds,
        It passed.   Light Sweeny, as it passed, went also from their
            view:
And, conscious only of her task, Lafinda bent anew
At Congal's side.   She bound his wounds, and asked him, 'Has
    thy heart
At all repented of its sins, unhappy that thou art?'
            'My sins,' said Congal, 'and my deeds of strife and blood-
                shed seem
No longer mine, but as the shapes and shadows of a dream:

And I myself, as one oppressed with sleep's deceptive shows,
Awaking only now to life, when life is at its close.'
      'Oh, grant,' she cried, with tender joy, 'Thou, who alone
        canst save,
That this awaking be to light and life beyond the grave !'

      'Twas then the long-corroded links of life's mysterious
      chain
Snapped softly ; and his mortal change passed upon Congal Claen.

THE BURIAL OF KING CORMAC [1]

'CROM CRUACH and his sub-gods twelve,'
    Said Cormac, 'are but carven treene ;
The axe that made them, haft or helve,
    Had worthier of our worship been.

' But He who made the tree to grow
    And hid in earth the iron-stone,
And made the man with mind to know
    The axe's use, is God alone.'

Anon to priests of Crom was brought—
    Where, girded in their service dread,
They minister'd on red Moy Slaught—
    Word of the words King Cormac said.

They loosed their curse against the King—
    They cursed him in his flesh and bones—
And daily in their mystic ring
    They turn'd the maledictive stones,

Till, where at meat the monarch sate,
    Amid the revel and the wine,
He choked upon the food he ate,
    At Sletty, southward of the Boyne.

---

[1] There is a Christian legend which tells that Cormac MacArt, who ruled Ireland in the third century, had an early intuition of the true faith and turned away from Paganism. Thereupon the priests of the great idol Crom Cruach cursed him, and he died, but charged that he should be buried at Rosnaree, and not at the great royal cemetery of Brugh (Newgrange) ; which came about as the poem relates.

High vaunted then the priestly throng,
　And far and wide they noised abroad,
With trump and loud liturgic song,
　The praise of their avenging god.

But ere the voice was wholly spent
　That priest and prince should still obey,
To awed attendants o'er him bent
　Great Cormac gather'd breath to say :

'Spread not the beds of Brugh for me
　When restless death-bed's use is done ;
But bury me at Rosnaree,
　And face me to the rising sun.

'For all the Kings who lie in Brugh
　Put trust in gods of wood and stone ;
And 'twas at Ross that first I knew
　One, Unseen, who is God alone.

'His glory lightens from the East ;
　His message soon shall reach our shore ;
And idol-god and cursing priest,
　Shall plague us from Moy Slaught no more.'

Dead Cormac on his bier they laid.
　'He reign'd a king for forty years,
And shame it were,' his captains said,
　'He lay not with his royal peers.

'His grandsire, Hundred-Battle, sleeps
　Serene in Brugh ; and all around
Dead kings in stone sepulchral keeps
　Protect the sacred burial ground.

'What though a dying man should rave
　Of changes o'er the Eastern sea ?
In Brugh of Boyne shall be his grave,
　And not in noteless Rosnaree.'

Then northward forth they bore the bier
   And down from Sletty side they drew,
With horseman and with charioteer,
   To cross the fords of Boyne to Brugh.

There came a breath of finer air,
   That touch'd the Boyne with ruffling wings ;
It stirr'd him in his sedgy lair,
   And in his mossy moorland springs.

And as the burial train came down
   With dirge and savage dolorous shows,
Across their pathway, broad and brown,
   The deep full-hearted river rose ;

From bank to bank through all his fords,
   'Neath blackening squalls he swell'd and boil'd,
And thrice the wondering Gentile lords
   Essay'd to cross, and thrice recoil'd.

Then forth stepp'd grey-hair'd warriors four ;
   They said : ' Through angrier floods than these
On link'd shields once our King we bore
   From Dread-Spear and the hosts of Deece.

' And long as loyal will holds good,
   And limbs respond with helpful thews,
Nor flood, nor fiend within the flood,
   Shall bar him of his burial dues.'

With slanted necks they stoop'd to lift ;
   They heaved him up to neck and chin ;
And, pair and pair, with footsteps swift,
   Lock'd arm and shoulder, bore him in.

'Twas brave to see them leave the shore ;
   To mark the deep'ning surges rise,
And fall subdued in foam before
   The tension of their striding thighs.

'Twas brave, when now a spear-cast out,
    Breast-high the battling surges ran ;
For weight was great, and limbs were stout
    And loyal man put trust in man.

But ere they reach'd the middle deep,
    Nor steadying weight of clay they bore,
Nor strain of sinewy limbs could keep
    Their feet beneath the swerving four.

And now they slide, and now they swim,
    And now, amid the blackening squall,
Grey locks afloat, with clutchings grim,
    They plunge around the floating pall ;

While as a youth with practised spear
    Through justling crowds bears off the ring,
Boyne from their shoulders caught the bier
    And proudly bore away the king.

At morning, on the grassy marge
    Of Rosnaree, the corpse was found ;
And shepherds at their early charge
    Entomb'd it in the peaceful ground.

A tranquil spot—a hopeful sound
    Comes from the ever youthful stream,
And still on daisied mead and mound
    The dawn delays with tenderer beam

Round Cormac Spring renews her buds ;
    In march perpetual by his side,
Down come the earth-fresh April floods,
    And up the sea-fresh salmon glide.

And life and time rejoicing run
    From age to age their wonted way ;
But still he waits the risen Sun,
    For still 'tis only dawning Day.

From AIDEEN'S GRAVE [1]

THEY heaved the stone ; they heap'd the cairn :
　　Said Ossian, ' In a queenly grave
We leave her, 'mong her fields of fern,
　　Between the cliff and wave.

' The cliff behind stands clear and bare,
　　And bare, above, the heathery steep
Scales the clear heaven's expanse, to where
　　The Danann Druids sleep.

' And all the sands that, left and right,
　　The grassy isthmus-ridge confine,
In yellow bars lie bare and bright
　　Amid the sparkling brine.

' A clear pure air pervades the scene,
　　In loneliness and awe secure ;
Meet spot to sepulchre a Queen
　　Who in her life was pure.

' Here, far from camp and chase removed,
　　Apart in Nature's quiet room,
The music that alive she loved
　　Shall cheer her in the tomb.

' The humming of the noontide bees,
　　The lark's loud carol all day long,
And, borne on evening's salted breeze,
　　The clanking sea-bird's song

' Shall round her airy chamber float,
　　And with the whispering winds and streams
Attune to Nature's tenderest note
　　The tenor of her dreams.

---

[1] Aideen was the wife of Oscar, son of Oisín, son of Finn. She died of grief after the slaying of Oscar and almost all the Fianna at the battle of Gabhra, when the tribes of Ireland rose against them, and was buried under the great cromlech on Howth.

'And oft, at tranquil eve's decline
  When full tides lip the Old Green Plain,
The lowing of Moynalty's kine
  Shall round her breathe again,

'In sweet remembrance of the days
  When, duteous, in the lowly vale,
Unconscious of my Oscar's gaze,
  She fill'd the fragrant pail,

'And, duteous, from the running brook
  Drew water for the bath ; nor deem'd
A King did on her labour look,
  And she a fairy seem'd.

' But when the wintry frosts begin,
  And in their long-drawn, lofty flight,
The wild geese with their airy din
  Distend the ear of night ;

'And when the fierce De Danann ghosts
  At midnight from their peak come down ;
When all around the enchanted coasts
  Despairing strangers drown ;

' When, mingling with the wreckful wail,
  From low Clontarf's wave-trampled floor
Comes booming up the burthen'd gale
  The angry Sand-Bull's roar ;

' Or, angrier than the sea, the shout
  Of Erin's hosts in wrath combined,
When Terror heads Oppression's rout,
  And Freedom cheers behind :

' Then o'er our lady's placid dream,
  Where safe from storms she sleeps, may steal
Such joy as will not misbeseem
  A queen of men to feel :

'Such thrill of free, defiant pride,
  As rapt her in her battle car
At Gavra, when by Oscar's side
  She rode the ridge of war,

  Exulting, down the shouting troops,
    And through the thick confronting kings
With hands on all their javelin loops
    And shafts on all their strings;

' Ere closed the inseparable crowds,
  No more to part for me, and show,
As bursts the sun through scattering clouds ;
  My Oscar issuing so.

'No more, dispelling battle's gloom,
  Shall son for me from fight return ;
The great green rath's ten-acred tomb
  Lies heavy on his urn.

'A cup of bodkin-pencilled clay
  Holds Oscar ; mighty heart and limb
One handful now of ashes grey :
  And she has died for him.

'And here, hard by her natal bower
  On lone Ben-Edar's side, we strive
With lifted rock and sign of power
  To keep her name alive ;

'That while, from circling year to year,
  Her Ogham-letter'd stone is seen,
The Gael shall say, "Our Fenians here
  Entomb'd their loved Aideen."'

THE FAIRY THORN

AN ULSTER BALLAD

'GET up, our Anna dear, from the weary spinning-wheel ;
  For your father's on the hill, and your mother is asleep ;
Come up above the crags, and we'll dance a Highland reel
  Around the fairy thorn on the steep.'

X

At Anna Grace's door 'twas thus the maidens cried,
    Three merry maidens fair in kirtles of the green ;
And Anna laid the *rock* and the weary wheel aside—
    The fairest of the four, I ween.

They're glancing through the glimmer of the quiet eve,
    Away in milky wavings of neck and ankle bare ;
The heavy-sliding stream in its sleepy song they leave,
    And the crags in the ghostly air.

And linking hand in hand, and singing as they go,
    The maids along the hillside have ta'en their fearless way,
Till they come to where the rowan trees in lonely beauty grow
    Beside the Fairy Hawthorn grey.

The Hawthorn stands between the ashes tall and slim,
    Like matron with her twin grand-daughters at her knee ;
The rowan berries cluster o'er her low head grey and dim
    In ruddy kisses sweet to see.

The merry maidens four have ranged them in a row,
    Between each lovely couple a stately rowan stem,
And away in mazes wavy, like skimming birds they go—
    Oh, never carolled bird like them !

But solemn is the silence of the silvery haze
    That drinks away their voices in echoless repose,
And dreamily the evening has stilled the haunted braes,
    And dreamier the gloaming grows.

And sinking one by one, like lark-notes from the sky
    When the falcon's shadow saileth across the open shaw,
Are hushed the maidens' voices, as cowering down they lie
    In the flutter of their sudden awe.

For, from the air above and the grassy ground beneath,
    And from the mountain-ashes and the old White-thorn between,
A power of faint enchantment doth through their beings breathe,
    And they sink down together on the green.

They sink together silent, and, stealing side to side,
  They fling their lovely arms o'er their drooping necks so fair ;
Then vainly strive again their naked arms to hide,
  For their shrinking necks again are bare.

Thus clasped and prostrate all, with their heads together bowed,
  Soft o'er their bosoms beating—the only human sound—
They hear the silky footsteps of the silent fairy crowd,
  Like a river in the air gliding round.

Nor scream can any raise, nor prayer can any say,
  But wild, wild the terror of the speechless three ;
For they feel fair Anna Grace drawn silently away—
  By whom, they dare not look to see.

They feel her tresses twine with their parting locks of gold,
  And the curls elastic falling, as her head withdraws ;
They feel her sliding arms from their trancèd arms unfold,
  But they dare not look to see the cause.

For heavy on their senses the faint enchantment lies
  Through all that night of anguish and perilous amaze ;
And neither fear nor wonder can ope their quivering eyes,
  Or their limbs from the cold ground raise.

Till out of Night the Earth has rolled her dewy side,
  With every haunted mountain and streamy vale below ;
When, as the mist dissolves in the yellow morning-tide,
  The maidens' trance dissolveth so.

Then fly the ghastly three as swiftly as they may,
  And tell their tale of sorrow to anxious friends in vain —
They pined away and died within the year and day,
  And ne'er was Anna Grace seen again.

The Fair Hills of Ireland

from the irish

A very close translation, in the original metre, of an Irish song of unknown authorship dating from the end of the seventeenth century. The refrain means ' O sad lament.'

A PLENTEOUS place is Ireland for hospitable cheer,
    Uileacán dubh O !
Where the wholesome fruit is bursting from the yellow barley ear,
    Uileacán dubh O !
There is honey in the trees where her misty vales expand,
And her forest paths in summer are by falling waters fann'd;
There is dew at high noontide there, and springs i' the yellow sand
    On the fair hills of holy Ireland.

Curl'd he is and ringleted, and plaited to the knee,
    Uileacán dubh O !
Each captain who comes sailing across the Irish Sea,
    Uileacán dubh O !
And I will make my journey, if life and health but stand,
Unto that pleasant country, that fresh and fragrant strand,
And leave your boasted braveries, your wealth and high command,
    For the fair hills of holy Ireland.

Large and profitable are the stacks upon the ground,
    Uileacán dubh O !
The butter and the cream do wondrously abound,
    Uileacán dubh O !
The cresses on the water and the sorrels are at hand,
And the cuckoo's calling daily his note of music bland,
And the bold thrush sings so bravely his song i' the forests grand
    On the fair hills of holy Ireland.

Lament for Thomas Davis

I WALKED through Ballinderry in the spring-time,
  When the bud was on the tree ;
And I said, in every fresh-ploughed field beholding
  The sowers striding free,

Scattering broadcast forth the corn in golden plenty
   On the quick seed-clasping soil,
'Even such, this day, among the fresh-stirred hearts of Erin,
   Thomas Davis, is thy toil !'

I sat by Ballyshannon in the summer,
   And saw the salmon leap ;
And I said, as I beheld the gallant creatures
   Spring glittering from the deep,
Thro' the spray, and thro' the prone heaps striving onward
   To the calm clear streams above,
' So seekest thou thy native founts of freedom, Thomas Davis,
   In thy brightness of strength and love !'

I stood on Derrybawn in the autumn,
   And I heard the eagle call,
With a clangorous cry of wrath and lamentation
   That filled the wide mountain hall,
O'er the bare deserted place of his plundered eyrie ;
   And I said, as he screamed and soared,
' So callest thou, thou wrathful-soaring Thomas Davis,
   For a nation's rights restored !'

And, alas ! to think but now, and thou art lying,
   Dear Davis, dead at thy mother's knee ;
And I, no mother near, on my own sick-bed,
   That face on earth shall never see :
I may lie and try to feel that I am not dreaming,
   I may lie and try to say, ' Thy will be done '—
But a hundred such as I will never comfort Erin
   For the loss of the noble son !

Young husbandman of Erin's fruitful seed-time,
   In the fresh track of danger's plough !
Who will walk the heavy, toilsome, perilous furrow
   Girt with freedom's seed-sheets now ?
Who will banish with the wholesome crop of knowledge
   The flaunting weed and the bitter thorn,
Now that thou thyself art but a seed for hopeful planting
   Against the Resurrection morn ?

Young salmon of the flood-tide of freedom
  That swells round Erin's shore !
Thou wilt leap against their loud oppressive torrent
  Of bigotry and hate no more :
Drawn downward by their prone material instinct,
  Let them thunder on their rocks and foam—
Thou hast leapt, aspiring soul, to founts beyond their raging
  Where troubled waters never come !

But I grieve not, eagle of the empty eyrie,
  That thy wrathful cry is still ;
And that the songs alone of peaceful mourners
  Are heard to-day on Erin's hill ;
Better far, if brothers' war be destined for us
  (God avert that horrid day, I pray !),
That ere our hands be stained with slaughter fratricidal
  Thy warm heart should be cold in clay.

But my trust is strong in God, who made us brothers,
  That He will not suffer those right hands
Which thou hast joined in holier rites than wedlock
  To draw opposing brands.
Oh, many a tuneful tongue that thou mad'st vocal
  Would lie cold and silent then ;
And songless long once more, should often-widowed Erin
  Mourn the loss of her brave young men.

Oh, brave young men, my love, my pride, my promise,
  'Tis on you my hopes are set,
In manliness, in kindliness, in justice,
  To make Erin a nation yet :
Self-respecting, self-relying, self-advancing,
  In union or in severance, free and strong—
And if God grant this, then, under God, to Thomas Davis
  Let the greater praise belong.

BOOK V

AUBREY DE VERE

THE family of the De Veres has followed high traditions in English poetry. The influence of Wordsworth, an intimate friend, is predominant in the work of Sir Aubrey and Mr. Aubrey de Vere; but, determined by the natural bent of their genius, both father and son achieved success in a form uncongenial to Wordsworth—the drama; while the poetic faculty was never more happily wedded to fine scholarship than in the TRANSLATIONS FROM HORACE of Mr. De Vere's elder brother, Sir Stephen.

To achieve high distinction in poetry it is before all things essential to maintain the balance between the intellectual and sensuous elements. Simple in theme and method, strong in its intellectual apprehension of life, nobly plain in diction, the poetry of the De Veres is deficient in the qualities which arrest popular attention; it is not sensuous enough, it is not passionate enough. Distinguished, too, by moral breadth and depth rather than by natural magic, it suffers amid the poetry of the day comparative neglect, and finds a narrow though appreciative audience. It may be claimed for it, and with justice, that if not throughout successful as art it is nevertheless conceived and executed in the school of the great masters; and where successful, it is successful in their manner. Read Sir Aubrey de Vere's SONNETS or his MARY TUDOR; read Mr. Aubrey de Vere's ALEXANDER or his 'Autumnal Ode,' and the impression received is that one is on elevated ground, on the higher slopes of Parnassus. We are not spoiled for

this poetry by reading in the books of Homer, of Dante, or of
Milton.

> Æschylus' bronze-throat, eagle bark for blood
> Has somewhat spoilt my taste for twitterings—

says Browning somewhere. The absence of largeness and
freedom, of far horizons and noble spaces, this we feel in the
company of the minor poets, but with the De Veres we are
among the mountains. Because neither Sir Aubrey nor Mr.
Aubrey de Vere found modern life rich in inspiring forces, and
each was touched less by the ideals of the present than by
those of the past, perhaps for this reason and because so much
of their work is dramatic in form and intention they have won no
large share of popular acceptance. It is not surprising that this
should be true of poetry characterised by its singular aloofness
from contemporary thought and feeling, characterised by its
impersonality, its dramatic method and character. This is poetry
whose themes are not chosen at the bidding of the poet's affections, but rather at the bidding of his genius. And when this
is said we have placed it, in conception and aim at least, in the
highest company. The lesser poet writes at the dictation of
his moods, but for Lucretius and Sophocles the sphere of
poetry is not delimited by the feelings that sway the inconstant
heart, making it an Æolian lyre responsive to all idle winds.

Not improbably, I think, Mr. De Vere would prefer to
be judged by his poems upon Irish subjects rather than by
any other part of his work. For in his old Irish lays, heroic
in theme, spiritual in significance, and in his poems which
enshrine the traditions of the Mediæval Church, Mr. De Vere is
most at home in spirit, and perhaps is at his best. Here he strikes
a note which falls upon the ear with a mingled solemnity and
joyousness, and seems to breathe the very air of that old
world of unconscious saintliness and glad romance. Whatever
of beauty or of good dwelt with the ages that found in religion
their joy as well as their peace is gathered into these legends ;
Cuchullin, Oisín and Ethell, Naisi and Deirdré, look out
upon us like the faces on some old tapestry, but far more

lifelike. Cuchullin in his war-car, calling the horses by their well-known names, and dashing through Eman's gateway as a storm ; Ethell, bard of Brian MacGuire, who sang of policy to chieftains and princes, of love to maids in the bower, and

> Of war at the feastings in bawn or grove ;

the lovers Naisi and Deirdré, self-forgetful, hand in hand, singing their passionate song of life and death—these are the true children of Ireland's golden age, called from the shores of dreamland to feed our hearts with the poetry of a nation's childhood.

It may be argued that the poetry of the De Veres is distinctively English, formed by English traditions, the product of English culture. It may be argued that it belongs to the classical school rather than to the school of romance. And indisputably in many of Mr. De Vere's finest and most characteristic passages we feel that he inherits in the line of Chaucer and of Dryden. Take this passage from his magnificent ' Autumnal Ode : '

> It is the Autumnal epode of the year :
>   The Nymphs that urge the seasons on their round,
> They to whose green lap flies the startled deer
>   When bays the far-off hound,
> They that drag April by the rain-bright hair,
> Though sun-showers doze her, and the rude winds scare,
>   O'er March's frosty bound,
> They by whose warm and furtive hand unwound
> The cestus falls from May's new-wedded breast,
> Silent they stand beside dead Summer's bier,
>   With folded palms and faces to the West,
> And their loose tresses sweep the dewy ground.

Nevertheless, Mr. De Vere is rightly ranked with the Irish poets. The profound sympathy with the Celtic nature, the insight into the Celtic heart, are there, and not a few unmistakable Celtic affinities, not a little of the Celtic charm. For some reason or other the Celtic imagination is less stirred by richness or picturesqueness in Nature than the Saxon imagination, dwells less in its happiest moments upon landscape luxuriant in leaf and flower, the valley with its lush pasture or the promise of the tilled glebe ; it is stirred rather by Nature in her severer aspects and by landscape of fewer elements—by the austere outline of cliff or mountain, the pure curve of the far rim of ocean. 'Delightful to be on Ben Eddar,' sings Columba in some charming verses—charming even in translation—written fifteen hundred years ago :

> Delightful to be on Ben Eddar
> Before going o'er the white sea ;
> The dashing of the wave against its face,
> *The bareness of its shore and its border.*

And in Celtic poetry likewise the emotions are purer, less complex, more elemental, more spiritual than in Saxon poetry. Simplicity, then, with full-heartedness—whether in joy or grief— a childlike transparency of soul, a courageous spirituality, these Celtic qualities Mr. De Vere's poetry preserves for us ; and because it preserves them his memory and his work are safe. He will be enrolled as a worthy successor to the bards of long ago, from Oiseen or

> That Taliessin once who made the rivers dance,
> And in his rapture raised the mountains from their trance.

W. MACNEILE DIXON.

Mr. Aubrey De Vere, third son of Sir Aubrey, was born at Curragh Chase in 1814 and died there in 1902. Besides a number of prose works, critical and miscellaneous, Mr. De Vere's poetical works were published in six volumes, 1884.

Later volumes issued by him were : LEGENDS AND RECORDS OF THE CHURCH AND THE EMPIRE, 1887; ST. PETER'S CHAINS, 1888; MEDIÆVAL RECORDS AND SONNETS, 1893. Two well-edited volumes of selections from his poetical writings have appeared, one by John Dennis (London, 1890) and one by G. E. Woodberry (New York, 1894).

THE SUN GOD

I SAW the Master of the Sun.   He stood
   High in his luminous car, himself more bright—
   An Archer of immeasurable might ;

On his left shoulder hung his quivered load,
Spurned by his steeds the eastern mountain glowed,
　Forward his eager eye and brow of light
He bent ; and, while both hands that arch embowed,
　Shaft after shaft pursued the flying Night.
No wings profaned that godlike form ; around
　His neck high held an ever-moving crowd
Of locks hung glistening ; while such perfect sound
Fell from his bowstring that th' ethereal dome
　Thrilled as a dewdrop ; and each passing cloud
Expanded, whitening like the ocean foam.

From THE BARD ETHELL

IRELAND, THIRTEENTH CENTURY

I

I AM Ethell, the son of Conn ;
　Here I live at the foot of the hill ;
I am clansman to Brian and servant to none ;
　Whom I hated I hate, whom I loved love still.
Blind am I.　On milk I live,
　And meat ; God sends it on each Saint's day,
Though Donald MacArt—may he never thrive !—
　Last Shrovetide drove half my kine away.

II

At the brown hill's base, by the pale blue lake
　I dwell, and see the things I saw ;
The heron flap heavily up from the brake,
　The crow fly homeward with twig or straw,
The wild duck, a silver line in wake,
　Cutting the calm mere to far Bunaw.
And the things that I heard, though deaf I hear :
From the tower in the island the feastful cheer,
The horn from the wood, the plunge of the stag,
With the loud hounds after him down from the crag.
Sweet is the chase, but the battle is sweeter ;
More healthful, more joyous, for true men meeter !

III

My hand is weak ; it once was strong.
  My heart burns still with its ancient fire.
If any man smite me, he does me wrong,
  For I was the Bard of Brian MacGuire.
If any man slay me—not unaware,
  By no chance blow, nor in wine and revel—
I have stored beforehand a curse in my prayer
  For his kith and kindred ; his deed is evil.

IV

There never was King, and there never will be,
In battle or banquet like Malachi !
The Seers his reign have predicted long ;
He honoured the Bards, and gave gold for song.
If rebels arose, he put out their eyes;
  If robbers plundered or burned the fanes
He hung them in chaplets, like rosaries,
  That others, beholding, might take more pains.
There was none to woman more reverent-minded,
  For he held his mother and Mary dear ;
If any man wronged them, that man he blinded,
  Or straight amerced him of hand or ear.
There was none who founded more convents—none :
  In his palace the old and the poor were fed ;
The orphan walked, and the widow's son,
  Without groom or page to his throne or bed.
In council he mused with great brows divine
And eyes like the eyes of the musing kine,
Upholding a Sceptre o'er which, men said,
Seven spirits of wisdom like fire-tongues played.
He drained ten lakes and he built ten bridges ;
  He bought a gold book for a thousand cows ;
He slew ten Princes who brake their pledges ;
  With the bribed and the base he scorned to carouse.
He was sweet and awful ; through all his reign
God gave great harvests to vale and plain ;
From his nurse's milk he was kind and brave ;
And when he went down to his well-wept grave

Through the triumph of penance his soul uprose
To God and the Saints.   Not so his foes !

V

The King that came after ! ah ! woe, woe, woe !
He doubted his friend and he trusted his foe ;
He bought and he sold ; his kingdom old
    He pledged and pawned to avenge a spite ;
No Bard or prophet his birth foretold ;
    He was guarded and warded both day and night :
He counselled with fools and had boors at his feast ;
He was cruel to Christian and kind to beast ;
Men smiled when they talked of him far o'er the wave,
Well paid were the mourners that wept at his grave.
God plagued for his sake his people sore :
    They sinned ; for the people should watch and pray,
That their prayers—like angels at window and door—
    May keep from the King the bad thought away !

X

I forgive old Cathbar, who sank my boat.
    Must I pardon Feargal, who slew my son ;
Or the pirate Strongbow, who burned Granote,
    They tell me, and in it nine priests, a nun,
And—worst—Saint Finian's crosier staff ?
At forgiveness like that I spit and laugh.
My Chief, in his wine-cups, forgave twelve men ;
And of these a dozen rebelled again !
There never was Chief more brave than he !
    The night he was born Loch Gur up-burst ;
He was Bard-loving, gift-making, loud of glee,
    The last to fly, to advance the first ;
He was like the top spray upon Uladh's oak,
    He was like the tap-root of Argial's pine ;
He was secret and sudden ; as lightning his stroke ;
    There was none that could fathom his hid design.
He slept not : if any man scorned his alliance
He struck the first blow for a frank defiance

With that look in his face, half night, half light,
Like the lake gust-blackened yet ridged with white.
There were comely wonders before he died :
The eagle barked and the Banshee cried ;
The witch-elm wept with a blighted bud ;
The spray of the torrent was red with blood ;
The Chief, returned from the mountain's bound,
Forgat to ask after Bran, his hound.
We knew he would die ; three days passed o'er ;
He died.   We *waked* him for three days more.
One by one, upon brow and breast
The whole clan kissed him.   In peace may he rest .

. . . . . .

XII

How long He leaves me—the great God—here !
  Have I sinned some sin, or has God forgotten ?
This year, I think, is my hundredth year :
  I am like a bad apple, unripe yet rotten.
They shall lift me ere long, they shall lay me—the clan—
By the strength of men on Mount Cruachan.
God has much to think of.   How much He has seen
And how much has gone by that once has been !
On sandy hills where the rabbits burrow
  Are raths of Kings men name not now ;
On mountain tops I have tracked the furrow,
  And found in forests the buried plough.
For one now living the strong land then
Gave kindly food and raiment to ten.
No doubt they waxed proud, and their God defied ;
  So their harvest He blighted or burned their hoard ;
  Or He sent them plague, or He sent the sword ;
  Or He sent them lightning ; and so they died
Like Dathi, the King, on the dark Alp's side.

XIII

Ah me ! that man who is made of dust
  Should have pride toward God !   'Tis a demon's spleen.
I have often feared lest God, the All-just,
  Should bend from heaven and sweep earth clean—

Should sweep us all into corners and holes,
Like dust of the house-floor, both bodies and souls.
I have often feared He would send some wind
In wrath, and the nation wake up stone-blind.
In age or in youth we have all wrought ill :
I say not our great King Nial did well,
Although he was Lord of the Pledges Nine,
    When, beside subduing this land of Eire,
He raised in Armorica banner and sign
    And wasted the British coast with fire.
Perhaps in His mercy the Lord will say :
' These men !   God's help !   'Twas a rough boy-play !
He is certain, that young Franciscan priest,
God sees great sin where men see least :
Yet this were to give unto God the eye—
Unmeet the thought !– of the humming fly.
I trust there are small things He scorns to see
In the lowly who cry to Him piteously.
Our hope is Christ.   I have wept full oft
    He came not to Eire in Oisin's time ;
Though love and those new monks would make men
        soft
    If they were not hardened by war and rhyme.
I have done my part : my end draws nigh :
I shall leave Old Eire with a smile and sigh :
She will miss not me as I missed my son :
Yet for her, and her praise, were my best deeds done.
Man's deeds ! man's deeds ! they are shades that fleet,
Or ripples like those that break at my feet :
The deeds of my Chief and the deeds of my King
Grow hazy, far seen, like the hills in spring.
Nothing is great save the death on the Cross.
    But Pilate and Herod I hate, and know
    Had Fionn lived then he had laid them low,
Though the world thereby had sustained great loss.
My blindness and deafness and aching back
With meekness I bear for that suffering's sake
And the Lent-fast for Mary's sake I love,
And the honour of Him the Man above !

My songs are all over now :—so best !
They are laid in the Heavenly Singer's breast,
Who never sings but a star is born :
May we hear His song in the endless morn !
I give glory to God for our battles won
    By wood or river, on bay or creek ;
For Norna—who died ; for my father, Conn ;
    For feasts, and the chase on the mountains bleak.
I bewail my sins, both unknown and known,
    And of those I have injured forgiveness seek.
The men that were wicked to me and mine—
Not quenching a wrong, nor in war or wine—
I forgive and absolve them all, save three :
May Christ in His mercy be kind to me !

THE WEDDING OF THE CLANS

I GO to knit two clans together,
    Our clan and this clan unseen of yore.
Our clan fears naught ; but I go, oh, whither?
    This day I go from my mother's door.

Thou, redbreast, singest the old song over,
    Though many a time hast thou sung it before ;
They never sent thee to some strange new lover
    To sing a new song by my mother's door.

I stepped from my little room down by the ladder—
    The ladder that never so shook before ;
I was sad last night, to-day I am sadder,
    Because I go from my mother's door.

The last snow melts upon bush and bramble,
    The gold bars shine on the forest's floor ;
Shake not, thou leaf ; it is I must tremble,
    Because I go from my mother's door.

From a Spanish sailor a dagger I bought me,
    I trailed a rose-bush our grey bawn o'er ;
The creed and the letters our old bard taught me ;
    My days were sweet by my mother's door.

My little white goat, that with raised feet huggest
  The oak stock, thy horns in the ivy frore ;
Could I wrestle like thee—how the wreaths thou tuggest !—
  I never would move from my mother's door.

Oh, weep no longer, my nurse and mother ;
  My foster-sister, weep not so sore ;
You cannot come with me, Ir, my brother—
  Alone I go from my mother's door.

Farewell, my wolf-hound, that slew MacOwing,
  As he caught me and far through the thickets bore,
My heifer Alb in the green vale lowing,
  My cygnet's nest upon Loma's shore.

He has killed ten Chiefs, this Chief that plights me,
  His hand is like that of the giant Balor ;
But I fear his kiss, and his beard affrights me,
  And the great stone dragon above his door.

Had I daughters nine, with me they should tarry ;
  They should sing old songs ; they should dance at my door
They should grind at the quern, no need to marry !
  Oh, when shall this marriage day be o'er ?

Had I buried, like Moirín, three mates already,
  I might say, Three husbands, then why not four ?
But my hand is cold, and my foot unsteady,
  Because I never was married before !

DIRGE OF RORY O'MORE

A.D. 1642

UP the sea-saddened valley, at evening's decline,
A heifer walks lowing—' the Silk of the Kine ; '
From the deep to the mountains she roams, and again
From the mountain's green urn to the purple-rimmed main.

What seek'st thou, sad mother ?   Thine own is not thine !
He dropped from the headland—he sank in the brine !
'Twas a dream ! but in dreams at thy foot did he follow
Through the meadow-sweet on by the marish and mallow !

Y

Was he thine? Have they slain him? Thou seek'st him, not
    knowing
Thyself, too, art theirs—thy sweet breath and sad lowing !
Thy gold horn is theirs, thy dark eye and thy silk,
And that which torments thee, thy milk, is their milk !

Twas no dream, Mother Land ! 'Twas no dream, Innisfail !
Hope dreams, but grief dreams not—the grief of the Gael !
From Leix and Ikerrin to Donegal's shore
Rolls the dirge of thy last and thy bravest—O'More !

SONG

I

WHEN I was young, I said to Sorrow:
  'Come and I will play with thee.'
    He is near me now all day,
    And at night returns to say :
  'I will come again to-morrow—
    I will come and stay with thee.'

II

Through the woods we walk together
  His soft footsteps rustle nigh me ;
    To shield an unregarded head
    He hath built a winter shed ;
  And all night in rainy weather
  I hear his gentle breathings by me.

SORROW

COUNT each affliction, whether light or grave,
  God's messenger sent down to thee ; do thou
  With courtesy receive him ; rise and bow ;
And, ere his shadow pass thy threshold, crave
Permission first his heavenly feet to lave ;
  Then lay before him all thou hast : allow
  No cloud of passion to usurp thy brow
Or mar thy hospitality ; no wave

Of mortal tumult to obliterate
The soul's marmoreal calmness ; grief should be—
Like joy—majestic, equable, sedate,
Confirming, cleansing, raising, making free ;
Strong to consume small troubles ; to commend
Great thoughts, grave thoughts, thoughts lasting to the end.

THE YEAR OF SORROW: IRELAND, 1849

SPRING

ONCE more, through God's high will, and grace
  Of hours that each its task fulfils,
Heart-healing Spring resumes her place,
  The valley throngs, and scales the hills.

In vain.   From earth's deep heart, o'ercharged,
  The exulting life runs o'er in flowers.
The slave unfed is unenlarged ;
  In darkness sleep a Nation's powers.

Who knows not Spring ?   Who doubts, when blows
  Her breath, that Spring is come indeed ?
The swallow doubts not ; nor the rose
  That stirs, but wakes not ; nor the weed.

I feel her near, but see her not ;
  For these with pain-uplifted eyes
Fall back repulsed, and vapours blot
  The vision of the earth and skies.

I see her not ; I feel her near,
  As, charioted in mildest airs,
She sails through yon empyreal sphere,
  And in her arms and bosom bears

That urn of flowers and lustral dews
  Whose sacred balm, o'er all things shed,
Revives the weak, the old renews,
  And crowns with votive wreaths the dead.

Once more the cuckoo's call I hear ;
 I know, in many a glen profound,
The earliest violets of the year
 Rise up like water from the ground.

The thorn, I know, once more is white ;
 And, far down many a forest dale,
The anemones in dubious light
 Are trembling like a bridal veil.

By streams released, that singing flow
 From craggy shelf through sylvan glades,
The pale narcissus, well I know,
 Smiles hour by hour on greener shades.

The honeyed cowslip tufts once more
 The golden slopes ; with gradual ray
The primrose stars the rock, and o'er
 The wood-path strews its milky way.

From ruined huts and holes come forth
 Old men, and look upon the sky.
The Power Divine is on the earth :
 Give thanks to God before ye die !

And ye, O children, worn and weak,
 Who care no more with flowers to play,
Lean on the grass your cold, thin cheek
 And those slight hands, and, whispering, say :

' Stern mother of a race unblest,
 In promise kindly, cold in deed,
Take back, O Earth, into thy breast,
 The children whom thou wilt not feed.'

SUMMER

Approved by works of love and might,
 The Year, consummated and crowned,
Hath scaled the zenith's purple height,
 And flings his robe the earth around.

Impassioned stillness, fervours calm,
  Brood, vast and bright, o'er land and deep ;
The warrior sleeps beneath the palm ;
  The dark-eyed captive guards his sleep.

The Iberian labourer rests from toil ;
  Sicilian virgins twine the dance ;
Laugh Tuscan vales in wine and oil ;
  Fresh laurels flash from brows of France.

Far off, in regions of the North,
  The hunter drops his winter fur ;
Sun-wakened babes their feet stretch forth ;
  And nested dormice feebly stir.

But thou, O land of many woes !
  What cheer is thine ?   Again the breath
Of proved Destruction o'er thee blows,
  And sentenced fields grow black in death.

In horror of a new despair
  His blood-shot eyes the peasant strains
With hands clenched fast, and lifted hair,
  Along the daily darkening plains.

Why trusted he to them his store ?
  Why feared he not the scourge to come ? '
Fool ! turn the page of History o'er—
  The roll of Statutes—and be dumb !

Behold, O People ! thou shalt die !
  What art thou better than thy sires ?
The hunted deer a weeping eye
  Turns on his birthplace, and expires.

Lo ! as the closing of a book,
  Or statue from its base o'erthrown,
Or blasted wood, or dried-up brook,
  Name, race, and nation, thou art gone !

The stranger shall thy hearth possess ;
 The stranger build upon thy grave.
But know this also—he, not less,
 His limit and his term shall have.

Once more thy volume, open cast,
 In thunder forth shall sound thy name ;
Thy forest, hot at heart, at last
 God's breath shall kindle into flame.

Thy brook, dried up, a cloud shall rise,
 And stretch an hourly widening hand,
In God's good vengeance, through the skies,
 And onward o'er the Invader's land.

Of thine, one day, a remnant left
 Shall raise o'er earth a Prophet's rod,
And teach the coasts, of Faith bereft,
 The names of Ireland and of God.

AUTUMN

Then die, thou Year—thy work is done ;
 The work, ill done, is done at last ;
Far off, beyond that sinking sun,
 Which sets in blood, I hear the blast

That sings thy dirge, and says : ' Ascend,
 And answer make amid thy peers,
Since all things here must have an end,
 Thou latest of the famine years.'

I join that voice.   No joy have I
 In all thy purple and thy gold ;
Nor in that ninefold harmony
 From forest on to forest rolled ;

Nor in that stormy western fire
 Which burns on ocean's gloomy bed,
And hurls, as from a funeral pyre,
 A glare that strikes the mountain's head ;

And writes on low-hung clouds its lines
  Of ciphered flame, with hurrying hand :
And flings, amid the topmost pines
  That crown the cliff, a burning brand.

Make answer, Year, for all thy dead,
  Who found not rest in hallowed earth :
The widowed wife, the father fled,
  The babe age-stricken from his birth !

Make answer, Year, for virtue lost ;
  For courage, proof 'gainst fraud and force,
Now waning like a noontide ghost ;
  Affections poisoned at their source !

The labourer spurned his lying spade ;
  The yeoman spurned his useless plough ;
The pauper spurned the unwholesome aid
  Obtruded once, exhausted now.

The roof-trees fall of hut and hall ;
  I hear them fall, and falling cry :
' One fate for each, one fate for all !
  So wills the Law that willed a lie.'

Dread power of Man ! what spread the waste
  In circles hour by hour more wide,
And would not let the past be past ?
  That Law which promised much, and lied.

Dread power of God, Whom mortal years
  Nor touch, nor tempt, Who sitt'st sublime
In night of night—oh, bid Thy spheres
  Resound, at last, a funeral chime !

Call up at last the afflicted race,
  Whom Man, not God, abolished.   Sore,
For centuries, their strife ; the place
  That knew them once shall know no more !

WINTER

Fall, snow, and cease not ! Flake by flake
    The decent winding-sheet compose ;
Thy task is just and pious ; make
    An end of blasphemies and woes !

Fall, flake by flake ! by thee alone,
    Last friend, the sleeping draught is given.
Kind nurse, by thee the couch is strown—
    The couch whose covering is from Heaven.

Descend and clasp the mountain's crest ;
    Inherit plain and valley deep.
This night on thy maternal breast
    A vanquished nation dies in sleep.

Lo ! from the starry Temple Gates
    Death rides, and bears the flag of peace ;
The combatants he separates ;
    He bids the wrath of ages cease.

Descend, benignant Power ! But, oh,
    Ye torrents, shake no more the vale !
Dark streams, in silence seaward flow !
    Thou rising storm, remit thy wail !

Shake not, to-night, the cliffs of Moher,
    Nor Brandon's base, rough sea ! Thou Isle,
The Rite proceeds ! From shore to shore
    Hold in thy gathered breath the while !

Fall, snow ! in stillness fall, like dew,
    On church's roof and cedar's fan ;
And mould thyself on pine and yew,
    And on the awful face of Man.

Without a sound, without a stir,
    In streets and wolds, on rock and mound,
O omnipresent Comforter,
    By Thee this night the lost are found !

On quaking moor and mountain moss,
  With eyes upstaring at the sky,
And arms extended like a cross,
  The long-expectant sufferers lie.

Bend o'er them, white-robed Acolyte !
  Put forth thine hand from cloud and mist ;
And minister the last sad Rite,
  Where altar there is none, nor priest ;

Touch thou the gates of soul and sense ;
  Touch darkening eyes and dying ears ;
Touch stiffening hands and feet, and thence
  Remove the trace of sins and tears !

And, ere thou seal those filméd eyes,
  Into God's urn thy fingers dip,
And lay, 'mid eucharistic sighs,
  The sacred wafer on the lip.

This night the Absolver issues forth ;
  This night the Eternal Victim bleeds.
O winds and woods, O heaven and earth,
  Be still this night ! The Rite proceeds !

THE LITTLE BLACK ROSE

THE Little Black Rose [1] shall be red at last ;
  What made it black but the March wind dry,
And the tear of the widow that fell on it fast ?
  It shall redden the hills when June is nigh !

The Silk of the Kine [1] shall rest at last ;
  What drove her forth but the dragon fly ?
In the golden vale she shall feed full fast,
  With her mild gold horn and her slow, dark eye.

The wounded wood-dove lies dead at last !
  The pine long-bleeding, it shall not die !
This song is secret. Mine ear it passed
  In a wind o'er the plains at Athenry.

---

[1] Mystical names of Ireland, frequently occurring in Gaelic poetry.

GEORGE SIGERSON

DR. SIGERSON in the Ireland of to-day stands forward a potent personality, to link in an embrace of amity the spirits of the Gall and of the Gael. Gall of the Gall himself, he is yet, as were also his ancestors, more Gaelic than the Gael ; and how thoroughly his ancestors had become one in soul and spirit with their new country the lament of the eighteenth-century poet for Francis Sigerson shows, for he describes the Suir as overflowing in its grief, the hills of Ireland as opening, and the Skellings as shrieking aloud 'A man has died'—all three bewailing.

> The handsome Hawk who towered the country o'er,
> Top-spray of all who sprang from Sigerson Mór.

And he himself has been true to his ancestry, for while no man has been more keen than he in investigating the history of his own forefathers, the Northmen, no man has at the same time done more to save and popularise the literature of the Irish Gael, the men whom his ancestors first met as their red-enemies. It is now close upon forty years ago since, in conjunction with old John O'Daly of Anglesea Street, Dublin, he took up the work which fell from the hands of Mangan, and in the second series of the POETS AND POETRY OF MUNSTER performed a task of immense service to the then neglected cause of native Irish literature, by publishing with metrical translations the text of nearly fifty Munster poems of great beauty. For close upon three decades he and John O'Daly held aloft almost single-handed the banner of the Irish Gael, and their efforts prepared the way for the great and real revival of the last three years. From the very earliest did Dr. Sigerson fall under the spell of that strange wild witch-soul which steals through Ireland under many names—whom some of our fathers have known as 'Moneen,' others as 'Sheela the Bright,' and others again as 'Kathleen' daughter of Houlihan—

and ever since his youth he has been her faithful attendant, proceeding in her cause from service to service, and finishing one task for her, only to take up another. For as leader-writer, essayist, land-reformer, scientist, poet, and lastly as President of the National Literary Society, Dr. Sigerson has performed for the 'Sean Bhean Bhocht' the part of many workers, and his home has been the rendezvous of those who loved her.

His recent book of translations from the Irish, THE BARDS OF THE GAEL AND GALL,[1] is really an extension into the past of his POETRY OF MUNSTER, and it is a contribution to the so-called Celtic Revival the importance of which it would be difficult to over-estimate. In this work he has given metrical translations of about one hundred and forty Irish poems, covering the ground from the earliest unrhymed chant ascribed to the first invading Milesian, down to the peasant songs of the last century. He has thus, for the first time, brought before the English reader a long gallery of poetic pictures, receding back into the past, and extending demonstrably over a period of one thousand two hundred years, and quite possibly over two thousand, and such as no other country in Europe except one can boast of. His merit as a translator is great, and his rhymed versions are the result of a subtle fusion of scholar and poet. To catch the music of Irish verse is extremely difficult ; it is perhaps easier to catch its spirit than its music ; but Dr. Sigerson has in many cases yoked both together with an extreme felicity. The heptasyllabic lines that prior to the seventeenth century were so beloved by the Irish are extremely hard to reproduce in English, which is far more suited to an octosyllabic measure ; but in scarcely any case has the translator allowed himself to be seduced from the severe path of scholarship, and his translations may be better relied on by the English reader for their accuracy than those of any other who has ever attempted to turn Irish into English verses. Indeed, this fidelity to his originals enormously enhances the value of the book for those who may consult it for other reasons than

[1] Fisher Unwin, 1897.

those of pure poetry. It is a book which is at present essential
to all who would form for themselves an idea of the Irish
literary past and of Irish versification.

As an original poet Dr. Sigerson is perhaps most distinctly a lyrist, as is natural to one who has come under the
native Irish spell. Many of his songs are written, like the
Gaelic ones, to Irish airs, and most of them lend themselves
naturally to music. The nobler characteristics of Irish verse,
which he has acquired from his lifelong acquaintance with the
Gaelic poets, tinge his own verses very appreciably—especially
the smoothness, the desire for recurrent or even interwoven
vowel sounds, and the love of alliteration, which when wholly
natural and devoid of any obtrusiveness, as they are here,
possess in themselves a subtle charm which is very Irish.
These characteristics will strike the careful reader in such
lyrics as 'Far-Away,' 'The Swans of Tir,' or 'The Roman
Tree ;' while they are wholly absent from the fine elegy on
Isaac Butt, with the severity of which they would not be in
keeping.

                                    DOUGLAS HYDE (AN CHRAOIBHIN).

George Sigerson, a native of Tyrone, was a descendant of a Norse-Irish
family, whose name, Filius Segeri, is on the oldest municipal roll of
Dublin (twelfth century). His studies in arts and medicine were chiefly
pursued in Paris, where he was a pupil of Claude Bernard, Duchenne (de
Boulogne), Charcot, Ranvier, Ball, and Béhier. His first medical treatise
was published at the instance of Duchenne ; he translated and edited the
first two volumes of Charcot, on DISEASES OF THE NERVOUS SYSTEM.
Darwin was interested in his biological work, and Tyndall observed that
his microscopic researches on the atmosphere revealed the true nature of
the organisms whose presence he himself had detected. As a sequel to his
work on the Dublin Mansion House Committee in 1880–81 (of which he
was named Medical Commissioner), he published a tract on the NEED AND
USE OF VILLAGE HOSPITALS in 1882. As a member of Lord Spencer's
Royal Commission on Prisons, in 1883–84, he aided in improving the dietary
(an improvement since followed in England) and the condition of weak-
minded prisoners, and in having a Medical Commissioner appointed. As a
sequel he published, in 1890, a work on THE TREATMENT OF POLITICAL
PRISONERS. He also published a book entitled MODERN IRELAND ; his
study of the LAND TENURES AND LAND CLASSES OF IRELAND was read

by Mr. Gladstone in proof, and convinced him on the subject of customary rights, which he embodied in his first Land Law. Having, when a student, given some versions of the Munster poets (second series), he in 1897 produced an Irish anthology, BARDS OF THE GAEL AND GALL: DONE INTO ENGLISH AFTER THE MODES AND METRES OF THE GAEL. He also prepared an analysis, with metrical examples, of the CARMEN PASCHALE of Sedulius, the first saint of Erin and her only epic poet. In 1913 his poem in blank verse, THE SAGA OF KING LIR, appeared. He was a Fellow of the Royal University, professor of Biology in University College, and President of the National Literary Society from 1893 until his death in 1925.

THE LOST TRIBUNE

TO THE MEMORY OF ISAAC BUTT

FAREWELL ! the doom is spoken.   All is o'er.
   One heart we loved is silent ; and one head,
Whose counsel guided Nations, guides no more ;
   A Man of the few foremost Men is dead.

With giant might of mind and mould of form
   He towered aloft ; with mightier love he bowed :
Strong not alone to dominate the storm,
   To brave the haughty, and rebuke the proud—

But strong to weep, to heed an infant's care,
   To gather sorrow to his heart ; nor scorn
To stoop from Fortune's brilliant ranks and share
   A weight of woe to which he was not born.

The secret of his greatness, there behold !
   More truly there than in th' unrivalled fence,
The vivid wit, the reason keen and bold,
   And all the power of peerless eloquence !

Mark yonder peasants who, in dumb despair,
   Kneel down to kiss the ruins of their home,
While beats the rain upon their hoary hair,
   Then turn to face the salt Atlantic foam ;

See, where yon massive dungeon walls surround
 The pale confessors of a country's cause,
Their grave, perchance, that plot of felon ground,
 Their name, their honour, branded by the laws—

These were his clients. Their defender he
 Whose genius, wielding justice as a glaive,
Delivered those from the strange bitter sea,
 And these from prison gyve and felon grave.

One chiefly served he, with chivalric faith ;
 One chiefly loved he, with devoted soul ;
His shield was spread between her breast and scathe ;
 His life was spent to save her life from dole.

Her fallen banner from the dust he raised,
 And proud advanced it, with uplifted brow,
Till the sun kissed it, and the Nations gazed—
 Whose was that Standard ? Answer, Erin, thou !

Farewell to all of personal joy that came
 Of seeing, 'mid these common days, a man
Titanic, victor of enduring fame,
 Whose immortality on earth began ;

Of that enlargement which the mind receives,
 The wider range, the deeper, subtler sense,
The higher flight of thought that upward cleaves,
 When near us moves a great Intelligence

But not farewell to him who hath outgrown
 The confines of mortality ; he survives
In every heart, and shall henceforth be known
 Long as his country loves, long as his Nation lives !

THE CALLING

O SIGH of the Sea, O soft lone-wandering sound,
Why callest thou me, with voice of all waters profound,
With sob and with smile, with lingering pain and delight,
With mornings of blue, with flash of thy billows at night ?

The shell from the shore, though borne far away from thy side,
Recalls evermore the flowing and fall of thy tide,
And so, through my heart thy murmurs gather and grow—
Thy tides, as of old, awake in its darkness, and flow.

O Sigh of the Sea, from luminous isles far away,
Why callest thou me to sail the impassable way?
Why callest thou me to share the unrest of thy soul—
Desires that avail not, yearnings from pole unto pole?

Still call, till I hear no voice but the voice of thy love,
Till stars shall appear the night of my darkness above,
Till night to the dawn gives way, and death to new life—
Heart-full of thy might, astir with thy tumult and strife.

Far-Away

As chimes that flow o'er shining seas
    When Morn alights on meads of May,
Faint voices fill the western breeze
    With whisp'ring songs from Far-Away.
        Oh, dear the dells of Dunanore,
            A home is odorous Ossory ;
        But sweet as honey, running o'er,
            The Golden Shore of Far-Away !

There grows the Tree whose summer breath
    Perfumes with joy the azure air ;
And he who feels it fears not Death,
    Nor longer heeds the hounds of Care.
        Oh, soft the skies of Seskinore,
            And mild is meadowy Mellaray ;
        But sweet as honey, running o'er,
            The Golden Shore of Far-Away !

There sings the Voice whose wondrous tune
    Falls, like diamond-showers above
That in the radiant dawn of June
    Renew a world of Youth and Love.
        Oh, fair the founts of Farranfore,
            And bright is billowy Ballintrae ;
        But sweet as honey, running o'er,
            The Golden Shore of Far-Away !

Come, Fragrance of the Flowering Tree,
Oh, sing, sweet Bird, thy magic lay,
Till all the world be young with me,
And Love shall lead us far away.
Oh, dear the dells of Dunanore,
A home is odorous Ossory ;
But sweet as honey, running o'er,
The Golden Shore of Far-Away !

The Blackbird's Song

from the irish : a.d. 850

An Irish scribe in the monastery of St. Gall, in Switzerland, while copying a Latin MS., heard a thrush's song in the woods outside his cell, and paused to indite these quatrains on the margin of his MS., where they were found by the Cavaliere Nigra, and published in Reliquie Celtiche, 1872. Note that at this early date (about 850) the Gaelic system of rhyming verse with its internal chimes is fully developed.

Great woods gird me now around,
With sweet sound Merle sings to me ;
My much-lined pages over
Sings its lover-minstrelsie.

Soft it sings its measured song,
Hid among the tree-tops green ;
May God on high thus love me,
Thus approve me, all unseen.

The Ruined Nest

author unknown

The original of this touching poem is found in ' the famous fourteenth-century manuscript known as the Lebor Breac,' writes Prof. Kuno Meyer, who first edited it and translated it for *The Gaelic Journal*, 1890. It was composed long before the fourteenth century.—*Translator's note.*

Sad is yonder blackbird's song,
Well I know what wrought it wrong ;
Whosoe'er the deed has done,
Now its nestlings all are gone.

Such a sorrow I, too, know
For such loss, not long ago ;
Well, O bird, I read thy state,
For a home laid desolate.

How thy heart has burned, nigh broke,
At the rude and reckless stroke ;
To lay waste thy little nest
Seems to cowboys but a jest.

Thy clear note called together
Flutt'ring young in new feather ;
From thy nest comes now not one—
O'er its mouth the nettle's gone.

Sudden came the callous boys,
Their deed all thy young destroys ;
Thou and I one fate deplore,
For my children are no more.

By thy side there used to be
Thy sweet mate from o'er the sea ;
The herd's net ensnared her head,
She is gone from thee—and dead.

O Ruler of high heaven,
Thou'st laid our loads uneven ;
For our friends on ev'ry side
'Mid their mates and children bide.

Hither came hosts of Faery
To waste our home unwary :
Though they left no wound to tell,
Brunt of battle were less fell.

Woe for wife—for children, woe !
I in sorrow's shadow go ;
Not a trace of them I had !
Hence my heavy heart is sad.

z

THE DIRGE OF CAEL

FROM THE IRISH : BY CRÉDÉ, HIS SPOUSE

The rhymes and metre of the original are given. It is taken from a Bodleian MS. of the fourteenth century.

MOANS the bay—
Billows gray round Ventry roar ;
Drowned is Cael MacCrimtann brave—
'Tis for him sob wave and shore.

Heron hoar
'Mid the moor of Dromatren,
Found the fox her young attack,
Bleeding, drove him back again.

Sore the sigh
Sobs the stag from Drumlis nigh ;
Dead the hind of high Drumsailin,
Hence the sad stag's wailing cry.

Wild the wail
From the thrush of Drumkeen's dale ;
Not less sad the blackbird's song,
Mourning long in Leitir's vale.

Woe is me !
Dead my Cael is, fair and free ;
Oft my arms would ward his sleep,
Now it is the deep, dark sea.

Woe, the roar
Rolling round from sea and shore ;
Since he fought the foreign foe,
Mine the woe for Cael no more.

Sad the sound,
From the beach and billows round ;
I have seen my time this day :
Change in form and face is found.

Ever raining,
Fall the plaining waves above ;
I have hope of joy no more,
Since 'tis o'er, our bond of love.

Dead, the swan
Mourns his mate on waters wan ;
Great the grief that makes me know,
Share of woe with dying swan.

Drowned was Cael MacCrimtann brave,
Now I've nought of life my own ;
Heroes fell before his glaive,
His high shield has ceased to moan.

THINGS DELIGHTFUL

FROM THE IRISH : OISIN

The original appeared in the Dean of Lismore's Book

SWEET is a voice in the land of gold,
Sweet is the calling of wild birds bold ;
Sweet is the shriek of the heron hoar,
Sweet fall the billows of Bundatrore.

Sweet is the sound of the blowing breeze,
Sweet is the blackbird's song in the trees ;
Lovely the sheen of the shining sun,
Sweet is the thrush over Casacon.

Sweet shouts the eagle of Assaroe,
Where the gray seas of MacMorna flow ;
Sweet calls the cuckoo the valleys o'er,
Sweet, through the silence, the corrie's roar.

Fionn, my father, is chieftain old
Of seven battalions of Fianna bold ;
When he sets free all the deerhounds fleet
To rise and to follow with him were sweet.

SOLACE IN WINTER

FROM THE IRISH : CAILTÉ *loquitur*

From SILVA GADELICA : Colloquy with the Ancients
Circa A.D. 1200

CHILL the winter, cold the wind,
Up the stag springs, stark of mind :
Fierce and bare the mountain fells—
But the brave stag boldly bells.

He will set not side to rest
On Sliav Carna's snowy breast ;
Echta's stag, also rousing,
Hears wail of wolves carousing.

Cailté I, and Diarmid Donn,
Oft, with Oscar apt to run,
When piercing night was paling
Heard rousing wolves a-wailing.

Sound may sleep the russet stag,
With his hide hid in the crag ;
Him, hidden, nothing aileth
When piercing night prevaileth.

I am aged now and gray,
Few of men I meet this day
But I hurled the javelin bold
Of a morning, icy cold.

Thanks unto the King of Heaven,
And the Virgin's Son be given :
Many men have I made still,
Who this night are very chill.

LAY OF NORSE-IRISH SEA-KINGS

FROM THE IRISH OF ARTUR MacGURCAICH, THE BLIND

Dean of Lismore's Book, pp. 117–151. Sweyn has been Gaelicised ' Suivne '
and ' Sweeney —but this is a confusion of the Norse with a somewhat similar
Gaelic name.—*Translator's note.*

FAIR our fleet at Castle Sweyn—
Glad good news for Innisfail !—
Never rode on bounding brine
Barks so fine with soaring sail.

Tall men urge the ships and steer
Our light, leaping, valiant van ;
Each hand holds a champion's spear—
Gay of cheer is ev'ry man.

Coats of black the warriors wear
On the barks with tree-mast tall ;
Broad the brown belts that they bear,
Norse and Nobles are they all.

Sword-hilts gold and iv'ry gleam
On our barks with banners high ;
Hung on hooks the bucklers beam,
Sheaves of spears are standing nigh.

Purple wings our ships expand
O'er the fleckt and flowing wave ;
'Mid the masts the champions stand
Fit for foray, mild and brave.

Blue is the sea surrounding
Prows o'er the billows bounding ;
Swords in their sheaths are glowing,
The lances thrill for throwing.

Fair are the forms reclining
On the cushioned couches high,
Wives in their beauty shining
'Neath the chequered canopy.

Silks in varied fold on fold
Clothe our king-ship sailing fast ;
Silks of purple splendour hold
Wells of wind at every mast.

There is seen no hardened hand—
Waist of worker belted tight ;
High-voiced heroes hold command,
Fond of music, play, and fight.

Ne'er did Finn or Fianna know
Gallant chiefs of deeds more grand,
Nor could Erinn braver show
Than this fair-haired battle band.

Swifter ship of ships there's none—
None shall go, and none has gone ;
Here comes nor sigh nor sorrow,
Night or noon, day or morrow.

Fleeter bark of barks ne'er fared—
Full of princely folk she goes ;
Gold with bards they've, gen'rous, shared
While the foam-topt ocean flows.

Who took this fleet together
Close to the high hill heather ?
Dauntless he ; he braves the blast—
Claims his right with upraised mast.

Sail the ship, Ion, son of Sweyn !
O'er the hard-backed brilliant brine ;
Raise aloft its conq'ring crown
O'er the billows' fret and frown.

Many welcomes, many smiles,
Greet our ship, 'mid Alba's isles ;
Bards, the narrow seas among,
Welcome us with harp and song.

Then we came to Castle Sweyn,
Like a bright hawk o'er the brine ;
By that rock we raised the fight,
Facing foes with fierce delight.

There we pierced the foreign foes
As the stinging serpent goes ;
Sore we smote them, men and lords,
With our thin, sharp, shearing swords.

Chanting Sweyn-son's battle-song,
All the surging seas along ;
Till the shore-rock, tall and black,
Over ocean sends it back.

Vain their spears and swords and darts,
Our brown bucklers hold our hearts ;
Rocky Rathlin,[1] rousing, hears
Singing of our swords and spears.

That thin sword is Europe's best,
That swift spear serves each behest ;
Where were shield safe in the world
When the victor weapon's hurled ?

Son of Sweyn, whose ways are wide,
These keen arms keeps at his side ;
Be it now the blind bard's care
Him to sing, strong, sage, and fair.

---

[1] An isle off the north coast of Ireland.

LOVE'S DESPAIR

FROM THE IRISH OF DIARMAD O'CURNAIN

O'Curnain was born in Cork in 1740, and died in Modeligo, Waterford, in the first quarter of the present century. He was a tall, handsome young farmer. He travelled to Cork to purchase wedding presents for his betrothed, but was met on his way home by the news that she had married a wealthy suitor. He flung all his presents into the fire, and, from the shock, lost his reason, which he never recovered. He was known to several persons recently alive.—*Translator's note.*

I AM desolate,
Bereft by bitter fate ;
No cure beneath the skies can save me,
No cure on sea or strand,
Nor in any human hand—
But hers, this paining wound who gave me.

I know not night from day,
Nor thrush from cuckoo gray,
Nor cloud from the sun that shines above thee—
Nor freezing cold from heat,
Nor friend—if friend I meet ;
I but know—heart's love !—I love thee.

Love that my life began,
Love that will close life's span,
Love that grows ever by love-giving ;
Love from the first to last,
Love till all life be passed,
Love that loves on after living !

This love I gave to thee,
For pain love has given me,
Love that can fail or falter never—
But, spite of earth above,
Guards thee, my Flower of love,
Thou Marvel-maid of life, for ever.

Bear all things evidence,
Thou art my very sense,

My past, my present, and my morrow !
   All else on earth is crossed,
   All in the world is lost—
Lost all, but the great love-gift of sorrow.

   My life not life, but death :
   My voice not voice—a breath ;
No sleep, no quiet—thinking ever
   On thy fair phantom face,
   Queen eyes and royal grace,
Lost loveliness that leaves me never.

   I pray thee grant but this :
   From thy dear mouth one kiss,
That the pang of death-despair pass over :
   Or bid make ready nigh
   The place where I shall lie,
For aye, thy leal and silent lover.

WHITLEY STOKES

Mr. Whitley Stokes was born in Dublin in 1830, and was the eldest son of William Stokes, M.D., Regius Professor of Medicine in Trinity College, Dublin. He was educated at Trinity College. A pupil of A. Cayley, H. M. Cairns, and T. Chitty, he was called to the English bar, and went in 1862 to India, where he became Secretary to the Government in the Legislative Department, Law Member of the Viceroy's Council, and President of the Indian Law Commission. It was at this time that Mr. Matthew Arnold, in his Celtic Literature, wrote of Mr. Whitley Stokes as ' one of the very ablest scholars formed in Zeuss's school, a born philologist —he now occupies, alas ! a post under the Government of India.' In spite of this disability, however, Mr. Stokes, besides The Anglo-Indian Codes and other legal works, produced editions and translations of ancient Irish texts which placed him at the head of Celtic scholarship in Europe, and revealed to Irish and English readers a great deal of what is best in ancient Irish literature. His translation of the tale of Deirdre, in Windisch and Stokes's IRISCHE TEXTE, Bd. II., has given us the noblest relic of that literature which yet survives in pure and unmutilated form. He published the Cornish dramas —THE PASSION (Berlin, 1862) and GUREANS AN BYS; OR, THE CREATION OF THE WORLD (1864), edited Old-Welsh and Old-Breton glosses; and contributed verse to *The Academy* and other periodicals. His Irish version of Lucan's BELLUM CIVILE was finished during the last year of his life. The following poems are founded on Celtic originals, but are not translations. Mr. Stokes was an honorary D.C.L. of Oxford, an honorary LL.D. of Dublin and Edinburgh, a Foreign Associate of the Institute of France, and an honorary member of the German Oriental Society. He died in 1909.

LAMENT FOR KING IVOR

Place.—The south-west coast of Ireland. *Time.*—The middle of the ninth century. *Author.*—The hereditary bard of a Kerry clan. *Cause of making.*—To lament his King, slain in battle with Danish Vikings.

THOU golden sunshine in the peaceful day !
　　Thou livid lightning in the night of war !
　　Hearing the onrush of thy battle-car,
Who could endure to meet thee in the fray ?

Who dared to see thine eyes aflame in fight,
　　Thou stormer through the whistling storm of darts ?
　　Pourer of panic into heroes' hearts !
Our hope, our strength, our glory, our delight !

Thy soul is striding down the perilous road ;
　　And, see, the ghosts of heathen whom thy spear
　　Laid low, arise and follow in their fear
Him who is braver than their bravest god !

Why is thy soul surrounded by no more
　　Of thine adoring clansmen ? 'You had been
　　Full worthy,' wouldst thou answer, hadst thou seen
The charge that drove the pirates from our shore.

But thou wast lying prone upon the sand,
  Death-wounded, blind with blood, and gasping : ' Go !
  Two swords are somewhat ; join the rest.   I know
Another charge will beat them from the land.'

So when the slaughter of the Danes was done,
  We found thee dead—a-stare with sunken eyes
  At those red surges, and bewailed by cries
Of sea-mews sailing from the fallen sun.

We kissed thee, one by one, lamenting sore :
  Men's tears have washed the blood-stain from thy brow ;
  Thy spear and sword and our dear love hast thou :
We have thy name and fame for evermore.

So sang the warriors to their clouded star,
  King Ivor, as they heapt his cairn on high ;
  A landmark to the sailor sailing by,
A warning to the spoiler from afar.

KING AILILL'S DEATH

FROM THE EARLY MIDDLE IRISH
Book of Leinster, fol. 214

I KNOW who won the peace of God,
  King Ailill, called ' the Beardless Man ;'
Who fought beyond the Irish Sea
  All day against a Connaught clan.

His host was broken : as he fled
  He muttered to his charioteer :
' Look back—the slaughter, is it red ?
  The slayers, are they drawing near ? '

The boy looks back.   The west wind blows
  Dead clansmen's hair against his face ;
He heard the war-shout of his foes,
  The death-cry of his ruined race.

The foes came darting from the height,
  Like pine trees down a flooded fall :
Like heaps of hay in spate, his clan
  Swept on or sank—he saw it all.

And spake : 'The slaughter is full red,
    But *we* may still be saved by flight.'
Then groaned the king : ' No sin of theirs
    Falls on my people here to-night :

' No sin of theirs, but sin of mine,
    For I was worst of evil kings ;
Unrighteous, wrathful, hurling down
    To death or shame all weaker things.

' Draw rein, and turn the chariot round :
    My face against the foeman bend ;
When I am seen and slain, mayhap
    The slaughter of my tribe will end.'

They drew, and turned.   Down came the foe,
    The king fell cloven on the sod ;
The slaughter then was stayed, and so
    King Ailill won the peace of God.

Man Octipartite

FROM THE MIDDLE IRISH

Cod. Clarend. (Mus. Brit.), vol. xv. fol. 7*a*, col. 1

Thus sang the sages of the Gael
    A thousand years ago well-nigh :
    ' Hearken how the Lord on high
Wrought man, to breathe and laugh and wail,
To hunt and war, to plough and sail,
    To love and teach, to pray and die ! '

Then said the sages of the Gael :

    ' Of parcels eight was Adam built.
    The first was earth, the second sea,
    The third and fourth were sun and cloud,
    The fifth was wind, the sixth was stone,
    The seventh was the Holy Ghost,
    The last, the Light which lighteth God.'

Then sang the sages of the Gael :

' Man's body, first, was built of earth
To lodge a living soul from birth,
And earthward home again to go
When Time and Death have spoken so.
Then of the sea his blood was dight
To bound in love and flow in fight.
Next, of the sun, to see the skies,
His face was framed with shining eyes.
From hurrying hosts of cloud was wrought
His roaming, rapid-changeful thought.
Then of the wind was made his breath
To come and go from birth to death.
And then of earth-sustaining stone
Was built his flesh-upholding bone.
The Holy Ghost, like cloven flame,
The substance of his soul became ;
Of Light which lighteth God was made
Man's conscience, so that unafraid
His soul through haunts of night and sin
May pass and keep all clean within.

' Now, if the earthiness redound,
He lags through life a slothful hound.
But, if it be the sea that sways,
In wild unrest he wastes his days.
Whene'er the sun is sovran, there
The heart is light, the face is fair.
If clouds prevail, he lives in dreams
A deedless life of gloom and gleams.
' If stone bear rule, he masters men,
And ruthless is their ransom then.
But when the wind has won command,
His word is harder than his hand.
The Holy Ghost, if He prevail,
Man lives exempt from lasting bale,
And, gazing with the eyes of God,
Of all he sees at home, abroad,

Discerns the inmost heart, and then
Reveals it to his fellow-men,
And they are truer, gentler, more
Heroic than they were before.

'But he on whom the Light Divine
Is lavished bears the sacred sign,
And men draw nigh in field or mart
To hear the wisdom of his heart.
For he is calm and clear of face,
And unperplexed he runs his race,
Because his mind is always bent
On Right, regardless of event.

'Of each of those eight things decreed
To make and mould the human breed,
Let more or less in man and man
Be set as God has framed His plan.
But still there is a ninth in store
(Oh grant it now and evermore !)—
Our Freedom, wanting which, we read,
    The bulk of earth, the strength of stone,
The bounding life o' the sea, the speed
    Of clouds, the splendour of the sun,
The never-flagging flight of wind,
    The fervour of the Holy Ghost,
    The Light before the angels' host,
Though all be in our frame combined,
Grow tainted, yea, of no avail.'

So sang the sages of the Gael.

JOHN TODHUNTER

DR. TODHUNTER's gifts and tastes are very various. While it
is not quite certain whether his versatility has been the most
favourable ally of his poetic genius, that it has contributed
charms to his poetic productions is unquestionable. Few

poets have been able to interpret the emotions of music in another art more effectively than he. His 'In a Gondola' (written in Trinity College Park, when he was an under-graduate) exhibits this power to a remarkable degree, and he has written no more genuine poems than the series in which he describes the essential characteristics of the music of Mendelssohn, Beethoven, and Rossini. In these poems he conducts the reader into a region of imagination to which no man who is not a poet ever finds his way alone. His eye for colour and form enables him to describe the objects of Nature with extreme minuteness—a faculty which recalls that of Keats, united with a manner which, no doubt, has been suggested by Keats. The rhythmic swing and verbal melody which abound in some of his poems make us miss them all the more in poems in which he seems deliberately to neglect them. His love of the stage, his intelligent appreciation of the greatest works of the greatest dramatists, and his eye for stage grouping and stage effects, have induced him to write dramas ; but there is little doubt that he has excelled most in his lyrical poems. His humour asserts itself most successfully—certainly most agreeably—in 'Laurella,' which, though closely following Paul Heyse's tale, is yet an original and delightful narrative poem. In this poem the difficult *ottava rima* is handled, frequently after the fashion of 'Beppo' and 'Don Juan,' with skill and dexterity ; and the narrative is so condensed, so well proportioned, and so well arranged, that one cannot help thinking that the author, if he had chosen, might have developed into one of the brightest and pleasantest of our story-tellers in verse. Until about the year 1888 he does not seem to have turned his attention to his native country. In his principal poems on Irish themes he has discarded rhyme in his regular lyrical measures—a dangerous experiment until something better and more pleasing to the ear can be provided as a substitute for it. Dr. Todhunter possesses a priceless gift, without which no man need ever hope to be a poet of the highest order—he is a *thinker* ; all that he has written in verse and prose bears upon it the attractive impress of a mind that has grown rich by reading and by thought, and refined by long self-culture ; and he has at times attained loftier altitudes in poetry than most Irish poets have been able to approach.

G. F. SAVAGE-ARMSTRONG.

Dr. John Todhunter, the elder son of an eminent Dublin merchant, was born in Dublin on December 30, 1839. Both his parents being members of the society of Friends, he received his early education at Quaker schools at Mountmellick and York. At the age of sixteen he was placed in a mercantile establishment in Ireland, but, emancipating himself from uncongenial employment, he entered Trinity College, Dublin, in 1861, with the intention of studying for the medical profession. After a college career of much distinction he took his degree of B.A. in 1865, M.B. in 1866, and M.D. in 1871, and in 1871 also a Diploma in State Medicine, which had been instituted in that year. After rambles and studies on the Continent he settled in Dublin, to practise, in 1870. Between 1870 and 1874 he was Assistant Physician to the Cork Street Fever Hospital in Dublin, and also Lecturer in English Literature at Alexandra College. He acted also as one of the Honorary Secretaries of the Dublin Sanitary Association. In 1874, resigning his appointments for the purpose of devoting himself exclusively to literature, he left Dublin, and resided chiefly in London until his death in 1916.

Among Dr. Todhunter's works are: LAURELLA AND OTHER POEMS, 1876; ALKESTIS (a Drama), 1879; A STUDY OF SHELLEY, 1880; THE TRUE TRAGEDY OF RIENZI, 1881; FOREST SONGS, 1881; HELENA IN TROAS (produced at Hengler's Circus as an imitation of a Greek play), 1885; THE BANSHEE AND OTHER POEMS, 1888; A SICILIAN IDYLL (produced at the theatre of the Club, Bedford Park, and at the Vaudeville), 1891; THE POISON-FLOWER (produced at the Vaudeville), 1891; THE BLACK CAT (produced by the Independent Theatre Society), 1893; A LIFE OF SARSFIELD, 1895; THREE BARDIC TALES, 1896; SOUND AND SWEET AIRS, 1905; TRIVIUM AMORIS AND THE WOOING OF ARTEMIS; and FROM THE LAND OF DREAMS.

MORNING IN THE BAY OF NAPLES

From LAURELLA

LIKE a great burst of singing came the day,
  After the dawn's soft prelude, from heaven's cave ;
Swooping to clasp the billowy-bosomed bay
  In his ecstatic arms, wooing each wave

To give him kiss for kiss.   His glorious way
  Was pioneered by the brisk winds, which gave
New life to the waking world, and filled each sense
With measureless desire and hopes immense.

In short, it was a most delicious morn —
  What clouds there were soared in the upper sky,
Or round the mountains died as they were born
  In the bright haze that clung mysteriously
To the dim coast.   An Amalthea's horn
  Of rathe delight seemed emptied from on high
On all the progeny of land and sea—
Shore-maidens sang and sea birds shrieked for glee.

There was a breath of fragrance in the air
  That stole upon the spirit like young love ;
An incense wafted from, you knew not where—
  From thymy dell and seaweed-scented cove.
Ocean and earth had found each other fair,
  And mingled their fresh lips—the tamarisk grove
Sighed for the kiss of the wave, and waves leapt up
To yield the winds dew for the myrtle's cup.

THE LAMENTATION FOR THE THREE SONS OF TURANN,
WHICH TURANN, THEIR FATHER, MADE OVER THEIR GRAVE

THE LITTLE LAMENTATION [1]

I

Low lie your heads this day,
My sons ! my sons,
Make wide the grave, for I hasten
To lie down among my sons.

II

Bad is life to the father
In the house without a son,
Fallen is the House of Turann,
And with it I lie low.

[1] From THREE IRISH BARDIC TALES, by John Todhunter, 1896.

A A

THE FIRST SORROW

I

The staff of my age is broken !
Three pines I reared in Dun-Turann :
Brian, Iuchar, Iucharba,
Three props of my house they were.

II

They slew a man to their wounding,
In the fierceness of their youth !
For Kian, the son of Cainté,
Their comely heads lie low.

III

A dreadful deed was your doing,
My sons ! my sons !
No counsel ye took with me
When ye slew the son of Cainté.

IV

A bad war with your hands
Ye made upon Innisfail,
A bad feud on your heads
Ye drew when ye slew no stranger.

V

And cruel was the blood-fine
That Lugh of the outstretched arm,
The avenging son of Kian,
Laid on you for his father.

VI

Three apples he claimed, a sow-skin,
A spear, two steeds and a war-car,
Seven swine, and a staghound's whelp,
A spit, three shouts on a mountain.

VII

A little eric it seemed
For the blood of Dé-Danaan ;
A paltry eric and foolish,
Yet there was death for the three !

THE SECOND SORROW

I

Crafty was Lugh, when he laid
The fine on the sons of Turann,
And pale we grew when we fathomed
The mind of the son of Kian.

II

Three apples of gold ye brought him
From the far Hesperian garden ;
Ye slew the King of Greece
For the skin that heals all wounds.

III

Ye took from the King of Persia
The spear more deadly than dragons ;
It keeps the world in danger
With the venom of its blade.

IV

Ye won from the King of Sicil
His horses and his war-car ;
The fleetness of wings their fleetness,
Their highway the land and the sea.

V

The King of the Golden Pillars
Yielded the swine to your challenge ;
Each night they smoked at the banquet,
Each morning they lived again.

VI

Ye took from the King of Iceland
His hound, like the sun for splendour ;
Ye won by your hands of valour
Those wonders, and brought them home.

VII

But short was the eric of Lugh
When your hearts grew hungry for Turann ;
For Lugh had laid upon you
Forgetfulness by his craft.

THE GREAT LAMENTATION

I

Death to the sons of Turann
Had Lugh in his crafty mind :
' Yet lacks of my lawful eric
The spit, three shouts on the mountain.'

II

The strength of the babe was left us
At the hearing of that word—
Brian, Iuchar, Iucharba,
Like dead men they fell down.

III

But Brian your courage kindled,
My sons ! my sons !
For the Island of Finchory
A year long ye searched the seas.

IV

Then Brian set the clearness
Of crystal upon his forehead,
And, his water-dress around him,
Dived through the waves' green gloom.

V

Days twice-seven was he treading
The silent gloom of the deep,
His lanterns the silver salmon,
To the sea-sunk Isle of Finchory.

VI

Soft shone the moony splendour
Of the magic lamps of Finchory ;
There sat in their hall of crystal
The red-haired ocean-wraiths.

VII

Twice-fifty they sat and broidered
With pearls their sea-green mantles ;
But Brian strode to their kitchen
And seized a spit from the rack.

VIII

Soft rippled their silvery laughter,
Like the laughter of summer wavelets :
'Strong is the son of Turann,
But stronger the weakest here.

IX

'And now, should we withstand thee,
No more shouldst thou see thy brothers.
Yet keep the spit for thy daring ;
Brian, we love the bold.'

. . . . .

SONG

BRING from the craggy haunts of birch and pine
Thou wild wind, bring,
Keen forest odours from that realm of thine,
Upon thy wing !

O wind, O mighty, melancholy wind,
            Blow through me, blow !
Thou blowest forgotten things into my mind
            From long ago.

BEETHOVEN

MUSIC as of the winds when they awake,
    Wailing, in the mid forest; music that raves
    Like moonless tides about forlorn sea-caves
On desolate shores, where swell weird songs and break
In peals of demon laughter ; chords athirst
    With restless anguish of divine desires—
    The voice of a vexed soul ere it aspires
With a great cry for light ; anon a burst
Of passionate joy—fierce joy of conscious might,
    Down-sinking in voluptuous luxury ;
Rich harmonies, full-pulsed with deep delight,
    And melodies dying deliciously
As odorous sighs breathed through the quiet night
    By violets.   Thus Beethoven speaks for me.

THE FATE OF THE SONS OF USNA.[1]

From THE FIRST DUAN : THE COMING OF DEIRDRE

SO Kings and Chiefs and Bards, in Eman of the Kings,
Feasted with Felimy ; and rank and order due
Were kept between them all, each Bard, or Chief, or King
Being marshalled to his place by stewards of the feast.
But Conchobar alone came armed into the hall.

And there the amber mead, crowning the golden cup,
Welcomed each noble guest.   There Conall Carnach sat,
Whose eyes, renowned in song, the blue eye and the brown,
Abashed his foes ; but now beamed kindly as he p'edged

---

[1] From THREE IRISH BARDIC TALES, 1896.   Deirdré was the Helen
of the Irish Iliad, and the story of her elopement with Naisi and the
vengeance taken by King Conchobar on the pair forms the most celebrated
of Irish bardic tales.

The man of glorious heart who laughed a realm away—
Fergus MacRoy ; who now pledged him again, and laughed,
With frank heart-easing roar, the laugh that all men loved.

So Fergus laughed, and looked a mighty man of men ;
Ruddy his face, and red the great beard on his breast,
Fergus, whose heart contained the laughter and the tears
Of all the world ; who held the freedom of his mood,
Love, and the dreaming harp that made the world a dream,
The comradeship of feasts, the wild joy of the chase,
Dearer than power ; Fergus, who sang in after-years
The raid of red Queen Meave, the wasting of the Branch,
Breaches in famous loves, long wars, and deaths renowned
Of many a feaster there ; where Conall now in mirth
Pledged his old friend, whose son ere long by him should fall.

And there Fardia felt the broad hand of his death
Laid on his shoulder now in comrade's love ; for there,
A friend beside his friend, unarmed Cuchullin sat,
Like a swift hound for strength and graceful slenderness,
In the first flower of his youth ; the colours of his face
Fresh as the dawning day, and in his clear blue eyes
The glad undaunted light of life's unsullied morn.

There in his royal state, a grave man among Kings,
Sat Conchobar, still, stern. The dark flame of his face
Tamed, as the sun the stars, all faces else : a face
Of subtle splendour ; brows of wisdom, broad and high,
Where strenuous youth had scored the runes of hidden power
Not easily read ; a mouth pliant for speech, an eye
Whose ambushed fires at need could terribly outleap
In menace or command, mastering the wills of men.

He wore upon him all the colours of a King
By ancient laws ordained : the three colours, the white,
Crimson, and black ; with these blending, by ancient law,
The four colours, the red, yellow, and green, and blue,
Enriched with gleaming gold. But subtly Conchobar
Loved to display the seven fair colours of a King
Inwoven and intertwined in traceries quaint and rare ;
And his keen eye would search the play of shimmering hues,

Even as his ear the turns and tricks of tuneful art
Of skilled harpers.   For craft of hand as craft of mind
Was ever his delight, and subtle as his mind
Ever his dress.   No King in splendour was his peer ;
Each looked a gaudy clown, at vie with Conchobar.
Over his chair of state four silver posts upheld
A silken canopy ; and by him were his arms :
' The Hawk,' his casting-spear, that never left his hand
But death sang in its scream ; and, in its jewelled sheath,
His sword, ' Flame of the Sea,' won by his sires, of yore,
From some slain Eastern King—the blade, with wizard spells,
Tempered in magic baths under the Syrian moon.
But in the House of Arms bode his long thrusting-spear,
' Spoil-winner ;' there, too, bode, far-famed in bardic song,
' The Bellower,' his great shield, seven-bossed, whose pealing voice,
Loud o'er the battle's roar, would call its vassal waves,
The wave of Toth, the wave of Rury, and the wave
Of Cleena, the three waves, to thunder on their shores,
Ireland's three magic waves, at danger of her King.

On the High-King's right hand sat Cathvah, that white peer
Of hoary Time, like Time wrinkled and hoar ; the beard
Upon his breast, the hair upon his druid head
Wintered with eld ; Cathvah, whose voice was like a sea's
For mystery and awe, and like the brooding sea
Blue were his druid eyes, and sad with things to come.

And on his left was set old Shancha of the Laws,
His Councillor ; none lived wiser in all the lore
Of statecraft, and the laws and customs of old time.
Thin was his shaven face ; deep under the black brows
Gleamed his keen eyes that weighed coldly each thing they saw ;
Long was his head and high, fringed round with silver hair ;
Smooth as an egg above, where baldness on the dome
Sat in grave state, yet looked no blemish where it sat.
These two after the King were honoured in the hall.

On wings of song flew by the hastening day, and song
Led in the hooded night, soft stealing on the feast ;
And without stint the wife of Felimy the Bard

Crowned the great horn with ale, with mead the golden cup,
To circle the great hall. Praised for her open hand,
She served with nimble cheer, though now her hour drew nigh.

But when the hearts of all were merry, and their brains
Hummed with the humming ale, and drowsily the harps
Murmured of deeds long done, till sleep with downy wing
Fanned heavy lids, a cry—a thin, keen, shuddering cry—
Rang eerily through the hall, dumbing all tongues, for lo !
Foreboding birth's dread hour, loud shrieked the babe unborn.

Then cheeks grew pale that ne'er in danger's grimmest hour
Failed of their wholesome red ; and ghastly looks met looks
As ghastly in the eyes of champions whose proud names
Were songs of valour.   First came loosing of the tongue
To Felimy. His words shook on the breath of fear :
'Woman, what woeful voice that rends my heart like steel,
Keenes from thee now ? ' His wife with trembling hands of prayer
Sank pale at Cathvah's feet : 'From what night-shrieking wraith,
O Druid, came that voice ?   A hand of ice is laid
Upon my heart : the *keene* comes to the house of death ! '

And Cathvah said : 'A child cries in the gate of birth
For terror of this world ; yet shall she be the queen
Of all this world for beauty. Ushered by fear she comes,
And " Dread " shall be her name ; Deirdré I name her now,
For dear shall Eri dree her beauty and her birth.'

Then, with her pangs upon her, the mother from the hall
Was hurried by her maids ; and ere they rose that night
A wail was in the house, for Death came to that birth,
And Deirdré's mother passed with the coming of her child.

Anon the aged crones that haunt with equal feet
The house of joy or tears, priestesses hoar like-skilled
In rites of death or birth, solemnly up the hall
Paced slow, bearing the babe ; and with a weeping word,
'Thy dead wife sends thee this,' laid it in its father's arms.
And Felimy bent down and, dazed with sudden grief,
Kissed it without a tear.   Then Cathvah took the child
And o'er its new-born head murmured his druid song :

THE DRUID SONG OF CATHVAH

I

O Deirdré, terrible child,
For thee, red star of our ruin,
Great weeping shall be in Eri—
Woe, woe, and a breach in Ulla !

II

The flame of thy dawn shall kindle
The pride of Kings to possess thee,
The spite of Queens for thy slander :
In seas of blood is thy setting.

III

War, war is thy bridesmaid,
Thou soft, small whelp of terror ;
Thy feet shall trample the mighty,
Yet stumble on heads thou lovest.

IV

The little heap of thy grave
Shall dwell in thy desolation ;
Sad songs shall wail over Eri
Thy dolorous name, O Deirdré !

To the nurse he gave the child.   In silence from the hall
Deirdré was borne.   Anon the vast hush of the night
Was filled with dreadful sound : the shield of Conchobar,
Raising its brazen voice within the House of Arms,
Bellowed ; and at its call a mighty voice they knew
Thundered from the far shore, the voice of the great Wave
Of Rury.   And the voice of the great Wave of Toth,
And the great Wave of Cleena, answered him from afar,
Thundering upon their shores at danger of their King.[1]

---

[1] According to the legend, the magic shield of Conchobar roared like
the sea when the king was in danger, and the seas of Erinn answered it,
thundering upon their beaches.

FAIRY GOLD

A BALLAD OF '48

BUTTERCUPS and daisies in the meadow,
    And the children pick them as they pass,
Weaving in the sunlight and the shadow
    Garlands for each little lad and lass ;
Weave with dreams their buttercups and daisies,
    As the poor dead children did of old.
Will the dreams, like sunshine in their faces,
    Wither with their flowers like Fairy Gold?

Once, when lonely in Life's crowded highway,
    Came a maiden sweet, and took my hand,
Led me down Love's green delightful byway,
    Led me dreaming back to Fairyland.
But Death's jealous eye that lights on lovers
    Looked upon her, and her breast grew cold,
And my heart's delight the green sod covers,
    Vanished from my arms like Fairy Gold !

Then to Ireland, my long-suffering nation,
    That poor hope life left me yet I gave ;
With her dreams I dreamed, her desolation
    Found me, called me, desolate by that grave.
Once again she raised her head, contending
    For her children's birthright as of old ;
Once again the old fight had the old ending,
    All her hopes and dreams were Fairy Gold.

Now my work is done and I am dying,
    Lone, an exile on a foreign shore ;
But in dreams roam with my love that's lying
    Lonely in the old land I'll see no more.
Buttercups and daisies in the meadows
    When I'm gone will bloom ; new hopes for old
Comfort her with sunshine after shadows,
    Fade no more away like Fairy Gold.

WILLIAM ALLINGHAM

In his beautiful and touching preface to Irish Songs and Poems, published in 1887, Allingham dwells upon his love for Ballyshannon, his native home—a place of primitive and kindly folk, a place of haunting loveliness. His heart clung to it always. He came to form friendships and interests and ways of life which might have turned him into a very English poet and man : he became intimate with Tennyson and Carlyle, with Rossetti, Patmore, Millais, and the Pre-raphaelites at large. Much of his work was influenced by these English artists, and he was probably more at home with them than with his own countrymen of letters. He was not bound to Ireland by any crusading passion of Nationalism : he even had something of that detachment which sometimes accompanies a devotion to art. But his early home kept him Irish at the heart. His most popular poem in Ireland is his 'Emigrant's Farewell'—that 'adieu to Ballyshannon and the winding banks of Erne' which is sung to-day by wandering singers who never heard of Allingham, and has become a classic lament among his own people. Though not of peasant stock, he had all the peasant's passion for the old home with its memories and associations, and in him it blossomed into poetry, poignant and simple and sincere. We are told that in twilight walks about Ballyshannon he would listen to girls singing old ballads at their cottage doors : if imperfect or crude, he would complete and correct them, have them printed in the old-fashioned broadsheet form, and have them sold or distributed about the district. Then, like Goldsmith in Dublin, but under happier conditions, he would listen delightedly to the sound of his own verses. Most of his Irish themes come from local legends and ways, from his loving knowledge of that countryside and shore 'on the extreme western verge of Europe,' as the moving preface to Irish Songs and Poems puts it. His longest work upon an Irish theme is a novel in verse, somewhat after the manner of Crabbe, though without his tragic power and with more of Goldsmith's gentleness. LAURENCE BLOOMFIELD IN IRELAND abounds in excellent portraits of Irish scenery and society. The great Russian writer, Turgenev, said upon reading it : ' I never understood Ireland before.' The poet himself said of it : ' Alas ! when all's done, who will like it ? Think of the Landlord and Tenant Question in flat decasyllabics ! ' Despite the poem's many incidental merits, that self-criticism is not unjust. In truth, Allingham's power was not in poems of any considerable length : he was a lyrist, and not an inspired writer of narrative or dramatic poems. ' Perfection,' he wrote, ' seems to me the most inalienable quality of a poem. From the chaos of incident and reflection arise the rounded worlds of poetry, and go singing on their way.' But, as Rossetti said of Allingham's ' Music Master,' the longer poems, though ' full of beauty and nobility,' are ' perhaps *too* noble or too resolutely healthy : ' the strenuous conscientiousness of composition results in some lack of charm. Tennyson, Rossetti, and Mr. Ruskin agreed in an ardent admiration of Allingham's lyrics, his flying or sighing snatches of song ; and the loveliest of these are among his DAY AND NIGHT SONGS, with which Mr. Ruskin was ' most delighted,' declaring that ' some of it is heavenly.' Here we find all his better qualities : his wistful, smiling Irish humour and sympathy with Irish character, with Irish ways and scenes ; his delicate love of Nature and earth's creatures, with children, and with the faëry world of fancy and myth ; his uncomplaining pensiveness at the memory of the past, of old time, ' little things ' that his heart remembers. *Sunt lacrimæ rerum et mentem mortalia tangunt* is very much the burden of his best singing : yet he can sing blithely enough of Kitty O'Hea, and Mary Donnelly, and ' Kate O'Belashanny,' or celebrate with artful homeliness of tone the good labours of country man and maid, of the toilers of the sea. ' Most comforting and gentle thoughts I had : ' so runs the last line of a very familiar poem, and it expresses the feeling with which most of Allingham's readers lay down his lyrics. For if these poems are often sad, it is with a sane and wholesome sadness. As Rossetti wrote to a friend in 1871 : 'another happy man, after all, seems to be Allingham, for all his want of "success." Nothing but the most absolute calm and enjoyment of outside Nature could account for so much gadding about on the soles of his two feet.' Not all his poems of action are failures : once or twice he has caught the fierce old Irish note of Ferguson. But we chiefly remember him as a poet whose aërial, Æolian melodies steal into the heart—a poet of twilight and the evening star, and the sigh of the wind over the hills and waters of an Ireland that broods and dreams. His music haunts the ear with its perfect simplicity of art, the cunning of its quiet cadences. Song upon song makes no mention, direct or indirect, of Ireland : yet an Irish atmosphere and temperament are to be felt in almost all. Hawthorne, who resembles Allingham, both in official position and in artistic quality and kind, described his looks as 'intelligent, dark, pleasing, and not at all John-Bullish.' As the outer aspect of the man, so his characteristic work—the work of a poet who was many things, but always and essentially an Irishman of the secluded west, with ancient visions and ponderings in his heart, and the gift of tears and smiles. He stands somewhat lonely and apart from the Irish poets of his time : he belonged to the minority in religious and political faith ; he was nothing of an Irish scholar, able to draw inspiration from Gaelic literature ; he lived in no centre of Irish literary society. He passed along his way alone, with a heart responding, a soul vibrating, to the voices of Nature and of tranquil lives : and to him those voices came in Irish. He wrote much ambitious work which may not live : he lacked concentrated strength and energy of imagination to succeed in the loftiest and most elaborate strains. But his lyric voice of singular sweetness, his Muse of passionate or pensive meditation, his poetic consecration of common things, his mingled aloofness and homeliness, assure him a secure place among the poets of his land and the Irish voices which never will fall silent. And though 'the Irish cause' receives from him but little direct encouragement or help, let it be remembered that Allingham wrote this great and treasurable truth :

> We're one at heart, if you be Ireland's friend,
> Though leagues asunder our opinions tend :
> There are but two great parties in the end.

LIONEL JOHNSON.

William Allingham was born, in 1824, at Ballyshannon, in the County Donegal. He had his early education at his native place, and at the age of fourteen became a clerk in the town bank, of which his father was manager. In this employment he passed seven dissatisfied years, during which his chief delight was in reading and in acquiring foreign literature. An opening was then found for him in the Customs Office, and after two years' preliminary training at Belfast he returned to Ballyshannon as Principal Officer. In 1847 he visited London for the first time, and the rest of his life was largely spent in England, where he received various official appointments. He retired from the Government service in 1870, when he became sub-editor, under Mr. Froude, of *Fraser's Magazine*. In 1874 he succeeded him as editor. Some years before he had been granted a pension for his literary services. In the same year (1874) he married, and he died at Hampstead in 1889. He was a fairly prolific writer, both in verse and prose : his first volume appeared in 1850, and there is a posthumous edition of his works in six volumes. The LETTERS OF DANTE GABRIEL ROSSETTI TO WILLIAM ALLINGHAM, edited and annotated by Dr. Birkbeck Hill, with a valuable introduction, record the chief facts of his life and literary friendships.

Allingham's principal volumes are : POEMS, 1850 ; DAY AND NIGHT SONGS, 1854 ; THE MUSIC MASTER, &C., 1855 (containing Rossetti's illustration of 'The Maids of Elfin-Mere' which moved Burne-Jones to become a painter); FIFTY MODERN POEMS, 1865 ; LAURENCE BLOOMFIELD IN IRELAND : A MODERN POEM, 1864 ; with SONGS, BALLADS, AND STORIES, 1877 ; EVIL MAY-DAY, 1883 ; ASHBY MANOR : A PLAY, 1883; FLOWER PIECES, 1888; LIFE AND PHANTASY, 1889 ; BLACKBERRIES, 1896.

ÆOLIAN HARP

> WHAT is it that is gone we fancied ours ?
> Oh, what is lost that never may be told ?—
> We stray all afternoon, and we may grieve
> Until the perfect closing of the night.

Listen to us, thou gray Autumnal Eve,
Whose part is silence.   At thy verge the clouds
Are broken into melancholy gold ;
The waifs of Autumn and the feeble flow'rs
Glimmer along our woodlands in wet light ;
Within thy shadow thou dost weave the shrouds
Of joy and great adventure, waxing cold,
Which once, or so it seemed, were full of m'ght.
Some power it was, that lives not with us now,
A thought we had, but could not, could not hold.
Oh, sweetly, swiftly pass'd !—air sings and murmurs ;
Green leaves are gathering on the dewy bough :
Oh, sadly, swiftly pass'd !—air sighs and mutters ;
Red leaves are dropping on the rainy mould.
Then comes the snow, unfeatured, vast, and white.
Oh, what has gone from us, we fancied ours ?

A Gravestone

FAR from the churchyard dig his grave,
On some green mound beside the wave ;
To westward, sea and sky alone,
And sunsets.   Put a massy stone,
With mortal name and date, a harp
And bunch of wild flowers, carven sharp ;
Then leave it free to winds that blow,
And patient mosses creeping slow,
And wandering wings, and footstep rare
Of human creature pausing there.

The Ban-Shee

A BALLAD OF ANCIENT ERIN

' HEARD'ST thou over the Fortress wild geese flying and crying ?
Was it a gray wolf's howl ? wind in the forest sighing ?

Wail from the sea as of wreck ? Hast heard it, Comrade ? ' ' Not
  so.
Here, all's still as the grave, above, around, and below.

' The Warriors lie in battalion, spear and shield beside them,
Tranquil, whatever lot in the coming fray shall betide them.
See, where he rests, the Glory of Erin, our Kingly Youth !
Closed his lion's eyes, and in sleep a smile on his mouth.'

' The cry, the dreadful cry ! I know it—louder and nearer,
Circling our Dūn—*the Ban-shee* !—my heart is frozen to hear her !
Saw you not in the darkness a spectral glimmer of white
Flitting away ?—I saw it !—evil her message to-night.

' Constant, but never welcome, she, to the line of our Chief ;
Bodeful, baleful, fateful, voice of terror and grief.
Dimly burneth the lamp--hush ! again that horrible cry !—
If a thousand lives could save thee, Tierna, thou shouldest not
  die.'

' Now ! what whisper ye, Clansmen ? I wake. Be your words
  of me ?
Wherefore gaze on each other ? I too have heard the Ban-shee.
Death is her message : but ye, be silent. Death comes to no man
Sweet as to him who in fighting crushes his country's foeman.

' Streak of dawn in the sky—morning of battle. The Stranger
Camps on our salt-sea strand below, and recks not his danger.
Victory !—that was my dream : one that shall fill men's ears
In story and song of harp after a thousand years.

' Give me my helmet and sword. Whale-tusk, gold-wrought, I
  clutch thee !
Blade, Flesh-Biter, fail me not this time ! Yea, when I touch
  thee,
Shivers of joy run through me. Sing aloud as I swing thee !
Glut of enemies' blood, meseemeth, to-day shall bring thee.

' Sound the horn ! Behold, the Sun is beginning to rise.
Whoso seeth him set, ours is the victor's prize,
When the foam along the sand shall no longer be white but red—
Spoils and a mighty feast for the Living, a carn for the Dead.'

B B

The Fairies

A CHILD'S SONG

Up the airy mountain,
   Down the rushy glen,
We daren't go a-hunting
   For fear of little men.
Wee folk, good folk,
   Trooping all together ;
Green jacket, red cap,
   And white owl's feather !

Down along the rocky shore
   Some make their home—
They live on crispy pancakes
   Of yellow tide-foam ;
Some in the reeds
   Of the black mountain-lake,
With frogs for their watch-dogs,
   All night awake.

High on the hill-top
   The old King sits ;
He is now so old and grey,
   He's nigh lost his wits.
With a bridge of white mist
   Columbkill he crosses,
On his stately journeys
   From Slieveleague to Rosses ;
Or going up with music
   On cold starry nights,
To sup with the Queen
   Of the gay Northern Lights.

They stole little Bridget
   For seven years long ;
When she came down again,
   Her friends were all gone.
They took her lightly back,
   Between the night and morrow ;

They thought that she was fast asleep,
  But she was dead with sorrow.
They have kept her ever since
  Deep within the lake,
On a bed of flag-leaves,
  Watching till she wake.

By the craggy hill-side,
  Through the mosses bare,
They have planted thorn-trees,
  For pleasure here and there.
Is any man so daring
  As dig them up in spite,
He shall find their sharpest thorns
  In his bed at night.

Up the airy mountain,
  Down the rushy glen,
We daren't go a-hunting
  For fear of little men.
Wee folk, good folk,
  Trooping all together;
Green jacket, red cap,
  And white owl's feather!

THE WINDING BANKS OF ERNE;
OR, THE EMIGRANT'S ADIEU TO BALLYSHANNON

A LOCAL BALLAD

I

ADIEU to Belashanny! where I was bred and born;
Go where I may, I'll think of you, as sure as night and morn—
The kindly spot, the friendly town, where every one is known,
And not a face in all the place but partly seems my own;
There's not a house or window, there's not a field or hill,
But, east or west, in foreign lands, I'll recollect them still.
I leave my warm heart with you, tho' my back I'm forced to
    turn—
So adieu to Belashanny, and the winding banks of Erne!

B B 2

II

No more on pleasant evenings we'll saunter down the Mall,
When the trout is rising to the fly, the salmon to the fall.
The boat comes straining on her net, and heavily she creeps.
Cast off ! cast off ! she feels the oars, and to her berth she
　　sweeps ;
Now fore and aft keep hauling, and gathering up the clew,
Till a silver wave of salmon rolls in among the crew.
Then they may sit, with pipes a-lit, and many a joke and ' yarn —
Adieu to Belashanny, and the winding banks of Erne !

III

The music of the waterfall, the mirror of the tide,
When all the green-hill'd harbour is full from side to side—
From Portnasun to Bulliebawns, and round the Abbey Bay,
From rocky Inis Saimer to Coolnargit sand-hills gray ;
While far upon the southern line, to guard it like a wall,
The Leitrim mountains clothed in blue gaze calmly over all,
And watch the ship sail up or down, the red flag at her stern—
Adieu to these, adieu to all the winding banks of Erne !

IV

Farewell to you, Kildoney lads, and them that pull an oar,
A lug-sail set, or haul a net, from the Point to Mullaghmore ;
From Killybegs to bold Slieve-League, that ocean-mountain
　　steep,
Six hundred yards in air aloft, six hundred in the deep,
From Dooran to the Fairy Bridge, and round by Tullen strand,
Level and long, and white with waves, where gull and curlew
　　stand ;
Head out to sea when on your lee the breakers you discern—
Adieu to all the billowy coast and winding banks of Erne !

V

Farewell, Coolmore ! Bundoran ! and your summer crowds that
　　run
From inland homes to see with joy th' Atlantic-setting sun ;
To breathe the buoyant salted air, and sport among the waves ;
To gather shells on sandy beach, and tempt the gloomy caves ;

To watch the flowing, ebbing tide, the boats, the crabs, the fish ;
Young men and maids to meet and smile, and form a tender
wish ;
The sick and old in search of health, for all things have their
turn—
And I must quit my native shore and the winding banks of
Erne !

VI

Farewell to every white cascade from the Harbour to Belleek,
And every pool where fins may rest, and ivy-shaded creek ;
The sloping fields, the lofty rocks, where ash and holly grow,
The one split yew-tree gazing on the curving flood below ;
The Lough, that winds through islands under Turaw mountain
green ;
And Castle Caldwell's stretching woods, with tranquil bays
between ;
And Breesie Hill, and many a pond among the heath and fern—
For I must say adieu—adieu to the winding banks of Erne !

VII

The thrush will call through Camlin groves the livelong summer
day ;
The waters run by mossy cliff, and bank with wild flowers gay ;
The girls will bring their work and sing beneath a twisted thorn,
Or stray with sweethearts down the path among the growing corn ;
Along the riverside they go, where I have often been—
Oh ! never shall I see again the days that I have seen !
A thousand chances are to one I never may return—
Adieu to Belashanny, and the winding banks of Erne.

VIII

Adieu to evening dances, when merry neighbours meet,
And the fiddle says to boys and girls : ' Get up and shake your
feet !'
To ' shanachus ' and wise old talk of Erin's days gone by—
Who trench'd the rath on such a hill, and where the bones
may lie
Of saint, or king, or warrior chief ; with tales of fairy power,
And tender ditties sweetly sung to pass the twilight hour.

The mournful song of exile is now for me to learn—
Adieu, my dear companions on the winding banks of Erne !

IX

Now measure from the Commons down to each end of the Purt,
Round the Abbey, Moy, and Knather—I wish no one any hurt ;
The Main Street, Back Street, College Lane, the Mall, and
  Portnasun,
If any foes of mine are there, I pardon every one.
I hope that man and womankind will do the same by me ;
For my heart is sore and heavy at voyaging the sea.
My loving friends I'll bear in mind, and often fondly turn
To think of Belashanny, and the winding banks of Erne.

X

If ever I'm a money'd man, I mean, please God, to cast
My golden anchor in the place where youthful years were pass'd ;
Though heads that now are black and brown must meanwhile
  gather gray,
New faces rise by every hearth, and old ones drop away—
Yet dearer still that Irish hill than all the world beside ;
It's home, sweet home, where'er I roam, through lands and waters
  wide.
And if the Lord allows me, I surely will return
To my native Belashanny, and the winding banks of Erne.

THE RUINED CHAPEL

By the shore, a plot of ground
Clips a ruin'd chapel round,
Buttress'd with a grassy mound,
  Where Day and Night and Day go by,
And bring no touch of human sound.

Washing of the lonely seas,
Shaking of the guardian trees,
Piping of the salted breeze ;
  Day and Night and Day go by,
To the endless tune of these.

Or when, as winds and waters keep
A hush more dead than any sleep,

Still morns to stiller evenings creep,
    And Day and Night and Day go by ;
Here the silence is most deep.

The empty ruins, lapsed again
Into Nature's wide domain,
Sow themselves with seed and grain
    As Day and Night and Day go by ;
And hoard June's sun and April's rain.

Here fresh funeral tears were shed ;
Now the graves are also dead ;
And suckers from the ash-tree spread,
    While Day and Night and Day go by
And stars move calmly overhead.

THERANIA

O UNKNOWN Belov'd One ! to the perfect season
    Branches in the lawn make drooping bow'rs ;
Vase and plot burn scarlet, gold, and azure ;
Honeysuckles wind the tall gray turret,
    And pale passion-flow'rs.
Come thou, come thou to my lonely thought,
        O Unknown Belov'd One.

Now, at evening twilight, dusky dew down-wavers,
    Soft stars crown the grove-encircled hill ;
Breathe the new-mown meadows, broad and misty ;
Through the heavy grass the rail is talking ;
    All beside is still.
Trace with me the wandering avenue,
        O Unknown Belov'd One.

In the mystic realm, and in the time of visions,
    I thy lover have no need to woo ;
There I hold thy hand in mine, thou dearest,
And thy soul is mine, and feels its throbbing,
    Tender, deep, and true :
Then my tears are love, and thine are love,
        O Unknown Belov'd One.

Is thy voice a wavelet on the listening darkness?
　　Are thine eyes unfolding from their veil?
Wilt thou come before the signs of winter—
Days that shred the bough with trembling fingers,
　　Nights that weep and wail?
Art thou Love indeed, or art thou Death,
　　　　　　　O Unknown Belov'd One?

STOPFORD AUGUSTUS BROOKE

BORN at Glendoen, Letterkenny, County Donegal, 1832.
B.A. Trinity College, Dublin, 1856 ; M.A. 1862. Entered the
Church of England, and was for some time Chaplain to the
British Embassy at Berlin. Mr. Brooke joined the Unitarian
body in 1880. His poetical works are : RIQUET OF THE TUFT
(1880); and POEMS (1888). He is author of a well-known
biography of the Rev. Frederick W. Robertson, of a HISTORY
OF EARLY ENGLISH LITERATURE, a study of Tennyson, and
several volumes of sermons, a book on Browning, two on
Shakespeare's plays, and two of miscellaneous essays on
poetry. He succeeded Sir Charles Gavan Duffy in 1899 as
President of the Irish Literary Society of London and died
in 1916.

THE NOBLE LAY OF AILLINN

AFTER AN IRISH TALE FROM THE ' BOOK OF LEINSTER'

PRINCE BAILÈ of Ulster rode out in the morn
　　To meet his love at the ford ;
And he loved her better than lands or life,
　　And dearer than his sword.

And she was Aillinn, fair as the sea,
　　The Prince of Leinster's daughter,
And she longed for him more than a wounded man,
　　Who sees death, longs for water.

They sent a message each to each :
   ' Oh, meet me near or far ;'
And the ford divided the kingdoms two,
   And the kings were both at war.

And the Prince came first to the water's pass,
   And oh, he thought no ill :
When he saw with pain a great grey man
   Come striding o'er the hill.

His cloak was the ragged thunder-cloud,
   And his cap the whirling snow,
And his eyes were the lightning in the storm,
   And his horn he 'gan to blow.

' What news, what news, thou great grey man ?
   I fear 'tis ill with me.'
' Oh, Aillinn is dead, and her lips are cold,
   And she died for loving thee.'

And he looked and saw no more the man,
   But a trail of driving rain.
'Woe ! woe !' he cried, and took his sword
   And drave his heart in twain.

And out of his blood burst forth a spring,
   And a yew-tree out of his breast ;
And it grew so deep, and it grew so high,
   The doves came there to rest.

But Aillinn was coming to keep her tryst,
   The hour her lover fell ;
And she rode as fast as the western wind
   Across the heathery hill.

Behind her flew her loosened hair,
   Her happy heart did beat ;
When she was 'ware of a cloud of storm
   Came driving down the street.

And out of it stepped a great grey man,
    And his cap was peaked with snow ;
The fire of death was in his eyes,
    And he 'gan his horn to blow.

'What news, what news, thou great grey man ?
    And is it ill to me ? '
'Oh, Bailè the Prince is dead at the ford,
    And he died for loving thee.'

Pale, pale she grew, and two large tears
    Dropped down like heavy rain,
And she fell to earth with a woeful cry,
    For she broke her heart in twain.

And out of her tears two fountains rose
    That watered all the ground,
And out of her heart an apple-tree grew
    That heard the water's sound.

Oh, woe were the kings, and woe were the queens,
    And woe were the people all ;
And the poets sang their love and their death
    In cottage and in hall.

And the men of Ulster a tablet made
    From the wood of Bailè's tree,
And the men of Leinster did the like
    Of Aillinn's apple-tree.

And on the one the poets wrote
    The lover-tales of Leinster,
And on the other all the deeds
    That lovers wrought in Ulster.

Now when a hundred years had gone
    The King of all the land
Kept feast at Tara, and he bade
    His poets sing a strand.

They sang the sweet unhappy tale,
  The noble Aillinn's lay.
' Go, bring the tablets,' cried the King,
  ' For I have wept to-day.'

But when he held in his right hand
  The wood of Bailè's tree
And in his left the tablet smooth
  From Aillinn's apple-tree,

The lovers in the wood who kept
  Love-longing ever true,
Knew one another, and at once
  From the hands of the king they flew.

As ivy to the oak they clung,
  Their kiss no man could sever—
Oh, joy for lovers parted long
  To meet, at last, for ever !

THE EARTH AND MAN

A LITTLE sun, a little rain,
  A soft wind blowing from the west,
And woods and fields are sweet again,
  And warmth within the mountain's breast.

So simple is the earth we tread,
  So quick with love and life her frame,
Ten thousand years have dawned and fled,
  And still her magic is the same.

A little love, a little trust,
  A soft impulse, a sudden dream,
And life as dry as desert dust
  Is fresher than a mountain stream.

So simple is the heart of man,
  So ready for new hope and joy ;
Ten thousand years since it began
  Have left it younger than a boy.

ALFRED PERCEVAL GRAVES

THERE is a story current, according to which Mr. A. P. Graves was once informed by a young gentleman whom he had casually met in a club-room that there was no one now living who could write really good and racy Irish songs —'such songs, for instance, as "Father O'Flynn."' Another would-be critic—a lady this time, doubtless otherwise well informed—was until corrected under the impression that Mr. Graves lived in the time of Queen Elizabeth. Nothing, I think, could afford more convincing testimony than do these anecdotes (for the authenticity of which the present writer can vouch) to the extent to which certain of Alfred Perceval Graves's songs and lyrics have passed into the general literary treasury of the Irish people and have been accepted as accurate embodiments of the national character in music and song.

Of these ballads and lyrics, mainly written for music and constituting no doubt the most popular and the most widely known portion of his literary work, I shall necessarily have something to say presently. But I wish to observe at the outset that to those who have studied Mr. Graves's work in its entirety, it is an inadequate estimate of his literary position which represents him as the successor of Samuel Lover, and which, having compared one or two of his songs with some of Lover's or with Charles Lever's 'Widow Malone,' dismisses him without further notice. Not only has he a distinctly individual note of his own, but there is in his work ample evidence of wider scope and greater variety. He may not have surpassed—perhaps he has not surpassed—his predecessors in the line which Lover made so peculiarly his own, and in which others have occasionally attained high excellence ; it is high enough praise, in this respect, to place him at their side. But he has also given us work which they could not have done—or, at least, which they did not do—and exercised an influence to which they did not aspire.

Let us remember, in developing this proposition, that this is an age in which the cultivation of literature in dialect has attained, throughout all Europe, dimensions hitherto unknown. No one who has not had occasion to look into the matter has any idea of the number of dialects in Germany and in Italy alone which have been raised during the past half-century from the despised position of vulgar *patois* to something like the dignity of written literature. In Provence—to change the field of observation—we should be able to find the most notable instance of this re-integration, were it not doubtful whether Provençal had ever forfeited its rank as a separate language, and whether therefore the parallel to be drawn should not be between the Provençal and the Gaelic movements. But innumerable other cases may be pointed out in which the dialect is in reality an ancient though a neglected branch—a poor cousin, so to speak—of the classical literary tongue, differing from the latter partly because it has preserved old forms and peculiarities which the language of the Court and the bookmen has suffered to fall into oblivion, partly because it has been influenced by the grammar, the idioms, and the vocabulary of another and often a more ancient language, with which it has come locally in contact. This is precisely the position of the Anglo-Irish dialect, which, as spoken and written to-day, shows clear traces not only of the English of Elizabethan and even earlier days, but also of the manner of thought, and consequently of construction and wording, resultant upon the familiarity of the speaker or of his ancestors with the ancient Celtic tongue.

The study of such a dialect is at once a matter of scientific importance, and one of great and often loving interest to the native of the land where it is spoken ; and the better an Irish-man speaks English, the more he is enabled to appreciate the resources and the raciness of what may be called (apart from Gaelic, which is a separate tongue) his native dialect. Certainly, the reproduction of Anglo-Irish in books written mainly in English began long ago, both in prose and in songs such as Lover's ; but however accurate the representation of the peasants' forms of speech, and however amusing the substance and brilliant the execution of such pieces may be (no one wishes to detract from their merit less than the present writer), there has, generally speaking, been an absence of serious effort in this line, so far as verse is concerned. It is in this connection that, without going so far as to number Mr. Graves among the greatest writers—those who create a literary vehicle or build up a language by individual effort—I claim for him the honourable distinction of having caused Anglo-Irish literature in verse to take a distinct step forwards. In 'The Girl with the Cows,' in his first volume, we have, so far as I know, the first instance of a really excellent long narrative in verse written in this dialect and, notwithstanding the racy humour of the style and manner of expression, of serious import.

Nevertheless, it is no doubt true that Mr. Graves owes a great part of his popularity to the fact that he has caught the ear of the public by the successful production of songs of the Irish peasantry not dissimilar to those on which Lover's reputation is founded ; nor is it in any way derogatory to his literary position to admit that many of his keenest admirers might not be so familiar with his verse as they are, had it not in many cases been wedded to beautiful and characteristic Irish music. This very fact constitutes, indeed, an essential portion of his achievement, and gives him a notable claim to the gratitude of his countrymen. The services which he has done to the cause of Irish music by rescuing from oblivion a large number of fine old airs would not perhaps require more than passing notice here, but for the fact that the words to which he has set them attain in many instances to a degree of literary merit not often found in work of this kind. The art of writing verse for music already existing—an inversion, as most poets are in the habit of thinking, of the natural order of affairs—is, no doubt, a trick easy enough to catch, if the writer is content to remain on that level of meaningless inanity and sham sentiment above which the ordinary drawing-room song does not usually attempt to soar. But to produce, under conditions much more difficult than most people are apt to suppose, work of this kind that shall be true literature—true poetry—is an achievement so difficult that but few have succeeded in it. Nor do I pretend that Mr. Graves has in every instance succeeded : that has not always been possible. The public has judged him by his best work, and the result is shown by the position to which he has attained.

In estimating, in their literary aspect, Mr. Graves's services to Irish music, it must here suffice to say that in the opinion of competent critics he has done more than any of Moore's successors to 'unbind the island harp;' and in his own sphere he is even more distinctly Irish than many of them. Mr. Graves knows and understands the peasantry of Ireland as but few writers of high merit and culture have known and understood them ; and he has given us in his popular songs and ballads a gallery of pictures in which the genial, passionate, lovable, and withal somewhat inconsequent Irish countryman is depicted merry-making, love-making, cutting capers, joking, lamenting, telling stories of the 'good people,' getting married, and dying, against backgrounds of Irish hills and lakes, rivers, and woods. And the great sea is there too, and the memory of those who have passed over it.

It is by such work as this that Mr. Graves's reputation is most likely to endure. Nevertheless it is not to be forgotten that much of it could not have been so well and daintily done had he not been a man of general culture, having a special devotion for the study of Irish character and of ancient Irish literature. He does not indeed (as his poetry testifies) hold that Irishmen should write only on Irish subjects and in what is called a Celtic manner ; that certain forms of verse are un-Irish ; and that the only high literary field for Celtic activity lies in the ancient mythology and in the heroic ages of the Celtic peoples. He cannot but be well aware that a literature bound (as none worthy of the name ever has been bound) by limitations so narrow and restrictions so arbitrary and paralysing would be destined only to a lingering inefficiency and a not distant extinction. But he fully recognises that there are periods in the development of every literature during which its national characteristics must be maintained by having recourse to the original fountains, to the national epos and to the local folklore so closely connected therewith. Therefore he has entered sympathetically into the movement known as the Celtic renascence, and while maintaining in those of his poems which are not written in dialect the purity of that English tongue in which of necessity the Celtic movement must mainly find expression to-day, he has given proof, in 'The Fairy Branch' and other pieces from the Gaelic, of his devotion to the study of that ancient literature the importance of which has of recent years come to be widely acknowledged. In the domain of folklore 'The Fairy Pig' is a good instance of his treatment of those popular tales, once so much despised and neglected, in which the gods of De Danaan legend, in their ancient greatness so far removed from the peasant's ken, have become the little dwellers in rath and lis, the 'good people' who play so real a part in the popular imagination.

Much of Mr. Graves's verse does not come under any of the categories already mentioned. In 'The Beautiful Bay,' for instance, he has given us an exquisite descriptive poem—no more Irish, in the perverse limited sense of the word, than is the echo-song in Tennyson's 'Princess,' which also owes its inspiration to the scenery of the County Kerry. Many other fine pieces of verse bear witness to his powers in wider fields ; yet it is doubtful whether his output in work of this kind would have entitled him to a higher position than has been attained by many a 'minor' English poet of the day. His reputation, not only among Irishmen, but among all who speak the English tongue, must finally rest upon those of his poems which treat of Irish subjects, and especially upon the songs and ballads in dialect—full, as many of them are, not only of quiet humour or of rollicking mirth, but also of an unobtrusive, yet deep and tender pathos.

GEORGE A. GREENE.

Born in Dublin, July 22, 1846, the son of the Right Rev. Charles Graves, D.D., Bishop of Limerick, Alfred Perceval Graves belongs to a distinguished literary family. He went to a school in the English lake country, but spent a good deal of his youth in the south-west of Ireland. Proceeding to the University of Dublin, he took his degree in 1871. He was for some time in the Home Office, and became private secretary to one of the chiefs in that department, but was subsequently appointed one of her Majesty's Inspectors of Schools, which position he held until 1910. His first volume, SONGS OF KILLARNEY, appeared in 1873, and was followed by IRISH SONGS AND BALLADS, 1880, which has passed through several editions, and by FATHER O'FLYNN AND OTHER IRISH LYRICS (largely a reprint) in 1889. The following were published in conjunction with musical accompaniments : SONGS OF OLD IRELAND (music arranged by Professor C. Villiers Stanford), Boosey & Co., 1883 ; IRISH SONGS AND BALLADS (*idem*), Novello, Ewer & Co., 1893 ; IRISH FOLK SONGS (the airs arranged by Mr. Charles Wood), Boosey & Co., 1897. Mr. Graves is the editor of SONGS OF IRISH WIT AND HUMOUR, 1884; of THE PURCELL PAPERS, by J. S. Le Fanu, three volumes, 1880; of THE IRISH SONG BOOK, Fisher Unwin, 1894 ; of THE BOOK OF IRISH POETRY, 1915; and of THE READER'S TREASURY OF IRISH PROSE AND VERSE (with Guy Roberts), 1915, etc. He is editor-in-chief of EVERY IRISHMAN'S LIBRARY. The Irish Poems of Alfred Perceval Graves in two volumes came out in 1908, and in 1930 he published his autobiography, TO RETURN TO ALL THAT. As a lecturer on Irish literature and music and for twelve years honorary secretary and for two terms president of the Irish Literary Society, Mr. Graves has played his part in the Irish literary and musical renascence of his day.

From THE GIRL WITH THE COWS

So he trassed away dreamin' of Nora na Mo,
While the mist it crept down to the valleys below
Unknownst to O'Neale, for each inch of the way
He'd have travelled as surely by night as by day.
Still an' all at long last on the edge of a bog
There puffed in his face such a powderin' fog
That he gave a great start and looked doubtin'ly down,
To be sure he'd made off the right track to the town ;
And he just then could see to the left of his path,
Roundin' out of the vapour, the ould Irish rath,
And says he wid a smile : ' Why, I might be a hound
For facin' so fair for the Barony's bound.

But I'd best hurry on, then, or—Mother Machree !—
It's in dread for me out in the mist but you'll be.'
So he started to run, when he heard from above
The voice of the girl that had stolen his love :
' *Magrina, magrina, magrinashin oge !*
Come hither, my Laidir ; come, Kitty, you rogue ;
Come up, Blackbird ; come, Snow, to the beautiful house.'
' 'Tis the Colleen na Mo,' he said, ' callin' her cows.'

But her voice sounded sadly and strange in his ear,
And the heart of O'Neale began knockin' for fear,
And he looked and he saw, risin' up from below,
The Shadow of the Shape of the Colleen na Mo,
Growin' greater for ever, till a monster of black,
Like the Spirit of Death, it stood out of the track ;
And O'Neale knew the warnin'—and shouted, ' *Stand back,*
Stand back for your life !' But the Shadow went still,
Wid its arms wavin' wild on the brow of the hill ;
Then it trembled, and balanced, and staggered, and fell,
Down, down wid the moan of a muffled death-bell.

    .   .   .   .   .

' Come, Jack, we'll go down to the foot of the rock,
And protect the poor corpse from the ravenous flock ; '
And he coaxed him to come, but the dog wouldn't stir,
So alone down the clift Pat went searchin' for her.

But as he was goin', a far hullahoo
Rose out of the distance, and into his view
Red torches came wavin' their way up the hill,
And he laughed a wild laugh, through his wanderin' will,
And he cried : ' *Is it wake-lights yez are drawin' near ?*
Hurry up, then, and show me the corpse of my dear.'
And the red lights approached, and a voice wid the light :
' *Who are ye in distress on the mountain to-night ?'*
And he answered : ' *Come up, for our name it is Death*
Wid the eagle above and the white-worm beneath ;
But the death-lights that hover by night o'er the grave
Will restore us our dead when your torches can save.'

'What is it, O'Neale, man ?   How wildly you rave ! '
And the hand of Murt Shea, the best friend that he had,
Was lovingly laid on the arm of the lad.
'Oh, Murt, give me hould of that splinter,' he said,
'And let me look down on the face of the dead ;
For Nora Maguire, Murt, my own secret love,
Has fallen from the clift of Coomassig above.'
' Is it she, wirra ! wirra ! the pride of us all ?
Do you say that the darlin's been killed by a fall ?
Ologone, my poor Pat, and you loved her at heart.'

Then O'Neale groaned again : ' Sure, I've searched every part
And no sign of her here at the foot of the clift.'
And the rest they come up, and the bushes they sift,
But sorra a trace to the right or the left.

Then O'Neale shouted : ' Come, every man of ye lift
His fire altogether.'   And one said : ' I see
Somethin' hangin' high up from the juniper-tree.'
''Tis herself ! ' shouted Pat, wid his hand to his brow.
' How far from the top is that juniper bough ? '
' Ten foot of a fall,' said a mountain gossoon.
' Wid no tussocks betune them ? '
                              ' Wid nothin' betune.
' Have yez e'er a rope handy, boys ? '
                              ' Divle a rope !
And not nearer nor Sneem for the likes you could hope.
' Come hither, gossoon, and be off wid this splinter,
For 'tis you know the mountain ; away widout hinder
To the nearest good haggard, and strip the sugane,
Not forgettin' a sop of the finest finane.
Brustig, brustig, alanah ! ' and hardly the rest
Had followed O'Neale up the vapoury crest
To the spot that the faithful, wise hound wouldn't pass,
When the boy he was back wid the hayropes and grass.

Then says Pat, leanin' down wid a splinter of light :
' God bless the good dog !—after all he was right.
Ten foot underneath us—she's plainly in sight.
Now give hither the ropes, and hould on while I twist.'
So he caught the suganes up like threads in his fist,

C C 2

And twined them and jined them a thirty-foot length,
Fourplait to a thickness of terrible strength ;
Then roped it around the two biggest boys there,
To see was it fit for supportin' a pair.
And he easily lifted the two through the air,
Up and down, till he'd proved it well able to bear.
'Now make the rope fast to me, boys, while I go
Down the side of the clift for the Colleen na Mo.
Livin' or dead—tho' I'm hopeful for all,
There's life in her still—tho' she's kilt from the fall.'

Then he turns to one side, and he whispers Murt Shea :
'If I'm killed from the clift of Coomassig to-day,
Come promise me faithful you'll stand to the mother
Like a son, till she's help from the sister and brother.
And give her this kiss, and I'll meet her again
In the place where's no poverty, sorrow, or pain.'
And he promised—and all then shook hands wid O'Neale,
And he cheered them and said : ' Have no dread that we'll fail,
For I'd not be afear'd—why, to balance the Pope
Himself from the clift by so hearty a rope.'

So a torch in his hand and a stick in his teeth,
And his coat round his throat, the boys lowered him beneath.
And all but Murt Shea, then, they couldn't make out
The coat round his throat and the stick in his mout'.

But it wasn't for long they'd the doubt in their mind,
For they saw his torch quenched wid a noise like the wind,
And ' Steady above !' came his voice from below.
Then heavy wings flapped wid a scream and a blow.
''Tis the eagles,' they cried, ' at the Colleen na Mo.'
But an old man amongst them spoke up and he said :
''Tis the eagles, for sartin—but not at the dead ;
For they'll not touch the corpse.   Murther ! but for the mist,
'Tis I could have told you that this was their nest.
It's O'Neale that they're at—pull him back, or they'll tear
The poor boy to pieces below in the air ;'
And they shouted together the eagles to scare.

And they called to O'Neale from the edge of the height :
' She's dead, Pat—she's dead ; never mind her to-night,
But come back, or the eagles'll pick out your sight.'
And they made for to pull ; but he cries, ' If you do,
I give you my oath that I'll cut the rope through.'
And they b'lieved him, and waited wid hearts beatin' loud,
Screechin' down at the birds through the vapoury cloud,
Showerin' splinters for ever to give the boy light,
And warnin' him watch to the left or the right,
As each eagle in turn it would fly at his head,
Till he dropped one below in the darkness for dead,
And the other flew off wid a yell through the night.
Then they felt the rope slacken as he crossed to the bough,
Then tighten again—and he called to them 'Now !'
And they knew that the dangerous moment was come ;
So wid wrist draggin' shoulder, tight finger to thumb,
And tooth crushing tooth in the silence of death,
They drew up the two from the blackness beneath.

The Limerick Lasses

' HAVE you e'er a new song,
 My Limerick Poet,
To help us along
 Wid this terrible boat
 Away over to Tork ? '
Arrah ! I understand
 For all of your work
 'Twill tighten you, boys,
To cargo that sand
To the overside strand
 Wid the current so strong,
 Unless you've a song—
A song to lighten and brighten you, boys.
 Be listenin' then,
 My brave Kerry men,
 And the new song,
 And the true song
Of the Limerick lasses 'tis I will begin.

O Limerick dear,
It's far and it's near
I've travelled the round of this circular sphere ;
Still an' all to my mind
No colleens you'll find
As lovely and modest, as merry and kind,
As our Limerick lasses ;
Our Limerick lasses—
So lovely and modest, so merry and kind.
So row,
Strong and slow,
Chorusing after me as we go :—
Still an' all to my mind
No colleens you'll find
As lovely and modest, as merry and kind,
As our Limerick lasses ;
Our Limerick lasses—
So lovely and modest, so merry and kind.

O your English colleen
Has the wonderful mien
Of a goddess in marble, all grand and serene ;
And, though slow to unbend,
Win her once for your friend,
And—no alter or falter—she's yours to the end.
But oh ! row,
Strong and slow,
Chorusing after me as we go :—
Still an' all to my mind
No colleens you'll find
As lovely and modest, as merry and kind,
As our Limerick lasses ;
Our Limerick lasses—
So lovely and modest, so merry and kind.

Of the French demoiselle
Delighted I'll tell,
For her sparkle and grace suit us Irishmen well ;

And taken complete,
From her head to her feet,
She's the perfectest picture of polish you'll meet.
But oh ! row,
Strong and slow,
Chorusing after me as we go :—
Still an' all to my mind
No colleens you'll find
As lovely and modest, as merry and kind,
As our Limerick lasses ;
Our Limerick lasses—
So lovely and modest, so merry and kind.

O Donna of Spain, ˙
It's the darlingest pain
From your dark eyes I've suffered again and again,
When you'd gracefully glide
Like a swan at my side,
Or sing till with rapture the woodbird replied.
But oh ! row,
Strong and slow,
Chorusing after me as we go :—
Still an' all to my mind
No colleens you'll find
As lovely and modest, as merry and kind,
As our Limerick lasses ;
Our Limerick lasses—
So lovely and modest, so merry and kind.

Now, my Maryland girl,
With your sunshiny curl,
Your sweet spirit eyes, and complexion of pearl ;
And the goodness and grace
That illumine your face,
You're the purtiest approach to my Limerick lass.
For oh ! row,
Strong and slow,
Chorusing after me as we go :—

Still an' all to my mind
No maiden you'll find
As lovely and modest, as merry and kind,
As our Limerick lasses ;
Our Limerick lasses—
So lovely and modest, and merry and kind.

THE IRISH SPINNING-WHEEL

SHOW me a sight
Bates for delight
An ould Irish wheel wid a young Irish girl at it.
Oh no !
Nothing you'll show
Aquals her sittin' an' takin' a twirl at it.

Look at her there—
Night in her hair,
The blue ray of day from her eye laughin' out on us !
Faix, an' a foot,
Perfect of cut,
Peepin' to put an end to all doubt in us.

That there's a sight
Bates for delight
An ould Irish wheel wid a young Irish girl at it—
Oh no !
Nothin' you'll show
Aquals her sittin' an' takin' a twirl at it.

See ! the lamb's wool
Turns coarse an' dull
By them soft, beautiful weeshy white hands of her.
Down goes her heel,
Roun' runs the wheel,
Purrin' wid pleasure to take the commands of her.

Then show me a sight
Bates for delight
An ould Irish wheel wid a young Irish girl at it.

Oh no !
Nothin' you'll show
Aquals her sittin' an' takin' a twirl at it.

Talk of Three Fates,
Seated on sates,
Spinnin' and shearin' away till they've done for me !
You may want three
For your massacree,
But one Fate for me, boys—and only the one for me !

And isn't that fate
Pictured complate—
An ould Irish wheel with a young Irish girl at it ?
Oh no !
Nothin' you'll show
Aquals her sittin' an' takin' a twirl at it.

IRISH LULLABY

I'D rock my own sweet childie to rest in a cradle of gold on a bough
of the willow,
To the *shoheen ho* of the wind of the west and the *lullalo* of the
soft sea billow.
Sleep, baby dear,
Sleep without fear,
Mother is here at your pillow.

I'd put my own sweet childie to sleep in a silver boat on the
beautiful river,
Where a *shoheen* whisper the white cascades, and a *lullalo* the
green flags shiver.
Sleep, baby dear,
Sleep without fear,
Mother is here with you for ever.

Shoheen ho ! to the rise and fall of mother's bosom 'tis sleep has
bound you,
And, O my child, what cosier nest for rosier rest could love have
found you ?
Sleep, baby dear,
Sleep without fear,
Mother's two arms are clasped around you.

FATHER O'FLYNN

OF priests we can offer a charmin' variety,
Far renowned for larnin' and piety ;
Still, I'd advance ye widout impropriety,
 Father O'Flynn as the flower of them all.

CHORUS

 Here's a health to you, Father O'Flynn,
 Sláinte, and *sláinte*, and *sláinte* agin ;
  Powerfulest preacher, and
  Tinderest teacher, and
 Kindliest creature in ould Donegal.

Don't talk of your Provost and Fellows of Trinity,
Famous for ever at Greek and Latinity,
Faix ! and the divels and all at Divinity—
 Father O'Flynn 'd make hares of them all !
 Come, I vinture to give ye my word,
 Niver the likes of his logic was heard,
  Down from mythology
  Into thayology,
 Troth ! and conchology if he'd the call.

CHORUS

 Here's a health to you, Father O'Flynn,
 Sláinte, and *sláinte*, and *sláinte* agin ;
  Powerfulest preacher, and
  Tinderest teacher, and
 Kindliest creature in ould Donegal.

Och ! Father O'Flynn, you've the wonderful way wid you,
All ould sinners are wishful to pray wid you,
All the young childer are wild for to play wid you,
 You've such a way wid you, Father avick !
 Still, for all you've so gentle a soul,
 Gad, you've your flock in the grandest control,
  Checking the crazy ones,
  Coaxin' onaisy ones,
 Liftin' the lazy ones on wid the stick.

CHORUS

Here's a health to you, Father O'Flynn,
Sláinte, and *sláinte*, and *sláinte* agin ;
    Powerfulest preacher, and
    Tinderest teacher, and
    ·Kindliest creature in ould Donegal.

And though quite avoidin' all foolish frivolity
Still, at all seasons of innocent jollity,
Where was the play-boy could claim an equality
    At comicality, Father, wid you?
      Once the Bishop looked grave at your jest,
      Till this remark set him off wid the rest :
        ' Is it lave gaiety
        All to the laity ?
    Cannot the clargy be Irishmen too ?'

CHORUS

Here's a health to you, Father O'Flynn,
Sláinte, and *sláinte*, and *sláinte* agin ;
    Powerfulest preacher, and
    Tinderest teacher, and
    Kindliest creature in ould Donegal.

Fan Fitzgerl

Wirra, wirra ! ologone !
Can't ye lave a lad alone,
Till he's proved there's no tradition left of any other girl—
    Not even Trojan Helen
    In beauty all excellin'—
Who's been up to half the divlement of Fan Fitzgerl ?

    Wid her brows of silky black
    Arched above for the attack,
Her eyes they dart such azure death on poor admirin' man ;
    Masther Cupid, point your arrows,
    From this out, agin the sparrows,
For you're bested at Love's archery by young Miss Fan.

See what showers of goolden thread
Lift and fall upon her head,
The likes of such a trammel-net at say was niver spread ;
For whin accurately reckoned,
'Twas computed that each second
Of her curls has cot a Kerryman and kilt him dead.

Now mintion, if ye will,
Brandon Mount and Hungry Hill,
Or Ma'g'llicuddy's Reeks renowned for cripplin' all they can ;
Still the countryside confisses
None of all its precipices
Cause a quarter of the carnage of the nose of Fan.

But your shatthered hearts suppose
Safely steered apast her nose,
She's a current and a reef beyant to wreck them rovin' ships.
My maning it is simple,
For that current is her dimple,
And the cruel reef 'twill coax ye to 's her coral lips.

I might inform ye further
Of her bosom's snowy murther,
And an ankle ambuscadin' through her gown's delightful whirl ;
But what need, when all the village
Has forsook its peaceful tillage
And flown to war and pillage all for Fan Fitzgerl ?

HERRING IS KING

Let all the fish that swim the sea,
Salmon and turbot, cod and ling,
Bow down the head and bend the knee
To herring, their king !—to herring, their king !
Sing, *Thugamar féin an samhradh linn*,
'Tis we have brought the summer in.[1]

The sun sank down, so round and red,
Upon the bay, upon the bay ;

---

[1] The second line of the refrain translates the first, which is pronounced *Hugamar fain an sowra linn.*

The sails shook idly overhead—
  Becalmed we lay, becalmed we lay.

    Sing, *Thugamar féin an samhradh linn*,
    'Tis we have brought the summer in.

Till Shawn the eagle dropped on deck,
  The bright-eyed boy, the bright-eyed boy ;
'Tis he has spied your silver track,
  Herring, our joy—herring, our joy.

    Sing, *Thugamar féin an samhradh linn*,
    'Tis we have brought the summer in.

It was in with the sails and away to shore,
  With the rise and swing, the rise and swing
Of two stout lads at each smoking oar,
  After herring, our king—herring, our king.

    Sing, *Thugamar féin an samhradh linn*,
    'Tis we have brought the summer in.

The Manx and the Cornish raised the shout,
  And joined the chase, and joined the chase,
But their fleets they fouled as they went about,
  And we won the race, we won the race.

    Sing, *Thugamar féin an samhradh linn*,
    'Tis we have brought the summer in.

For we turned and faced you full to land,
  Down the *góleen* long, the *góleen*[1] long,
And after you slipped from strand to strand
  Our nets so strong, our nets so strong.

    Sing, *Thugamar féin an samhradh linn*,
    'Tis we have brought the summer in.

Then we called to our sweethearts and our wives,
  ' Come, welcome us home—welcome us home,'
Till they ran to meet us for their lives
  Into the foam, into the foam.

    Sing, *Thugamar féin an samhradh linn*,
    'Tis we have brought the summer in.

---

[1] Creek.

Oh, the kissing of hands and waving of caps
From girl and boy, from girl and boy,
While you leapt by scores in the lasses' laps,
Herring, our joy—herring, our joy.

Sing, *Thugamar féin an samhradh linn,*
'Tis we have brought the summer in.

FRANCIS A. FAHY

BORN at Kinvara, County Galway, 1854, and entered the Civil Service in London (Board of Trade Department) 1873. Mr. Fahy took an active part in various Irish literary movements in London, especially in the formation of the Southwark Irish Literary Club and the Irish Literary Society which grew out of it. He wrote a play, THE LAST OF THE O'LEARYS, at the age of sixteen, which was performed in his native town. He also contributed verses marked by much humour and grace to many Irish periodicals. His songs, of which a large number are well-known favourites in concert-rooms, have the merit of being eminently singable. A volume of his IRISH SONGS AND POEMS appeared in 1887.

THE DONOVANS

IF you would like to see the height of hospitality,
The cream of kindly welcome, and the core of cordiality :
Joys of all the olden time – you're wishing to recall again ?
Come down to Donovans, and there you'll meet them all again.

Céad míle fáilte they'll give you down at Donovans,
As cheery as the springtime and Irish as the *cannawaun,*[1]
The wish of my heart is, if ever I had any one—
That every luck that lightens life may light upon the Donovans.

As soon as e'er you lift the latch, the little ones are meeting you ;
Soon as you're beneath the thatch, oh ! kindly looks are greeting
   you ;

---

[1] Bog-cotton.

Scarcely are you ready to be holding out the fist to them,
When down by the fireside you're sitting in the midst of them.
   Céad míle fáilte they'll give you down at Donovans, &c.

There sits the *cailín deas* [1]—oh! where on earth's the peer of her?
The modest face, the gentle grace, the humour and the cheer of
   her—
Eyes like the summer skies when twin stars beam above in them,
Oh! proud will be the boy that's to light the lamp of love in them.
   Céad míle fáilte they'll give you down at Donovans, &c.

Then when you rise to go, it's 'Ah, then, now sit down again!'
'Isn't it the haste you're in?' and 'Won't you soon come round
   again?'
Your *caubeen* and your overcoat you'd better put astray from them,
'Twill take you all your time to try and tear yourself away from them,
   Céad míle fáilte they'll give you down at Donovans, &c.

IRISH MOLLY O

OH! fairer than the lily tall, and sweeter than the rose,
As modest as the violet in dewy dell that blows;
With heart as warm as summer noon, and pure as winter snow—
The pride of Erin's isle is she, dear Irish Molly O!

No linnet of the hazel grove than she more sweetly sang,
No sorrow could be resting where her guileless laughter rang,
No hall of light could half so bright as that poor cabin glow
Where shone the face of love and grace of Irish Molly O!

But fever's breath struck down in death her father strong and
   brave,
And who should now his little ones from want and sorrow save?
'Oh, never fear, my mother dear, across the seas I'll go,
And win for ye a new home there,' said Irish Molly O!

And far away 'mid strangers cold she toiled for many a year,
And no one heard the heart-wrung sigh or saw the silent tear,
But letters fond the seas beyond would kind and constant go,
With gold won dear, and words of cheer, from Irish Molly O!

---

[1] Pretty girl.

And one by one she sent for all the loved ones o'er the foam,
And one by one she welcomed them to her fond heart and home,
And last and best her arms caressed the aged head of snow—
' Oh, mother, we'll be happy now ! ' said Irish Molly O !

Alas ! long years of toil and tears had chilled her young heart's
　　glow,　.
And grief and care had blanched her hair and stilled her pulse's
　　flow,
And when the spring bade wild birds sing and buds in beauty blow—
They made your grave where willows wave, poor Irish Molly O !

THE OULD PLAID SHAWL

NOT far from old Kinvara, in the merry month of May,
When birds were singing cheerily, there came across my way,
As if from out the sky above an angel chanced to fall,
A little Irish *cailín* in an ould plaid shawl.

She tripped along right joyously, a basket on her arm ;
And, oh ! her face, and, oh ! her grace, the soul of saint would
　　charm ;
Her brown hair rippled o'er her brow, but greatest charm of all
Was her modest blue eyes beaming 'neath her ould plaid shawl.

I courteously saluted her—' God save you, miss,' says I ;
' God save you, kindly sir,' said she, and shyly passed me by ;
Off went my heart along with her, a captive in her thrall,
Imprisoned in the corner of her ould plaid shawl.

Enchanted with her beauty rare, I gazed in pure delight,
Till round an angle of the road she vanished from my sight ;
But ever since I sighing say, as I that scene recall,
' The grace of God about you and your ould plaid shawl.'

I've heard of highway robbers that, with pistols and with knives,
Make trembling travellers yield them up their money or their
　　lives,
But think of me that handed out my heart and head and all
To a simple little *cailín* in an ould plaid shawl !

Oh ! graceful the mantillas that the signorinas wear,
And tasteful are the bonnets of Parisian ladies fair,
But never cloak or hood or robe, in palace, bow'r, or hall,
Clad half such witching beauty as that ould plaid shawl.

Oh ! some men sigh for riches, and some men live for fame,
And some on history's pages hope to win a glorious name ;
My aims are not ambitious, and my wishes are but small—
You might wrap them all together in an ould plaid shawl.

I'll seek her all through Galway, and I'll seek her all through
    Clare,
I'll search for tale or tidings of my traveller everywhere,
For peace of mind I'll never find until my own I call
That little Irish *cailín* in her ould plaid shawl.

MALACHY RYAN

A SCHOOLMASTER in County Carlow. He subsequently
became librarian in the Record Office, Dublin. He published
a volume of poems—ELSIE LEE, THE WHITETHORN TREE,
AND OTHER POEMS—in 1872.

ROSE ADAIR

'TWAS in green-leafy springtime,
  When the birds on every tree
Were breakin' all their little hearts
  In a merry melody ;
An' the young buds hung like tassels
  An' the flowers grew everywhere—
'Twas in green-leafy springtime
  I met sweet Rose Adair.

    O Rose Adair ! O Rose Adair !
      You are the radiant sun,
    The blossomed trees, an' scented breeze,
      An' song-birds all in one.

I met her sowin' mushrooms
  With her white feet in the grass ;
'Twas eve—but mornin' in the smile
  Of my sweet *cailín deas ;*
An' I kissed her—oh, so secretly
  That not a one should know—
But the roguish stars they winked above
  An' the daisies smiled below.

The Father in confession, Rose,
  Won't count that love a sin
That with a kiss taps at the heart
  An' lets an angel in ;
'Twas so love entered into mine
  An' made his dwellin' there—
If *that's* a sin, the Lord forgive
  Your beauty, Rose Adair !

If springtime never came at all
  To chase the winter's frown,
Her smile would coax the flowers up
  An' charm the sunshine down ;
There's not a perfumed breeze that blows
  Or bird that charms the air,
But stole its sweetness from the lips
  Of lovely Rose Adair.

The leaves will fall in autumn,
  An' the flowers all come to grief,
But the green love in my heart of hearts
  Will never shed a leaf !
For the sunshine of your bonny eyes
  Will keep it green and fair,
An' your breath will be its breeze-o'-spring,
  O, lovely Rose Adair.

PATRICK JAMES COLEMAN

BORN at Ballaghadereen, County Mayo, in 1867. He matriculated at London University, and later came to America and went into journalism. The following poem is singularly close to the soil, and characteristic of certain phases of Irish feeling.

SEED-TIME

I

THE top o' the mornin' to you, Mick,
   Isn't it fine an' dhry an' still?
Just an elegant day, avic,
   To stick the toleys on Tullagh hill.
The field is turned, an' every clod
   In ridge an' furrow is fresh an' brown ;
So let's away, with the help o' God,
   By the heel o' the evenin' we'll have them down.

     As long as there's plenty o' milk to churn,
       An' plenty o' pyaties in ridge an' furrow,
     By the winter fire we'll laugh to scorn
       The frown o' famine an' scowl o' sorrow.

II

There's a time to work, an' a time to talk ;
   So, Patsy, my boy, your pratin' shtop !
By Midsummer Day, blossom an' stalk,
   We'll feast our eyes on a right good crop.
Oh, the purple blossoms, so full o' joy,
   Burstin' up from our Irish loam,
They're bether than gold to the peasant, boy ;
   They crown him king in his Irish home !

     As long as the cows have milk to churn,
       With plenty o' pyaties in ridge an' furrow,
     By the winter hearth we'll laugh to scorn
       The frown o' famine an' scowl o' sorrow.

III

A year ago we wor full o' hope,
  For the stalks wor green by the First o' May,
But the brown blight fell over field an' slope,
  An' the poreens rotted by Lady Day.
You'd dig a ridge for a creel in vain ;
  But He left us still our dacint friends ;
If it comes again we won't complain—
  His will be done !—it's the besht He sends !
    As long as we've plenty o' milk to churn,
      An' plenty o' pyaties in ridge an' furrow,
    By the winter fire we'll laugh to scorn
      The frown o' famine an' scowl o' sorrow.

IV

An' whin the turf's in the haggard piled,
  We'll come, plase God ! with our spades and loys ;
It's busy ye'll be, then, Brigid, my child,
  Fillin' the baskets behind the boys.
So shtick thim deep in Ould Ireland's clay—
  It's nearly dusk, an' there's work galore ;
It's time enough in the winter to play,
  When the crop is safe on our cabin floor.
    As long as the cows have milk to churn,
      With plenty o' pyaties in ridge an' furrow,
    By the winter hearth we'll laugh to scorn
      The frown o' famine an' scowl o' sorrow.

PATRICK JOSEPH McCALL

MR. P. J. McCALL was born in Dublin, 1861, and educated at the Catholic University School, Leeson Street. His volumes of poems (besides excellent translations from the Irish) contain much racy and original verse, chiefly descriptive of peasant life in the County Wexford. There are no literary echoes in his work ; it springs straight from the soil ; and though Mr. McCall does not deal in tragedy or romance, he puts before us the humour,

the gaiety, the daily toil, and the half serious, half sportive
love-making of the Irish peasant with refreshing fidelity and
absence of rhetorical sentiment. Among his books are :
Irish Nóiníns (Daisies), 1894 ; and Songs of Erinn, 1899.

Old Pedhar Carthy from Clonmore

If you searched the county o' Carlow, ay, and back again,
  Wicklow too, and Wexford, for that matter you might try,
Never the equal of Old Pedhar would you crack again'—
  Never such another would delight your Irish eye !
Mirth, mime, and mystery, all were close combined in him,
  Divelment and drollery right to the very core,
As many tricks and turns as a two-year-old you'd find in him—
  In Old Pedhar Carthy from Clonmore !
        Old Pedhar, Old Pedhar, Old Pedhar Carthy !
        Old Pedhar Carthy from Clonmore !

Shure, whene'er the *bouchals* used to have a game o' ' Forty-five,'
  Pedhar was the master who could teach them how to play ;
Bring a half-crown—though you lost it, yet, as I'm alive,
  You'd be a famous player to your distant dying day.
Scornful grew his look if they chanced to hang your king or queen ;
  Better for your peace o' mind you'd never crossed his door ;
' You to play cards ! ' would he mutter in sarcasm keen—
  Old Pedhar Carthy from Clonmore !
        Old Pedhar, Old Pedhar, Old Pedhar Carthy !
        Old Pedhar Carthy from Clonmore !

Politics he knew better than the men in Parliament,
  And the wars in Europe for the past half-century ;
If you were to hear him with Cornelius Keogh in argument,
  Arranging every matter that was wrong in history !
Ah ! but if the talking ever travelled back to ' Ninety-eight,'
  Then our Pedhar's diatribes grew vehement and sore.
Rebel in his heart, how he hated to have long to wait !—
  Old Pedhar Carthy from Clonmore !
        Old Pedhar, Old Pedhar, Old Pedhar Carthy !
        Old Pedhar Carthy from Clonmore !

The mischief for tricks, he was never done inventing them ;
   Once he yoked Dan Donohoe's best milker to the plough—
At the Fair of Hacketstown there was no circumventing him ;
   He'd clear a crowd of *salachs*,[1] and you never could tell how !
The Ryans and the Briens and their factions were afraid of him ;
   For Pedhar's fighting kippeen could command a ready score.
Woe to the boys that spoke *cruked*, undismayed of him—
   Of Old Pedhar Carthy from Clonmore !

      Old Pedhar, Old Pedhar, Old Pedhar Carthy !
      Old Pedhar Carthy from Clonmore !

But the times grew bad, and the people talked so well and wise,
   Fighting left poor Ireland, and mad mischief had its head ;
Pedhar, left alone, began to muse and to soliloquise,
   Until the dear old fellow couldn't bear to leave the bed.
But when dead and buried all the neighbours felt his bitter loss—
   The place in Pedhar's absence such a look of sorrow wore—
They sighed and cried in turn from great Eagle Hill to Cameross
   For Old Pedhar Carthy from Clonmore !

      Old Pedhar, Old Pedhar, Old Pedhar Carthy !
      Old Pedhar Carthy from Clonmore !

      Old Pedhar, Old Pedhar, Old Pedhar Carthy !
      Old Pedhar Carthy from Clonmore !

HERSELF AND MYSELF

AN OLD MAN'S SONG

'TWAS beyond at Macreddin, at Owen Doyle's weddin',
   The boys got the pair of us out for a reel.
Says I : 'Boys, excuse us.'   Says they : 'Don't refuse us.'
   'I'll play nice and aisy,' says Larry O'Neill.
So off we went trippin' it, up an' down steppin' it—
   Herself and Myself on the back of the doore ;
Till Molly—God bless her !—fell into the dresser,
   An' I tumbled over a child on the floore.

---

        [1] Untidy people, tinkers, &c.

Says Herself to Myself : ' We're as good as the best o' them.'
Says Myself to Herself : ' Shure, we're betther than gold.'
Says Herself to Myself : ' We're as young as the rest o' them.'
Says Myself to Herself : ' Troth, we'll never grow old.'

As down the lane goin', I felt my heart growin'
    As young as it was forty-five years ago.
'Twas here in this *bóreen* I first kissed my *stóireen*—
    A sweet little colleen with skin like the snow.
I looked at my woman—a song she was hummin'
    As old as the hills, so I gave her a *pogue* ;[1]
'Twas like our old courtin', half sarious, half sportin',
    When Molly was young, an' when hoops were in vogue.

When she'd say to Myself : ' You can coort with the best o' them.'
    When I'd say to Herself : ' Sure, I'm betther than gold.'
When she'd say to Myself : ' You're as wild as the rest o' them.'
    And I'd say to Herself : ' Troth, I'm time enough old.'

LADY GILBERT (ROSA MULHOLLAND)[2]

A POPULAR and gifted Irish poetess and novelist born in
Belfast about 1855.   She is the author of a long list of novels
and books of verse, among which are VAGRANT VERSES
(1886); SPIRIT AND DUST (1908); and DREAMS AND REAL-
ITIES (1916) finished shortly before her death, as well as a
life of her husband, Sir John T. Gilbert (1905).

SONG

THE silent bird is hid in the boughs,
    The scythe is hid in the corn,
The lazy oxen wink and drowse,
    The grateful sheep are shorn ;
Redder and redder burns the rose,
    The lily was ne'er so pale,
Stiller and stiller the river flows
    Along the path to the vale.

---

[1] *Pogue* : **kiss.**   [2] See also p. **179.**

A little door is hid in the boughs,
　　A face is hiding within ;
When birds are silent and oxen drowse
　　Why should a maiden spin ?
Slower and slower turns the wheel,
　　The face turns red and pale,
Brighter and brighter the looks that steal
　　Along the path to the vale.

Saint Brigid

'MID dewy pastures girdled with blue air,
　　Where ruddy kine the limpid waters drink,
Through violet-purpled woods of green Kildare,
　　'Neath rainbow skies, by tinkling rivulet's brink,
O Brigid, young, thy tender, snow-white feet
　　In days of old on breezy morns and eves
Wandered through labyrinths of sun and shade,
　　　　Thy face so innocent-sweet
　　Shining with love that neither joys nor grieves
Save as the angels, meek and holy maid !

With white fire in thy hand that burned no man,
　　But cleansed and warmed where'er its ray might fall,
Nor ever wasted low, or needed fan,
　　Thou walk'dst at eve among the oak-trees tall.
There thou didst chant thy vespers, while each star
　　Grew brighter listening through the leafy screen.
Then ceased the song-bird all his love-notes soft,
　　　　His music near or far,
　　Hushing his passion 'mid the sombre green
To let thy peaceful whispers float aloft.

And still from heavenly choirs thou steal'st by night
　　To tell sweet Avès in the woods unseen,
To tend the shrine-lamps with thy *flambeau* white
　　And set thy tender footprints in the green.
Thus sing our birds with holy note and pure,
　　As though the loves of angels were their theme ;

Thus burn to throbbing flame our sacred fires
With heats that still endure ;
Thence hath our daffodil its golden gleam,
From thy dear mindfulness that never tires !

KATHARINE TYNAN-HINKSON

WHEN in 1885 the little volume entitled LOUISE DE LA VALLIÈRE was given to the world, not a few lovers of modern poetry perceived that here was the voice of a new and a real singer. Faults it would have been doubtless easy to find, but they were the faults of youth. Where, for instance, so many and so various were the metres essayed, it would be strange for a young writer not to fail occasionally in the striking of the first chord ; the metre is sometimes not, in the first line, inevitable and unmistakable, and the reader may stumble for a moment before he finds it. Here and there, again, in Mrs. Tynan-Hinkson's work a rhyme may be found which will not find acceptance east of St. George's Channel. Having made these reservations, we have in LOUISE DE LA VALLIÈRE not only a promise that has been since fulfilled, but an achievement well worthy of note for its own sake. Greater experience in metrical training has long since corrected such roughnesses as are to be expected in an early work, and the most captious critic will not find fault with the technical workmanship of THE WIND IN THE TREES. And apart from this point—a minor one, doubtless, when compared with the great essentials of poetry, inspiration, sincereness, insight, and real melody— Miss Tynan's subsequent work has placed her among the foremost women writers in English verse of the present day.

There are three notes immediately and distinctly discernible in Mrs. Tynan-Hinkson's poetry which demand special observation—love of country ; a religious feeling at once deep, sincere, and glowing ; and an intimate appreciation of the beauty and essence of external Nature. The first of these need not

detain us long ; it is obvious on perusal.   Mrs. Hinkson is
Irish in many of her subjects and in much of her style, and
her work is pervaded with a healthy patriotism such as can
hardly offend either those of another nationality or those of
her compatriots who differ from her upon points of present
interest and pressure.   She loves the real Ireland as well as
that of romance, and in (for instance) the pathetic verses
entitled ' An Island Fisherman ' gives a picture of the home-
tragedies of the poor of to-day as faithful to truth and Nature
as the piece called ' Waiting ' in her first published volume is
to the glory and glamour of an Ireland that has passed away.
But if this be a charm appealing especially to her compatriots,
in her devotional moods she represents and interprets, as few
others now living do, the yearnings and the mental struggles,
the temptations, fears, and hopes of the Christian soul, not
only for the Church to which she belongs, but for an audience
larger still, inasmuch as that which has found utterance in her
religious verse is concerned with the central truths of Christianity and its essential operation.   In the ' Chapel of the
Grail,' the ' Rock of Ages,' the ' Angel of the Annunciation,'
this devout and reverent spirit is expressed in artistic form, and
the charm of language throughout enables one to understand
how to her at least ' there remaineth therefore a rest to the
people of God.'

The critics have already pointed out the special fascination
which St. Francis exercises upon Mrs. Hinkson's mind as
shown in her poetry.   This influence indeed is obvious, and
it would have been strange had it been absent.   For that
gentlest and most lovable figure among the saints of the
Mediæval Church must necessarily make a peculiar appeal to
the spirit of a writer so full of reverent admiration for all the
creatures of God ; so imbued with a loving observation of the
beauties of Nature, whether exhibited on a broad and grand
scale, as in the great landscapes, or in closer detail in bird,
insect, flower, and leaf.   It is in this latter sphere indeed that
to my mind Mrs. Hinkson rises to her highest point.   She
loves the creatures, and therefore understands them and is able

to depict them so well. I have spoken of 'the essence of external Nature ;' what I am endeavouring to express by the phrase is the life that is in Nature, and that not every one perceives, because to see it one must have reverence and love —reverence for the great spiritual forces that imbue external Nature, and love for the small things that are so beautiful, and even glorious, when one watches them with an understanding eye. I have tried to avoid the mention of Wordsworth in this connection, because to my mind Mrs. Hinkson has come to this inner understanding of Nature by another path than his ; but of course it is an understanding of the same kind. Other poets have had it ; it is a part—almost, though not quite, an essential part—of the poetic insight, innate but trained by observation. Take, for instance, the murmur and rustle of that living thing, the rain ; how variously will two different poets, of diverse genius, take note of it ! In his beautiful verses ' Il pleure dans mon cœur Comme il pleut sur la ville' Verlaine has the lines :

> O bruit doux de la pluie
> Par terre et sur les toits !
> Pour un cœur qui s'ennuie
> O le chant de la pluie !

The rain is already falling ; we are treating of its effect on the cast-down spirit of a poet caged and confined in prison-cells. We are in a city; the rain falls on roof and pavement. Compare with this Mrs. Hinkson's short poem called ' Drought : '

> Little voices complain,
> The leaves rustle before the rain.
>
> .   .   .   .
>
> Only the trembling cry
> Of young leaves murmuring thirstily.
> Only the moan and stir
> Of little hands in the boughs I hear,
> Beckoning the rain to come
> Out of the evening, out of the gloom.

Here the rain has not yet fallen ; its sister-creatures are calling, yearning for it. The voices are the voices of the country;

we are in the broad free air of heaven. The human touch is here also, but it does not come till all the rest is realised :

> And hearts that complain.
> The leaves rustle before the rain.

Both passages are beautiful ; in both a few lines suffice to draw the picture, a few notes to make the music and waken the emotion ; but the results are quite different.

Mrs. Hinkson is at her best out of doors. She exults in the beauty of Nature ; nothing is too small, too near the sod for observation, for love and song. In THE WIND IN THE TREES the piece called ' Leaves,' somewhat akin to that just now quoted, is full of subdued expression and fine suggestion, and yet it is radiant with colour. For Mrs. Hinkson has a keen sense of natural colour ; naturally therefore she delights in it ; colour is the music of the eye. To one who interprets the leaves so well, what songs have not the flowers to sing? Her own, therefore, are full of natural colour ; they are full also of the perfumes of flower and field, and of the voices of the birds. Of these last the short poem entitled ' Larks ' is only one instance. It is the silence of Nature that is dreadful, and the exact word is found by the poet, as (in ' Cruel Winter ')

> The dear song-thrush is dead,
> The valley hath instead
>   Only the silence.
> The silence *aches* all day
> In hills and valleys gray . . .

I must not leave without mention the songs of pathos and affection, many of them touching and sweet, which are to be found scattered through Mrs. Hinkson's volumes. I could wish, perhaps, that the author had exercised a little more literary economy ; in so considerable an output not everything can be at the same high level. Yet sometimes the fault may lie with the reader or the critic. Thus, I have not spoken of the Miracle Plays, because I am not quite sure of myself, holding as I do that the mediæval religious drama has not been

successfully revived by any writer, even the greatest. Mrs.
Hinkson certainly possesses the first necessary quality for such
work, the right devotional spirit ; but I am disposed to cavil
at the form (or else, perhaps, at the title). 'The play—the play's
the thing,' and in English—at all events, in this dying century—I doubt whether dramatic action and the dramatic spirit
can be rendered in lyrical measures such as Mrs. Hinkson has
here adopted. But this is the opinion of one who holds that
Calderon and Metastasio cannot be translated into the English
tongue without considerable loss. Every language has its
limitations ; yet it is sometimes well to strive against them, in
the hope of ultimately broadening them, even but a little.
Mrs. Hinkson has done gallant service in several spheres ; but
it will have been perceived that the present writer's preference
is for those delightful swift glances into Nature and Nature's
secrets of which THE WIND IN THE TREES is full ; this at
least is a booklet from which I would not willingly spare a
page. It holds the secrets of the birds, the leaves, and the
flowers ; and the human voice, too, is deep and touching—the
voice of the Irish poetess :

> Oh, green and fresh your English sod
>   With daisies sprinkled over ;
> But greener far were the fields I trod,
>   And the honeyed Irish clover.
>
> Oh, well your skylark cleaves the blue
>   To bid the sun good-morrow ;
> He has not the bonny song I knew
>   High over an Irish furrow.
>
> And often, often, I'm longing still,
>   This gay and golden weather,
> For my father's face by an Irish hill
>   And he and I together.

GEORGE A. GREENE.

Born in Dublin in the early sixties, Miss Katharine Tynan was for
some time at school at a Dominican convent in Drogheda, which, however,
she left at the age of fourteen : the rest of her education was gained at
home, and mainly by her own energy and love of study, to which her

father allowed full scope. With the exception of a few visits to London, Miss Tynan remained at home until her marriage in 1893 with Mr. Henry Hinkson, ex-Scholar of Trinity College, Dublin, and himself a well-known writer. She settled in London with her husband, and was engaged in constant literary work until her death in 1931. Her poetical output began in 1885 with the publication of LOUISE DE LA VALLIÈRE AND OTHER POEMS (Kegan Paul & Co.), which was followed by SHAMROCKS, 1887; BALLADS AND LYRICS, 1892 (same publishers); CUCKOO SONGS (John Lane, 1894); MIRACLE PLAYS (*idem*, 1896); A LOVER'S BREAST-KNOT (Elkin Mathews, 1897); THE WIND IN THE TREES (Grant Richards, 1898); POEMS BY KATHARINE TYNAN (1901); INNOCENCIES : A BOOK OF VERSE (1905); LAUDS (1909); IRISH POEMS (1913); FLOWER OF YOUTH (1915); THE HOLY WAR (1916); and COLLECTED POEMS (1930). Mrs. Tynan-Hinkson also edited an anthology, THE WILD HARP (1923).

LARKS

ALL day in exquisite air
The song clomb an invisible stair,
Flight on flight, story on story,
Into the dazzling glory.

There was no bird, only a singing,
Up in the glory, climbing and ringing,
Like a small golden cloud at even,
Trembling 'twixt earth and heaven.

I saw no staircase winding, winding,
Up in the dazzle, sapphire and blinding,
Yet round by round, in exquisite air,
The song went up the stair.

DAFFODIL

WHO passes down the wintry street?
Hey, ho, daffodil !
A sudden flame of gold and sweet.

With sword of emerald girt so meet,
And golden gay from head to feet.

How are you here this wintry day?
Hey, ho, daffodil !
Your radiant fellows yet delay.

No windflower dances scarlet gay,
Nor crocus-flame lights up the way.

What land of cloth o' gold and green,
      Hey, ho, daffodil !
Cloth o' gold with the green between,

Was that you left but yestere'en
To light a gloomy world and mean ?

King trumpeter to Flora queen,
      Hey, ho, daffodil !
Blow, and the golden jousts begin.

SUMMER-SWEET

HONEY-SWEET, sweet as honey smell the lilies,
    Little lilies of the gold in a ring ;
Little censers of pale gold are the lilies,
    That the wind, sweet and sunny, sets a-swing.

Smell the rose, sweet of sweets, all a-blowing !
    Hear the cuckoo call in dreams, low and sweet !
Like a very John-a-Dreams coming, going.
    There's honey in the grass at our feet.

There's honey in the leaf and the blossom,
    And honey in the night and the day,
And honey-sweet the heart in Love's bosom,
    And honey sweet the words Love will say.

AUGUST WEATHER

DEAD heat and windless air,
    And silence over all ;
Never a leaf astir,
    But the ripe apples fall ;
Plums are purple-red,
    Pears amber and brown ;
Thud ! in the garden-bed
    Ripe apples fall down.

Air like a cider-press
  With the bruised apples' scent ;
Low whistles express
  Some sleepy bird's content ;
Still world and windless sky,
  A mist of heat o'er all ;
Peace like a lullaby,
  And the ripe apples fall.

AN ISLAND FISHERMAN

I GROAN as I put out
  My nets on the say,
To hear the little *girshas* shout,
  Dancin' among the spray.

Ochone ! the childher pass
  An' lave us to our grief ;
The stranger took my little lass
  At the fall o' the leaf.

Why would you go so fast
  With him you never knew ?
In all the throuble that is past
  I never frowned on you.

The light o' my old eyes !
  The comfort o' my heart !
Waitin' for me your mother lies
  In blessed Innishart.

Her lone grave I keep
  From all the cold world wide,
But you in life an' death will sleep
  The stranger beside.

Ochone ! my thoughts are wild :
  But little blame I say ;
An ould man hungerin' for his child,
  Fishin' the livelong day.

You will not run again,
　Laughin' to see me land.
Oh, what was pain an' throuble then,
　Holdin' your little hand?

Or when your head let fall
　Its soft curls on my breast ?
Why do the childher grow at all
　To love the stranger best ?

LUX IN TENEBRIS

AT night what things will stalk abroad,
　What veiled shapes, and eyes of dread !
With phantoms in a lonely road
　And visions of the dead.

The kindly room when day is here,
　At night takes ghostly terrors on ;
And every shadow hath its fear,
　And every wind its moan.

Lord Jesus, Day-Star of the world,
　Rise Thou and bid this dark depart
And all the east, a rose uncurled,
　Grow golden at the heart !

Lord, in the watches of the night,
　Keep Thou my soul ! a trembling thing
As any moth that in daylight
　Will spread a rainbow wing.

WINTER EVENING

BUT the rain is gone by, and the day's dying out in a splendour ;
　There is flight as of many gold wings in the heart of the sky :
God's birds, it may be, who return from their ministry tender,
　Flying home from the earth, like the earth-birds when darkness
　　is nigh.

E E

Gold plumes and gold feathers, the wings hide the roseate faces,
  But a glimmer of roseate feet breaks the massing of gold :
There's gold hair blowing back, and a drifting of one in clear
    spaces,
  A little child-angel whose flight is less sure and less bold.

They are gone, they are flown, but their footprints have left the
    sky ruddy,
  And the night's coming on with a moon in a tender green sea,
And my heart is fled home, with a flight that is certain and steady
  To her home, to her nest, to the place where her treasure shall
    be—
Across the dark hills where the scarlet to purple is waning ;
  For the birds will fly home, will fly home, when the night's
    coming on.
But hark ! in the trees how the wind is complaining and straining,
  For the birds that are flown it may be, or the nests that are
    gone.

WAITING

IN a grey cave, where comes no glimpse of sky,
  Set in the blue hill's heart full many a mile,
Having the dripping stone for canopy,
  Missing the wind's laugh and the good sun's smile,
I, Fionn, with all my sleeping warriors lie.

In the great outer cave our horses are,
  Carved of grey stone, with heads erect, amazed,
Purple their trappings, gold each bolt and bar,
  One fore-foot poised, the quivering thin ears raised :
Methinks they scent the battle from afar.

A frozen hound lies by each warrior's feet—
  Ah, Bran, my jewel ! Bran, my king of hounds !
Deep-throated art thou, mighty-flanked, and fleet ;
  Dost thou remember how with giant bounds
Didst chase the red deer in the noontide heat ?

I was a king in ages long ago,
　A mighty warrior, and a seer likewise,
Still mine eyes look with solemn gaze of woe
　From stony lids adown the centuries,
And in my frozen heart I know, I know.

A giant I, of a primeval race,
　These, great-limbed, bearing helm and shield and sword,
My good knights are, and each still, awful face
　Will one day wake to knowledge at a word—
O'erhead the groaning years turn round apace.

Here with the peaceful dead we keep our state ;
　Some day a cry shall ring adown the lands :
'The hour is come, the hour grown large with fate.'
　He knows who hath the centuries in His hands
When that shall be—till then we watch and wait.

The queens that loved us, whither be they gone,
　The sweet, large women with the hair as gold,
As though one drew long threads from out the sun ?
　Ages ago, grown tired, and very cold,
They fell asleep beneath the daisies wan.

The waving woods are gone that once we knew,
　And towns grown grey with years are in their place :
A little lake, as innocent and blue
　As my queen's eyes were, lifts a baby face
Where once my palace towers were fair to view.

The fierce old gods we hailed with worshipping,
　The blind old gods, waxed mad with sin and blood,
Laid down their godhead as an idle thing
　At a God's feet, whose throne was but a Rood ;
His crown, wrought thorns ; His joy, long travailing.

Here in the gloom I see it all again,
　As ages since in visions mystical
I saw the swaying crowds of fierce-eyed men,
　And heard the murmurs in the judgment hall.
Oh, for one charge of my dark warriors then !

E E 2

Nay, if He willed, His Father presently
   Twelve star-girt legions unto Him had given.
I traced the blood-stained path to Calvary,
   And heard far off the angels weep in heaven ;
Then the Rood's arms against an awful sky.

I saw Him when they pierced Him, hands and feet,
   And one came by and smote Him, this new King,
So pale and harmless, on the tired face sweet ;
   He was so lovely and so pitying,
The icy heart in me began to beat.

Then a strong cry—the mountain heaved and swayed
   That held us in its heart, the groaning world
Was reft with lightning and in ruins laid,
   His Father's awful hand the red bolts hurled,
And He was dead—I trembled, sore afraid.

Then I upraised myself with mighty strain
   In the gloom, I heard the tumult rage without,
I saw those large dead faces glimmer plain,
   The life just stirred within them and went out,
And I fell back, and grew to stone again.

So the years went – on earth how fleet they be !
   Here in this cave their feet are slow of pace,
And I grow old, and tired exceedingly,
   I would the sweet earth were my dwelling-place—
Shamrocks and little daisies wrapping me !

There I should lie, and feel the silence sweet
   As a meadow at noon, where birds sing in the trees ;
To mine ears should come the patter of little feet,
   And baby cries, and croon of summer seas,
And the wind's laughter in the upland wheat.

Meantime o'erhead the years were full and bright,
   With a kind sun, and gold wide fields of corn ;
The happy children sang from morn to night,
   The blessed church bells rang, new arts were born,
Strong towns rose up and glimmered fair and white.

Once came a wind of conflict, fierce as hail,
　　And beat about my brows : on the eastward shore,
Where never since the Vikings' dark ships sail,
　　All day the battle raged with mighty roar ;
At night the Victor's fair dead face was pale.

Ah ! the dark years since then, the anguished cry
　　That pierced my deaf ears, made my hard eyes weep,
From Erin wrestling in her agony,
　　While we, her strongest, in a helpless sleep,
Lay, as the blood-stained years trailed slowly by.

And often in those years the East was drest
　　In phantom fires, that mocked the distant dawn,
Then blackest night—her bravest and her best
　　Were led to die, while I slept dumbly on,
With the whole mountain's weight upon my breast.

Once in my time it chanced a peasant hind
　　Strayed to this cave.　I heard, and burst my chain,
And raised my awful face stone-dead and blind,
　　Cried, ' Is it time ? ' and so fell back again.
I heard his wild cry borne adown the wind.

Some hearts wait with us.　Owen Roe O'Neill,
　　The kingliest king that ever went uncrowned,
Sleeps in his panoply of gold and steel
　　Ready to wake, and in the kindly ground
A many another's death-wounds close and heal.

Great Hugh O'Neill, far off in purple Rome,
　　And Hugh O'Donnell, in their stately tombs
Lie, with their grand fair faces turned to home.
　　Some day a voice will ring adown the glooms :
' Arise, ye Princes, for the hour is come ! '

And these will rise, and we will wait them here,
　　In this blue hill-heart in fair Donegal ;
That hour shall sound the clash of sword and spear,
　　The steeds shall neigh to hear their masters' call,
And the hounds' cry shall echo shrill and clear.

St. Francis and the Wolf

This wolf for many a day
 Had scourged and trodden down
 The folk of Agobio town ;
Old was he, lean and grey.

Dragging a mildewed bone,
 Down from his lair he came,
 Saw in the sunset flame
Our Father standing alone.

Dust on his threadbare gown,
 Dust on his blessed feet,
 Faint from long fast and heat,
His light of life died down.

This wolf laid bare his teeth,
 And growling low there stood ;
 His lips were black with blood,
His eyes were fires of death.

So for a spring crouched he ;
 But the Saint raised his head—
 ' Peace, Brother Wolf,' he said,
' God made both thee and me.'

And with the Cross signed him :
 The wolf fell back a-stare,
 Sat on his haunches there,
Forbidding, black and grim.

' Come nearer, in Christ's Name,'
 Said Francis, and, so bid,
 Like a small dog that's chid,
The fierce beast fawning came.

Trotting against his side,
 And licked the tender hand
 That with soft touch and bland
Caressed his wicked hide.

' Brother,' the Saint said then,
  ' Who gave thee leave to kill ?
  Thou hast slain of thine own will
Not only beasts, but men.

'And God is wroth with thee :
  If thou wilt not repent,
  His anger shall be sent
To smite thee terribly.

' See, all men hate thy name,
  And with it mothers fright
  The froward child by night.
Great are thy sin and shame.

' All true dogs thee pursue ;
  Thou shouldst hang high in air
  Like a thief and murderer,
Hadst thou thy lawful due.

'Yet, seeing His hands have made
  Even thee, thou wicked one
  I bring no malison,
But blessing bring instead.

' And I will purchase peace
  Between this folk and thee
  So love for hate shall be,
And all thy sinning cease.

' Say, wilt thou have it so ? '
  Thereat, far off, we saw
  The beast lift up his paw,
His great tail wagging go.

Our Father took the paw
  Into his blessed hand,
  Knelt down upon the sand,
Facing the creature's jaw.

That were a sight to see :
   Agobio's folk trooped out ;
   They heard not all that rout,
Neither the beast nor he.

For he was praying yet,
   And on his illumined face
   A shamed and loving gaze
The terrible wolf had set.

When they came through the town,
   His hand that beast did stroke,
   He spake unto the folk
Flocking to touch his gown.

A sweet discourse was this ;
   He prayed them that they make
   Peace, for the Lord Christ's sake,
With this poor wolf of His ;

And told them of their sins,
   How each was deadlier far
   Than wolves or lions are,
Or sharks with sword-like fins.

Afterwards some came near,
   Took the beast's paw and shook,
   And answered his sad look
With words of honest cheer.

Our Father, ere he went,
   Bade that each one should leave
   Some food at morn and eve
For his poor penitent.

And so, three years or more,
   The wolf came morn and even—
   Yea, long forgiven and shriven,
Fed at each townsman's door ;

And grew more grey and old,
　Withal so sad and mild,
　Him feared no little child
Sitting in the sun's gold.

The women, soft of heart,
　Trusted him and were kind :
　Men grew of equal mind,
None longer stepped apart.

The very dogs, 'twas said,
　Would greet him courteously,
　And pass his portion by,
Though they went on unfed.

But when three years were gone
　He came no more, but died ;
　In a cave on the hillside
You may count each whitening bone.

And then it came to pass
　All gently of him spake,
　For Francis his dear sake,
Whose Brother Wolf this was.

ROSE KAVANAGH

Born at Killadroy, County Tyrone, on June 23, 1859, and
died of consumption on February 26, 1891. She was a contributor of poems and stories to the Irish papers, &c., and a
bright future was predicted for her. Her early death caused
widespread regret among readers of Irish literature, and a deep
sense of loss to the personal friends to whom her sweet and noble
character had endeared her.

St. Michan's Churchyard

INSIDE the city's throbbing heart
One spot I know set well apart
From life's hard highway, life's loud mart.

Each Dublin lane and street and square
Around might echo ; but in there
The sound stole soft as whispered prayer.

A little, lonely, green graveyard,
The old churchyard its solemn guard,
The gate with naught but sunbeams barred ;

While other sunbeams went and came
Above the stone which waits the name
His land must write with Freedom's flame.[1]

The slender elm above that stone,
Its summer wreath of leaves had thrown
Around the heart so quiet grown.

A robin the bare boughs among,
Let loose his little soul in song—
Quick liquid gushes fresh and strong !

And quiet heart, and bird and tree,
Seemed linked in some strange sympathy
Too fine for mortal eye to see—

But full of balm and soothing sweet,
For those who sought that calm retreat ;
For aching breast and weary feet.

Each crowded street and thoroughfare
Was echoing round it—yet in there
The peace of Heaven was everywhere !

---

[1] Referring to the grave of Robert Emmet.

ALICE FURLONG

MISS FURLONG'S small volume of poems, ROSES AND RUE, when it appeared in 1899, attracted much recognition from the leading organs of literary criticism. Her poetry has delicacy, pathos, and music, and much power of drawing a vivid picture in few words. The authoress was born in County Dublin about 1875, and has written much in prose and verse for *The Irish Monthly* and other periodicals, as well as being the author of several novels and many short stories.

THE DREAMER

A WIND that dies on the meadows lush,
Trembling stars in the breathless hush!—
The maiden's sleeping face doth bloom
A sad, white lily in the gloom.

Along the limpid horizon borne
The first gold breathing of the morn!—
A lovely dawn of dreams doth creep
Athwart the darkness of her sleep.

In the dim shadow of the eaves
A quiet stir of lifted leaves!
As in the old, beloved days,
She wandereth by happy ways.

With half-awakened twitterings,
The young birds preen their folded wings!
She giveth a forget-me-not
To him who long ago forgot.

Athwart the meadow, dewy-sweet,
A wind comes wandering on light feet!
For her the wind is from the south,
His kiss is kind upon her mouth.

In the bird's house of emerald
The sun is weaving webs of gold!
He *never* coldly went apart!
She *never* broke her passionate heart!

Pipeth clear from the orchard close
A thrush in the bowers of white and rose !
She waketh praying : ' God is good,
With visions for my solitude.'

For full delight of birds and flowers
The long day spins its golden hours.
She serves the household destinies ;
The dream is happy in her eyes.

JANE BARLOW

MISS JANE BARLOW'S admirable sketches of peasant-life in
Ireland have in a few years gained for her a well-deserved reputation among the Irish writers in prose of the present generation ; it may be doubted indeed whether any one has to the
same extent sounded the depths of Irish character in the
country districts and touched so many chords of sympathy,
humour, and pathos.   Of her work in verse, with which I have
here to do, a portion, and that perhaps the most significant,
falls into the same category.   BOGLAND STUDIES (among
which ' Terence Macran ' may be included) are indeed, save
for the metrical form, just another volume of the IRISH IDYLLS
which have charmed and delighted so many readers.   It is not
merely the peasant dialect that is faithfully and picturesquely
reproduced, but the working of the rural mind and the emotions of the heart, fully and sympathetically understood ; so
much so that in the eight studies thus classed together it
has become inevitable that in each case the narrator should
be the peasant himself or herself.   It is because the author
has so completely succeeded in identifying herself with her
characters that the language employed by them as means of
expression is so veritably and vividly Irish, natural, and not
put on.   Thus the flashes of wit, the neat turns of phrase, the
quick and apt similes, the quaint and picturesque form and
colour of language, strike the reader not only as characteristic,

unmistakable Irish sayings, exactly such as are to be caught
flying in every village, but they arise naturally out of the
thought. One recognises that at that juncture the peasant
would have said either what he is made to say, or something
very like it, and bearing the same individual semblance.
Hence while such passages are eminently quotable, they lose
somewhat by quotation apart from their context. It is because
the individual and the environment have between them created
the psychological moment that the peasant's quaint philosophy
breaks out so aptly in such passages as

For it's aisier risin' a quarrel than sthrikin' a match on a wall ;

or

So thinks I to meself ; but sure, musha, wan's thoughts is like beads off a
thread,
Slippin' each after each in a hurry : an' so I kep' considherin' on ;

or

Thin the bugle rang out—Och, I've ne'er heard the like, yet wan aisy
can tell
They'd ha' lep' all the locked gates of Heaven to ride with that music
to Hell ;

or again

'T is the same as if God an' the Divil tuk turns to be ownin' the earth.

It would be hypercritical to examine the metre too closely;
the narrative comes rushing quickly, with sudden irregular
gusts, as one feels it would naturally come.

For my present purpose, that of selection, this unity and
continuity has one inconvenience ; the stories in BOGLAND
STUDIES are too long for one of them to be quoted here in its
entirety, and being in fact ' short stories ' they are too ably
written to permit of abbreviation, and extracts would be quite
unrepresentative of Miss Barlow's excellence in this line. I
can only hope that what I have said will cause readers to turn to
them with something of that zest which those who know her
prose writings do not need to have the critic's help in awaken-
ing. In TH' OULD MASTER we have a tragedy of the sea told

from the peasant's standpoint on land, the real tragedy being in the household of the kind old landlord during his long bereavement and before his long-absent son returns to die in the bay at home, for of this last cruel blow Fate, less cruel than would at first appear, spares him the knowledge. Yet the shadow deepens upon the land, for the new owner of the estate will be a stranger having no hold upon the affections of the peasantry, the expression of which forms the lighter side of the picture. The ruling class appears in a far less favourable light in ' Past Praying for ; or, The Souper's Widow,' where the crime of the dead ' souper' lay in accepting, on condition of attending at Sunday service, the relief distributed by the parson – accepting it not for himself, for he died leaving it untouched, but for his family, perishing around him in the dread years of famine. In ' Walled Out' and in ' Last Time at M'Gurk's ' we have two excellent studies of peasant philosophy ; in ' Terence Macran ' a delightful and at the same time pathetic picture of one of the old hedge-schools of Ireland. But the most dramatic of these stories is that entitled ' By the Bog-hole.' The hero and heroine, next-door neighbours in the same boreen, are children together, Jimmy's special care as a boy being to see that Nelly does not fall into the bog-hole,

> So ugly and black,
> Wid its sides cut wall-sthraight wid the spade, an' the wather like midnight below,
> Lyin' far out of reach.

They grow up together, but just as Jimmy becomes aware of what is stirring in his heart a handsome, gaudy young soldier steps round the end of the turf-stack, 'and himself was just Felix Magrath comin' home to his father's on leave.' This is the first breath of the ill-wind of Fate. Felix is pleasant, plausible, full of stirring stories of strange lands 'where the curiousist things ye could think do be plenty as turf-sods in stacks,' and of course Nell listens to him, 'small blame to her ; ' and equally of course Jimmy thinks of provoking him to a quarrel, being cursed by all the torments of jealousy. But, though he believes his superior strength would give him the victory, Jimmy puts the temptation from him, and determines to sacrifice his own happiness to Nelly's. And at this very moment Felix is bidding farewell to her, for it turns out he has a wife at the Curragh ; and in the brief scene that follows he takes a step back, forgetting the bog-hole is near at hand. When Jimmy comes up, he is only in time to save Nelly from flinging herself into the black waters after her false lover, and when she faints, and recovers consciousness only to go out of her mind, it is clear enough to the villagers now arriving on the scene that Jimmy has murdered his rival before his sweetheart's eyes : a conclusion supported by the girl's ravings. How he rises to the height of this last fierce trial I leave the reader to ascertain for himself.

Another portion of Miss Barlow's work falls into a different category, and though not so obviously Irish in subject is excellent in quality, and treats of a subject which probably finds its best expression in Celtic lands—that of fairy lore. This is a branch of study which has of late years attracted the attention of all lovers of literature, as distinguished from literary form. Together with its kindred sciences of mythology and folklore, it provides us with the nearest glimpses now obtainable of the primitive imagination of man, upon which almost all imaginative literature, even the greatest, is primarily founded. We need not—cannot—be faithless to or forgetful of ' the glory that was Greece and the grandeur that was Rome,' the light wherewith Dante illumined the darkness of ages, the ' spacious times of great Elizabeth,' the triumphal march-music of French and German literature ; yet often from the *crambe repetita* of classical learning, from its meticulous criticism, from the stifling atmosphere of over-culture, from the mists and mire of decadence, one turns with relief to the broad skies and the fresh breezes of a simpler age and a less sophisticated humanity, in whose root-thoughts are the germs of later and more gorgeous imaginings. So Miss Barlow turns from the ' Batrachomyomachia ' to ' The End of Elfintown,' and gives us a delightful glimpse of fairyland, of the troubles which descended on the race of the elves, of the passing of Oberon, and the twilight of the lesser gods.

GEORGE A. GREENE.

Miss Jane Barlow was born in Clontarf, County Dublin. She spent much of her life at Raheny in the same county, and published in verse: BOGLAND STUDIES (Fisher Unwin, 1891; enlarged edition, Hodder & Stoughton, 1893); THE BATTLE OF THE FROGS AND MICE—a metrical version of the 'Batrachomyomachia' (Methuen, 1894); THE END OF ELFINTOWN (Macmillan, 1894); GHOST-BEREFT (1901) and THE MOCKERS (1908); besides scattered poems in various periodicals, among which may be mentioned TERENCE MACRAN : A HEDGE-SCHOOL STUDY, a story in verse in the style and metre of BOGLAND STUDIES, originally published in *The Journal of Education* for May, 1894, and since reprinted in ESSAYS AND MOCK ESSAYS (Arnold). Miss Barlow's prose works are more numerous, and include : IRISH IDYLLS (Hodder & Stoughton, 1892); KERRIGAN'S QUALITY (same publishers, 1894); STRANGERS AT LISCONNEL—a second series of Irish Idylls (same publishers, 1895); MAUREEN'S FAIRING and MRS. MARTIN'S COMPANY, both in the 'Irish Library' (Dent, 1895 and 1896); A CREEL OF IRISH STORIES (Methuen, 1897); and FROM THE EAST UNTO THE WEST (same publishers, 1898). Miss Barlow died in 1917.

MISTHER DENIS'S RETURN

FROM 'TH' OULD MASTER'

AN' the thought of us each was the boat; och, however'd she stand it at all,

If she'd started an hour or two back, an' been caught in the thick o' that squall?

Sure, it's lost she was, barrin' by luck it so chanced she'd run under the lee

O' Point Bertragh or Irish Lonane; an' 'twas liker the crathurs 'ud be

Crossin' yonder the open, wid never a shelter, but waves far an wide

Rowlin' one on the other till ye'd seem at the feet of a mad mountain-side.

An' the best we could hope was they'd seen that the weather'd be
turnin' out quare,

An' might, happen, ha' settled they wouldn't come over, but bide
where they were.

Yet, begorrah ! 'twould be the quare weather entirely, as some of
us said,

That 'ud put Misther Denis off aught that he'd fairly tuk into his
head.

Thin Tim Duigan sez : 'Arrah, lads, whist ! afther sailin' thro'
oceans o' say

Don't tell *me* he's naught better to do than get dhrowned in our
dhrop of a bay.'

An' the words were scarce out of his mouth, whin hard by, thro' a
dhrift o' the haze,

The ould boat we beheld sthrivin' on in the storm—och, the yell we
did raise !

An' it's little we yelled for, bedad ! for next instant there under
our eyes,

Not a couple o' perch from the pier-end, th' ould baste she must
take an' capsize.

Och ! small blame to thim all if we'd never seen sight of a one o'
thim more,

Wid the waves thumpin' thuds where they fell, like the butt-ends
o' beams on a door ;

An' the black hollows whirlin' between, an' the dhrift flyin' over
thim thick,

'S if the Divil had melted down Hell, an' was stirrin' it up wid a
stick.

But it happint the wave that they met wid was flounderin'
sthraight to the strand,

An' just swep' thim up nate on its way, till it set thim down safe
where the sand

Isn't wet twice a twelvemonth, no hurt on thim all, on'y dhrippin'
an' dazed.

And one come to his feet nigh me door, where that mornin' me
heifer had grazed,

An', bedad ! 'twas himself, Misther Denis, stood blinkin' and shakin'
the wet

F F

From his hair : ' Hullo, Connor!' sez he, ' is it you, man?' He'd never forget

One he'd known. But I'd hardly got hould of his hand, an' was wishin' him joy,

Whin, worse luck, he looked round an' he spied Widdy Sullivan's imp of a boy

That a wave had tuk off of his feet, an' was floatin' away from the beach,

An' he screechin' an' sthretchin' his arms to be saved, but no help was in reach.

An' as soon as the young master he seen it, he caught his hand out o' me own :

' Now, stand clear, man,' sez he ; ' would ye have me be lavin' the lad there to dhrown?'

An' wid that he throd knee-deep in foam-swirls. Ochone! but he gev us the slip,

Runnin' sheer down the black throat o' Death, an' he just afther 'scapin' its grip ;

For the wild says come flappin' an' boomin' an' smotherin' o'er him, an' back

In the lap o' their ragin' they swep' him as light as a wisp o' brown wrack.

An' they poundin' the rocks like sledge-hammers, an' clatterin' the shingle like chains ;

Ne'er the live sowl they'd let from their hould till they'd choked him or bet out his brains,

Sure an' certin. And in swung a wave wid its welthers o' wather that lept

Wid the roar of a lion as it come, an' hissed low like a snake as it crept

To its edge, where it tossed thim, the both o' them. Och ! an' the little spalpeen

Misther Denis had gript be the collar, he jumped up the first thing we seen,

While young master lay still—not a stir—he was stunned wid a crack on the head—

Just a flutter o' life at his heart—but it's kilt he was, kilt on us dead.

The Flitting of the Fairies
From The End of Elfintown

*   *   *   .*   *   *

THEN Oberon spake the word of might
That set the enchanted cars in sight ;
But lore I lack to tell aright
   Where these had waited hidden.
Perchance the clear airs round us rolled
In secret cells did them enfold,
Like evening dew that none behold
   Till to the sward 'tis slidden.

And who can say what wizardise
Had fashioned them in marvellous wise,
And given them power to stoop and rise
   More high than thought hath travelled ?
Somewhat of cloud their frames consist,
But more of meteor's luminous mist,
All girt with strands of seven-hued twist
   From rainbow's verge unravelled.

'T is said, and I believe it well,
That whoso mounts their magic selle,
Goes, if he list, invisible
   Beneath the broadest noonlight ;
That virtue comes of Faery-fern,
Lone-lived where hill-slopes starward turn
Thro' frore night hours that bid it burn
   Flame-fronded in the moonlight ;

For this holds true—too true, alas !
The sky that eve was clear as glass,
Yet no man saw the Faeries pass
   Where azure pathways glisten ;
And true it is—too true, ay me—
That nevermore on lawn or lea
Shall mortal man a Faery see,
   Though long he look and listen.

Only the twilit woods among
A wild-winged breeze hath sometimes flung
Dim echoes borne from strains soft-sung
    Beyond sky-reaches hollow ;
Still further, fainter up the height,
Receding past the deep-zoned night—
Far chant of Fays who lead that flight,
    Faint call of Fays who follow :

(*Fays following.*)   Red-rose mists o'erdrift
           Moth-moon's glimmering white,
           Lit by sheen-silled west
           Barred with fiery bar ;
           Fleeting, following swift,
           Whither across the night
           Seek we bourne of rest?

(*Fays leading.*)   Afar.

(*Fays following.*)   Vailing crest on crest
           Down the shadowy height,
           Earth with shores and seas
           Dropt, a dwindling gleam.
           Dusk, and bowery nest,
           Dawn, and dells dew-bright,
           What shall bide of these ?

(*Fays leading.*)   A dream.

(*Fays following.*)   Fled, ah ! fled, our sight.
           Yea, but thrills of fire
           Throbbed adown yon deep,
           Faint and very far
           Who shall rede aright?
           Say, what wafts us nigher,
           Beckoning up the steep?

(*Fays leading.*)   A star.

(*Fays following.*)   List, a star ! a star !
           Oh, our goal of light !
           Yet the winged shades sweep,
           Yet the void looms vast.

Weary our wild dreams are :
When shall cease our flight
Soft on shores of sleep?
(*Fays leading.*)   At last.

DORA SIGERSON (MRS. CLEMENT SHORTER)

THAT divine discontent with the colourless realisms and the banalities of life which overcomes at uncertain periods the soul of every poet, has been much with Miss Sigerson ; but it exhibits itself more in her earlier and less mature than in her later and more objective poems. It is not the joy bells of Nature, but its funeral sounds that strike first upon her listening ear. Her earliest volume is tinged with a profound melancholy—a melancholy which to some extent runs through her later ones also, though in them it does not obtrude nor convey the same feeling of recurrent depression. She weighs life in her balances, and finds it wanting. The very Hill of Fame, upon which life's fortunate ones are crowned, raises in her only a shudder—for is it not built upon the bones of the dead ? The shadows of the unfathomed mysteries of life and death hang heavily over all.

White rose must die, all in the youth and beauty of the year.

That is the recurrent burden of many of her songs, the prevailing note of her earlier music. Life as it unfolds itself is cruelty and disillusion. No Prince Charming can ever recover for her her fairy-land. Everything must end in death, and the shadow feared of man is not to be got rid of.

So for the luxury of the flesh, wrap it in fur of fox, that it be warm,
In the bear's coat, sheltering its nakedness from storm ;
Give wine for its hot veins, fame for its throne, and laughter for its lips,
All ends in one eclipse.
Sunshine or snows,
We gain a grave, and afterwards—God knows !

The barren and meaningless conventionalities of life disgust her. They help to make existence less endurable than it might be if dealt with in a more rational manner. Under the constant fret of petty conventionalities 'the world becomes a weariness, life's current choked with straws,' and she longs for a man's freedom to leave it all behind, and come face to face with Nature 'when the sky is black with thunder and the sea is white with foam.' But the actualities of life tie her down, fetter her, disappoint her, nor can she claim the personal freedom of action that is a man's birthright.

> Alas ! to be a woman, and a nomad's heart in me.

Of the poet, of the dreamer to whom his dream is the one reality of earth, whose bubble is blown only to be burst, and who yet continues to dream because he can do naught else, she sings with much of the insight of a kindred nature.

> Alone among his kind he stands alone,
>   Torn by the passions of his own sad heart,
>   *Stoned by continual wreckage of his dreams*,
>   He in the crowd for ever is apart.

Is not this the very language of De Musset in his glorious address to his fellow poet Lamartine ?

> Désir, crainte, colère, inquiétude, ennui,
>   Tout passe et disparaît, tout est fantôme en lui.
>   Son misérable cœur est fait de telle sorte
>   *Qu'il faut incessamment qu'une ruine en sorte.*

This feeling of depression however is suffused with, and to some extent counteracted by, a strong religious faith and a belief in the soul's immortality. In this respect she has the closest affinities with her friends Katharine Tynan and Miss Furlong, and one of her most powerful poems is that in which, in her last volume, she describes the disastrous influence of an Agnostic husband upon the heart of a believing girl fresh from her convent.

In her second and third volumes Miss Sigerson (now Mrs. Clement Shorter) has struck out into new paths, and largely sought for her inspiration outside of her own feelings and experience. She has turned herself with signal success to ballad-poetry, and in many of her pieces, especially in her second volume, she has sought inspiration from Irish motives and dealt with Irish superstitions. Her very absence from Ireland has made her—a phenomenon which we may often witness—more Irish than if she had never left it, and we can overhear in more than one poem the cry of the Connacht fiddler :

> Dá brázraíõe anír mé i zceánc lán mo õaoine
> D' imceóċaõ an aoir õíon, a'r beiõinn anír óz.

As a ballad-writer Mrs. Shorter has been successful, chiefly because she is unconventional. Almost all English ballads more or less consciously imitate those splendid folk-tales in verse that are the glory of the Lowlands of Scotland ; but the tricks and turns of speech and thought that are in them so delightful, because they are so natural, become at the present moment affectation or worse, and no skill can atone for a conscious unreality of style or expression. Mrs. Shorter's merit is simplicity combined with directness, and the ballads in her second volume are not mere tales in verse, but have almost all of them an underlying *motif*, and exemplify truths of deep psychical import. In her later ballads the mere story or tale itself seems to have attracted her to versification, which, however skilfully done, does not, I think, always possess the interest of her earlier work, in which the tale evidently counted for less than the eternal truth or feeling which it exemplified.

DOUGLAS HYDE (AN CRAOIBHIN).

Mrs. Clement Shorter, the eldest daughter of Dr. George Sigerson, was born in Dublin. In 1895 she married Clement Shorter. Among her books are : VERSES, 1893 ; THE FAIRY CHANGELING, 1898 ; BALLADS AND POEMS, 1899 ; THE WOMAN WHO WENT TO HELL, 1902 ; COLLECTED POEMS, 1907 ; THE TROUBADOUR, 1910 ; NEW POEMS, 1912 ; MADGE LINSEY, 1913 ; LOVE OF IRELAND, 1916. Mrs. Shorter died in 1918. Several posthumous volumes have appeared : THE SAD YEARS, 1918 ; A LEGEND OF GLENDOLOUGH, 1919 ; SIXTEEN DEAD MEN AND OTHER POEMS OF EASTER WEEK, 1919 ; THE TRICOLOUR, 1922.

Cean Duv Deelish

Cean duv deelish, beside the sea
I stand and stretch my hands to thee
    Across the world.
The riderless horses race to shore
With thundering hoofs and shuddering, hoar,
    Blown manes uncurled.

Cean duv deelish, I cry to thee
Beyond the world, beneath the sea,
    Thou being dead.
Where hast thou hidden from the beat
Of crushing hoofs and tearing feet
    Thy dear black head ?

Cean duv deelish, 'tis hard to pray
With breaking heart from day to day,
    And no reply ;
When the passionate challenge of sky is cast
In the teeth of the sea and an angry blast
    Goes by.

God bless the woman, whoever she be,
From the tossing waves will recover thee
    And lashing wind.
Who will take thee out of the wind and storm,
Dry thy wet face on her bosom warm
    And lips so kind ?

I not to know !   It is hard to pray,
But I shall for this woman from day to day.
    Comfort my dead,
The sport of the winds and the play of the sea.
I loved thee too well for this thing to be,
    O dear black head !

The Wind on the Hills

    Go not to the hills of Erin
      When the night winds are about ;
    Put up your bar and shutter,
      And so keep the danger out.

For the good-folk whirl within it,
    And they pull you by the hand,
And they push you on the shoulder,
    Till you move to their command.

And lo ! you have forgotten
    What you have known of tears,
And you will not remember
    That the world goes full of years ;

A year there is a lifetime,
    And a second but a day ;
And an older world will meet you
    Each morn you come away.

Your wife grows old with weeping,
    And your children one by one
Grow grey with nights of watching,
    Before your dance is done.

And it will chance some morning
    You will come home no more ;
Your wife sees but a withered leaf
    In the wind about the door.

And your children will inherit
    The unrest of the wind ;
They shall seek some face elusive,
    And some land they never find.

When the wind is loud, they sighing
    Go with hearts unsatisfied,
For some joy beyond remembrance,
    For some memory denied.

And all your children's children,
    They cannot sleep or rest,
When the wind is out in Erin
    And the sun is in the West.

A Rose will Fade

You were always a dreamer, Rose—red Rose,
　As you swung on your perfumed spray,
Swinging, and all the world was true,
Swaying, what did it trouble you?
　A rose will fade in a day.

Why did you smile to his face, red Rose,
　As he whistled across your way?
And all the world went mad for you,
All the world it knelt to woo.
　A rose will bloom in a day.

I gather your petals, Rose—red Rose,
　The petals he threw away.
And all the world derided you;
Ah! the world, how well it knew
　A rose will fade in a day!

The One Forgotten

There is a belief in some parts of Ireland that the dead are allowed to return to earth on November 2 (All Souls' Night), and the peasantry leave food and fire for their comfort, and set a chair by the hearth for their resting before they themselves retire to bed.

A spirit speeding down on All Souls' Eve
　From the wide gates of that mysterious shore
Where sleep the dead, sung softly and yet sweet.
　'So gay a wind was never heard before,'
The old man said, and listened by the fire;
　And, ''Tis the souls that pass us on their way,'
The young maids whispered, clinging side by side—
　So left their glowing nuts awhile to pray.

Still the pale spirit, singing through the night,
　Came to this window, looking from the dark
Into the room; then passing to the door
　Where crouched the whining dog, afraid to bark,

Tapped gently without answer, pressed the latch,
　　Pushed softly open, and then tapped once more.
The maidens cried, when seeking for the ring,
　　' How strange a wind is blowing on the door ! '

And said the old man, crouching to the fire :
　　' Draw close your chairs, for colder falls the night ;
Push fast the door, and pull the curtains to,
　　For it is dreary in the moon's pale light.'
And then his daughter's daughter with her hand
　　Passed over salt and clay to touch the ring,
Said low : ' The old need fire, but ah ! the young
　　Have that within their hearts to flame and sting.'

And then the spirit, moving from her place,
　　Touched there a shoulder, whispered in each ear,
Bent by the old man, nodding in his chair,
　　But no one heeded her, or seemed to hear.
Then crew the black cock, and so, weeping sore,
　　She went alone into the night again ;
And said the greybeard, reaching for his glass,
　　' How sad a wind blows on the window-pane ! '

And then from dreaming the long dreams of age
　　He woke, remembering, and let fall a tear :
' Alas ! I have forgot—and have you gone ?—
　　I set no chair to welcome you, my dear.'
And said the maidens, laughing in their play :
　　' How he goes groaning, wrinkle-faced and hoar.
He is so old, and angry with his age—
　　Hush ! hear the banshee sobbing past the door.'

ALL SOULS' NIGHT

O MOTHER, mother, I swept the hearth, I set his chair and the
　　white board spread,
I prayed for his coming to our kind Lady when Death's sad doors
　　would let out the dead ;
A strange wind rattled the window-pane, and down the lane a dog
　　howled on ;
I called his name, and the candle flame burnt dim, pressed a hand
　　the door-latch upon.

Deelish ! Deelish ! my woe for ever that I could not sever coward
  flesh from fear.

I called his name, and the pale Ghost came ; but I was afraid to
  meet my dear.

O mother, mother, in tears I checked the sad hours past of the
  year that's o'er,

Till by God's grace I might see his face and hear the sound of his
  voice once more ;

The chair I set from the cold and wet, he took when he came from
  unknown skies

Of the land of the dead, on my bent brown head I felt the reproach
  of his saddened eyes ;

I closed my lids on my heart's desire, crouched by the fire, my
  voice was dumb :

At my clean-swept hearth he had no mirth, and at my table he
  broke no crumb.

Deelish ! Deelish ! my woe for ever that I could not sever coward
  flesh from fear.

His chair put aside when the young cock cried, and I was afraid
  to meet my dear.

A Ballad of Marjorie

'What ails you that you look so pale,
  O fisher of the sea ?'
''Tis for a mournful tale I own,
  Fair maiden Marjorie.'

'What is the dreary tale to tell,
  O toiler of the sea ?'
'I cast my net into the waves,
  Sweet maiden Marjorie.

'I cast my net into the tide
  Before I made for home :
Too heavy for my hands to raise,
  I drew it through the foam.'

What saw you that you look so pale,
Sad searcher of the sea?'
A dead man's body from the deep
My haul had brought to me!'

'And was he young, and was he fair?'
'Oh, cruel to behold!
In his white face the joy of life
Not yet was grown a-cold.'

'Oh, pale you are, and full of prayer
For one who sails the sea.'
Because the dead looked up and spoke,
Poor maiden Marjorie.'

'What said he, that you seem so sad,
O fisher of the sea?'
(Alack! I know it was my love,
Who fain would speak to me!)

'He said: "Beware a woman's mouth—
A rose that bears a thorn."'
'Ah, me! these lips shall smile no more
That gave my lover scorn.'

'He said: "Beware a woman's eyes;
They pierce you with their death."'
'Then falling tears shall make them blind
That robbed my dear of breath.'

'He said: "Beware a woman's hair—
A serpent's coil of gold."'
'Then will I shear the cruel locks
That crushed him in their fold.'

'He said: "Beware a woman's heart
As you would shun the reef."'
'So let it break within my breast,
And perish of my grief.'

' He raised his hands ; a woman's name
    Thrice bitterly he cried.
My net had parted with the strain ;
    He vanished in the tide.'

'A woman's name !   What name but mine,
    O fisher of the sea ? '
'A woman's name, but not your name,
    Poor maiden Marjorie.'

STEPHEN LUCIUS GWYNN

BORN in 1865 in the County Donegal, Stephen Gwynn was
educated at St. Columba's College and at Oxford.   He has
published several novels, two or three biographies, as well as
books of history, critical studies, essays, travel, and anthologies.   His COLLECTED POEMS came out in 1923.   Mr. Gwynn
settled in London as a free-lance writer, but returned to Ireland in 1903 and made entry into Irish politics.   In 1906 he
was elected to Parliament.   He served in France during the
War.

OUT IN THE DARK

OH, up the brae, and up and up, beyont the fairy thorn,
It's there they hae my baby laid, that died when he was born.
Afore the priest could christen him to save his soul, he died ;
It never lived at all, they said—'twas livin' in my side.
For many a day an' many a night, an' weary night and day,
I kent him livin' at my heart, I carena what they say.
For many a day an' many a night I wearied o' unrest,
But now I'm sore to hae my wean back hidden in my breast.
He'll sure be thinkin' long for me, an' wearyin' his lone
Up in thon corner by the whins wi' neither cross nor stone ;
Ay, tho' I'd died wi' him itself, they wouldna let us be—
The corner o' a field for him, the holy ground for me ;
The poor, wee, helpless, Christless wean—Och ! Mary, Mother mild,
Sure, ye were unbaptised yoursel', have pity on a child.

Th' are many a wean that lies wi' him, and none that got a name,
Th' are many a wife, hard put till it, was glad that dead they came;
Ay, many a man that scarcely minds a child o' his lies there ;
But, och ! it's cruel hard to quit the first you'd ever bear.
The graves are all that tiny that they'd hardly raise a mound,
And couples o' a Sunday do be coortin' on thon ground,
An' th' are none that thinks upon them ; but my heart'll be there
    still,
On the sod among the bracken an' the whins upon the hill.
I'd be feared to come o' night there, for the hill is fairy ground,
But th' are, maybe, more nor fairies dancin' in the fairy round—
Och, an' if I only thought it ! sure, I'd let them do their worst,
An' I'd go to see my baby, tho' I be to be accursed.
But I'll never reach my wean now, neither here nor in the sod,
An' I'm betther wi' the Christians an' the souls that's saved for
    God ;—
Och, to feel his fingers on me an' to clasp him when he smiled !
Sure, ye'd think there'd be one heaven for the mother an' the child.

MATER SEVERA

WHERE the huge Atlantic swings heavy water eastward,
    Ireland, square to meet it, shoulders off the seas ;
Wild are all her coasts with stress of cliff and billow,
    On her northern moorland is little sheltered ease.

Well is with the salmon, ranger of her rivers :
    Well is with the mackerel shoaling in each bay,
Dear is all the land to the lonely snipe and curlew :
    Ay, but for its manfolk ! a bitter lot have they.

Thankless is the soil : men trench, and delve, and labour
    Black and spongy peat amid barren knowes of stone :
Then to win a living overseas they travel,
    And their women gather, if God pleases, what was sown.

Harvesters, a-homing from the golden tilth of England,
    Where they sweat to cope with increase of teeming years,
Find too oft returning, sick with others' plenty,
    Sunless autumn dank upon green and spindling ears.

Or a tainted south wind brings upon the root-crop
  Stench of rotting fibre and green leaf turning black :
Famine, never distant, stalks nearer now and nearer,
  Bids them rake like crows amid mussel-beds and wrack.

Bleak and grey to man is the countenance of Nature ;
  Bleak her soil below him, bleak her sky above ;
Wherefore, then, by man is her rare smile so cherished?
  Paid her niggard bounty with so lavish love ?

Not the slopes of Rhine with such yearning are remembered ;
  Not your Kentish orchards, not your Devon lanes.
'Tis as though her sons for that ungentle mother
  Knew a mother's tenderness, felt a mother's pains.

Many an outward-bound, as the ship heads under Tory,
  Clings with anguished eyes to the barren Fanad shore.
Many a homeward-bound, as they lift the frowning Foreland,
  Pants to leap the league to his desolate Gweedore.

There about the ways God's air is free and spacious :
  Warm are chimney-corners there, warm the kindly heart.
There the soul of man takes root, and through its travail
  Grips the rocky anchorage till the life-strings part.

FRANCES WYNNE

THE daughter of Mr. Alfred Wynne of Collon, County Louth,
and author of a small volume of poems, entitled WHISPER !
(1890), marked by an impulsive tenderness and a natural grace
of style. Her powers both in prose and in poetry were developing with much promise when her early death occurred in 1894.
She had married in 1892 her cousin the Rev. Henry Wynne.

A LESSON IN GEOGRAPHY

AWAY from the town, in the safe retreat
Of a rare old garden, sunny and sweet,
Four little happy children played
In and out of the light and shade,

Through a long summer's blissful prime,
Once on a time.
Between the garden borders neat
The gravel-walks stretched warm and wide.
The diligent brown-coated bees
Were ever astir
Among the roses and lavender
And the great dark pansies, yellow-eyed,
And the faint sweet-peas.
But the children on their tireless feet
Flitted about in the pleasant heat
Like the butterflies,
Nor even cared to stray outside
Their Paradise.
Round the old garden was a wall ;
Snapdragons crowded along the ledge,
Crimson and tall,
And in every niche and crevice small
Tiny mosses uncurled.
And though the children would often try,
And even stand on tip-toe to look,
They could hardly see over the top at all.
But there was one corner not quite so high
And above it, against the farthest edge
Of the beautiful sky—
(The part that was golden and green and red
In the evenings, when they were going to bed)—
A row of poplars shook and shook ;
And the children said
The poplars must be the end of the world.

On one of those happy summer days—
When the garden borders were all ablaze,
And the children for once felt too hot to play,
Though all their lessons were done,
But lay
On the grass and watched a delicate haze
Quiver across the brooding blue

Up to the sun—
Something happened strange and new.
For a beggar pushed open the garden door
And stood in the flooding sunshine bright
Full in the wondering children's sight,
A pale-faced woman, young and footsore,
With a baby boy on her arm.
Her ragged dress was all powdered grey
With the dust of the road.
She fixed a long bewildered gaze
On the quaint old garden gay,
Then, with a sudden smile and a nod,
She pointed in rapt delight
To the place where, cool and shimmering white,
The lilies shone—
Touched the baby and said, 'Ah! plaze,
If it wudn't do them flowers no harm,
Childhren, will yiz give him wan
For the love o' God?'
The children started, an awe-struck band,
At the stranger pair.
Then the youngest ran, and with one bold twist
Of his firm little wrist
He wrenched a thick lily stem in two,
And put it, with all its blossoms fair,
In the beggar baby's hand.
'Ah! acushla,' the woman said, 'there's few
In this hard world like you.
I've a long, long way to thravel yet,
Beyond them high threes over there,
But I'll not forget
To pray for you and yours everywhere,
Never fear.
Good evenin' an' God love ye, dear.'

'She's gone,' said Cissy; 'how queer she spoke!'
Whispered Dickie: 'O Tom, you've broke
The best lily: whatever shall you do

When gardener sees the empty space
There where it grew,
And father has to be told ? '
' It was for the love of God, you see,
I did it,' said Tom : ' so maybe He
Won't let them scold.'
' We know now,' said Will,
' There's world the other side of that hill.'

'MOIRA O'NEILL'

MANY of the early poems of ' Moira O'Neill ' made their first
appearance in *Blackwood* and *The Spectator*, and were brought
together in 1900 in SONGS OF THE GLENS OF ANTRIM.
Among her prose stories are THE ELF-ERRANT and AN EASTER
VACATION. Her poetry is Irish of the Irish—tender, wistful,
hovering on the borderland between tears and laughter, and
as musical as an old Gaelic melody. It springs straight from
life, a genuine growth of the Antrim glens.

CORRYMEELA

OVER here in England I'm helpin' wi' the hay,
An' I wisht I was in Ireland the livelong day ;
Weary on the English hay, an' sorra take the wheat !
Och ! Corrymeela an' the blue sky over it.

There's a deep dumb river flowin' by beyont the heavy trees,
This livin' air is moithered wi' the hummin' o' the bees ;
I wisht I'd hear the Claddagh burn go runnin' through the heat
Past Corrymeela wi' the blue sky over it.

The people that's in England is richer nor the Jews,
There's not the smallest young gossoon but thravels in his shoes !
I'd give the pipe between me teeth to see a barefut child,
Och ! Corrymeela an' the low south wind.

Here's hands so full o' money an' hearts so full o' care,
By the luck o' love ! I'd still go light for all I did go bare.

'God save ye, colleen dhas,' I said : the girl she thought me wild !
Far Corrymeela, an' the low south wind.

D'ye mind me now, the song at night is mortial hard to raise,
The girls are heavy goin' here, the boys are ill to plase ;
When ones't I'm out this workin' hive, 'tis I'll be back again—
Aye, Corrymeela, in the same soft rain.

The puff o' smoke from one ould roof before an English Town !
For a *shaugh* wid Andy Feelan here I'd give a silver crown,
For a curl o' hair like Mollie's ye'll ask the like in vain,
Sweet Corrymeela, an' the same soft rain.

JOHNEEN

Sure, he's five months, an' he's two foot long,
        Baby Johneen ;
Watch yerself now, for he's terrible sthrong,
        Baby Johneen.
An' his fists 'ill he up if ye make any slips,
He has finger-ends like the daisy-tips,
But he'll have ye attend to the words of his lips,
        Will Johneen.

There's nobody can rightly tell the colour of his eyes,
        This Johneen ;
For they're partly o' the earth an' still they're partly o' the skies,
        Like Johneen.
So far as he's thravelled he's been laughin' all the way,
For the little soul is quare an' wise, the little heart is gay ;
An' he likes the merry daffodils—he thinks they'd do to play
        With Johneen.

He'll sail a boat yet, if he only has his luck,
        Young Johneen ;
For he takes to the wather like any little duck,
        Boy Johneen ;
Sure, them are the hands now to pull on a rope,
An' nate feet for walkin the deck on a slope,
But the ship she must wait a wee while yet, I hope,
        For Johneen.

For we couldn't do wantin' him, not just yet—
   Och, Johneen,
'Tis you that are the daisy, an' you that are the pet,
   Wee Johneen.
Here's to your health, an' we'll dhrink it to-night,
Sláinte gal, avic machree! live an' do right!
Sláinte gal avourneen! may your days be bright,
   Johneen!

LOOKIN' BACK

WATHERS o' Moyle an' the white gulls flyin',
 Since I was near ye what have I seen?
Deep great seas, an' a sthrong wind sighin'
 Night and day where the waves are green.
Struth na Moile, the wind goes sighin'
 Over a waste o' wathers green.

Sternish an' Trostan, dark wi' heather
 High are the Rockies, airy-blue;
Sure, ye have snows in the winter weather,
 Here they're lyin' the long year through.
Snows are fair in the summer weather,
 Och, an' the shadows between are blue!

Lone Glen Dun an' the wild glen-flowers,
 Little ye know if the prairie is sweet.
Roses for miles, an' redder than ours,
 Spring here undher the horses' feet—
Aye, an' the black-eyed gold sun-flowers,
 Not as the glen-flowers small an' sweet.

Wathers o' Moyle, I hear ye callin'
 Clearer for half o' the world between,
Antrim hills an' the wet rain fallin'
 Whiles ye are nearer than snow tops keen:
Dreams o' the night an' a night wind callin',
 What is the half o' the world between?

DOUGLAS HYDE

Dr. Hyde's best work as an Irish poet has been done either in the Gaelic language or in translations from modern Gaelic, in which he has rendered with wonderful accuracy the simplicity and tenderness of the peasant bards of the West, together with the beautiful metrical structure of their verses. He has devoted his life to the collection and publication of Gaelic songs and folk-tales, and to the organisation of a movement for the preservation of the ancient language. There is probably no contemporary name in Irish literature which is better known (on purely literary grounds) to the Irish people, and which has become more endeared to them than that of Douglas Hyde.

Douglas Hyde, LL.D., M.R.I.A., was born in County Sligo in 1860 and is a descendant of the Castle Hyde family of Cork. After a brilliant career in Trinity College, Dublin, he settled down to Gaelic studies. He has published collections of folk-tales and of poetry (Love-Songs of Connacht, 1893 ; Songs Ascribed to Raftery, 1903, and The Religious Songs of Connacht, 1906) ; and in 1899 produced a Literary History of Ireland which may be reckoned as the first attempt to write a comprehensive and connected history of Gaelic literature, and several plays in Gaelic. Dr. Hyde was President of the Gaelic League for twenty-two years.

My Love—Oh ! she is my Love

from the irish

She casts a spell—oh ! casts a spell,
Which haunts me more than I can tell,
Dearer, because she makes me ill,
Than who would will to make me well.

She is my *store*—oh ! she my *store*,
Whose grey eye wounded me so sore,
Who will not place in mine her palm,
Who will not calm me any more.

She is my pet—oh ! she my pet,
Whom I can never more forget,
Who would not lose by me one moan,
Nor stone upon my cairn set.

She is my *roon* [1]—oh ! she my *roon*,
Who tells me nothing, leaves me soon ;
Who would not lose by me one sigh,
Were death and I within one room.

She is my dear—oh ! she my dear,
Who cares not whether I be here,
Who would not weep when I am dead,
Who makes me shed the silent tear.

Hard my case—oh ! hard my case.
How have I lived so long a space ?
She does not trust me any more,
But I adore her silent face.

She is my choice—oh ! she my choice,
Who never made me to rejoice,
Who caused my heart to ache so oft,
Who put no softness in her voice.

Great my grief—oh ! great my grief,
Neglected, scorned beyond belief,
By her who looks at me askance,
By her who grants me no relief.

She's my desire—oh ! my desire,
More glorious than the bright sun's fire ;
Who were than wind-blown ice more cold,
Had I the boldness to sit by her.

She it is who stole my heart,
But left a void and aching smart ;
And if she soften not her eye,
Then life and I shall shortly part.

---

[1] *Rúin* : secret treasure, love.

Ringleted Youth of my Love

FROM THE IRISH

Ringleted youth of my love,
   With thy locks bound loosely behind **thee,**
You passed by the road above,
   But you never came in to find me.
Where were the harm for you
   If you came for a little to see me?
Your kiss is a wakening dew
   Were I ever so ill or so dreamy.

If I had golden store
   I would make a nice little *boreen* [1].
To lead straight up to his door—
   The door of the house of my *storeen* [2]—
Hoping to God not to miss
   The sound of his footfall in it ;
I have waited so long for his kiss
   That for days I have slept not a minute.

I thought, O my love ! you were so—
   As the moon is, or sun on a fountain,
And I thought after that you were snow—
   The cold snow on top of the mountain—
And I thought after that you were more
   Like God's lamp shining to find me,
Or the bright star of knowledge before,
   And the star of knowledge behind me.

You promised me high-heeled shoes,
   And satin and silk, my *storeen,*
And to follow me, never to lose,
   Though the ocean were round us roaring ;
Like a bush in a gap in a wall
   I am now left lonely without thee,
And this house I grow dead of, is all
   That I see around or about me.

---

[1] Path.   [2] Little treasure.

My Grief on the Sea

FROM THE IRISH

My grief on the sea,
    How the waves of it roll !
For they heave between me
    And the love of my soul !

Abandoned, forsaken,
    To grief and to care,
Will the sea ever waken
    Relief from despair ?

My grief and my trouble !
    Would he and I were
In the province of Leinster,
    Or county of Clare !

Were I and my darling—
    Oh, heart-bitter wound !—
On board of the ship
    For America bound !

On a green bed of rushes
    All last night I lay,
And I flung it abroad
    With the heat of the day.

And my love came behind me—
    He came from the South ;
His breast to my bosom,
    His mouth to my mouth.

Little Child, I call Thee

FROM THE IRISH

Little child, I call thee fair,
    Clad in hair of golden hue,
Every lock in ringlets falling
    Down, to almost kiss the dew.

Slow grey eye and languid mien,
  Brows as thin as stroke of quill,
Cheeks of white with scarlet through them,
  Och ! it's through them I am ill.

Luscious mouth, delicious breath,
  Chalk-white teeth, and very small,
Lovely nose and little chin,
  White neck, thin—she is swan-like all.

Pure white hand and shapely finger,
  Limbs that linger like a song ;
Music speaks in every motion
  Of my sea-mew warm and young.

Rounded breasts and lime-white bosom,
  Like a blossom touched of none,
Stately form and slender waist,
  Far more graceful than the swan.

Alas for me ! I would I were
  With her of the soft-fingered palm,
In Waterford to steal a kiss,
  Or by the Liss whose airs are balm.

THE ADDRESS OF DEATH TO TOMAS DE ROISTE
FROM THE IRISH

I AM the Death who am come to you
Adam I smote and Eve I slew ;
All have died or shall die by me
Who have been or who shall be,
Until the meeting on that great hill,
Where the world must gather—for good, for ill,
And judgment will fall upon every one
For the things he has thought and things he has done.

I am active as the mind,
And swifter than the rush of wind
That lifts the sea-gull off the lake,
And faster than goat in a mountain brake,
Swifter than the sounding tide,
Or the plunge of the bark with its long black side

That furrows the wave when the cold sea wind
Rings in its whistling sails behind.
Swifter am I than the bird on the bough
Or the fish with the current that darts below ;
Swifter than the heavens high,
Or the cold clear moon in the star-bright sky,
Or the grey gull o'er the water,
Or the eagle that stoops when it scents the slaughter.
I am swifter than the pour
Of heavy waves on ocean shore,
Swifter than the doubling race
Of the timid hare with the hounds in chase.
I mount upon the back of kings
Standing by their pleasant things,
By the banqueting-board where the lamps are bright,
Or the lonely couch in the lonely night—
I am a messenger tried and true ;
Wherever they travel, I travel too.

From the land of the End I have tidings wan—
I love no woman, I like no man,
Nor high, nor low, nor young, nor old :
I snatch the child from its mother's fold,
I tear the strong man from his wife,
And I come to the nurse for the infant's life ;
I take from the month-old child the father,
The widow's son to myself I gather,
With her who was married yesternight,
And the wretch that wails for his doleful plight ;
I seize the hero of mighty deed,
And pull the rider from off his steed,
The messenger going his rapid road,
And the lord of the house from his proud abode,
And the poor man gleaning his pittance of corn.
And the white-necked maiden nobly born,
And the withered woman old and bare,
And the handsome youth so strong and fair,
From the hunt or the dance or the feast I bear.

T. W. ROLLESTON

BORN 1857 in the King's County. Educated at St. Columba's College, near Dublin, and Trinity College, Dublin. Mr. Rolleston's prose works include THE TEACHING OF EPICTETUS, 1886; A LIFE OF LESSING, 1889; various essays and translations in German; THE HIGH DEEDS OF FINN, a group of Irish sagas, 1910; MYTHS AND LEGENDS OF THE CELTIC RACE, 1911. His poems appeared in *The Spectator* and *The Academy*, etc., and in 1909 SEA SPRAY: VERSES AND TRANSLATIONS came out. He died in 1920.

THE DEAD AT CLONMACNOIS

FROM THE IRISH OF ENOCH O'GILLAN

IN a quiet water'd land, a land of roses,
    Stands Saint Kieran's city fair :
And the warriors of Erin in their famous generations
    Slumber there.

There beneath the dewy hillside sleep the noblest
    Of the clan of Conn,
Each below his stone with name in branching Ogham
    And the sacred knot thereon.

There they laid to rest the seven Kings of Tara,
    There the sons of Cairbré sleep—
Battle-banners of the Gael, that in Kieran's plain of crosses
    Now their final hosting keep.

And in Clonmacnois they laid the men of Teffia,
    And right many a lord of Breagh ;
Deep the sod above Clan Creidé and Clan Conaill,
    Kind in hall and fierce in fray.

Many and many a son of Conn, the Hundred-Fighter,
    In the red earth lies at rest ;
Many a blue eye of Clan Colman the turf covers,
    Many a swan-white breast.

THE LAMENT OF MAEV LEITH-DHERG,

FOR CUCHORB : SON OF MOGHCORB, KING OF IRELAND

From an extremely ancient Irish poem in the BOOK OF LEINSTER, fol. 24. See O'Curry's MANUSCRIPT MATERIALS OF IRISH HISTORY, p. 480. This Maev is not the warrior-goddess of Connacht, but a Queen of Ireland in times approaching the historic, about A.D. 20. Cucorb ('Chariot-Hound') was slain on Mount Leinster on the borders of Wexford.

RAISE the Cromlech high !
   MacMoghcorb is slain,
And other men's renown
   Has leave to live again.

Cold at last he lies
   Neath the burial-stone ;
All the blood he shed
   Could not save his own.

Stately-strong he went,
   Through his nobles all
When we paced together
   Up the banquet-hall.

Dazzling white as lime
   Was his body fair,
Cherry-red his cheeks,
   Raven-black his hair.

Razor-sharp his spear,
   And the shield he bore,
High as champion's head—
   His arm was like an oar.

Never aught but truth
   Spake my noble king ;
Valour all his trust
   In all his warfaring.

As the forkéd pole
   Holds the roof-tree's weight,
So my hero's arm
   Held the battle straight.

Terror went before him,
  Death behind his back ;
Well the wolves of Erinn
  Knew his chariot's track.

Seven bloody battles
  He broke upon his foes ;
In each a hundred heroes
  Fell beneath his blows.

Once he fought at Fossud,
  Thrice at Ath-finn-Fail ;
'Twas my king that conquered
  At bloody Ath-an-Scail.

At the Loundary Stream
  Fought the Royal Hound,
And for Bernas battle
  Stands his name renowned.

Here he fought with Leinster—
  Last of all his frays—
On the Hill of Cucorb's Fate
  High his Cromlech raise.

SONG OF MAELDUIN.

THERE are veils that lift, there are bars that fall,
There are lights that beckon, and winds that call—
        Good-bye !
There are hurrying feet, and we dare not wait,
For the hour is on us—the hour of Fate,
The circling hour of the flaming gate—
        Good-bye—good-bye—good-bye !

Fair, fair they shine through the burning zone—
The rainbow gleams of a world unknown ;
        Good-bye !
And oh ! to follow, to seek, to dare,
When, step by step, in the evening air
Floats down to meet us the cloudy stair !
        Good-bye—good-bye—good-bye !

The cloudy stair of the Brig o' Dread
Is the dizzy path that our feet must tread—
  Good-bye !
O children of Time—O Nights and Days,
That gather and wonder and stand at gaze,
And wheeling stars in your lonely ways,
  Good-bye—good-bye—good-bye !

The music calls and the gates unclose,
Onward and onward the wild way goes—
  Good-bye !
We die in the bliss of a great new birth,
O fading phantoms of pain and mirth,
O fading loves of the old green earth—
  Good-bye—good-bye—good-bye !

THOMAS BOYD

THOMAS BOYD, a native of County Louth, published his first book, POEMS, in 1906 in a regular and limited edition (O'Don-aghue & Co., Dublin). His very striking poem, ' To the Lea-nán Sidhe,' shows a genius akin to that of George Darley and eminently Celtic in character.

To THE LEANÁN SIDHE [1]

WHERE is thy lovely perilous abode ?
 In what strange phantom-land
Glimmer the fairy turrets whereto rode
 The ill-starred poet band ?

Say, in the Isle of Youth hast thou thy home,
 The sweetest singer there,
Stealing on wingéd steed across the foam
 Through the moonlit air ?

Or, where the mists of bluebell float beneath
 The red stems of the pine,
And sunbeams strike thro' shadow, dost thou breathe
 The word that makes him thine ?

---

[1] ' The Fairy Bride.' Pronounced *Lenawn Shee.*

Or by the gloomy peaks of Erigal,
  Haunted by storm and cloud,
Wing past, and to thy lover there let fall
  His singing-robe and shroud?

Or, is thy palace entered thro' some cliff
  When radiant tides are full,
And round thy lover's wandering, starlit skiff,
  Coil in luxurious lull?

And would he, entering on the brimming flood,
  See caverns vast in height,
And diamond columns, crowned with leaf and bud,
  Glow in long lanes of light,

And there, the pearl of that great glittering shell
  Trembling, behold thee lone,
Now weaving in slow dance an awful spell,
  Now still upon thy throne?

Thy beauty! ah, the eyes that pierce him thro'
  Then melt as in a dream;
The voice that sings the mysteries of the blue
  And all that Be and Seem!

Thy lovely motions answering to the rhyme
  That ancient Nature sings,
That keeps the stars in cadence for all time,
  And echoes thro' all things!

Whether he sees thee thus, or in his dreams,
  Thy light makes all lights dim;
An aching solitude from henceforth seems
  The world of men to him.

Thy luring song, above the sensuous roar,
  He follows with delight,
Shutting behind him Life's last gloomy door,
  And fares into the Night.

THE KING'S SON

WHO rideth thro' the driving rain
   At such a headlong speed?
Naked and pale he rides amain
   Upon a naked steed.

Nor hollow nor height his going bars,
   His wet steed shines like silk ;
His head is golden to the stars,
   And his limbs are white as milk.

But lo, he dwindles as a light
   That lifts from a black mere !
And as the fair youth wanes from sight
   The steed grows mightier.

What wizard by the holy tree
   Mutters unto the sky,
Where Macha's flame-tongued horses flee
   On hoofs of thunder by ?

Ah, 'tis not holy so to ban
   The youth of kingly seed ;
Ah, woe, the wasting of a man
   That changes to a steed !

Nightly upon the Plain of Kings
   When Macha's day is nigh
He gallops ; and the dark wind brings
   His lonely human cry.

LIONEL JOHNSON

IF I were asked to say what distinguishes the little school of
contemporary Irish poets, I would say they believe, with a
singular fervour of belief, in a spiritual life, and express this
belief in their poetry. Contemporary English poets are

interested in the glory of the world, like Mr. Rudyard Kipling ;
or in the order of the world, like Mr. William Watson ; or in the
passion of the world, like Mr. John Davidson ; or in the pleasure
of the world, like Mr. Arthur Symons.   Mr. Francis Thompson,
who has fallen under the shadow of Mr. Coventry Patmore,
the poet of an older time and in protest against that time, is
alone preoccupied with a spiritual life ; and even he, except at
rare moments, has less living fervour of belief than pleasure in
the gleaming and scented and coloured symbols that are the
footsteps where the belief of others has trodden.   Ireland,
which has always believed in a spiritual life, is creating in
English a poetry which, whatever be its merits, is as full of
spiritual ardour as the poetry that praised in Gaelic 'the Ever-
Living Living Ones,' and 'the Country of the Two Mists,' and
'the Country of the Young,' and 'the Country of the Living
Heart.'

  'A. E.' has written an ecstatic pantheistic poetry which
reveals in all things a kind of scented flame consuming them
from within.   Miss Hopper, an unequal and immature poet,
whose best verses are delicate and distinguished, has no clear
vision of spiritual things, but makes material things as frail
and fragile as if they were already ashes, that we stirred
in some mid-world of dreams, as 'the gossips' in her poem
'stir their lives' red ashes.'   Mrs. Hinkson, uninteresting at
her worst, as only uncritical and unspeculative writers are uninteresting, has sometimes expressed an impassioned and
instinctive Catholicism in poems that are, as I believe, as
perfect as they are beautiful, while Mr. Lionel Johnson has in
his poetry completed the trinity of the spiritual virtues by
adding Stoicism to Ecstasy and Asceticism.   He has renounced
the world and built up a twilight world instead, where all the
colours are like the colours in the rainbow that is cast by
the moon, and all the people as far from modern tumults as
the people upon fading and dropping tapestries.   He has so
little interest in our pains and pleasures, and is so wrapped up
in his own world, that one comes from his books wearied and
exalted, as though one had posed for some noble action in a

strange *tableau vivant* that cast its painful stillness upon the mind instead of the body. He might have cried with Axel, 'As for living, our servants will do that for us.' As Axel chose to die, he has chosen to live among his books and between two memories—the religious tradition of the Church of Rome and the political tradition of Ireland. From these he gazes upon the future, and whether he write of Sertorius or of Lucretius, or of Parnell or of 'Ireland's dead,' or of '98, or of St. Columba or of Leo XIII., it is always with the same cold or scornful ecstasy. He has made a world full of altar lights and golden vestures, and murmured Latin and incense clouds, and autumn winds and dead leaves, where one wanders remembering martyrdoms and courtesies that the world has forgotten.

His ecstasy is the ecstasy of combat, not of submission to the Divine will; and even when he remembers that 'the old Saints prevail,' he sees the 'one ancient Priest' who alone offers the Sacrifice, and remembers the loneliness of the Saints. Had he not this ecstasy of combat, he would be the poet of those peaceful and unhappy souls, who, in the symbolism of a living Irish visionary, are compelled to inhabit when they die a shadowy island Paradise in the West, where the moon always shines, and a mist is always on the face of the moon, and a music of many sighs is always in the air, because they renounced the joy of the world without accepting the joy of God.

W. B. YEATS

Lionel Johnson was born about 1867, and died in 1902, as the result of an accident. He was educated at Winchester and Oxford. Early in the nineties he gained recognition in the London literary world for his brilliant critical articles. POEMS was published in 1895.

WAYS OF WAR

A TERRIBLE and splendid trust
    Heartens the host of Innisfail :
Their dream is of the swift sword-thrust,
    A lightning glory of the Gael.

Croagh Patrick is the place of prayers,
    And Tara the assembling-place :
But each sweet wind of Ireland bears
    The trump of battle on its race.

From Dursey Isle to Donegal,
    From Howth to Achill, the glad noise
Rings : and the heirs of glory fall,
    Or victory crowns their fighting joys.

A dream ! a dream ! an ancient dream !
    Yet, ere peace come to Innisfail,
Some weapons on some field must gleam,
    Some burning glory fire the Gael.

That field may lie beneath the sun,
    Fair for the treading of an host :
That field in realms of thought be won,
    And armed minds do their uttermost :

Some way to faithful Innisfail
    Shall come the majesty and awe
Of martial truth, that must prevail
    To lay on all the eternal law.

Te Martyrum Candidatus

AH, see the fair chivalry come, the companions of Christ !
    White Horsemen, who ride on white horses, the Knights of God !
They for their Lord and their Lover who sacrificed
    All, save the sweetness of treading where He first trod !
These through the darkness of death, the dominion of night,
    Swept, and they woke in white places at morning tide :
They saw with their eyes, and sang for joy of the sight,
    They saw with their eyes the Eyes of the Crucified.

Now, whithersoever He goeth, with Him they go :
    White Horsemen, who ride on white horses—oh, fair to see !
They ride where the Rivers of Paradise flash and flow,
    White Horsemen, with Christ their Captain : for ever He !

THE DARK ANGEL

DARK Angel, with thine aching lust
   To rid the world of penitence :
Malicious Angel, who still dost
   My soul such subtile violence !

Because of thee, no thought, no thing,
   Abides for me undesecrate :
Dark Angel, ever on the wing,
   Who never reachest me too late !

When music sounds, then changest thou
   Its silvery to a sultry fire ;
Nor will thine envious heart allow
   Delight untortured by desire.

Through thee, the gracious Muses turn
   To Furies, O mine Enemy !
And all the things of beauty burn
   With flames of evil ecstasy.

Because of thee, the land of dreams
   Becomes a gathering-place of fears ;
Until tormented slumber seems
   One vehemence of useless tears.

When sunlight glows upon the flowers,
   Or ripples down the dancing sea,
Thou with thy troop of passionate powers
   Beleaguerest, bewilderest me.

Within the breath of autumn woods,
   Within the winter silences,
Thy venomous spirit stirs and broods,
   O Master of impieties !

The ardour of red flame is thine,
   And thine the steely soul of ice ;
Thou poisonest the fair design
   Of Nature with unfair device.

Apples of ashes, golden bright ;
　　Waters of bitterness, how sweet !
O banquet of a foul delight,
　　Prepared by thee, dark Paraclete !

Thou art the whisper in the gloom,
　　The hinting tone, the haunting laugh ;
Thou art the adorner of my tomb,
　　The minstrel of mine epitaph.

I fight thee, in the Holy Name !
　　Yet what thou dost is what God saith.
Tempter ! should I escape thy flame,
　　Thou wilt have helped my soul from Death —

The second Death, that never dies,
　　That cannot die, when time is dead ;
Live Death, wherein the lost soul cries,
　　Eternally uncomforted.

Dark Angel, with thine aching lust !
　　Of two defeats, of two despairs :
Less dread, a change to drifting dust,
　　Than thine eternity of cares.

Do what thou wilt, thou shalt not so,
　　Dark Angel ! triumph over me :
Lonely unto the Lone I go ;
　　Divine, to the Divinity.

THE CHURCH OF A DREAM

SADLY the dead leaves rustle in the whistling wind,
　　Around the weather-worn, grey church, low down the vale ;
　　The Saints in golden vesture shake before the gale ;
The glorious windows shake, where still they dwell enshrined ;
Old Saints, by long dead, shrivelled hands long since designed ;
　　There still, although the world autumnal be, and pale,
　　Still in their golden vesture the old saints prevail ;
Alone with Christ, desolate else, left by mankind.
Only one ancient Priest offers the sacrifice,
　　Murmuring holy Latin immemorial ;

Swaying with tremulous hands the old censer full of spice,
  In grey, sweet, incense clouds ; blue, sweet clouds mystical ;
To him in place of men, for he is old, suffice
  Melancholy remembrances and vesperal.

THE AGE OF A DREAM

IMAGERIES of dreams reveal a gracious age ;
  Black armour, falling lace, and altar lights at morn.
The courtesy of Saints, their gentleness and scorn,
Lights on an earth more fair than shone from Plato's page ;
The courtesy of knights, fair calm and sacred rage ;
  The courtesy of love, sorrow for love's sake borne.
  Vanished, those high conceits ! Desolate and forlorn,
We hunger against hope for that lost heritage.

Gone now, the carven work ! Ruined, the golden shrine !
No more the glorious organs pour their voice divine ;
  No more rich frankincense drifts through the Holy Place ;
Now from the broken tower, what solemn bell still tolls,
Mourning what piteous death? Answer, O saddened souls !
  Who mourn the death of beauty and the death of grace.

NORA HOPPER

MODERN poetry grows weary of using over and over again the
personages and stories and metaphors that have come to us
through Greece and Rome, or from Wales and Brittany
through the Middle Ages, and has found new life in the Norse
and German legends. The Irish legends, in popular tradition
and in old Gaelic literature, are more numerous and as beautiful, and alone among great European legends have the beauty
and wonder of altogether new things. May one not say, then,
without saying anything improbable, that they will have a pre·
dominant influence in the coming century, and that their
influence will pass through many countries?

The latest of a little group of contemporary writers, who have begun to found their work upon them, as the Trouveres founded theirs upon the legends of Arthur and his knights, is Miss Nora Hopper, whose two books, though they have many of the faults of youth, have at their best an extraordinary delicacy and charm. I got BALLADS IN PROSE when it came out, two or three years ago, and it haunted me as few new books have ever haunted me, for it spoke in strange wayward stories and birdlike little verses of things and of persons I remembered or had dreamed of; it did not speak with the too emphatic manner that sometimes mars the more powerful stories Miss Fiona Macleod has told of like things and persons, but softly—more murmuring than speaking. Even now, when the first enchantment is gone and I see faults I was blind to, I cannot go by certain brown bogs covered with white tufts of bog-cotton—places where the world seems to become faint and fragile—without remembering the verses her Daluan—a kind of Irish Pan—sings among the bogs; and when once I remember them, they run in my head for hours—

> All the way to Tir na n'Og are many roads that run,
> But the darkest road is trodden by the King of Ireland's son.
> The world wears on to sundown, and love is lost and won,
> But he recks not of loss or gain, the King of Ireland's son.
> He follows on for ever, when all your chase is done,
> He follows after shadows—the King of Ireland's son.

One does not know why he sings it, or why he dies on November Eve, or why the men cry over him 'Daluan is dead—dead! Daluan is dead!' and the women, 'Da Mort is king,' for 'Daluan' is but Monday and 'Da Mort' is but Tuesday; nor does one well know why any of her best stories, 'Bahalaun and I,' 'The Gifts of Aodh and Una,' 'The Four Kings,' or 'Aonan-nan Righ,' shaped itself into the strange, drifting, dreamy thing it is, and one is content not to know. They delight us by their mystery, as ornament full of lines, too deeply interwoven to weary us with a discoverable secret, delights us with its mystery; and as ornament is full of strange beasts and trees and flowers, that were once the symbols of great religions, and are now mixing one with another, and changing into new shapes, this book is full of old beliefs and stories, mixing and changing in an enchanted dream. Their very mystery, that has left them so little to please the mortal passionate part of us, which delights in the broad noonlight men need if they would merely act and live, has given them that melancholy which is almost wisdom.

A great part of QUICKEN BOUGHS was probably written before BALLADS IN PROSE ; for, though it is all verse, it has few verses of the same precise and delicate music as those scattered among the stories in the earlier book. But 'Phyllis and Damon' is perfect in its kind, while 'The Dark Man' gives beautiful words to that desire of spiritual beauty and happiness which runs through so much modern true poetry. It is founded upon the belief, common in Ireland, that certain persons are, as it is called, 'away' or more with the fairies than with us, and that 'dark' or blind people can see what we cannot.

W. B. YEATS.

Nora Hopper was born in 1871 and married W. H. Chesson, a well-known writer, in 1901. She died in 1906. Her volumes are : BALLADS IN PROSE, QUICKEN BOUGHS, SONGS OF THE MORNING, and SELECTED POEMS.

THE FAIRY FIDDLER

'TIS I go fiddling, fiddling,
  By weedy ways forlorn :
I make the blackbird's music
  Ere in his breast 'tis born ;
The sleeping larks I waken
  'Twixt the midnight and the morn.

No man alive has seen me,
  But women hear me play
Sometimes at door or window,
  Fiddling the souls away—
The child's soul and the colleen's—
  Out of the covering clay.

None of my fairy kinsmen
  Make music with me now :
Alone the raths I wander,
  Or ride the whitethorn bough ;
But the wild swans they know me,
  And the horse that draws the plough.

THE DARK MAN

ROSE O' THE WORLD, she came to my bed
And changed the dreams of my heart and head ;
For joy of mine she left grief of hers,
And garlanded me with a crown of furze.

Rose o' the World, they go out and in,
And watch me dream and my mother spin :
And they pity the tears on my sleeping face
While my soul's away in a fairy place.

Rose o' the World, they have words galore,
And wide's the swing of my mother's door :
And soft they speak of my darkened eyes—
But what do they know, who are all so wise ?

Rose o' the World, the pain you give
Is worth all days that a man may live—
Worth all shy prayers that the colleens say
On the night that darkens the wedding-day.

Rose o' the World, what man would wed
When he might dream of your face instead ?—
Might go to his grave with the blessed pain
Of hungering after your face again ?

Rose o' the World, they may talk their fill,
For dreams are good, and my life stands still
While their lives' red ashes the gossips stir ;
But my fiddle knows—and I talk to her.

Phyllis and Damon

Phyllis and Damon met one day .
    (Heigho !)
Phyllis was sad, and Damon grey,
Tired with treading a separate way.

Damon sighed for his broken flute :
    (Heigho !)
Phyllis went with a noiseless foot
Under the olives stript of fruit.

Met they, parted they, all unsaid?
    (Heigho !)
Ah ! but a ghost's lips are not red ;
Damon was old and Phyllis dead.
    (Heigho !)

ALTHEA GYLES

Miss Althea Gyles may come to be one of the most important of the little group of Irish poets who seek to express
indirectly through myths and symbols, or directly in little
lyrics full of prayers and lamentations, the desire of the soul
for spiritual beauty and happiness. She has done, besides the
lyric I quote, which is charming in form and substance, a small
number of poems full of original symbolism and spiritual
ardour, though as yet lacking in rhythmical subtlety. Her
drawings and book-covers, in which precise symbolism never
interferes with beauty of design, are as yet her most satisfactory
expression of herself.

W. B. Yeats.

Sympathy

The colour gladdens all your heart ;
    You call it Heaven, dear, but I—
Now Hope and I are far apart—
    Call it the sky.

I know that Nature's tears have wet
 The world with sympathy ; but you,
Who know not any sorrow yet,
 Call it the dew.

WILLIAM LARMINIE

It is difficult in an anthology to do justice to poetry whose charm does not lie so much in the beauty of exceptional passages as in a continuous elevation of thought. I believe Mr. Larminie's verse, now almost unknown, will find many readers, and that his two longest poems—'Fand' and 'Moytura'— will be permanently remembered. It is difficult to understand why this writer, who has many and great gifts as an imaginative poet, should have been so coldly received. With the general public the irregular form and the unusual metres may explain the neglect, for the Gaelic assonance has in much of his verse been substituted for rhyme. But the few who persevered beyond the first pages, long enough to allow the cadences to become familiar, have found a growing charm such as we experience on a misty morning when we go out and feel the sun's rays slowly warming and pervading the world w.th clear cool light. I confess this austere poetry at its best holds my imagination almost as much as that of any contemporary writer. It is not always beautiful in expression, though it is full of dignity. The poet certainly does not 'look upon fine phrases like a lover.' He is much more concerned with the substance of his thought than with the expression. He leads us into his own spirit by ways which are often rugged ; but at the end, as we close the pages, we are on a mountain-top and the stars are very near. He is a mystic, but his mysticism is never incoherent and is always profoundly philosophical ; and those who perhaps would look in poetry for other verbal effects of sound and colour may at least read for this with interest and pleasure the dramatic poem 'Moytura.' Here the battle fought between the De Danann gods and the Fohmors becomes the eternal war between light and darkness, and the Celtic legend is interwoven with wonderful skill into more universal hopes and traditions. For sustained imaginative power this poem is not surpassed by anything in modern Irish poetry, and I cannot read it without an excitement of the spirit. Mr. Larminie's method of treatment of Irish traditions is indeed very different from that of other contemporary artists who have handled them. He has experimented in a style of his own which is sometimes disagreeable, but often has a novel charm, and suggests that, used by a more skilful artist in words, the assonance might very well replace rhyme. Even where Mr. Larminie fails most to express himself with charm, a spiritual depth and originality in his thought is evident : and I might describe him as a poet by saying that the spirit is indeed kingly, but without the purple robe which should be the outer token of his lofty rank.

A. E.

Mr. William Larminie was a native of Mayo, and lived most of his life near Dublin. His early and lamented death took place in 1899. His publications are GLANLUA AND OTHER POEMS, 1889 ; WEST IRISH FOLK TALES AND ROMANCES, 1893 ; FAND AND OTHER POEMS, 1892.

THE SPEECH OF EMER

This fragment is from 'Fand.' Cuhoolin has been lured from his home by the wiles of the goddess Fand ; his wife Emer discovers him, and pleads with him as follows :

HEED her not, O Cuhoolin, husband mine ;
Delusive is the bliss she offers thee—
Bliss that will to torment turn,
Like one bright colour for ever before thine eyes,
Since of mortal race thou art.
Man is the shadow of a changing world ;
As the image of a tree
By the breeze swayed to and fro
On the grass, so changeth he ;
Night and day are in his breast ;

Winter and summer, all the change
Of light and darkness and the seasons marching ;
Flowers that bud and fade,
Tides that rise and fall.
Even with the waxing and the waning moon
His being beats in tune ;
The air that is his life
Inhales he with alternate heaving breath ;
Joyous to him is effort, sweet is rest ;
Life he hath and death.

Then seek not thou too soon that permanence
Of changeless joy that suits unchanging gods
In whom no tides of being ebb and flow.
Out of the flux and reflux of the world
Slowly man's soul doth gather to itself,
Atom by atom, the hard elements—
Firm, incorruptible, indestructible —
Whereof, when all his being is compact,
No more it wastes nor hungers, but endures
Needing not any food of changing things,
But fit among like-natured gods to live,
Amongst whom, entering too soon, he perishes,
Unable to endure their fervid gaze.
Though now thy young, heroic soul
Be mate for her immortal might,
Yet think : thy being is still but as a lake
That, by the help of friendly streams unfed,
Full soon the sun drinks up.
Wait till thou hast sea-depths—
Till all the tides of life and deed,
Of action and of meditation,
Of service unto others and their love,
Shall pour into the caverns of thy being
The might of their unconquerable floods.
Then canst thou bear the glow of eyes divine.
And like the sea beneath the sun at noon
Shalt shine in splendour inexhaustible.

Therefore be no more tempted by her lures—
Not that way lies thine immortality :
But thou shalt find it in the ways of men,
Where many a task remains for thee to do,
And shall remain for many after thee,
Till all the storm-winds of the world be bound.

EPILOGUE TO FAND

Is there one desires to hear
If within the shores of Eirè
Eyes may still behold the scene
Fair from Fand's enticements?

Let him seek the southern hills
And those lakes of loveliest water
Where the richest blooms of spring
Burn to reddest autumn :
And the clearest echo sings
Notes a goddess taught her.

Ah ! 'twas very long ago,
And the words are now denied her :
But the purple hillsides know
Still the tones delightsome,
And their breasts, impassioned, glow
As were Fand beside them.

And though many an isle be fair,
Fairer still is Inisfallen,
Since the hour Cuhoolin lay
In the bower enchanted.
See ! the ash that waves to-day,
Fand its grandsire planted.

When from wave to mountain-top
All delight thy sense bewilders,
Thou shalt own the wonder wrought
Once by her skilled fingers,
Still, though many an age be gone,
Round Killarney lingers.

Consolation

Yes, let us speak, with lips confirming
　　The inner pledge that eyes reveal—
Bright eyes that death shall dim for ever,
　　And lips that silence soon shall seal.

Yes, let us make our claim recorded
　　Against the powers of earth and sky,
And that cold boon their laws award us—
　　Just once to live and once to die.

Thou sayest that fate is frosty nothing,
　　But love the flame of souls that are :
' Two spirits approach, and at their touching,
　　Behold ! an everlasting star.'

High thoughts, O love : well, let us speak them !
　　Yet bravely face at least this fate :
To know the dreams of us that dream them
　　On blind, unknowing things await.

If years from winter's chill recover,
　　If fields are green and rivers run,
If thou and I behold each other,
　　Hangs it not all on yonder sun ?

So while that mighty lord is gracious
　　With prodigal beams to flood the skies,
Let us be glad that he can spare us
　　The light to kindle lovers' eyes.

And die assured, should life's new wonder
　　In any world our slumbers break,
These the first words that each will utter :
　　' Beloved, art thou too awake ? '

The Sword of Tethra

From Moytura

The sword of Tethra, one of the Kings of the Fohmors, is captured by the sun-god Lu.   This sword is Death.

The Sword :   I am the breath of Tethra, voice of Tethra,
The tongue of an utterance harsh :
I am the beat of the heart
Of the inmost darkness, that sends
Night to the world's far ends.
I am the raven of Tethra, mate of Tethra, slave of Tethra :
My joy is the storm
That strews the ground with the fruit—
Half-living, bleeding, and bruised—
From life's tree shaken.
I desire the flame of battle ;
I desire gore-spouting wounds ;
Flanks that are gashed, trunks that are headless
Heads that are trunkless in piles and in mounds ;

    *   *   *   *   *

Do you seek to bind me, ye gods,
And the deeds of me only beginning ?
Shall I gloat over triumphs achieved
When the greatest remains for the winning ?
Ye boast of this world ye have made,
This corpse-built world ?
Show me an atom thereof
That hath not suffered and struggled,
And yielded its life to Tethra ?
The rocks they are built of the mould,
And the mould of the herb that was green,
And the beast from the herb,
And man from the beast,
And downward in hurried confusion,
Through shapes that are loathsome,
Beast, man, worm, pellmell,
What does it matter to me ?

All that have lived go back to the mould,
To stiffen through ages of pain
In the rock-rigid realms of death.

Ah, ah !
Loose me, ye gods !
I stifle, I faint in your hands :
Your presence benumbs me :
An effluence from you exhales,
Life deadly to death,
The poison whereof overcomes me,
And it is not my doom to perish ;
Gods ye have slain that were brave and mighty,
But Tethra ye never shall slay.
　　Lu : We will not loose thee till thou be subdued—
Thy venom quenched a little ; till thy song
In milder music sheathe its jagged edge,
And choose a smoother speech that shall not rend.
　　The Sword : Ah, ah ! I gash ! Alas, alas !
That even of me should soft things be averred ;
I am the song unheard,
Shall ofttimes lure men's falt'ring souls away ;
Soft as from summer's eve the tender light
Stolen by northern night,
My gentle call they gladly shall obey :
From them regretful tears shall flow not,
But eyes shine bright with hope to see the land they
　　know not.
Loose me ! loose me !

STANDISH JAMES O'GRADY

Mr. Standish O'Grady was born in 1846 at Castletown
Berehaven, and was educated in Tipperary and at Trinity
College, Dublin, where he won a classical scholarship, and took
his degree in 1868. He was called to the Bar, and practised
that profession for a time, but ultimately devoted himself to

literature and journalism. In 1900 he was owner and editor of the *Kilkenny Moderator* and of the *All-Ireland Review*. He died in 1928. His HISTORY OF IRELAND: MYTHICAL PERIOD appeared in 1878, and though totally unrecognised at the time, except by one or two English journals such as *The Spectator*, it proved to be one of the epoch-making books of modern Irish literature, re-creating as it did for English readers the heroic character of Cuchullin, and revealing a buried world of legendary splendour and romance. Something of the same kind Mr. O'Grady did in the sphere not of legend but of authentic history in his FLIGHT OF THE EAGLE, 1897, a tale of Elizabethan Ireland. Other important works of Mr. O'Grady's (who must not be confounded with the distinguished Irish scholar, Mr. Standish Hayes O'Grady) are FINN AND HIS COMPANIONS, 1892; THE COMING OF CUCULAIN, 1894; and ULRICK THE READY, 1896. A collected edition of his works with a preface by A. E. has appeared.

Mr. O'Grady is understood to have burned a pile of poetry. These waifs have escaped destruction, and appear to have in them much of the bardic *afflatus* which fills the mythical and Elizabethan romances of the same author.

LOUGH BRAY

NOW Memory, false, spendthrift Memory,
　　Disloyal treasure-keeper of the soul,
This vision change shall never wring from thee
　　Nor wasteful years effacing as they roll.
O steel-blue lake, high cradled in the hills !
　　O sad waves, filled with little sobs and cries !
White glistening shingle, hiss of mountain rills,
　　And granite-hearted walls blotting the skies,
Shine, sob, gleam, gloom for ever ! Oh, in me
　　Be what you are in Nature—a recess—
To sadness dedicate and mystery,
　　Withdrawn, afar, in the soul's wilderness.
Still let my thoughts, leaving the worldly roar
Like pilgrims, wander on thy haunted shore.

I GIVE MY HEART TO THEE

I

I GIVE my heart to thee, O mother-land—
I, if none else, recall the sacred womb.
I, if none else, behold the loving eyes
Bent ever on thy myriad progeny
Who care not nor regard thee as they go,
O tender, sorrowing, weeping, hoping land !
I give my heart to thee, O mother-land.

II

I give my heart to thee, O father-land,
Fast-anchored on thine own eternal soul,
Rising with cloudy mountains to the skies.
O proud, strong land, unstooping, stern of rule,
Me rule as ever ; let me feel thy might ;
Let me go forth with thee now and for aye.
I give my heart to thee, O father-land.

III

I give my heart to thee, heroic land—
To thee or in thy morning when the Sun
Flashed on thy giant limbs—thy lurid noon—
Or in thy depth of night, fierce-thoughted one—
Wrestling with phantoms of thy own wild soul,
Or, stone-still, silent, waiting for the dawn,
I give my heart to thee, heroic land.

IV

I give my heart to thee, ideal land,
Far-soaring sister of the starry throng.
O fleet of wing, what journeyings are thine,
What goal, what god attracts thee ?   What unseen
Glory reflected makes thy face a flame ?
Leave me not ; where thou goest, let me go.
I give my heart to thee, ideal land.

'A. E.'

SOME dozen years ago a little body of young men hired a room in Dublin, and began to read papers to one another on the Vedas and the Upanishads and the Neo-Platonists, and on modern mystics and spiritualists. They had no scholarship, and they spoke and wrote badly, but they discussed great problems ardently and simply and unconventionally, as men perhaps discussed great problems in the mediæval Universities. When they were scattered by their different trades and professions, others took up the discussions where they dropped them, moving the meetings, for the most part, from back street to back street; and now two writers of genius— 'A. E.' and 'John Eglinton'—seem to have found among them, without perhaps agreeing with them in everything, that simplicity of mind and that belief in high things, less common in Dublin than elsewhere in Ireland, for whose lack imagination perishes. 'John Eglinton' in TWO ESSAYS ON THE REMNANT and in the essays he has published in the little monthly magazine they print and bind themselves, analyses the spiritual elements that are transforming and dissolving the modern world; while 'A. E.,' in HOMEWARD: SONGS BY THE WAY and in THE EARTH BREATH, repeats over again the revelation of a spiritual world that has been the revelation of mystics in all ages, but with a richness of colour and a subtlety of rhythm that are of our age. Plotinus wrote : ' In the particular acts of human life it is not the interior soul and the true man, but the exterior shadow of the man alone, which laments and weeps, performing his part on the earth, as in a more ample and extended scene, in which many shadows of souls and phantom forms appear ;' and so these poems cry out that ' for every deep filled with stars ' there ' are stars and deeps within,' and that ' our thought' is but ' the echo of a deeper being,' and that ' we kiss because God once for beauty sought amid a world of dreams,' and that we rise by ' the symbol charioted' ' through loved things ' to ' love's own ways.' They are full of the sadness that has fallen upon all mystics, when they have first come to understand that there is an invisible beauty from which they are divided by visible things. How can one be interested in the rising and in the setting of the sun, and in the work men do under the sun, when the mistress that one loves is hidden behind the gates of death, and it may be behind a thousand gates beside—gate beyond gate?

> What of all the will to do?
>   It has vanished long ago,
> For a dream-shaft pierced it through
>   From the Unknown Archer's bow.
>
> What of all the soul to think?
>   Some one offered it a cup
> Filled with a diviner drink;
>   And the flame has burned it up.
>
> What of all the hope to climb?
>   Only in the self we grope
> To the misty end of time:
>   Truth has put an end to hope.

It is this invisible beauty that makes the planets 'break in woods and flowers and streams' and 'shake' the winds from them 'as the leaves from off the rose,' and that 'kindles' all souls and lures them 'through the gates of birth and death,' and in whose heart we will all rest when 'the shepherd of the ages draws his misty hordes away through the glimmering deeps to silence' and to 'the awful fold.' But this invisible beauty kindles evil as well as good, for its shadow is 'the fount of shadowy beauty' that pours out those things 'the heart,' the merely mortal part of us, 'would be,' and 'chases' them in 'endless flight.' All emotions are double, for either we choose 'the shadowy beauty,' and our soul weeps, or the invisible beauty that is 'our high ancestral self,' and the body weeps.

These poems, the most delicate and subtle that any Irishman of our time has written, seem to me all the more interesting because their writer has not come from any of our seats of literature and scholarship, but from among sectaries and

visionaries whose ardour of belief and simplicity of mind have
been his encouragement and his inspiration.

W. B. Yeats.

‘A. E.’ (George Russell) was born in Lurgan in 1867. Among his
books of poems are: Homeward: Songs by the Way, 1894; The
Earth Breath, 1897; Collected Poems, 1913; Voices of the Stones,
1925, and Vale and Other Poems, 1930.

Sacrifice

Those delicate wanderers—
  The wind, the star, the cloud—
Ever before mine eyes,
  As to an altar bowed,
Light and dew-laden airs
Offer in sacrifice.

The offerings arise :
  Hazes of rainbow light,
Pure crystal, blue, and gold,
  Through dreamland take their flight ;
And ’mid the sacrifice
God moveth as of old.

In miracles of fire
  He symbols forth His days ;
In gleams of crystal light
  Reveals what pure pathways
Lead to the soul’s desire,
The silence of the height.

Dana [1]

I am the tender voice calling ‘Away,’
Whispering between the beatings of the heart,
And inaccessible in dewy eyes
I dwell, and all unkissed on lovely lips,
Lingering between white breasts inviolate,
And fleeting ever from the passionate touch
I shine afar, till men may not divine

---

[1] Dana is the ‘ Mater Deorum ’ of the Celtic mythology.

Whether it is the stars or the beloved
They follow with rapt spirit.   And I weave
My spells at evening, folding with dim caress,
Aerial arms, and twilight-dropping hair,
The lonely wanderer by shore or wood,
Till filled with some vast tenderness he yields,
Feeling in dreams for the dear mother heart
He knew ere he forsook the starry way,
And clings there pillowed far above the smoke
And the dim murmur from the dûns of men ;
I can enchant the trees and rocks, and fill
The dumb brown lips of earth with mystery,
Make them reveal or hide the god.   I breathe
A deeper pity than all love, myself
Mother of all, but without hands to heal,
Too vast and vague—they know me not !   But yet
I am the heartbreak over fallen things,
The sudden gentleness that stays the blow ;
And I am in the kiss that warriors give
Pausing in battle, and in the tears that fall
Over the vanquished foe ; and in the highest
Among the Danann gods I am the last
Council of mercy in their hearts, where they
Mete justice from a thousand starry thrones.

SYMBOLISM

Now when the giant in us wakes and broods,
    Filled with home-yearnings, drowsily he flings
From his deep heart high dreams and mystic moods,
    Mixed with the memory of the loved earth-things ;
Clothing the vast with a familiar face,
Reaching his right hand forth to greet the starry race.

Wondrously near and clear the great warm fires
    Stare from the blue ; so shows the cottage light
To the field labourer whose heart desires
    The old folk by the nook, the welcome bright
From the housewife long parted from at dawn—
So the star villages in God's great depths withdrawn.

Nearer to Thee, not by delusion led,
  Though there no house-fires burn nor bright eyes gaze ;
We rise, but by the symbol charioted,
  Through loved things rising up to Love's own ways ;
By these the soul unto the vast has wings,
And sets the seal celestial on all mortal things.

JANUS

IMAGE of beauty, when I gaze on thee,
Trembling I waken to a mystery ;
How through one door we go to life or death,
By spirit kindled or the sensual breath.

Image of beauty, when my way I go,
No single joy or sorrow do I know ;
Elate for freedom leaps the starry power,
The life which passes mourns its wasted hour.

And, ah ! to think how thin the veil that lies
Between the pain of hell and paradise !
Where the cool grass my aching head embowers,
God sings the lovely carol of the flowers.

CONNLA'S WELL [1]

A CABIN on the mountain-side hid in a grassy nook,
With door and window open wide, where friendly stars may look,
The rabbit shy can patter in, the winds may enter free—
Who throng around the mountain throne in living ecstasy.

And when the sun sets dimmed in eve, and purple fills the air,
I think the sacred hazel-tree is dropping berries there,
From starry fruitage waved aloft where Connla's well o'erflows ;
For, sure, the immortal waters run through every wind that blows.

---

[1] 'Sinend, daughter of Lodan Lucharglan, son of Ler, out of the Land of Promise, went to Connla's Well, which is under sea, to behold it. That is a well at which are the hazels of wisdom and inspirations, that is, the hazels of the science of poetry, and in the same hour their fruit and their blossom and their foliage break forth, and then fall upon the well in the same shower, which raises upon the water a royal surge of purple.' THE VOYAGE OF BRAN, p. 214.

I think, when night towers up aloft and shakes the trembling dew,
How every high and lonely thought that thrills my spirit through
Is but a shining berry dropped down through the purple air,
And from the magic tree of life the fruit falls everywhere.

OUR THRONES DECAY

I SAID my pleasure shall not move ;
    It is not fixed in things apart ;
Seeking not love—but yet to love—
    I put my trust in mine own heart.

I knew the fountain of the deep
    Wells up with living joy, unfed ;
Such joys the lonely heart may keep,
    And love grow rich with love unwed.

Still flows the ancient fount sublime —
    But ah ! for my heart, shed tears, shed tears !
Not it, but love, has scorn of time —
    It turns to dust beneath the years.

THE THREE COUNSELLORS

IT was the fairy of the place,
    Moving within a little light,
Who touched with dim and shadowy grace
    The conflict at its fever height.

It seemed to whisper ' Quietness,'
    Then quietly itself was gone :
Yet echoes of its mute caress
    Were with me as the years went on.

It was the warrior within
    Who called : 'Awake ! prepare for fight !
Yet lose not memory in the din ;
    Make of thy gentleness thy might ;

' Make of thy silence words to shake
    The long-enthronéd kings of earth :
Make of thy will the force to break
    Their towers of wantonness and mirth.'

It was the wise all-seeing soul
  Who counselled neither war nor peace :
' Only be thou thyself that goal
  In which the wars of Time shall cease.'

INHERITANCE

As flow the rivers to the sea
  Adown from rocky hill or plain,
A thousand ages toiled for thee
  And gave thee harvest of their gain ;
And weary myriads of yore
Dug out for thee earth's buried lore.

The shadowy toilers for thee fought,
  In chaos of primeval day,
Blind battles with they knew not what ;
  And each before he passed away
Gave clear articulate cries of woe :
Your pain is theirs of long ago.

And all the old heart-sweetness sung,
  The joyous life of man and maid
In forests when the earth was young,
  In rumours round your childhood strayed :
The careless sweetness of your mind
Comes from the buried years behind.

And not alone unto your birth
  Their gifts the weeping ages bore,
The old descents of God on earth
  Have dowered thee with celestial lore :
So, wise, and filled with sad and gay,
You pass into the further day.

THE MEMORY OF EARTH

IN the wet dusk silver sweet,
  Down the violet-scented ways,
As I moved with quiet feet
  I was met by mighty days.

On the hedge the hanging dew
  Glassed the eve and stars and skies ;
While I gazed a madness grew
  Into thundered battle-cries.

Where the hawthorn glimmered white,
  Flashed the spear and fell the stroke—
Ah, what faces pale and bright
  Where the dazzling battle broke !

There a hero-hearted queen
  With young beauty lit the van :
Gone ! the darkness flowed between
  All the ancient wars of man.

While I paced the valley's gloom,
  Where the rabbits pattered near,
Shone a temple and a tomb
  With the legend carven clear :

' *Time put by a myriad fates*
  That her day might dawn in glory;
Death made wide a million gates
  So to close her tragic story.'

WILLIAM BUTLER YEATS

FEW poets have revised and retouched their work more than
Mr. Yeats, and this may perhaps be one cause of the singular
unity of the impression which it leaves upon the mind. In
the final edition of his poems, where much is altered and much
early work struck out altogether, one sees naturally but little
sign of the immature and experimental stages which every
poet must go through. He appears to have struck the rock,
and the water flowed ; we do not see it led with pain and toil
from distant sources, through miry channels, and by feeble
streamlets into its true bed. Nor is this merely because

Mr. Yeats has pruned away his early work so remorselessly. His first printed poem was THE ISLAND OF STATUES, which appeared in *The Dublin University Review* in the summer of 1885, when the writer was just nineteen years old. It is a drama of magic and enchantment, full of weird and picturesque effects, and, though a little weak in its handling of long metres, containing some of the most musical and beautiful verse Mr. Yeats has ever written. Act II. Sc. 3 opens thus :

'THE ISLAND.—Flowers of manifold colour are knee-deep before a gate of brass, above which, in a citron-tinctured sky, glimmer a few stars. At intervals come mournful blasts from the horns among the flowers.'

Then follows the exquisite lyric included in his last volume under the title of ' The Cloak, the Boat, and the Shoe : '

> ' What do you weave so fair and bright ? '
> ' The cloak I weave of sorrow.'

Lines like these are also quite in the spirit of Mr. Yeats's later work :

> A foolish word thou gavest me !
> For each within himself hath all
> The world, within his folded heart
> His temple and his banquet hall.

And these :

> Hear thou, O daughter of the days,
>
> *   *   *   *   *   *
>
> Thou shalt outlive thine amorous happy time,
> And dead as are the lovers of old rime
> Shall be the hunter-lover of thy youth.
> Yet ever more, through all thy days of ruth,
> Shall grow thy beauty and thy dreamless truth.
> As a hurt leopard fills with ceaseless moan
> And aimless wanderings the woodlands lone,
> Thy soul shall be ; though pitiless and bright
> It is, yet it shall fail thee day and night
> Beneath the burden of the infinite,
> In those far years, O daughter of the days.

In lines such as the following there is perhaps a reminiscence of Shelley :

> Sad lady, cease !
> I rose, I rose
> From the dim wood's foundation—
> I rose, I rose
> Where in white exultation
> The long lily blows. . . .

But on the whole it may be said that Mr. Yeats's note was from the very beginning both singularly strong and singularly original. His published works, at any rate, tell no story of any period of discipleship. It is remarkable that his passion for Ferguson's poetry, which he gave expression to in his first published prose work, and which brought a powerful and enduring influence into his literary development, never coloured his style and manner of expression in the slightest degree.

The influence in question was that of the ancient Celtic literature and mythology, which Mr. Yeats has apprehended in a deeper and more intimate sense than even Ferguson. That great writer may count as the earliest of those who have contributed to what I think can fairly be described as the supreme task of Irish literature in the present day—the task of leading that literature to strike its roots into the Gaelic past, and not into the mighty tradition of England. Ferguson did this by re-telling in noble verse the old Gaelic myths and heroic tales. But he still remains a man of the nineteenth century, telling us about gods and heroes of the prime. With Mr. Yeats, however, the gods and heroes are no longer far-off—they are here among us, 'forms more real than living man.' They are even so melted into the imagination of the poet that they emerge from it not as 'symbols' of ideas (as the phrases of modern mysticism have it), but the very ideas themselves. Niam and Caolte and Cleena of the Wave are no mere symbols, no devices of the intellect to represent the unintelligible—they have an intensity of spiritual life comparable only to that which, in effect, beings of the same order possess in ancient Irish myth.

It is fortunate indeed that Irish mythology, in attracting Mr. Yeats's imagination, laid hold of something which that mythology had never found before—a great artist to absorb and interpret it. This is a new thing in Irish literature. The Gaelic bards and sagamen had the creative touch and musical utterance, but next to no sense of the profound rhythms of life and thought. Moore was an accomplished mechanician of verse, but could rarely produce anything outside his regular stock of tunes. Ferguson had the 'grand manner,' but not always the sustained and arduous intensity of poetic passion informing every vibrating line; and Mangan, who had this intensity at times, fell—like many Irish poets of high natural endowment— too easily into the trivial and commonplace both in thought and diction. Mr. Yeats, however, with a certain reservation which I shall refer to later, is an artist *pur sang*. Though he has deemed much of his work not worth republishing, I do not think he has ever written one feeble or worthless passage—one that is not alive with the life of the imagination, and that does not re-echo in some degree the music at the heart of things. He has in this way set a shining example to Irish writers of this and following generations—he has set the standard of achievement at a height that the strongest may only attain, as Mr. Yeats attained it, by strenuous, unflinching toil and an ear ever open to the whisper of perfection.

But what of the substance, the matter, conveyed to us by all this beautiful art? This is not an indifferent question. It cannot be answered by saying that Mr. Yeats's verse lives and shines and sings, and is sufficiently criticised when we show that it does so. Art is to help us to live—not to live well or ill, but simply to live. If, however, it induces bewildered or unnatural or unwholesome moods, it is not helping us towards life—but towards death. On the other hand, life is more vast and varied than any one individual or any one epoch can know. The poet may be a pioneer on its dim frontiers, as well as a cultivator of its rich fields of traditional and familiar toil. Mr. Yeats's work is for the most part done on the frontier of life. He has followed up doubtful gleams, interpreted mysteries, made himself a philosophy of dreams. The reader, however, who bestows upon Mr. Yeats's poetry the attention it deserves, will perceive that his mind is no mere Eolian harp answering to the faint breathings of a wind from another world. Behind Mr. Yeats's 'wizard song' a keen, questioning, co-ordinating intellect is at work—like Baudelaire he tills his plot of ground 'avec le fer de la raison.' It is ill translating the philosophy of a poet, which he reveals poetically, into scientific language ; but it may perhaps be said, without overstraining the attempt to formalise and define, that Mr. Yeats—like the Oriental mystics who formulated their creed, and the Celtic mystics who did not, regards the outer world as a creation of spiritual activity— bids us cultivate the inward life, the inward vision, as the sure path to truth and peace. The profound and beautiful poem named 'The Two Trees,' which is included in the selection here given, seems to me to contain as much of his scheme of thought as can be put into form so compressed. The idea is of course in itself neither new nor rare ; but what is rare is Mr. Yeats's firm grasp of it, his rich and subtle illustration of it, the new and beautiful vesture of imagination he has found for it.

Mr. Yeats has still, it may be hoped, a long literary career before him, and many new fields of work to enter upon. But it may be observed that the ground he has already covered is not wanting in extent and variety. Poems like 'Father Gilligan' or 'The Old Pensioner' or the 'Fiddler of Dooney' show a command of simple objective emotion which may yet be developed in work of what is called a more 'popular' charac- ter than Mr. Yeats has so far done. Some love-poems, more- over, such as 'When you are Old' or 'The Cloths of Heaven,' have for all their rare and spiritual grace a strain of human passion more intense than that of many lyrists who have won fame by singing of nothing but love. Whether these qualities will ever yield work of great tragic power is a question that the future must decide. Mr. Yeats's dramatic experiments appear to testify to some impulse in this direction. His first published work and his second were both in dramatic form, and his

Countess Cathleen and the Land of Heart's Desire are not only dramas, but have attained the natural end of a drama —that of being acted. Yet I do not know that Mr. Yeats's dramatic work forms, so far, an exception to the general rule that good drama can only be written by poets both gifted with the dramatic imagination and intimately familiar with the stage. In dramatic composition Mr. Yeats appears to be moving about in worlds not realised. There are, no doubt, dramatists of the 'literary' school, who seem to ignore the fact that in assuming dramatic form a poem also assumes certain stringent laws and responsibilities foreign to other forms of poetry. I grant that if d'Annunzio, for instance, is a dramatist, so is Mr. Yeats ; and I grant also that a sort of pageant accompanied by recitative may be a legitimate and interesting form of art, so long as it is kept strictly within its own conventions. Yet I cannot but think that Mr. Yeats's dramatic enterprises are a step in the wrong direction, or rather I should say a step for which a certain training and discipline are needed that his talent has not hitherto undergone.[1]

This is one reservation I have to make in my admiration for a poet whom I consider the first of the English-writing poets of his own day. Another, and a much slighter one, concerns itself with his occasional use of terms which are purely symbolic and not vitalised by the imagination. Probably Mr. Yeats has caught this habit from his study of Blake—Blake, who might have left volumes of immortal verse had not his intellect mastered his imagination and led him into limitless deserts of dry symbolism. Mr. Yeats's imagination, as I have already said, is usually supreme in these matters ; it burns up the symbol, and a winged creature soars singing from the flame. But the mystic in him is sometimes, especially in his later work, found adoring the mere stigmata of mysticism ; and then one thinks with dismay that a finer and stronger genius than Blake's may some day lose itself in that dreary waste inhabited by Los and Orc and Enitharmion.

But these forebodings soon vanish when one hears again

---

[1] Since 1899, when these words were written, Mr. Yeats's dramatic power has developed considerably.—T. W. R.

K K

the 'lake water lapping' on the shores of Innisfree, or the murmuring of the bell-branch which Mr. Yeats has taken from the hand of nameless singers who moved the heart of Ireland a thousand years ago—

> It charmed away the merchant from his guile,
> And turned the farmer's memory from his cattle,
> And hushed in sleep the roaring ranks of battle,
> For all who heard it dreamed a little while.

T. W. ROLLESTON.

W. B. Yeats was born in Dublin, June 13, 1866, the eldest son of J. B. Yeats, R.H.A., a well-known Irish artist. He was educated chiefly at the High School, Harcourt Street, Dublin, but spent much of his early life in the County Sligo, where his grandparents lived. In 1885 he published THE ISLAND OF STATUES, a romantic drama, in *The Dublin University Review*. MOSADA, a short dramatic piece, was published in the same year as a brochure by Sealy, Bryers and Walker, Dublin. About the beginning of the century, with the help of Lady Gregory and others, he founded the Abbey Theatre of Dublin. Among his books of poetry are: THE WANDERINGS OF OISIN, 1889; THE WIND AMONG THE REEDS, 1889; IN THE SEVEN WOODS, 1903; THE GREEN HELMET, 1910; THE WILD SWANS OF COOLE, 1919; THE TOWER, 1928. His plays include THE COUNTESS KATHLEEN, 1892; THE LAND OF HEART'S DESIRE, 1894; THE SHADOWY WATERS, 1900; CATHLEEN NI HOULIHAN, 1902; DEIRDRE, 1907; FOUR PLAYS FOR DANCERS, 1921; PLAYS IN PROSE AND VERSE, 1923. His works are published in six volumes including LATER POEMS, PLAYS AND CONTROVERSIES, PLAYS IN PROSE AND VERSE, ESSAYS, EARLY POEMS AND STORIES, REVERIES OVER CHILDHOOD AND YOUTH, and THE TREMBLING OF THE VEIL.

THE HOSTING OF THE SIDHE

THE host is riding from Knocknarea
  And over the grave of Clooth-na-bare ;
  Caolte tossing his burning hair,
And Niamh calling : *Away, come away :*
Empty your heart of its mortal dream.
  The winds awaken, the leaves whirl round,
  Our cheeks are pale, our hair is unbound,
Our breasts are heaving, our eyes are a-gleam,

Our arms are waving, our lips are apart;
And if any gaze on our rushing band,
We come between him and the deed of his hand—
We come between him and the hope of his heart.
The host is rushing 'twixt night and day,
And where is there hope or deed as fair?
Caolte tossing his burning hair,
And Niamh calling: *Away, come away.*

MICHAEL ROBARTES REMEMBERS FORGOTTEN BEAUTY

WHEN my arms wrap you round, I press
My heart upon the loveliness
That has long faded from the world;
The jewelled crowns that kings have hurled
In shadowy pools, when armies fled;
The love-tales wove with silken thread
By dreaming ladies upon cloth
That has made fat the murderous moth;
The roses that of old time were
Woven by ladies in their hair;
The dew-cold lilies ladies bore
Through many a sacred corridor,
Where such grey clouds of incense rose
That only the gods' eyes did not close:
For that pale breast and lingering hand
Come from a more dream-heavy land—
A more dream-heavy hour than this.
And when you sigh from kiss to kiss
I hear white Beauty sighing, too,
For hours when all must fade like dew,
But flame on flame, deep under deep,
Throne over throne, where in half-sleep
Their swords upon their iron knees
Brood her high lonely mysteries.

THE ROSE OF THE WORLD

WHO dreamed that beauty passes like a dream?
　　For these red lips, with all their mournful pride,
　　Mournful that no new wonder may betide,
Troy passed away in one high funeral gleam,
　　And Usna's children died.

We and the labouring world are passing by :
　　Amid men's souls, that waver and give place,
　　Like the pale waters in their wintry race,
Under the passing stars, foam of the sky,
　　Lives on this lonely face.

Bow down, archangels, in your dim abode :
　　Before you were, or any hearts to beat,
　　Weary and kind one lingered by His seat ;
He made the world to be a grassy road
　　Before her wandering feet.

THE LAKE ISLE OF INNISFREE

I WILL arise and go now, and go to Innisfree,
　　And a small cabin build there, of clay and wattles made ;
Nine bean rows will I have there, a hive for the honey-bee,
　　And live alone in the bee-loud glade.

And I shall have some peace there, for peace comes dropping
　　　　slow,
　　Dropping from the veils of the morning to where the cricket
　　　　sings
There midnight's all a-glimmer, and noon a purple glow,
　　And evening full of the linnet's wings.

I will arise and go now, for always night and day
　　I hear lake water lapping with low sounds by the shore ;
While I stand on the roadway, or on the pavements grey,
　　I hear it in the deep heart's core.

WHEN YOU ARE OLD

WHEN you are old and grey and full of sleep,
  And nodding by the fire, take down this book,
  And slowly read, and dream of the soft look
Your eyes had once, and of their shadows deep ;

How many loved your moments of glad grace,
  And loved your beauty with love false or true !
  But one man loved the pilgrim soul in you,
And loved the sorrows of your changing face.

And bending down beside the glowing bars
  Murmur, a little sadly, how love fled
  And paced upon the mountains overhead,
And hid his face amid a crowd of stars.

A DREAM OF A BLESSED SPIRIT

ALL the heavy days are over ;
  Leave the body's coloured pride
Underneath the grass and clover,
  With the feet laid side by side.

One with her are mirth and duty ;
  Bear the gold-embroidered dress,
For she needs not her sad beauty,
  To the scented oaken press.

Hers the kiss of Mother Mary,
  The long hair is on her face ;
Still she goes with footsteps wary,
  Full of earth's old timid grace :

With white feet of angels seven
  Her white feet go glimmering ;
And above the deep of heaven,
  Flame on flame and wing on wing.

The Lamentation of the Old Pensioner

I had a chair at every hearth,
  When no one turned to see,
With ' Look at that old fellow there
  And who may he be?'
And therefore do I wander now,
  And the fret lies on me.

The roadside trees keep murmuring—
  Ah ! wherefore murmur ye,
As in the old days long gone by,
  Green oak and poplar tree?
The well-known faces are all gone,
  And the fret lies on me.

The Two Trees

Beloved, gaze in thine own heart,
  The holy tree is growing there ;
From joy the holy branches start,
  And all the trembling flowers they bear.
The changing colours of its fruit
  Have dowered the stars with merry light ;
The surety of its hidden root
  Has planted quiet in the night ;
The shaking of its leafy head
  Has given the waves their melody,
And made my lips and music wed,
  Murmuring a wizard song for thee.
There, through bewildered branches, go
  Winged Loves borne on in gentle strife,
Tossing and tossing to and fro
  The flaming circle of our life.
When looking on their shaken hair,
  And dreaming how they dance and dart,
Thine eyes grow full of tender care :
  Beloved, gaze in thine own heart.

Gaze no more in the bitter glass
   The demons, with their subtle guile,
Lift up before us when they pass,
   Or only gaze a little while ;
For there a fatal image grows,
   With broken boughs and blackened leaves,
And roots half hidden under snows
   Driven by a storm that ever grieves.
For all things turn to barrenness
   In the dim glass the demons hold—
The glass of outer weariness,
   Made when God slept in times of old.
There, through the broken branches, go
   The ravens of unresting thought ;
Peering and flying to and fro,
   To see men's souls bartered and bought.
When they are heard upon the wind,
   And when they shake their wings, alas !
Thy tender eyes grow all unkind :
   Gaze no more in the bitter glass.

THE ISLAND OF SLEEP

From THE WANDERINGS OF OISÍN

FLED foam underneath us and round us, a wandering and milky
   smoke,
  High as the saddle-girth, covering away from our glances the
    tide ;
And those that fled, and that followed, from the foam-pale distance
   broke ;
  The immortal desire of immortals we saw in their faces, and
    sighed.

I mused on the chase with the Fenians, and Bran, Sgeolan
   Lomair,
  And never a song sang Niam, and over my finger-tips
Came now the sliding of tears and sweeping of mist-cold hair
  And now the warmth of sighs, and after the quiver of lips.

Were we days long or hours long in riding, when rolled in a grisly
　　peace,
　　An isle lay level before us, with dripping hazel and oak ?
And we stood on a sea's edge we saw not ; for whiter than new-
　　washed fleece
　　Fled foam underneath us and round us, a wandering and milky
　　smoke.

And we rode on the plains of the sea's edge—the sea's edge barren
　　and grey,
　　Grey sand on the green of the grasses and over the dripping trees,
Dripping and doubling landward, as though they would hasten
　　away
　　Like an army of old men longing for rest from the moan of the
　　seas.

But the trees grew taller and closer, immense in their wrinkling
　　bark ;
　　Dropping—a murmurous dropping—old silence and that one
　　sound ;
For no live creatures lived there, no weasels moved in the dark ;
　　Long sighs arose in our spirits, beneath us bubbled the ground.

And the ears of the horse went sinking away in the hollow night,
　　For, as drift from a sailor slow drowning the gleams of the world
　　and the sun,
Ceased on our hands and our faces, on hazel and oak leaf, the
　　light,
　　And the stars were blotted above us, and the whole of the world
　　was one.

Till the horse gave a whinny ; for, cumbrous with stems of the
　　hazel and oak,
　　A valley flowed down from his hoofs, and there in the long grass
　　lay,
Under the starlight and shadow, a monstrous slumbering folk,
　　Their naked and gleaming bodies poured out and heaped in the
　　way.

And by them were arrow and war-axe, arrow and shield and
blade ;
  And dew-blanched horns, in whose hollow a child of three years
  old
Could sleep on a couch of rushes, and all inwrought and inlaid,
  And more comely than man can make them with bronze and
  silver and gold.

And each of the huge white creatures was huger than fourscore
men ;
  The tops of their ears were feathered, their hands were the claws
  of birds,
And, shaking the plumes of the grasses and the leaves of the
mural glen,
  The breathing came from those bodies, long-warless, grown
  whiter than curds.

The wood was so spacious above them that He who had stars for
His flocks
  Could fondle the leaves with His fingers, nor go from His dew-
  cumbered skies ;
So long were they sleeping, the owls had builded their nests in
their locks,
  Filling the fibrous dimness with long generations of eyes.

And over the limbs and the valley the slow owls wandered and
came,
  Now in a place of star-fire, and now in a shadow-place wide ;
And the chief of the huge white creatures, his knees in the soft
star-flame,
  Lay loose in a place of shadow ; we drew the reins by his side.

Golden the nails of his bird-claws, flung loosely along the dim
ground ;
  In one was a branch soft-shining, with bells more many than
  sighs,
In midst of an old man's bosom ; owls ruffling and pacing around
  Sidled their bodies against him, filling the shade with their eyes.

And my gaze was thronged with the sleepers ; no, neither in
    house of a cann
  In a realm where the handsome are many, or in glamours by
    demons flung,
Are faces alive with such beauty made known to the salt eye of
    man,
  Yet weary with passions that faded when the seven-fold seas
    were young.

And I gazed on the bell-branch, sleep's forbear, far sung by the
    Sennachies.
  I saw how those slumberers, grown weary, there camping in
    grasses deep,
Of wars with the wide world and pacing the shores of the wander-
    ing seas,
  Laid hands on the bell-branch and swayed it, and fed of un-
    human sleep.

Snatching the horn of Niam, I blew a lingering note ;
  Came sound from those monstrous sleepers, a sound like the
    stirring of flies.
He, shaking the fold of his lips, and heaving the pillar of his
    throat,
  Watched me with mournful wonder out of the wells of his eyes.

I cried, ' Come out of the shadow, cann of the ails of gold !
  And tell of your goodly household and the goodly works of your
    hands,
That we may muse in the starlight and talk of the battles of old.
  Your questioner, Oisín, is worthy ; he comes from the Fenian
    lands.'

Half open his eyes were, and held me, dull with the smoke of their
    dreams ;
  His lips moved slowly in answer, no answer out of them came ;
Then he swayed in his fingers the bell-branch, slow dropping a
    sound in faint streams
  Softer than snow-flakes in April and piercing the marrow like
    flame.

Wrapt in the wave of that music, with weariness more than of
 earth,
 The moil of my centuries filled me ; and gone like a sea-covered
  stone
Were the memories of the whole of my sorrow and the memories
 of the whole of my mirth,
 And a softness came from the starlight and filled me full to the
  bone.

In the roots of the grasses, the sorrels, I laid my body as low ;
 And the pearl-pale Niam lay by me, her brow on the midst of
  my breast ;
And the horse was gone in the distance, and years after years 'gan
 flow ;
 Square leaves of the ivy moved over us, binding us down to our
  rest.

And, man of the many white croziers, a century there I forgot
 How the fetlocks drip blood in the battle, when the fallen on
  fallen lie rolled ;
How the falconer follows the falcon in the weeds of the heron's
 plot ;
 And the names of the demons whose hammers made armour for
  Conhor of old.

And, man of the many white croziers, a century there I forgot
 That the spear-shaft is made out of ashwood, the shield out of
  ozier and hide ;
How the hammers spring on the anvil, on the spear-head's burning
 spot ;
 How the slow blue-eyed oxen of Finn low sadly at evening tide.

But in dreams, mild man of the croziers, driving the dust with their
 throngs,
 Moved round me, of seamen or landsmen, all who are winter
  tales ;
Came by me the canns of the Red Branch, with roaring of laughter
 and songs,
 Or moved as they moved once, love-making or piercing the
  tempest with sails.

Came Blanid, MacNessa, tall Fergus, who feastward of old time
    slunk,
    Cook Barach, the traitor ; and warward, the spittle on his beard
    never dry,
Dark Balor, as old as a forest, car-borne, his mighty head sunk
    Helpless, men lifting the lids of his weary and death-making eye.

And by me, in soft red raiment, the Fenians moved in loud streams,
    And Grania, walking and smiling, sewed with her needle of bone.
So lived I and lived not, so wrought I and wrought not, with
    creatures of dreams,
    In a long iron sleep, as a fish in the water goes dumb as a stone.

BOOK VI

SIR AUBREY DE VERE

SIR AUBREY DE VERE, among whose schoolfellows at
Harrow were Byron and Sir Robert Peel, was, like his friend
Wordsworth, from childhood a lover of the mountains and the
woods, and the Rotha was for him a stream of inspiration
more sweet than Castaly. An Irishman by birth, his natural
sympathies found expression in the fine series of sonnets—
described by Wordsworth as 'the most perfect of our age '—
dealing with events in Irish history and scenes of Irish landscape ; while to the country of his earlier ancestors he paid a
noble poetic tribute in MARY TUDOR, a drama worthy comparison
with the Histories of the sixteenth and seventeenth centuries.
In the delineation of Queen Mary we possess a portrait the
most arresting that the modern drama has to offer—a portrait at
once human and royal, at once tragic and convincing. 'The
author of MARY TUDOR,' says Mr. De Vere, ' used to affirm that
most of the modern historians had mistaken a part, and that
the smaller part, of the sad Queen's character for the whole of
it.' Presented by Sir Aubrey de Vere, the contrasted figures
of the lonely Mary, distraught indeed, but no impossible
Fury, and of the gentle-hearted Jane Grey, innocent victim of
an unkind destiny, must take their place in the gallery of
English Queens painted by the masters. Since no room can
be found for selections from the De Vere dramas, a single
passage from MARY TUDOR may rightly be given here. Lady

Jane, a few moments before her execution, takes her last farewell of her weeping mother.

> What shall I give thee ?—they have left me little—
> What slight memorial through soft tears to gaze on ?
> This bridal ring—the symbol of past joy ?
> I cannot part with it ; upon this finger
> It must go down into the grave.   Perchance
> After long years some curious hand may find it,
> Bright, like our better hopes, amid the dust,
> And piously, with a low sigh, replace it.
> Here, take this veil, and wear it for my sake.
> And take this winding-sheet to him, and this
> Small handkerchief, so wetted with my tears,
> To wipe the death-damp from his brow.   This kiss—
> And this—my last—print on his lips, and bid him
> Think of me to the last, and wait my spirit.
> Farewell, my mother !   Farewell, dear, dear mother !
> These terrible moments I must pass in prayer—
> For the dying—for the dead !   Farewell ! farewell !

Sir Aubrey de Vere in this play—and it is no slight dramatic achievement—enlists our sympathies for Jane Grey, yet gives us to feel that with Mary we visit higher heights and lower depths of tragedy.   Both in MARY TUDOR and Mr. Aubrey de Vere's ALEXANDER THE GREAT the weight of a great subject is fully sustained, the action is spaciously planned, the verse moves with stately grace.   But our age has set its face against the drama, and it may perhaps be counted fortunate that in a literary form so popular as the sonnet the De Veres have graven for themselves a lasting memorial.   There are sonnets by father and by son that anthologies centuries hence will reproduce.   Sonnets like Sir Aubrey's entitled 'The Shannon,' or 'Spanish Point,' or 'The Rock of Cashel,' or Mr. De Vere's 'Sorrow' or 'The Sun God,' must remain among our permanent poetical treasures.

W. MACNEILE DIXON.

Sir Aubrey de Vere, Bart., born 1788, was the eldest son of Sir Vere Hunt, of Curragh Chase, County Limerick, Ireland.   His father afterwards took the name of De Vere as a descendant of De Vere, fifteenth Earl of

Oxford. He published JULIAN THE APOSTATE, a drama, 1822 ; THE DUKE
OF MERCIA, an historical drama, and THE LAMENTATIONS OF IRELAND,
1823 ; THE SONG OF FAITH, DEVOUT EXERCISES AND SONNETS, 1842.
MARY TUDOR, an historical drama (written 1844), was published after the
author's death, and without his final revision, in 1847. He died in 1846.

GOUGANE BARRA

NOT beauty which men gaze on with a smile,
 Not grace that wins, no charm of form or love,
 Dwelt with that scene. Sternly upon my view
And slowly—as the shrouding clouds awhile
Disclosed the beetling crag and lonely isle—
 From their dim lake the ghostly mountains grew,
 Lit by one slanting ray. An eagle flew
From out the gloomy gulf of the defile,
Like some bad spirit from Hades. To the shore
 Dark waters rolled, slow-heaving, with dull moan ;
 The foam-flakes hanging from each livid stone
Like froth on deathful lips ; pale mosses o'er
 The shattered cell crept, as an orphan lone
 Clasps his cold mother's breast when life is gone.

LIBERTY OF THE PRESS

SOME laws there are too sacred for the hand
 Of man to approach : recorded in the blood
 Of patriots, before which, as the Rood
Of faith, devotional we take our stand ;
Time-hallowed laws ! Magnificently planned
 When Freedom was the nurse of public good,
 And Power paternal : laws that have withstood
All storms, unshaken bulwarks of the land !
Free will, frank speech, an undissembling mind,
 Without which Freedom dies and laws are vain,
  On such we found our rights, to such we cling ;
In them shall power his surest safeguard find.
 Tread them not down in passion or disdain ;
  Make man a reptile, he will turn and sting.

The Rock of Cashel

ROYAL and saintly Cashel ! I would gaze
  Upon the wreck of thy departed powers
  Not in the dewy light of matin hours,
Nor the meridian pomp of summer's blaze,
But at the close of dim autumnal days,
  When the sun's parting glance, through slanting showers,
  Sheds o'er thy rock-throned battlements and towers
Such awful gleams as brighten o'er Decay's
Prophetic cheek.   At such a time methinks
  There breathes from thy lone courts and voiceless aisles
A melancholy moral ; such as sinks
  On the lone traveller's heart amid the piles
Of vast Persepolis on her mountain stand,
Or Thebes half buried in the desert sand.

The Shannon

RIVER of billows, to whose mighty heart
  The tide-wave rushes of the Atlantic Sea ;
  River of quiet depths, by cultured lea,
Romantic wood or city's crowded mart ;
River of old poetic founts, which start
  From their lone mountain-cradles, wild and free,
  Nursed with the fawns, lulled by the woodlark's glee,
And cushat's hymeneal song apart ;
River of chieftains, whose baronial halls,
  Like veteran warders, watch each wave-worn steep,
Portumna's towers, Bunratty's royal walls,
  Carrick's stern rock, the Geraldine's grey keep—
River of dark mementoes ! must I close
My lips with Limerick's wrong, with Aughrim's woes ?

Spanish Point

THE waters—O the waters !—wild and glooming,
  Beneath the stormy pall that shrouds the sky,
On, through the deep'ning mist more darkly looming,
  Plumed with the pallid foam funereally,

Onward, like death, they come, the rocks entombing !
  Nor thunder-knell is needful from on high ;
Nor sound of signal gun, momently booming
  O'er the disastrous deep ; nor seaman's cry !
And yet, if aught were wanting, manifold
  Mementoes haunt those reefs ; how that proud Host
Of Spain and Rome so smitten were of old,
  By God's decree, along this fatal coast,
And over all their purple and their gold,
Mitre and helm and harp, the avenging waters rolled !

JOHN KELLS INGRAM

DR. INGRAM was born in 1823, in the County Donegal, and educated at Newry School, and in Trinity College, Dublin. He became a Fellow of Trinity in 1846, and was an Honorary LL.D. of Glasgow University. He held in Trinity College the offices of Professor of Greek, Professor of English Literature, Senior Lecturer and Vice-Provost, and he was President of the Royal Irish Academy and a Commissioner for the Publication of the Ancient Laws and Institutions of Ireland. Owing to advancing age he laid down all these offices in 1899, but left behind him an enduring record of work well done for the interests of Irish intellect and scholarship. He died in 1907. His principal published works relate to political economy ('Work and the Workman'—an address to the Trades Union Congress in 1880—and the articles on 'Political Economy' and 'Slavery' in the ENCYCLOPÆDIA BRITANNICA, ninth edition).

The famous lyric, written in Dr. Ingram's student days, 'The Memory of the Dead' (see Book III., 'Poets of *The Nation*'), was for the first time formally acknowledged when Dr. Ingram published a volume of poems in 1900; but its authorship had long been an open secret. The quatrain, printed in the following selection, 'Each nation master at its

L L

own fireside,' may perhaps be taken as representing his later views on the Irish National Question.

The best of Dr. Ingram's sonnets, in his volume SONNETS AND OTHER POEMS, belong to a sequence, and cannot, as a rule, be taken out of their context without loss. Noble in thought and expression, they seem to carry with them the air of great literature, and they make us regret that their author has given us so little verse, and that little so late.

SONNET

On reading the Sonnet by R. C. D., entitled ' In Memoriam G. P. C.,' in ' Macmillan's Magazine.'

In *Macmillan's Magazine* for April 1881 there appeared a sonnet by Archbishop Trench on the death of Sir George Pomeroy Colley on Majuba Hill. The following sonnet, signed ' J. K. I.,' appeared in *The Academy* of April 2:

YES ! mourn the soul, of high and pure intent,
Humane as valiant, in disastrous fight
Laid low on far Majuba's bloody height !
Yet not his death alone must we lament,
But more such spirit on evil mission sent
To back our broken faith with arméd might
And the unanswered plea of wounded Right
Strike dumb by warfare's brute arbitrament.
And while these deeds are done in England's name,
Religion, unregardful, keeps her cell :
The tuneful note that wails the dead we hear ;
Where are the sacred thunders that should swell
To shame such foul oppression, and proclaim
Eternal justice in the nation's ear ?

SOCIAL HEREDITY

MAN is no mushroom growth of yesterday.
His roots strike deep into the hallow'd mould
Of the dead centuries ; ordinances old
Govern us, whether gladly we obey

Or vainly struggle to resist their sway :
Our thoughts by ancient thinkers are controll'd,
And many a word in which our thoughts are told
Was coined long since in regions far away.
The strong-soul'd nations, destin'd to be great,
Honour their sires and reverence the Past ;
They cherish and improve their heritage.
The weak, in blind self-trust or headlong rage,
The olden times' transmitted treasure cast
Behind them, and bemoan their loss too late.

NATIONALITY

Each nation master at its own fireside—
The claim is just, and so one day 'twill be ;
But a wise race the time of fruit will bide,
Nor pluck th' unripen'd apple from the tree.

WILLIAM ALEXANDER

THREE pieces are here given as specimens of the stately verse
of William Alexander, whose eloquence, learning, and character made his name one of the most cherished and honoured
in the whole history of his Church.   Though perhaps rarely
characterised by the concentrated force of the poetry which
springs from a native gift, assiduously cultivated, nevertheless the cultivated imagination of Dr. Alexander, his feeling
for the glory of Nature, his rich but never overloaded rhetoric,
and the occasional strains of a wistful pathos which reveal a
sensitive human spirit—all these qualities make his poetic
contribution to Irish literature one of high worth and distinction.

Dr. Alexander was born at Derry, 1824, and educated at Tunbridge
and Oxford.   In 1850, when rector of Termonamongan, in the diocese of
Derry, he was married to Miss Cecil Frances Humphreys, who was
destined to aid in winning distinction for her new name.   After holding

L L 2

cures at Upper Fahan and at Strabane he became, in 1867, Bishop of
Derry and Raphoe, and in 1897 was called to the Primacy of All Ireland.
His poetical publications are THE DEATH OF JACOB, 1858 ; SPECIMENS,
POETICAL AND CRITICAL, 1867 ; LYRICS OF LIFE AND LIGHT (by W.
A. and others), 1878 ; ST. AUGUSTINE'S HOLIDAY, 1886.

AMONG THE SAND-HILLS

FROM the ocean half a rood
　To the sand-hills long and low
　Ever and anon I go ;
Hide from me the gleaming flood,
　Only listen to its flow.

To those billowy curls of sand
　Little of delight is lent—
　As it were a yellow tent,
Here and there by some wild hand
　Pitch'd, and overgrown with bent ;

Some few buds like golden beads
　Cut in stars on leaves that shine
　Greenly, and a fragrance fine
Of the ocean's delicate weeds,
　Of his fresh and foamy wine.

But the place is music-haunted.
　Let there blow what wind soever—
　Now, as by a stately river,
A monotonous requiem's chanted ;
　Now you hear great pine woods shiver.

Frequent when the tides are low
　Creep for hours sweet sleepy hums.
　But when in the spring tide comes,
Then the silver trumpets blow
　And the waters beat like drums.

And the Atlantic's roll full often,
　Muffled by the sand-hills round,
　Seems a mighty city's sound,
Which the night-wind serves to soften
　By the waker's pillow drown'd.

Seems a salvo—state or battles—
  Through the purple mountain gaps
  Heard by peasants ; or perhaps
Seems a wheel that rolls or rattles ;
  Seems an eagle's wing that flaps ;

Seems a peal of thunder, caught
  By the mountain pines and tuned
  To a marvellous gentle sound ;
Wailings where despair is not—
  Hearts self-hushing some heart-wound.

Still what winds there blow soever,
  Wet or shine, by sun or star,
  When white horses plunge afar,
When the palsied froth-lines shiver,
  When the waters quiet are ;

On the sand-hills where waves boom,
  Or, with ripples scarce at all,
  Tumble not so much as crawl,
Ever do we know of whom
  Cometh up the rise and fall.

Need is none to see the ships,
  None to mark the mid-sea jet
  Softening into violet,
While those old pre-Adamite lips
  To those boundary heaps are set.

Ah ! we see not the great foam
  That beyond us strangely rolls,
  Whose white-wingèd ships are souls
Sailing from the port called Home,
  When the signal-bell Death tolls.

And we catch not the broad shimmer,
  Catch not yet the hue divine
  Of the purpling hyaline ;
Of the heaving and the glimmer
  Life's sands cheat our straining eyne.

But by wondrous sounds not shut
From those sand-hills, we may be
Sure that a diviner sea
Than earth's keels have ever cut
Floweth from eternity.

INSCRIPTION

ON THE STATUE ERECTED TO CAPTAIN BOYD IN
ST. PATRICK'S CATHEDRAL, DUBLIN

OH ! in the quiet haven, safe for aye,
If lost to us in port one stormy day,
Borne with a public pomp by just decree,
Heroic sailor ! from that fatal sea,
A city vows this marble unto thee.
And here, in this calm place, where never din
Of earth's great waterfloods shall enter in,
Where to our human hearts two thoughts are given—
One Christ's self-sacrifice, the other Heaven—
Here is it meet for grief and love to grave
The Christ-taught bravery that died to save,
The life not lost, but found beneath the wave.

VERY FAR AWAY

ONE touch there is of magic white,
  Surpassing southern mountain's snow,
That to far sails the dying light
  Lends, where the dark ships onward go
Upon the golden highway broad
That leads up to the isles of God.

One touch of light more magic yet,
  Of rarer snow 'neath moon or star,
Where, with her graceful sails all set,
  Some happy vessel seen afar,
As if in an enchanted sleep
Steers o'er the tremulous stretching deep.

O ship ! O sail ! far must ye be
　Ere gleams like that upon ye light.
O'er golden spaces of the sea,
　From mysteries of the lucent night,
Such touch comes never to the boat
Wherein across the waves we float.

O gleams more magic and divine,
　Life's whitest sail ye still refuse,
And flying on before us shine
　Upon some distant bark ye choose.
—By night or day, across the spray,
That sail is very far away.

CECIL FRANCES ALEXANDER

Mrs. Alexander's hymns and religious verse have made her name as a poetess very widely known. Her poems on secular themes have perhaps been less heard of, but they show, together with a certain weakness in constructive power, much force and picturesqueness of diction and touches of keen pathos. Her poetic development was evidently much influenced by her husband's work, but she occasionally commanded an accent of passion rendered with a penetrating simplicity which was all her own. Her poem on the leaguer of Derry is a fine example of her mastery of language and rhythm.

Cecil Frances Humphreys was born in Dublin about 1825; a daughter of Major John Humphreys, a Norfolk man by birth, who became a land-owner in Tyrone and in Wicklow. She came early under the religious influence of Dr. Hook, Dean of Chichester, and subsequently of Keble, who edited her HYMNS FOR LITTLE CHILDREN. She married William Alexander—then rector of Termonamongan—in 1850, and died in 1895. Her poems were collected and edited by her husband (POEMS, by C. F. Alexander, 1896).

The Siege of Derry

' O MY daughter ! lead me forth to the bastion on the north,
    Let me see the water running from the green hills of Tyrone,
Where the woods of Mountjoy quiver above the changeful river,
    And the silver trout lie hidden in the pools that I have known.

' There I wooed your mother, dear ! in the days that are so near
    To the old man who lies dying in this sore-beleaguered place ;
For time's long years may sever, but love that liveth ever,
    Calls back the early rapture—lights again the angel face.

' Ah, well ! she lieth still on our wall-engirdled hill,
    Our own Cathedral holds her till God shall call His dead ;
And the Psalter's swell and wailing, and the cannon's loud assailing,
    And the preacher's voice and blessing, pass unheeded o'er her
        head.

' 'Twas the Lord who gave the word when His people drew the
        sword
    For the freedom of the present, for the future that awaits.
O child ! thou must remember that bleak day in December
    When the 'Prentice-Boys of Derry rose up and shut the gates.

' There was tumult in the street, and a rush of many feet—
    There was discord in the Council, and Lundy turned to fly,
For the man had no assurance of Ulstermen's endurance,
    Nor the strength of him who trusteth in the arm of God Most
        High.

' These limbs, that now are weak, were strong then, and thy cheek
    Held roses that were red as any rose in June—
That now are wan, my daughter ! as the light on the Foyle water
    When all the sea and all the land are white beneath the moon.

' Then the foemen gather'd fast—we could see them marching
        past—
    The Irish from his barren hills, the Frenchmen from his wars,
With their banners bravely beaming, and to our eyes their seeming
    Was fearful as a locust band, and countless as the stars.

And they bound us with a cord from the harbour to the ford,
 And they raked us with their cannon, and sallying was hot ;
But our trust was still unshaken, though Culmore fort was taken,
 And they wrote our men a letter, and they sent it in a shot.

They were soft words that they spoke, how we need not fear their
  yoke,
 And they pleaded by our homesteads, and by our children
  small,
And our women fair and tender ; but we answered : " No
  surrender ! "
 And we called on God Almighty, and we went to man the wall.

' There was wrath in the French camp ; we could hear their
  Captain's stamp,
 And Rosen, with his hand on his cross'd hilt, swore
That little town of Derry, not a league from Culmore ferry,
 Should lie a heap of ashes on the Foyle's green shore.

' Like a falcon on her perch, our fair Cathedral Church
 Above the tide-vext river looks eastward from the bay—
Dear namesake of St. Columb, and each morning, sweet and
  solemn,
 The bells, through all the tumult, have call'd us in to pray.

' Our leader speaks the prayer—the captains all are there—
 His deep voice never falters, though his look be sad and grave.
On the women's pallid faces, and the soldiers in their places,
 And the stones above our brothers that lie buried in the nave.

' They are closing round us still by the river ; on the hill
 You can see the white pavilions round the standard of their
  chief ;
But the Lord is up in heaven, though the chances are uneven,
 Though the boom is in the river whence we look'd for our relief.

' And the faint hope dies away at the close of each long day,
 As we see the eyes grow lustreless, the pulses beating low ;
As we see our children languish.   Was ever martyr's anguish,
 At the stake or in the dungeon, like this anguish that we know ?

'With the foemen's closing line, while the English make no sign,
  And the daily lessening ration, and the fall of staggering feet,
And the wailing low and fearful, and the women, stern and tearful,
  Speaking bravely to their husbands and their lovers in the
    street.

'There was trouble in the air when we met this day for prayer,
  And the joyous July morning was heavy in our eyes ;
Our arms were by the altar as we sang aloud the Psalter,
  And listen'd in the pauses for the enemy's surprise.

'"Praise the Lord God in the height, for the glory of His might !"
  It ran along the arches and it went out to the town :
"In His strength He hath arisen, He hath loos'd the souls in
    prison,
  The wrong'd one He hath righted, and raised the fallen-down."

'And the preacher's voice was bold as he rose up then and told
  Of the triumph of the righteous, of the patience of the saints,
And the hope of God's assistance, and the greatness of resistance,
  Of the trust that never wearies and the heart that never faints.

'Where the river joins the brine, canst thou see the ships in line ?
  And the plenty of our craving just beyond the cruel boom ?
Through the dark mist of the firing canst thou see the masts
    aspiring,
  Dost thou think of one who loves thee on that ship amidst the
    gloom ?'

She was weary, she was wan, but she climb'd the rampart on,
  And she look'd along the water where the good ships lay afar :
'Oh ! I see on either border their cannon ranged in order,
  And the boom across the river, and the waiting men-of-war.

'There's death in every hand that holds a lighted brand,
  But the gallant little *Mountjoy* comes bravely to the front.
Now, God of Battles, hear us ! Let that good ship draw near us.
  Ah ! the brands are at the touch-holes—will she bear the
    cannon's brunt ?

'She makes a forward dash.   Hark ! hark ! the thunder-crash !
    O father, they have caught her—she is lying on the shore.
Another crash like thunder—will it tear her ribs asunder ?
    No, no ! the shot has freed her—she is floating on once more.

' She pushes her white sail through the bullets' leaden hail—
    Now blessings on her captain and on her seamen bold !—
Crash ! crash ! the boom is broken ; I can see my true love's
        token—
    A lily in his bonnet, a lily all of gold.

' She sails up to the town, like a queen in a white gown
    Red golden are her lilies, true gold are all her men.
Now the *Phœnix* follows after—I can hear the women's laughter,
    And the shouting of the soldiers, till the echoes ring again.'

       *   *   *   *   *   *

She has glided from the wall, on her lover's breast to fall,
    As the white bird of the ocean drops down into the wave ;
And the bells are madly ringing, and a hundred voices singing,
    And the old man on the bastion has joined the triumph stave :

' Sing ye praises through the land ; the Lord with His right hand,
    With His mighty arm hath gotten Himself the victory now.
He hath scattered their forces, both the riders and their horses.
    There is none that fighteth for us, O God ! but only Thou.'

THE IRISH MOTHER'S LAMENT

  ' She watched for the return of her son from America in her house by the
Foyle, near Derry.'

> ' THERE'S no one on the long white road
>   The night is closing o'er ;
> O mother ! cease to look abroad
>   And let me shut the door.
>
> ' Now here and there a twinkling light
>   Comes out along the bay ;
> The little ships lie still and white,
>   And no one comes this way.'

She turned her straining eyes within ;
  She sighed both long and low.
' Shut up the door ; take out the pin,
  Then, if it must be so.

' But, daughter, set the wick alight,
  And put it in the pane ;
If any should come home to-night,
  He'll see it through the rain.

' Nay, leave the pin beneath the latch ;
  If some one push the door,
Across my broken dreams I'll hear
  His footstep on the floor.'

She crouched within the ingle nook,
  She spread her fingers sere,
Her failed eyes had a far-off look,
  Despite her fourscore year.

And if in youth they had been fair,
  'Twas not the charm they had,
Not the old beauty lingering there,
  But something weird and sad.

The daughter, in the firelight pale,
  A woman grey and wan,
Sat listening, while half dream, half wail,
  Her words went wandering on ;

' O river that dost never halt
  Till down beyond the bar
Thou meet'st the breakers green and salt
  That bore my lads afar—

' O sea betwixt our slighted isle
  And that wide bounteous West
That has such magic in her smile
  To lure away our best—

' Bring back, bring back the guiding keel ;
    Bring fast the home-bound ship ;
Mine eyes look out ; I faint to feel
    The touch of hand and lip.

' And is that land so much more fair,
    So much more rich that shore
Than this, where, prodigal of care,
    I nursed the sons I bore ?

' I nursed them at my yielding breast,
    I reared them at my knee,
They left me for the golden West ;
    They left me for the sea.

' With hungry heart, and eyes that strove
    In vain their eyes to meet,
And all my lavish mother's love
    Beat backward to my feet—

' Like that broad stream that runs, and raves,
    And floweth grandly out,
But the salt billows catch its waves,
    And fling them all about —

' The bitter world washed out my claim ;
    In childhood it was dear,
But youth forgets, and manhood came,
    And dashed it far and near.

' But when I think of the old time,
    Soft fingers, eyes that met,
In spite of age, in spite of clime,
    I wonder they forget.

' And if they live, their life is strong ;
    Forgotten here I die ;
I question with my heart, and long,
    And cannot answer why,

'Till by Christ's grace I walk in white
    Where His redeemèd go,
And know the reason of God's right,
    Or never care to know.

'But out-bound ships come home again;
    They sail 'neath sun and moon.
Put thou the candle in the pane;
    They may be coming soon.'

'Calm lie the lights below the town;
    There's not a ship in sight;
O mother! cease, and lay you down;
    They will not come to-night.'

Dreams

Beyond, beyond the mountain line,
    The grey-stone and the boulder,
Beyond the growth of dark green pine,
    That crowns its western shoulder,
There lies that fairy-land of mine,
    Unseen of a beholder.

Its fruits are all like rubies rare;
    Its streams are clear as glasses;
There golden castles hang in air,
    And purple grapes in masses,
And noble knights and ladies fair
    Come riding down the passes.

Ah me! they say if I could stand
    Upon those mountain ledges,
I should but see on either hand
    Plain fields and dusty hedges;
And yet I know my fairy-land
    Lies somewhere o'er their edges.

EDWARD DOWDEN

THE younger generation of literary students owes so much to the critical work of Edward Dowden that it is impossible to wish away any part of it. Yet the readers of his verse must feel that the hours he has spent with the sovereign lady of poesy have been, alas ! too few ; that his distinction as a prose-writer has been bought at almost too great a price. For he has not written his poetry as with his left hand ; here he has not in any degree tutored himself to speak, but speaks in his own natural voice and in his native tongue.

There are among the poets of our time some whose music assails the ear with more insistence ; there is none who more surely enters and subdues the heart. Like the poetry of Andrew Marvell, it is not for the multitude, but for him who

> Can burst joy's grape against his palate fine.

It puts forth its own flower and fruit ; it creates its own world, awakens its own mood. And as a poet it is with Marvell that, if comparison is needful, Professor Dowden may best be compared. He recalls to us Marvell's fine simplicity, his unfailing sense for the beautiful, his pervading spirituality, his touch of resolute aloofness from the haste and fever of life, his glad and serious temper, his unaffected charm of phrase and movement. Like Marvell's, this is but a small island of poetry ; but the human spirit may inhabit here. Over it bends the same sky as over the great continents ; across it blow the same winds, and on its shores break the everlasting seas.

W. MACNEILE DIXON.

Professor E. Dowden, LL.D., was born in Cork, 1843, and educated at Trinity College, Dublin. At one time he was Professor of English Literature in Dublin University. He died in 1913. He produced much prose work, including a life of Southey and a volume of 'Studies in Literature.' His SHAKESPERE: HIS MIND AND ART (1874) marked an epoch in Shakesperean studies in England. It was the first work of importance in which the results of textual research in Shakespere's plays and poems were turned fruitfully to the uses of æsthetic criticism. Professor Dowden's POEMS appeared first in 1876, and a later edition came out in 1913.

ON THE HEIGHTS

HERE are the needs of manhood satisfied !
Sane breath, an amplitude for soul and sense,
The noonday silence of the summer hills,
And this embracing solitude ; o'er all
The sky unsearchable, which lays its claim—
A large redemption not to be annulled—
Upon the heart ; and far below, the sea
Breaking and breaking, smoothly, silently.
What need I any further ?   Now once more
My arrested life begins, and I am man
Complete with eye, heart, brain, and that within
Which is the centre and the light of being ;
O dull ! who morning after morning chose
Never to climb these gorse and heather slopes
Cairn-crowned, but lost within one seaward nook
Wasted my soul on the ambiguous speech
And slow eye-mesmerism of rolling waves,
Courting oblivion of the heart.   True life
That was not which possessed me while I lay
Prone on the perilous edge, mere eye and ear,
Staring upon the bright monotony,
Having let slide all force from me, each thought
Yield to the vision of the gleaming blank,
Each nerve of motion and of sense grow numb,
Till to the bland persuasion of some breeze
Which played across my forehead and my hair
The last volition would efface itself,
And I was mingled wholly in the sound
Of tumbling billow and upjetting surge,
Long reluctation, welter and refluent moan,
And the reverberating tumultuousness
'Mid shelf and hollow and angle black with spray.
Yet under all oblivion there remained
A sense of some frustration, a pale dream

Of Nature mocking man, and drawing down—
As streams draw down the dust of gold—his will,
His thought, and passion, to enrich herself—
The·insatiable devourer.
                              Welcome Earth,
My natural heritage ! and this soft turf, .
These rocks, which no insidious ocean saps,
But the wide air flows over, and the sun
Illumines. Take me, mother, to thy breast ;
Gather me close in tender, sustinent arms ;
Lay bare thy bosom's sweetness and its strength
That I may drink vigour and joy and love.
O infinite composure of the hills,
Thou large simplicity of this fair world,
Candour and calmness, with no mockery,
No soft frustration, flattering sigh or smile
Which masks a tyrannous purpose ; and ye Powers
Of these sky-circled heights, and Presences
Awful and strict, I find you favourable,
Who seek not to exclude me or to slay,
Rather accept my being, take me up
Into your silence and your peace. Therefore
By him whom ye reject not, Gracious Ones,
Pure vows are made that haply he will be
Not all unworthy of the world ; he casts
Forth from him, never to resume again,
Veiled nameless things, frauds of the unfilled heart,
Fantastic pleasures, delicate sadnesses,
The lurid and the curious and the occult,
Coward sleights and shifts, the manners of the slave,
And long unnatural uses of dim life.
Hence with you ! Robes of angels touch these heights
Blown by pure winds, and I lay hold upon them.
Here is a perfect bell of purple heath,
Made for the sky to gaze at reverently,
As faultless as itself, and holding light,
Glad air and silence in its slender dome ;
Small, but a needful moment in the sum
Of God's full joy—the abyss of ecstasy

O'er which we hang as the bright bow of foam
Above the never-filled receptacle
Hangs seven-hued, where the endless cataract leaps.
Oh ! now I guess why you have summoned me,
Headlands and heights, to your companionship.
Confess that I this day am needful to you !
The heavens were loaded with great light, the winds
Brought you calm summer from a hundred fields,
All night the stars had pricked you to desire,
The imminent joy at its full season flowered,
There was a consummation, the broad wave
Toppled and fell.   And had ye voice for this ?
Sufficient song to unburden the urged breast ?
A pastoral pipe to play ? a lyre to touch ?
The brightening glory of the heath and gorse
Could not appease your passion, nor the cry
Of this wild bird that flits from bush to bush.
Me therefore you required, a voice for song,
A pastoral pipe to play, a lyre to touch.
I recognise your bliss to find me here ;
The sky at morning, when the sun upleaps,
Demands her atom of intense melody,
Her point of quivering passion and delight,
And will not let the lark's heart be at ease.
Take me, the brain with various subtile fold,
The breast that knows swift joy, the vocal lips ;
I yield you here the cunning instrument
Between your knees ; now let the plectrum fall !

ABOARD THE 'SEA-SWALLOW'

THE gloom of the sea-fronting cliffs
    Lay on the water, violet-dark ;
The pennon drooped, the sail fell in,
    And slowly moved our bark.

A golden day ; the summer dreamed
    In heaven and on the whispering sea,
Within our hearts the summer dreamed ;
    The hours had ceased to be.

Then rose the girls with bonnets loosed,
   And shining tresses lightly blown,
Alice and Adela, and sang
   A song of Mendelssohn.

Oh ! sweet and sad and wildly clear,
   Through summer air it sinks and swells,
Wild with a measureless desire
   And sad with all farewells.

OASIS

LET them go by—the heats, the doubts, the strife ;
   I can sit here and care not for them now,
Dreaming beside the glimmering wave of life
   Once more—I know not how.

There is a murmur in my heart ; I hear
   Faint—oh ! so faint—some air I used to sing ;
It stirs my sense ; and odours dim and dear
   The meadow-breezes bring.

Just this way did the quiet twilights fade
   Over the fields and happy homes of men,
While one bird sang as now, piercing the shade,
   Long since—I know not when.

EDMUND JOHN ARMSTRONG

THE elder brother of George Francis Savage-Armstrong (q.v.),
by whom the story of his short life has been written and his
literary remains collected (1877). His fine character and
brilliant intellect appear to have made a deep impression on his
contemporaries, and his death at the age of twenty-three was
accompanied with a widespread regret and sense of loss such as
rarely attend the passing-away of so young a writer. Armstrong
was born in Dublin in 1841, and entered Trinity College, Dublin,
in 1859. Though apparently of strong physique, and, like his

brother, a great lover of outdoor life, he was attacked by consumption and died in 1865.

Mr. E. J. Armstrong's POEMS have been posthumously published.

THE BLIND STUDENT

ON Euripides' plays we debated,
    In College, one chill winter night ;
A student rose up, while we waited
    For more intellectual light.
As he stood, pale and anxious, before us,
    Three words, like a soft summer wind,
Went past us and through us and o'er us—
    A whisper low-breathed : ' He is blind ! '

And in many a face there was pity,
    In many an eye there were tears ;
For his words were not buoyant or witty,
    As fitted his fresh summer years.
And he spoke once or twice, as none other
    Could speak, of a woman's pure ways—
He remembered the face of his mother
    Ere darkness had blighted his days.

ADIEU

I HEAR a distant clarion blare
    The smouldering battle flames anew ;
A noise of onset shakes the air—
    Dear woods and quiet vales, adieu !

Weird crag, where I was wont to gaze
    On the far sea's aërial hue,
Below a veil of glimmering haze
    At morning's breezy prime—adieu !

Clear runnel, bubbling under boughs
    Of odorous lime and darkling yew,
Where I have lain on banks of flowers
    And dreamed the livelong noon—adieu !

And, ah ! ye lights and shades that ray
  Those orbs of brightest summer blue,
That haunted me by night and day
  For happy moons—adieu ! adieu !

From FIONNUALA

WITH heaving breast the fair-haired Eileen sang
The mystic, sweet, low-vowelled Celtic rhyme
Of Fionnuala and her phantom lover,
Who wooed her in the fairy days of yore
Beneath the sighing pines that gloom the waves
Of Luggalà and warbling Anamoe—
And how he whispered softly vows of love,
While the pale moonbeam glimmered down and lit
The cataract's flashing foam, and elves and fays
Played o'er the dewy harebells, wheeling round
The dappled foxglove in a flickering maze
Of faint aërial flame ; and the wild sprites
Of the rough storm were bound in charmèd sleep—
And how the lovely phantom lowly knelt,
And pleaded with such sweet-tongued eloquence,
Such heavenly radiance on his lips and eyes,
That Fionnuala, blushing, all in tears,
Breaking the sacred spell that held her soul,
Fell on his bosom and confessed her love—
And how the demon changed, and flashed upon her
In all his hideous beauty, and she sank
In fearful slumbers, and, awaking, found
Her form borne upward in the yielding air ;
And, floating o'er a dark blue lake, beheld
The reflex of a swan, white as the clouds
That fringe the noonday sun, and heard a voice,
As from a far world, shivering through the air :
' Thou shalt resume thy maiden form once more
When yon great Temples, piled upon the hills
With rugged slabs and pillars, shall be whelmed
In ruin, and their builders' names forgot ! '—
And how she knew her phantom lover spoke,

And how she floated over lake and fell
A hundred years, and sighed her mournful plaint
Day after day, till the first mass-bell pealed
Its silvery laughter amid Erin's hills,
And a young warrior found her, with the dew
Of morning on her maiden lips, asleep
In the green woods of warbling Anamoe,
And wooed and won her for his blushing bride.

GEORGE FRANCIS SAVAGE-ARMSTRONG

MR. ARMSTRONG is one of the most fertile of Irish writers of the present day. He has given himself to poetry in that spirit of single-hearted devotion in which great works are achieved ; and his array of volumes—containing dramas, lyrics, narrative poems, odes, meditations, and what not—represent a strenuous attempt to pay what Baudelaire calls the poet's ransom by the harvest of his art.

The earliest years of Mr. Armstrong were spent in the southern part of the County Wicklow, and as in the case of his elder brother, Edmund J. Armstrong (q.v.), whom he accompanied in endless rambles and explorations

          . . . Along the stormful shore,
Roaming underneath the lonely woodlands' branches old and hoar,
Where the golden rills of Wicklow foaming
Flash from rock to rock through many a dark ravine,
Where the crags above the hollows and the lakes in splendour lean,

this region with its singular and pathetic beauty was the true nursing-mother of his poetic gift. The following passage from a letter which I am permitted to quote gives the clue to the character of his whole poetic work : 'The love of Nature led in my brother's case and in mine to the love of poetry. At the age of twelve I had read all Shakespeare's plays and a vast deal of other poetry and prose besides. I used to spend hours, with a book of poetry in my hand, in the tops of tall trees, reading, or on the side of the Dublin or Wicklow mountains, alone ; or my brother and I together would scale a mountain, with a volume of Byron or Scott or Wordsworth or Coleridge or Keats or Shelley, and lie in the heather, reading aloud alternately poem after poem.'   All his life long, but especially in the years from about 1864 to 1877, Mr. Armstrong—as his readers might per-ceive—has been a devoted lover of the knapsack and the ' open road,' and has tramped not only over a great part of his own country, but through Normandy and Brittany, the Riviera, Switzerland, Italy, and even Greece, Turkey, and Bulgaria. The effect of his devotion both to poetry and to open-air life may be clearly traced in Mr. Armstrong's work.   It shows fine culture and acquaintance with the highest models, and it brings with it also something far more precious—a breath from the hills, the odour of pines, the gleam of mountain torrents, the sunlight on leagues of heather.   Mr. Armstrong has travelled much, both in the outward world and in that inner one of thought and study, and from every place that he has visited in both worlds some glimpse of the scenery of his life is reflected in his verse.   But he seems to have taken everywhere with him, and preserved in all its buoyancy, the early youthful delight in exploration and in the physical con-tact with wild Nature.   The distinct note, the original flavour, of Mr. Armstrong's poetry appears to be formed by the union of his ornate and stately diction with the peculiar freshness and directness of his pictures of outdoor life.   These pictures have the true quality of the *plein air*—they are not memories or dreams of Nature, but experiences, won by the toil that deepens the breath and braces the muscle upon the mountain-side, and that reader must have surely left his youth of body and spirit long behind in whose veins they do not stir the roving blood.

But though Mr. Armstrong's renderings of the life of Nature form, to my mind, the most original and valuable part of his work, he is also a poet of human thought and passion, and has produced in that province a great deal of masterly work. His three-volumed drama, or trilogy, on ' Saul,' ' David,' and

'Solomon,' was perhaps a piece of misdirected labour—for these figures have become symbols to us, and as human characters in a drama of action they do not appear to live— yet one cannot but admire the strenuous artistic impulse in which such a work was conceived and executed. These dramas—like the author's earlier work UGONE, founded on a passionate Italian story—are designed with thoughtfulness and skill, and wrought out with accomplished craftsmanship. But it is in poems—half narrative, half reflective—like 'Through the Solitudes' or 'Lugnaquillia,' where the poet's mind is free to roam at will and follow up any pleasant path that may present itself, that Mr. Armstrong's art is seen at its best. It is true that in the pure analysis of passion (as in the striking poem 'Sundered Friendship,' which won the enthusiastic praise of Sainte-Beuve) and in the region of pure philosophic meditation, to which he has devoted a complete volume, ONE IN THE INFINITE, Mr. Armstrong has won laurels which the critic cannot overlook. But he seems most at home and most original when the outward and the inward life play into and stimulate each other, and the bulk of his work is conceived on this plane :

> Yet the Indefinite, Awful, Infinite
> Vibrates about me, and these scenes have grown
> The tokens of Its life and of Its power,
> And, yielding to the pulses of Its might,
> And worshipping before Its viewless throne,
> My spirit widens towards a larger light.
> So may that Voice still speak from hill, wave, flower,
> Love, to thy heart and mine.

Yet with all this love and reverence for external Nature Mr. Armstrong's feeling towards it differs markedly from that of the new Celtic school, in that it is not mingled with the least trace of mysticism. Nature with him is always one thing ; God is another ; self a third. To the mystic the scenery of the inward and of the outward life are indistinguishably blended, just as they are in the old Celtic literature from which the Irish mystical poetry of to-day has sprung. Mr. Armstrong's poetry shows no sign in this or any other way of the influence of the Celtic literary tradition. It is simple and objective in its conception, and forms the most important body of poetic work which has been produced outside the Celtic tradition since the time when Ferguson and Mangan began to lead the waters from that ancient source into the channels of modern Irish verse.

T. W. ROLLESTON.

George Francis Savage-Armstrong, M.A., D.Litt., was born in the County Dublin, 1845 ; son of the late Edmund J. Armstrong, a descendant of the Irish branch of the Armstrongs of Mangerton. Mr. Armstrong's mother was a daughter of the Rev. Henry Savage, of Glastry, County Down. On the death of a maternal uncle in 1891, Mr. Armstrong assumed the additional surname of Savage, as representative of the Glastry branch of the Savages of the Ards, the most ancient of the Anglo-Norman families of Ulster. He was educated, partly by private tuition, in the Channel Islands—whither he had accompanied his elder brother, Edmund J. Armstrong (q.v.)—and at Trinity College, Dublin, where among other distinctions he won the Vice-Chancellor's prize for English verse with a poem on ' Circassia.' His first literary work was the editing of his brother Edmund's POEMS. This was shortly followed, in 1869, with a volume of POEMS, LYRICAL AND DRAMATIC, which won the warm commendations of many distinguished critics, including Sainte-Beuve. The tragedy UGONE followed next (1871), and after this the TRAGEDY OF ISRAEL (1872–1876). Mr. Armstrong next turned to a fresh edition of his brother's writings, accompanied with a ' Life and Letters.' A GARLAND FROM GREECE was the fruit of a tour in that country undertaken in 1877. Next, after a long break, came STORIES OF WICKLOW (1886), the fulfilment of an early poetic project which was to have been carried out in concert with the author's brother ; VICTORIA REGINA, a ' Jubilee Song' (1887) ; a satire entitled MEPHISTOPHELES IN BROADCLOTH (1888) ; ONE IN THE INFINITE (1891) ; the Trinity College, Dublin, TERCENTENARY ODE (1892), set to music by Sir Robert Stewart ; a poem for the Diamond Jubilee (1898), written in a very successful adaptation of the Anglo-Saxon verse. He also contributed prose articles to various magazines; wrote an interesting volume on the family history of the Savages of the Ards, and in 1901 published BALLADS OF DOWN. He was a Fellow of the Royal University. In 1871 Mr. Armstrong was appointed to the post of Professor of English Literature in the Queen's College, Cork. He died in 1906 at the age of sixty-one.

THE SCALP

STERN granite Gate of Wicklow, with what awe,
　　What triumph, oft (glad children strayed from home)
　　We passed into thy shadows cool, to roam
The Land beyond, whose very name could draw
A radiance to our faces ; till we saw,
　　With airy peak and purple mountain-dome,
　　And lawn and wood and blue bay flecked with foam.
The Land indeed—fair truth without one flaw !
Never may I with foot of feeble age
　　Or buoyant step of manhood pass thy pale
　　　And feel not still renewed that awe, that joy
(Of the dim Past divinest heritage)—
　　Seeking the sacred realm thou dost unveil,
　　　Earth's one spot loved in love without alloy !

A WICKLOW SCENE [1]

FROM THE SUMMIT OF LUGNAQUILLIA

FOR many a mile the tawny mountains heaved
In rough confusion.　Here among the heaths
A brown dull tarn reflected the heaven's blue,
Or the slow-moving shadow of a cloud
Darkened a cliff or valley.　Northward far
Slieve-Cullinn, dwindled to an arrowy point,
Lifted his rosy peak beyond grey Djouce,
That in a cleft amid the summer woods
Showed, nestling, Luggela ; and near us ran
The Avonbeg by Fananierin's base
Away to mingle with bright Avonmore ;
And low amid Ovoca's wooded vale
We traced the wedded waters to the sea ;
Then, turning, watched beneath in wide Imahl
Far-winding Slaney glittering in the noon,
And fashioned for our fancies in the haze
Faint in the West the rims of Galteemore.

---

[1] From ' Lugnaquillia' (STORIES OF WICKLOW).

Wicklow [1]

YES, this is Wicklow ; round our feet
    And o'er our heads its woodlands smile ;
Behold it, love—the garden sweet
    And playground of our stormy isle.

II

Look round thee from this wooded height
    Where, girdled in its sheltering trees,
Our home uprears its turrets bright—
    Our own dear home of rest and peace.

III

Is it not fair—the leafy land?
    Not boasting Nature's sterner pride,
Voluptuous beauty, scenes that stand
    By minds immortal deified ;

IV

Yet fraught with sweet resistless spells
    That wake a deep, a tranquil love,
The witchery of the ferny dells,
    The magic of the murmuring grove.

V

The ever-present varying sea,
    The graceful Peaks, the violet hills,
The fruitful lawn and flowery lea,
    The breezy moors, the golden rills.

VI

A land with every delicate tint
    Of fleeting shadow, wandering light
Rich as the rainbows when they glint
    O'er its own bays ere falls the night.

[1] From ' De Verdun of Darragh ' (STORIES OF WICKLOW).

VII

Here all the year the mountains change
  From month to month, from hour to hour ;
Now rosy-flushed, now dim and strange,
  Now sparkling from the sunlit shower.

VIII

Now far in moving clouds withdrawn,
  Or gilt with yellowing fern and larch,
Or smit with crimson beams of dawn,
  Or silvered with the sleets of March.

IX

Fair when the first pale primrose shines,
  The first gay moth the furze has kissed ;
When under Little Giltspear's pines
  The bluebells seem an azure mist ;

X

When summer robes with all her leaves
  The rough ravine, the lakelet's shore ;
Or when the reaper piles his sheaves
  Beside the pools of Avonmore ;

XI

When the brown bee on Croghan bites
  In eager haste the heathbell through,
And children climb Gleneely's heights
  To gather fraughans fresh with dew ;

XII

When grouse lie thick in lonely plots
  On Lugnaquillia's lofty moor,
And loud the sportsmen's echoing shots
  Ring from the rocks of Glenmalure.

XIII

Fair when the woodland strains and creaks
  As loud the gathering whirlwinds blow,
And through the smoke-like mists the Peaks
  In warm autumnal purples glow ;

XIV

When madly toss the bracken's plumes
  Storm-swept upon the seaward steep,
As far below them foams and fumes
  On beach and cliff the wrathful deep,

XV

Till cloud and tempest, creeping lower,
  Old Djouce's ridges swathe in night,
And down through all his hollows pour
  The foaming torrents swoln and white ;

XVI

Or when o'er Powerscourt's leafless woods,
  With crests that down the tempest lean,
Bend, braving winter's fiercest moods,
  The pines in all their wealth of green.

XVII

A tract of quiet pastoral knolls ;
  Of farms ; of gardens breathing balm ;
Grey beaches where the billow rolls
  With wandering voice in storm or calm ;

XVIII

Of sombre glen and lonely lake,
  Of ivied castles, ruined fanes,
Wild paths by crag and skyey brake,
  And dewy fields and bowery lanes ;

XIX

With glimpses sweet and prospects wide
   Of sea and sky from wood or scar,
And faint hills glimmering from the tide
   That tell of other realms afar.

XX

A spot that owns the priceless charm
   Of gentle human hearts and minds—
A people whom the roughest storm
   True to its kindlier impulse finds ;

XXI

A kindly folk in vale and moor,
   Unvext with rancours, frank and free
In mood and manners—rich with poor
   Attuned in happiest amity ;

XXII

Where still the cottage door is wide,
   The stranger welcomed at the hearth,
And pleased the humbler hearts confide
   Still in the friend of gentler birth ;

XXIII

A land where alway God's right hand
   Seems stretching downward to caress
His wayward children as they stand
   And gaze upon its loveliness.

THROUGH THE SOLITUDES

I

IT was long past the noon when I pushed back my chair
   In the hostel, slung knapsack on shoulder, and walked
Through the low narrow room where the folk from the fair
   Old peasants deep-wrinkled, sat clustered and talked

In their guttural Gaelic ; and out through the stalls
    Girt with marketers laughing, and groups here and there
Of maidens blue-eyed, hooded figures in shawls
    Of scarlet, and wild mountain lads in long hair,
Rude carts, and rough ponies with creels, gaily passed
    Up the street ; through the starers and bargainers prest ;
And asked of an idler my way ; and at last
    Struck out on the hill-road that winds to the west.

II

And I thought, as I strode by the last heavy cart
    Moving earlier home than the rest (wife and child
Sitting close on the trusses of straw, and apart
    On the road, cracking whip, chatting loud, laughing wild,
The husband and sire in knee-breeches and shoes),
    Though it was of the first of such journeys to me
Since my life's friend was lost, yet I dared not refuse
    The gift of good angels that even, the free
Glad heart in my breast, the delight in my soul,
    As I greeted the hill-tops, and saw down below
The sea winding in from afar, heard the roll
    Of the stream on the rocks, felt the autumn air blow
Through my hair as I moved with light step on the way :
    And I said, ' Let me drink to the dregs the black cup
Of pain when 'tis nigh ; but if joy come to-day,
    Let me drain the last drop of the dæmon-wine up.'
Then I journeyed along through the moorlands, and crossed
    The mad stream by the bridge at the crest of the creek,
And wound up the mountain to northward, and lost
    All sight of the village and hill-folk.

III

A bleak
Heavy cloud, dull and inky, crept over the sun
    And blackened the valleys.

IV

In under the hills
Ran the road, among moors where the myrtle stood dun,
  And the heather hung rusted.   The voice of the rills
Was choked in grey rushes.   No footstep was nigh.
One rush-covered hut smoked aloft.   Not a bird
Or a bee flittered by me.   The wind seemed to die
  In the silence and sadness.   No blade of grass stirred.
Not a tuft of the bog-cotton swayed.   Lone and rude
  Grew the path ; and the hills, as I moved, stood **apart**
And opened away to the drear solitude.

V

Then a sorrow crept writhingly over my heart
And clung there—a viper I dared not fling off.
  The sound of dear voices sang soft in my ear
To mock me, dear faces came smiling to scoff
  At my loneliness, making the drearness too drear.
Up the track, now to right, now to left as I c'omb,
  Weird visions came thronging in thick on the brain—
Of days long forgotten, of friends, of a home
  By death desolated, of eyes that in vain
Gazed out for a soul that no more would come back,
  Of one face far away drawing out my life's love
Very strangely that day to it.
                    Everywhere, b'ack,
  Storm-shattered, the mountains loomed lonely above.
A horror, a sickness slipt down through my blood.
  All my thoughts, all my dreams, all that memory's load,
All the terror of loneliness, broke like a flood
  Over body and soul, and I shrank from the road.

VI

I cowered at the frown of the mountains that hung
  On this side and that ; and the brown dreary waste ;
The barren grey rocks far aloft ; for they wrung
  My soul with dim fears ; and I yearned but to taste

The sweets of companionship, yearned to return
  To the far-away village ; to hear once again
The buzz of kind voices about me ; to spurn
  The sadness and horror, the fear and the pain.
Then I bent down my head as I moved, and my mind
  Ran out in vague musings :
                   ' If God laid His hand
On my life now, and suddenly, swiftly consigned
  My soul, at a breath, to the dim spirit-land—
Guiding on to a world that at best would be strange,
  Would be sad in its joys, in its sweetness unsweet
To a mind rent away in so awful a change
  From a world of bright faces, the park and the street,
And the room, and the glances of languishing eyes,
  The smiles of red lips, and the touch of soft arms,
The gay merry laughters, the happy love-sighs—
  And I found myself out in a region of storms,
Out beating my way through the waste, with one star
  In dark heavens to lead me ; through regions unknown,
Dim regions of midnight outstretching afar ;
  A bodiless soul on its journey alone :
Ah, methinks I would yearn for a land such as this,
  For a cloud that but darkens the *sun*, for the strife
With dim dreams, for the heights that shut out the near bliss
  Of dear home for a little . . . O life of my life,
My lost one, thou stay of my childhood, my youth,
  Thou fount of my joys in the days that are gone,
Where, where in the darkness, the regions of drouth,
  The realm of the dead, art thou journeying on ?
Is it strange to thee now, that new being of thine ?
  Dost thou fear in the midst of the darkness, and yearn
To be back in the sweet human throngs, in the shine
  Of the bird-waking sun, 'mid the soft eyes that burn
With love and with bliss ? . . art thou lonely as I ?
  Art thou sad in a world that belieth its God
In its pitiless coldness ?' . . Then up to the sky
  I lifted my face, and I cried unto God.

N N

VII

And when back from the dream I had come, every rock
  Had a livelier tinge, and the frown from the heaven
Had faded, the mountains no more seemed to lock
  My lone life in their folds out of hate, and the even
Grew cheery, grew sweet, and a light wind upsprung
  'Mid the grasses, and fanned me, and wooed me to roam
Through the moorland to seaward, and blissfully sung
  In music as soothing as whispers of home.
And at last when the sun had gone down to his sleep,
  And I caught the Atlantic's loud roar from the west,
Saw the flare of the lighthouse, and wound to the deep,
  All awe of the wilds had died out in my breast.

GAY PROVENCE

I

O'ER Provence breathing, nimble air,
  Blown keen by dale and sea,
Who throws the throbbing bosom bare,
  And bathes himself in thee,

II

Who feels thee clear on cheek and brows,
  And quaffs thee through the lips,
With love and light and music glows
  From foot to finger-tips.

III

He lives a king, in court and hall,
  'Mid wail of wildering lyres ;
A priest, by carven cloister-wall
  Or dim cathedral-choirs ;

IV

A knight, with airy lance in rest,
  That rides in lonely vale ;
A page, by queenly hand caressed,
  By gate or vineyard-pale.

V

He loiters in a golden light,
   Is led with dulcet lure
By ghostly town, by towered height,
   A tuneful troubadour.

VI

He pines for soft imagined eyes
   Where fictive fervour beams,
And wooes with phantom tears and sighs
   The faëry dame of dreams.

VII

O'er Provence breathing, nimble air,
   Blown keen by dale and sea,
O subtle, playful spirit rare,
   O wanton witchery,

VIII

Well, well I love that land of thine,
   Its peaks and ferny caves,
And fields of olive, orange, vine,
   Blue bays, and breaking waves!

WILLIAM WILKINS

A PERFECTLY genuine ardour; a keen delight in Nature; a
hearty self-abandonment to emotion and imagination; a
fearless frankness in the utterance of personal thought and
feeling; often a power of calling up a vivid picture by means
of a single felicitous original phrase; a good deal of rhythmic
fervour; a fine sympathy with the varied activities of humankind; a cultivated intellectuality, are among the poetic
qualities which lift Mr. Wilkins out of the ranks of the versifiers,
and entitle him to a place among the poets. He has not to
wander the world over in search of subjects for his song, or to

go back for material to the crudities of a remote antiquity. He finds poetry in the objects that are nearest to him and in the life of the actual present ; in the pursuits and aspirations of his fellow-students ; in the moonlit quadrangles of his college ; in the whirl of the city by which he is surrounded ; in the blue Irish hills which draw him away to their solitudes ; in the sea that breaks upon familiar Irish shores. It was these aptitudes and these habits which made his University in his college days look forward with interest to his future as a poet, and which still encourage us to expect from him strong, virile, healthy poetry, ennobled by the reflections of a maturer intellect and moulded with the perfection of a more practised art.

G. F. SAVAGE-ARMSTRONG.

Mr. William Wilkins was born in the garrison of Zante, Ionian Islands, on August 21, 1852, the son of the late Dr. William Mortimer Wilkins, who was surgeon to the 41st Regiment, and served in the Peninsula and in India. Having received his early education at Dundalk Grammar School, under Dr. Flynn, he entered Trinity College, Dublin, where his career was brilliant. At college at the same time with him were his two brothers—George, at one time a Fellow of Trinity, and Charles, who died in 1878 at the early age of twenty-two, and in whose memory has been established the prize known as the ' Wilkins Prize.' In his first year at college Mr. Wilkins won the Vice-Chancellor's Prize for English verse by a poem on the subject of Columbus, and the following year he made a name for himself as a poet by his earliest contributions to *Kottabos*. Equally distinguished in Modern Literature and in Mathematics, Mr. Wilkins graduated with the best degree of his year in 1878. In the following year he was appointed headmaster of the High School, Dublin.

SONGS OF STUDY was published in 1881.

From ACTÆON

IT was on the Mount Cithæron, in the pale and misty morn,
That the hero, young Actæon, sounded the hunter's horn.
Princeliest of pursuers of the flying roe was he,
Son of great Aristæus and Theban Autonoë.
Oak-like in massy stature and carriage of kingly limb—
Lo ! the broad, brave grace, and the fleet, fine might of manhood's
fair prime in him,

Grandly brow'd as a sea-cliff with the curling waves at its base,
And its storm-haunted crest a tangle of deep ripe weeds and grass.
And many an Arcadian maiden thought not of a maiden's pride,
But looked on the youth with longing, and watch'd as he went,
  and sighed ;
And Ægië had proffer'd a jewel that a queen might carefully keep
For a favouring smile of the hunter and a touch of his beardless
  lip ;
But never on dame or damsel had his falcon glance made stay,
And he turn'd from the love-sick Ægië, and toss'd her gifts away.

For where was so soft a bower, or where so goodly a hall,
As the dell where the echoes listen'd to the noise of the waterfall ?
And where was there cheek of woman aş lovely to soul and sense
As the gracious hues of the woodlands in depths of the stately
  glens ?
And where were there eyes or tresses as gloriously dark or bright
As the flood of the wild Alpheus as it pour'd from the lonely
  height ?

So the hero, young Actæon, fled far from the girl-fill'd house,
To rove with the beamy spear-shaft through the budded forest
  boughs.
And sweeter than smiles of Ægië or sheen of her rippling hair
Were the heads of his great hounds fawning, or snuffing the
  morning air ;
And to tread by the precipices that down from his feet shore
  clean ;
And to mark where the dappled leopard was couch'd in the long
  ravine ;
And to look at the eagle wheeling up peak-ward, and hear him
  scream ;
And to plant strong steps in the meadows, and plash through the
  babbling stream ;
And to hurl the spear in the thicket, and draw the bow in the
  glade,
And to rush on the foaming fury of the boar by the dogs
  embayed ;

And ever in midland valley to smell the leaves and the grass,
Or the brine-scent blown o'er the headlands high up to the bare
    hill-pass,
Where, lovelier far than Æglë or her eyes' bright witchery,
Was Morning, born of the marriage of silent Sky and Sea.

So the hunter, young Actæon, to the Mount Cithæron came,
And blew his horn, in the dank, white morn, to startle the sleeping
    game ;
Nor thought, as the pealing echoes were clatter'd from crag to
    crag,
That Fate on his trace held him in chase, as a huge hound holds
    a stag.

By rock and by rift and runnel, by marsh and meadow and
    mound,
He went, with his dogs beside him, and marvell'd no game was
    found ;
Till the length of the whole green gorge and the grey cliffs
    gleaming on high
Rang and re-echoed with horns and the musical hunting-cry ;
And the hounds broke out of the cover, all baying together in
    tune ;
And the hart sprang panting before them along up the lawns dew-
    strewn ;
And a bevy of buskin'd virgins, dove-breasted, broke from the
    bowers,
With spears half-poised for the hurling, and tresses tangled with
    flowers ;
Their lips, rose-ruddy, disparted to draw their delightsome breath
For the chase, and the cheer thereof ringing the rapture of dealing
    death—
The fine heads eagerly lifted, the pitiless fair eyes fix'd ;
The cheeks, flower-fresh, flush'd flower-like—rich lily, rich rose
    commix'd ;
The slender feet flying swiftly, the slight shapes rushing like reeds
When the Thracian breezes of winter descend on the marshy
    meads ;
So swept they along like music, and wilder'd Actæon stood
Till the last of the maiden rangers was lost in the leaning wood.

       *   *   *   *   *   *

Disillusion

'Say a day without the ever.'
As You Like It.

YOUR proud eyes give me their wearied splendour ;
    Your cold loose touch and your colder smile
The truth to my jealous heart surrender :
    You tire, having loved me a little while.
Ah ! well, my sweet, I was sure you would,
    For I knew you false when I saw you fair.
I have watched and watched for your altered mood,
    And have schooled me so that I shall not care.

The knoll's blue bonnet, the dell's green mantle,
    The mid-wood hollow where waters run,
The bare, stained shore, with its white surf-sandal,
    The sudden smile of the gallant sun—
Will change not, be you or sweet or bitter :
    A heart after all is hard to break ;
But the world at sweetest were surely sweeter
    If only sweet for your own sweet sake.

Yea, I know right well, if our love were sterling
    We had drained the earth and the skies of joy ;
But I— God wot—and you too, my darling,
    No rare fair flower of girl and boy :
How should we rise to such exaltation
    As climbs from a cloud a splendid star ?
How live—how love with such perfect passion,
    We—who are only what others are ?

Magazine Fort, Phœnix Park, Dublin

INSIDE its zig-zag lines the little camp is asleep,
    Embalm'd in the infinite breath of the greensward, the river, the
        stars.
Round the staff, the yellow leopards of England, weary of wars,
Curl and uncurl, to the murmurous voice of the greenwood deep.

On the lonely terrace their watch the shadowy sentinels keep,
 Each bayonet a spire of silver—high over the silvery jars
 Of the streamtide, swooning in starlight adown its foam-fretted
  bars
To the city, that lies in a shroud as of ashes under the steep.
 To the south are the hills everlasting ; eastward the sea-capes
  and isles ;
 Inland, the levels of emerald stretch for a hundred miles.

———————

GEORGE ARTHUR GREENE

OF a distinguished Anglo-Irish stock, George Arthur Greene
was born at Florence on February 21, 1853, in that Casa
Capponi in which Lever, a family friend, had written his
CHARLES O'MALLEY. His father, the Rev. H. Greene, had
been for many years British Chaplain at Pisa and Lucca, and
most of his own youth was spent in Italy.

 Educated first at a French school in Florence, and then at
the Instituto di Studi Superiori in that city, he afterwards
entered Dublin University, and there obtained the highest
distinctions in the Romance Languages as well as in English
Literature. He was in 1876 appointed Professor of English
Literature in the Alexandra College, Dublin. Later he settled in London.

 As vice-chairman of the committee of the Irish Literary
Society of London he became one of the leaders of the new
Irish literary movement, by contributing valuable papers and
addresses on Irish history to its proceedings, and he turned
his linguistic talent to the study of Irish, throwing himself
actively into the work of the newly established Irish Texts
Society. His contributions to the two volumes of the Rhymers'
Club and to DUBLIN VERSES BY MEMBERS OF TRINITY
COLLEGE gained him acceptance as a song-writer and son-
neteer of fine poetic quality.

In 1893 was published his ITALIAN LYRISTS OF TO-DAY. These translations possess the interest of being in the original metres used by some thirty Italian writers living at the time of their publication.

ARTS LOUGH

GLENMALURE, COUNTY WICKLOW

LONE lake, half lost amidst encircling hills,
    Beneath the imprisoning mountain-crags concealed,
    Who liest to the wide earth unrevealed,
To whose repose the brief and timorous rills

Bring scarce a murmur—thou whose sight instils
    Despair, o'er whom his dark disdainful shield
    Abrupt Clogherna 'gainst the sun doth wield,
And thy dim face with deepening shadow fills—

O poet soul ! companionless and sad,
    Though half the daytime long a death-like shade
    Athwart thy depths with constant horror lies,

Thou art not ever in dejection clad,
    But showest still, as in a glass displayed,
    The limitless, unfathomable skies.

ON GREAT SUGARLOAF

WHERE Sugarloaf with bare and ruinous wedge
    Cleaves the grey air to view the darkening sea,
    We stood on high, and heard the northwind flee
Through clouds storm-heavy fallen from ledge to ledge.

Then sudden ' Look ! ' we cried.   The far black edge
    Of south horizon oped in sunbright glee,
    And a broad water shone, one moment free,
Ere darkness veiled again the wavering sedge.

Such is the Poet's inspiration, still
  Too evanescent ! coming but to go :
Such the great passions showing good in ill,

Quick brightnesses, love-lights too soon burnt low ;
  And such man's life, which flashes Heaven's will
Between two glooms a transitory glow.

The Return

ITALIAN lakes, transparent blue,
  Where, mirrored in the waters deep,
  The wraith of every hill asleep
Dreams all the day-time through :

And heights of Alp with winter hoar,
  And olivets of Apennine,
  Where the grey, twisted woods incline
Down to the dark seashore :

Valdarno with its rounding hills
  That hem it from the invading north,
  Whence o'er Morello bursting forth
The tramontana shrills :

Maremma shores all fever-pale,
  Where slow the evening mist outspread
  Covers the coast from head to head,
And poisons every vale ;

Cyclopean cities, silent, vast,
  Stretched, all one wilderness of stones,
  Like some colossal mammoth's bones
From a forgotten past :

And Rome the great, eternal, dread,
  Whose feet stand in the depths of Time,
  Grown old in fame and still sublime,
She lifts her meteor head

Like Memnon's statue, grandly dumb,
   Standing for ever bold, erect,
   With open eyes that still expect
The sunrise that shall come—

Rome the Republic—Empire—she
   The footstool of three hundred Popes—
   Rome of the newer, wider hopes
That pulse through Italy—

Aye, Rome the eternal city, throned
   Upon the seven sacred hills,
   And by the people's patient wills
Made new, her crimes atoned :

O unforgotten southern skies !
   Though now I plough the northward sea,
   The white-winged memories fly with me,
The young hopes re-arise.

And yet, though sweet the sunburnt South
   When daylight ebbs o'er west and east,
   The North shall not obtain the least
Of praises from my mouth ;

For, now returned from golden lands,
   I see Night lift her misty shroud,
   And through the veil of morning cloud
The sun strikes northern sands ;

I hail with joy the early ray
   That gleams o'er valleys thrice more dear ;
   My pulse beats quicker as I hear
Up from Killiney Bay

The whisper of familiar rills ;
   And sudden tremors veil mine eyes
   As, at a turn, before me rise,
Long sought, the Wicklow Hills.

LINES

SURELY a Voice hath called her to the deep—
  The deep of heaven, star calling unto star :
Surely she passed but through the vale of sleep
  That hideth from our hearts the things that are.

Surely the ringing music of the spheres
  Sounds richlier to-day by one pure voice :
Ah ! though we mourn its silence with our tears,
  The stars we hear not, hearing it, rejoice.

WILLIAM KNOX JOHNSON,

Author of TERRA TENEBRARUM (1897), from which this poem
is taken ; a native of County Kildare, at one time a Civil
Servant in Benares.   Mr. Johnson has published a striking
but unequal poem on the ' Death of Mangan,' and has written
an admirable criticism on him as an interpreter of the Celtic
genius to English readers.

AN ANNIVERSARY

HOW sweetly keen, how stirred the air !
  The woods are thrilled at touch of spring ;
Along the road from Château Vert
  Gaily the thrushes sing.

No stranger here I come to-day !
  I know the river winding slow,
This haze of blue, with green and grey ;
  And all the flowers I know.

With you I plucked them ; now, alone.
  The slope is starred with shaken flame
Three times the daffodils have blown
  Since we together came.

A fire was in our souls ; we spoke
  Of Fate, the evil reign of things
How good men ever spurn the yoke
  That tyrant Nature brings.

' She knows no God ; her law is hate.
  Brave deed and duty still remain ;
Justice and Love we must create,
  Whose quest of Love is vain.'

My hope was set across the seas ;
  I'd till a land with freer men,
Where greed no more the heart should freeze,
  And Pity rule again.

In widening current from our shore
  The great gulf-stream of joy should flow ;
Nations, their lethargy past o'er,
  Should feel the answering glow !

Three years ! and under dusking skies
  To-night you cross the stream with me.
I cannot turn, those ardent eyes,
  That eager mien to see.

I dare not look upon your face
  Our dreams I sold for daily bread
I mingle with the accursed race,
  Dead—with the living dead !

Yet hear !—ah no ! far northward now
  In Aran of the mighty wave
The thunder of the surges slow
  Rolls round your ocean grave.

High on the rocky spur you lie,
  A splendour floods the solemn west,
The voices of the sea go by,
  And night is thine—and rest.

W. E. H. LECKY

Mr. Lecky is well known as the historian of the eighteenth century whose deep research and unwavering rectitude in dealing with the stormy history of his own country have set so high an example to future writers. He was born in County Dublin, 1838. He was educated in Trinity College, and in 1895 was elected to represent his University in Parliament. He died in 1903. His Poems were published in 1891.

Undeveloped Lives

Not every thought can find its words,
　Not all within is known ;
For minds and hearts have many chords
　That never yield their tone.

Tastes, instincts, feelings, passions, powers,
　Sleep there unfelt, unseen ;
And other lives lie hid in ours—
　The lives that might have been.

Affections whose transforming force
　Could mould the heart anew ;
Strong motives that might change the course
　Of all we think and do.

Upon the tall cliff's cloud-wrapt verge
　The lonely shepherd stands,
And hears the thundering ocean surge
　That sweeps the far-off strands ;

And thinks in peace of raging storms
　Where he will never be—
Of life in all its unknown forms
　In lands beyond the sea.

So in our dream some glimpse appears,
    Though soon it fades again,
How other lands or times or spheres
    Might make us other men ;

How half our being lies in trance,
    Nor joy nor sorrow brings,
Unless the hand of circumstance
    Can touch the latent strings.

We know not fully what we are,
    Still less what we might be ;
But hear faint voices from the far
    Dim lands beyond the sea.

THE SOWER AND HIS SEED

HE planted an oak in his father's park
    And a thought in the minds of men,
And he bade farewell to his native shore,
    Which he never will see again.
Oh, merrily stream the tourist throng
    To the glow of the Southern sky ;
A vision of pleasure beckons them on,
    But he went there to die.

The oak will grow and its boughs will spread,
    And many rejoice in its shade,
But none will visit the distant grave,
    Where a stranger youth is laid ;
And the thought will live when the oak has died,
    And quicken the minds of men,
But the name of the thinker has vanished away,
    And will never be heard again.

THE 'KOTTABISTAI'

An anthology of Anglo-Irish verse would be incomplete if it did not include within it some selections representative of an interesting literary movement in Trinity College, Dublin, which has been marked by the publication of successive numbers of a college magazine entitled *Kottabos*, between the year 1874 and the present day. *Kottabos* owed its origin, and much of its lustre, to the eminent classical scholar, Professor Robert Yelverton Tyrrell, F.T.C.D., who for many years acted as its editor. It was primarily a magazine of Greek and Latin compositions written by Trinity College men, but it was open also to contributions, from the same source, of original English verse and of English verse-translations. In such a miscellany we could not expect to find the productions of many born poets. Born poets are not numerous in any generation, and when they do appear they are seldom gregarious ; they are disposed to 'dwell apart ;' their utterances are not often of the kind that fits them to take a place side by side with the productions of the 'elegant trifler' in verse. To *Kottabos* some writers of unmistakable kinship with the genuine poets did occasionally contribute ; but these cannot be numbered with the typical 'Kottabistai.' The typical 'Kottabistai' have been men of culture and scholarship, who have written English verse at that period of life at which men are most enthusiastic, most emotional, most enamoured of beauty, most ambitious, most receptive, and most imitative. *Kottabos* encouraged a taste for English verse-writing, just as it encouraged a taste for Greek and Latin verse-writing ; and between the accomplished contributor of English verse and the accomplished contributor of Greek and Latin verse there was generally a close affinity. Many of the English verse-compositions—like some by Mulvany, Martley, Mr. S. K. Cowan, and Professor Tyrrell—were excellent parodies ; many—like some by Professor Dowden, Dr. Todhunter, and Professor Tyrrell—were deliberate and acknowledged studies

of the styles of eminent masters ; many—like some by
De Burgh, Dr. Todhunter, Mr. Newcomen, Mr. George
Wilkins, and Mr. Rolleston—were clever translations ; many
were unconscious imitations of poets who happened at the
moment to be in vogue. Often the lyrics were humorous and
very amusing ; often they contained just enough spontaneous
personal emotion to be very nearly genuine poems ; occasionally
they *were* genuine poems. A few of the early contributors to
Kottabos have proved that the poetic impulse of their college
days was not transient ; their poetical individuality has shown
itself to be strong and persistent ; and to these must be
assigned separate places in every anthology of modern Irish
verse. On the other hand, some who did very good and even
promising work in those days have gone to the grave without
having accomplished anything better ; and some had not yet
had time to prove whether their early fervour was the enduring
spirit of poetry or not. From these two latter classes, with
hesitation and with diffidence, and not without a misgiving
that writers as worthy have been omitted, the names of Charles
Pelham Mulvany, John Martley, Professor Palmer, and Percy
Somers Payne have been selected.

G. F. SAVAGE-ARMSTRONG.

CHARLES PELHAM MULVANY

CHARLES PELHAM MULVANY was born in Dublin on May 20,
1835. He was educated in Dublin, and took his degree of
B.A. at Trinity College in 1856. For a time he was a surgeon
in the Royal Navy, but subsequently entered Holy Orders,
and went to reside in Canada, where he died after a very
chequered career on May 31, 1885. Besides his many
contributions to *Kottabos,* he published verses in *The Nation,*
The Irish Metropolitan Magazine, and, we believe, in *The
College Magazine,* which he edited.

Mulvany's works are :—LYRICS OF HISTORY AND OF LIFE

o o

(1880) ; A HISTORY OF BRANT, ONTARIO (1883) ; TORONTO, PAST AND PRESENT (1884) ; HISTORY OF THE NORTH-WEST REBELLION OF 1885 (1886).

Mulvany is less of a poet than of a clever and humorous parodist. His serious poems are often pervaded by a melan-choly not unlike Edgar Allan Poe's. They generally begin well, but, like the productions of most writers of his degree, fall off towards the close.

G. F. S.-A.

MESSALINA SPEAKS

Two sides to a story! One of mine
Points the lash of each poison'd line
Of the famed Sixth Satire, our sex's shame
Pilloried in a woman's name.
Smooth flows the verse ; and the scorpion muse,
Rich in the rhetoric of the stews,
Lingers each phase of vice to tell,
Licking the foulness she loves so well.

Who knows not the picture Aquinas paints—
(The Satirist's picture, not the Saint's)—
The palace left at the midnight hour,
The orgies in lewd Lycisca's bower,
When over the bosom, bedeck'd with gold,
That cushion'd an Emperor, hot eyes rolled,
That foul life's license of lust and wine—
This tale the world has heard.   Hear mine!

I was no Empress—not mine that praise,
'Born in the purple,' of Rome's last days—
To cringe to eunuch or slave, and fret
In a prison of courtly etiquette ;
But a Roman woman, whose grandsire died,
As he fought and revell'd, at Sulla's side—
Not more his heiress in name and land
Than in passionate heart and strong right hand.

Mine the strength of the ancient Roman stamp,
That swam the Tiber from Tarquin's camp—

Aye, even the courage to match that one
Who saved the city and doom'd her son,
Or hers who wept not her jewels twain
Lavish'd and lost for Rome in vain,
Unmoved in her love's imperial pride
When Freedom totter'd and Gracchus died.

Or welcome had been a calmer life,
The sweet home-ways of the Roman wife,
Who spun the wool by the household fire,
While her boys were piling the pine-blaze higher,
At the hour of rest, when the day fulfils,
And the sun is low on the Sabine hills.
Such life, such scenes, our Rome had then
For the mothers and mates of her bravest men.

What manner of hero had I for mate?
That pedant prince of the servile State,
Bold with grammarians war to wage,
Skill'd in the lore of Numa's age,
With whom faint heart and folly came,
A double curse, to the Claudian name,
Yet more cursed to me, whom Fortune gave
To a freedman's client, a eunuch's slave.

What cared I then for my place of pride,
To empire wed, as the world is, wide?
Though where I passed, to my service vow'd,
Thirty legions their eagles bow'd,
That life I brook'd not.   Soul-surfeit came—
Wild quest of pleasures that know not shame,
Such passion-madness as, ere the end,
To those they ruin the good Gods send.

For the Gods ordain, since earth began,
By perfect conditions the perfect man.
Vice comes or virtue, good comes or sin,
From the world without to the world within.
Life's form must vary, itself the same—
Cornelia's pride, Messalina's shame,
Through all whose passion, condemn who will,
One voice of womanhood pleadeth still.

JOHN MARTLEY

JOHN MARTLEY, the third son of Mr. Henry Martley, Q.C., afterwards a Judge of the Landed Estates Court, Ireland, was born in Dublin on May 15, 1844. He was educated at Cheltenham College ; at St. Columba's College, Rathfarnham ; and at Trinity College, Dublin, where he took his degree of B.A. in 1866. In 1875 he was called to the Irish Bar, but, obtaining an appointment in the Landed Estates Court, he did not practise. He wrote both for *Kottabos* and for *Froth*, a Dublin periodical (1879). He married Miss Frances Howorth, sister of Mr. H. Howorth, M.P., and died of consumption on August 25, 1882.

Martley's work is : FRAGMENTS IN PROSE AND VERSE (published posthumously, 1883).

Martley, like Mulvany, excelled as a parodist ; but his parodies lack the completeness and the original surprises of Mulvany's. His serious poems have the same tendency to lose force and power as they advance. He manifests a higher culture, a greater tenderness, and a purer taste than Mulvany ; and his skill in versification is sometimes, though not always, masterly.

G. F. S.-A.

THE VALLEY OF SHANGANAGH

WRITTEN FOR THE AIR ' THE WEARING OF THE GREEN '

IN the Valley of Shanganagh, where the songs of skylarks teem,
And the rose perfumes the ocean-breeze, as love the hero's dream,
'Twas there I wooed my Maggie. In her dark eyes there did
    dwell
A secret that the billows knew, but yet could never tell.

Oh ! light as fairy tread her voice fell on my bounding heart ;
And like the wild bee to the flower still clinging we would part.
' Sweet Valley of Shanganagh,' then I murmur'd, ' though I die,
My soul will never leave thee for the heaven that's in the sky ! '

In the Valley of Shanganagh, where the sullen sea-gulls gleam,
And the pine-scent fills the sighing breeze as death the lover's
    dream,
'Twas there I lost my Maggie.   Why that fate upon us fell
The powers above us knew, perhaps, if only they would tell.

Oh ! like the tread of mournful feet it fell upon my heart,
When, as the wild bee leaves the rose, her spirit did depart.
In the Valley still I linger, though it's fain I am to die,
But it's hard to find a far-off heaven when clouds are in the sky.

A Budget of Paradoxes

Child in thy beauty ; empress in thy pride ;
Sweet and unyielding as the summer's tide ;
Starlike to tremble, starlike to abide.

Guiltless of wounding, yet more true than steel
Gem-like thy light to flash and to conceal ;
Tortoise to bear, insect to see and feel.

Blushing and shy, yet dread we thy disdain ;
Smiling, a sunbeam fraught with hints of rain ;
Trilling love-notes to freedom's fierce refrain.

The days are fresh, the hours are wild and sweet,
When spring and winter, dawn and darkness meet ;
Nymph, with one welcome, thee and these we greet.

ARTHUR PALMER

Born in Canada about 1842 ; scholar of Trinity College,
Dublin, 1861 ; Fellow, 1867 ; Professor of Latin, 1880, Mr.
Palmer won high distinction in the world of learning by his
editions of Ovid (Heroides) and Propertius.   He died in 1897.
His contributions to Kottabos, whether in English or the
classical tongues, show a peculiar delicacy as well as dignity of

phrase ; and some of his Latin lines, such as *In tacitis silvis altum finivit amorem*, for Keats's ' There in the forest did his great love cease,' dwell in the memory like certain lines of Virgil.

T. W. R.

EPICHARIS

TAC. 'ANN.' XV. 57

MOTIONLESS, in a dark, cold cell in Rome,
A woman, bruised and burnt, but breathing still,
Lay all alone, and thus her weak, wan lips
Whisper'd to high Jove from that dungeon floor :
' I am a poor weak woman, O ye gods,
And now I ask forgiveness, lying here
(I have no strength to rise upon my knees),
For all the heavy sins that I have done.
Remember, O just gods, that this is Rome,
And I a woman, and the weakest born.
Could such a woman, nursed in such a city,
Live righteously, as high-born maidens live ?
A poor, fair slave, on Rome's waste ocean thrown,
I had but Heaven to turn to in distress,
And Heaven always turn'd away from me.
But if I have offended by my life,
Oh, let me make atonement by my death !
I bore the torture yesterday, kind gods,
Bravely, and would have died before a word
Escaped me ; but my cunning torturers,
Seeing the ensign of my ally—Death—
Advancing swiftly, seeing me still dumb,
Released me, hoping that another trial
Would quell me, and I fear, I fear it may—
For, oh, the pain was horrible !   But yesterday
A sort of trance was on me all the time
That let me triumph over any pain,
And made me secretly deride the fools
For wasting all their cruel toil in vain.
But to begin the agony again !—
The burning bricks, the red-hot plates, the scourge—

Kind gods, assist me ! let me not die a traitor !
Take from me this weak breath, or give me means
To stop it, so men may say when I am gone :
" This was a poor, weak woman, but no traitor ! "
And so, perhaps, when poor Epicharis
Is cast away, without a grave or name,
Some man who fears the gods, and loves not traitors,
May come and lay a penny on my lips,
That I may want not Charon's passage-fee,
Nor flit for ever by the bank of Styx.'
She ceased for very weakness, but her words
Mounted as high as heaven from the stones,
And on the moment Nero's messengers
Came in to lead her to the torment-room ;
But finding that she could not stand, they brought
A litter, and so bore her through the streets.
And thus the gods granted the harlot's prayer ;
For in the litter's roof she spied a ring,
And quickly loosed the band that bound her waist,
And did it round her neck, and through the ring,
And, calling up her torture-broken strength,
Crush'd out her little life—a faithful girl !
And on the soldiers bore her through the streets,
Until they reach'd the hall of doom, and there
Open'd the litter's door, and she was gone ;
More nobly dead, though a freedwoman,
Than many a Roman swoln with pedigree.[1]

PERCY SOMERS PAYNE

SON of the Rev. Somers Payne, of Upton, County Cork. He
died in 1874, aged twenty-four. He contributed to *Kottabos*
two or three poems marked by an intensity and sincerity of
feeling, and a certain creative power, which gave promise of
high distinction.

T. W. R.

---

[1] *Cf.* Juv. SAT. viii : ' Tumes alto Drusorum stemmate.'

Rest

SILENCE sleeping on a waste of ocean—
　　Sun-down—westward traileth a red streak—
One white sea-bird, poised with scarce a motion,
　　Challenges the stillness with a shriek—
Challenges the stillness, upward wheeling
　　Where some rocky peak containeth her rude nest ;
For the shadows o'er the waters they come stealing,
　　And they whisper to the silence : ' There is Rest.'

Down where the broad Zambesi River
　　Glides away into some shadowy lagoon
Lies the antelope, and hears the leaflets quiver,
　　Shaken by the sultry breath of noon—
Hears the sluggish water ripple in its flowing ;
　　Feels the atmosphere, with fragrance all opprest ;
Dreams his dreams ; and the sweetest is the knowing
　　That above him, and around him, there is Rest.

Centuries have faded into shadow,
　　Earth is fertile with the dust of man's decay ;
Pilgrims all they were to some bright El-dorado,
　　But they wearied, and they fainted, by the way.
Some were sick with the surfeiture of pleasure,
　　Some were bow'd beneath a care-encumber'd breast ;
But they all trod in turn Life's stately measure,
　　And all paused betimes to wonder, ' Is there Rest ? '

Look, O man ! to the limitless Hereafter,
　　When thy Sense shall be lifted from its dust,
When thy Anguish shall be melted into Laughter,
　　When thy Love shall be sever'd from its Lust.
Then thy spirit shall be sanctified with seeing
　　The Ultimate dim Thulé of the Blest,
And the passion-haunted fever of thy being
　　Shall be drifted in a Universe of Rest.

BOOK VII

THE poems given in this section are representative of the work of the poets of the generation next W. B. Yeats' and A. E.'s. These poets were given their inspiration and material by the Gaelic Language Revival movement, which had the effect of turning the minds of the writers of that generation towards the countryside—they were the discoverers of 'folk' Ireland, and back of their work is a knowledge of folk-poetry in Gaelic and English. They left aside mythology and legend, and tried to render aspects of the life that they saw around them. John M. Synge, when he bade adieu to Angus, Maeve, and Fand, spoke for the poets of this movement. Synge, however, belonged to the generation of Yeats and A. E., although younger by a few years. His poems were written and published during the later movement. The Hon. Emily Lawless, too, belonged to an older generation ; the poems of hers that are given here were published after her contemporaries had done their typical work, and they are related to the poetry that came out of the Gaelic revival through the passionate feeling that is reflected in them for the fighting men of the Gaelic dispersal of the seventeenth century. James Joyce is the exceptional figure of this genera-tion, his inspiration and his form coming from English and Elizabethan sources.

JOSEPH CAMPBELL

JOSEPH CAMPBELL was born in Belfast in 1881, and is not only a poet but an artist and playwright. He made the illustrations for THE RUSHLIGHT (1906), a volume of his own poems, and did sixteen pencil drawings for MEARING STONES, leaves from his notebook while on a tramp in Donegal. Writing under the

Gaelic form of his name (Seosamh MacCathmhaoil), he has published half a dozen books of verse, the most striking of which are THE MOUNTAINY SINGER, first published in Dublin in 1909, and IRISHRY, 1913. Mr. Campbell is now (1932) director of the School of Irish Studies in Fordham University, New York.

THE BLIND MAN AT THE FAIR

O TO be blind!
To know the darkness that I know.
The stir I hear is empty wind,
The people idly come and go.

The sun is black, though warm and kind,
The horsemen ride, the streamers blow
Vainly in the fluky wind,
For all is darkness where I go.

The cattle bellow to their kind,
The mummers dance, the jugglers throw,
The thimble-rigger speaks his mind—
But all is darkness where I go.

I feel the touch of womankind,
Their dresses flow, as white as snow;
But beauty is a withered rind,
For all is darkness where I go.

Last night the moon of Lammas shined,
Rising high and setting low;
But light is nothing to the blind—
All, all is darkness where they go.

White roads I walk with vacant mind,
White cloud-shapes round me drifting slow,
White lilies waving in the wind—
And darkness everywhere I go.

THE OLD WOMAN

As a white candle
In a holy place,
So is the beauty
Of an aged face.

As the spent radiance
Of the winter sun,
So is a woman
With her travail done.

Her brood gone from her
And her thoughts are still
As the waters
Under a ruined mill.

PADRAIC COLUM

PADRAIC COLUM was born in County Longford on December 8, 1881. He was brought up in the counties of Longford and Cavan, and as he grew up he absorbed folk-lore and popular songs until he became fairly steeped in the traditional native culture of the Irish people. He joined the National Theatre movement in Dublin, and learned to know and admire George Russell (A. E.), William Butler Yeats, Lady Gregory, and the rest of that group. It was at this time that his first poems and essays appeared in the journal which Arthur Griffith was conducting. His plays were among the first to be produced by the Irish Theatre. 'Broken Soil' (1903) was given when he was only twenty-one. He intended to write a series of plays for the Irish Theatre—a sort of human comedy of Ireland—but a disagreement on the question of policy led to his withdrawal from the group that directed the theatre. Meanwhile he was writing verse (published in the volume called WILD EARTH, 1907) that marked a new departure in Irish poetry. He was one of the founders of the *Irish Review* in 1911, and its sole editor during 1912–1913. His three most recent books—all published in 1930—are CROSS ROADS IN IRELAND, a travel volume describing his country from both the historical and visual points of view ; OLD PASTURES, a book of verse ; and ORPHEUS : MYTHS OF THE WORLD, containing folk-legends from all nations. Among his other books are : THE BOY WHO KNEW WHAT THE BIRDS SAID, 1918 ; DRAMATIC LEGENDS AND OTHER POEMS, 1922 ; CASTLE CONQUER, 1923 ; and THE ROAD ROUND IRELAND, 1926.

For some years Mr. Colum and his wife have made their home in America, usually returning to Ireland for part of each year. Padraic Colum typifies the best in the Irish Renaissance. To hear him talk on Irish poetry, or give a reading from his own poems or tales, is to fall under the spell of all Ireland.

THE DEER OF IRELAND

AN old man said, ' I saw
The chief of the things that are gone ;
A stag with head held high,
A doe, and a fawn ;

' And they were the deer of Ireland
That scorned to breed within bound :
The last ; they left no race
Tame on a pleasure-ground.

' A stag, with his hide all rough
With the dew, and a doe and a fawn ;
Near by, on their track on the mountain
I watched them, two and one,

' Down to the Shannon going—
Did its waters cease to flow,
When they passed, they that carried the swiftness,
And the pride of long ago ?

'The last of the troop that had heard
Finn's and Oscar's cry;
A doe and a fawn, and before
A stag with head held high!'

MEN ON ISLANDS

CAN it be that never more
Men will grow on Islands?
Ithaka and Eriskey,
Iceland and Tahiti!
Must the engines he has forged
Raven so for spaces,
That the Islands dwindle down,
Dwindle down!—
Pots that shelve the tap-root's growth?
Must it be that never more
Men will flower on Islands?
Crete and Corsica, Mitylene,
Aran, and Iona!

THE LANDING

THE great ship lantern-girdled,
The tender standing by;
The waning stars cloud-shrouded,
The land that we descry!

That pale land is our homeland,
And we are bound therefor;
On her lawns and in her coppice
No birds as yet make stir.

But birds are flying round us,
The white birds of the sea—
It is the breeze of morning,
This that comes hummingly.

And like the talk that comes from
A room where a babe is born,
Such clearness and such mystery
Are in words said on the morn,

Where, like a nation cloven,
In two our ranks divide:
One half on the high ship's bulwark,
One half by the tender's side;

Where, like a people sundered,
Who yet have each other's hail,
Faces look down from the bulwarks,
And look up from the tender's rail;

And names are called and spoken—
" Nancy," " Mary," " Owen!"
" Good-bye, and keep your promise!"
" Farewell to you, my son!"

They are more spirit-stirring
Than any words that are
Remembered from the spokesmen
Of any avatar!

" Oh, all I had to tell you!"
" Ellen," " Michael," " Joan"—
" Good-bye, and God be with you!"
" And can it be you're gone!"

The great ship lantern-girdled,
Her engines thresh, immerse—
The great ship that had station
Takes motion for her course.

Her little course the tender,
Our little ship, goes on—
The stars they are fast waning,
But we'll land ere 'tis the dawn!

Green, greener grows the foreland
Across the slate-dark sea,
And I'll see faces, places
That have been dreams to me!

JAMES JOYCE

JAMES JOYCE was born in Dublin on February 2, 1882. After
attending the Jesuit institution, Clongowes Wood College, and
Belvedere College, Joyce received his degree from the Royal
University in Dublin. Padraic Colum describes the Joyce of
those days: "Joyce, when I knew him first, was a student in
the old Royal University. . . . He was tall and slender then,
with a Dantesque face and steely blue eyes. His costume, as
I see him in my mind's eye now, included a peaked cap and
tennis shoes more or less white." After graduation from the
Royal University, Joyce determined to leave Ireland. He
went to Paris, where he stayed for about a year (1903–1904),
studying medicine at the University of Paris. He was called
back to Dublin in 1904 by the death of his mother. There he
wrote the stories which make up DUBLINERS and started work
on his first novel, A PORTRAIT OF THE ARTIST AS A YOUNG MAN,
which he did not complete until ten years later. CHAMBER
MUSIC (1907) was his first published volume ; it is a collection
of lyrics. In 1904 he married, and he and his wife left Ireland
for the Continent. In Trieste Joyce taught English at the
Berlitz School, and later at the Commercial Academy. In
1914 DUBLINERS—his book of short stories—was published,
and he completed the writing of A PORTRAIT OF THE ARTIST.
War was declared and Joyce became a free prisoner in
Trieste—a British citizen living in Austrian territory. He was
forced to give up his job at the Commercial Academy, and
moved to Zürich. There he found friends among the Irish
exiles and helped to found a company of "Irish Players,"
which gave the first performance of his play, " Exiles." In

1919 the Joyces returned for a while to Trieste, where they lived with Joyce's brother. Soon they went on to Paris, where they have remained. In 1922 Joyce's monumental work, ULYSSES, was published in Paris. Its sale is forbidden in Great Britain and the United States, and hundreds of copies have been burned by the authorities. In 1927 POMES PENNYEACH was published.

CHAMBER MUSIC

XIV

My dove, my beautiful one,
Arise, arise!
The nightdew lies
Upon my lips and eyes.

The odorous winds are weaving
A music of sighs;
Arise, arise,
My dove, my beautiful one!

I wait by the cedar tree,
My sister, my love.
White breast of the dove,
My breast shall be your bed.

The pale dew lies
Like a veil on my head.
My fair one, my fair dove,
Arise, arise!

XXXV

All day I hear the noise of waters
Making moan,
Sad as the seabird is when going
Forth alone
He hears the winds' cry to the waters'
Monotone.

The grey winds, the cold winds are blowing
> Where I go.
I hear the noise of many waters
> Far below.
All day, all night, I hear them flowing
> To and fro.

SHE WEEPS OVER RAHOON

RAIN on Rahoon falls softly, softly falling,
Where my dark lover lies.
Sad is his voice that calls me, sadly calling,
At grey moonrise.

Love, hear thou
How soft, how sad his voice is ever calling,
Ever unanswered, and the dark rain falling,
Then as now.

Dark, too, our hearts, O love, shall lie and cold
As his sad heart has lain
Under the moongrey nettles, the black mould
And muttering rain.

A MEMORY OF THE PLAYERS IN A MIRROR AT MIDNIGHT

THEY mouth love's language.   Gnash
The thirteen teeth
Your lean jaws grin with.   Lash
Your itch and quailing, nude greed of the flesh.
Love's breath in you is stale, worded or sung,
As sour as cat's breath,
Harsh of tongue.

This grey that stares
Lies not, stark skin and bone.
Leave greasy lips their kissing. None
Will choose her what you see to mouth upon.
Dire hunger holds his hour.
Pluck forth your heart, salt blood, a fruit of tears,
Pluck and devour!

CHAMBER MUSIC, London, Jonathan Cape; POMES PENNYEACH, Paris,
Shakespeare & Co.

EMILY LAWLESS

THE Honorable Emily Lawless, daughter of the third Lord
Cloncurry, was born in 1845. Her childhood was spent largely
in the west of Ireland, where she early showed her tremendous
interest in the natural sciences by indulging in moth hunts before dawn, and so forth. Her literary career began when she
was forty-one with the publication of HURRISH, a story of the
peasants of Galway. This novel won instant praise. Her
second book, GRANIA, published in 1892, was likewise most
successful. She was praised by Gladstone, Meredith, Swinburne, and countless other celebrities of her day. Miss Lawless
was Irish first, and interested in politics secondly. She was a
Unionist, for she believed that her countrymen were not yet
ready for self-government. In 1902 her book of verse, THE
WILD GEESE, came out, with a preface by Stopford Brooke;
in 1909 THE POINT OF VIEW was privately printed for the bene-
fit of the Galway fishermen, and in 1914, the year after her
death, THE INALIENABLE HERITAGE was published.

SPAIN

YOUR sky is hard and dazzling blue,
Your earth and sands are a dazzling gold,
And gold or blue is the proper hue,
You say for a swordsman bold.

In the land I have left the skies are cold,
The earth is green, the rocks are bare,
Yet the devil may hold all your blue and gold
Were I only once back there !

SPAIN: A DRINKING SONG

MANY are praised, and some are fair ;
But the fairest of all is *She*,
And he who misdoubts let him have a care,
For her liegemen sworn are we !
Then Ho! for the land that is green and grey,
The land of all lands the best,
For the South is bright and the East is gay,
But the sun shines last in the West,
        The West !
The sun shines last in the West !

A queen is she, though a queen forlorn,
A queen of tears from her birth,
Ragged and hungry, woeful and worn,
Yet the fairest Fair on the earth.
Then here's to the land that is green and grey,
The land of all lands the best !
For the South is bright and the East is gay,
But the sun shines last in the West,
        The West !
The sun shines last in the West !

From THE INALIENABLE HERITAGE, by Emily Lawless. (Privately printed.)

FRANCIS LEDWIDGE

FRANCIS LEDWIDGE was born in County Meath, Ireland, in 1891, of Irish peasant stock. His brief life was intensely romantic. He was at various times a farmer, a grocer's clerk, a scavenger, an experimenter in hypnotism, and, at the end, a

soldier. He served as a lance-corporal in the Royal Inniskil-
ling Fusiliers, and was killed on the Flanders front in July, 1917,
at the age of twenty-six. Discovered and sponsored by Lord
Dunsany, Ledwidge published two volumes of verse during his
lifetime—SONGS OF THE FIELDS (1916) and SONGS OF PEACE
(1917). Both books (as well as the posthumous LAST SONGS)
were incorporated in COMPLETE POEMS (1919) with Lord
Dunsany's original introductions.

TO A LINNET IN A CAGE

WHEN Spring is in the fields that stained your wing,
    And the blue distance is alive with song,
And finny quiets of the gabbling spring
    Rock lilies red and long.
At dewy daybreak, I will set you free
    In ferny turnings of the woodbine lane,
Where faint-voiced echoes leave and cross in glee
    The hilly swollen plain.

In draughty houses you forget your tune,
    The modulator of the changing hours,
You want the wide air of the moody noon,
    And the slanting evening showers.
So I will loose you, and your song shall fall
    When morn is white upon the dewy pane,
Across my eyelids, and my soul recall
    From worlds of sleeping pain.

From SONGS OF THE FIELDS, by Francis Ledwidge. Published by Herbert
Jenkins, Ltd., London, 1916.

A LITTLE BOY IN THE MORNING

HE will not come, and still I wait.
He whistles at another gate
Where angels listen. Ah, I know
He will not come, yet if I go
How shall I know he did not pass
Barefooted in the flowery grass?

The moon leans on one silver horn
Above the silhouettes of morn,
And from their nest sills finches whistle
Or stooping pluck the downy thistle.
How is the morn so gay and fair
Without his whistling in its air?

The world is calling, I must go.
How shall I know he did not pass
Barefooted in the shining grass?

THE HOMECOMING OF THE SHEEP

THE sheep are coming home in Greece,
Hark the bells on every hill!
Flock by flock, and fleece by fleece,
Wandering wide a little piece
Through the evening red and still,
Stopping where the pathways cease,
Cropping with a hurried will.

Thro' the cotton-bushes low
Merry boys with shouldered crooks
Close them in a single row.
Shout among them as they go
With one bell-ring o'er the brooks.
Such delight you never know
Reading it from gilded books.

Before the early stars are bright,
Cormorants and sea-gulls call,
And the moon comes large and white
Filling with a lovely light
The ferny curtained waterfall.
Then sleep wraps every bell up tight
And the climbing moon grows small.

From SONGS OF PEACE, by Francis Ledwidge. Published by Herbert
Jenkins, Ltd., London, 1917.

THOMAS MacDONAGH

THOMAS MACDONAGH was executed in Dublin as one of the leaders of the Irish Rebellion of 1916—closing his career in the midst of a tragedy similar to that which inspired his play, "When the Dawn Is Come" (1908). An officer who witnessed the execution of the leaders of the Rebellion is quoted as saying, "They all died well, but MacDonagh died like a prince." Thomas MacDonagh was born in Cloughjordan, a town in the County Tipperary. He became a teacher in a college in Kilkenny and later in Fermay, and finally in Padraic Pearse's school in Dublin. His knowledge of Irish was fluent, and it was he who taught Joseph Plunkett, so that he might matriculate at the National University. SONGS OF MYSELF (1910) came out after four years in Dublin, where he had gone to see one of his plays produced. His LYRICAL POEMS, published in Dublin by the *Irish Review* in 1913, contains all that he wished to preserve of his verse outside of the poems contained in SONGS OF MYSELF. In the fall of 1913, he joined with Joseph Mary Plunkett and took over the *Irish Review*. James Stephens says of him: "I do not think that Thomas MacDonagh had any other ambition than to write good verse and to love his friends, and the pleasure he found in these two arts was the sole profit I ever knew him to seek or to get. . . . One could quarrel with Mac Donagh, but not for more than three minutes at a time, and if he were ruffled, the mere touch of a hand or the wind of a pleasant word appeased him instantly. I have seldom known a man in whom the instinct of friendship was so true, nor one who was so prepared to use himself in the service of a friend. (See THE POETICAL WORKS OF THOMAS MACDONAGH, with an Introduction by James Stephens.) There was a strange dualism in Thomas MacDonagh—the professor of English Literature who lectured daily as if he had no other thought in the world, and the patriot who was one of the most ardent leaders in the political movement of his day.

It is said that he suffered from a too great facility in writing verse; and that he would often alter a complete poem over and over again until he felt that it approached the poem of his imagination.

JOHN-JOHN

I DREAMT last night of you, John-John,
    And thought you called to me;
And when I woke this morning, John,
    Yourself I hoped to see;
But I was all alone, John-John,
    Though still I heard your call:
I put my boots and bonnet on,
    And took my Sunday shawl,
And went, full sure to find you, John,
    To Nenagh fair.

The fair was just the same as then,
    Five years ago to-day,
When first you left the thimble-men
    And came with me away;
For there again were thimble-men
    And shooting galleries,
And card-trick men and Maggie men
    Of all sorts and degrees,—
But not a sight of you, John-John,
    Was anywhere.

I turned my face to home again,
    And called myself a fool
To think you'd leave the thimble-men
    And live again by rule,
And go to Mass and keep the fast
    And till the little patch:
My wish to have you home was past
    Before I raised the latch
And pushed the door and saw you, John,
    Sitting down there.

How cool you came in here, begad,
   As if you owned the place !
But rest yourself there now, my lad,
   'Tis good to see your face ;
My dream is out, and now by it
   I think I know my mind :
At six o'clock this house you'll quit,
   And leave no grief behind ;—
But until six o'clock, John-John,
     My bit you'll share.

My neighbours' shame of me began
   When first I brought you in ;
To wed and keep a tinker-man
   They thought a kind of sin ;
But now this three year since you're gone
   'Tis pity me they do,
And that I'd rather have John-John,
   Than that they'd pity you.
Pity for me and you, John-John,
     I could not bear.

Oh, you're my husband right enough,
   But what's the good of that?
You know you never were the stuff
   To be the cottage cat,
To watch the fire and hear me lock
   The door and put out Shep—
But there now, it is six o'clock
   And time for you to step.
God bless and keep you far, John-John!
     And that's my prayer.

A Woman

Time on her face has writ
   A hundred years,
And all the page of it
   Blurred with his tears ;

Yet in his holiest crypt
Treasuring the scroll,
Keeps the sweet manuscript
Fair as her soul.

From POEMS BY THOMAS MACDONAGH. Published by The Talbot Press, Dublin, 1916.

ALICE MILLIGAN

ALICE MILLIGAN was born in Omagh, County Tyrone. She wrote for the *Irish National Press* for some years under the *nom de plume*, Iris Olkyrn. She has an unusual gift for ballad poetry, and most of her ballads are founded on native history and legend. She has written Irish plays for the Irish Literary Theatre, and she has identified herself with Irish National feeling in its widest sense.

THE DARK PALACE

THERE beams no light from thy hall to-night,
    O House of Fame;
No mead-vat seethes and no smoke upwreathes
    O'er thy hearth's red flame;
No high bard sings for the joy of thy kings,
    And no harpers play;
No hostage moans as thy dungeon rings,
    As in Muircherteach's day.

Fallen! fallen! to ruin all in
    Thy covering mould;
The painted yew, and the curtains blue,
    And the cups of gold;
The linen, yellow as the corn when mellow,
    That the princes wore;
And the mirrors brazen for your queens to gaze in—
    They are here no more.

The sea-bird's pinion thatched Gormlai's grianan;
    And through windows clear,
Without crystal pane, in her Ard-righ's reign,
    She looked from here;
There were quilts of eider on her couch of cedar;
    And her silken shoon
Were as green and soft as the leaves aloft
    On a bough in June.

Ah, woe unbounded, where the harp once sounded
    The wind now sings;
The grey grass shivers where the mead in rivers
    Was outpoured for kings;
The min and the mether are lost together
    With the spoil of the spears;
The strong dun only has stood dark and lonely
    Through a thousand years.

But I'm not in woe for the wine-cup's flow,
    For the banquet's cheer.
For tall princesses with their trailing tresses
    And their broidered gear;
My grief and my trouble for this palace noble,
    With no chief to lead
'Gainst the Saxon stranger on the day of danger,
    Out of Aileach Neid!

SEUMAS O'SULLIVAN

SEUMAS O'SULLIVAN, born in 1879, is a Dublin man whose
real name is James Starkey. He began to write his verse
during the time that he was a member of the group that fos-
tered the Irish Theatre. His poems are, in subject and music,
for the most part far removed from the workaday world. The
title of one of his books, THE TWILIGHT PEOPLE, admirably
suggests the quiet tone of his writing. Padraic Colum has

said of him : " Seumas O'Sullivan has interpreted perfectly
one mood of the Irish country, the mood that comes with the
slow, haunted Irish twilight." And A. E. (George Russell)
has called him " the literary successor to those old Gaelic
poets who were fastidious in their verse, who loved little in
this world but some chance light in it which reminded them of
fairy-land." THE TWILIGHT PEOPLE (1905) was followed
by VERSES SACRED AND PROFANE (1908); THE EARTH LOVER
(1909); SELECTED LYRICS, with a preface by A. E. (1910),
and THE POEMS OF SEUMAS O'SULLIVAN with an Introduction
by Padraic Colum, AN EPILOGUE TO THE PRAISE OF ANGUS
(1914).

THE SHEEP

SLOWLY they pass
In the grey of the evening
Over the wet road,
A flock of sheep.
Slowly they wend
In the grey of the gloaming,
Over the wet road
That winds through the town.
Slowly they pass,
And gleaming whitely
Vanish away
In the grey of the evening.
Ah, what memories
Loom for a moment,
Gleam for a moment,
And vanish away,
Of the white days
When we two together
Went in the evening
Where the sheep lay ;
We two together,
Went with slow feet
In the grey of the evening

Where the sheep lay.
Whitely they gleam
For a moment and vanish
Away in the dimness
Of sorrowful years ;
Gleam for a moment,
All white, and go fading
Away in the greyness
Of sundering years.

The Herdsman

O HERDSMAN, driving your slow twilight flock
By darkening meadow and hedge and grassy rath,
The trees stand shuddering as you pass by ;
The suddenly falling silence is your path.

Over my heart too, the shadows are creeping,
But on my heart for ever they will lie :
O happy meadows and trees and rath and hedges,
The twilight and all its flock will pass you by.

From POEMS BY SEUMAS O'SULLIVAN. Published by Maunsel & Co.,
Dublin, 1912.

The Others

FROM our hidden places
By a secret path
We troop in the moonlight
To the edge of the green rath.

There the night through
We take our pleasure
Dancing to such a measure
As earth never knew.

To song and dance
And lilt without a name
So sweetly breathéd
'Twould put a bird to shame.

And many a young maiden
Is there of mortal birth
Her young eyes laden
With dreams of earth.

And many a youth entrancéd
Moves slowly in the wildered round,
His brave lost feet enchanted
In the rhythm of elfin sound.

Music so forest wild
And piercing sweet would bring
Silence on blackbirds singing
Their best in the ear of Spring.

And now they pause in their dancing
And look with troubled eyes
Earth's straying children
With sudden memory wise.

They pause, and their eyes in the moonlight
With faery wisdom cold,
Grow dim and a thought goes fluttering
In hearts no longer old.

And then the dream forsakes them
And sighing, they turn anew
As the whispering music takes them
To the dance of the elfin crew.

Oh, many a thrush and a blackbird
Would fall to the dewy ground
And pine away in silence
For envy of such a sound.

So the night through
In our sad pleasure
We dance to many a measure
That earth never knew.

From An Epilogue by Seumas O'Sullivan.   Published by Maunsel & Co.,
Dublin, 1914.

PADRAIC PEARSE

PADRAIC PEARSE and his friends, Thomas MacDonagh and Joseph Plunkett, were the three poets who were foremost to take up arms to assert Ireland's Declaration of Independence. All three were executed in April 1916 as leaders of the Irish Rebellion. Padraic Pearse was the first of the younger group to be recognised by the Gaelic League. He learned Irish in one of the few schools where it was then taught, and took up Irish studies in University College, then part of the Old Royal, and now part of the new National, University. He graduated from University College and was called to the Bar. Meanwhile he had mastered the language, and had learned about Gaelic life by living for long spaces of time in a cottage he owned in one of the poorest districts of West Connacht. It was in Dublin that he organised St. Enda's School for boys. Two years later he opened a girls' school organised along similar lines—the whole atmosphere of both being Gaelic. He wrote in Gaelic and his book was called SUAN-TRAIDHE AGUS GOLTRAIDHE—SONGS OF SLUMBER AND OF SORROW (1912).

IDEAL

Translated by Thomas MacDonagh

NAKED I saw thee,
O beauty of beauty!
And I blinded my eyes
For fear I should flinch.

I heard thy music,
O sweetness of sweetness!
And I shut my ears
For fear I should fail.

I kissed thy lips
O sweetness of sweetness!
And I hardened my heart
For fear of my ruin.

I blinded my eyes
And my ears I shut,
I hardened my heart,
And my love I quenched.

I turned my back
On the dream I had shaped,
And to this road before me
My face I turned.

I set my face
To the road here before me,
To the work that I see,
To the death that I shall meet.

JOSEPH MARY PLUNKETT

JOSEPH MARY PLUNKETT belonged to a Catholic branch of a
family whose name appeared in Irish history for six hundred
years. He was the son of the Count and Countess Plunkett,
and was born in Dublin in November 1887. He attended
the Catholic University School, Belvedere College, and was
an omnivorous reader. When he was eighteen he followed
the two years' philosophy course at Stonyhurst College. This
made a strong impression on him, and mystical philosophy
influenced his writings. He was obliged by ill health to
spend a great deal of his short life in inactivity, and to winter
abroad. He and his mother spent one winter travelling in
Italy, Sicily, and Malta, and another winter was spent in
Algiers where he studied the Arabic literature and language.
Before he went to Algiers he met Thomas MacDonagh,
who was teaching at the time at St. Enda's School, which he
had helped P. H. Pearse to start. MacDonagh taught him
Irish for his matriculation at the National University. He
later became editor, with MacDonagh, of the *Irish Review*.
In 1911 his book of verse, THE CIRCLE AND THE SWORD,

was published. The Irish Theatre was started in 1914 by
a partnership consisting of Edward Martyn, Thomas Mac-
Donagh, and Joseph M. Plunkett. Its purpose, as opposed
to that of the Abbey Theatre, was to produce Irish plays other
than peasant plays. Toward the last six months of his life
Plunkett disagreed with the other directors for not abiding
by the spirit of the agreement, and disassociated himself from
the theatre. He was an ardent participator in the Volunteer
movement, and like his friend, MacDonagh, was executed in
Dublin as one of the leaders of the Irish Rebellion of 1916.
THE POEMS OF JOSEPH MARY PLUNKETT, published in 1916
after his death, contains the best of his verse

THE SPARK

BECAUSE I used to shun
Death and the mouth of Hell,
And count my battles won
When I should see the sun
The blood and smoke dispel.

Because I used to pray
That living I might see
The dawning light of day
Set me upon my way,
And from my fetters free ;

Because I used to seek
Your answer to my prayer,
And that your soul should speak
For strengthening of the weak
To struggle with despair ;

Now I have seen my shame
That I should thus deny
My soul's divinest flame ;
Now I shall shout your name ;
Now I shall seek to die.

By any hands but these
In battle or in flood,
On any lands or seas ;
No more shall I spare ease,
No more shall I spare blood.

When I have need to fight
For heaven or your heart,
Against the powers of light,
Or darkness I shall smite
Until their might depart ;

Because I know the spark
Of God has no eclipse,
Now Death and I embark,
And sail into the dark
With laughter on our lips.

JAMES STEPHENS

JAMES STEPHENS was born in Dublin in February 1882 of
parents in moderate circumstances ; he grew up with but little
formal education and at an early age began to earn his own
living. He became a typist in a solicitor's office and his
parents encouraged him to study law. But he has said : " It
is not much work that I did. I thought in those days that
maybe I'd be a poet. All day I used to sit and think about
big words. By big I mean high-sounding words like 'honour' and 'noble' and 'courage,' and I spent most of my time
scribbling them down." Some of his musings and "scrib-
blings" were sent to a Dublin journal where they were
published under the title JOTTINGS OF A PHILOSOPHER. They
attracted the attention of A. E. (George Russell) and he
called at the solicitor's office to see the young writer, and
then began the friendship which still continues. The JOT-

TINGS were to become the base of James Stephens' fame, for with some elaboration they became the now celebrated classic that defies classification, THE CROCK OF GOLD (1912). Three years before this his first book of poems, INSURRECTIONS, had appeared (1909). Of its inception he has said, "One day while I was waiting for somebody to come and take me out, I picked up a volume of Browning from the table. I read and read. I thought, 'This stuff makes sense,' and then I thought, 'I can do this too.' The next thing I read was Blake, and he drove me clean mad. I was like a man drunk. I began to write verse immediately, and one month from that day my first book was published." Other volumes of verse by Stephens are: THE HILL OF VISION, 1912; SONGS FROM THE CLAY, 1915; THE ROCKY ROAD TO DUBLIN, 1915; GREEN BRANCHES, 1916; REINCARNATIONS, 1918; A POETRY RECITAL, 1925; COLLECTED POEMS, 1926; and STRICT JOY AND OTHER POEMS, 1931. His prose includes THE CROCK OF GOLD, 1912; THE CHARWOMAN'S DAUGHTER, 1912; HERE ARE LADIES, 1913; THE DEMI-GODS, 1914; IRISH FAIRY TALES, 1920; DEIRDRE, 1923; IN THE LAND OF YOUTH, 1924; ETCHED IN MOONLIGHT, 1928. James Stephens' home is in Dublin, where he lives with his wife and his children. For some years he served as assistant to the Director of the National Gallery of Ireland, a position which fortunately allowed him much leisure, but now he devotes his entire time to his writings. He has made several visits to America, and occasionally he goes to London and Paris, but he always returns happily to the Ireland which he so competently interprets for the world.

THE COOLIN

COME with me, under my coat,
And we will drink our fill
Of the milk of the white goat,
Or wine if it be thy will.

And we will talk, until
Talk is a trouble, too,
Out on the side of the hill;
And nothing is left to do,

But an eye to look into an eye;
And a hand in a hand to slip;
And a sigh to answer a sigh;
And a lip to find out a lip!

What if the night be black!
Or the air on the mountain chill!
Where the goat lies down in her track,
And all but the fern is still!

Stay with me, under my coat!
And we will drink our fill
Of the milk of the white goat,
Out on the side of the hill!

THE DAISIES

In the scented bud of the morning-o,
When the windy grass went rippling far!
I saw my dear one walking slow
In the field where the daisies are.

We did not laugh, and we did not speak,
As we wandered happily, to and fro;
I kissed my dear on either cheek,
In the bud of the morning-o!

A lark sang up, from the breezy land,
A lark sang down, from a cloud afar;
As she and I went, hand in hand,
In the field where the daisies are.

BESSIE BOBTAIL

As down the road she wambled slow,
She had not got a place to go;
She had not got a place to fall
And rest herself—no place at all:
She stumped along, and wagged her pate;
And said a thing was desperate.

Her face was screwed and wrinkled tight
Just like a nut—and, left and right,
On either side she wagged her head
And said a thing; and what she said
Was desperate as any word
That ever yet a person heard.

I walked behind her for a while,
And watched the people nudge and smile:
But ever, as she went, she said,
As left and right she swung her head,
—*Oh, God He knows!   And, God He knows!*
And surely God Almighty knows!

From COLLECTED POEMS, by James Stephens.   Published by The Macmillan Company, New York, 1926.

JOHN M. SYNGE

JOHN M. SYNGE was born on the 16th of April, 1871, at Newtown Little, near Dublin—the son of a barrister.   He attended the private schools in Dublin and in Bray, but not being very strong, he left school when he was fourteen and studied thereafter with a tutor.   In 1888 he entered Trinity College, Dublin; he won prizes in Hebrew and in Irish in Trinity term in 1892, and took his B.A. degree in December 1892.   While at Trinity he studied music at the Royal Irish

Academy of Music. When he left college he was undecided about a career, but was inclined to make music his profession. He went, therefore, to Germany to study music, but in 1894 he gave this up and went to Paris, with the thought of devoting himself to writing. For the next few years he spent much of his time in France, writing constantly, but without marked success. It was in 1898 that he made his first visit to the Aran Islands. During that visit he began the first draft of the notes which afterwards grew to be his book, THE ARAN ISLANDS. His writings up to this time had been more or less imitative, being chiefly reflections from, and upon, what had most struck him in his readings. While he was in Paris in 1899, he met William Butler Yeats, who, having seen some of his work, suggested that it might be wise for him to give up writing criticism, and go again to the Aran Islands to study the life there. He followed Mr. Yeats' advice, and made five or six visits of some duration to the Aran Islands in the years from 1899 to 1902. Meanwhile he worked on THE ARAN ISLANDS, and on his three early one-act plays, " The Tinker's Wedding," " Riders to the Sea," and " The Shadow of the Glen." About once a year when the Abbey Theatre—of which he was one of the advisers—toured in England, he came with it. His activities, outside of this, are vague for that period. Little can be said except that he passed most of the time in Ireland, writing and rewriting. His general health was never robust, and in May 1908 he underwent a serious operation, after which his health was, unfortunately, not improved. He passed the last few months of his life trying to finish his play " Deirdre," and writing some of his few poems. He died in a private nursing home in Dublin on the 24th of March, 1909. THE WORKS OF JOHN M. SYNGE in four volumes, published in 1910, contains all the published plays and books, and certain selections from his criticisms. His most famous play is probably " The Playboy of the Western World " (1905). A volume of his POEMS AND TRANSLATIONS, written between 1891 and 1908, appeared in 1909. John Masefield in a penetrating word picture of him published under the title : " John M. Synge : A Few Personal Recollections," tells us that he worked slowly and carefully, usually composing directly on a typewriter, and doing a good deal of rewriting. He calls Synge a man interested in life rather than ideas, and says : " Those who want to know what Synge was should read his poems. The poems are the man speaking."

THE PASSING OF THE SHEE *

AFTER LOOKING AT ONE OF A. E.'S PICTURES

ADIEU, sweet Angus, Maeve, and Fand,
Ye plumed yet skinny Shee,
That poets played with hand in hand
To learn their ecstasy.

We'll stretch in Red Dan Sally's ditch,
And drink in Tubber fair,
Or poach with Red Dan Philly's bitch
The badger and the hare.

QUEENS *

SEVEN dog-days we let pass
Naming Queens in Glenmacnass,
All the rare and royal names
Wormy sheepskin yet retains ;
Etain, Helen, Maeve, and Fand,
Golden Deirdre's tender hand ;
Bert, the big-foot, sung by Villon,
Cassandra, Ronsard found in Lyon.
Queens of Sheba, Meath, and Connaught,
Coifed with crown, or gaudy bonnet;
Queens whose finger once did stir men,
Queens were eaten of fleas and vermin,
Queens men drew like Monna Lisa,
Or slew with drugs in Rome and Pisa.

We named Lucrezia Crivelli,
And Titian's lady with amber belly,
Queens acquainted in learned sin,
Jane of Jewry's slender shin ;
Queens who cut the bogs of Glanna,
Judith of Scripture, and Glorianna,
Queens who wasted the East by proxy,
Or drove the ass-cart, a tinker's doxy.
Yet these are rotten—I ask their pardon—
And we've the sun on rock and garden ;
These are rotten, so you're the Queen
Of all are living, or have been.

From WORKS OF J. M. SYNGE, Vol. II. Published by Maunsel & Co., Dublin, 1910.

INDEX TO FIRST LINES

INDEX OF AUTHORS

Printed in the United States of America.

1776: July 4, Declaration of Independence; Hopkins, "Dialogue Concerning the Slavery of the Africans"

1777: Vermont abolishes slavery

1780: Population of the United States: 2,781,000; Pennsylvania abolishes slavery

1783: Treaty of Paris

1784: Methodist Episcopal Church formed, adopting a rule for the freeing of members' slaves (suspended in six months)

1787: Northwest Ordinance, prohibiting slavery in the Northwest Territory; Jefferson, *Notes on Virginia; The Federalist* (1787-1788)

1789: Constitution of the United States adopted; French Revolution begins

1790: Population of the United States: 3,929,214

1791: Haitian uprising under L'Ouverture; Bill of Rights

1792: Brackenridge, *Modern Chivalry*

1793: Haitian proclamation of freedom; first Fugitive Slave Law; Eli Whitney invents the cotton gin

1794: First convention of Abolition Societies meets in Philadelphia; Act to prohibit American vessels from supplying slaves to another country; Dwight, *Greenfield Hill*

1800: Population of the United States: 5,308,483; Capital moved to Washington

1801: Haitian declaration of independence

1802: Lydia Maria Child (1802-1880)

1803: Louisiana Purchase; Ralph Waldo Emerson (1803-1882), Boston

1804: Nathaniel Hawthorne (1804-1864), Salem, Massachusetts

1807: John Greenleaf Whittier (1807-1892), Haverhill, Massachusetts; Henry Wadsworth Longfellow (1807-1882), Portland, Maine

1780: First African Baptist Church, Richmond, founded

1786: New York African free school established

1787: Free African Society organized by Absalom Jones and Richard Allen

1789: *The Interesting Narrative of the Life of Olaulah Equiano, or Gustavus Vassa, the African*

1790: Negro Population: 757,208 (19.3%)

1794: Richard Allen and Absalom Jones' *A Narrative of the Black People during the Late Awful Calamity in Philadelphia;* Zoar Methodist Episcopal Church organized in Philadelphia

1796: Varick establishes colored Methodist Episcopal church in New York City

1797: George Moses Horton (1797-c. 1883), Northampton County, North Carolina

1800: Negro Population: 1,002,037 (18.9%); Gabriel insurrection, Henrico County, Virginia

1808: Further importation of slaves prohibited

1809: Abraham Lincoln (1809-1865), Kentucky; Edgar Allan Poe (1809-1849), Boston

1810: Population of the United States: 7,239,881; Theodore Parker (1810-1860), Lexington, Massachusetts; Elihu Burritt (1810-1879), New Britain, Connecticut

1810: Negro Population: 1,377,808 (19%); Charles Remond (1810-1873), Salem, Massachusetts

1811: Harriet Beecher Stowe (1811-1896), Litchfield, Connecticut

1811: Daniel A. Payne (1811-1893), Charleston, South Carolina

1812: War of 1812

1812: Martin R. Delany (1812-1885), Charlestown, Virginia

1813: Battle of Lake Erie

1814: Hartford Convention; Treaty of Ghent

1815: Lundy organizes the Union Humane Society, St. Clairsville, Ohio; Richard Henry Dana, Jr. (1815-1881), Cambridge Massachusetts; *North American Review* founded

1816: African Methodist Episcopal Church organized in Philadelphia

1817: American Colonization Society organized; First Seminole War; Henry David Thoreau (1817-1862), Concord, Massachusetts

1817: Frederick Douglass (1817-1895), Talbot County, Maryland

1819: Florida purchased; Congress empowers President to use navy to suppress slave trade; Walt Whitman (1819-1892), Huntington, Long Island; James Russell Lowell (1819-1891), Cambridge, Massachusetts; Herman Melville (1819-1891), New York City

1820: Negro Population: 1,771,656 (18.4%); George B. Vashon (1820-1878)

1821: African Methodist Episcopal Zion church organized in New York; William Still (1821-1902), Burlington County, New Jersey

1820: Population of the United States: 9,638,453

1822: Denmark Vesey insurrection, Charleston, South Carolina

1821: Liberian colony established; Lundy begins *The Genius of Universal Emancipation,* Mt. Pleasant, Ohio

1825: Frances E. W. Harper (1825-1911), Baltimore

1824: Samuel Bowles establishes the Springfield *Republican*

1826: James Russwurm graduates from Bowdoin; James Bell (1826-1902), Gallipolis, Ohio

1827: Captain and Mrs. Basil-Hall in America

1827: *Freedom's Journal,* edited by Samuel Cornish and John Russwurm, founded

1828: Tariff of Abominations

1829: Lundy and Garrison editing the *Genius of Universal Emancipation* in Baltimore

1829: Oblate Sisters of Providence founded in Baltimore by Dominican refugee; David Walker, *Appeal;* Horton, *Hope of Liberty*

1830: Population of the United States: 12,866,020; Weld begins his antislavery campaign

1831: Garrison founds *The Liberator*; Weld converts Birney to the antislavery position

1832: South Carolina's Ordinance of Nullification; Kennedy, *Swallow Barn*

1832-1835: Removal of Florida and Georgia Indians

1833: American Anti-slavery Society organized; Rev. Dr. Furman of South Carolina proclaims slaveholding established by Holy Scripture; Prudence Crandall's school closed, Canterbury, Connecticut; Captain Hamilton, *Men and Manners in America*; Mrs. Child's *Appeal in Favor of That Class of Americans Called Africans*

1834 Lane Seminary debates; British emancipation of slaves; *Southern Literary Messenger* founded

1835: Finney called to Oberlin College, where students, regardless of sex or color, were to be educated; Noyes Academy, New Canaan, New Hampshire, destroyed by mob violence for accepting Negro students; Taney appointed chief justice; antislavery mails seized and burned at Charleston; Seminole War, 1835-1842; Garrison mobbed; De Tocqueville, *Democracy in America*; Longstreet, *Georgia Scenes*; Simms, *The Yemassee*

1836: People of the District of Columbia present memorial to Congress asking for the abolition of slavery in their territory; Tucker, *The Partisan Leader*

1837: Elijah P. Lovejoy killed by proslavery mob in Alton, Illinois; Wendell Phillips makes his first antislavery speech in protest; Harriet Martineau, *Society in America*; Emerson,

1830: Negro Population: 2,328,642 (18.1%); James M. Whitfield (1830-1870), Boston, Massachusetts

1831: First convention of people of color, Philadelphia; Southampton insurrection led by Nat Turner

1833: Robert Purvis attends first Anti-slavery Convention

1837: James McCune Smith returns to New York from the University of Glasgow

"The American Scholar";
Whittier, *Abolition Poems*

1838: First gag resolution, banning antislavery petition discussion; Whittier begins to edit *The Pennsylvania Freeman*; Philadelphia mob destroys Lundy's Pennsylvania Hall

1839: Liberty Party holds convention at Warsaw, N. Y.; *Amistad* case

1840: Population of the United States: 17,069,453; Liberty Party casts 7,069 votes; *The Dial* founded; Brisbane, *Social Destiny of Man*

1841: *Creole* case and Giddings Resolutions; Brook Farm (1841-1846); Greeley founds the New York *Tribune*; David Lee Child and Mrs. Lydia Maria Child begin editing the *National Anti-Slavery Standard*

1842: Dickens in America; Longfellow, *Poems on Slavery*; Hawthorne, *Twice-Told Tales*; Sidney Lanier (1842-1881), Macon, Georgia

1843: Wesleyan Methodist Connection, opposing slavery and intoxicating liquors, organized; Whittier, "Massachusetts to Virginia," after Latimer fugitive slave case

1844: Whittier, *Voices of Freedom*; Georgia Washington Cable (1844-1925), New Orleans

1845: Methodist Episcopal Church, South, organized; Southern Baptist Convention organized; Texas annexed; Irish immigration as result of famine in Ireland; Mowatt, *Fashion*; Lowell begins to write for *The Pennsylvania Freeman*

1846: Wilmot Proviso; Mexican War (1846-1848); Melville, *Typee*; Hooper, *Adventures of Simon Suggs*

1847: Free and Independent Republic of Liberia established

1848: Lowell becomes corresponding editor of the *National Anti-Slavery Standard;* publishes

1838: Douglass escapes from slavery; David Ruggles establishes the *Mirror for Liberty,* first Negro magazine; William Whipper establishes the *National Reformer* in Philadelphia; Remond begins career as antislavery lecturer

1839: Samuel Ringgold Ward becomes minister of the Congregational Church and agent for the American Anti-slavery Society

1840: Negro Population: 2,873,648 (16.8%); Remond goes to London for the World Antislavery Convention

1841: Daniel Payne, "An Original Poem Composed for the Soirée of the Vigilant Committee of Philadelphia"; Garrison meets Douglass at Nantucket antislavery meeting

1842: Congregation of the Sisters of the Holy Family established at New Orleans

1843: William Wells Brown becomes lecturer for the Western New York Anti-slavery Society; Delany's *Mystery* (1843-1847) established in Pittsburgh; Garnet delivers "An Address to the Slaves of the United States of America" at Buffalo

1845: Douglass goes to England to lecture; first edition of the *Narrative of the Life of Frederick Douglass*

1846: *Correspondence between the Rev. Samuel H. Cox . . . and Frederick Douglass, a Fugitive Slave,* first extant Douglass pamphlet

1847: Douglass' *North Star* begins publication; *Narrative of William W. Brown* published by the Massachusetts Anti-slavery Society; Still begins to work with the Pennsylvania Anti-slavery Society

1848: W. W. Brown, *Antislavery*

Biglow Papers; Foster, *Songs of the Sable Harmonists*; Joel Chandler Harris (1848-1908), Eatonton, Georgia

1849: California Gold Rush; German immigration as result of Revolution of 1848; Melville, *Mardi*

1850: Population of the United States: 23,191,876; Fugitive Slave Law and Compromise of 1850; slave trade prohibited in the District of Columbia after January 1, 1851; Hawthorne, *The Scarlet Letter*; Lafcadio Hearn (1850-1894), Leucadia, Greece; Charles Egbert Craddock (1850-1922), Murfreesboro, Tennessee; *Harper's* founded

1851: Christiana (Pa.) riot; Shadrach case, both involving fugitive slaves; Melville, *Moby Dick*; Hawthorne, *The House of Seven Gables*; Whittier, "Ichabod"; *Uncle Tom's Cabin* begins in *The National Era*

1852: *Uncle Tom's Cabin* produced as a play in Troy, New York; Mrs. Eastman, *Aunt Phyllis' Cabin*

1853: *A Key to Uncle Tom's Cabin;* Lieber, *On Civil Liberty*; Thomas Nelson Page (1853-1922), Hanover Co., Va.; Irwin Russell (1853-1879), Port Gibson, Mississippi

1854: Kansas-Nebraska Bill; Anthony Burns's rendition; Fitzhugh, *Sociology for the South*; Mrs. Hentz, *The Planter's Northern Bride*

Harp; Ward establishes the *Impartial Citizen,* in Syracuse

1849: W. W. Brown goes to Britain as a lecturer, delivering more than a thousand addresses in five years; *The Life of Josiah Henson . . .; Narrative of Henry Box Brown;* Harriet Tubman escapes from slavery; G. W. Williams (1849-1891), Pennsylvania; Archibald H. Grimké (1849-1930), Charleston, South Carolina

1850: Negro Population: 3,638,808 (15.7%); *Narrative of Sojourner Truth, Northern Slave;* Francis J. Grimké (1850-1938), Charleston, South Carolina

1851: Douglass breaks with Garrison, joins the Liberty Party; Delany enters Harvard Medical School; William Nell, *Services of Colored Americans in the Wars of 1776 and 1812;* Albery A. Whitman (1851-1902), Kentucky

1852: W. W. Brown's *Three Years in Europe* published in England; Delany, *The Condition, Elevation, Emigration, and Destiny of the Colored People of the United States . . .; Christian Recorder* begins publication

1853: W. W. Brown's *Clotel, or the President's Daughter,* first novel by an American Negro; Ward goes to England to lecture for the Anti-slavery Society of Canada; Crummell goes to Liberia after graduating from Queen's College, Cambridge; Whitfield, "America," *Autographs of Freedom*

1854: Colored Colonization Convention; Lincoln University founded as Ashmun Institute; Douglass delivers *Claims of the Negro Ethnologically Considered* at Western Reserve commencement; W. W. Brown manumitted

1855: Massachusetts citizens purchase Anthony Burns for $1300; Lowell appointed to Harvard; Whitman, *Leaves of Grass*; Longfellow, *The Song of Hiawatha*; Melville, *Benito Cereno*

1855: Douglass, *My Bondage and My Freedom*; Ward, *The Autobiography of a Fugitive Negro* (London); Ward goes to Jamaica; W. W. Brown, *Sketches of Places and People Abroad*; Nell, *The Colored Patriots in the American Revolution*

1856: Battle of Ossawatomie; Brooks attacks Sumner; first Republican National Convention, Philadelphia; Mrs. Stowe's *Dred*

1856: Wilberforce founded by the Methodist Episcopal Church; Rogers, *Repeal of the Missouri Compromise Considered*; Charles Chesnutt (1856-1932), Cleveland

1857: Dred Scott decision; *Atlantic Monthly* founded, Lowell editing the magazine to 1861; Whittier, *Collected Poems*

1858: Lincoln-Douglas debates; crew of the *Echo*, slave ship seized by U. S. brig *Dolphin*, freed by grand jury in Columbia, S. C.

1858: Brown, *The Escape,* first play by a Negro author; National Colonization Convention in Cleveland; Booker T. Washington (1858-1915), Hales Ford, Virginia

1859: John Brown at Harper's Ferry; Mrs. Child asks permission to nurse Brown; last slave ship, *The Clothilde*, lands in Mobile Bay; Boucicault, *The Octoroon*, playing in New York; Darwin, *Origin of the Species*; Helper, *The Impending Crisis*

1859: *Echo* slaves returned to Liberia. Delany, *Blake, or the Huts of America; The Rev. J. W. Loguen, as a Slave and as a Freeman;* Hamilton's *Anglo-African Magazine* begins publication

1860: Population of the United States: 31,443,790; Lincoln elected president; South Carolina secedes; Child-Mason-Wise correspondence; Hamlin Garland (1860-1940), Wisconsin

1860: Negro Population: 4,441,830 (14.1%)

1861: Civil War (1861-1865)

1861: Mary Peake establishes school at Fortress Monroe, Virginia, out of which Hampton Institute grew; Joseph S. Cotter, Sr. (1861-   ), Bardstown, Kentucky

1862: Antietam; Freedmen's Relief Association; *Artemus Ward: His Book*; O. Henry (1862-1910), Greensboro, N. C.

1863: Emancipation Proclamation; West Virginia admitted to the Union, establishes public schools for Negroes; Gettysburg and Lincoln's Gettysburg Address; Vicksburg

1863: W. W. Brown, *The Black Man . . .;* Kelly Miller (1863-1939), Winnsboro, South Carolina

1864: Sherman in Georgia; Locke, *Nasby Papers*

1865: Lincoln's Second Inaugural Address; Appomattox; assassination of Lincoln; Freedmen's Bureau established; Thirteenth Amendment; Phillips con-

1865: Delany commissioned a major in the Union army; Shaw, Atlanta, Wayland (Virginia Union) founded

tinues Anti-Slavery Society; E. L. Godkin founds *The Nation*; Whitman, *Drum Taps*

1866: Civil Rights Act; Tennessee re-admitted; race riots in New Orleans; Locke, *Swingin' round the Circle*

1867: Reconstruction begins; Ku Klux Klan organized; Alaska purchased; T. W. Higginson, "Negro Spirituals," *Atlantic Monthly*; W. F. Allen *et al.*, *Slave Songs of the United States*; Helper, *Nojoque*

1868: Fourteenth Amendment; Johnson impeached

1869: Union Pacific completed; Mark Twain, *Innocents Abroad*

1870: Population of the United States: 39,818,449; Fifteenth Amendment; Enforcement Act; Ku Klux Klan; organization of Standard Oil Company; American Anti-slavery Society comes to an end; *Scribner's* founded; Higginson, *Army Life in a Black Regiment*; Frank Norris (1870-1902), Chicago

1871: Whitman, *Democratic Vistas*; Howells becomes editor of the *Atlantic*; Stephen Crane (1871-1900), Newark, New Jersey; Theodore Dreiser, (1871-), Terre Haute, Indiana

1872: Horace Greeley dies; Twain, *Roughing It*; Gertrude Stein (1872-), Baltimore

1873: Warner and Twain, *The Gilded Age*

1874: Civil Rights act; W. C. T. U. founded; Vicksburg, Mississippi, race riots; Amy Lowell (1874-1925), Brookline, Massachusetts; Ellen Glasgow (1874-), Richmond, Virginia

---

1866: Fisk University founded

1867: Howard University chartered; Talladega, Morehouse, Johnson C. Smith founded; W. W. Brown, *The Negro in the American Rebellion;* W. E. B. DuBois (1868-), Great Barrington, Massachusetts

1868: J. W. Menard, elected to Congress from Louisiana, refused seat by the House; G. W. Williams organizes student body at Howard on a military basis; Mrs. Keckley, *Behind the Scenes*

1869: Douglass founds the *New National Era* (1869-1872), Washington; Clark, Morgan founded; Langston dean of the Howard Law School; James D. Corrothers (1869-1919), Cass County, Michigan

1870: Negro Population: 4,880,009 (12.7%); Colored Methodist Episcopal Church organized at Jackson, Tennessee; Hiram R. Revels elected to the United States Senate from Mississippi

1871: Fisk Jubilee Singers make first concert tour

1872: Douglass' Rochester house and papers destroyed by fire; *Southern Workmen* founded at Hampton; Still, *The Underground Railroad;* Elliot's Emancipation Oration; Paul Laurence Dunbar (1872-1906), Dayton, Ohio; James Weldon Johnson (1872-1930), Jacksonville, Florida

1873: Crummell returns from Liberia as rector of St. Luke's, Washington; Mrs. Harper, *Sketches of Southern Life;* Bennett College founded

1874: G. W. Williams graduates from Newton Theological Seminary; W. W. Brown, *The Rising Son*

1875: Robert Frost (1875-   ), San Francisco; J. E. Spingarn (1875-1940), New York City

1876: Harrison-Tilden election; Twain, *Tom Sawyer*; Jack London (1876-1916), San Francisco; Ole Rölvaag (1876-1931), Norway; Sherwood Anderson (1876-1941), Camden, Ohio; Willa Cather (1876-   ), Winchester, Virginia

1877: Withdrawal of federal troops from the South; Morgan, *Ancient Society*; Page, "Uncle Gabe's White Folks," *Scribner's*; Lanier, *Poems*

1878: Hearn's Creole Sketches begin to appear in New Orleans newspapers; Carl Sandburg, Galesburg, Illinois, and Upton Sinclair, Baltimore (1878-   ).

1879: Cable, *Old Creole Days*; Tourgee, *A Fool's Errand*; Cooke, *Stories of the Old Dominion*; George, *Progress and Poverty*; Vachel Lindsay (1879-1931), Springfield, Illinois

1880: Population of the United States: 50,155,783; Harris, *Uncle Remus: His Songs and Sayings*; Tourgee, *Bricks without Straw*

1881: American Federation of Labor organized; Howells leaves the *Atlantic Monthly*; Cable, *Madame Delphine*; Henry James, *Portrait of a Lady*; Carl Schurz joins *The Nation* staff

1882: John F. Slater Fund created; Twain, *Life on the Mississippi*; Howells, *A Modern Instance*; Whitman, *Specimen Days*

1883: Civil Rights Act invalidated; opening of Brooklyn Bridge; Pulitzer purchases *World*; Howe, *The Story of a Country Town*; L. F. Ward, *Dynamic Sociology*; Sumner, *What Social Classes Owe to Each Other*

1884: Slaughter-House Cases: first opinion indicating the use to

1875: Knoxville College founded; Blanche K. Bruce of Mississippi elected to the United States Senate; Carter G. Woodson (1875-   ), Buckingham County, Virginia

1877: Whitman, *Not a Man and Yet a Man*

1878: Flipper, *The Colored Cadet at West Point;* William Stanley Braithwaite, (1878-   ), Boston

1879: Negro exodus to Kansas; T. Thomas Fortune goes to New York, edits *The Rumor* (later, The New York *Globe*); *The Washington Bee* founded

1880: Negro Population: 6,580,793 (13.1%); W. W. Brown, *My Southern Home*

1881: Booker T. Washington opens Tuskegee Institute; Spelman College founded; *Life and Times of Frederick Douglass;* Scarborough, *First Lessons in Greek*

1882: Benjamin G. Brawley (1882-1939), Columbia, South Carolina

1883: G. W. Williams, *History of the Negro Race*

1884: Whitman, *The Rape of Florida*

which the Fourteenth Amendment was to be put in protecting business; Twain, *Huckleberry Finn*; Page, "Marse Chan" in *Century Magazine*; Craddock, *In the Tennessee Mountains*

1885: Howells, *The Rise of Silas Lapham*

1886: Haymarket Riot; Howells in "The Editor's Easy Chair," *Harper's*; H. James, *The Bostonians*

1887: Founding of the Catholic University of America; Page, *In Ole Virginia*

1887: Chesnutt publishes "The Goophered Grapevine," is admitted to bar in Cleveland; William J. Simmons' biographical dictionary, *Men of Mark;* Fortune begins to edit *The New York Age*

1888: Daniel Hand fund created; Cable, *The Negro Question*; Russell, *Poems*; Allen, "Two Gentlemen of Kentucky"; Bellamy, *Looking Backward*

1888: Bishop Payne, *Recollections of Seventy Years*

1889: John D. Rockefeller makes his first gift to the University of Chicago

1890: Population of the United States: 62,947,714; Mississippi constitution points way to disfranchisement of Negroes; William James, *The Principles of Psychology*; Riis, *How the Other Half Lives*; Grady, *The New South*

1890: Negro Population: 7,488,676 (11.9%)

1891: Beginnings of the Populist Party; eleven Italians lynched in New Orleans; deaths of Lowell and Melville; Smith, *Colonel Carter of Cartersville*; Allen, "King Solomon of Kentucky"; Garland, *Main Travelled Roads*

1891: Schomburg comes to America; Langston takes seat in the House of Representatives; A. H. Grimké, *Life of Charles Sumner;* Penn, *The Afro-American Press*

1892: Homestead, Pennsylvania, and Coeur d'Alene, Idaho, strikes; deaths of Whitman and Whittier; Howells, *An Imperative Duty*

1892: John H. Murphy founds the Baltimore *Afro-American*

1893: Chicago World's Fair; Grace King, *Balcony Stories*; Turner, "The Significance of the Frontier in American History"; Ward, *The Psychic Factors of Civilization*

1893: Dunbar, *Oak and Ivy*

1894: Coal strike; Coxey's Army; Pullman and railroad strikes; first motion picture; Twain, *Pud-*

1894: Langston, *From the Virginia Plantation to the National Capital*

d'nhead Wilson; Kate Chopin, *Bayou Folk*

1895: Cuban rebellion; Crane, *Red Badge of Courage*

1896: Plessy v. Ferguson: Louisiana jim-crow law upheld by the Supreme Court

1897: Alaska gold rush; Glasgow, *The Descendant*

1898: Spanish-American War; Hawaiian Islands annexed; Puerto Rico and the Philippines annexed; Wilmington, North Carolina, riots; Markham, "The Man with the Hoe"

1899: Philippine insurrection; Burton, *Old Plantation Hymns*; Norris, *McTeague*; Veblen, *The Theory of the Leisure Class*

1900: Population of the United States: 75,994,575; Boxer Rebellion, China; Long and Belasco, *Madame Butterfly*; Dreiser, *Sister Carrie*

1901: Hay-Pauncefote treaty; Norris, *The Octopus*; Carnegie, *The Gospel of Wealth*; Cable, *The Cavalier*

1902: John D. Rockefeller establishes the General Education Board; anthracite coal mine strike; Virginia constitution disfranchising Negroes; Riis, *The Battle with the Slum*; Dixon, *The Leopard's Spots*

1903: Panama revolts from Colombia; Wright brothers fly their plane at Kitty Hawk, North Carolina

1895: Bob Cole, *A Trip to Coontown*, first musical produced and managed by Negroes; Alice Moore (Dunbar-Nelson), *Violets and Other Tales;* Williams and Walker arrive in New York (Tony Pastor's); Booker T. Washington delivers his Atlanta Exposition Address (September)

1896: DuBois, *The Suppression of the African Slave Trade;* DuBois goes to Atlanta as professor of economics and history; Dunbar, *Lyrics of Lowly Life*

1897: Crummell founds the American Negro Academy in Washington; Tanner completes "The Resurrection of Lazarus"; D. W. Davis, *Weh Down Souf';* Scarborough, "Negro Folk-Lore and Dialect"

1898: Cook and Dunbar, *Clorindy;* Cotter, *Links of Friendship;* Dunbar, *Folks from Dixie, The Uncalled*

1899: Chesnutt, *The Conjure Woman, The Wife of His Youth, Frederick Douglass;* Dunbar, *Lyrics of the Hearthside;* DuBois, *The Philadelphia Negro*

1900: Negro Population: 8,833,994 (11.6%); Chesnutt, *The House behind the Cedars;* Dunbar, *The Love of Landry, The Strength of Gideon;* Washington, *Up from Slavery,* begins in the *Outlook*; *The Chicago Defender* founded; first meeting of the National Negro Business League, Boston

1901: Monroe Trotter founds the *Boston Guardian*; Whitman, "The Octoroon"; Chesnutt, *The Marrow of Tradition;* Dunbar, *The Fanatics, The Sport of the Gods* (in *Lippincott's*)

1902: Dunbar, Cook, Shipp and Rogers, *In Dahomey*

1903: Dubois, *Souls of Black Folk;* Dunbar, *Lyrics of Love and Laughter, In Old Plantation Days*

1904: Page, *The Negro, the Southerner's Problem*; Steffens, *The Shame of the Cities*; Glasgow, *The Deliverance*

1905: Industrial Workers of the World organized; Federal Council of Churches organized; London, *The War of the Classes*; Dixon, *The Clansman*

1906: San Francisco earthquake and fire; segregation of Japanese children in San Francisco schools; Atlanta, Georgia, and Brownsville, Texas, riots; construction of Panama Canal begins; Henry Adams, *The Education of Henry Adams*; Sinclair, *The Jungle*

1907: William James, *Pragmatism*; Sumner, *Folkways*; Rauschenbusch, *Christianity and the Social Crisis*

1908: Springfield, Illinois, riots; *Social Creed of the Churches*

1909: North Pole reached by Peary and Henson; Commission to investigate Liberian affairs; Stein, *Three Lives*; Sheldon, *The Nigger*

1910: Population of the United States: 93,402,151; Carnegie Corporation chartered; Lomax, *Cowboy Songs*; Moody, *The Faith Healer*; Robinson, *The Town down the River*

1912: Roosevelt forms the Progressive Party; first Rosenwald aid to rural schools; Harriet Monroe founds *Poetry: a Magazine of Verse*

1913: Department of Labor created; Smith-Lever bill; grandfather clause, disfranchising Negroes, held unconstitutional; Max Eastman edits *The Masses* (later, *The Liberator*)

1914: Lindsay, *The Congo and Other Poems*; Amy Lowell, *Sword Blades and Poppy Seeds*; *The Little Review* founded

1915: Panama Canal opened; *Lusitania* sunk; Ford's Peace Ship; *Some Imagist Poets, 1915;* Masters,

1904: Braithwaite, *Lyrics of Life and Love;* Dunbar, *The Heart of Happy Hollow*

1906: James Weldon Johnson consul in Venezuela; Williams and Walker in *Abyssinia;* Allen, *Rhymes, Tales and Rhymed Tales;* Cotter, *Caleb, the Degenerate;* DuBois, "Litany of Atlanta"

1907: Locke graduates from Harvard, wins Rhodes scholarship for Pennsylvania; Braithwaite, *The House of Falling Leaves;* Williams and Walker in *Bandanna Land*

1908: Cole and Johnson write and play in *Red Moon*

1909: Miller, *Race Adjustment;* founding of the National Association for the Advancement of Colored People

1910: Negro Population: 9,827,763 (10.7%); DuBois made director of publicity, editor of *The Crisis* for the N. A. A. C. P.; first edition of Brawley, *The Negro in Literature and Art in the United States*

1911: National Urban League organized; Bert Williams joins *Ziegfeld Follies*; DuBois, *The Quest of the Silver Fleece*

1912: McKay comes to America to study at Tuskegee; J. W. Johnson, *The Autobiography of an Ex-Colored Man*

1913: Harriet Tubman dies, Auburn, New York; Dunbar, *Complete Poems*

1914: N. A. A. C. P. exposes and blocks anti-intermarriage, segregation laws in the District of Columbia, and bill to exclude Negroes from the army and the navy; Cromwell, *The Negro in American History;* W. C. Handy, "St. Louis Blues"; Mamie Smith makes the first blues recording

1915: Booker T. Washington dies; first Spingarn Medal for achievement presented to E. E. Just:

Spoon River Anthology; New Republic founded; D. W. Griffith's motion picture, The Birth of a Nation

1916: Virgin Islands purchased; Mexican border clashes; Dewey, Democracy and Education; Sandburg, Chicago Poems; Amy Lowell, Men, Women, and Ghosts

1917: United States enters World War I; Smith-Hughes bill; East St. Louis race riots; Julius Rosenwald Fund established; Torrence, Three Plays for a Negro Theatre

1918: Wilson's fourteen points; Armistice; Sandburg, Cornhuskers; Joyce's Ulysses appearing in The Little Review

1919: Chicago, Washington riots; Sherwood Anderson, Winesburg, Ohio; Frank, Our America; Mencken, The American Language; Veblen, The Higher Learning in America

1920: Population of the United States: 105,710,620; Nineteenth Amendment ratified; Sandburg, Smoke and Steel; Anderson, Poor White; O'Neill, The Emperor Jones

1921: Tulsa race riots; Dos Passos, Three Soldiers; Robinson, Collected Poems

1922: T. S. Eliot, The Waste Land; Sinclair Lewis, Babbitt; Eugene O'Neill, The Hairy Ape; Tate, Ransom, Davidson found The Fugitive; Gonzales, The Black Border

Association for the Study of Negro Life and History founded; J. W. Work, Folk Songs of the American Negro

1916: Tenth Cavalry and Twenty-fourth Infantry with Pershing's Mexican punitive force; J. W. Johnson becomes secretary of the N. A. A. C. P.; first issue of the Journal of Negro History, Woodson as editor; Locke, Race Contacts and Inter-racial Relations

1916-1919: Great migration of Southern Negroes to Northern industrial centers

1917-1918: 367,710 Negroes inducted into the military service; 1400 officers commissioned

1918: Walter White joins N. A. A. C. P. staff; Miller, The Appeal to Conscience

1919: Washington, Chicago race riots; Pan-African Congress, Paris; Claude McKay's "If We Must Die," in The Liberator; Fletcher Henderson's first Roseland Orchestra, first large Negro band to play Broadway

1920: Negro Population: 10,463,131 (9.9%); "King" Oliver organizes his Creole Jazz Band; DuBois, Darkwater

1921: C. S. Johnson becomes director of research and publicity for the National Urban League; Frazier in Denmark; McKay goes to Russia; Handy, Loveless Love; Sissle and Blake, Shuffle Along; Gilpin plays The Emperor Jones; J. W. Johnson, The Book of American Negro Poetry; Brawley, A Social History of the American Negro

1922: Garvey's Universal Negro Improvement Association reaching height of its influence; Shuffle Along reaches Broadway, first of a series of popular musicals; first edition of Woodson, The Negro in Our History; McKay, Harlem

AMERICAN SCENE

1923: District of Columbia minimum wage law held unconstitutional; Frank, *Holiday;* Cather, *A Lost Lady;* O'Neill, *All God's Chillun Got Wings*

1924: *The American Mercury* founded; Green, *In Abraham's Bosom;* E. Dickinson, *Complete Poems;* Peterkin, *Green Thursday*

1925: Scopes (evolution) trial, Dayton, Tennessee; Dos Passos, *Manhattan Transfer;* Dreiser, *An American Tragedy;* Lewis, *Arrowsmith;* Glasgow, *Barren Ground;* Anderson, *Dark Laughter;* Van Vechten, *Nigger Heaven;* Heyward, *Porgy,* and *Mamba's Daughters;* Gaines, *The Southern Plantation;* Odum and Johnson, *The Negro and His Songs*

1926: Hemingway, *The Sun Also Rises;* Mumford, *The Golden Day;* Sheldon and MacArthur, *Lulu Belle;* Odum and Johnson, *Negro Workaday Songs;* Sandburg, *Abraham Lincoln, The Prairie Years*

1927: Sacco and Vanzetti executed; great Mississippi flood; Roberts, *My Heart and My Flesh;* Adams, *Congaree Sketches;* Peterkin, *Black April;* Theatre Guild's *Porgy;* Rölvaag, *Giants in the Earth;* Sandburg, *The American Songbag;* Parrington, *Main Currents in American Thought,* Vols. I and II; Beard and Beard, *The Rise of American Civilization*

1928: Benet, *John Brown's Body;* Peterkin, *Scarlet Sister Mary;* Odum, *Rainbow Round My Shoulder;* Bradford, *Ol' Man Adam an' His Chillun;* White, *American Negro Folk-Songs*

1929: Collapse of the New York stock market, followed by business depression; Botkin edits first *Folk-Say: A Regional Miscellany;* Bynner, *Indian Earth;* Wolfe, *Look Homeward,*

NEGRO WORLD

Shadows; G. D. Johnson, *Bronze*

1923: *Opportunity: Journal of Negro Life* begins publication, C. S. Johnson, editor; Toomer, *Cane*

1924: *Crisis* and *Opportunity* prizes for creative expression announced; Miller, *The Everlasting Stain;* Fauset, *There Is Confusion;* Miller and Lyles in *Runnin' Wild;* DuBois, *The Gift of Black Folk*

1925: Garvey imprisoned; Sweet trial (residential segregation case), Detroit; Locke edits Harlem number of the *Survey Graphic, The New Negro;* Johnson and Johnson, *The Book of American Negro Spirituals;* Cullen, *Color;* White, *Fire in the Flint;* Louis Armstrong's Hot Five recording

1926: Florence Mills in *Blackbirds;* Handy and Niles, *Blues;* Jessye, *My Spirituals;* Hughes, *The Weary Blues;* White, *Flight,* Walrond, *Tropic Death*

1927: Garvey deported; J. W. Johnson, *God's Trombones;* Hughes, *Fine Clothes to the Jew;* Charles S. Johnson (ed.), *Ebony and Topaz;* Wesley, *Negro Labor in the United States;* Louis Armstrong organizes own band, playing at the Sunset, Chicago; Duke Ellington opens at the Cotton Club, Harlem

1928: Fisher, *The Walls of Jericho;* McKay, *Home to Harlem;* DuBois, *Dark Princess;* Fauset, *Plum Bun;* Larsen, *Quicksana*

1929: Cullen, *The Black Christ;* McKay, *Banjo;* Thurman, *The Blacker the Berry*

Angel; Green, *The House of Connelly;* Rice, *Street Scene*

1930: Population of the United States: 122,775,046; *I'll Take My Stand;* Connelly, *The Green Pastures;* Gold, *Jews without Money*

1931: Faulkner, *Sanctuary;* MacLeish, *Conquistador;* O'Neill, *Mourning Becomes Electra;* Rourke, *American Humor;* Stribling, *The Forge;* Caldwell, *American Earth*

1932: Reconstruction Finance Corporation established; World War veterans' "Bonus March" on Washington; F. D. Roosevelt elected; Faulkner, *Light in August*

1933: Depression measures of the New Deal: banks closed by Presidential order, Civilian Conservation Corps, Civilian Works Authority, Farm and Unemployment Relief bills, T. V. A. bill, National Industrial Recovery Act, Home Owners' Loan bill; Stribling, *The Store;* Stein, *Autobiography of Alice B. Toklas;* Barnes, *The Antislavery Impulse*

1934: *Culture in the South;* Young, *So Red the Rose;* Mumford, *Technics and Civilization;* Josephson, *The Robber Barons;* March, *Come in at the Door;* Peters and Sklar, *Stevedore;* Wexley, *They Shall Not Die*

1935: Works Progress Administration established, including the Federal Arts Projects; National Labor Relations Board; Social Security Act; N. R. A. declared unconstitutional; First American Writers' Congress; Cohn, *God Shakes Creation;* Wolfe, *Of Time and the River;* Caldwell, *Kneel to the Rising Sun;* Odets, *Waiting for Lefty;* Gershwin, *Porgy and Bess;* J. A. and Alan Lomax, *American Ballads and Folk Songs*

1930: Negro Population: 11,891,143 (9.7%); J. W. Johnson, *Saint Peter Relates an Incident and Black Manhattan;* Hughes, *Not Without Laughter;* C. S. Johnson, *The Negro in American Civilization*

1931: Fauset, *The Chinaberry Tree;* Bontemps, *God Sends Sunday; The Journal of Negro Education* founded; Spero and Harris, *The Black Worker*

1932: Defection from the Republican party in the Hoover-Roosevelt campaign; Brown, *Southern Road;* McKay, *Gingertown;* Fisher, *The Conjure Man Dies;* first Negro detective novel

1933: First Scottsboro trials; J. W. Johnson, *Along This Way;* McKay, *Banana Bottom;* Fauset, *Comedy, American Style*

1934: Hughes, *The Ways of White Folks;* C. S. Johnson, *The Shadow of the Plantation;* J. W. Johnson, *Negro Americans, What Now?*

1935: Harlem race riots; beginning of the "swing" fad; Davis, *Black Man's Verse;* Hurston, *Mules and Men;* Henderson, *Ollie Miss;* Bontemps, *Black Thunder;* Hughes's *Mulatto* begins longest run enjoyed by play by a Negro

1936: Agricultural Adjustment Act declared unconstitutional; C.I.O. unions suspended; Dos Passos, *The Big Money;* Eliot, *Collected Poems;* publication of *The Dictionary of American English* begins; Brooks, *The Flowering of New England;* Lomax and Lomax, *Negro Folk Songs as Sung by Lead Belly;* Shaw, *Bury the Dead;* Faulkner, *Absalom, Absalom!*

1936: Brawley, *Paul Laurence Dunbar;* Harris, *The Negro as Capitalist;* Lee, *River George*

1937: "Sit-down" strikes; Saxon, *Children of Strangers;* Steinbeck, *Of Mice and Men;* Benton, *An Artist in America;* Dollard, *Caste and Class in a Southern Town*

1937: Hurston, *Their Eyes Were Watching God;* Turpin, *These Low Grounds*

1938: Mumford, *The Culture of Cities;* Blitzstein, *The Cradle Will Rock; These Are Our Lives;* Meade, *The Back Door;* Caldwell, *Southways;* MacLeish, *Land of the Free*

1938: Gaines v. University of Missouri provides for equal educational facilities; Brawley, *Negro Builders and Heroes;* Wright, *Uncle Tom's Children*

1939: World War II; Steinbeck, *The Grapes of Wrath;* Sandburg, *Abraham Lincoln, The War Years; Mamba's Daughters* produced; Hobson, *American Jazz Music;* Sargent, *Jazz: Hot and Hybrid;* Ramsey and Smith, *Jazzmen*

1939: Turpin, *O Canaan!;* Frazier, *The Negro Family in the United States;* DuBois, *Black Folk, Then and Now*

1940: Population of the United States: 131,669,275; F. D. Roosevelt re-elected for a third term; Cather, *Sapphira and the Slave Girl;* McCullers, *The Heart Is a Lonely Hunter;* Adamic, *From Many Lands;* Faulkner, *The Hamlet;* Hemingway, *For Whom the Bell Tolls;* Caldwell, *Trouble in July*

1940: *Phylon* established with DuBois as editor; American Youth Commission volumes; *The Negro in Virginia;* Wright, *Native Son;* DuBois, *Dusk of Dawn;* Hughes, *The Big Sea;* McKay, *Harlem; Negro Metropolis*

1941: Mitchell vs. Interstate Commerce Commission, Illinois Central Railroad, Chicago, Rock Island and Pacific Railway Company, et cetera; Locke, *The Negro in Art;* Richard Wright, *Twelve Million Black Voices;* William Attaway, *Blood on the Forge;* Davis and Gardiner, *Deep South*

INDEX

OF AUTHORS AND SELECTIONS